Information Systems Security

Information Systems Security
A Practitioner's Reference

Philip E. Fites, MBA, CDP
Martin P. J. Kratz, B. Sc., LLB

VNR VAN NOSTRAND REINHOLD
New York

Library of Congress Catalog Card Number 93-15895
ISBN 0-442-00180-0

I⟨T⟩P   Van Nostrand Reinhold is a division of International Thomson Publishing Company. ITP logo is a trademark under license.

Printed in the United States of America

Van Nostrand Reinhold
115 Fifth Avenue
New York, New York 10003

International Thomson Publishing GmbH
Konigswinterer Str. 518
5300 Bonn 3
Germany

International Thomson Publishing
Berkshire House, 168-173
High Holborn, London WC1V 7AA
England

International Thomson Publishing Asia
38 Kim Tian Rd., #0105
Kim Tian Plaza
Singapore 0316

Thomas Nelson Australia
102 Dodds Street
South Melbourne 3205
Victoria, Australia

International Thomson Publishing Japan
Kyowa Building, 3F
2-2-1 Hirakawacho
Chiyada-Ku, Tokyo 102
Japan

Nelson Canada
1120 Birchmount Road
Scarborough, Ontario
M1K 5G4, Canada

16 15 14 13 12 11 10 9 8 7 6 5 4 3 2 1

Library of Congress Cataloging-in-Publication Data

Fites, Philip E.
     Information systems security: a practitioner's reference / Philip Fites, Martin P. J. Kratz
          p.   cm.
     Bibliography: p.
     Includes index.
     ISBN 0-442-00180-0
     1. Computer security. I. Kratz, Martin P. J. II. Title
     QA76.9.A25F536 1993
     005.8—dc20   93-15895
                                                                         CIP

Contents

ACKNOWLEDGMENTS ix

ACRONYMS xiii

INTRODUCTION xvii

   Organization of this Book xvii

   Background xvii

   Existing Programs xviii

   (ISC)2 xviii

   The Consortium Approach xviii

   Groups that Formed the Consortium xix

   Code of Ethics xix

   Code of Good Practice xx

THE BODY OF KNOWLEDGE xxiii

   Informatics Background Knowledge xxiv

OVERVIEW xxvii

   I. . Development of Security Program xxvii

   II. . Risk Analysis xxix

   III. Contingency Planning xxx

   IV. Legal Issues for Managers xxx

   V. System Validation and Verification (Accreditation) xxxi

   VI. Information Systems Audit xxxi

1. ACCESS CONTROL 1

   1.1 Ownership, Accountability, and Controls 1

   1.2 User Authentication and Password Management 2

   1.3 Access Control Administration 8

   1.4 Computer Access Control Software 13

   References 18

2. CRYPTOGRAPHY 21

   2.1 Definitions and Characteristics 21

   2.2 Public Key and Private Key; Key Characteristics 25

   2.3 Key Management 27

   2.4 Link level, End-to-End 28

   2.5 Block Mode, Cipher Block Chaining, Stream Ciphers
       (Synchronous and Self-synchronous) 29

   2.6 Cryptanalysis and Strength of Ciphers
       (Theoretically Secure, Computationally Secure) 31

   2.7 Error Detection and Correction Features of Encryption Methods 32

   2.8 Implementations: DES, RSA 33

   2.9 Applications: MAC, X9.9, Digital Signature, Cryptographic Checksum 44

   2.10 Advantages and Disadvantages 46

   References 47

3. RISK MANAGEMENT 49

   3.1 Asset Identification and Valuation 54

   3.2 Threat and Exposure Assessment 69

   3.3 Safeguards and Countermeasures 87

   3.4 Perception and Communication of Risk 92

   References 93

4. BUSINESS CONTINUITY PLANNING 95
    4.1 Backups and Procedures 96
    4.2 Catastrophe, Contingency, and Continuation .105
    4.3 Contingency and Disaster Planning 105
    4.4 Security and Controls in Off-site Backup and Facilities 109
    4.5 Business and DP Insurance 110
    4.6 Software Escrow Arrangements 112
    References 112

5. DATA CLASSIFICATION 113
    5.1 Elements and Objectives of a Classification Scheme 120
    5.2 Criteria for Classifying Data 120
    5.3 Statistical Inference 121
    5.4 Government Clearances and Data Sensitivities .124
    5.5 Procedures and Management for a Classification Scheme 126
    References 127

6. SECURITY AWARENESS 129
    6.1 Components of EDP Security: Administrative and Organizational Controls 129
    6.2 Organizational and Administrative Controls 131
    6.3 Personnel Considerations 137
    References 145

7. COMPUTER AND SYSTEM SECURITY 147
    7.1 Secure Operating Systems 160
    7.2 Present Guidelines and Standards, Trusted computing base 163
    7.3 Design Principles for Secure Systems 168
    7.4 Common Flaws and Penetration Methods 170
    7.5 Computer Virus Code 175
    7.6 Countermeasures 179
    References 179

8. TELECOMMUNICATIONS SECURITY 181
    8.1 Telecommunications Fundamentals 187
    8.2 Types of Attack 192
    8.3 Electronic Emissions and TEMPEST 196
    8.4 Communications 197
    8.5 Network Design 203
    8.6 Locus of attack 208
    References 218

9. ORGANIZATION ARCHITECTURE 219
    9.1 Responsibility Areas, System Security Officer .227
    9.2 Common Forms of Organizations 232
    9.3 Organizational Considerations for Computer Security Incident Response 247
    9.4 Management of Information Technology and Services 250
    References 252

10. LEGAL/REGULATORY 255
    10.1 Introduction 258
    10.2 Laws As Tools for Computer Security 260
    10.3 Constitutional Structure 262
    10.4 Broad Categories of Law 262
    10.5 Federal Computer Crime Laws 266
    10.6 State Computer Crime Laws 270

10.7 Model Computer Crime Bills. 272
10.8 Introduction to Civil Law. 272
10.9 Introduction to Criminal Law. 287
10.10 Control of Strategic Materials 289
10.11 Transborder Data Flows. 290
10.12 Privacy of Data—OECD Guidelines. 291
References. 294

11. INVESTIGATION. 297
11.1 Evidence—Proof in Court. 300
11.2 Authorized Use and a Computer Use Policy. 304
11.3 Computer Abuse Checklist 305
11.4 Review of Documents. 306
11.5 Review of the Abuser's Alleged Conduct 307
11.6 The Information Security Specialist's Role 308
References. 311

12. APPLICATION PROGRAM SECURITY **313**
12.1 Software Controls: Development. 317
12.2 Software Controls: Maintenance 320
12.3 Assurance 322
12.4 Formal Specification and Verification .323
12.5 Database Systems Security 325
12.6 Integrity Controls 331
12.7 Accounting and Auditing. 334
12.8 Specific Controls. 349
References. 350

13. PHYSICAL SECURITY 353
13.1 Site Location and Construction. 358
13.2 Physical Access 360
13.3 Power 360
13.4 Air Conditioning 362
13.5 Water Exposures and Problems 363
13.6 Fire Prevention 363
13.7 Fire Protection. 364
13.8 Tape and Media Libraries, Retention Policies 366
13.9 Document (Hard-Copy) Libraries 367
13.10 Waste Disposal. 368
13.11 Off-site Storage. 370
13.12 Physical Attack Parameters 370
References. 371

14. OPERATIONS SECURITY 373
14.1 Organization of Computer Operations. .378
14.2 Separation of Duties. 383
14.3 Controls at Interfaces 385
14.4 Media Controls 387
14.5 Backup Procedures 388
14.6 Console Capabilities. 388
14.7 Personnel Controls 389
14.8 Documentation Controls 390
References. 390

15. INFORMATION ETHICS 393
   15.1 Ethical Decision-making 393
   15.2 Professional Societies 396
   15.3 Canadian System Security Centre 401
   15.4 National Computer Security Center 402
   15.5 National Institute of Standards and Technology 402
   15.6 Professional Certifications 403
   References 408

16. POLICY DEVELOPMENT 411
   16.1 Formal Security Policy Considerations 415
   16.2 Informal Security Policy 416
   16.3 Publication and Staff Acknowledgment 418
   16.4 Model Computer Security Policies 418
   References 427

APPENDIX A: REFERENCES 429
APPENDIX B: ATTACKS 437
   B.1 General Definitions 437
   B.2 Cryptography Attacks 438
   B.3 Communications Attacks 439
   B.4 Attacks on Data and Databases 441
   B.5 Operating System Attacks 443
   B.6 Malicious Code 444
   B.7 Console and Operations Room Attacks 446
   B.8 Physical Attacks 448
APPENDIX C: SECURITY VIDEOS 449
INDEX 459

Acknowledgments

DEFINITIONS

The formal definitions used in this text are from a draft Canadian Dictionary of Information Technology Security being prepared by the System Security Centre of the Communications Security Establishment. The dictionary was published in 1992 and is available from the Canadian Standards Association or the Communications Security Establishment. Where available, references to the international standards and U.S. Government documents that contain the original sources of definitions are given.

The list of sources below contains an abbreviation in parentheses preceding each source. In the chapter opening sections, this abbreviation is appended t/o each definition to facilitate reference to original sources.

(AFR 205-16)	Air Force Regulation 205-16, (draft).
(AFR 700-10)	Air Force Regulation 700-10, *Information System Security* of 3/15/85.
(AR 380-380)	Army Regulation 380-380, *Automation Security* of 3/3/85.
(A-123)	Office of Management and Budget Circular A-123, *Internal Control Systems* of 10/28/81.
(A-130)	Office of Management and Budget Circular A-130, *Management of Federal Information Resources* of 12/12/85.
(BBD)	*The Bulletin Board Dictionary*, anon., no date.
(Cohen)	*Computer Viruses*, Ph.D. Thesis 1986, Dr. Fred Cohen.
(CSC-STD-001-83)	CSC-STD-001-83, *DOD Trusted Computer System Evaluation Criteria* of 8/15/83.
(CSC-STD-002-85)	CSC-STD-002-85, *DOD Password Management Guideline* of 4/12/85.
(CSC-STD-003-85)	CSC-STD-003-85, *DOD Computer Security Requirements* of 6/25/85.
(CSC-STD-004-85)	CSC-STD-004-85, *Technical Rationale Behind CSC-STD-003-85* of 6/25/85.
(CSC-STD-005-85)	CSC-STD-005-85, *DOD Magnetic Remanence Security Guideline* (FOUO) of 11/15/85.
(DCID 1/16-1)	Director of Central Intelligence Directive 1/16-1, *Security Policy on Intelligence Information in Automated Data Processing Systems and Networks, Computer Security Manual* (C) of 1/4/83.
(DCID 1/16-1, Sup.)	Supplement to DCID 1/16-1 titled: *Uniform Safeguards for the Protection of 'Critical Systems' Processing Intelligence Information* (S) of 12/84.
(DODD 5200.1-R)	Department of Defense Directive 5200.1-R, *Information Security Program Regulation* of 6/86.
(DODD 2040.2)	Department of Defense Directive 2040.2, *International Transfers of Technology, Goods, Services and Munitions* of 1/17/84.
(DODD 3200.12)	Department of Defense Directive 3200.12, *DOD Scientific and Technical Information Programs* of 2/15/83.

(DODD 5200.28)	Department of Defense Directive 5200.28 (draft).
(DODD 5200.28M)	Department of Defense Directive 5200.28M, *ADP Security Manual* of 1/73.
(DODD 5200.28-STD)	Department of Defense Standard 5200.28-STD, *Department of Defense Trusted Computer System Evaluation Criteria* of 12/85.
(DODD 5215.1)	Department of Defense Directive 5215.1, *Computer Security Evaluation Center* of 10/25/82.
(DODD 5230.24)	Department of Defense Directive 5230.24, *Distribution Statements on Technical Documents* of 11/20/84.
(DODD 5230.25)	Department of Defense Directive 5230.25, *Withholding of Unclassified Technical Data from Public Disclosure* of 11/6/84.
(DODD 7040.6)	Department of Defense Directive 7040.6, *Internal Control Systems* of 3/24/82.
(DODI 5215.2)	Department of Defense Instruction 5215.2, *Computer Security Technical Vulnerability Reporting Program (CSTVRP)* 9/2/86.
(DOE 5635.1A)	Department of Energy Order 5635.1A, *Control of Classified Documents and Information* (draft).
(DOE 5636.2A)	Department of Energy Order 5636.2A, *Security Requirements for Classified Automated Data Processing Systems* (draft).
(ed.)	The editors.
(ET)	Expert/Risk – Denver
(FIPS PUB 39)	Federal Information Processing Standards Publication 39, *Glossary for Computer Systems Security*, National Bureau of Standards of 2/15/76.
(FIPS PUB 112)	Federal Information Processing Standards Publication 112, *Password Usage*, National Bureau of Standards of 5/30/85.
(GAO)	General Accounting Office, *Survey of Computer and Telecommunications Based Information Systems Security in the Civil Sector of the Federal Government*, no date.
(IC)	Internet Crash
(ISO 7498-2)	*Information Processing Systems—Open Systems Interconnection—Basic Reference Model—Part 2: Security Architecture*, ISO 7498-2: 1989 (E), International Standards Organization, 1989.
(JL)	Llaurado, J. D., *Breaches of Computer Security*, International Journal of Biomedical Computing, v. 14, no. 3, pp. 87-93, March, 1983.
(MA)	MAPLESS and Uncertainty.
(MK)	Milan Kuchta, Communications Security Establishment, Ottawa.
(MS)	Michael Shain, private communication, 1/9/87.
(MTR-8201)	Mitre Corporation Technical Report MTR-8201, *Trusted Computer Systems-Glossary* of 3/87.
(NCSC-WA-001-85)	National Computer Security Center, *COMPUSECese: Computer Security Glossary*, 2nd edition, (draft).
(NSDD-145)	National Security Decision Directive 145, *National Policy on Telecommunications and Automated Information System Security* of 12/17/84.

(OPNAVINST 5239.1A)	Office of Navy Operations Instruction 5239.1A, *Department of the Navy Automatic Data processing Security Program* of 3/8/82.
(PC/PCIE)	Prevention Committee, President's Council on Integrity and Efficiency, *Computers: Crimes, Clues, and Controls* (NTIS No. PB86-221850) of 3/86.
(RM)	Risk Management
(TC)	Conlon, Theresa, *Parker's Guide to Hackers' Lexicon*, Computer Decisions, July 15, 1985.
(WB)	Banks, William W., et al., *Security Checklist for Computer Based Information Systems for the Air Force Logistics Command*, Lawrence Livermore National Laboratory (FOUO), (LINL No. UCAR-10135), October 1985.

PERSONAL ACKNOWLEDGMENTS

The material in Chapter 10 and Chapter 11 is adapted from papers written by Thomas Richards, Ph.D., University of North Texas, and Corey D. Schou, Ph.D., Idaho State University, as well as Philip E. Fites, MBA, CDP, Fites & Associates Management Consultants Ltd. and Martin P., J. Kratz, LLB, Bennett, Jones Verchere,[1] Edmonton Canada.

Many other people provided assistance, advice and guidance in the creation of this book. Particular thanks are due to (in alphabetical order):

- Mr. Charles Cresson Wood, Sausalito, California
- Ms. Chris Grisonich, Van Nostrand Reinhold
- Mr. Kim Hay and E. J. Lindeburg, Edmonton, Alberta
- Ms. Dianne Littwin, Van Nostrand Reinhold
- Mr. F. Lynn McNulty and the staff at NIST
- Dr. Evie Nemeth and Mr. Alex Popiel, University of Colorado
- Ms. Barbara Stephens, Colorado Department of Transportation
- Mr. Leslie Stephens, Arvada, Colorado
- Mr. Robert Verrett, Communications Security Establishment
- Ms. Denise Weatherwax, After V Systems

---

[1]Martin Kratz is the partner responsible for the Bennett, Jones Verchere law firm's advanced technology and intellectual property groups. His practice largely involves the protection, enforcement, and commercializing of innovative developments in the computer, electronics, and telecommunications industries.

Acronyms

The discipline of information systems security is rich in acronyms, and many are included in this book. Where an acronym first appears, it is defined, and all acronyms are in the index. The acronyms that abbreviate various publications from which definitions are excerpted are listed in the *Acknowledgments* section. To assist the reader further, this section lists other acronyms and what they abbreviate.

Acronym	Unabbreviated text
ACF-2	Name of an access-control security package
ACK	ACKnowledged (a code in communications protocols)
ACP	Access Control Package
ADP	Automated Data Processing
AIS	Automated Information system
AM	Amplitude Modulation
ASIS	American Society for Industrial Security
BCS	British Computer Society
CASE	Computer-Assisted System Engineering
CATV	CAble TeleVision
CCITT	Committee Consultativ International Telefon et Telegraf
CD	Compact Disk
CD-ROM	Compact Disk/Read-Only Memory
CDI	Constrained Data Item
CDP	Certified Data Processor (a designation sponsored by ICCP)
CERT	Computer Emergency Response Team (also an organization in the U.S.)
CICA	Canadian Institute of Chartered Accountants
CICS	Name of a mainframe communication software system
CIPS	Canadian Information Processing Society
CISA	Certified Information Systems Auditor
CISSP	Certified Information Systems Security Practitioner
COMSEC	Communications Security
COPS	Name of a software package (developed at Purdue University) for evaluating UNIX environments for potential security problems
CTCPEC	Canadian Trusted Computer Product Evaluation Criteria
CPSR	Computer Professionals for Social Responsibility
CPU	Central Processing Unit
CSA	Canadian Standards Association
CSE	Communications Security Establishment (Canada)
CSI	Computer Security Institute
CSIRC	Computer Security Incident Response Capability
CSMA/CA	Carrier Sense Multiple Access with Collision Avoidance
CSMA/CD	Carrier Sense Multiple Access with Collision Detection

CSP	Certified Systems Professional (a designation sponsored by ICCP)
DASD	Direct Access Storage Device
DBMS	DataBase Management System
DES	Data Encryption Standard
DOS	Name of a popular personal computer operating system (also an obsolete main-frame operating system)
DPMA	Data Processing Management Association
DSO	Departmental Security Officer (see also SSO)
EDI	Electronic Data Interchange
EDP	Electronic Data Processing
EDPAF	EDP Auditors' Foundation
EFT	Electronic Funds Transfer
EMI	ElectroMagnetic Interference
EMP	ElectroMagnetic Pulse
FBCS	Fellow of the British Computer Society
FC	Federal Criteria for Information Technology Security
FDM	Frequency-Division Multiplexing
FECP	Front-End Communications Processor
FEP	Front-End Processor (see FECP)
FIPS	Federation of Information Processing Societies
FM	Frequency Modulation
GAAP	Generally Accepted Accounting Principles
IBM	International Business Machines Corporation
ICCP	Institute for Certification of Computer Professionals
IEEE	Institute of Electrical and Electronic Engineers
IFIP	International Federation for Information Processing
InfoSec	Information Security, or Information Systems Security
InterNet	A large computer communications network based in North America (with thousands of nodes, many scattered across the globe)
(ISC)²	International Information Systems Security Certification Consortium, Inc.
ISDN	Integrated Services Digital Network
ISO	International Standards Organization
ISP	Information Systems Professional (a designation sponsored by CIPS in Canada)
ISSA	Information Systems Security Association
ISU	Idaho State University
ITSEC	Information Technology Security Evaluation Criteria
IVP	Integrity Verification Procedure
JCL	Job Control Language
LAN	Local Area Network
MAC	Message Authentication Code
MBWA	Management by Walking Around

MCI	Name of a U.S. telecommunications company
MIPS	Millions of Instructions Per Second
modem	Modulator/demodulator
MSAT	Name for a Canadian communications satellite project scheduled for launch in the mid 1990s
MULTICS	Name of a computer operating system
MVS	Name of a mainframe operating system
NAK	Not AcKnowledged (a code in communications protocols)
NCCD	National Center for Computer Crime Data
NCSC	National Computer Security Center (U.S.)
NIST	National Institute of Standards and Technology
NWT	Northwest Territories (Canada)
OECD	Organization of Economic Cooperation and Development
OMB	Office of Management and Budget (U.S. Government)
OS/2	Name of a popular personal computer operating system
OSI	Open Systems Interconnect (a standard of ISO, often referred to as ISO/OSI)
PABX	Private Automatic Branch Exchange
PBX	Private Branch Exchange
PCM	Pulse Code Modulation
PIN	Personal Identification Number
RACF	Name of an access-control security package
RCMP	Royal Canadian Mounted Police
RFI	Radio Frequency Interference
RSA	An encipherment technique; the letters are the initials of the inventors' last names (Rivest, Shamir, and Adleman)
SAFE	Security and Audit Field Evaluation (a study conducted in the 1970s)
SIG-CP	Data Processing Management Association—Special Interest Group for Certified Professionals
SIG-CS	Data Processing Management Association—Special Interest Group for Computer Security
SOG-IS	EC Senior Officials Group for the Security of Information Systems
SRI	Stanford Research International
SSO	System Security Officer
TCB	Trusted computing base
TCSEC	Trusted Computer System Evaluation Criteria
TCP	Transmission Control Protocol
TDM	Time-Division Multiplexing
TEMPEST	The name applied to a group of (classified) standards relating to electronic emanations.
TOC/TOU	Time Of Check *versus* Time Of Use (sometimes TOCTU)
TOP-SECRET	Name of an access-control security package

TP	Transformation Procedure
TSO	Name of a time-sharing mainframe operating system
UCC	Uniform Commercial Code
UDI	Unconstrained Data Item
UL	Underwriter's Laboratory (U.S.)
UNIX	Name of a popular computer operating system
UPS	Uninterruptible Power Supply
VAX	Name of a computer
VDT	Video Display Terminal
VMS	Name of a computer operating system (The same acronym is used by different manufacturers to refer to different systems.)
VTOC	Volume Table Of Contents
WAN	Wide Area Network
WORM	Write Once, Read Many (times)
X.25	A communications protocol

Introduction

ORGANIZATION OF THIS BOOK

This book is organized into an Introduction and presentation of the International Information Systems Security Certification Consortium, Inc. [(ISC)²] "Common Body of Knowledge," an overview, then 16 chapters and 3 appendices. A glossary of acronyms follows the Acknowledgments section at the beginning of the book.

The first twelve chapters follow the topics outlined in the Common Body of Knowledge. Topics of System Program Security, item 13 in the Common Body of Knowledge, are covered in other locations, notably Chapters 2, 7 and 15. These topics include hazards to which the system program may be exposed; the mechanisms available to protect it; security functions that should be assigned to the system program; and issues of operating system design and implementation such as access control and security administration. Chapters 13 to 16 correspond to the Common Body of Knowledge topic areas 14 through 17. References specific to each topic follow each chapter. The first appendix collects all references in alphabetical order. The second appendix collects the varied kinds of attacks addressed in the text body into one place for easy cross-reference. The third appendix contains a list of security visual training aids and sources.

BACKGROUND

This manual is intended to serve as a professional-level reference to many different topics for the information systems security professional. Few if any other publications cover as broad a range of security topics at the level of detail contained in this review manual. A secondary purpose of this text is to aid those who wish to review the professional knowledge necessary to perform successfully on the Certified Information Systems Security Practitioner (CISSP) examination. In support of the secondary objective it is appropriate first to review briefly some of the events that led to the formation of (ISC)² and the program to develop and administer the CISSP certification examination.

Recent developments in the worldwide business community have prompted a considerable increase in management awareness of the value of computer and information security. The integration of executive information systems, electronic data interchange, artificial intelligence and expert systems has propelled computing from the back office to the front lines of business operation and strategy. To remain competitive in the more complex world markets, business leaders must use these new information technology tools as an integral component in their operation and strategy. And these are only a few of the encouraging highlights.

On a discouraging note, exposures within the information technology community have jeopardized the effective use of these systems. Computer theft through illicit hacker networks, the spread of computer virus code, increased cases of computer fraud, extortion, and terrorism have demonstrated the increased vulnerability that accompanies the benefits in an environment of information based strategic planning, operations, and communications.

Legislation (*e.g.* the Computer Security Act of 1987 in the United States) has created the need for more qualified computer security personnel than ever before. Today nearly all business applications in whole or in part are developed by or for computer equipment of some kind. Just the number of personal computers in use is in the tens of millions. They exist in stand-alone configurations, in networked workstations, linked to mainframe computers, or in conjunction with manufacturing, distribution, or laboratory equipment. Increased use of supercomputers, shared computing facilities and high-speed local, national, and international networks will continue to lead to more and more use of computers. As we come to depend increasingly on this technology, our vulnerability also increases. The need for professionals certified in information systems security is growing along with the expansion and growing complexity of computer usage.

EXISTING PROGRAMS

In 1992, several programs existed to attempt to qualify and quantify the knowledge and experience required for computer security practitioners. The Certified Information Systems Auditor (CISA) and Institute for Certification of Computer Professionals (ICCP) programs include some questions designed to test and evaluate the general knowledge of the computer auditor, information systems manager, programmer, or analyst in the field of computer security.[1] This knowledge is essential to those practitioners in fulfilling their responsibilities; however, they are seldom the individuals assigned the full-time responsibility for computer security. These programs do not address information security as the primary objective. Information security includes many specialized knowledge sets that are not required for a more generalized certification program. Examples of these include trusted computer concepts, access controls, encryption, and contingency planning concepts. In addition, because information systems security requires a direct linkage with other business areas, a program that specializes in information security must address related topics such as records management, building design, and financial controls.

(ISC)[2]

Leading computer industry professional groups with an interest in information system security addressed this need in 1988 and 1989. The International Information system security Certification Consortium, Inc., or (ISC)[2], was formed as a cooperative effort by representatives of several organizations interested in a professional level certification program for information systems security certification. The mission of (ISC)[2] is straightforward:

To support a program for the certification of information systems security professionals.

(ISC)[2] was established in July 1989 as a non-profit corporation with a mission to develop a process including a comprehensive examination to certify individuals in the information systems security specialty.

THE CONSORTIUM APPROACH

The number of data processing organizations and the proliferation of letters certifying, qualifying, and otherwise designating skill levels has become so complex it is difficult to keep track of all the players. For years, computer and information systems security has been in the shadow of

---

[1]ICCP added a specialty examination module in information security in 1992.

other information technology fields. Some work was started by several of the Consortium members several years ago toward certification of computer security practitioners. This work was conducted independently and largely without knowledge of each others' efforts. After discovering the each other's work, the groups felt it was in their best interest to combine and offer a single examination leading to the awarding of a single certificate designation, the Certified Information Systems Security Practitioner (CISSP). The Consortium approach involves many organizations, avoids the wasted effort of competing programs, and helps to ensure the acceptance of the certification. To realize the benefits of support from multiple organizations, (ISC)^2 the Consortium was created. (ISC)^2 is a nonprofit corporation chartered in the Commonwealth of Massachusetts dedicated solely to its stated mission. It operates independently of all computer security groups, companies, and organizations.

GROUPS THAT FORMED THE CONSORTIUM

(ISC)^2 was formed by representatives from the following groups (listed alphabetically):

Canadian Information Processing Society (CIPS)

Computer Security Institute (CSI)

Data Processing Management Association—Special Interest Group for Certified Professionals (DPMA SIG-CP)

Data Processing Management Association—Special Interest Group for Computer Security (DPMA SIG-CS)

Idaho State University (ISU)

Information Systems Security Association (ISSA)

International Federation for Information Processing (IFIP)

Representatives for each of these groups hold positions as officers or members of the board of directors, although in their capacity as (ISC)^2 representatives they are committed solely to the goals of (ISC)^2. These individuals are volunteers, without compensation.

Control and overview of the Consortium takes place through the vehicle of an Advisory Committee. Positions on the Advisory Committee are held by representatives of the groups who formed the consortium, recognized industry experts selected by the board of directors, and representatives of organizations that qualify as significant corporate contributors.

CODE OF ETHICS

(ISC)^2 CODE OF ETHICS FOR
CERTIFIED INFORMATION SYSTEMS SECURITY PRACTITIONERS

All information systems security professionals who are certified by (ISC)^2 recognize that such certification is a privilege that must be both earned and maintained. In support of this principle, all Certified Information Systems Security Practitioners commit to fully support this Code of Ethics and the Code of Good Practice. Certified professionals who willfully violate any of the aforementioned shall be subject to action by a peer review panel that may result in revocation of certification.

Individuals certified by (ISC)[2] agree to abide by the following:

In the course of my professional activities I shall conduct myself in accordance with high standards of moral, ethical, and legal behavior. I will never knowingly commit or be party to an unlawful or unethical act that negatively affects my professional reputation or that of my profession.

I shall support efforts to promote an understanding and acceptance of prudent information security standards, procedures, and practices throughout the public, private, and academic sectors of our global community.

I shall provide loyal and competent service to my employers and clients. I will work diligently to enhance my knowledge of the various interrelated disciplines and technologies associated with my profession.

I shall execute my responsibilities in a manner consistent with the highest standards of my profession. I will strive to offer only recommendations or opinions that can be objectively substantiated and will maintain the confidentiality of all the information within my possession that is so identified.

CODE OF GOOD PRACTICE

In addition to a Code of Ethics, a true profession is characterized by other guidelines that define a set of behaviors which the public should expect of professionals. One such set of guidelines is a Code of Good Practice, along with mechanisms for reporting and resolving problems (reporting, sanctions, appeal processes and such). (ISC)[2] has not yet approved a Code of Good Practice. Preliminary work has been completed, however; a committee was formed, and produced a draft of a Code, which is reproduced here with the permission of (ISC)[2].

(Proposed)
(ISC)[2]
CODE OF GOOD PRACTICE

The following expands upon the Code of Ethics and provides the Certified Information Systems Security Practitioner with more specific guidance concerning his or her professional responsibilities.

1. Professional Conduct

1.1 I recognize that I alone am fully accountable for my actions and accept responsibility for them.

1.2 I will support the laws of any community or nation where I practice my profession. If an ethical or moral conflict does arise, I will actively pursue any peaceable means necessary to correct the perceived injustice.

1.3 I will support my employer's or client's policies and standards. If an ethical, moral, or legal conflict does arise, I will work with management to resolve my concerns but will refuse to comply with any flawed directive.

1.4 I will always be cognizant of and try to avoid conflict of interest situations. If a conflict does arise, I will promptly notify the appropriate personnel.

1.5 I will refuse to promulgate statements about an individual, organization, product, or service that cannot be objectively substantiated.

1.6 I will promptly report any known violations of the (ISC)^2 Code of Ethics or Code of Good Practice to the Chairman of the Ethics Committee and fully assist in any ensuing investigation.

2. Promote Information Security

2.1 I will assist in developing and then support prudent information security policies, standards, practices, and procedures.

2.2 I will work to ensure that such policies, standards, practices, and procedures are appropriately current, effective, and cost efficient.

2.3 I will provide assistance for developing appropriate information security related legislation and will support its enactment.

2.4 I will assist in the development of educational and training programs designed to increase student knowledge of information security subjects and their responsibilities as users.

2.5 I will support efforts to increase the level of information security awareness both within and outside my place of business.

2.6 When requested, I will assist any recognized standards body in drafting information security standards.

3. Professional Competence

3.1 I will achieve at least the minimum amount of continuing education and professional development that is required to maintain my certification.

3.2 As is legally and ethically permissible, I will make reasonable attempts to assist other information security professionals and share my experiences with them.

3.3 I will continually strive to have excellent working relationships with all individuals and groups within my place of business that are associated with the information security program.

3.4 I will claim to have expertise only in those areas where I possess the necessary qualifications.

4. Professional Execution of Duties

4.1 I will adhere to all generally accepted information security standards in the performance of my responsibilities.

4.2 I will ensure that my work is adequately documented.

4.3 I will safeguard the assets of my employer or client to the best of my ability.

4.4 I will strive to provide my employers and clients with recommendations and/or opinions that are objective and apolitical.

4.5 I will protect confidential information that has been entrusted to me from unauthorized disclosure or compromise.

4.6 I will work to ensure that appropriate information security and integrity mechanisms are implemented and functioning properly.

4.7 I will keep management apprised of significant information security threats and appropriate countermeasures.

The Body of Knowledge

Professions are characterized in part by a body of knowledge, shared by the members of the profession, and used in their work. It is usually abstract, stable, and technology-free. It is independent of necessary skills, tasks, or activities. Its language facilitates communication among the members.

The existence of such a common body of knowledge is necessary, but not sufficient, evidence of the existence of the profession. Habitual knowledge of the body is a requirement for inclusion in the profession.

This text is patterned after the boundaries of the information systems security body of knowledge, and the subject areas identified by the (ISC)^2 Common Body of Knowledge Committee. For each area it provides a description, identifies what a professional is expected to know about it, and presents an outline of specific skills and knowledge. Illustrative examples, discussion, and references are provided.

The outline for this text is based on two documents:

- Draft *Computer Security Certification Body of Knowledge*, prepared for the Data Processing Management Association Special Interest Group for Computer Security (SIG-CS) October 1988 by Fites & Associates Management Consultants Ltd.
- *Information System Security Common Body of Knowledge*, prepared for (ISC)^2 by the Common Body of Knowledge Committee, October, 1989

In deciding what to include in the body of knowledge, the Common Body of Knowledge Committee relied upon its expectations of its members. That is, if the members expected certain knowledge of each other, but would not expect that knowledge of those not in the field, then that knowledge was identified as part of the body. If the members would not expect certain knowledge of each other, or would expect it of those not in the field, then it was excluded.

The committee identified the following areas of knowledge as included within the field of information systems security:

1. Access Control
2. Cryptography
3. Risk Management
4. Business Continuity Planning
5. Data Classification
6. Security Awareness
7. Computer and System Security
8. Telecommunications Security
9. Organization Architecture
10. Legal and Regulatory Considerations
11. Investigation
12. Application Program Security (change control, etc.)

13. System Program Security
14. Physical Security
15. Operations Security
16. Information Ethics
17. Policy Development

The chapters in this book are organized according to these topics; the first few paragraphs in each chapter are adapted from the (ISC)[2] Common Body of knowledge.

INFORMATICS BACKGROUND KNOWLEDGE

As a prerequisite to the specialized knowledge needed to claim a professional certification in Information Systems Security, it is necessary that candidates be familiar with a number of more general topics in management and information processing. These include:

1. *Computer hardware*, including microcomputers, minicomputers, and mainframe computers. This includes also some knowledge of the history of the development of computers. The requirement is not for a detailed in-depth knowledge, but for enough to support effective research and understanding of issues and practices in use.

2. *Computer software*, as for hardware: a base of knowledge including system life cycle, development methods, controls, and exposures during the processes involved.

3. *Telecommunications concepts*, as for hardware and software: sufficient knowledge to be able to consider effectively such security exposures as in LANs, WANs, common carriers, and so forth. Candidates need to be aware of what roles are played in networks by various components such as FECPs, modems, various types of transmission lines, and similar considerations.

4. *Physical environment and security*: Candidates must be aware of the more common exposures and protective mechanisms.

5. *Data architecture, database management, data access methods*: A knowledge of at least the basic elements of how data are stored is necessary before intelligent security planning can be undertaken. Records management concepts for physical as well as electronic data formats are included here.

6. *Law and legislation*: A basic understanding of the operation of the legal system in the local jurisdiction is needed to serve as support for the more specialized legal knowledge needed for security matters, fraud investigation, and so forth.

7. *Accounting and auditing*: Candidates require exposure to accounting concepts before such security issues as audit trails and proper system and accounting controls can be understood.

8. *Management and organizational issues* must be understood by the candidate in a general sense before the specific impacts of security principles, security policies, personnel management, and similar security issues can be examined.

As an approximation, the level of general knowledge appropriate before certification as an information systems security practitioner would correspond to possession of a CDP, CISA, CSP, FBCS, or ISP designation. Given this base, the following outline expands on the items with which candidates for a computer security certification should possess some familiarity.

It is recognized that few if any professionals will claim detailed knowledge in all of these areas; however, all Certified Information Systems Security Practitioners (CISSP) should at least be aware of all of these topics as areas of relevance to their professional practice.

Overview

Information Systems Security at a corporate management level includes elements described in the following outline. This outline is adapted with permission from the module "Corporate Security Management," in the publication *Information Security Modules*, Dr. Corey D. Schou (ed.), Idaho State University, 1990. The material is the "capstone" of a series of computer security modules developed during and after a workshop at Idaho State University in June, 1988; the module's purpose—bringing together specialized security concerns and presenting a corporate perspective—serves as an excellent introduction to this text.[1]

The 16 sections that follow this Overview expand on the overview from the perspective of the information security professional as contrasted with that of senior management.

I. DEVELOPMENT OF SECURITY PROGRAM

Every corporation has a responsibility to itself, to its clientele, and to society in general, to have good control of its information systems. Internal operations rely on accurate and timely data and information; personal data about employees and clients must be kept confidential; much of the corporation's competitive position may depend on controlling the information it has. All these and other factors imply that a corporate security plan is an important element of proper operation of the corporation.

A. Objectives

A corporation needs a general security policy; the Computer Security Act of 1987 requires that such an effort be made. The policy must be developed and supported by management at all levels of the organization, from the highest to employees at the operational levels. Critical elements of the development process for a corporate security plan, as for any other planning process, include defining objectives, defining policies that will support those objectives, and devising plans that will implement the policies. The responsibility for defining objectives and policies rests at the highest level, the senior management and board of directors; lower levels of management devise plans and implementation strategies; people at all levels must be aware of their individual responsibilities.

Three things are required by the Computer Security Act of 1987:

- Sensitive systems and data must be identified
- Plans for ensuring security and control of such systems must be created
- Personnel training programs must be developed and in place

These factors form a basis for beginning to create a corporate security plan. Other laws such as the Privacy Act of 1974 and the Foreign Corrupt Practices Act impose requirements upon corporations to ensure control and security of their information systems. The most compelling argument from the corporation's standpoint is that confidential data may give a competitive advantage. This advantage may be lost if controls break down, with the consequent possibility of the firm's demise if legal requirements have been violated materially.

---

[1]The publication became available from NIST in late 1991.

Each corporation has its own strategic imperatives; objectives for a corporate security plan will follow from these combined with the guidance offered by applicable legislation.

B. Policies

The board of directors and senior management of a corporation must set strategic objectives for the management of corporate security; policies to guide implementation are also a senior level responsibility. It is the responsibility of the Board and through them management to ensure effective communication of policies. Specific examples of policies will change from company to company, but most will include statements like "This firm is committed to ethical and professional behavior."

C. Connectivity, Corporate Structure, and Security.

1. Connectivity Defined

One of the major thrusts of the development of computers in the past 40 years has been growing ease of use and growing interconnection of systems. Today, major manufacturers are marketing computers that use compatible operating systems from microcomputers to mainframes (UNIX or DOS). PostScript is a language accepted by more and more laser printers and by almost all new typesetting machines: It is becoming a standard language for describing marks on paper. Word processors are available that accept files from IBM-compatible machines into Macintosh computers and vice versa. Networks may span continents or simply connect rooms.

The total phenomenon—compatible operating systems, compatible languages, communications, and so on—refers to "connectivity." This exceeds mere communications. It is a holistic effect that computers simply become more pervasive and easy to use. Connectivity means something more than the pieces: Much as a telephone network, the utility simply is used, with the user unaware of details of the pieces such as DOS, or such as satellite protocols in the case of long-distance telephone.

2. Effect on Corporate Structure

Connectivity of computer systems makes it much easier to support a physically and/or organizationally decentralized form of corporate structure. The principle of moving decision making as close as possible to the point where workers actually accomplish things is easier to implement with connected computers. There are many reasons a decentralized structure may be chosen (see any text on organization structure for examples); connectivity makes it simple.

3. Security Considerations

When planning the basic structure of the organization the Board of Directors and senior management should be aware that there are security risks involved in moving to greater connectivity. Connectivity has security implications. One may purchase a personal computer, write one's own software for everything wanted, and never communicate with another system; this computer is almost totally immune to things like computer viruses. Connectivity refers to a system in which there are communications exposures, exposures due to programs created in an unsecured environment, such as a personal computer, then moved into a formerly secure environment, such as a mainframe, and many other exposures.

Details of the exposures are covered in other chapters. In the context of corporate security management it is important to recognize that increased connectivity implies increased exposure.

D. Plans

Plans to implement security policies depend on the level of management involved. Operations management may be concerned with things such as physical access to a computer room; user department management may be concerned with correct use of application systems; human resources management may be concerned with proper training programs and career path counseling; and so on. Items that must be included somewhere in any effective set of security plans include:

- Access controls (proper identification, authentication of user protection from computer crime)
- Data security program: Most data security programs are based on the fact that a corporation depends on its computer system.
- Data labeling: a method for safeguarding sensitive data to the degree of control necessary for protection desired by the corporation
- Human resources planning: hiring properly qualified people and ensuring good employee-management relations and effective training programs
- Contingency planning for avoidance and recovery from problems
- Understanding of and provision for legal requirements

E. Responsibilities

- Board of directors and senior management: Define corporate security objectives
- Senior management and board of directors: Define policies to achieve corporate security objectives, and ensure that mechanisms for communicating those policies are in place. This may include tying both compensation and promotion of managers to success in meeting the corporate security objectives
- Middle management (*e.g.*, Human resources manager, DP manager, plant management): Define procedures for staff to follow to ensure that the policies are implemented properly
- Employees: Responsible for ensuring that elements under their own control are carried out according to policy and procedures to maintain effective control and security

II. RISK ANALYSIS

The actual development of a plan needs to begin with some form of risk analysis (see Chapter 3.) At the least, sensitive systems and data need to be identified; the value of these systems needs to be estimated; and threats, such as listed below, have to be identified. Without some notion of the risks faced and the value of assets exposed, any security plan really is created in a vacuum and cannot be very effective.

Many kinds of risks can be identified, and these vary depending on individual situations. Some of the ones that will be found in a typical plan include:

- Sabotage (Trojan horse, trap door, time bomb, virus, worm)
- Environmental: fire, flood, power outage, etc.
- Errors (input entry mistakes, poor quality control in system development, etc.)

Many methods have been developed to quantify risk analysis data. Various metrics, including so-called "fuzzy metrics," may be used. The purpose of the metrics and other methods is to reduce inexact opinions to a form that permits adding up exposures and determining a dollar figure.

Formal methods include estimating the probability of loss, multiplying by the value of the exposed asset, and adding these numbers (see Chapter 3, for example). In practice, this approach tends to lead to a sea of numbers that loses all real meaning ("paralysis by analysis"); the ease with which computers produce numbers has not helped this problem.

The two main purposes of risk analysis are:

- Assure that no significant intentional or accidental threat to the information system is overlooked
- Assure that cost-benefit analysis allows management to avoid spending more to control an exposure than the cost of the potential loss

III. CONTINGENCY PLANNING

The key elements of a contingency plan are "protect, detect, and recover."

A contingency plan is a plan based on fact that disaster can happen: The organization must design a plan to accommodate the survival of organizational operations in the event of flood, fire, earthquake, electrical disturbance, or other unexpected events that can disrupt the organization's systems. Risk analysis should offer guidance as to how likely various contingencies are, and what resources to invest in providing such recovery methods as off-site systems, backups and so on. See Chapter 4 for details on contingency planning.

Every effective contingency plan must consider backing up data files!

The most critical things about a contingency plan are that:

- It exists.
- It is communicated to employees.
- It is tested regularly.

IV. LEGAL ISSUES FOR MANAGERS

Managers, particularly more-senior managers, must deal with the external environment. Many problems that have occurred in information systems have led to legislation. Issues that have to be addressed by senior levels of the organization include potential legal problems and requirements (see Chapters 10 and 11 for details). These include the following:

A. Licenses

Application software for microcomputers, and even for large installations, normally is licensed rather than owned. Terms of the license must be followed, or the organization risks serious legal problems.

B. Fraud/Misuse

Fraud is straightforward; corporate security planning must include allowance for possible fraud by employees, contractors, customers, or non-associated people.

Misuse includes penetration by unauthorized users, unauthorized copying, negligence, and similar exposures.

C. Privacy

The organization may have legal or other responsibilities to safeguard data about customers, employees, or others from disclosure.

D. Copyright

Related to licensing, some organizations may need to be very careful about copyright (publishers and educational institutions are obvious candidates here).

E. Trade Secrets

One method open to organizations to protect their confidential data is through trade secret legislation. The corporate security plan should identify circumstances, if any, where trade secrets may be appropriate. Use of trade secret to protect confidentiality imposes certain legal requirements on the organization, and these have to be identified as part of the overall plan.

F. Employee Agreements

Among the issues involved in protecting trade secrets is the need to ensure that employees are aware that they are secrets. This usually is accomplished through an employment contract (plus other administrative actions of the organization's operations). A typical contract includes clauses limiting employee use or disclosure of corporate data after the employee leaves. The corporate security plan needs to address clauses needed in employee contracts.

V. SYSTEM VALIDATION AND VERIFICATION (ACCREDITATION)

Contingency plans must be tested; similarly, it is critical that all aspects of the corporate security plan be tested. Does the plan meet the originally identified needs; does it work as planned. Accreditation occurs when a responsible manager "signs off," that is, attests that the system is in conformance with the plan. The appropriate signing authority will depend on the portion of the plan in question.

VI. INFORMATION SYSTEMS AUDIT

The information systems audit is a way to have an outside entity assess the organization's corporate security (and other information systems) plan. The information systems security auditor should attest that the plan meets accepted standards or that it does not, and in either case should identify strengths and weaknesses.

Information Systems Security

1. Access Control

Access control is the collection of mechanisms that permits the managers of a system to exercise a directing or restraining influence over the behavior, use, and content of the system. This control is employed to achieve the security objectives of the system, such as data integrity and confidentiality.

The knowledge includes:

- Functions, such as:
  - user identification
  - password creation and administration
  - authentication (based upon knowledge, tokens, biometrics or behavior)
  - control
  - administration
  - logs and journals
  - alarms, signals, reports

- Implementations, to include two or more systems (for example, RACF, ACF-2, TOP-SECRET)
- Good practices, for example:
  - rule of least privilege
  - segregation of incompatible functions and responsibilities
  - ownership
  - accountability
  - reconciliation and other controls

- Systems and environments

1.1 OWNERSHIP, ACCOUNTABILITY, AND CONTROLS

1.1.1 Ownership and Custodianship of Data

The notions of ownership and custody of data, although fairly simple, are basic to consideration of access control and accounting controls.

Two definitions related to ownership of data follow:

Owner of data

1. The statutory authority responsible for a particular type or category of information or the individual or organization responsible for the actual data contained therein. (DODD 5200.28)
2. The individual or group that has responsibility for specific data types and that is charged with the communication of the need for certain security-related handling procedures to both the users and custodians of this data. (WB)

The first, from Department of Defense regulations, is the more general. The second concentrates more specifically on security aspects, and includes the responsibility for communicating information about the security status of the data.

In each definition, a phrase like "individual or organization" is used. This is where ownership can become complex: As data move through an organization and are altered or manipulated, ownership may change. This is primarily a procedural matter and outside the scope of technical security measures. However, it is essential that ownership of data or information be clear in order to assign accountability.

When data are entrusted to others for processing, the issue of custodianship of data becomes a key procedural mater. Although ownership may not change through a series of processing steps (for example, processing a payroll run), custodianship frequently changes very often. The custodian of data has a responsibility to the owner to ensure continued integrity and security of the data.

Custodian of Data

The individual or group that has been entrusted with the possession of, and responsibility for, the security of specified data. (WB)

1.1.2 Accountability

Again we present two definitions of accountability. The first is more general and might apply to processes in operating systems as well as to persons. The second, again from Department of Defense regulations, concentrates on people.

Accountability

1. The property that ensures that the actions of an entity may be traced uniquely to the entity. (ISO 7498-2)
2. The property which enables activities on an ADP system to be traced to individuals who can then be held responsible for their activities. (DOE 5636.2A)

1.1.3 Reconciliation and Other Controls

This sub-section is inserted to maintain consistency with the (ISC)[2] Common Body of Knowledge. Topics of reconciliation and other controls are addressed in Chapter 12. Segregation of incompatible functions and responsibilities is also addressed in Chapter 12.

1.1.4 Rule of Least Privilege

In the design of security systems, both technical and procedural, the rule of least privilege is basic.

Least Privilege

This principle requires that each subject be granted the most restrictive set of privileges needed for the performance of authorized tasks. The application of this principle limits the damage that can result from accident, error, or unauthorized use. (NCSC-WA-001-85; CSC-STD-001-83)

1.2 USER AUTHENTICATION AND PASSWORD MANAGEMENT

Identification of an authorized user is done by means of some name or equivalent known to the system. The issue of how to ensure that someone identifying him or herself to the system actually is the user identified is *authentication*. Authentication is done by means of three standard dimensions: something the user *knows* (such as a password or PIN); something the user *holds* (such as a key or an identification card); or some *characteristic* that applies only to the authorized user (fingerprints, or movement patterns while writing, for example).[1]

Authentication may be defined[2] as:

A positive identification, with a degree of certainty sufficient for permitting certain rights or privileges to the person or thing positively identified. (DCID 1/16-1; DCID 1/16-1, Sup.)

Each of the dimensions is examined below. Combining more than one dimension significantly increases the likelihood of correct authentication in much the same way that using different protection methods in various layers of protection improves overall security.

1.2.1 Knowledge-Based Authentication

The most common method of authentication is use of something that the user knows, and only the user knows. The most common examples are passwords and the related Personal Identification Number (PIN). The principle is that the valid user knows the password or PIN and no other person does; therefore, a correct password or PIN is an authentication.

A variation on the use of passwords is to use the results of mathematical calculations, or memorized sentences, or similar tactics. The virtue is that the degree of certainty increases, mostly because there are more possible sentences, for example, than there are, say, six-character passwords.

The primary failure of knowledge-based authentication is the disclosure of the knowledge. As discussed in section 1.2.4, people allowed to choose their own passwords often choose easily guessed passwords; people who must memorize nonsense sentences, phrases, or even words tend to write them down and lose the written copy; and so forth. In any security situation, passwords are a very weak authentication mechanism.

1.2.2 Token-Based Authentication

One solution to the problem of password management is to add a second authenticator: a token of some sort. This may be a key that unlocks a terminal or computer, a "key card" containing various kinds of information stored magnetically, or even a "smart card" that forms part of the hardware itself. Thus, something that one possesses is an authenticator.

Use of such a token in combination with another authentication mechanism improves security. Without other mechanisms, tokens are subject to loss and, like passwords, can be used by anyone who holds them.

1.2.3 Characteristic-Based Authentication

A solution to the problem posed by things-known and things-held—that whoever knows or holds them will be authenticated, whether properly or not—is to use some characteristic possessed by the valid user and not by any possible imitator.

---

[1]The discussion following is in terms of computer information systems. Those with a *penchant* for spy novels will recognize many of the same authentication methods in use in non-computer-related situations, such as passwords and identification phrases to be given on challenge by a guard or to identify a fellow espionage agent, tokens like the famous "cricket" noisemakers used during the Normandy invasion, and biometrics like fingerprints and photographs.

[2]Authentication also has a specific meaning in the context of data transmission; see Chapter 2 for treatment of this aspect.

The general term for the field involving use of characteristics for authentication is biometrics, which may be defined as:

The use of specific quantities that reflect unique personal characteristics (such as a fingerprint, an eye blood vessel print, or a voice print) to validate the identity of users. (WB)

A significant problem in biometric authentication is to set criteria tight enough to deny access to those without the proper characteristic match, yet allow access to those who should be authenticated. The problem may be clear if one considers voice identification. A person's voice patterns vary depending on things like illness (a cold or influenza), various kinds of stress, and so forth. It is difficult or impossible to distinguish between, for example, stress caused by shortness of breath (running in from a rainstorm for instance) and stress caused by being in a hostage situation and under threat. Similar problems limit the use of such biometrics as the time pattern of strokes on a keyboard.

There are other problems with biometric systems. For example, in order to examine a retinal blood vessel pattern the eye must be pressed against a reader of some sort; transmission of diseases of the eye can be a problem with this sort of system. It may be important that recognition systems respond quickly, which is difficult with complex pattern matching such as fingerprint, voice or retina-print authentication. Rapid response often is correlated with a high level of false positives or false negatives.

Biometric methods used in authentication include manual or computerized recognition of:

- fingerprints
- retina prints (patterns of blood vessels at the back of any eye)
- combinations of hand measurements such as length of fingers and width of palms (geometric characteristics)
- voice patterns
- timing patterns of keystrokes on a terminal
- photographs
- time of day or schedule

1.2.4 Passwords

One of the easiest and most effective access control methods (in non-critical situations) is passwords. The user is assigned an identification and then is assigned or creates a password; the system will not allow log-on, file access, or access to password-protected resources, without the correct identification and password. Most multi-user systems have this capability. Often it is not used or is used improperly.

1.2.4.1 General Discussion

Some general rules about passwords should be obvious but are often violated:

- Do not allow repeated attempts. Disconnect after some small number of unsuccessful tries.
- Log unsuccessful sign-on attempts and system disconnections.
- Make sure someone reviews the log and follows up on patterns.

- Never write down a password and account together, never tape a password to a terminal, to the phone list on a desk "pull-out shelf," in a file folder labeled "passwords," or in any other obvious place.
- Select unusual passwords that are several characters long; preferably at least eight characters. Use mixed alphabetic and numeric data for passwords to make them harder to guess. (*Any* actual word [in any language] may be in a spelling dictionary, and a microcomputer can be programmed to try using words from such a dictionary as password guesses.) Do not use the user identification account number or personal names.
- Change passwords frequently.
- Passwords should be easy to remember but hard to guess correctly.
- Never tell anyone else your password; change it immediately after the other's use if there is a legitimate need to tell someone else.
- Do not allow others to watch while you key in a password.
- The system should not display the password; the screen should display nothing at all or overstrike characters or some other means to be sure the identification is not visible.
- Job streams that are not stored in a secure manner should not contain sign-on information. This applies particularly to personal computers, where it is common to store such data in "macros" so the user presses only one key for commonly accessed services. (It once was common to see card decks containing a sign-on card, with identification and password information, stored in a publicly accessible area along with the output from the run; sign-on information in macros or scripts is a more modern equivalent.)
- Passwords assigned to users must be sent via secure transmission methods.
- Password tables should be encrypted.

Passwords are convenient, relatively cheap ways to improve on system access security, when used properly. In practice, their use helps, but people defeat the system by carelessness or improper use in all too many instances. The organizational climate should stress proper use of passwords, and reminders need to be frequent.

Passwords may be chosen in any of a number of ways. Today, most systems allow users to choose their own. If the user chooses the password, it should be chosen to be unusual. Lists with titles like "The One Hundred Most Common Passwords" are published in many places; reproducing such a list and posting it may discourage users from trying their own "unique" ideas. One method that yields reasonably good passwords that are hard to guess, is:

1. Choose two words or numbers that are easy to remember.
2. Using some rule, combine them. One possible rule is to use alternate letters.

Using this method, one might select, say "1066" (or some other easily remembered date) and "ABCD." The resulting password would be A1B0C6D6, which is much less obvious than either of the easily remembered sequences. Other sequences—for instance, height and maternal grandmothers' maiden initials—may serve the need to be easily remembered but create a good password when combined.

In principle, passwords created by the system using a random number generator are more secure; in practice, people are less likely to remember nonsense, and thus more likely to write down the password. The same applies to long passwords: the longer, the more theoretically secure but the more difficult to remember. The method described in the previous paragraph has the virtue that the resulting password looks like nonsense and is hard to guess, but the components and combining rule are easy for the user to remember; thus the user is less likely to write it down.

If the system generates a password, it must be communicated to the user somehow. The transmission channel is subject to compromise, from human error (lost mail) to eavesdropping through communication taps. Whether using system-generated passwords is a good idea depends on the circumstances. In this analysis, issues related to password generation and management are nearly identical to key generation and management in an encryption system. Sections 2.2 and 2.3 examine this area in more detail.

1.2.4.2 *Passwords and Combinatorial Mathematics*

The selection of a password involves several issues. Ease of remembering is one. Length (time) of validity is another. The basic mathematics of password choice is that of combinatorial mathematics.

For the following discussion,[3] assume the following variable definitions:

A is the number of characters in the alphabet used to generate passwords

G is the total number of guesses that can be made during the lifetime of the password
  $(G = R \times L)$

L is the maximum lifetime that a password is a valid authenticator

M is the password length

P is the probability that a password can be guessed within its lifetime (without limits on the number of guesses)

R is the number of guesses possible per unit of time

S is the password space (the total number of unique passwords possible with a given algorithm)

For most real-world situations, the maximum alphabet is that recognized by a computer, less any characters reserved for control sequences. This may be about 32 symbols to about 224 symbols. Restricting the alphabet to the English alphabet of 26 symbols severely limits the number of passwords. The number is further limited by a restriction that no password be found in any spelling dictionary. Therefore, so-called "special characters" should be used within passwords.

Password Space

The number of unique passwords possible is:

$$S = A^M$$

This number is a maximum assuming random generation. If an algorithm generates non-randomly, the maximum number of *M*-character passwords possible from an alphabet of *A* characters may be smaller.

The password space expands exponentially when the alphabet increases; therefore, it is of considerable advantage to use a larger alphabet.

Guessing Passwords

---

[3]Adapted from *Department of Defense Password Management Guideline*, CSC-STD-002-85, April 12, 1985.

The probability of guessing a password during its lifetime, assuming continuous guessing over time, is:[4]

$$P = (L \times R) / S = G / S$$

This allows derivation of the necessary password space to ensure a certain maximum probability of guessing a password:

$$S = G / P$$

Given a desired probability, one may vary the number of guesses per unit of time R ($G = L \times R$) or the length L to determine the necessary space.

Password Length

The length needed for the password is given by the formula:

$$M = (\log S) / (\log A)$$

(M is rounded up to the nearest whole number to finalize the password length.)

1.2.4.3 One-Time Passwords

In a security situation, passwords, pass phrases, and so forth cannot be considered reliable authenticators. The essential problem is that when establishing a link to a system, one must enter (in cleartext[5]) an identification and a password; this then must be processed. While in transit, the cleartext identification plus password is available for eavesdropping. Even if the work station is an intelligent station and performs encryption at the local site, an encrypted valid authenticator is available for eavesdropping[6] and later spoofing.[7]

One solution to the eavesdropping problem is a "one-time password" (actually in current implementations a variation of the token mechanism). It is defined:

> One-time passwords [are] those that are changed after each use [and] are useful when the password is not adequately protected from compromise during log-in (*e.g.*, the communication line is suspected of being tapped). (FIPS PUB 112)

The principle is that a password is valid only one time and never again (subject to random number statistics within the password space). To implement such a mechanism, a token is provided to the user; the token generates a password in synchrony with the remote site, and the two must match to ensure authentication. One current instance of such synchronization involves a token with a chip that includes a clock; the clock is synchronized with the primary system and the token and the system generate a password based on the time. A similar scheme in another implementation uses a token whose chip communicates with the primary system to ensure synchrony. This second scheme is somewhat less secure, as there is a possibility of compromise in the communication channel.

---

[4]The derivation of this equation is based on combinatorial mathematics, specifically the formula $_nC_r = (n-1)C(r-1) + (n-1)C_r$. Details are in Appendix F of the DoD guideline CSC-STD-002-85, or in any book on probability and statistics.

[5]Cleartext is the normal language you would type in. It is defined more precisely in Chapter 2.

[6]The local station could perform all validation, but it still must be identified to the remote station and the problem continues with the same logical form if a different physical form.

[7]*Spoofing* here is recording the encrypted material and then later playing it back, to try to masquerade as the legitimate user. More precise definitions of spoofing, masquerade, and similar terms are in Chapter 7 and Appendix B.

This solution is superficially identical to the "smart card" solution referred to above, with one important difference: cost. A "smart card" or key card solution would require a card reader for every potential work station, thus either imposing enormous costs on organizations, or severely limiting the work stations available to the user. Neither is desirable in an environment where the value-added feature of connectivity can exceed the value of data at *any* single locus. A token that generates a password in synchrony with the remote site involves a cost once per user, and then once at the local site, rather than a cost once per potential work station.

1.2.4.4 Password Encryption

All passwords should be encrypted once they are entered in cleartext form by the user. This includes any storage in system tables, and before any data transmission. Obviously, this may not be feasible; for example, connecting to a remote computer includes sending cleartext identification and password signals to the processor, unless there is on-site authentication ("intelligent terminal"). Ideally, the encryption should be one-way and mathematically impossible to reverse, so that cleartext passwords cannot be derived from a table of encrypted passwords.

Encryption is only partial protection. Although the password table may be encrypted, a penetration attempt may be made using encrypted versions of spelling dictionaries, lists of common passwords, and so forth. Such attacks have been successful, particularly when done by means of copying the encrypted password table and then attempting access using the results in the place of a "spelling dictionary." Any link involving a communications channel is subject to eavesdropping (particularly in networks[8]); any authentication information on such a link, whether encrypted or not, may be copied and used in a spoofing attack, as noted in the previous section.

1.3 ACCESS CONTROL ADMINISTRATION

The following checklist, reproduced with permission from ISSA, covers most of the issues relevant in the administration of access control.

This material is abstracted from a memo distributed at the November 13, 1985, chapter meeting of the Information System Security Association's (ISSA) Special Interest Group (SIG) on Access Control Systems Administration. The coordinator was Charles Cresson Wood.

Password-Based Computer Access Control Systems; Policies, Procedures, Standards and Related Control Ideas

This paper concisely lists policies, procedures, and related control ideas germane to the successful installation and administration of RACF, ACF-2, VMSECURE, TOP SECRET and related access control packages. Control ideas are described in a generic fashion, and are meant to be applicable to all access control packages. Nevertheless, these control ideas may be inapplicable to specific operating environments due to Access Control Program (ACP) features implemented/available, nature of the business controlled, overlap with already-installed controls, etc. This material is not comprehensive, but is intended to be of value to those individuals charged with ACP administration.

The SIG decided to approach the topic assuming the parties involved had already decided that their organization needs a password-based access control system. Thus, cost/benefit analysis

---

[8]*See* the discussions in Chapters 2 and 8

of the pros/cons of ACPs, the selection of one ACP over others, and the associated management approval of the selected ACP were outside the scope of this work.

The scope of this paper and the interests of the SIG are defined by the areas appearing in the following list. Each of the subsequently presented controls is a member of one of these categories.

ACP Control Categories

1.   Prerequisites to the successful implementation of an ACP
2.   Sources of training for administrators and users
3.   Log review, monitoring events, and preparing reports
4.   Accounts administration (opening, closing, transfers, suspensions, temporary accounts, etc.)
5.   System design considerations

Section 1: Prerequisites to the Successful Implementation of an ACP

1.   Use unique user-IDs and passwords for every user (including ACP administrators and, in some cases, computers and processes).
2.   Establish and enforce standard dataset/system-resource naming conventions (facilitates use of ACP rules).
3.   Document objectives for the installation of an ACP, including threats to be addressed.
4.   Provide a detailed project plan including realistic estimates of required resources and management approval of same.
5.   Identify the specific person(s) responsible for the effort.
6.   Be sure to prepare a system resource risk ranking and phase-in plan.
7.   List the resources that will be protected (terminals, CICS transactions, etc.).
8.   Define the target environment and how the ACP fits in with other security measures.
9.   Produce a shift in systems security perspectives resulting in support from top management and users.
10. Establish data-sensitivity classification standards (and perhaps data-criticality classification standards as well) and indicate how they will be used with the ACP.
11. Prohibit passwords from being stored as terminal function keys or stored on disks with auto-log-in programs.
12. Assume that both dial-up and hard-wired lines will be used, even if only hard-wired lines are currently employed.
13. Advertise the security approach provided by the ACP and the fact that a genuine service will be delivered.
14. Severely restrict the use of powerful systems utilities that can overcome or circumvent the ACP.
15. Do not make exceptions for certain user groups such as vendor maintenance personnel and systems programmers (or at least do so with great restraint and suspicion).
16. Make sure that a production program change control procedure is installed and working effectively.
17. Keep focusing on the big picture and don't get bogged down in technical details.
18. Make sure that data owners/custodians/users are identified and acquainted with their ACP-related responsibilities.

Section 2: Sources of Training for Administrators and Users

For Administrators:

1. Manuals
2. Vendor-supplied classes
3. Testing the ACP via prototype applications
4. User groups
5. Newsletters
6. Professional Associations
7. Consultants
8. Installing the system in "warn mode" only (without actually locking anyone out of access to a resource) and monitoring the results

For Users:

1. User guides (includes a definition of user responsibilities
2. Classes held by data security administrator
3. On-line manuals (do not reveal info that might be an undue exposure)
4. Videotaped classes (duration of 10 minutes or thereabouts recommended)
5. Reference cards
6. Security sections in user manual/guide
7. Policies, procedures, guidelines in the security manual and other documents
8. Non-disclosure agreement signed by employees when they are hired
9. User agreements specifying security responsibilities and procedures

Section 3: Reviewing Logs, Monitoring Systems Security Relevant Events, and Preparing Reports

1. On a timely (daily) basis, review reports and promptly follow-up on any suspicious or significant security-relevant events.
2. Define who will review which ACP reports; make specific individuals accountable for taking action on significant items in these reports.
3. Clearly define to users what constitutes an ACP security violation and what corresponding penalties exist.
4. Whenever possible, (perhaps write programs to be able to) use summaries and condensations of activity, rather than having to wade through long listings.
5. Protect logs so that it is extremely difficult to tamper with or destroy them.
6. Make a hard copy of the security log in addition to a disk or tape copy; if there is some dispute about log alterations, the hard copy may be of assistance.
7. Among the data to log should be: successful activity, changes in rules (changes in ID status, in profiles, etc.), unsuccessful attempts, use of remote diagnostic capabilities, use of debugging tools, full trace of certain IDs or types of IDs, and log-in via dial-up lines.
8. Don't log anything the ACP administrator does not intend to respond to or use.
9. Decide which ACP reports should be kept secret (contents and perhaps even existence).
10. Prepare a policy regarding the use of ACP logs for non-access-control activities that might entail an invasion of privacy or some other abuse (*e.g.,* employee performance measurement, punctuality checking, etc.).

Section 4: Accounts Administration

1. Establish a (preferably automated) connection with the personnel application system(s) to promptly and automatically determine when people terminate and/or change responsibilities.

2. Provide a mechanism that notifies ACP administrative staff of user personnel suspensions and that triggers user-ID suspension.

3. Don't rock the boat too much when installing an ACP. Cut-over systems programming IDs first, applications programming IDs next, and then other users' IDs. Likewise, implement controls over production datasets first, then production applications, and then operating system datasets. (Use a phased approach.)

4. Establish a hierarchy of security administration personnel and related IDs so that access privileges and related responsibilities can be delegated as may be necessary in the event of an emergency.

5. Automate the process of making ACP-related data access rules by reviewing existing JCL and procedure libraries.

6. If possible, group user-IDs together so that certain rules can be applied across the board, saving administration time and decreasing the probability of error.

7. To the extent possible, let data owners, custodians, and users decide what systems resources should be protected.

8. When a user ID is cancelled or suspended, make sure involved datasets are not removed/erased but are appropriately handled (create a form that allows DP to be notified of appropriate handling procedures).

9. Provide the facility for ACP administrator to cancel a pending job, a session, as well as an ID, as might be needed to combat hackers.

10. Define ID suspension criteria such as: number of log-in attempts exceeds a certain threshold, user did not change password within certain time frame, user attempted to access resources not authorized for him/her, dormant account, etc.

11. Avoid sabotage of administrator accounts by disabling the suspension of these accounts in response to a certain number of incorrect log-in attempts. Provide option for alarms and/or temporary suspension of an ID (*e.g.*, for 15 minutes) while such an attack is in progress.

12. Provide 24-hour backup technical coverage or other procedures such as beeper notification so that quick technical response is available. (Assumes 24-hour-a-day computer operation).

13. Create a master ACP database that reflects privileges on all machines controlled by a certain ACP, to prevent profile updates from having to be made on each machine.

14. Make sure that all managers are familiar with and comply with procedures to be used for duress terminations (such as immediate revocation of user IDs).

15. Management should explicitly communicate to systems programmers that the ACP installation and maintenance is a high priority, and that they should treat it accordingly; in too many shops, it is given insufficient systems programming resources and attention.

16. Establish a standard procedure for determining that a telephone request for a password comes from the user who is entitled to know the password; a question about the user's mother's maiden name (also appearing on the account request form) may suffice.

17. Establish a policy to verify the signature on an account request form by either having someone who is familiar with the approving manager's signature review the form, or call the manager to make sure the account should be initialized.

18. When protecting production jobs, make sure that any operators do not have the privileges assigned to the job that is executing, and make sure that the operator(s) don't have access to the jobs' password(s). Operator in this case refers to both the person running the machine and any employees involved in setting up or submitting the production JCL.

19. ACP administrators should not be able to gain access to any passwords (except their own), although they may be able to issue new user-IDs/passwords.

20. Bring the ACP up on a test system before it is applied to a production system; this is particularly easy to do in those environments where different machines are used for these operating environments.

21. If circumstances (such as very high turnover) indicate that management is not willing to have one user-ID/password for each individual use, then special shared/restricted-privilege IDs may be used in the event that management agrees to take responsibility for abuses.

22. There should be a checklist for terminating employees to make sure that IDs are disabled, badges and keys returned, etc.

23. A policy should be adopted in which the user-ID/password combination is used as the sole basis for privilege checking (as opposed to user identification) on all machines; the job name or some other identifier should not be used for this purpose. Biometrics, magnetic cards, and other user identification approaches could act in conjunction with the user-ID/password to identify users.

24. A policy regarding the level of management approval necessary for the granting of a user-ID and privileges should be established, and managers should not be permitted to authorize themselves in this process.

25. There should be an express process for granting user-IDs under special rush circumstances; such IDs should be temporary, expire in a short while, and the users should be required to go through a regular request procedure; all activity with these temporary IDs should be thoroughly logged.

26. A group of special temporary IDs established in advance for the use of operators, systems programmers, and application developers should be established; the privileges of these IDs should be defined well in advance so that there need not be undue privilege determination delays and so that mistakes are not made in the wake of an emergency (don't let the use of such IDs become a usual practice).

27. Special procedures should be established in the event that the ACP is out of commission; these procedures should include database restoration, fail-safe/fail-soft routines, denial of certain privileges while the ACP is not available. Such procedures and their impacts should be thoroughly studied in advance of their use.

28. ACP administration staff should be part of the disaster recovery planning effort.

29. A specific policy regarding the confidentiality of user-IDs should be established. Should they be public easy-to-remember and used for electronic message (mail) systems, or should they be confidential and difficult to guess? If confidential, electronic mail can be sent to the person's name, and a systems table can translate that into a user-ID.

Section 5: System Design Considerations

1. Any password that is new or reset by the ACP administrator should expire upon first use by the user, forcing him/her to enter a new password.

2. Password construction standards should be established and machine-enforced. These should include repeated password disallowed, change of password required at certain intervals, no proper words in dictionary, no readily identifiable personal data (*e.g.*, license plate number), require multiple words all run together, minimum number of characters, no repeating characters (*e.g.*, AAAA etc.). [See FIPS Pub. 112 - Password Usage]

3. Passwords should not be displayed in readable form (echo-off on CRT screens, overstrike characters on hard copy, etc).

4. Passwords should always be encrypted in storage, and when a password is provided by a user, that password should be encrypted and then matched to a value on file.

5. Although some ACPs don't support it, certain users should be locked into a certain mode of interaction with the machine. This may be implemented via an auto-execute routine or C-lists under TSO that, for instance, keeps such users in a particular application.

6. Some modification to systems utilities may be required and should be investigated prior to ACP installation. For instance, IBM's MVS ASM2, a DASD management utility used to archive/scratch datasets, needs to be modified to restore RACF profiles.

7. If possible, use "standard vanilla" (unmodified) operating system on the target machine, otherwise systems programming may be very busy evaluating vendor operating system updates and trying to decide which of these enhancements are consistent with in-house code and should accordingly be installed.

8. As a goal to work towards, each user should have only one user-ID for all systems at a firm, and this ID should be used throughout a network.

9. Although not yet done at many firms, procedures to consistently and securely handle single users' access to several machines and the secure movement of data among these machines needs to be addressed.

10. Although not done at most firms, policies and procedures need to consistently handle data whatever machine it resides upon (based upon its sensitivity and perhaps criticality as well). This problem is made worse by the fact that few microcomputers and minicomputers are protected by an ACP.

11. Install a two-tier network access scheme whereby the first level checks to see which computers the user will be permitted to connect with, and the second level checks privileges on a particular host to which he/she has been connected.

12. To facilitate administration, user-IDs should be the same across all machines if the same users are involved (standards for user-ID construction are needed).

13. To handle concurrent log-ons, a message for all users logging onto an account already in use which informs them of the other uses of the ID; this message should also go to the user who was already logged-on.

14. Concurrent log-ons from geographically separate locations should be prohibited (same room OK as this is probably the same user); this can only be supported if the system is aware of the terminal locations (many are not, particularly if dial-up lines are used without terminal IDs).

15. To spot unauthorized usage, the user should receive at log-on time a message indicating the last session's log-out time, the duration of the session, the involved network node, and related particulars.

1.4 COMPUTER ACCESS CONTROL SOFTWARE

One way to implement access control in computer systems is to use access control software designed for the purpose. Three general points are significant:

- Unless the operating system is inherently secure (see Chapter 7), no access control package can ensure security.
- The commercial packages available all require modifications to operating system software during installation.
- Access control *per se* does not improve control of data *integrity*.[9]

The implication of the first two points is that adding an access control package will not improve security of a poorly-designed operating system. It probably will *decrease* security because it adds complexity and requires changes that are subject to human error. The third point emphasizes that access control is not the same as data integrity control. Integrity normally is not a concern of access control software.

Nevertheless, since these packages do offer at least an appearance of increased security, and since they do not require massive changes such as replacing the operating system with a secure system, they are popular. In some cases, "native" operating systems offer little or no access control capability, so the appearance of improved security sometimes may be a reality. Collectively, ACF-2, RACF, Top Secret, and VMSECURE have been installed on several thousand IBM systems worldwide.[10]

The form of access control defined in the Trusted Computing Base series (the "rainbow series," Trusted Computer System Evaluation Criteria [TCSEC]) is covered in some detail in Chapter 7 and elsewhere as appropriate. This is a U.S. government standard, particularly Department of Defense. It is being used as a guideline for other U.S. government departments as the Computer Security Act of 1987 exerts more influence on government operations. As more government operations use this model for a reference, commercial organizations dealing with U.S. government agencies are being encouraged strongly to meet the TCSEC guidelines. This is driving changes in the commercial market, and the packages outlined in the following subsections are changing rapidly. Current comparisons are published from time to time. The Stuart Henderson articles in the *Computer Security Journal* in 1989 are a recent example.

The access control software packages described in the following are currently commercially available packages. In various implementations, some are certified under the TCSEC as high as C2 or B1.

1.4.1 IBM Mainframe Systems

A list of commonly seen access control packages on IBM mainframe systems would include:

- ACF-2 (Computer Associates International, Garden City, NJ)
- Omniguard (OnLine Software International, Fort Lee, NJ)
- RACF (IBM Corporation, White Plains, NY)
- Top Secret (Computer Associates)
- VMSECURE (Systems Center, Reston, VA)

---

[9]Dr. F. Cohen in his Ph.D. thesis reports experiments proving that virus code will bypass access control software in a short time, even with correct implementations of some of the access control packages outlined below: an *integrity* issue.

[10]Precise data are impossible, as some vendors will not release data about numbers of installations.

This list of access control software packages is for IBM systems. Access control packages are most common for IBM systems for several reasons. Some are:

- There are many IBM installations.
- Some early versions of IBM operating systems were weak in the area of access control, and an add-on package was needed.
- Software bundling practices often meant that access control was not included with the basic operating system.
- More recent operating systems, especially for minicomputers and networks (see 1.4.2 below), have been designed from the start with security as a consideration, and there is less need for add-on packages in newer systems.

1.4.1.1 General Descriptions

All of these access control packages function around three primitives: entities, requests for access, and resources. Typically, tables are maintained that list defined entities, the types of access permitted, and the resources that may be accessed. An "entity" in this sense may be a user, a specific input device, a program, a process in the computer, or any other definable thing that can request resources. A "resource" is some capability provided by the computer or some entity to which access is desired. This could include output capabilities, print spools, any dataset, system utility programs, or anything else defined by the installer of the security software. An "access" could be an attempt to read from or write to a dataset, execute a load module, or any other action typical of the operation of a program.

A simple scheme might define tables of:

- users
- types of access in terms such as read, write, scratch, execute, link/load, copy or delete
- resources such as datasets, load modules, source code, executable programs, input or output capabilities

A typical package implementing these simple tables would then have another set of tables that defines which types of access to which resources are available to which users, and any password or other control mechanisms that must be met to grant the accesses. These tables typically are stored as some form of disk dataset. (VMSECURE uses the VM system facilities and stores things in a different fashion, due to the virtual machine concept of the operating system design.)

In practice, complex operating systems and access control software include many methods of controlling such activities. The basic principles all are definable in terms of the four sets of tables.

Clearly, the tables defining users and so forth are sensitive. A system penetrator could masquerade as a legitimate user if the penetrator could read the tables, or particularly if the penetrator could change any information. Encryption schemes are used by all packages to minimize this risk. Further, failures occur; if the tables are lost due to hardware or software problems, it must be possible to re-create them quickly or the system will be unusable.

All of the packages noted above have extensive provisions for protection of the tables and for recovery in the case of problems.

1.4.1.2 Changes to Operating System Software

Each of these packages must be installed in such a way that system resource requests are channelled through the security software before the operating system grants the request. This involves "patches," changes to parts of the operating system. Some of the packages can install these patches automatically; some require manual intervention. All permit manual intervention. Most also provide the ability to define user exits. For example, random password generation is not provided by all packages; however, all packages permit a user exit that can link into a password-provider of the organization's choice. Similarly, some packages allow user exits to permit enforcement of customized (generally more stringent) controls in addition to the normal controls provided by the access control software.

1.4.1.3 Strengths of Access Control Software Packages

One of the strengths of the access control software packages is provision of relatively easy-to-use means to add, alter, and delete users and resources. This may be done by defining groups of users or in several other ways. Changes to capabilities can be applied to many users with simple commands affecting groups. Some of the packages permit the use of "wild card" characters, so that a single command may affect, for example, all users whose IDs contain the characters "AC."[11] Thus, the administrative load of managing a system with thousands of users and keeping security status current is significantly lessened.

Another valuable capability of these packages is report generation. Each package provides abilities to define custom reports and each package provides numerous standard reports. Using these reports, the security administrator can determine the status of users, unusual requests that may represent penetration attempts, and so forth. Some of the packages have the capability of "real-time" reporting, so that a penetration attempt may be monitored as it is happening.

1.4.1.4 Caveats

Although these access control software packages all are subject to the basic principle that one cannot secure an insecure system by adding access control, more pragmatic concerns commonly limit the effectiveness of security provided. These are basically organizational and procedural issues, and must be addressed as a management problem rather than a technical problem.

Each system must be installed, typically in a weak mode at first. After appropriate testing and experience, stronger features are implemented as appropriate. It is common to observe systems where features that were needed during the testing phase are retained during the supposedly more secure operational phase. Often, privileges are retained due to organizational position rather than the principle of least privilege. Also, it is common for users to resist the decrease in ease-of-use of the system as more complete controls are applied. Clearly, solutions to such problems lie in the realm of education and management, rather than technical areas.

There is reason for caution about TCSEC classes claimed by these access control software packages. There have been marketing claims by some vendors that their package has been *submitted* for certification at some level. Level C2 is about the highest that has found commercial acceptance; higher levels begin to impose severe constraints on how non-military organizations usually want to use their information system resources. Thus, certification at one level does not imply suitability for a specific organization. Further, certifications at a given level are for an exact implementation, both of the access control software package and of the operating system on

---

[11]Some packages explicitly do not provide wild card facilities, under the philosophy that such features are a security exposure whose benefits are smaller than the increased risks.

which it is installed, and on the management of that combination. Other versions of the same operating system or access control software would have to be evaluated separately and might not achieve the same rating. Any changes to the operating system, even seemingly minor maintenance upgrades, may invalidate the classification, unless the changed combination of operating system, access control software, and management are re-evaluated.

1.4.2 UNIX, VAX, Network Software

Few comprehensive access control software packages exist for minicomputers. To some extent, this is related to typical use in environments where security is not a major concern (such as academic environments). More important, minicomputer operating systems were developed after mainframe systems had illustrated the need for security. Typical minicomputer systems provide fairly good access control capabilities as part of the basic operating system; add-ons simply aren't needed. For example, VAX VMS is similar to IBM's VM/CMS, partly due to the VAX architecture and partly due to the learning curve noted.[12]

Some access control packages exist for microcomputers. Microcomputers inherently are not secure; they were designed as single-user machines and access control was not a design consideration. When microcomputers are in an environment that involves several people sharing the same machine, access control becomes an issue. Various encryption methods can offer some amelioration of a basically intractable problem, but stand-alone microcomputers are and will remain basically non-secure computing environments.

When microcomputers are linked into networks, the security problem begins to resemble that of mainframes. Network software has built-in security capabilities, typically implemented along much the same lines as one of the access control software packages outlined above. Examples include Novell Netware and Banyan Vines. Again, since access control is built-in, few automated packages are commercially available. Security software for networks tends to concentrate on unfulfilled needs, such as system performance monitoring.

UNIX can be considered an "oddball" due to the variety of UNIX versions, the centrality of the *superuser* concept, and typical environments where UNIX is used.

UNIX was developed originally to support on-line software (particularly operating system and compiler) development. It excels at linking many people together in this kind of development environment. However, UNIX is decades old, and several variations have proliferated. As a generalization, UNIX systems are not secure.

UNIX is becoming more widely accepted in environments that differ from the original design concepts, for example in the commercial world. To a great extent, this is due to a combination of its superb handling of networks and the reasonably large base of application software available. Efforts are underway to standardize on one version of UNIX and integrate it with the ISO/OSI standards. The use of UNIX in commercial and other situations where security needs exceed those of academic or development environments has generated a demand for secure UNIX. Variations of UNIX that have been certified C2 exist, and at least one variation has been submitted for B1 certification. Since the superuser capability is both a major part of the UNIX philoso-

---

[12]As any computing science student can attest, VAX VMS and UNIX are well-supplied with security holes as well as built-in capabilities. As security incidents increase, academic system managers are changing what has been a rather lackadaisical approach to security. However, in a learning environment some restrictions that might be acceptable in business are serious constraints on the basic purpose of the environment.

phy and a significant security problem, such certified variations operate quite differently than the more popular variations of UNIX. There are compatibility problems, and it is debatable whether these variations can be called UNIX in any real sense.

An entire book could be devoted to UNIX security, and an entire book has been. Garfinkel and Spafford's book *Practical UNIX Security* is an excellent reference.

REFERENCES

Bell, D. E., and L. J. La Padula, "Secure Computer Systems: Unified Exposition and MULTICS Interpretation," MTR-2997, rev. 1, Mitre Corporation, Bedford, MA, November, 1973-June, 1974 vols. I-III.

Blanc, Robert P., Ed., "An Analysis of Computer Security Safeguards for Detecting and Preventing Intentional Computer Misuse," National Bureau of Standards Special Publication 500-25, 1978.

Computer Associates, ACF-2 documentation and manuals.

Computer Control Guidelines Second Edition, Canadian Institute of Chartered Accountants (CICA), February, 1986.

"Computer Security Guidelines For Implementing the Privacy Act of 1974," National Bureau of Standards, FIPS-PUB-41, U.S. Department of Commerce, Springfield, VA, May 30, 1975, p. 3.

Department of Defense, *Password Management Guideline*, CSC-STD-002-85, Fort George G. Meade MD, 12 April, 1985.

Fisher, Royal, *Information Systems Security*, Prentice-Hall, Englewood Cliffs, NJ, 1984.

Garfinkel, Simon and Eugene Spafford, *Practical UNIX Security*, O'Reilly & Associates, Inc., 632 Petaluma Avenue, Sebastopol, CA, 95472, 1991.

"Guidelines on User Authentication Techniques for Computer Network Access Control," FIPS Publication 83, U.S. Department of Commerce/National Bureau of Standards, Washington DC, September, 1980.

Henderson, Stuart C., "A Comparison of Data Access Control Packages: Part I," *Computer Security Journal*, Computer Security Institute, Vol. IV # 2, 1989; and ". . .: Part II," Vol. V # 1, 1989.

IBM, *OS/VS2 MVS RACF General Information*, document GC28-0722-xx (xx is the number of the current release).

IBM, *RACF Auditor's Guide System Reference Library*, document SC28-1342-xx.

IBM, *RACF GAC and Generics Use*, document GG22-9375-xx.

IBM, *RACF Security Administrator's Guide*, document SC28-1340-xx.

IBM, *RACF 1.8.1 Overview*, July 1988

Landreth, Bill, with Howard Rheingold, *Out of the Inner Circle: A Hacker's Guide to Computer Security*, Microsoft Press, Bellevue, WA (Distributed by Simon & Schuster).

Lobel, J., *Foiling the System Breakers: Computer Security and Access Control*, McGraw-Hill, NY, 1986

Martin, James, *Security, Accuracy, and Privacy in Computer Systems*, Prentice-Hall, Inc., Englewood Cliffs, NJ, 1973.

Parker, Donn B., *Computer Security Management*, Reston Publishing Company, Inc., Reston, VA, 1981.

Password Usage, Federal Information Processing Standards Publication 112, National Bureau of Standards 5/30/85.

Systems Center, Inc., *VMSECURE Directory Manager's Guide*, Reston, VA, August, 1989.

Systems Center, Inc., *VMSECURE Rules Facility Guide*, Reston, VA, August, 1989.

Systems Center, Inc., *VMSECURE System Administrator's Guide and Reference*, Reston, VA, August, 1989.

Systems Center, Inc., *VMSECURE Messages and Codes*, Reston, VA, August, 1989.

Wood, Helen M., "The Use of Passwords for Controlled Access to Computer Resources," National Bureau of Standards Special Publication, 500-9, 1977.

2. Cryptography

Cryptography can be described as the use of secret codes to provide for the integrity and confidentiality of data.

The knowledge includes:

- Applications and uses
- Factors affecting relative strength, for example:
    - complexity
    - secrecy
    - characteristics of the key (*e.g.,* symmetry, length, percentage of weak keys, ease of key generation or selection, etc.)
    - other
- Implementations (*e.g.,* DES, RSA, CCEP)
- Applications (*e.g.,* message authentication, digital signatures, digital envelopes, FIMA (X9.9), STU)
- Administration and management (for example, key distribution issues)
- Error detecting and correcting features of encryption methods

Aspects of these topics also are addressed in Chapter 7, "Computer and System Security" and Chapter 8, "Telecommunications Security."

2.1 DEFINITIONS AND CHARACTERISTICS

2.1.1 Definitions

Encryption is the process of using an "encryption unit" and an *encryption key* to change *plaintext,* or the normally-understandable information, into *ciphertext,* which (hopefully) is not readable without the encryption unit's inverse and a key. *Decryption* is the process of changing the ciphertext into plaintext. The encryption unit can be anything from pencil and paper, to computer software and/or chips, to special-purpose devices (one of the most famous is the "enigma" device used by the Germans in World War II and captured by the Allies).

Historically, any information that people have had to send to someone else along channels that are not secure has been encrypted in some fashion before transmission. This information could be anything from credit or financial data, to personal private information, to military communications. Because of the inherent vulnerability of data communication channels on public carriers, particularly microwave and satellite transmissions, and because of technological advances, encryption has become a cost-effective way to ensure secure data transmission.

More formally, definitions include:

Ciphertext

Data produced through the use of *encipherment.* The semantic content of the resulting data is not available.

Note: *Ciphertext* may itself be input to *encipherment*, such that super-enciphered output is produced. (ISO 7498-2)

Cleartext

Intelligible data, the semantic content of which is available. (ISO 7498-2)

Code System

1. Any system of communication in which groups of symbols are used to represent plain text elements of varying length.
2. In the broadest sense, a means of converting information into a form suitable for communications or encryption, for example, coded speech, Morse Code, teletypewriter codes.
3. A cryptographic system in which cryptographic equivalents (usually called code groups) typically consisting of letters, digits, or both in meaningless combinations are substituted for plain text elements which may be words, phrases, or sentences.

Cryptography

1. The art or science concerning the principles, means, and methods for rendering plain text unintelligible and for converting encrypted messages into intelligible form. (FIPS PUB 39)
2. The discipline which embodies principles, means, and methods for the transformation of data in order to hide its information content, prevent its undetected modification, and/or prevent its unauthorized use.

Note: Cryptography determines the methods used in encipherment and decipherment. An attack on a cryptographic principle, means, or method is cryptanalysis. (ISO 7498-2)

Data Encrypting Key

A cryptographic key used for encrypting (and decrypting) data. (FIPS PUB 112)

Data Encryption Standard (DES)

An unclassified crypto algorithm adopted by the National Institute of Standards and Technology for public use. (NCSC-WA-001-85)

Data Integrity

The property that data has not been altered or destroyed in an unauthorized manner. (ISO 7498-2)

Decipher

See decipherment.

Decipherment

The reversal of a corresponding reversible *encipherment*. (ISO 7498-2)

Decrypt

To convert, by use of the appropriate key, encrypted (encoded or enciphered) text into its equivalent plaintext. (FIPS PUB 39)

See also decipherment.

Digital Signature

Data appended to, or a cryptographic transformation (see *cryptography*) of, a data unit that allows a recipient of the data unit and protect against forgery, *e.g.*, by the recipient. (ISO 7498-2)

Encipher

To convert plain text into an unintelligible form by means of a cipher system. (FIPS PUB 39; AR 380-380)

Encipherment

The cryptographic transformation of data (see *cryptography*) to produce *ciphertext.*

Note: Encipherment may be irreversible, in which case the corresponding decipherment process cannot feasibly be performed. (ISO 7498-2)

Encode

To convert plain text into an unintelligible form by means of a code system. (FIPS PUB 39; AR 380-380)

Encrypt

To convert plain text into unintelligible form by means of a cryptosystem. (AFR 700-10; AR 380-380; FIPS PUB 39)

Encryption

The process of transforming data to an unintelligible form in such a way that the original data either cannot be obtained (one-way encryption) or cannot be obtained without using the inverse decryption process (two-way encryption). (FIPS PUB 112)

See encipherment

End-to-End Encryption

Encipherment of data within or at the source end system, with the corresponding *decipherment* occurring only within or at the destination end system. (See also link-by-link encipherment.) (ISO 7498-2)

Key

A sequence of symbols that controls the operations of *encipherment* and *decipherment*. (ISO 7498-2)

Key Management

The generation, storage, distribution, deletion, archiving and application of keys in accordance with a *security policy*. (ISO 7498-2)

Link Encryption

1. The application of on-line crypto-operations to a link of a communications system so that all information passing over the link is encrypted in its entirety. (FIPS PUB 39)
2. End-to-end encryption within each link in a communications network. (FIPS PUB 39)

Link-by-link Encipherment

The individual application of encipherment to data on each link of a communications system. (See also end-to-end encipherment.)

   NOTE: The implication of link-by-link encipherment is that data will be in cleartext form in relay entities. (ISO 7498-2)

Notarization

The registration of data with a trusted third party that allows the later assurance of the accuracy of its characteristics such as content, origin, time, and delivery. (ISO 7498-2)

One-Way Function

A mathematical process that involves the transformation of data, usually with encryption-related routines, into a quantity that cannot then be used to recover the original data. (WB)

Plaintext

Intelligible text or signals that have meaning and which can be read or acted upon without the application of any decryption. (FIPS PUB 39; AR 380-380)

   See also Cleartext.

Repudiation

Denial by one of the entities involved in a communication of having participated in all or part of the communication. (ISO 7498-2)

Traffic Analysis

The inference of information from observation of traffic flows (presence, absence, amount, direction, and frequency). (ISO 7498-2)

Traffic Padding

The generation of spurious instances of communication, spurious data units, and/or spurious data within data units. (ISO 7498-2)

2.1.2 General Cryptographic System Characteristics

All cryptographic systems must satisfy three requirements to be acceptable for general use in automated information systems:[1]

1.   The enciphering and deciphering transformations must be efficient for all keys.
2.   The system must be easy to use.
3.   The security of the system should depend only on the secrecy of the keys and not on the secrecy of the enciphering or deciphering transformations.

   In addition to these general characteristics, there are two sets of requirements that must be

---

[1]This list and the next two lists regarding secrecy and authenticity are adapted from Denning, *Cryptography and Data Security*.

satisfied: *secrecy* and *authenticity*.[2] *Secrecy* requirements are defined in terms of feasible computation:

1. It should be computationally infeasible to determine the deciphering transformation systematically from intercepted ciphertext, even if the corresponding plaintext is known.
2. It should be computationally infeasible to determine plaintext systematically from intercepted ciphertext.

The effect of these two requirements is that, without the key(s), an analyst cannot decipher encrypted messages. Further, even if one message somehow is deciphered, the work needed to decipher another message remains the same since the deciphering algorithm remains unknown. These two requirements must continue to be satisfied regardless of the length or number of messages intercepted.

In order for a cryptography system to be acceptable for general use, it also must be impossible for a cryptanalyst to substitute a false ciphertext for a correct one without detection. This leads to two further *authenticity* requirements:

1. It should be computationally infeasible to determine the enciphering transformation systematically for a given ciphertext, even if the corresponding plaintext is known.
2. It should be computationally infeasible to find ciphertext systematically such that the deciphered ciphertext is a valid plaintext message.

As with secrecy, these two requirements must hold regardless of the number or length of intercepted ciphertext messages.

Two points are important with respect to the security and authenticity requirements. First, the word "systematically" is used to allow for the possibility of a "lucky guess." Although one successful guess may lead to one instance of a breakdown of security of authenticity, it should not be possible to do this repeatedly—that is, systematically. Second, the term "computationally infeasible" is a mathematical concept grounded in the theory of computing and in number theory. In practice, this means that mathematicians consider that very great effort, perhaps thousands of years of supercomputer time, would be needed to crack the coding. Section 2.6 contains further discussion of this point. This sort of analysis is risky, as new developments in mathematics can offer new ways to crack codes and invalidate such analyses.

These and other concepts are examined in this chapter.

2.2 PUBLIC KEY AND PRIVATE KEY; KEY CHARACTERISTICS

Two basic encryption systems are common today: *public key* and *private key*. In a private key system, encryption and decryption are done using the same key. The key must be kept secret. Anyone with the key can both encrypt and decrypt data. In a public key system, two keys are used, one to encrypt and one to decrypt. The two keys are related mathematically in a way that cannot be determined using "reasonable" computational methods. The terms *symmetric key* and *asymmet-*

---

[2]Care is needed in the use of terminology in information security, and the word *authenticity* is an example. In this context, the meaning relates to data integrity. In the discussion in Chapter 1, the context was more related to determination of authorized users.

ric key also are used to denote private key and public key systems, respectively. Since the private key system has only one key, used both for encipherment and deciphering, it is a symmetric key system; the use of two separate keys makes a public key system asymmetric.

Thus, the encryption key in a public key system may be published; anyone can encrypt and send messages to whomever owns the decrypting key but only the owner of the decrypting key can read any such encrypted data. This has the advantage that only one copy, or a small number of copies, of the private key needs to be kept secure. As well, anyone can *send* encrypted data using the public key (enhancing convenience) but only a receiver possessing the private key can read the message (retaining privacy.) Another characteristic of a public key system is that to receive encrypted messages from anyone, only two keys are needed; in a private key system, each pair of communicators requires a different key unless everyone is to be able to read all messages. The most commonly used public key system is the RSA scheme, discussed in section 2.5.

Typically, a public key system is mathematically complex, and the processes of selecting keys and doing the actual encipherment are time-consuming. Even with various mathematical methods that ease the calculation problem, the public key systems available in 1993 are considerably more complex to use than most private key systems. Thus, one tries to use public key techniques where keys don't change frequently and the amount of data to be enciphered is small. Private key systems, particularly ones that appear to have been designed with computer processing in mind (such as DES), can be several orders of magnitude faster than public key systems.

DES, a symmetric system, and RSA, an asymmetric system, are examined later in this chapter.

2.2.1 Key Selection

It probably should be superfluous to note that selection of enciphering keys is critical to the strength of the enciphered messages. Unfortunately, as with the very similar case of password selection, people seldom have been very good at selecting strong keys. The discussion of password selection in the last half of Chapter 1 (and elsewhere) applies as well to encryption keys.

The basic principles of selection of passwords apply to encryption keys: no words in a spelling dictionary, no personal data, no similarly easy-to-guess keys, no obvious patterns in keys, change keys frequently, and so forth.

Since the notion of randomly selected keys or passwords is encountered repeatedly, we will add another caution. Computer-generated "random numbers" are not truly *random* numbers, but are pseudo-random numbers. This can be demonstrated easily by generating a "random number" using some seed, then trying the same random number function again with the same seed. In most computer implementations, the same number will result.

A more subtle problem with computer-generated pseudo-random numbers lies in the deterministic nature of the algorithms and how computers work. (No finite algorithm can generate truly random numbers.) This problem can be illustrated by generating two large sets of pseudo-random numbers. The sets should each contain 50 to 100,000 or so numbers. Then choose an x coordinate from one set and a y coordinate from the other and plot the point. When this is done for many numbers, a scatter diagram results. Depending on the specific pseudo-random number generator used, non-random behavior may be visible, sometimes in the form of diagonal bands of differing density in the plot. These bands indicate areas of non-randomness. This is illustrated for one random number generator in Figure 2.1. This is an example of second-order correlation.

Modern pseudo-random number generators usually pass more stringent tests than the one which produced the illustration, including nth order correlation; however, it is best to check to be sure.

One way to avoid this problem is simply to toss a coin to generate the bits of a key (0 for heads and 1 for tails, or vice versa.) For DES, 56 coin tosses of a fair coin will produce 56 random bits for a key.

Figure 2.1. Pseudo-random Numbers[3]

2.3 KEY MANAGEMENT

Key management refers to the hardware, software, and procedures associated with generating, distributing, and using encryption keys. Given enciphering and deciphering algorithms that fit the requirements of ease-of-use, security, and authentication, the greatest exposure in a cryptographic system centers around keys. If the security of the key management system is not at least as great as that of the rest of the cryptography system, then the system may not be trustworthy. In a public key system, the public key of course need not be protected. In a private or public key system, at least one key must be protected.

Clearly, the facility that generates keys must be subjected to the highest feasible security measures. This may be accomplished by various combinations of encipherment of keys and operations within the generating facility, and other procedural measures. Security of the key generation facility may be strengthened by implementations using hardware rather than software. (The DES, discussed in section 2.8.1, specifies an algorithm implemented in hardware.)

The key generation facility may differ, depending on whether the application is an individual protecting data in a file or files, a secure site, a network protecting data transmission, or a mainframe installation. In the case of a file, one key is generated and used, and it has a relatively long lifetime. Typically, this key remains valid for the lifetime of the data file or files, and is distributed once per intended recipient. The coin toss mentioned earlier may be appropriate for such an environment.

For a network or mainframe, for highest security a key must be generated for each packet of information leaving a secure environment. This key must be communicated to the intended recipient somehow. Once used, the key usually is of no further value. The lifetime of this sort of key can be very short, depending on the frequency of data communication in the environment. Many keys must be generated and distributed, frequently. An alternative that lessens the workload and

---

[3]Greenberger, M., "Method in Randomness," *Communications of the ACM*, vol 8 #3, March, 1965, p. 177.

exposures associated with many keys is to use a *session key*. In this instance, a key is established for each work session (terminal log-on session, for example); it is used throughout the session, and the distribution problem is limited to once per session rather than once per packet.

The next step in key management is distribution of keys. In the instance of an individual protecting data files, simply storing the key separately from the system, and distributing the key to the intended recipient by means different from the channel for distributing the ciphertext, normally should provide adequate security. Use of cipher block chaining (see section 2.5.2) can strengthen this process.

The problem is more complex for networks of computers, or systems that involve communication channels combined with high frequencies of key generation and change. Typically, a hierarchy of keys will be used. A master key (changed at least annually) is generated, then stored in ROM or similar secure hardware facility. Sub-master keys are generated using the master key, at the behest of users. The lifetime of a sub-master key should be determined based on the needs of the specific environment; one month is a common time. The sub-master key is always encrypted once generated (using the master key). A third level of key hierarchy is the session key, which is used only during a particular session as noted above. The session key also is encrypted once generated. A fourth level of hierarchy would add a key for each packet of data communicated.

In such a hierarchical scheme, it is common to use a public key method to encipher the keys used in a private key application. For example, the RSA algorithm may be used to encipher DES keys, and the DES keys used to encipher actual data for transmission. This combines the advantages of public key (stronger and better understood enciphering and simpler key distribution) and private key systems (speed of use). Because two different methods are used, the effort to break such a distribution system is much greater than if only a single method were involved.

Few other general statements are appropriate on this topic. For more detailed and theoretical treatments, the Denning reference at the end of this chapter is recommended (pages 165-185). Two other books address key management in some detail: Meyer & Matyas, *Cryptography*, and Davies & Price, *Security for Computer Networks*.

2.4 LINK LEVEL, END-TO-END

There are two basic extremes of encryption in a communications network: link-by-link and end-to-end.[4] For the following discussion, *node* refers to a location (for example, a computer, terminal, front-end processor, program, or switching system) where data may be input, stored, encrypted, processed, decrypted, routed, or output; *link* refers to any communication line (for example, a public carrier, data bus, even a removable diskette) or other method of transferring data between nodes.

Figures 2.2 and 2.3 illustrate these extremes. One message passing along one channel is used to simplify illustration. (In an application, the next part of a complete message could pass along entirely different links and nodes to reach the same destination.) In these figures, M is the original message, E is an encryption algorithm, and D is an decryption algorithm. $E(M)$ is an encrypted message. $E_1, E_2, \ldots, E_n$ and $D_1, D_2, \ldots, D_n$ refer to encryption or description schemes

---

[4]The next two figures are adapted from Denning, *Cryptography and Data Security*. Areas where data are in un-encrypted form and thus much more vulnerable are highlighted.

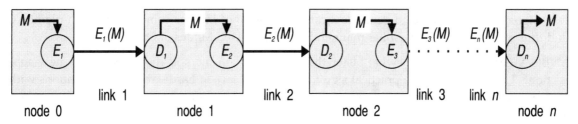

Figure 2.2. Link Encryption

employed in nodes *1, 2, . . ., n*. Parts of the network where the original plaintext message exists, and is therefore vulnerable to compromise, are shaded.

In link encryption (Figure 2.2), the user need only know the key(s) necessary to access the nearest node. Each node may decrypt, process, route, output, or otherwise manipulate, and then encrypt data. All data on a link are encrypted, but data may or may not be in plaintext form within a node. The user has no control over this and must depend on the security of the node for security of transmitted data.

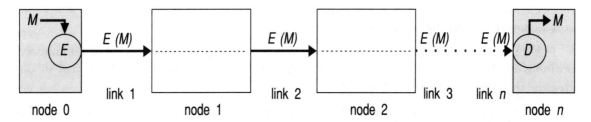

Figure 2.3. End-to-End Encryption

In end-to-end encryption (Figure 2.3), the user must have an encryption key for each intended recipient, and each pair of communicators must have a means of exchanging keys and protocols for transmission. The data are never in plaintext form except at the originating and receiving end. The user avoids most risks of interception during transmission at the cost of risks associated with management of numerous keys and protocols. Also, since the nodes and links must assign addresses somehow, a traffic analysis attack is somewhat more likely to succeed. Again, the user has no control over how addresses may be assigned or enciphered by the links or nodes.

In practice, some combination of link and end-to-end encryption will be found in most communication links, with details depending on the security needs of the users and characteristics of the links.

2.5 BLOCK MODE, CIPHER BLOCK CHAINING, STREAM CIPHERS (SYNCHRONOUS AND SELF-SYNCHRONOUS)

There are two basic modes of encipherment: block ciphers and stream ciphers.

2.5.1 Block Mode

In *block mode,* a message is broken into successive blocks, typically of the same length. (Ending blocks are padded to the same length. This ensures that an attacker sees blocks of uniform size and cannot gain useful data simply by observing message length.) Each successive block is encrypted using the same key. The DES algorithm is a block cipher, with a block size of 64 bits. (The

DES algorithm can be used to generate a random stream of bits for combination with plaintext, and thus operate in a stream cipher manner. See FIPS 81, DES Modes of Operation.)

Block enciphering is somewhat faster than either stream method discussed in the next subsection. (This may have little practical significance in the case of hardware implementations with higher data rates than available transmission rates.) Transmission or other errors affect only a single block.

Block ciphers may be more subject to cryptanalysis than stream ciphers. First, the same block of plaintext will yield the same ciphertext. Therefore, a guessing attack based on expected occurrence of things like spaces or keywords in a programming language (see known-plaintext attack, section 2.6) has a higher probability of success than with a stream cipher. Because blocks are independently enciphered, replay and substitution (insertion or deletion of blocks) are easier as well. Block chaining and cipher block chaining are strategies to increase the difficulty of these kinds of attacks.

2.5.2 Cipher Block Chaining

Block chaining and cipher block chaining link blocks together, so that vulnerability to attacks involving insertion, deletion and substitution is lessened.

In *block chaining*, some of the bits of the previous block of ciphertext are inserted into unused positions of the current block. This substantially reduces vulnerability, but at the cost of decreasing the available message bits per block.

In *cipher block chaining*, an entire block of ciphertext is fed back through a register to be exclusive-Ored with the next plaintext block. The result is then passed through the encipherment transform using the single key. The effect of this is somewhat like a self-synchronous stream cipher (next section) in that each block is dependent on all preceding blocks. Thus, the final block is usable as a checksum, as is the last portion of a self-synchronous cipher ciphertext message. Cipher block chaining avoids the loss of usable bits in block chaining, while statistically distributing the plaintext message content across the entire ciphertext.

2.5.3 Stream Ciphers

A *stream cipher* breaks the message into successive characters or smaller units (bits) and enciphers each character with an element from a *key stream*.

A *synchronous* stream cipher is one in which the key stream is generated independently of the stream. The key stream must be truly random, and it should be at least as long as the message. (If the key stream is periodic, the behavior of the cipher approaches a block cipher for short periods, and of a true stream cipher for longer periods.)

If a character is lost during transmission, the sender and receiver must re-synchronize their key generators to recover from the problem.

In a *self-synchronous* stream cipher, each key element is derived from some fixed number of preceding ciphertext characters. This avoids the problem of re-synchronization after a transmission problem, since the cipher re-synchronizes by itself after receipt of the fixed number of correct ciphertext characters.

Since the key and the resulting ciphertext are dependent on preceding parts of the message, the last part of a self-synchronous stream cipher message stream depends upon the entire preceding message. This means that the final portion can be used as a form of checksum to ensure complete message transmittal.

The second autokey Vigenère cipher (once considered unbreakable and now not considered strong) is a self-synchronous cipher in the sense that each character of the key is computed from the preceding ciphertext character.

2.6 CRYPTANALYSIS AND STRENGTH OF CIPHERS (THEORETICALLY SECURE, COMPUTATIONALLY SECURE)

The definition of *cryptanalysis* is:

> The analysis of a cryptographic system and/or its inputs and outputs to derive the confidential variables and/or sensitive data including *cleartext*. (ISO 7498-2)

In essence, the cryptanalyst tries to break the coding of ciphertext that was not meant for him or her. Many attack methods have been found useful. Some are within the general realm of computer security literature and are only mentioned below. (General attack methods that have been used to penetrate information systems are covered in section 7.5.1.) Some attacks are specialized within cryptanalysis and are described in somewhat more detail.

It is doubtful whether the concept of "theoretically secure" is meaningful in cryptography. Given unlimited resources, the only unbreakable cipher is one using a non-repeating random key stream, where the number of keys equals or exceeds the number of possible messages. This is called a *one-time pad*. Unfortunately, since information systems deal with human activities, even such a one-way cipher is susceptible to several attacks involving statistical methods. Thus the only meaningful definition of strength of a cipher is *computationally secure*.

As noted at the end of section 2.1, the term "computationally infeasible" is a mathematical concept grounded in the theory of computing and in number theory. For example, public key systems proposed are based on "difficult" problems, such as factoring large numbers or computing discrete logarithms. There is no proof that factoring large numbers is infeasible; however, mathematicians have been trying to find better ways to accomplish this for some 2,000 years with little success, so the problem is considered difficult.[5] Some of the other problems on which proposed public key systems are based have been proven to be "NP-complete," a concept from the theory of complexity in computer science mathematics. Formal analysis of the complexity of a cipher system is difficult and beyond the scope of this book.

In practice, "computationally infeasible" means that mathematicians consider that the computation effort needed to break the cipher exceeds available resources. This sort of analysis is risky, as new developments in mathematics can offer new ways to crack codes and thus can invalidate such analyses. As well, the notion of "available resources" changes with the exponential growth in capability of computer technology. Many calculations barely feasible on a supercomputer ten years ago are routine on personal computers today.

More precisely, a cipher's strength can be measured in terms of a work function. This function typically yields the number of operations necessary to decipher ciphertext. Obviously, the num-

---

[5]If tomorrow, some graduate student were to discover an efficient method for finding prime factors of large numbers, the RSA public key system would be useless. The student would also become quite famous.

ber of operations varies depending on the algorithm chosen for the attack. Therefore, the work factor depends not only on the strength of the cipher, but also on the method chosen to attack the cipher.

As one example, there are 2^{56} possible keys in the DES algorithm. One measure of the strength of DES is the number of operations necessary to generate half the possible keys (on the average, half of all possible keys would have to be tried before success). This measure assumes that the rather simplistic means of exhaustive search is chosen. It also assumes that the optimum DES implementation is used; errors in implementation can significantly affect the strength. Other strategies for attacking DES or another cipher algorithm are possible, although none has been published that requires less work than exhaustive search.

Strategies common in cryptanalysis include:

- *Ciphertext-only attack*

  The analyst has only the ciphertext from which to determine the key.

- *Known-plaintext* attack

  The cryptanalyst knows some plaintext-ciphertext pairs. For instance, if the ciphertext represents a computer program, one may reasonably expect that words like *begin, end, do, while, if, then,* and so forth appear with some frequency. More precisely, the analyst may *know* that the first portion of the ciphertext relates to a sign-on message and contains the characters "LOGON".

- *Chosen-plaintext attack*

  The analyst is able to obtain ciphertext corresponding to selected plaintext. This is the most favorable case for the analyst. One way to obtain such plaintext-ciphertext pairs is to insert elements into a database, then observe the changes in the stored ciphertext.

- *Chosen-ciphertext attack*

  With public-key systems, the inverse of the chosen-plaintext attack becomes feasible. The analyst may be able to deduce the private key.

Other cryptographic attacks include things like masquerading, playback, spoofing, traffic analysis, and insertion/deletion of blocks or records. These are addressed in section 7.5.

2.7 ERROR DETECTION AND CORRECTION FEATURES OF ENCRYPTION METHODS

Perhaps the most basic error-detection function of an encryption scheme is: If you can decipher a message successfully, there were no errors. Other error-detection features can be built into an encryption transform. One example is the parity bits that are included in the DES algorithm. The 64 bits used for the key include 56 bits for the key itself, and 8 bits to indicate parity.

It is not a purpose of this text to explore error-detecting and error-correcting codes in any detail. One feature of encryption schemes is the parity checks in the DES algorithm. Others include the capability to use the final block of a ciphertext in a cipher block or cipher block chain mode, or portion of ciphertext in a self-synchronous stream cipher, as a form of checksum to verify complete and correct transmission of the ciphertext. The "re-synchronization" aspect of self-synchronous ciphers may be considered in some sense an error-correcting feature of these types of encryption transforms.

Authentication and digital signatures are discussed in section 2.9. While these are not intended as error-detecting or error-correcting codes, one thing that they must do is to indicate any changes to a message. They thus add to the error-detection capability of the enciphering transform when in use.

2.8 IMPLEMENTATIONS: DES, RSA

2.8.1 Data Encryption Standard (DES)

Because it is reasonably secure and is in the public domain, DES has come into widespread use. As the security professional should understand details of a common encipherment scheme, the Data Encryption Standard is reproduced below. DES is an example of a symmetric, or public key system.

The Data Encryption Standard (DES)[6] shall consist of the following Data Encryption algorithm to be implemented in special purpose electronic devices. These devices shall be designed in such a way that they may be used in a computer system or network to provide cryptographic protection to binary coded data. The method of implementation will depend on the application and environment. The devices shall be implemented in such a way that they may be tested and validated as accurately performing the transformations specified in the following algorithm.

Introduction

The algorithm is designed to encipher and decipher blocks of data consisting of 64 bits under control of a 64-bit key.[7] Deciphering must be accomplished by using the same key as for enciphering, but with the schedule of addressing the key bits altered so that the deciphering process is the reverse of the enciphering process. A block to be enciphered is subjected to an initial permutation IP, then to a complex key-dependent combination and finally to a permutation which is the inverse of the initial permutation IP^{-1}. The key-dependent computation can be simply defined in terms of a function f, called the cipher function, and a function KS, called the key schedule. A description of the computation is given first, along with details as to how the algorithm is used for encipherment. Next, the use of the algorithm for decipherment is described. Finally, a definition of the cipher function f is given in terms of primitive functions which are called the selection functions S_i and the permutation function P. S_i, P, and KS of the algorithm are included.

The following notation is convenient: Given two blocks L and R of bits, LR denotes the block consisting of the bits of L followed by the bits of R. Since the concatenation is associative $B_1B_2 \ldots B_8$, for example, denotes the block consisting of the bits of B_1 followed by the bits of $B_2 \ldots$ followed by the bits of B_8.

Enciphering
A sketch of the enciphering computation is given in Figure 2.4.

---

[6]The material describing DES is reproduced from *Federal Information Processing Standards Publication 46-1* (FIPS 46-1), January 22, 1988, available from the National institute of Standards and Technology (NIST) or from National Technical Information Services (NTIS) of the U.S. Department of Commerce, Springfield, VA 22161.

[7]Blocks are composed of bits numbered from left to right, i.e., the leftmost bit of a block is one.

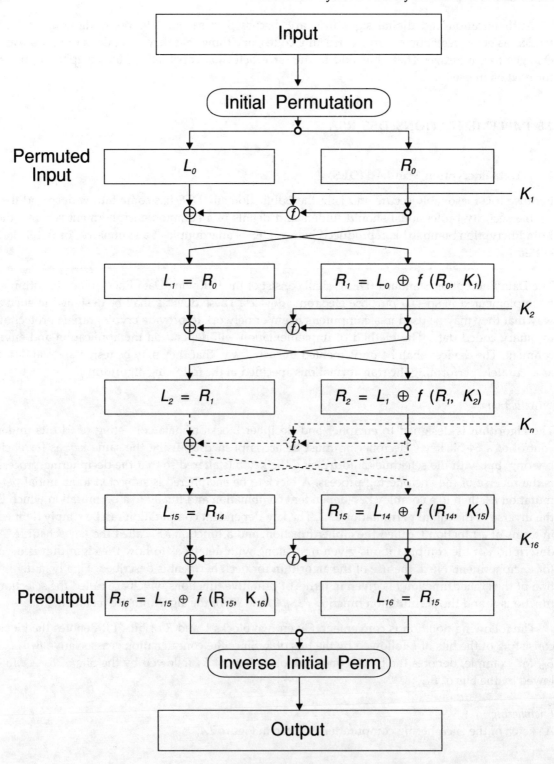

Figure 2.4. Enciphering Computation

The 64 bits of the input block to be enciphered are first subjected to the following permutation:

$$\underline{IP}$$

58	50	42	34	26	18	10	2
60	52	44	36	28	20	12	4
62	54	46	38	30	22	14	6
64	56	48	40	32	24	16	8
57	49	41	33	25	17	9	1
59	51	43	35	27	19	11	3
61	53	45	37	29	21	13	5
63	55	47	39	31	23	15	7

That is, the permuted input has bit 58 of the input as its first bit, bit 50 as its second bit, and so on with bit 7 as its last bit. The permuted input block is then the input to a complex key-dependent computation described below. The output of that computation, called the preoutput, is then subjected to the following permutation which is the inverse of the initial permutation:

$$\underline{IP^{-1}}$$

40	8	48	16	56	24	64	32
39	7	47	15	55	23	63	31
38	6	46	14	54	22	62	30
37	5	45	13	53	21	61	29
36	4	44	12	52	20	60	28
35	3	43	11	51	19	59	27
34	2	42	10	50	18	58	26
33	1	41	9	49	17	57	25

That is, the output of the algorithm has bit 40 of the preoutput block as its first bit, bit 8 as its second bit, and so on, until bit 25 of the preoutput block is the last bit of the output.

The computation which uses the permuted input block as its input to produce the preoutput block consists, but for a final interchange of blocks, of 16 iterations of a calculation that is described below in terms of the cipher function f which operates on two blocks, one of 32 bits and one of 48 bits, and produces a block of 32 bits.

Let the 64 bits of the input block to an iteration consist of a 32-bit block L followed by a 32-bit block R. using the notation defined in the introduction, the input block is then LR.

Let K be a block of 48 bits chosen from the 64-bit key. Then the output $L'R'$ of an iteration with input LR is defined by:

(1) $L' = R$

$R' = L \oplus f(R,K)$

where $\oplus$ denotes bit-by-bit addition modulo 2.

As remarked before, the input of the first iteration of the calculation is the permuted input block. If $L'R'$ is the output of the 16th iteration, then $R'L'$ is the preoutput block. At each iteration a different block K of key bits is chosen from the 64-bit key designated by KEY.

With more notation we can describe the iterations of the computation in more detail. Let KS be a function which takes an integer n in the range from 1 to 16 and a 64-bit block KEY as input and yields as output a 48-bit block K_n which is a permuted selection of bits from KEY.

That is

(2) $K_n = KS(n, KEY)$

with K_n determined by the bits in 48 distinct bit positions of *KEY*. *KS* is called the key schedule because the block *K* used in the *n*th iteration of (1) is the block K_n determined by (2).

As before, let the permuted input block be *LR*. Finally, let L_0 and R_0 be respectively *L* and *R* and let L_n and R_n be respectively *L'* and *R'* of (1) when *L* and *R* are respectively L_{n-1} and R_{n-1} and *K* is K_n; that is, when *n* is in the range from 1 to 16:

(3) $L_n = R_{n-1}$
     $R_n = L_{n-1} \oplus f(R_{n-1}, K_n)$

The preoutput block is then $R_{16}L_{16}$.

The key schedule *KS* of the algorithm is described in detail below. The key schedule produces the 16 K_n which are required for the algorithm.

Deciphering

The permutation IP^{-1} applied to the preoutput block is the inverse of the initial permutation *IP* applied to the input. Further, from (1) it follows that:

(4) $R = L'$
     $L = R' \oplus f(L', K)$

Consequently, to *decipher* it is only necessary to apply the *very same algorithm to an enciphered message block*, taking care that at each iteration of the computation *the same block of key bits K is used* during decipherment as was used during encipherment of the block. Using the notation of the previous section, this can be expressed by the equations:

(5) $R_{n-1} = L_n$
     $L_{n-1} = R_n \oplus f(L_n, K_n)$

where now $R_{16}L_{16}$ is the permuted input block for the deciphering calculation and L_0R_0 is the preoutput block. That is, for the decipherment calculation with $R_{16}L_{16}$ as the permuted input, K_{16} is used in the first iteration, K_{15} in the second, and so on, with K_1 used in the 16th iteration.

The Cipher Function f

A sketch of the calculation of $f(R,K)$ is given in Figure 2.5.

Let *E* denote a function which takes a block of 32 bits as input and yields a block of 48 bits as output. Let *E* be such that the 48 bits of its output, written as 8 blocks of 6 bits each, are obtained by selecting the bits in its inputs in order according to the following table:

E Bit-Selection Table

32	1	2	3	4	5
4	5	6	7	8	9
8	9	10	11	12	13
12	13	14	15	16	17
16	17	18	19	20	21
20	21	22	23	24	25

| 24 | 25 | 26 | 27 | 28 | 29 |
| 28 | 29 | 30 | 31 | 32 | 1 |

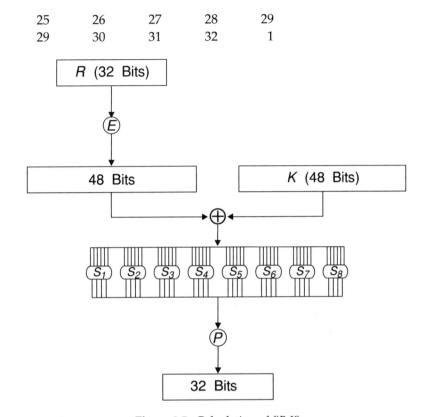

Figure 2.5. Calculation of $f(R,K)$

Thus the first three bits of $E(R)$ are the bits in position 32, 1 and 2 of R while the last 2 bits of $E(R)$ are the bits in positions 32 and 1.

Each of the unique selection functions $S_1, S_2, \ldots, S_8$ takes a 6-bit block as input and yields a 4-bit block as output and is illustrated by using a table containing the recommended S_1:

$$S_1$$

Row No.	Column Number															
	0	1	2	3	4	5	6	7	8	9	10	11	12	13	14	15
0	14	4	13	1	2	15	11	8	3	10	6	12	5	9	0	7
1	0	15	7	4	14	2	13	1	10	6	12	11	9	5	3	8
2	4	1	14	8	13	6	2	11	15	12	9	7	3	10	5	0
3	15	12	8	2	4	9	1	7	5	11	3	14	10	0	6	13

If S_1 is the function defined in this table and B is a block of 6 bits, then $S_1(B)$ is determined as follows: The first and last bits of B represent in base 2 a number in the range 0 to 3. Let that number be i. The middle 4 bits of B represent in base 2 a number in the range 0 to 15. Let that number be j. Look up in the table the number in the ith row and jth column. It is a number in the range of 0 to 15 and is uniquely represented by a 4-bit block. That block is the output $S_1(B)$ of S_1 for the input B. For example, for input 011011 the row is 01, that is row 1, and the column is determined by 1101, that is column 13. In row 1 column 13 appears 5 so that the output is 0101. Selection functions $S_1, S_2, \ldots, S_8$ of the algorithm appear below.

The permutation function P yields a 32-bit output from a 32-bit input by permuting the bits of the input block. Such a function is defined by the following table:

$$P$$

16	7	20	21
29	12	28	17
1	15	23	26
5	18	31	10
2	8	24	14
32	27	3	9
19	13	30	6
22	11	4	25

The output $P(L)$ for the function P defined by this table is obtained from the input L by taking the 16th bit of L as the first bit of $P(L)$, the 7th bit as the second bit of $P(L)$, and so on until the 25th bit of L is taken as the 32nd bit of $P(L)$. The permutation function P of the algorithm is repeated below.

Now let $S_1, S_2, \ldots, S_8$ be eight distinct selection functions, let P be the permutation function and let E be the function defined above.

To define $f(R,K)$, we first define $B_1, \ldots, B_8$ to be blocks of 6 bits each for which:

(6) $B_1 B_2 \ldots B_8 = K \oplus E(R)$

The block $f(R,K)$ is then defined to be

(7) $P(S_1(B_1)S_2(B_2) \ldots S_8(B_8))$

Thus $K \oplus E(R)$ is first divided into the 8 blocks as indicated in (6). Then each B_i is taken as an input to S_i and the 8 blocks $S_1(B_1)$, $S_2(B_2)$, $\ldots S_8(B_8)$ of 4 bits each are consolidated into a single block of 32 bits which forms the input to P. The output (7) is then the output function f for the inputs R and K.

Primitive Functions for the Data Encryption Algorithm

The choice of the primitive functions KS, $S_1, S_2, \ldots, S_8$, and P is critical to the strength of an encipherment resulting from the algorithm. Specified below is the recommended set of functions, describing $S_1, S_2, \ldots, S_8$ and P in the same way they are described in the algorithm. For the interpretation of the tables describing these functions, see the discussion in the body of the algorithm, in the preceding sections.

The primitive functions $S_1, S_2, \ldots, S_8$ are:

$$S_1$$

14	4	13	1	2	15	11	8	3	10	6	12	5	9	0	7
0	15	7	4	14	2	13	1	10	6	12	11	9	5	3	8
4	1	14	8	13	6	2	11	15	12	9	7	3	10	5	0
15	12	8	2	4	9	1	7	5	11	3	14	10	0	6	13

$$S_2$$

15	1	8	14	6	11	3	4	9	7	2	13	12	0	5	10
3	13	4	7	15	2	8	14	12	0	1	10	6	9	11	5
0	14	7	11	10	4	13	1	5	8	12	6	9	3	2	15

| 13 | 8 | 10 | 1 | 3 | 15 | 4 | 2 | 11 | 6 | 7 | 12 | 0 | 5 | 14 | 9 |

S_3

10	0	9	14	6	3	15	5	1	13	12	7	11	4	2	8
13	7	0	9	3	4	6	10	2	8	5	14	12	11	15	1
13	6	4	9	8	15	3	0	11	1	2	12	5	10	14	7
1	10	13	0	6	9	8	7	4	15	14	3	11	5	2	12

S_4

7	13	14	3	0	6	9	10	1	2	8	5	11	12	4	15
13	8	11	5	6	15	0	3	4	7	2	12	1	10	14	9
10	6	9	0	12	11	7	13	15	1	3	14	5	2	8	4
3	15	0	6	10	1	13	8	9	4	5	11	12	7	2	14

S_5

2	12	4	1	7	10	11	6	8	5	3	15	13	0	14	9
14	11	2	12	4	7	13	1	5	0	15	10	3	9	8	6
4	2	1	11	10	13	7	8	15	9	12	5	6	3	0	14
11	8	12	7	1	14	2	13	6	15	0	9	10	4	5	3

S_6

12	1	10	15	9	2	6	8	0	13	3	4	14	7	5	11
10	15	4	2	7	12	9	5	6	1	13	14	0	11	3	8
9	14	15	5	2	8	12	3	7	0	4	10	1	13	11	6
4	3	2	12	9	5	15	10	11	14	1	7	6	0	8	13

S_7

4	11	2	14	15	0	8	13	3	12	9	7	5	10	6	1
13	0	11	7	4	9	1	10	14	3	5	12	2	15	8	6
1	4	11	13	12	3	7	14	10	15	6	8	0	5	9	2
6	11	13	8	1	4	10	7	9	5	0	15	14	2	3	12

S_8

13	2	8	4	6	15	11	1	10	9	3	14	5	0	12	7
1	15	13	8	10	3	7	4	12	5	6	11	0	14	9	2
7	11	4	1	9	12	14	2	0	6	10	13	15	3	5	8
2	1	14	7	4	10	8	13	15	12	9	0	3	5	6	11

The primitive function P is:

P

16	7	20	21
29	12	28	17
1	15	23	26
5	18	31	10
2	8	24	14
32	27	3	9
19	13	30	6
22	11	4	25

Recall that K_n, for $1 \leq n \geq 16$, is the block of 48 bits in (2) of the algorithm. Hence, to describe KS, it is sufficient to describe the calculation of K_n from KEY for $n = 1, 2, \ldots, 16$. That calculation is illustrated in Figure 2.6. To complete the definition of KS it is therefore sufficient to describe the two permuted choices, as well as the schedule of left shifts. One bit in each 8-bit byte of the KEY may be utilized for error detection in key generation, distribution, and storage. Bits 8, 16, . . ., 64 are for use in assuring that each byte is of odd parity.

PC-1

57	49	41	33	25	17	9
1	58	50	42	34	26	18
10	2	59	51	43	35	27
19	11	3	60	52	44	36
63	55	47	39	31	23	15
7	62	54	46	38	30	22
14	6	61	53	45	37	29
21	13	5	28	20	12	4

The table has been divided into two parts, with the first part determining how the bits of C_0 are chosen, and the second part determining how the bits of D_0 are chosen. The bits of KEY are numbered 1 through 64. The bits of C_0 are respectively bits 57, 49, 41, . . ., 44 and 36, of KEY, with the bits of D_0 being bits 63, 55, 47, . . ., 12, and 4 of KEY.

With C_0 and D_0 defined, we now define how the blocks C_n and D_n are obtained from the blocks C_{n-1} and D_{n-1}, respectively, for $n = 1, 2, \ldots, 16$. That is accomplished by adhering to the following schedule of left shifts for the individual blocks:

Iteration Number	Number of Left Shifts
1	1
2	1
3	2
4	2
5	2
6	2
7	2
8	2
9	1
10	2
11	2
12	2
13	2
14	2
15	2
16	1

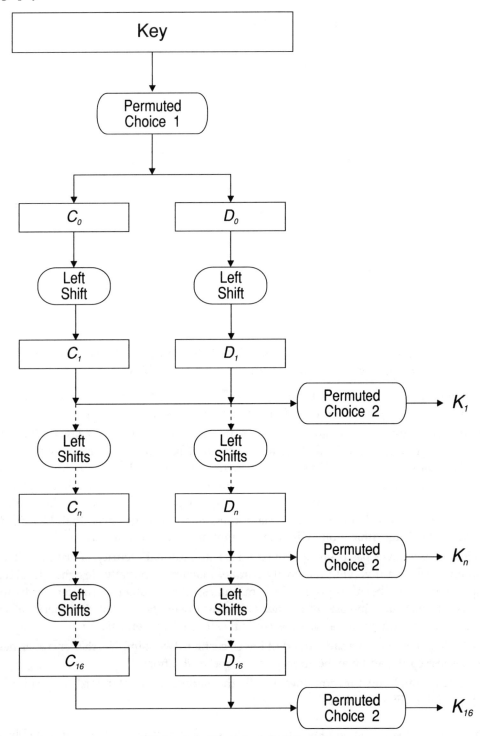

Figure 2.6. Key Schedule Calculation

Permuted choice 1 is determined by the following table:

For example, C_3 and D_3 are obtained from C_2 and D_2, respectively, by two left shifts, and C_{16} and D_{16} are obtained from C_{15} and D_{15}, respectively, by one left shift. In all cases, by a single left shift is meant a rotation of the bits one place to the left, so that after one left shift the bits in the 28 positions are the bits that were previously in positions 2, 3, . . ., 28, 1.

Permuted choice 2 is determined by the following table:

PC-2

14	17	11	24	1	5
3	28	15	6	21	10
23	19	12	4	26	8
16	7	27	20	13	2
41	52	31	37	47	55
30	40	51	45	33	48
44	49	39	56	34	53
46	42	50	36	29	32

Therefore, the first bit of K_n is the 14th bit of C_nD_n, the second bit the 17th, and so on with the 47th bit the 29th, and the 48th bit the 32nd.

Discussion

As noted above, since the Data Encryption Standard is in the public domain many implementations exist. Several points are significant in evaluating the use of DES:

- The standard specifies an implementation in *hardware*. Most commercially available implementations are *software*, and thus do not follow the standard precisely.

- Although the algorithms are published, there are restrictions under U.S. law on the export of devices conforming to the DES standard. A prudent security practitioner will ensure that these laws are not violated. This may mean that, for example, it is unlawful to carry a portable computer to some countries if that computer contains programs that implement the DES algorithm. One such program is PCSECURE, a program provided with a file utility package from Central Point Software. Many other such packages exist that, like PCTOOLS, include the DES algorithm along with other common tools. Caution is advised.

- DES is not, and never has been, approved for use in national security or critical military applications. Schemes involving massively parallel machines specially designed to break DES encipherment have been proposed. Such machines, like all other computer hardware, will decrease dramatically in cost over time. This may lower the cost of decipherment enough that, for example, financial transactions could be attacked cost-effectively.

- As with decipherment, the same trend of lower-cost hardware implies that encipherment also becomes less costly, and may be appropriate in more situations.

- Key selection and the functions defined in the tables of the standard are critical to the strength of the DES algorithm.

There are several keys that are known to be weak. For example, the key whose 56 bits are all 1s enciphers any message to itself, giving no protection at all. Other weak keys are a key of all 0s, or a key that is 28 0s followed by 28 1s (after removing parity bits), or 28 1s followed by 28 0s. Of course, no key with such an obvious pattern should be used in any case. At least seven other weak keys are known to exist; their patterns are less obvious and the weakness derives from subtleties in the interactions of the S tables.

DES has been subjected to a great deal of academic attention since its introduction. (To some extent, this is due to the fact that the developers of DES have never released any of the bases for developing DES, nor confirmed academic speculations about findings.) The standard emphasizes that selection of keys is critical, and also notes that the substitution tables are sensitive.

DES is not complex mathematically; its strength comes from simple permutations and substitutions, repeated many times to yield a result. The contents of the substitution functions define how the substitutions are to be performed, and are critical. Analysis has shown that these so-called S-boxes (the substitution functions S_1 through S_8) are essentially ideal for their purpose, and that any change in their contents severely impacts the strength of DES.

2.8.2 RSA

The concept of two-key cryptography systems was introduced in 1976.[8] It is called *public key encryption*; each user has a public key and a private key, and two users can communicate if they know only each other's public keys. The public key, or transformation, is registered with a directory. Anyone may encipher a message using the public key, but only the recipient can decipher it, since the private key is required to decipher.

The public key is derived from the private key by a one-way transformation. It must be computationally infeasible to derive the private key from the public key, or even to find a transformation equivalent to the private transformation. Several problems in mathematics that are considered difficult have been exploited to create public key systems, including computing discrete logarithms and finding prime factors of large numbers.

The most common public key system is the RSA system, named for its authors Rivest, Shamir, and Adleman.[9] A message block M in the interval $[0, n\text{-}1]$ is enciphered into ciphertext C by computing the exponential

$C = M^e \bmod n$,

where e and n are the keys to the transformation. The ciphertext is restored to plaintext by the transformation

$M = C^d \bmod n$

The enciphering and deciphering transformations are based on Euler's generalization of Fermat's Theorem, which states that for every M relatively prime to n:

$M^{\phi(n)} \bmod n = 1$

(ϕ is the Euler totient function.) This property implies that if e and d satisfy the relation *ed mod $\phi(n)$* = 1, then the enciphering and deciphering equations given above are mutual inverses.

In the RSA encryption scheme, the modulus n is the product of two large prime numbers p and q, $n = pq$. Thus, $\phi(n) = (p\text{-}1)(q\text{-}1)$. Rivest, Shamir, and Adleman recommend picking d relatively prime to $\phi(n)$ in the interval $[\max(p, q)+1, n\text{-}1]$; e is computed using the equation:

$e = inv(d, \phi(n))$

[8]Diffie, W. and M. Hellman, "New Directions in Cryptography," *IEEE Transactions on Information Theory*, Vol. IT-22(6), p. 644-654, November, 1976.

[9]First published in Rivest, R. L., A. Shamir, and L. Adleman, "A Method for Obtaining Digital Signatures and Public-Key Cryptosystems," *Communications of the ACM*, vol. 21(2), p. 120-126, February, 1978.

If this returns $e < \log_2 n$, then a new value of d should be picked to ensure that every encrypted message is subjected to some wrap-around.

Since $\phi(n)$ cannot be determined without knowing the prime factors p and q, d can be kept secret even if e and n are public.

The security of the system depends on the difficulty of factoring n into p and q, and on careful selection of these prime numbers. Rivest, Shamir, and Adleman suggested using 100-digit numbers for p and q. This would give a work factor approximating several hundred thousand years at the fastest speeds available in today's computers. Doubling the number of digits of p and q would give a time something like one hundred thousand times as large as the best current estimate of the age of the universe. Again, the caution about "computationally infeasible" is appropriate: A breakthrough in number theory leading to faster means of factoring large numbers could completely invalidate these work factor approximations. Recently, the authors have recommended doubling the number of digits, citing both developments in computer technology and a new method for factoring large numbers.

The computations involved in selecting keys and in enciphering data are be complex, and are not practical for manual use. However, using mathematical properties of modular arithmetic and a method known as "computing in Galois fields," RSA is quite feasible for computer use. As noted in the discussion of key management, RSA and other public key schemes are much slower than permutation and substitution schemes like DES. This limits their potential for such uses as scrambling video signals in television, due to the high speeds and large amounts of data required.

The RSA scheme is patented in the United States and cannot be used in the U.S. without a license. Since it was published prior to granting of the patent, it may be used without payment of royalties in other countries with different patent laws. Many of these countries are in Europe; thus it may not be surprising that RSA is more popular in Europe than in the U.S.

2.9 APPLICATIONS: MAC, X9.9, DIGITAL SIGNATURE, CRYPTOGRAPHIC CHECKSUM

Applications of cryptography to information systems include the obvious instances of keeping confidential data secret. This may apply to data transmission along a network, over broadcast waves or satellites, or physically in the form of magnetic or other storage media.

An application that has seen increased importance since 1989 is integrity protection of programs, particularly from viruses and other malicious code. One form of protection is to use the cryptographic checksum noted for chained block ciphers and self-synchronous stream ciphers. An executable version of the program known to be free from undesired modifications is taken as a basis. A checksum of some sort is calculated and stored. Then the checksum is re-calculated each time the program is invoked. If the current checksum matches the stored one, the program may be considered not to be infected by a virus or whatever, and it is allowed to run. Use of cryptographic checksums provides a much stronger assurance of continued file integrity than a simpler, and well-known, checksum algorithm might. Although the algorithm for a cryptographic checksum may be as well-known as more common varieties, the key(s) used will not be known. The problem of modifying a file and retaining the same checksum thus has acquired a significantly higher work factor.

Another class of applications of cryptography includes the need to ensure that a message that is received was sent by the proper parties and has not been altered during transmission. This need extends in some instances to a requirement to ensure that the message was sent, was received, and has not been altered even by the receiver. The general term for this kind of use of cryptographic techniques is message authentication code (MAC); the specific technology from cryptography usually is a digital signature.

A digital signature in computerized information systems serves much the same function as a handwritten signature in common person-to-person transactions. More precisely, if R is the recipient, S is the sender, and M is the message, then a digital signature must satisfy three requirements:

- R must be able to validate S's signature on M.
- It must be impossible for anyone to forge S's signature.
- If S should claim not to have signed a message, it must be possible for a third party to resolve a dispute between R and S (repudiation).

Use of a public key encryption scheme can provide a simple means of implementing a digital signature. S merely enciphers M using the private transformation to decipher M. R can verify that M is unchanged and from S by enciphering using the public transformation. If M is restored, then the digital signature is correct. A judge or other third party can repeat the same test using the public key, thus resolving a dispute. There are technical problems involved in using some public key systems (in the example, the message cannot be both secret and validated), and the problems differ, depending on the system under consideration.

Digital signatures in conventional systems like DES are more complex. Since both parties must have the same key to encipher and decipher a message, forgery is possible. Variations involving trusted third parties holding additional keys have been proposed. (For example, a third party holds one of a pair of keys from each of S and R. One key is private, one is shared between R and S. The private key is held by the third party. Various methods of using the private key by the third party can meet the requirements for digital signatures.)

Several standards involving message authentication codes and digital signatures now exist. FIPS 113, *Computer Data Authentication*, specifies a Data Authentication Algorithm based on DES. ANSI X9.9 (FIMA, relating to transmission of financial information) specifies a MAC computed in the same manner as the Data Authentication Code specified in FIPS 113.) A proposal for a Digital Authentication Standard was published by the National Institute of Standards and Technology in the U.S. in the summer of 1992; its fate remains to be determined, and it is the subject of considerable controversy.

In April, 1993, NIST published a proposal for a hardware device, called a "Clipper Chip," to implement a new encryption scheme suitable for use in communications devices. Without going into available details of the scheme itself, it is a private-key system with a "key escrow" provision. Here, key escrow means that two separate organizations (not identified in the announcement) each will hold part of a key for every chip; with both parts of the key, all messages enciphered by the chip can be deciphered. The intention is that it should be possible for authorized law enforcement agencies to obtain a court order for access to the escrow keys in circumstances controlled by the equivalent of search warrants. The stated reason for this escrow feature is that law enforcement agencies should be able to decipher drug dealers' traffic.

The Clipper Chip concept is very controversial, and it may not succeed. The notion of key escrow so that official agencies can decipher traffic raises issues of rights to privacy and freedom of speech. For example, it is speculated that the Clipper Chip cannot succeed unless other, stronger, cryptosystems are outlawed, which might be both unconstitutional in the U.S. and unenforceable as well. The security of the encryption itself depends upon secrecy of an algorithm, which is not considered appropriate in cryptography. The length and other characteristics of the keys to be generated have led to criticism of the strength of the encipherment. Security of processes for manufacturing and distributing the chips, including controls on seeds used in creating the master keys to be held in escrow, have been questioned.

Some of these issues have been raised in Europe as well. There, the A5 encipherment scheme, which is believed to be a very strong cryptosystem, has been implemented as a standard for telecommunications. Belatedly, governments in some countries have objected to routine use of encipherment methods not breakable by national security agencies, and there is a (retroactive) effort under way to implement weaker schemes that can be broken. These often are called A5(1), A5(2) and so forth, where A5(1) is the original strong system, and others are weaker. In a sense, this controversy is the dual of the controversy over the Clipper Chip; here governments object to a system that is too strong and, in the Clipper Chip case, private individuals object to one that is too weak.

2.10 ADVANTAGES AND DISADVANTAGES

The obvious advantage of any good encryption scheme is that the coded material cannot be used without the key. This means that, for example, one need not worry about someone tapping the telephone line or intercepting the microwave signal—the intercepted transmission is useless without the key. Similarly, encrypted data on diskettes are not at risk of disclosure unless the key is obtained along with the diskette. In essence, encrypted data in any form and on any medium, assuming DES or an equivalent or better coding scheme is used, reasonably may be considered not to be subject to disclosure or to use by unauthorized people, in nonmilitary situations.

Encryption does have disadvantages. If the key is lost, the data or whatever will not be available to the authorized user. The penetration effort shifts emphasis to the key: People must remember to keep that key confidential. (Personal Identification Numbers [P. I. N.] are issued by banks along with cards that will access automated teller equipment; an amazing percentage of people write their PINs *on the card*—thus destroying any security offered by use of PINs.) Thus key management (section 2.3) becomes a much more important part of managing data security.

The biggest potential disadvantage of encryption probably is performance degradation. To use any data or program that is encrypted, information first must be encoded, then stored or transmitted, then, later, decoded; in principle, this can slow a system down by as much as a factor of three. If the system has reasonable performance in the first place, this may not be too much of a problem, but it certainly *can* be a problem. Encrypted data may take more storage than plaintext; this can be a problem if storage is at a premium.

Somehow, the key needed to read encrypted data must be given to the intended user. The method of communicating such keys must be extremely secure, or encryption using the keys is useless. However, far fewer keys need to be transmitted, and transmitted less often, than encrypted data. Protection that would not be cost-effective in bulk can be cost-effective for infrequent short messages such as keys.

The best advice on encryption would be to be sure that extremely sensitive material (for example, tables of passwords and authorization codes, or encryption keys during transmission) is encrypted. Most material is not that sensitive and probably should not be encrypted. Use of the risk analysis methods outlined in Chapter 3 should identify the really sensitive material.

This advice will change as costs change and the cost-effectiveness of encryption changes. Costs are dropping and more software implementations of algorithms such as DES are seen, and in the near future it may be cost-effective to encrypt basically everything.

In some cases, there may be no option: For example, United States law required banks with automated teller devices to utilize DES or better encryption by 1989. Sometimes the no-option works the other way: It may be unlawful to take any computer containing a DES chip into a country considered unfriendly under U.S. law, for example.

Encryption increasingly is being seen as necessary for protection of privacy in applications such as cellular telephones, and for security in such areas as financial transactions, electronic data interchange (EDI), and other commercial applications. Applications of cryptography will continue to raise issues of privacy and national security. Another possible issue is that of non-tariff trade barriers is different governments mandate (or forbid) different cryptosystems as standards. Clearly, this is an area that will be active for years to come.

REFERENCES

Beker, Henry and Fred Piper, *Cipher Systems*, John Wiley & Sons, New York, 1982.

Bosworth, Bruce, *Codes, Ciphers and Computers*, Hayden Book Company, New York, 1982.

Brandstad, Dennis K., Ed., *Computer Security and the Data Encryption Standard*, National Bureau of Standards Special Publication 500-27, 1978.

Computer Data Authentication, Federal Information Processing Standards Publication 113, National Institute of Standards and Technology, Washington, DC.

Data Encryption Standard, Federal Information Processing Standards Publication 46-1, National Institute of Standards and Technology, Washington, DC, 1988.

Davies, D. W. and W. L. Price, *Security for Computer Networks*, John Wiley & Sons, New York, 1984.

DES Modes of Operation, Federal Information Processing Standards Publication 81, National Institute of Standards and Technology, Washington, DC, 1980.

Deavours, Cipher A., and Louis Kruh, *Machine Cryptography and Modern Cryptanalysis*, Artech House, Dedham, MA, 1985.

Denning, Dorothy Elizabeth Robling, *Cryptography and Data Security*, Addison-Wesley Publishing Company, Reading, MA, 1983.

Diffie, W. and M. Hellman, "New Directions in Cryptography," *IEEE Transactions on Information Theory*, Vol. IT-22(6), p. 644-654, November, 1976.

"Financial Institution Message Authentication X9.9," American National Standards Committee X9- Financial Services, American Bankers Association, Washington, DC, April 13, 1982.

Greenberger, M., "Method in Randomness," *Communications of the ACM*, vol 8 #3, March, 1965, p. 177.

"Guidelines for Implementing and Using the NBS Data Encryption Standard," FIPS Publication 74, U.S. Department of Commerce/National Bureau of Standards, Washington, DC, April, 1981.

Katzen, Harry J., *The Standard Data Encryption Algorithm*, Petrocelli Books, New York, 1977.

Message Authentication Code (MAC) Validation Systems Requirements and Procedures, NBS Special Publication 500-156, NIST, Washington, DC, 1988.

Meyer, Carl H., and Stephen M. Matyas, *Cryptography: A New Dimension in Computer Security*, John Wiley & Sons, New York, 1982.

Rhee, Man Y., *Error Correction Coding Theory*, McGraw-Hill, New York, 1990.

Rivest, R. L., A. Shamir, and L. Adleman, "A Method for Obtaining Digital Signatures and Public-Key Cryptosystems," *Communications of the ACM*, vol. 21(2), p. 120-126, February, 1978.

Shannon, C. E. "Communication Theory of Secrecy Systems," *Bell System Technical Journal*, October 1949.

3. Risk Management

The term *risk management* is used to describe the ideas, models, abstractions, methods, and techniques that are employed to control risk.

The knowledge includes:

- Risk assessment (or analysis, quantitative and qualitative)
- Risk reduction
- Selection, justification, and application of protective measures
- Risk acceptance
- Risk assignment (insurance)

Practitioners are expected to know:

- The principles of risk assessment
- The underlying mathematics
- The indications, uses, and applications of formal risk assessment methods
- The limitations of such methods
- The principle mechanisms for dealing with risk

For example:

- Identify risk prevention, reduction, assignment, and acceptance; give examples.
- Order or rank internal *versus* external, accidental *versus* intentional, modification *versus* disclosure; dishonest *versus* disgruntled, etc.
- Contrast effective *versus* efficient.
- Contrast hazard, vulnerability, exposure, risk.
- Contrast probability and rate of occurrence.
- Contrast quantitative *versus* qualitative risk analysis.
- Rank hazards by damage or rate of occurrence, *e.g.*, fire *versus* water, error *versus* malice, etc.
- Rank protective measures by effectiveness or efficiency, *e.g.*, supervision *versus* access control.
- Contrast acceptance *versus* assignment; recognize examples of each; suggest applications of each.
- Apply principles of cost-benefit analysis.
- Apply automated risk analysis systems.
- Compute annual loss expectancy.

DEFINITIONS

As in most chapters, some standard definitions are presented here. These are explored in this chapter and often reviewed to contrast differing expressions from different sources, or expanded upon or added to.

Annual Loss Expectancy

The ALE of an ADP system or activity is the expected yearly dollar value loss from the harm to the system or activity by attacks against its assets. (OPNAVINST 5239.1A)

Asset

1. Any software, data, hardware, administrative, physical, communications, or personnel resource within an ADP system or activity. (OPNAVINST 5239.1A)
2. An individual entity of the internal environment that must be protected from all types of peril. (ET)
3. An item whose compromise, as the result of an event, causes a financial loss to its owner. (RM)

Asset Category

A grouping of individual asset items. (RM)

Attack

The realization of a threat. How often a threat is realized depends on such factors as the location, type, and value of information being processed. Thus, short of moving the system or facility or radically changing its mission, there is usually no way that the level of protection can affect the frequency of attack. The exceptions to this are certain human threats where effective security measures can have a deterrent effect. The fact that an attack is made does not necessarily mean that it will succeed. The degree of success depends on the vulnerability of the system or activity and the effectiveness of existing countermeasures. (OPNAVINST 5239.1A)

Availability

That computer security characteristic that ensures the computer resources will be available to authorized users when they need them. This characteristic protects against denial of service. (AFR 205-16)

Denial of Service

The prevention of authorized access to resources or the delaying of time-critical operations. (ISO 7498-2)

Detection

The process of identifying the occurrence of an event and possibly the agent involved—the purpose of some protective mechanisms. (RM)

Exposure

1. A specific instance of the condition of being unduly exposed to losses resulting from the occurrence of one or more threat events. (WB)
2. A numerical evaluation of the degree of vulnerability of an asset to an event or threat. Computed in terms of statistically expected cost per time unit. (RM)

Passive Threat

The threat of unauthorized disclosure of information without changing the state of the system. (ISO 7498-2)

Peril

1. A generic form of misadventure to which certain classes of entities of the internal environment may be prone; for example, destruction, theft. (ET)
2. A number of different problems that assets of various types might experience. For computer systems, these are frequently taken to be theft, destruction, disclosures, contamination, and interruption. (RM)

Prevention

The process of inhibiting agents from performing events—the purpose of some protective mechanisms. (RM)

Risk

1. The loss potential that exists as the result of threat-vulnerability pairs. Reducing either the threat or the vulnerability reduces the risk. (AFR 205-16; AFR 700-10)
2. The uncertainty of loss expressed in terms of probability of such loss. (AR 380-380)
3. The probability that a particular threat will exploit a particular vulnerability of the Automated Information System or telecommunications system. (NCSC-WA-001-85)

Risk Analysis

1. An analysis of system assets and vulnerabilities to establish an expected loss from certain events based on estimated probabilities of occurrence. (AR 380-380; FIPS PUB 39)
2. The process of identifying security risks, determining their magnitude, and identifying areas needing safeguards; sometimes called *risk assessment*. (NCSC-WA-001-85; DODD 5200.28)

Risk Assessment

1. A study of the vulnerabilities, threats, likelihood, loss or impact, and theoretical effectiveness of security measures. Managers use the results of a risk assessment to develop security requirements and specifications. (AFR 205-16)
2. The process of evaluating threats and vulnerabilities, known and postulated, to determine expected loss and establish the degree of acceptability to system operations. (AR 380-380)
3. An analysis of system assets and vulnerabilities to establish an expected loss from certain events based on estimated probabilities of the occurrence of those events. The purpose of a risk assessment is to determine if countermeasures are adequate to reduce the probability of loss or the impact of loss to an acceptable level. (OPNAVINST 5239.1A)

Risk Management

1. An element of managerial science concerned with the identification, measurement, control, and minimization of uncertain events. An effective risk-management program encompasses

the following four phases:

a) Risk assessment, as derived from an evaluation of threats and vulnerabilities

b) Management decision

c) Control implementation

d) Effectiveness review. (AR 380-380)

2. The total process of identifying, controlling, and minimizing uncertain events affecting Automated Information System (AIS) resources. It includes risk analysis, cost benefit analysis, selection, implementation, test and evaluation of safeguards, and overall security review. (NCSC-WA-001-85; DODD 5200.28)

Safeguard

An entity (possibly a physical object, a procedure, or software) used to prevent, lessen the impact of, assist in the detection of, or in the recovery from risks. (ET)

Scenario Analysis

An information systems vulnerability assessment technique in which various possible attack methods are identified and the existing controls are examined in light of their ability to counter such attack methods. (WB)

Security Safeguards

The protective measures and controls that are prescribed to meet the security requirements specified for an AIS. Those safeguards may include, but are not necessarily limited to hardware and software security features, operations procedures, accountability procedures, access and distribution controls, management constraints, personnel security, physical structures, areas, and devices. (DODD 5200.28; NCSC-WA-001-85)

Sensitivity

The characteristic of a resource which implies its value or importance, and may include its vulnerability. (ISO 7498-2)

Sensitivity and Criticality

A method developed to describe the value of an information system by taking into account the cost, capability, and jeopardy to mission accomplishments or human life associated with the system. (AFR 700-10)

Sensitivity Assessment

A study of the data to determine level of protection required. (AFR 205-16)

Threat

1. The means through which the ability or intent of a threat agent to adversely affect an automated system, facility, or operation can be manifest. Categorize and classify threats as follows:

Categories	Classes
Human	Intentional

	Unintentional
Environmental	Natural
	Fabricated

(AFR 205-16; AFR 700-10)

2. Any circumstance or event with the potential to cause harm to a system in the form of destruction, disclosure, modification of data, and/or denial of service. (NCSC-WA-001-85)

Threat Agent

A method used to exploit a vulnerability in a system, operation, or facility. (NCSC-WA-001-85)

Threat Analysis

A methodology for determining the areas of vulnerability within a system and the result of emplacing countermeasures to counteract perceived threats to assets. (RM)

Threat Event

A specific type of threat event as often specified in a risk-analysis procedure. Examples are the neighboring river overflows its banks and submerges the adjacent data processing center under ten feet of water, and an ex-employee throws a Molotov cocktail into the organization's off-site data storage facility. (WB)

Threat Monitoring

The analysis, assessment and review of audit trails and other data collected for the purpose of searching out system events which may constitute violations or attempted violations of system security. (NCSC-WA-001-85)

Vulnerability

1. A weakness in system security procedures, hardware design, internal controls, etc., which could be exploited to gain unauthorized access to classified or sensitive information. (NCSC-WA-001-85)
2. A weakness in the physical layout, organization, procedures, personnel, management, administration, hardware, or software that may be exploited to cause harm to the ADP system or activity. The presence of a vulnerability does not in itself cause harm; a vulnerability is merely a condition or set of conditions that may allow the ADP system or activity to be harmed by an attack. (OPNAVINST 5239.1A)

Vulnerability Assessment

1. A measurement of vulnerability which would include:

   a) The susceptibility of a particular system to a specific attack.

   b) The opportunity available to a threat agent (methods or things which may be used to exploit a vulnerability (such as fire)) to mount that attack. A vulnerability is always demonstrable but may exist independently of a known threat. In general, a description of a vulnerability takes account of those factors under friendly control. (AR 380-380)

2. A review of the susceptibility to loss or unauthorized use of resources, errors in reports and information, illegal or unethical acts, and adverse or unfavorable public opinion. Vulnerability assessments do not identify weaknesses or result in improvements. They are the mechanism with which an organization can determine quickly the potential for losses in its different programs or functions. The schedule of internal control reviews should be based on the results of the vulnerability assessments. (DODD 7040.6)

3.1 ASSET IDENTIFICATION AND VALUATION

3.1.1 Processing Valuation

Since an asset is something of value, let us consider value analysis next. A computer system, or any other system, presumably has value to a business. If not, it should be scrapped, or never created in the first place. The "processing value" analysis considers what it is worth to the business to have this thing done: From the viewpoint of the user, *and without regard to how the activity is to be performed*, what is the value of the activity. Preferably, this value should be expressed in dollars and cents. The instructor presumably teaches students, who pay the institution for the service. What is this value to the institution? Notice that here, the instruction perhaps could have been delivered by video tape, or laser disc, or by satellite hookup from another city. We are asking at the moment only about the value of the service. Having established a value, we can then say that this service is an asset, and the value of having it performed is whatever we determined it to be in the analysis. Only the user of the service has the background to assign a value; for security purposes, the more senior the user, the more useful the value assigned is likely to be.

In data processing systems, the value analysis should be performed in terms of three properties:

1. Availability
2. Confidentiality
3. Integrity

In the first instance, what is the value of continued *availability* of the service? Or, turned around, what would happen if the service disappeared entirely? (The computer center burned down, for example.) If the payroll run takes five hours, is normally started at 11:00 A.M. on payday, and checks must be delivered by 5:00 P.M. the same day, then the maximum acceptable downtime is probably less than one hour. The value of this service could well be the continued existence of the business, or large legal fees due to violation of a union contract and resulting strike, or similar high figures.

Confidentiality refers to the need to keep data or information from being public. If all the organization's data and information could be published without problems, then there might be no need of confidentiality. In practice, this is rarely, if ever, true. In Canada and the United States, privacy laws require employers to be reticent about personal information of employees. Most financial figures for a company are at least sensitive. For example, a competitor might pay well indeed to know the exact budget allocated to advertising a specific product. Medical records are highly protected in most jurisdictions. One way to get an idea how much the confidentiality attribute of an asset is worth is to imagine how much money a person or group would pay to have the information, or the cost of the loss of the business, if there is a legal requirement to observe privacy.

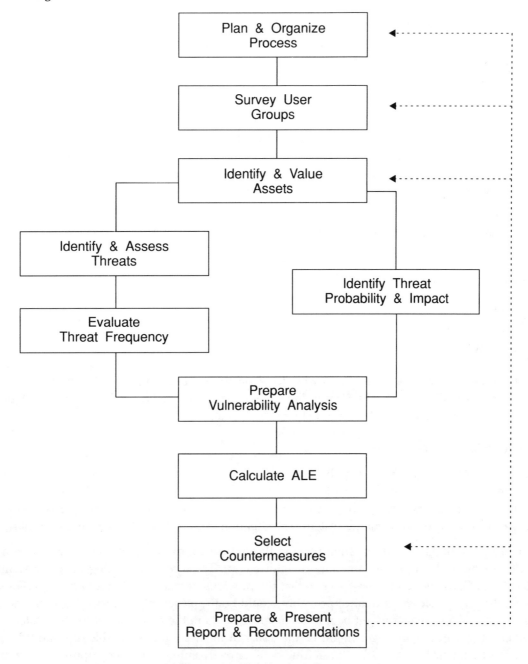

Figure 3.1. Risk Analysis Process

The third property of the assets in an information system under consideration is *integrity*. Integrity of data or processes is the property that relates to their authenticity, accurateness, and completeness. Has there been an unannounced change in a credit limit? Has all information been reported to the credit granter? Is the information that was reported accurate as well as authentic and complete? It is perhaps easiest to comprehend the value of integrity when a tangible asset is under discussion. For example, if a bank cannot depend on account balances, it could sustain a very large loss through paying checks that are not covered. In an inventory, the potential loss is the amount of material that could be diverted between physical inventory counts. In a more general information system, the loss of goodwill of clients could be a cost. For a newspaper, unreliable data used as backing for a damaging story could incur substantial legal liabilities.

Through looking at value analysis we have examined the three characteristics of an asset in an information system and we have discussed some examples of how one would set a value on an asset. The three characteristics are *availability*, *confidentiality*, and *integrity*. The general rule for setting a value on an asset is that the user or owner of the asset must be the one to do it (with the help of professionals to be sure). Let us look first at considerations in selecting a risk management team, and then at two classifications of assets, and at some representative assets in each of the classifications.

While "asset" has not been defined other than as "something of value to the business," we have identified a starting point for identification of assets and properties to be examined:

Start by determining the processing value of the service in question.

Examine the properties of

1. availability
2. confidentiality
3. integrity

This gives a sufficient picture of "asset" to begin the valuation process. Examination of the valuation process has resulted in identifying some of the people who need to be involved; next, we expand upon this to look at the risk management team.

3.1.2 Risk Management Team

Value analysis is not a particularly difficult activity, but it does require that fundamental questions be answered carefully by people who have the appropriate background to know the answers. On the data processing group's side, the key team member clearly is that person who has final responsibility for securing the system. The situation from the users' side is more complex.

Every piece of data or information passing through an information system has an *owner* and someone who is *responsible* for the data or information. The *owner* may delegate responsibility; delegation of ownership of course means that the previous owner is no longer involved. For example, the vice president of finance probably would be the *owner* of all accounting data; the accounts receivable manager might be *responsible* for the data in the accounts receivable system. At another level, the A/R manager might be the *owner* of the accounts receivable data, and the supervisor of data entry responsible for getting data correctly entered into a computer. In the final analysis, the *owner* must be involved in the value attribution. Since data and information may be changed as they pass through the information system, the persons who hold the ownership and responsibility positions may also change; thus several people may need to be involved on the users' side where only the person with final responsibility is necessary from the data processing department. As stated previously, the more senior the people involved, the better the results are likely to be as answers to fundamental questions about the value of a particular asset to the ongoing organization.

In summary then, the following people must be members of the risk analysis team:

- Data Processing: Person with final responsibility for securing the system

- Users: Owner(s) of data and information [or their delegates]

Many other team members may be desirable for technical expertise or other reasons, but these two groups *must* be involved or the security effort is doomed to irrelevance.

3.1.3 Classification of Assets

There are many ways to classify assets. Classification schemes like "secret" and so forth are of great interest in access control considerations, and are examined in Chapter 5. Here we are concerned with valuation and risk analysis, and we use the accounting distinction between "tangible" and "intangible" assets. In essence:

> *Tangible* assets are measurable in dollars and cents.
>
> *Intangible* assets are not easily measured in dollars and cents.

This distinction is somewhat arbitrary; greater effort at measurement, or more data to work with, often will allow a measurement in dollars. For example, Johnson & Johnson probably considers the brand name Tylenol to be an intangible asset because its value was very difficult to measure. Since the discovery of packages with broken seals and poisoned capsules added in 1982 and 1986, and the resulting product redesign, the asset is easier to measure, as it has at least the value of the money spent on advertising and management time in allaying public fears and redesigning the product to be more tamper resistant. Of course, much effort was spent; it seems likely that Johnson & Johnson would prefer to have had the value remain intangible rather than spend the money that was invested. The point here is that even "intangible" assets often can have dollar values applied, if enough effort is invested. The risk management team and senior management must trade off measurement effort against value achieved; in asset valuation for security purposes, being out by a factor of two normally is not a problem so long as relative sizes are maintained.

A second, related classification is *physical versus logical* assets. A physical asset is also a tangible asset. Many logical assets are intangible. An example could be a computer program stored on a "floppy disk." The physical value of the storage medium is likely about $2. The logical value of the arrangement of data (the "program") may be hundreds of thousands of dollars. It would be difficult to measure this value precisely; the usual way is to estimate how long it would take to recreate the program, or how long it took to create it in the first place. In this case, the *intrinsic* value of the medium has an *acquired* value added to it.

Much, or most, of the value of assets in an information system very well may be represented by intangible logical assets. The value of a document in computer-readable format, such as this one, is at least the cost of having it re-entered from a paper backup, assuming all computer readable forms are lost. If the paper backup were lost as well, it would have to be created again, likely from memory, by a senior person who did the original creation. The value of data in an accounts receivable subsystem could be as high as the total of all bad accounts, or of all purchases not yet billed. More about actual asset values is discussed below.

There are two main ways to classify assets that are of interest in security work: tangible/intangible, and physical/logical. *Tangible* assets have easily measured dollar values; *intangible* assets are not easily measured in dollars. *Physical* assets are those you can "feel;" *logical* assets are such things as data and the arrangement of things. Most physical assets are tangible as well. To some extent, the amount of effort expended on measurement can change an asset from intangible to tangible; if you spend enough, most intangible assets can be given dollar values with high confidence.

3.1.4 Subclassifications of Assets

3.1.4.1 People, Skills, and Procedures

In discussions and seminars on computer security, participants often are asked to identify the single most-important asset requiring protection. Is it the mainframe computer hardware? The program library? Or whatever? Surprisingly, many make several guesses before they reach the correct answer: "people." (More senior staff generally get the right answer the first time.) An organization can be defined as a group of *people* gathered to accomplish a *purpose* that they cannot accomplish individually. Machines do not have purposes; people do. Without the people, all other assets are irrelevant. In security, people may have reasons to penetrate, and they nearly always deal with people in a penetration attempt.

Both philosophically and practically, then, the protection of human life is the one overriding concern in any intelligent security plan. The fire extinguisher exists, not to put out the fire, but to ensure a clear path to safety for people in the computer room. Industrial safety is a field with an extensive literature; computer operations are not so different as to require much special treatment in a work of this type.

The skills, training, and experience of people are assets. It costs money to find new people and to train them. Examples of people in the information security arena include:

- Operators
- Programmers
- Analysts
- Managers
- Secretarial staff
- Security staff
- Custodial staff
- Vendors
- Customers

All of these and others, depending on the installation, must be considered both as assets and also as threats or exposures.

Figure 3.2 is one of the familiar "pyramid" representations showing the approximate relationship of four major types of asset and their cost. The cost or value of the people in the organization, their training and experience, and their familiarity with procedures is by far the most significant (and also the most often ignored in evaluating a change to a new system). This observation naturally leads to another asset, procedures and procedure manuals, as well as documentation for systems, programs, equipment, and all else.

3.1.4.2 Physical and Environmental

Here, we are looking at physical assets besides such things as computer hardware, which is treated separately. A list of physical, tangible assets could include:

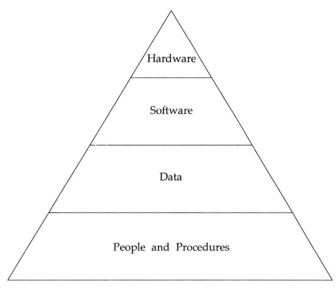

Figure 3.2. Investment Triangle

- **Facilities**
  Building, back-up storage area, equipment rooms, air conditioning rooms, office space
- **Support**
  Fire system, electricity, air conditioning, communications, fuel oil for backup power, water
- **Supplies, Material, and Furniture**
  Re-usable tapes, disks, diskettes, tape cartridges, expendable paper, forms, waste paper, blank checks, desks, chairs, containers, bookcases, filing cabinets

Physical, intangible assets do exist, despite the blanket comment earlier. A "prime location" such as Colorado Springs, Colorado, can make the job of attracting people to come to work with a company a much easier task. This would be an intangible asset, although the site location is clearly physical.

Of course, this list is nowhere near exhaustive and will vary depending on location. In Yellowknife, NWT (an isolated city of 10,000 in the Canadian Arctic), retail stores with computer-controlled cash registers have boxes between the machine and the power supply. Due to special problems with utility power reliability and "cleanness," some sort of filter is universal there. In Edmonton, Alberta, and many other major cities, such devices are rare since the power supply is quite dependable and "clean." Other major centers, especially in the U.S.. Eastern Seaboard area, experience brownouts or other power supply problems; in those locations, the boxes between the machines and the wall plug are again common. Thus, local considerations affect the items on the list and their value.

3.1.4.3 Communications

Communications could be listed under "Physical and Environmental"; however, as computer and other technologies grow, communications is assuming an increasing part of a computer center's value and costs[1]. Basic telephone is one thing; Local Area Networks, Distributed Data

---

[1]See Chapter 8 for a detailed exploration of telecommunications security.

Processing, satellite communications and other capabilities are quite another. Therefore, it is appropriate to consider communications facilities separately. Physical tangible assets might include:

- Front-end processors (specialized computers programmed to act as an interface between mainframe computers and communications channels)
- Concentrators (a *concentrator* normally takes input from many low-speed channels and combines it into one high-speed channel leading to the front-end processor)
- Terminals
- Modems
- Communication lines (coaxial cable or optical fibers, for example)
- Data encryption hardware
- Satellite uplinks and downlinks
- Private branch exchange (PBX and PABX) equipment

All of these assets could be included in a complex voice/data communications system for a transnational company; or a small company might use only telephone and public carriers.

3.1.4.4 Hardware

The hardware area is the one most people associate immediately with the notion of a physical asset to be considered in an information system security program. It is probably the smallest, and probably also the area of the least total dollar investment. Hardware includes media such as paper, tapes, and so on, both re-usable and expendable; these have been mentioned above. Equipment includes:

- Processors
- Disk drives
- Tape drives
- Printers
- Terminals
- Cabling
- Spare parts

The equipment probably varies as much as anything, except software and data, from place to place. Perhaps some installations still have card readers and card punches. Certainly some have mass storage devices.

3.1.4.5 Software

Software, particularly applications software, is different in each information system. (This is changing with the mass retail sale of identical copies of such programs as Lotus 1-2-3 and other proprietary software.) A list of common software would include:

- Operating system (MS-DOS, UNIX, or whatever)
- Utilities (sorts, editors, . . .)
- Compilers
- Communications software

- Database software (Cullinet's IDMS, IBM's SQL, dBASE, . . .)[2]
- Teleprocessing software (IBM's CICS and CMS, . . .)
- Application software
- Catalogued procedure libraries

Each item has some value, if only in availability. Without the operating system, all other software is useless, even though the operating system may have been included "free" with the hardware.

3.1.4.6 Data and Information

The things that vary most from place to place naturally are data and information. It is somewhat pointless to attempt any sort of exhaustive listing of such variable items. Note, however, that data and information are assets of considerable value. Computer-readable data is worth *at least* as much as it would cost to re-enter it (that is, recapture or recreate it, if possible). Over time, this dominates the cost of hardware and software. Some types of data commonly found are:

1. Databases (Nexis, for example, contains full text of numerous U.S. newspapers and would be enormously expensive to recreate, if it is even possible.)
2. On-line files (whatever is more or less current)
3. Off-line files
4. Input files (alteration could leave an opening for fraud.)
5. Output files
6. Audit trails and logs (loss could make recovery, or fraud detection, impossible.)
7. Indexes (Just as a telephone book is more valuable with letter-of-the-alphabet tabs, most data are closer to usable information with a table of contents.)
8. Contents of memory (lost if power is lost and the data were not yet saved)

3.1.4.7 Goodwill

Goodwill refers to a company or organization or individual's reputation among the clientele. While it is difficult or impossible to attach a dollar value to goodwill, the way potential or actual customers view an organization is a critical determinant of its success or failure. The most senior level of management usually has the best idea of the value of the organization's goodwill.

3.1.5 Determining values for assets

3.1.5.1 Acquired and Intrinsic Values

The notions of intrinsic and acquired value are significant both in accounting terms and for risk-analysis purposes. In determining asset values, it is necessary to be sure that these concepts are very clear, and that they are kept separate. For security purposes, protecting a blank diskette worth perhaps $2 is a very different problem from protecting a program on the diskette, which could be worth $100,000.

---

[2]dBASE may be a poignant illustration of how asset valuation can change, and also of the risks of litigation regarding copyright. When Ashton-Tate lost in court, they lost their copyrights, and thus the value of dBASE (and of Ashton-Tate as a corporation) changed significantly.

The *intrinsic* value of an asset is normally the cost of replacing the physical component, or what the physical component could be sold for. A diskette has an intrinsic value of perhaps $2. A five-year-old used computer may have a negative intrinsic value; you could have to pay for someone to take it away and dispose of it. The intrinsic value of a procedures manual may be $20 in copying and paper costs. However, intrinsic value is not the whole story. An asset also has an *acquired* value. When information is put onto that diskette, the diskette has an intrinsic value *plus* an acquired value. When people become used to new procedures and training programs are in place, the procedures manual has an intrinsic value and a very large acquired value as well. As an organization becomes used to one way of doing things, the system itself gains an acquired value. The first major step is when parallel testing is complete and the doubling of effort is stopped; the system then has no backup and a large acquired value component is added. As people get more and more comfortable with using the new system, the training, experience, and familiarity add further to the acquired value of the system. Sudden loss of availability after a few years can become catastrophic; the acquired value is thus extremely large. The five-year-old computer may still be in use to process the payroll; loss of availability at the wrong time could be catastrophic.

It helps ease the analysis process when standard forms (such as illustrated in Figure 3.3) are used; they are easier to combine in later stages, and they help ensure that things do not get overlooked. A form might contain:

3.1.5.2 Purpose of Assigning Value to Assets

Once the value of various services to the company has been determined, it is fairly straightforward to identify the assets involved in providing the services. The analysis of processing value was done without regard to the methods used to provide the service. When asset valuation is done, assets involved in providing the service as it is done now are identified, classified according to physical/logical and tangible/intangible categories, and by subcategory. It then is necessary to attach a value to each of the identified assets. Recall that the purpose of this exercise is to identify security exposures and the value of the assets that may be exposed, so that an intelligent security program can be designed. We are *not* trying to get an exact value of the business; in fact, it often is sufficient simply to know that one asset is worth more than another (you protect the more valuable one).

With this in mind, there are probably thousands of ways to ascribe a value to an asset. Some are difficult to use; some are expensive to use; some may not be possible or practical. The purpose of the valuation in security analysis is to rank assets and to get a reasonable idea of how much it is worth investing to protect them. The valuation process is part of the cost of the security system, and normally low cost outweighs greater precision. The ultimate result of all this work is to make sure that appropriate effort is invested to protect assets, but not so much that the cost of the security exceeds the expected loss in case of an incident.

3.1.5.3 How to Measure Asset Values

With the purpose of asset valuation for security in mind, consider first how to measure the value of an asset; that is, what units of measure to use. The traditional unit is dollars.

The arguments for using dollars as a measure are many and powerful. First, it is a universal measure. A given number of dollars has the same value everywhere within a single economy. Reducing everything to this universal measure means it is easy to make comparisons. This is probably the most important argument for using dollars and cents. Second, using this measure forces people to expend more care on determining a value; therefore, the resulting values are more likely to be reasonably accurate. Third, since a business's success or failure is measured in dollar terms, people are comfortable with thinking about assets in terms of dollars.

On the other hand, it can be very difficult to reduce some kinds of intangible assets to dollar values. It may be necessary to use statistical techniques or other methods involving estimation. Eventually, not only does the cost of estimating go up, but the final result comes to depend on very subjective assumptions and may not be any better than simpler estimating methods.

Designing a security system involves accurate relative rankings. No system can protect everything perfectly; it is necessary to trade off cost against value and priority. Rather than expend extraordinary efforts to come up with dollar figures, it may be sufficient to use *scalar* measures. The most commonly proposed is simple orders of magnitude. An example is:

Asset Valuation
Acquired Value Worksheet

Date Valued: _____

Revised: No._____

                Date_____

Page __ of __

ASSET

Intrinsic Value:_____

ACQUIRED VALUES

1. Integrity

        VALUE:_____

Justification:

2. Availability

        VALUE:_____

Justification:

3. Confidentiality

        VALUE:_____

Justification:

Figure 3.3. Asset Valuation—Acquired Value Worksheet

Table 3.1. Scale for Asset Valuation in Dollars

Scalar Number	*Value in Dollars*
0	$1 or less
1	up to $10
2	$100
3	$1,000
4	$10,000
.	.
.	.
8	$100,000,000

In this scale, the number assigned is based on a power of 10 ("order of magnitude"). If the asset has any value between, say, $10,000 and $100,000, it will get the scalar value 5. This is a very wide scale, but most people will be able to give a firm estimate within an order of magnitude. If more precision is needed, other power bases can be used. If the Naperian logarithm base e (2.7182818 . . .) is used, we could construct a table like this:

Table 3.2. Scale for Asset Valuation in Dollars

Scalar Number	Dollar Value
0	below $300
1	up to $700
2	up to $2,000
3	up to $5,000
4	$15,000
5	$40,000
6	$110,000
7	$300,000
8	$800,000
9	$2,200,000
.	.
.	.
.	.

In this table, each range limit grows by a factor of about 2.7183 rather than by a factor of 10. This allows people still to "guess" reliably, but gives smaller intervals and thus more precision.

Scales like this can be used in two ways. First, people can be asked to estimate a loss as "between 500 and 1,000 dollars," or whatever interval is of interest. The guess is then recorded as a scalar (in this case, 3 or 1, depending on which of the above two tables were used). The scalars are then used in further calculations, which simplifies the arithmetic. A second way to use such a table is to ask people to rank exposures relative to a known exposure. If they ranked event B as "about 100 times as bad as event A," then (assuming powers of 10), if A were a $100,000 problem, B would be a $10,000,000 problem. Using this method, one arrives at (very conservative) dollar figures, which again are used in further calculation.

The main disadvantage of using scalars to get a relative ranking is that corporate management normally are conditioned and trained to think in dollars; the scalar rankings will not have the same impact as dollars would.

Dollar values are best, since they allow comparison and people are comfortable with them. If it is expensive or impractical to get exact dollars, scalar estimation methods are one way to convert "guesses" into dollar values. More sophisticated weighted entry table methods can also be used; these are beyond the scope needed here.

3.1.5.4 Criticality and Sensitivity

We begin this section by repeating two definitions from the beginning of the chapter:

Sensitivity

The characteristic of a resource which implies its value or importance, and may include its vulnerability. (ISO 7498-2)

Sensitivity and Criticality

A method developed to describe the value of an information system by taking into account the cost, capability, and jeopardy to mission accomplishments or human life associated with the system. (AFR 700-10)

The definition of *sensitivity* from the International Standards Organization (ISO) is more general than the specific valuation method defined in Air Force regulations. However, the principles of such analysis do not vary within commercial and military or national security arenas, merely the consequences of security incidents.

3.1.5.4.1 Criticality

The term *criticality* typically is used to refer to analysis relating to items that are critical to an operation, in the sense that a security incident involving these items can cause major impacts on the organization. Some such impacts could be:

- Loss of human life
- Business impact, such as major destruction of corporate assets or other events that interrupt the normal course of business significantly
- Revenue losses
- Embarrassment
- Legal problems

These dimensions are not independent. For example, loss of life probably also will be associated with destruction of assets and with legal problems. One reason for differences in treatment of information security between government and commercial sectors is that in the government arena, consequences of incidents involving critical assets are more likely to include loss of life, national prestige, or even national existence. More attention to security is appropriate given the greater costs of some types of incident.

The most significant difference between the commercial and government arenas in risk analysis and management is that due to the greater exposures in government (and, especially, military), more assets are critical. Also, efforts at perpetrating security problems often may be better funded and more focused than typical commercial espionage. Again, military situations are the most problematic, as human life and national security may be involved, on both sides of the security effort.

3.1.5.4.2 Sensitivity

Sensitivity typically refers to information that must not be disclosed lest it lose value or provide significant advantage to a competitor. In the commercial arena, issues that must be examined in evaluating sensitivity of assets include:

- Privacy
- Trade secrets
- Planning information
- Financial data

In national security and military environments, much the same issues are relevant. As with criticality, the environment includes intelligent, well-funded penetration attempts. The consequences of disclosure of sensitive information also may be far greater in the non-commercial areas.

3.1.5.4.3 Sources

Four sources of information about sensitivity and criticality of assets are of major relevance:

- Senior management
- Clients
- Users
- MIS

This list is approximately in order of the value of sources sensitivity and criticality information. It is a major part of the responsibility of senior management to be aware of the sensitivity and criticality of assets entrusted to their care, as this affects the allocation of organizational resources. Another major part of senior managements' role is strategic planning; they must be aware of the value of information to their organization (and thus conversely to their competitors) in order to plan effectively.

Users of organization assets may have a good perspective on the sensitive and criticality of assets they use in the course of their normal work. The professional should ensure that input is obtained from users in a properly conducted risk analysis. In general, one should not expect users to have much feel for strategic implications of the information or assets they use. Quite simply, this is not part of their job.

An asset often overlooked in this sort of analysis is clients. In a commercial environment, the clients of an organization are those for whom the corporation ultimately works. Particularly in the case of issues of privacy, the best source of the criticality of client information is the client.

Other than very senior personnel who also are involved in more general corporate activities, people in Management Information Systems (or whatever the name is in a specific organization) typically are not a good source of data in a sensitivity and criticality analysis. The major exception to this observation is in the area of assets critical to the operation of corporate information handling, where MIS people typically are very well-versed. It may be hoped that this situation will change; however, it has not changed significantly in the experience of the authors, which spans the time from 1964 to the present.

3.1.5.4.4 Levels: Military; National Security; Commercial

The qualitative differences among the three levels of risk evaluation and management are small. However, there is a quantitative difference great enough to amount to a qualitative difference.

In the commercial arena, the basis is financial; while human life may be involved, it is relatively rare. Most problems are from human error. Industrial espionage exists, but it is seldom well-financed. Sabotage also exists, but also seldom is well-financed or focused.

In the national security arena, issues of human error are joined with very well-financed and directed security threats as governments engage in all manner of espionage and sabotage. The basic dimensions of sensitivity and criticality analysis are much as above, but the degree of effort by penetrators and the potential losses to security incidents justify the investment of much more effort in security issues.

In military situations, the notes in the previous paragraph are emphasized even further, and the range of threat is greater. The same principles apply.

3.1.5.5 Asset Valuation: Standard Accounting

With the purpose of asset valuation in mind, and noting the possibility of using differing metrics, the easiest way to value assets relates to normal accounting practices. This will work only for tangible assets whose value is "on the books," that is, valued in the accounting records of the company according to Generally Accepted Accounting Principles (GAAP). Then the value of the asset simply can be looked up:

- Locate the book value of the asset.
- Locate the accumulated depreciation.

Add the two, and you have an idea of the loss. Depending on the depreciation method used, you may also have an idea of replacement cost.

3.1.5.6 Asset Valuation: Replacement Cost

Probably the main virtue of the previous method is that it is fast; for tangible assets, the numbers are already there, and there is little difficulty or cost in getting to them. Many accountants would caution that adding book value to depreciation does not necessarily give a good measure of replacement cost. There are accounting and other techniques that allow fairly good estimation of replacement costs. One that often works well at minimal cost is to call up a vendor and ask what the cost of asset A is today. For tangible assets, this works well for security purposes. Note that this issue is more complex in practice; one would not necessarily replace item A with an identical item today: The business may have changed, item A could be obsolete, etc. Accountants have devised ways to cope with this sort of problem. Recall again, that exact dollars are not usually needed in security analysis. Most estimates should be rounded to the nearest $1,000 or even the nearest $10,000; don't spend too much time on small numbers.

3.1.5.7 Asset Valuation: Loss Of Availability

Frequently, an asset with a relatively low cost ("intrinsic value") may be vital to the continued operation of the business. Loss of its availability represents a very large cost. The risk evaluation team should ensure that loss of availability is considered as a cost in each asset that is valued. Concerned personnel may be able to estimate these losses clearly; or estimating methods such as the scalars shown previously may be used.

3.1.5.8 Asset Valuation: Estimating Methods

The procedures of identifying processing values, identifying assets, and valuing assets lead to a considerable amount of data. These data should be collected in a standardized format so they will be available for further calculation. Many sources show forms for this purpose. All of the forms are very similar, with entries for assets, intrinsic value, and the acquired value components of availability, integrity, and confidentiality. Such a layout is found in Figure 3.4.

Filling in the asset, intrinsic value, and acquired value components columns will leave the data gathered in a format that is concise and useful for the fourth step in the risk management process, combining threat assessments with the asset valuation to calculate dollar exposures and priorities. Each asset is named in the first column. Then the intrinsic value is entered. The acquired values of integrity, availability, and confidentiality are filled in last. Repeat this for each asset.

As an example, a diskette (*asset*) may have an intrinsic value of $2. One possibility is a diskette with a word processor on it. (One also could list the intrinsic value as the cost of the software plus diskette, perhaps $450.) Its acquired values will vary from time to time. It has an acquired value of availability that might be equal to the down time incurred by the operator while a new diskette is obtained, say, $125. (If the diskette contains custom programmed macros, then the programming cost would be added to the availability.) The value of integrity in this case would be about the same—if it doesn't retain integrity, the word processor won't work and the software has to be replaced. The acquired value of confidentiality in this case probably is zero.

General Value Analysis of System Assets

ASSET	INTRINSIC VALUE	ACQUIRED VALUE		
		AVAILA-BILITY	INTEGRITY	CONFIDEN-TIALITY

Figure 3.4. Asset Valuation Worksheet

3.1.6 Use of Asset Analysis Results; Limitations—Lack of Data, Interpretation

There are two primary uses for the results obtained from this asset analysis process:

1. A picture of the total investment by the firm is gained. Since much of the material has been reduced to dollars, senior management and others accustomed to thinking in dollar terms will get an appreciation (frequently, a *new* and *different* appreciation) of the amount at risk.
2. The figures derived are used as input to calculations leading to the final risk management assessment.

The asset analysis could show that there are no really valuable assets to be protected, and thus it is a waste of resources to go further in the risk management process. More commonly, it alerts senior management to the fact that some very valuable parts of the business are exposed and need to be looked at very carefully. The total value of the assets related to information systems frequently comes as a great surprise to management, with a resulting desire to carry on in the process, at a rather high priority.

In some form, the process of valuing services, identifying assets, and valuing assets must be undergone before one can plan a rational security system. However, for a smaller organization, often the basic data are unavailable. Statistical techniques that work well for large samples do not always work well for small samples. There is little actual difficulty in most of the asset identification and valuation process described previously; however, if done properly the result is a lot of data. The total risk assessment process does involve a substantial amount of arithmetic and detail work. It is probably impractical for a small organization to attempt a full-fledged risk analysis unless computer support is available.

It is important to avoid "paralysis by analysis" while still doing a thorough job of asset identification and valuation. Too much detail is as bad as too little:

- It is hard to value the "small stuff."
- The cost of the risk analysis rises.
- The result can be an overwhelming sea of numbers.

3.2 THREAT AND EXPOSURE ASSESSMENT

3.2.1 Threats, vulnerabilities, and exposures defined

Many factors, some unique to EDP systems, singly and especially in combination make computer systems particularly vulnerable to threats. A particular characteristic of EDP systems is the density of information. A problem that is not unique is what must be characterized simply as poor management. (See also Chapter 10 for comments on legislative efforts related to these factors.) There are six areas of special interest:

- Density of information
- Accessibility of systems
- Complexity
- Electronic vulnerability
- Media vulnerability
- Human factors

The first factor is density of information. A diskette contained in a package about 1/16" thick and about 3-1/2" square may contain the equivalent of 50 to over 5,000 pages of textual information. It is easy for someone to slip several of these into a shirt pocket and carry out information and programs that may be worth hundreds or thousands of dollars. This exposure will increase with technological advances; optical storage, for example, permits densities much greater than presently achievable with the magnetic diskette described. One diskette the size of an audio CD disk can hold many thousands of pages of information. Similarly, anyone with a computer has access to a great deal of information and can affect it very quickly. When a terminal may be connected from anywhere in the world where there is a telephone system, the problem of securing information is not in the same class as simply putting a lock on the file-room door.

The second factor is that computer systems traditionally have been designed to be as accessible as possible to a wide range of people. As noted earlier, with communications included, the physical location of the people no longer matters very much. This accessibility means many exposures exist that were minimal or nonexistent in manual paper-based systems.

The third factor is complexity. It is not unusual to find operating systems or applications programs containing millions of instructions, far more than any single human being can comprehend as a whole. Worse, while it is simple to demonstrate that an error does exist, there is no universal way to prove that errors do *not* exist. Technically sophisticated people ("hackers") have taken advantage of errors to penetrate these complex, dense systems that are accessible from anywhere.

Computer systems function using electronic signals. These signals can be detected and interpreted from outside the systems. Outside sources such as radio transmitting towers or police radar in a speed trap can interfere with the internal working of unshielded computer systems.

The information-dense medium of magnetic disks mentioned previously is also subject to problems not commonly considered. For example, placing the diskette on top of a home television receiver, or beside a ringing telephone, may subject the information to corruption from unintended magnetic impulses. The fact that the information is not easily read by people without equipment can be a good thing—it lessens the exposure to casual "eavesdropping." The same characteristic means, however, that people may have control over sensitive information without realizing it.

The sixth and final area where EDP systems are particularly vulnerable must be laid at the feet of DP management. As of 1992, most senior DP managers started in a technical position. Many have reached management positions with little or no proper training in management. It is not unusual to find a high degree of implicit trust and responsibility placed on personnel at junior levels without commensurate management control and accountability. This sort of human exposure is probably the greatest vulnerability associated with the EDP environment. It is essentially poor management (and here is a reason why effective security is not greatly concerned with technical factors in system security, but spends so much time on non-computer areas such as procedures).

The word "threat" in casual conversation is used in relation to people with intent to do something bad to something else. In security and control analysis, this word has taken on a slightly different meaning. To the security specialist the word "threat" does not refer so much to a person, as to a *situation* where some (unknown and unspecified) person *could* do something undesirable.

To be precise:

A *threat* is any circumstance or event with the potential to cause harm to a system in the form of destruction, disclosure, modification or data, and/or denial of service. (NCSC-WA-001-85)

The difference in usage is perhaps unfortunate, as it tends to cause management to consider security personnel to be paranoid when they refer to "threats." The word should be avoided (unless used with the more "standard" meaning) in reports to management.

The word "vulnerability," used as a noun in the context of security analysis, addresses the same area as "threat." The vulnerability is the exposure or weakness; the threat is the ability to take, or the act of taking, advantage of a vulnerability. This word will recur in the following text, for example when discussing possible exposures to threats from personnel as related to their normal job responsibilities.

The word "exposure" has a semi-technical meaning when used in a context such as "calculating exposures." In this context, we are talking about a dollar value that is assigned to the result of identifying an asset, a threat, and a likelihood and combining these three data. This dollar value serves two functions: to rank exposures, and to allow the risk manager to select security measures that control exposure without costing more than the exposure itself. In more casual discussion, "exposure" and "vulnerability" are more or less interchangeable.

3.2.2 Methodologies for Threat Assessment

In risk management, it is critical not to ignore threats, *however unlikely they seem*. A very small chance of an event that would kill the business still must be considered. Only if the likelihood is truly zero—for instance, communications risk in a system with no communications capability—is it valid to ignore the threat entirely. As was mentioned when discussing asset valuation, one of the goals of a methodology for selecting threats must be to be sufficiently complete without the analysis costing more than the exposure that might be avoided.

A starting point for a methodology is to consider either the properties of *threats* or the properties of *assets*. In the first case, what are the threats—for example, earthquake, fire, nuclear disaster, or police radar. The exposed assets are then identified and the analysis proceeds. A second approach is to identify properties of assets, and then determine which potential threats relate to those properties. This approach is the basis chosen by the RCMP [RCMP 1982], and followed in this text.

Whichever approach is taken, the analysis must relate threats and assets to perform the exposure calculation; the two approaches thus converge in the end.

3.2.2.1 Properties of Threats

Threats may be categorized as actions undertaken by agents, for a motive. The agents may be persons, hardware, software, communications, procedures, or acts of God; the motive may be accidental or intentional; the action may be disclosure, modification, or destruction of data.

The purpose of this list, and generally of all such lists, is similar to that seen in asset analysis: to create a list that is:

- sufficient
- not redundant
- not too long

Of course, all possible combinations of such a list still lead to an enormous number of questions. A methodology remains necessary to select a reasonable and sufficient set from within the set generated by such a list. In EDP systems in the classical sense, the IBM "SAFE" methodology of 11 control points helps to accomplish the selection. More detail of this particular tool is presented in section 3.2.4.3 when specific means of getting threat information are examined.

3.2.2.2 Properties of Assets

A second approach to limiting the nearly infinite number of possible threats to be considered starts from the perspective of assets. Earlier, assets were classified as tangible/intangible, physical/logical, and properties were discussed:

Intrinsic Value, Acquired Value, Availability, Confidentiality, and Integrity

Using this as a basis, related threat classes can be defined as they affect the properties of assets:

Motive	Property Affected	Class of Threat
	Availability	1. Destruction
Accidental		
	Availability	2. Interruption
	Availability	3. Removal or loss
	Confidentiality	4. Disclosure
Intentional		
	Integrity	5. Corruption

There are now five classes of threat, doubled by the basic concepts of deliberate or accidental to ten, to consider. Here, we examine each asset already identified, then consider what threats (if any) will deliberately or accidentally lead to destruction, loss, disclosure, corruption, or interruption (of services). The methodology of the IBM SAFE study (see 3.2.4.3 in this chapter) can be of use when this stage is reached, for assets may change as they pass control points. Using the control points also provides a useful second check on the asset and ownership identifications already done, as whenever an asset passes a control point it should change ownership, and may change its character as well.

3.2.2.3 Combining Properties: The Cost Exposure Matrix

Whatever starting point is chosen, threats and assets must be considered together in order to create a list of exposures for further progress in the risk management process. A tool that helps with the merging, suggested by the RCMP [RCMP 1982] and used in this text, is the "Cost Exposure Matrix" form. In this form, the data already gathered can be combined in a reasonably compact manner. The form is used twice: first, to identify the likelihood of a threat in one or more of the ten categories; then with the asset values to calculate the exposure represented by the threats identified. More detail on estimation of likelihood is given in section 3.2.3.

Consider the form in Figure 3.5.

Column 1:   Asset

The assets have been identified and categorized according to a rule such as:

1. Software
2. Hardware
3. Data and information
4. People and procedures
5. Communications
6. Physical and environmental

Each asset is listed here. For this first time around, no dollar values are inserted.

Column 2:   Destruction

The total loss of the asset involved. Enter the likelihood of destruction (in this case, deliberate destruction) into this cell.

Column 3:   Disclosure

If the asset involved is such that it should or must not be disclosed, enter the likelihood of disclosure in this cell.

Column 4:   Removal

Enter the likelihood of removal of the asset in this cell. Note that removal implies that the asset still exists, but is (temporarily or otherwise) not available.

Column 5:   Corruption

Corruption refers to the unauthorized modification of software, data, or EDP equipment. Enter the likelihood of this threat in this cell.

Column 6:   Interruption

Interruption refers mainly to services. Enter the likelihood of an interruption here.

Note that some of these threat classes are not independent (more about that in section 3.3). For example, destruction also implies removal and interruption. More than one entry may be in each row in this form.

Column 7 and 8:   Accidental or Deliberate

Accidental and deliberate threats require quite different security measures for protection. Therefore, these columns are provided to give the full ten threat classes.

When this form has been filled in for all assets identified in the earlier steps in the risk management process, we have two pieces of data that can be combined to yield information: a complete list of assets to be protected, and a summary of the likelihood of each being affected by each of the ten threat classes considered. The remaining step to get to an exposure analysis is merely to multiply the likelihoods by the values of the assets. Before this is done, it will be worthwhile to examine some probability concepts as they relate to threat likelihoods and exposure calculations.

Use of a form such as the Cost Exposure Matrix Worksheet (Figure 3.6) will help in organizing the data to be summarized in the matrix.

Total Cost Exposure					
Threats	Accidental	Interruption			
		Corruption			
		Removal			
		Disclosure			
	⑧	Destruction			
	Deliberate	Interruption	⑥		
		Corruption	⑤		
		Removal	④		
		Disclosure	③		
	⑦	Destruction	②		
Asset			①		

Figure 3.5. Cost Exposure Matrix

COST EXPOSURE MATRIX WORKSHEET

DATE _____

No. _____

ASSET Affected: REVISED: Date _____

Page ____ of _____

Basic Classification of Threat:

Accidental   _____   Deliberate   _____

Interruption   _____

Corruption   _____

Removal   _____

Disclosure   _____

Destruction   _____

Nature of Threat:

Likelihood of Threat: _____ times per _____

Potential Loss:

Justification for Loss Calculation:

Description of Existing Control if any:

Figure 3.6. Cost Exposure Worksheet

3.2.3 Probability Concepts

In essence, risk evaluation amounts to determining the value of an asset V (from the "General Values Analysis of System Assets" form, Figure 3.4) and the likelihood of loss L in some time period, and multiplying the two: $V * L$ gives the expected loss. One then designs safeguards that minimize this expected loss at the lowest practical cost. Assets have been assigned values (the V) and threats have been assigned likelihoods (the L). Before exposure calculation is treated (the $V * L$), it is wise to look more carefully at what has been called "likelihood."

3.2.3.1 Definitions

Mathematically, the thing that has been called "likelihood" previously actually is related to a "probability." Precisely, it is a multiplier calculated by estimating the probability of one occurrence of an event and multiplying by the frequency with which the event occurs in a given time period.

The probability is a way to assign a numeric value to the likelihood. As it happens, this numeric probability is not a good measure to use in threat analysis: It turns out that people on the whole are very poor at estimating probabilities. (This is one reason casino owners get rich.) A much better approach usually is to ask people how often something might happen. One may then use tables to relate "how often" to a probability so as to get a number for the likelihood and permit calculation of $V * L$ (see the tables and discussion in the next section).

The concept of "independent events" needs to be introduced here. Mathematically, this can get somewhat involved; it is sufficient here to define two or more events as independent if they do not affect one another. In the coin-tossing example, any two coin tosses are independent of one another. (This is one reason people guess badly—if five heads in a row have been thrown, the probability of a head next time is still 0.5.) In doing risk analysis, the end result involves adding together costs of various potential threats. This is mathematically valid *only* if the threats are independent. A fire or an earthquake may be unlikely, but are usually considered as though independent. However, earthquakes *cause* fires; if the earthquake happens first, the fire probably happens next. (The reverse of course is not true for fires and earthquakes.) The process of treating assets first, then examining the threats that may affect them, while following the objective of keeping lists complete and non-overlapping, maximizes independence of the threats identified. In filling out the Cost Exposure Matrix, some threats will wind up listed several times, as they affect each asset; one effect of this is to approximate the correct mathematical treatment for including non-independent events. Readers who wish to pursue the mathematics of probability further are referred to any standard introductory text in probability or statistics.

3.2.3.2 Tables of Probability Values

People generally can make fairly good estimates in terms of "how often should we expect this to happen?" Since most budgeting decisions are related to a yearly budget period, it is useful to create a table that relates "how many times per year" to a loss multiplier L. The final calculation of $V * L$ will then yield an expected loss per year, and one may easily compare this exposure to the cost per year of the proposed safeguard(s). One such table is given in Table 3.3. This table lists some subjective notions of "how often," then puts a fractional equivalent beside it, and in the third column what is in principle a probability figure. Using the "Cost/Loss Multiplier" from the table as a probability in the $V * L$ equation above can be easier than using more formal probabilities. If different intervals are appropriate in a specific situation, another table similar to this can be constructed easily with a calculator, as this one was.

Table 3.3. Annualized Loss Multiplier Table

Subjective Frequency	Fractional Equivalent	Cost/Loss Multiplier
Never	–	0.0
Once in 300 Years	1/300	0.00333
Once in 200 years	1/200	0.005
Once in 100 years	1/100	0.01
Once in 50 years	1/50	0.02
Once in 25 years	1/25	0.04
Once in 5 years	1/5	0.20
Once in 2 years	1/2	0.50
Yearly	1/1	1.0
Twice a year	1/.5	2.0
Four times a year	1/.25	4.0
Once a month	12/1	12.0
Twice a month	12/.5	24.0
Once a week	52/1	52.0
Once a day	365/1	365.0
Twice a day	365/.5	730.0
Ten times a day	365/.1	3650.0
Hourly	8760/1	8760.0
Once a minute	525,600/1	525600.0

As an example, consider a public timesharing system that has an average of 2,000 users signed onto terminals (somewhere) at any given time. It may not be unreasonable to assume that there is a constant risk of exposure to at least one of those 2,000 users (exposure to 1 of 2,000 gives a probability $P = .0005$; L = number of users times probability of exposure $(2,000 * P) = 1$ event per minute; if there were 4,000 users, it might be 2 per minute). The multiplier of 500,000+ may be entirely appropriate in this case. That is, *if the system were entirely unprotected*, a loss might well occur every minute or so. Even a small loss, (say $V = \$0.50$ each time an event occurs) half a million times per year, adds up to a large exposure ($V * L$ = about \$250,000).

The recommendation that follows from the material presented in sections 3.2.3.1 and 3.2.3.2, is to estimate likelihood in terms of "how often per year"; then look up a multiplier and enter the multiplier in the appropriate likelihood cell in the Cost Exposure Matrix form. This would be roughly equivalent to estimating the probability, then multiplying by the frequency, to get a multiplier to enter into the form.

When this is done, the $V * L$ calculation can be done for the final step in risk analysis. In section 3.2.4, several ways to arrive at the "how often per year" are presented.

3.2.3.3 Fuzzy Metrics

Fuzzy metrics are based around the concepts of *fuzzy sets*, first described in a 1965 paper by Lofti A. Zadeh[3]. In essence, the concepts of fuzzy sets are an attempt to formalize mathematically the natural language tendency to speak of things in terms of *possibilities*. Rather than the discrete numbers of probability, human languages tend to refer to a range of possibilities, using concepts

---

[3]Zadeh, Lofti A., "Fuzzy Sets," *Information and Control*, vol. 8 (1965), p. 338-353.

like *very, somewhat, a little,* and so forth. Limited research[4] has suggested that human beings who estimate risks and other imprecise metrics, particularly in complex or inherently imprecise applications, may estimate as much as 20 to 30 percent more accurately when they use the familiar fuzzy terms than when they attempt to assign numbers to such risks.

Tables 3.1 and 3.2 presented some suggested scalar metrics that in effect map human terms like "once in a while" into numeric values. These values then are used in calculations of risk. The reader should notice serious reservations and *caveats* about use of this sort of estimation. Information security is one of the areas in which issues and interrelationships are complex and estimates are inherently imprecise, and for which fuzzy sets have been explored. *Fuzzy sets* and *fuzzy metrics* are mathematical concepts that have been implemented in automated risk management models. When validated over some years of actual experience, they may offer a solution to some of the problems inherent in use of such simple-minded metrics.

Simplifying, a *fuzzy set* is defined in terms of *degree of membership*, rather than absolute "member or not-member" two-valued logic. In the limiting cases of degree 0 or degree 1, fuzzy set theory reduces to normal set theory (thus fuzzy set theory *includes* classical set theory.) Intermediate degrees of membership in the interval [0,1] correspond to natural language concepts like "little," "very," or "somewhat."

A fuzzy metric then simply is (as closely as a system designer chooses) the natural language term such as "little," or whatever. The implementer of the automated tool is responsible for management and manipulation of the fuzzy metrics and presentation of a useful result.

The utility of results produced using fuzzy metrics has not been proven over a large base of experience. Much of the value lies in those tools that permit a question like, "What factors were most important in determining this result as presented?" When such a question is easy to ask, the automated tool can handle far more complex interrelationships than are feasible manually, and can serve as a major aid to a security analyst. section 3.2.3.5 discusses the use of automated packages further.

A quite readable review of issues in using fuzzy sets for information security management is found in Kurt J. Schmucker's book *Fuzzy Sets, Natural Language Computations, and Risk Analysis.* This book also contains a carefully annotated bibliography of further readings.

3.2.3.4 Expected Values versus Worst Case

Once calculations have been performed and acceptable risk evaluations obtained, two primary approaches are common: *Expected value* and *Worst case.*

One may invest in security based on the expected value of losses in the absence of the investment. This is easy to justify to management. It fits with the sort of financial analysis methods taught in management education and accounting education programs, and thus is considered understandable by management.

As noted in the previous sub-section, expected value may not be the best method of choosing how to invest. Information security management has the uncomfortable characteristic that the

---

[4]For example, Hersh, H. M. and Caramazza, A., "A Fuzzy Set Approach to Modifiers and Vagueness in Natural Language," *Journal of Experimental Psychology: General,* vol. 105, no. 3, 1976, p. 254-276; —, —, and Brownell, H. H., "Effects of Context on Fuzzy Membership Functions," in *Advances in Fuzzy Set Theory and Applications,* Gupta, M. M., Ragade, R. K., and Yager, R. R. (Eds.), New York, Elsevier North-Holland, 1979.

"weak link in the chain" is the controlling factor. That is, however improbable a threat may be, even *one* breach of security may seriously compromise the entire system. Fuzzy metrics are one way to attack this characteristic; another (rather simpler in concept) is *worst case* analysis.

In a worst case analysis, the amount to invest in security management is based on the *worst* thing that can happen. This may be a very improbable event that would lead to destruction of life or property or merely to major loss of business. Typically, military or national security situations are more likely to use worst-case analysis than a commercial enterprise. The usual result is far more security investment than in an expected value approach.

No universal rules apply to how much to invest in information security. Theoretically, use of fuzzy metrics should be far better than expected value approaches. Practically, it may be harder to convince senior managers to invest using fuzzy metrics as a basis. Worst case approaches invariably involve "judgment calls:" in the extreme, should the "worst case" include nuclear attack, or perhaps the sun going nova? Where does one draw a line?

3.2.3.5 Automated Packages

In a review manual of this sort, it is inappropriate to examine automated packages in detail. The primary reason is that this field changes so quickly that anything set down here would be obsolete before the publication date of this book. Some general considerations of automated packages that attempt to assist in a complete risk analysis include:

- As computer hardware costs continue their exponential decrease, the capability of packages is changing dramatically. Methods like so-called "expert systems" are becoming feasible for microcomputer-based packages. There is not sufficient experience with such automated tools to justify their sole, or even primary, application in a security analysis.
- Current packages as a group tend to be similar to spreadsheets or database managers in that they permit automated management and manipulation of data gathered, and production of various kinds of reports with relative ease. A risk is producing volumes of reports that really have little utility (the "paralysis by analysis" referred to elsewhere).
- Current packages may contain various methods of assigning weights to differing threats and vulnerabilities and calculating some sort of overall metric. There is insufficient history of use of these packages to justify placing great reliance on risk metrics calculated this way.

In general then, due to the rapid fluctuation in this area and the known limitations of current packages, a prudent recommendation would be to use automated packages mostly for their utility in organizing data. Any metrics calculated should serve at best as a guide to areas deserving further attention, and never as a primary guide to investment of limited resources.

There is one significant exception to the previous comments. The class of automated packages that examine networks or specific operating system installations for known vulnerabilities can be very useful indeed. The COPS package from CERT and others, for example, examines an implementation of a UNIX environment and highlights instances of installation characteristics that have been proven to increase security risks. The security practitioner then may invest time in analyzing the degree of risk and where to invest resources in the most effective countermeasures. Similar packages are available for analyzing networks of microcomputers, and for minicomputer and mainframe systems.

These tools can be extremely useful in saving much human effort in analyzing hardware and software setups, which otherwise usually involves poring through massive volumes of paper in the form of system operating records. Computers are far better than humans at this kind of analysis. Some packages can monitor and record actual operating characteristics in real-time, a task normally impossible for human beings.

It is important to keep in mind that use of such packages addresses only narrow technical aspects of the risk-analysis problem (an important reason for their relative reliability and value).

3.2.4 Sources of Threat Information

There are many ways to gather and delineate information about threats that may affect an organization. In this section, we look at:

1. Vulnerability analysis, particularly issues related to personnel
2. Threat scenarios
3. Control point analysis
4. History
5. Research, especially questionnaires
6. Sources outside the organization

3.2.4.1 Vulnerability Analysis

One source of threat information is analysis of vulnerabilities in the organization. This occasionally is referred to as "sensitivity analysis." Sensitivity analysis more correctly relates to analysis of the components of a system for which a small change effects a large change in the system, or in the exposure level in this instance. Therefore, we use "vulnerability analysis" here.

In some cases, there may not be any past history to refer to in estimating threats. Worse, the situation may be an entirely new one, and thus no other organization's experience (even if available) would give a good guide. One technique, especially applicable to the selection of administrative and personnel control measures, is analyzing the vulnerabilities of the new system with respect to the people who will work in the system.[5] Briefly, one examines each job involved: The skills and training necessary to do the job, the access to the system necessary to do the job, the normal working conditions, and the assets that the job impacts, are analyzed. One typical result of such an analysis is given in Table 3.4, (updated for typical modern mainframe computer operations from Donn Parker's *Computer Security Management* [Parker 1981].)

Using this table, or a similar one developed for a specific organization, the probable exposures—that is, if a person in this position wanted to do harm, in what areas could harm be done—can be estimated. This identification could serve to guide the risk management effort to areas of greatest exposure. From the table, for instance, it is clear that only the EDP Auditor, Security Specialist, and Computer Systems Engineer can affect all areas considered. Further analysis will suggest that only the auditor and security person have the specialized knowledge actually to do anything significant. Thus, administrative and personnel controls should concentrate on the auditor and security specialist, both of whom know what to do to affect systems, know the safeguards in place, know how to hide acts, and have access to essentially everything.

---

[5]We concentrate on personnel and organizational vulnerabilities here, since people are by far the greatest security risk in most situations. Again we note that military and national security situations alter such relative risks.

Table 3.4. Job Exposures

Occupation	Physical	Operational	Programming	Electronic
User transaction and data-entry operator		X		
Computer operator	X	X	X	
Peripheral equipment operator	X	X		
Job-set-up clerk	X	X	X	
Data-entry & update clerk	X	X		
Tape librarian	X	X	X	
User tape librarian		X	X	
Systems programmer	X	X	X	
Application programmer	X	X	X	
User programmer		X	X	
Terminal engineer	X	X		X
Computer systems engineer	X	X	X	X
Communications eng./operator	X	X		X
Facilities engineer	X			X
Operations manager	X	X		
Database administrator	X	X	X	
Programming manager	X	X	X	
Security specialist	X	X	X	X
EDP auditor	X	X	X	X

It is important to examine such a table and ensure that it is customized for a specific situation. Some of the exposure categories may not exist, or may be different, depending on the way the organization manages its computer resources and what resources are available. In a distributed processing environment, for example, data-entry personnel may not present any physical risk since their only access to the computer is by means of communication lines. The degree of programming risk from a job-setup clerk or tape librarian changes if these people have no programming knowledge.

This analysis can be carried further to a risk level by occupation. Since this is essentially non-quantitative, one should avoid too many categories. The following table shows a ranking by asset exposure, with the highest risk referring to people who have great capabilities and access and also can affect important assets.

Table 3.5. Risk Level of Occupations Based on Asset Exposure

Greatest Risk
> EDP Auditor
> Security Specialist

Great Risk
> Computer Operator
> Data-entry and Update Clerk
> Operations Manager
> Systems Programmer

Moderate Risk
> Computer Systems Engineer
> Programming Manager

Limited Risk
> Application Programmer
> Communications Engineer/Operator
> Database Administrator
> Facilities Engineer
> Peripheral Equipment Operator
> Tape Librarian
> User Programmer
> User Transaction and Data-entry Operator

Low Risk
> Terminal Engineer
> User Tape Librarian

The security manager, for example, must have the skills, training, and access necessary to destroy the system in order to perform his or her work. This does *not* mean that the security manager *will* do this. Analyzing whether someone *could* do something is no guide as to whether they *will*. The exposure data available from this vulnerability analysis is most likely to be useful in designing administrative controls. (Perhaps dollar exposure figures could serve as a guide to how many dollars management should be willing to spend on having a "happy workplace," but this is at best a broad leap.) This analysis technique is useful mostly in identifying threats.

The vulnerability analysis presented here must be examined carefully for full applicability to any specific organization. In some contexts, for example national intelligence, risk levels will differ from those presented. A spy may be presumed to have capabilities that are not normally required for the job and that do not show on the resume. Particularly in small organizations, there may not be sufficient staff to separate duties as would be ideal, and some of the occupational classes noted in the table could be combined, leading to different exposures.

3.2.4.2 Scenarios

A technique that is useful when solid data are not available is scenarios. One creates a scenario depicting what a specific threat might be. An example (somewhat elaborate in this case) is creating "penetration teams" whose job it is to simulate terrorists and attempt to penetrate a nuclear power station. A more scenario-like example could be considering what a terrorist *might* do to disrupt some event (for example, hijack a jet and crash it into a stadium).

The scenario technique is useful in visualizing what *might* happen when no real data are available. It is highly subjective, but nonetheless is valuable in identifying potential threats and vulnerabilities. A scenario may help managers to visualize something not clearly understood. However, scenarios are risky. In the first place, normally they should be *extremely confidential*: There is no value to be gained by publishing a plan for terrorists which they may not have thought of themselves. Also, scenarios may unnecessarily alarm employees or others if they become public. It is questionable whether the use of scenarios outweighs the risks involved. If used, their use should be cleared in advance with senior management, and means to ensure confidentiality should be in place from the start.

3.2.4.3 Control Points/exposures

One tool that has considerable value at the detail level of identifying assets and threats, is "control point analysis." In this manual, the overall security problem is examined, and only a summary of this particular detailed technique is appropriate.

In 1972, IBM and others participated in a major data security study known as "SAFE" (Security and Audit Field Evaluation)[IBM 1972, Krauss 1972]. One result of this study has been the identification of control points relating to data in any information system. While the technique is relatively limited to data in a classical sense, it is certainly a useful way to approach the necessity to limit the infinity of possible threats. The accounting profession, particularly in the Canadian Institute of Chartered Accountants' *Computer Control Guidelines*, both the first and second editions [CICA 1986], has built on this technique, as well as updated recommended methods from time to time as technology has changed. (A summary of parts of the *Computer Control Guidelines* is in Chapter 12.)

Briefly, eleven control points were identified in the SAFE study:

(The author's comments are *italicized*.)

CP1:   Data Gathering

The manual creating and transporting of data.

CP2:   Data Input Movement

The manual movement of source documents to the data entry area in which the source documents are converted to machine-readable form.

(Note: In more modern systems this and some other control points may not even exist—direct screen entry or machine scanning often supersedes source documents now, for instance. Trade publications report a dramatic decline in data-entry positions in EDP departments between 1984 and 1987.)

CP3:   Data Conversion

The physical conversion of initial source documents to machine-readable form.

CP4:   Data Communication (input)

The transmission of machine-readable data.

CP5:   Data Receipt

The receipt and storage of data via communications or manual facilities.

CP6:   Data Processing

The execution of application programs to perform intended computations and their results.

CP7:   Data Preparation (output)

The preparation of data output media such as cards, paper tape, disks, diskettes, and microfilm for dissemination to the users.

CP8:   Data Output Movement

The manual movement of computer-produced output, in various media forms, to the output area to await user pick-up.

CP9:   Data Communication (output)

The direct transmission and/or delivery of output to the user.

CP10:   Data Usage

The use of data by the recipient, including the storage or location of data while it is being used.

CP11:   Data Disposition

The disposition of data after the period of usage, including the methods and locations of storage, length of time for storage, and final disposal, as appropriate.

This is a detailed tool that may be used either in the "threat-based" approach described earlier, or the "asset-based" approach recommended by the RCMP and this text. It is necessary to use some caution in applying this control point analysis: Many of the methods of data entry common today are materially different from those available in the early 1970s when the study was performed.

An alternate approach, which is similar in intent to the IBM "SAFE" approach, can be found in the Canadian Institute of Chartered Accountants' reviews of controls and auditing of data processing systems, noted above. This document is from the accounting standpoint, and covers areas beyond the "classical" view of data considered by the SAFE study.

As a comment on the use of the SAFE or CICA approaches: Recall that the involvement of the user management has been identified as being critical to the success of the risk management process. Recall also that it is poor practice to spend more money analyzing or controlling exposures than could be lost if the exposure became actual. It probably is best to engage the services of a professional with expertise in security and/or EDP auditing in applying these exhaustive techniques. Detailed techniques tend to the direction of "overcontrol" referred to earlier, unless used intelligently. Experienced professionals should possess the background to know when it is appropriate to "break the rules" by applying less than total controls, and when the rules must be applied rigorously regardless of apparent cost-ineffectiveness.

3.2.4.4 Past History

Clearly, the best source of good data about security exposures is history: If losses have occurred in the past, usually it is simple to quantify them and thus to have exact data on what this type of exposure entails. The history need not be only of a single organization. The Stanford Research International group (SRI) has compiled data about problems of organizations for a number of years. The newsletter of the Data Processing Management Association (DPMA) has published data about computer security experience in organizations based on surveys of some 40,000 DPMA members in Canada and the United States. The Information Systems Security Association (ISSA) quarterly magazine and the National Center for Computer Crime Data (NCCCD) also publish statistical information from time to time.

Probably the greatest disadvantage of past history is that one hopes a problem will not have occurred previously; security is concerned first with *prevention*. Also, in a small organization, there may not be a very large data base.

3.2.4.5 Questionnaires

One way to get information from many sources is to use a questionnaire.

The objectives of a survey first must be defined clearly and in writing. Then a sample must be chosen. Questions must be created; a pilot test is strongly advised to validate the questions; and considerations of time frame must be studied. Writing of questions that are precise and not subject to unexpected interpretations is as much an art as a science; the security professional should consider engagement of professionals in the field of test instrument design before embarking on the use of questionnaires.

The following table summarizes the virtues and faults of several data-gathering methods.

There are four primary means of gathering data:

- the interview
- the questionnaire
- observation
- research

Under the rubric "research" we will include sampling, documentation reviews, literature or database searches, and experimental testing situations. The following table discusses advantages and disadvantages of the various data-gathering methods.

	Advantages	*Disadvantages*
Interview	Informal and loosely structured	Time-consuming
	Permits nonverbal communications	May be impractical due to distance
	Permits investigative approach	Requires very narrow control responsibilities
	Permits sensitivity to the interviewee's mannerisms	Dependent on human relations ability
	Performed where the process is executed	Dependent on questioning techniques
	Permits immediate feedback	Dependent on handling risk and confrontation
Questionnaire	Concise	Imprecise language
	Easily tabulated	Over-structure of possible responses
	Inexpensive	Inflexible
	Structured	No guarantee of return
	Requires little time to complete	No guarantee of validity
	Minimizes risk via possible anonymity	No opportunity to expand on questions
		No opportunity to answer omitted questions
		No opportunity to volunteer information
		No incentive to respond
		No means to test reaction to questions
Observation	Done where the work is performed	May be hazardous, as most people dislike being watched while they work
	A first-hand observation of the process	People usually dislike having their performance measured in "real-time"
	An opportunity to deal with fact rather than opinion	Artificial timing—the work observed may not accurately represent most frequent difficulty
	An opportunity to perform measurements, or observe them being performed	Imprecise timing—the work may be subject to frequent interruptions
		People being observed are likely to be suspicious of the observer's qualifications.
Research	Allows preparation	A narrow perspective when taken alone

Provides the structure for future interviews and questionnaires	Information obtained is not necessarily current
Observations may be necessary	Experiments difficult to design and interpret, and expensive
Prevents "re-inventing the wheel"—the "problem" may have already been solved	

In summary, questionnaires probably are necessary to gather data from dispersed, varied sources. Their validity is suspect unless the designers have significant expertise in the design and administration of questionnaires. As with any other organizational intervention, merely distributing questionnaires or conducting interviews will impact the target population; such effects must be identified and considered in a research plan. It is recommended that professionals be engaged if the questionnaire route is seen to be appropriate.

3.2.4.6 Outside Sources

Several outside sources have been referred to already: the SRI data bank and various newsletters. These may be unique in their presentation of information about actual problems in DP organizations. Any one organization is unlikely to be able to get good information about the security failures of any other organization, unless it is someone like DPMA, ISSA, or SRI who are demonstrably related to the profession rather than to, for example, potential competitors.

Other sources of specific data include:

- Insurance companies for loss data
- Statistics Canada for such things as fire loss data
- U.S. Geological Survey for earthquake risk areas
- National weather bureaus for weather risk data
- Federal Bureau of Investigation (FBI), Royal Canadian Mounted Police (RCMP) or other police forces for criminal loss data
- U.S. Federal Information Processing Standards
- Electronic Data Processing Security Standards and Practices for Departments and Agencies of the Government of Canada (1992 update)
- Computer Security Institute publications
- Datapro Publications Computer Security Reference
- Data Processing Management Association Special Interest Group for Computer Security (SIG-CS) publications
- Information Systems Security Association publications

This list is not exhaustive. Unfortunately, the basic data needed often are not easily available, or even do not exist. This is why this section has concentrated on several techniques that help to get useful analysis in the absence of a database of basic information.

3.2.5 Calculating Exposures

Once all the preliminary work has been done, the Cost Exposure Matrix, which now contains likelihoods expressed as loss multipliers, is combined with the General Value Analysis of System Assets form to yield exposures. The essence is simply a multiplication—the "$V * L$" referred to in section 2.3. If the preliminary work was done with a computerized spreadsheet, this step may be done with only a few commands to the software.

There is nothing "fancy" about this step; it amounts to simple arithmetic.

The result is a second version of the Cost Exposure Matrix, with dollar figures in each cell and assets along the side. It is now a simple procedure to examine the form, select the greatest dollar exposures, and decide where time and money is best invested in designing and applying safeguards. The obvious way is to start applying the cheapest safeguard that avoids the greatest exposure, and work down until the budget is exhausted. (In some risk situations, particularly where espionage is involved, measures other than dollars come into play; however, they should have been incorporated earlier in the asset valuation process.)

If the time and other resources are available, it is a good idea to perform a simple sensitivity analysis on the resulting form. With a computerized spreadsheet, it is easy to vary the values assigned to important assets by perhaps plus or minus 20%, or by 50%, and examine the results. Usually, the relative ranking of the major exposures does not change when this is done, although small exposures may. If there is a material change in ranking among major exposures, more time should be spent on examining the assets involved to be sure that the best possible values have been obtained. Again, the risk analysis team must consider how much money to invest for better information; sensitivity analysis is *much* cheaper when it amounts to a few keystrokes in a computer than when it is done manually.

The approach just described can grow into a major analytical problem very quickly. Techniques such as "fuzzy metrics" (see, for example, [Schmucker 1984]), checklists presented by computer and sorted appropriately after filling in entries, and others have been developed to try to cope with the so-called "real world," in which very many things happen in complex patterns.

3.3 SAFEGUARDS AND COUNTERMEASURES

3.3.1 Types of Controls: Protection, Detection, Reaction

In this section, we consider the basic types and purposes of various controls.

3.3.1.1 Basic Purposes of Controls

There are three basic purposes that all controls are intended to address:

- *Prevent* exposures
- *Detect* attempted threats
- *Correct* the causes of threats

Many controls have elements of more than one of these basic purposes. The risk-management team should consider for each identified exposure how to prevent a problem, how to detect a problem if it happens, and what to do about making sure the problem will not recur. No asset is ever completely immune to harm, given enough will and resources on the part of threat agents. By setting up several layers of controls—preventive, detective, and corrective—the asset gets progressively safer. Keeping the basic purposes of controls in mind will help focus the risk management team.

3.3.1.2 Prevention

The first line of defense is protection, or prevention. Given that a problem is defined and may occur, risk management would include prevention of the known exposure. For example, it is known that without any controls, anyone could access a computer system and change someone else's data (if there is more than one person's data on the system). Therefore, some preventive measure is needed. One that has proven value is the use of account identification and password controls. Casual "potential threats" are deterred, and some prevention has been achieved.

Preventive controls generally have one or more of several characteristics:

- They are passive, and require no feedback:
  a fence
  a padlock
  a power-off switch

- They guide, or help things happen correctly:
  properly designed forms
  training programs
  employee awareness programs

- They are not impervious:
  "No Admittance" sign (this means *you*?)
  automatically closing door propped open
  password and account ID taped to terminal

- They reduce threat occurrence frequency:
  reference checks
  segregation of duties
  surprise audits (announced, but timing variable)

- They are transparent (people are not aware of them):
  fire-retardant materials
  anti-static mats and rugs
  shatterproof glass

- They are inexpensive:
  door lock
  employee identification badges
  signs (for example, speed limit)

The purpose of the protection, or preventive control, is to deter casual threats and slow down more determined threats. Several layers of preventive controls may add up to a rather effective protective mechanism.

However many layers of preventive controls there are, either sufficient determination or, more likely, unanticipated threats, can penetrate them. The frequency of occurrence should be much lower than for an uncontrolled situation, however.

3.3.1.3 Detection

Once the prevention is penetrated, the unwanted thing has occurred. The next step in controls is to detect this event. Detection systems indicate and/or verify an actual or attempted penetration. Examples include console printouts, alarms, video monitoring. Detective controls do one or more of the following:

- Trigger an alarm:
  smoke detector
  radar in a speed trap
  oil pressure warning light

- Register the event:
  console printout
  count errors in a batch
  photographs of intruders

- Stop further processing:
  batch may not be processed with errors
  disconnect terminal after three unsuccessful log-on attempts
  abort program on divide-by-zero

- Assess the situation:
  reasonableness checks (sales of skis in July; 25 hours a day in a time sheet)
  range checks (voltage 100 to 130)
  expectations (sign-on Sunday at 0300)

- Alert people:
  alarms
  warning lights
  error reports

- Test protection:
  hash totals, check digits
  authorization tables
  batch balancing

According to the RCMP, a detection system normally has four primary components:

- Sensors to detect the activity
- Communications to relay the fact of the event
- Assessment system to evaluate the needs of the situation
- Reporting system to announce the situation to the appropriate response force(s).

As a simple example, a smoke detector has a *sensor* to detect smoke, and a light or buzzer (*communications*) to relay the occurrence of an event. The detection system includes a person noticing the detector's activity and deciding what to do (*assessment*), which may include calling the fire department and reporting to management (*reporting system*).

The last point in the list emphasizes again that no control is perfect, and also raises the point that detection is linked with correction. Protective controls can be bypassed. Once this happens, the event should be detected, or the security is compromised. Detection should be linked with correction: There is not much value in knowing that breaches have occurred if nothing is done about it.

3.3.1.4 Containment

One form of control that does not fit neatly into the categories of protection, detection, and reaction, is *containment*. In a sense, containment includes elements of each kind of control. The essence is to limit the effect of a security incident. This may be done by system design that inherently limits side effects (such as high "cohesion" and high "modularity" in computer systems design). This would be a protective control in a sense. Usually, early detection improves chances of containing a problem, and there is an element of detective control as well. To the extent that the security system actually does something to contain the extent of an incident, this represents a reactive control.

Many of the strategies of safeguards have containment as a primary or secondary goal.

3.3.1.5 Reaction or Correction

Once a threat has occurred and has been detected, something should be done about it. Doing nothing is also a decision: Someone should have analyzed the situation and decided that it is cheaper not to correct the problem. The purpose of the communication and reporting components of a detection system is to ensure that someone does something—reacts, or corrects the situation.

Some attributes of corrective controls are:

- They involve action to resolve a problem
  automatic error correction (spelling checker)
  call the police forces
  review employment policies

- They are expensive
  parallel operation
  police forces
  quality control group
  change control group

Less can be said in general about corrective or reactive measures than about prevention and detection, as appropriate reactions vary according to the threat and assets, and the security policies of an organization.

3.3.2 Countermeasures

Another aid to the risk-management team, in addition to the basic purposes of controls, is some set of tools—basic strategies—that the risk-analysis team can "mix and match" in designing safeguards. Any security system may, as was noted previously, contain several "layers" (and indeed, layers of protection is one of the basic strategies). It is helpful to have several standard strategies to choose from, once assets and types of controls desired are gathered. At least six strategies have stood the test of time:

- Avoid the exposure.
- Split the target.
- Put the asset in a highly visible position.
- Hide the asset.
- Combine several assets.
- Use of multiple strategies: "Rings of Protection."

Sometimes, the easiest way to control an exposure is to *avoid* it. If there is a great concern that outsiders will intercept communications in the computer system, the problem can be avoided by not providing communications. If there is danger of legal problems from illicit copying of software, do not provide diskette drives so copies cannot be made or removed. Perhaps the most general expression of this is "don't ask for trouble." (A frequent example relates to walking in Central Park in New York at night.) This basic strategy can be useful; of course, it is not always appropriate (communications exposure may be impractical to avoid since communication is an important value-added part of many computer systems, and essential for electronic mail, for example).

The second basic strategy is to *split the asset*. A rifle is merely an expensive club without its bolt and ammunition; store the rifle, the bolt, and the ammunition in three places and the asset may be very well protected. Similarly, an encrypted file is useless without the key; store them separately. The disadvantage of this basic strategy is that separate security systems may be much more expensive than a single one. As well, *use* of the asset may be unreasonably difficult (storing rifles, bolts, and ammunition separately does not help fast response to a surprise attack, for example).

A third strategy is to *expose* the asset, in the sense that it is put into an area that is highly visible and under continuous normal surveillance. Convenience stores typically use several strategies: Entrances and approaches are well-lit, most money goes immediately into a safe and the safe is visible from the street, clerks are on a raised dais to have better vision and also to be psychologically more imposing. A portable computer in an occupied office is not in much danger of theft, as long as the office remains occupied.

The opposite of the third strategy is to *hide* the asset. There are two basic variations: the "purloined letter" method, and "invisibility." In the first case, a valuable asset is mixed in with many other valueless assets that are superficially similar. A potential threat agent would have to identify which one is worthwhile. In "invisibility," the asset is hidden, for instance at another location, or inside a building in a room without windows. There are many variations on either basic hidden-asset approach.

The fifth strategy is to *combine* assets. A disadvantage of splitting the target is that separate security systems can be expensive. By combining several assets in one place, better security can be provided at lower total cost.

The final strategy is *rings of protection*, or layers of protection, or the "onion skin" method (Figure 3.7). This has been referred to several times previously because it is an excellent basic strategy. Multiple layers of protection are provided, ideally with different strategies in each layer. In an operating system, the first layer might be account and password; the second layer, access

ESSENTIAL COMPONENTS OF SECURITY

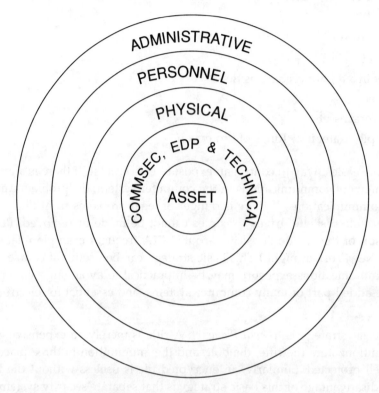

Figure 3.7. Rings of Protection Concept

control tables; a third layer, passwords on individual files; and a fourth layer perhaps a physical switch that must be thrown by an operator to permit access at all. Very few threats, accidental or deliberate, would penetrate four such layers, particularly since different methods are needed in layers 1, 2, and 4.

3.4 PERCEPTION AND COMMUNICATION OF RISK

In the preceding material, we have referred repeatedly to most people's poor estimation of risks. To some extent, this is a human characteristic. To some extent, this is inherent in information security analysis, where complex interrelationships prevail and probability assessment is neither precise nor the best estimating method. To some extent, this is a human characteristic.

People quite simply are not good at estimating risk in general. After seven consecutive "heads," the probability of a head on the next coin toss remains almost exactly 0.5 (not precisely 0.5, as the coin could balance on edge). Situations involving conditional probabilities present surprises to people without training in probability mathematics. Even when trained in probability concepts, most people cannot effectively handle decisions and evaluations in complex situations. For example, many people are extremely concerned about residence near a nuclear power station, despite the far better safety record in North America of the nuclear power industry than any other method of generating power.

An important part of the security practitioner's responsibilities thus has to be education. Staff need to be educated in how to evaluate risks. Where the evaluation process is too complex for reasonable expectation, the professional has a responsibility to evaluate risks as well as feasible and to communicate this evaluation to affected personnel.

REFERENCES

"Checklist for Computer Center Self-Audits," AFIPS Press, Washington, DC, 1979.

"EDP Threat assessments: Concepts and Planning Guide," *RCMP Security Information Publications* # 2, January, 1982.

Fites, Philip. E., Martin P. J. Kratz, and Alan F. Brebner, *Control and Security of Computer Information Systems*, W. H. Freeman/Computer Science Press, 1989.

"Guidelines for Automatic Data Processing Physical Security and Risk Management," FIPS Publication 31, U.S. Department of Commerce/National Bureau of Standards, Washington, DC, June, 1974.

Hersh, H. M. and A. Caramazza, "A Fuzzy Set Approach to Modifiers and Vagueness in Natural Language," *Journal of Experimental Psychology: General*, vol. 105, no. 3, 1976, p. 254-276

Hersh, H. M., A. Caramazza, and H. H. Brownell, "Effects of Context on Fuzzy Membership Functions," in *Advances in Fuzzy Set Theory and Applications*, Gupta, M. M., Ragade, R. K., and Yager, R. R. (eds.), New York, Elsevier North-Holland, 1979.

"Human Error," AD-689 365, U.S. Department of Commerce, Springfield, VA.

Krauss, Leonard L. and Aileen MacGahan, *Computer Fraud and Countermeasures*, Prentice-Hall, Englewood Cliffs, NJ, 1979.

Martin, James, *Security, Accuracy, and Privacy in Computer Systems*, Prentice-Hall, Inc., Englewood Cliffs, NJ, 1973.

National Technical Information Service, *Risk Analysis Methodology*, AD-A072-249, Dept. of Commerce, Springfield, VA, 1979.

Parker, Donn B., "Safeguards Selection Principles," *Computer Security*, IFIP, 1984.

Parker, Donn B., *Computer Security Management*, Reston Publishing Company, Inc., Reston, VA, 1981.

Reed, Susan K., "Automatic Data Processing Risk Assessment," National Bureau of Standards NBSIR 77-1228, 1977.

Schmucker, Kurt J., *Fuzzy Sets, Natural Language Computations, and Risk Analysis*, Computer Science Press, Reston, VA, 1984.

Zadeh, Lofti A., "Fuzzy Sets," *Information and Control*, vol. 8 (1965), p. 338-353.

4. Business Continuity Planning

Business continuity planning is the preparation of specific action to preserve the business in the face of major disruptions to normal business operations. It deals with natural and man-made events with low rates of occurrence but with devastating consequences if not dealt with promptly and effectively. These include fire, wind, storm, earthquake and other natural events; and mischief, vandalism, sabotage, riot, war, and other man-made events.

The professional is expected to know:

- Planning and analysis methods
- Relative rates of occurrence of disabling events
- The availability and use of planning tools and aids
- The identification of business success factors and critical capabilities (critical or key success factors)
- Alternative means of accomplishing objectives
- Alternative sources of supply
- Legal and regulatory requirements

For example, the professional would be expected to:

- Be able to establish a planning system for dealing with contingencies
- Recommend the use of available planning and documentation tools
- Distinguish between strategies and tactics for dealing with contingencies
- Distinguish between operational and catastrophic contingencies
- Distinguish between disaster recovery and business continuity
- Distinguish between back-up, recovery and restoration
- Be able to identify critical applications and business success factors
- Advise management on critical business functions
- Estimate threats and vulnerabilities
- Recommend strategies for the continuation of critical applications in the absence of critical services and resources
- Recommend strategies for the timely recovery and restoration of critical services
- Advise management on the availability and merits of available and applicable services and offerings (catering, cleaning, leasing, sites, etc.)
- Advise managers and directors on their responsibilities under national and regional (for example, state or provincial) law

DEFINITIONS

Backup Procedures

The provisions made for the recovery of data files and program libraries, and for restart or replacement of ADP equipment after a system failure or disaster. (AR 380-380; FIPS PUB 39)

Catastrophe

An event which causes significant restructuring of an environment. (MK)

Contingency Management

Management of all the actions to be taken before, during, and after a disaster (emergency condition), along with documented, tested procedures which, if followed, will ensure the availability of critical ADP systems and which will facilitate maintaining the continuity of operations in an emergency situation. (DOE 5636.2A)

Contingency Plan

A plan for emergency response, backup operations, and post-disaster recovery maintained by an ADP activity as part of its security program. A comprehensive consistent statement of all the actions (plans) to be taken before, during, and after a disaster (emergency condition), along with documented, tested procedures which, if followed, will ensure the availability of critical ADP resources and which will facilitate maintaining the continuity of operations in an emergency situation. (OPNAVINST 5239.1A; NCSC-WA-001-85)

Continuity of Operations

The maintenance of essential services for an information system after a major failure at an information center. The failure may result from natural causes (such as fire, flood or earthquakes) or from deliberate events (such as sabotage). (GAO)

Criticality

1. A concept related to the mission the automated system supports and the degree that the mission is dependent upon the system. This degree of dependence corresponds to the effect on the mission in the event of denial of service, modification, or destruction of data or software. (AFR 205-16)
2. A parameter indicating the degree of dependence of the organization on an asset. (RM)

Hot-Standby

Equipment and other information system components that are electrically activated and so configured such that production operations can be quickly and easily switched to such components. (WB)

Recovery Procedures

The actions necessary to restore a system's computational capability and data files after a system failure or penetration. (FIPS PUB 39; AR 380-380; NCSC-WA-001-85)

4.1 BACKUPS AND PROCEDURES

4.1.1 Importance for recovery

Magazine advertisements, articles, books, and computer manuals all emphasize that data files should be backed up. This means that in addition to the copy in use at any given time, at least one other copy should be available in case something goes wrong. Exactly what to back up, and exactly how often, can vary enormously. Backing up files costs time, media, and money. An on-line database system may require easily as much (or more) computer resources keeping audit trail and backup copies as it does actually processing.

How often should backups be made? There is no easy or universal answer to this question. In the days of sequential systems using magnetic tapes, the "grandfather, father, son" file management procedure was a standard and nearly universal. It is not so easy now. The "volatility" of the file—how often it is changed and how fragile it is—must be considered, as well as the value and the size of the file.

4.1.2 Data

From risk-analysis results, the value of the data should be fairly clear. For any given situation, the costs of producing backups can be calculated exactly. The probability of loss will have been estimated. A rough rule of thumb is that the probability of loss P, times the cost of recreating lost data V, is an upper limit for how much to spend ($) on backups: ($ < P * V$). Some examples follow, using common situations, which may serve as a guide.

One thing that is very common is the entering of data into a file. This may be a programmer typing a program, a word-processor operator entering a document, someone entering accounting data, or any of many other similar activities. It is a good idea to save files frequently. If anything happens to the power, even for a fraction of a second, or if the communication line used "drops," or *anything* that interrupts whatever is under way occurs, whatever hasn't been saved will be lost. Usually, it takes only seconds to tell the program to save the file. The file representing about 25% of this text has just been saved; it is about 325,000 characters and took 6 seconds to save on a personal computer. If the power were to go down, only this and the previous sentence would have to be re-entered; over 1/2 hour of time would be saved. Random Access Memory (RAM) is volatile, and the disk to which the file was saved doesn't lose data when the power "blips." (Some personal computers use "nonvolatile" memory and this paragraph doesn't apply, but they are special-purpose units today.)

Notice that there is a trade-off; the power supply did *not* fail, and a cost of 6 seconds of "wasted" time has been incurred. A "backup procedure" that implied saving this file four times per hour would cost 0.1 minute * 4 = 0.4 minutes per hour, or about 3.2 minutes daily, or 16 minutes weekly. If failures are rare, that could be a rather high cost, higher than the cost of re-entry if a failure occurs only once per week. This issue of frequency of backups is addressed in more detail in section 4.1.4 below. The actual backup procedure used includes periodic saving of parts of the file that have changed (*not* the entire file); full saves whenever a break is taken or the computer is left to itself for a minute or two; and copying to removable media prior to lunch and daily breaks.

The disk containing this part of the book is non-volatile—that is, if the power is turned off, the data still will be there. However, some kinds of power problems can destroy disks. Various system "bugs" can cause data on disks to be lost. At least daily, data on a disk in a computer should be copied onto a *removable* storage medium; in the case of this work station, a diskette. If this is done, and the diskette is stored in another room, the computer could be destroyed and only one day of work would be lost. Such destruction is very rare, but it can and does occur.

Removable media themselves can be destroyed. It is a good idea to keep two or more copies. The second copy might as well be in a different location; then a fire in the office or home will not result in loss of all the data. In one example, the backup procedure was to save at least hourly, copy onto diskette daily, and make a second backup weekly. The second copy was stored in another building. Once, a hardware problem caused the internal disk to "crash" *while a daily backup was being made*. The copy in RAM, the copy on the internal disk, and the copy being made to diskette all were lost. Until things were returned to normal, there was only *one* copy of data that would have taken at least a week to recreate. The backup procedure was changed to require a third copy, so that there would never be a time when only one copy existed.

In a larger installation, a more formal backup procedure should exist, probably involving transport of significant volumes of material to a site away from the computer center. While the grandfather/father/son rotation leads to two backups, perhaps with some other "family member" being a third backup off site, there still is a reason to have yet another backup: the transport process itself. While unlikely, it is possible that some computer problem could destroy the current (son) and most recent backup (father) files, at the same time the oldest backup (grandfather) is being destroyed in a traffic accident. If a fourth backup is stored at the off-site facility, recovery is still possible.

This discussion has presented some very common situations as examples, with reasons for maintaining as many as three copies in addition to the one currently in use. Note that there is an implied catastrophe plan in keeping one copy in a separate location (see also sections 4.1, 4.3, and 14.5); even total destruction of the computer does not mean total loss of data. A new computer can be brought in, and processing continued with a minimum number of problems.

At the other end of the scale, an on-line database, in use 24 hours a day, cannot be backed up as simply. It is impractical to stop everything, take a copy (which may cost hours of time), and restart. What is done in most cases is to keep a "running" copy, with duplicates of every transaction and the "before" image of the affected records; thus, in case of a problem, the effects of the transaction can be reproduced. The recovery process can get very complex, to the point that a modern on-line database *cannot* have complete backup protection (it would take more time and resources to ensure backup than it takes to do the work). One scheme sometimes used, to minimize the amount of information that has to be stored and processed to be able to do a backup, is a program (part of the database management system) which "browses" through the database, and makes a copy of everything that has been changed since the last "look" (or perhaps, in the last hour, or some other rule).[1] This limits the loss to data changed since the program last copied it, and thus limits the cost of recovery.

In critical situations, duplicate computers may be used, both doing the same work; if one fails, the other takes up the load while the first is repaired. In extreme situations there may be more than two: The space shuttle uses *three* main computers; if anything goes wrong with one, there still is a backup. Obviously, this is very expensive, but the consequences of total failure include billions of dollars and loss of human life. Similar considerations apply in hospitals and medical applications, air traffic control, and other situations where lives are at stake.

The principles are that backups need to be made; the cost of backups should not exceed the expected cost of replacing lost data; files (or in some systems, pieces of files) changed often need to be backed up often, as do files that are important or exposed to high risk.

4.1.3 Manuals and Documentation

Many programs and systems are practically useless without the manuals that tell people how to use them. Any system that needs to be maintained—and that is all systems—will be almos'

---

[1] This program is an example of a worm, used for a benign purpose. See Chapter 7 for more detail on w

possible to alter without the *documentation* relating to programs, systems, operating procedures, and so on. Consider the effects on a computer operation if the copies of the manual in use, containing handwritten and undocumented notes, and the operator who wrote the notes, both are lost in a disaster, and the backup copies are six months out of date. Contingency plans must include keeping backup copies of the *manuals*. If the manuals contain sensitive information, then the same security controls that apply to the originals must also be applied to the copies (see section 4.3).

Procedures must be set up to ensure that the backup copies of manuals are updated to stay current with the copies in use. This is especially important for the Security Officer to look into: In very many organizations, the copies *in use*, especially system and program documentation, are not kept very current, much less *backup* copies. Outdated manuals can be literally worse than useless. The Security Officer can do the organization a favor, not only in the unlikely case of a real disaster, but in saving personnel training time, by helping to ensure that manuals exist, are current, and have current backup copies.

4.1.4 Backup Frequency

The discussion of backups during data entry in a microcomputer environment touched on the issue of frequency of backups. Operations vary widely. The only general rule that can be given is that frequency is determined by the following:

- the criticality and rate of change of the data;
- the cost of making backup copies;
- the cost of re-creating or recovering data; and
- the expected frequency of data loss incidents.

Assessment of these factors should be part of the creation of a contingency plan. Data relating to cost should be available from the risk assessment exercise described in Chapter 3.

4.1.4.1 Criticality and Rate Of Change

The two definitions from the beginning of this chapter cover the gamut of the concept of *criticality*:

> A concept related to the mission the automated system supports and the degree that the mission is dependent upon the system. This degree of dependence corresponds to the effect on the mission in the event of denial of service, modification, or destruction of data or software. (AFR 205-16)

> A parameter indicating the degree of dependence of the organization on an asset. (RM)

In the first definition, the *concept* is highlighted. The second definition emphasizes the nature of criticality as a *parameter* to be included in risk management and the preparation of a contingency plan.

Many factors affect the degree to which data are critical to an organization. For example, data that represent creative output, such as the words in this text, may be difficult or impossible to re-create precisely. Therefore, such data are more critical than those which could simply be re-entered from input forms. (In this case, multiple backups that ensure *recovery*, rather than re-creation, are strongly indicated.)

Another factor that affects backup planning (and to some extent criticality of data) is rate of change of the data. Clearly, data that seldom change do not need to be copied as often as data that change daily or more frequently. The worm program described for on-line backups has this consideration built in. Old data tend to lose value as time progresses. No general rules can be given, as technical details of the processes of creating backups may dictate frequent copies even of slow-to-change data.

4.1.4.2 *Cost of Backups* versus *Cost of Re-creation*

The cost of making backup copies usually can be determined with a high degree of precision. Although it may be necessary to use benchmarks and statistical methods in some situations (see the next section on on-line systems), this is essentially a mechanical task involving arithmetic. The cost of re-creation may be more difficult to determine.

Recovery of data from backups normally is the lowest-cost alternative. No re-entry is needed, and issues such as creative output or real-time data do not arise. This is a significant reason for backing up data being the preferred strategy.

It may be impossible to re-create data that represent creative output or the results of real-time processes. The phrasing of an author may not be possible to reproduce, even for the author. Real-time processes that produce data may not be possible of repetition. Data loss during generation of an encryption key stream (see Chapter 2) may cause loss not only of the encipherment process, but also of any enciphered messages (this depends on the cryptography system in use). (In these instances, backups are the only alternative. In real-time processing, tandem processing may be the only alternative, as the data may need to be *used* in real-time as well as generated in real-time. In some instances the processes involved can be designed to be self-correcting; an example would be a self-synchronous stream cipher.) For such data, backups, if possible, are the only alternative. The question of cost of re-creation does not arise.

For data that can be re-created, several cost factors are relevant:

- Personnel costs for locating original input documents
- Personnel costs for re-entry
- Costs of equipment for re-entry
- Costs of machine time for re-entry
- Costs related to the unavailability of the data until re-entry is complete

Personnel costs are fairly straightforward. Original records that document the costs of original entry may exist. The original costs, if available, probably are the best estimate of re-entry costs in any significant data re-entry operation. Although learning curve effects exist, they may not still apply. Overtime pay may be a factor. If the re-entry operation is more extensive than merely re-entering a day (or some short period) of transactions, then costs for setting up and management of the recovery also must be considered. In some cases, this may include hiring and management of temporary staff, or arrangements for alternative office space.

Costs of equipment and machine time for data re-entry are separate items due to the nature of contingency planning. Depending on the severity of the incident that caused a need for data recovery, normal equipment, office space, or personnel may be unavailable. Even if normal conditions apply otherwise, there may be insufficient staff or computing capacity to handle day-to-day operations and data re-creation or recovery simultaneously. Contingency planners need to consider several cases, from simple erroneous erasure of data to disasters that materially affect the entire organization. Arrangements for alternate or supplemental equipment and computer capacity may be necessary to achieve recovery or re-entry.

Costs related to unavailability of data are the most difficult to estimate. Although these may well be the greatest costs of an incident, only one general rule can be given: contingency planners must give careful attention to such consequential damages.

Having determined backup costs and several cases of costs for data recovery or re-entry, the planners are in a position to evaluate costs of backups *versus* recovery or re-entry of data. Probabilistic and statistical methods outlined in Chapter 3 should be applied to the costs of recovery, then compared with costs for various backup alternatives. For instance, if re-creation costs for one year are:

- $150,000 for a disaster of probability 1%
- $25,000 for a significant incident of probability 10%
- $5,000 for normal incidents related to equipment failure, with probability 50%
- $1,000 for minor incidents to be expected during normal operations (probability 100%)

then the expected cost of recovery would be $7,500. Backup procedures whose total annual cost does not exceed $7,500 would be appropriate.

Two points need to be mentioned here:

- Criticality of some data may mandate backup procedures whose costs exceed figures obtained in this fashion, at least for data whose loss or corruption would materially impact the mission of the organization; and
- Insurance (see section 4.5) coverage may affect the expected cost of recovery. For example, low-probability events could be insured through a broker rather than self-insured as implied in the previous discussion.

4.1.5 On-line Systems

On-line systems, particularly those that must function 24 hours a day, or those that simply are very large, present special problems. In effect, a continuously functioning system always operates in real-time mode in terms of data creation. The communications network that supports operations must be maintained or recovered, as well as data center operations. Few if any large systems have sufficient excess capacity to support sufficient backups to recover; even if they could, the system cannot be shut down to restore without major consequences. These and other considerations require special attention to be given to alternative plans for backups.

In principle, an on-line system can make a backup copy of the state of the system at some intervals, then maintain continuous records of all transactions, including before and after images of affected entities. With such data, the state of the system can be restored in case of an interruption. (Such before-and-after records also normally include date, time, and origin information and fulfill auditing needs as well.)

In practice, considerable (expensive) excess computing capacity (particularly storage) is required to maintain such system audit records, and considerable excess capacity is required to effect such a restoration. Many on-line systems simply cannot be halted to make a copy of the system state or to restore it without major disruptions.

Solutions to these problems are as varied as major networks. In some instances, the ideal can be approached or achieved by shutting down the system periodically. During processing, system audit information is maintained. During the shutdown a copy of the system state is made and the state change data are cleared. Normally, the previous state and the state change data will be saved, generally under some variation of the grandfather, father, son backup paradigm. Another variation is continuous backups, perhaps performed by a worm program that migrates through the system making copies of all files that have changed recently.

When a shutdown is not feasible, tandem processing is about the only solution. The second (or *n*th) processor in effect provides the necessary excess capacity to perform such recoveries and to save system states and transition data. In critical applications, such tandem capability should involve separate sites so that all processing will not be interrupted even in case of a major disaster. (This naturally adds more communications networks to the reliability equations.)

Network management software that monitors activity in such systems may provide data that will allow contingency planners to calculate (statistically) various parameters regarding backup frequency and cost *versus* risk tradeoffs.

4.1.6 Equipment

Although the discussion in this section might seem to fit more precisely with the topics covered in Chapter 13, Physical Security, environmental control and power supply backup are covered here, as they relate directly to contingency planning and backup measures.

4.1.6.1 Air Conditioning

"Air conditioning," for most people, means "cooling." For computers, it might be better to speak of "environmental control," as heating and humidity control may be needed as well. Much of this is a normal responsibility of operations management, who will work with manufacturers in setting up a reasonable environment for the equipment. Some security involvement is advisable, however.

Some computers require no special cooling equipment. Some require a great deal of cooling. Personal computers normally require only "room temperature," with no special considerations. This is becoming true of more and more computer equipment; however, large mainframes have required many tons of air conditioning capacity in the past, and some still do. Some supercomputers rely on liquefied gases, such as nitrogen, to function at all. The consequences of loss of air conditioning capability differ as well, from "basically, none" to destruction of sensitive equipment.

Details of need for, and appropriate supply of, air conditioning capability will be specified by the manufacturer, and should be adhered to. The Security Officer should be involved in the process, at least to ensure that someone has asked, "What happens if the air conditioning goes down?" Some computers may be able to function without cooling at least long enough to be shut down "gracefully." Some can be damaged very quickly. Security considerations include being sure what the behavior of the organization's computer is, and planning accordingly. Backup power supply for the cooling may be advisable and may be necessary for computers that *must* continue to run. An uninterruptible power supply (see the next section) is not much use if there is no power for air conditioning, and it is not a good idea to assume that the cooling will continue to run unless explicit backup power has been provided for.

One idea, which provides enough cooling capacity to allow a graceful shutdown, is simply to use two or more cooling units. That way, if one fails, or needs maintenance, the other provides at least partial capacity. Whether both (or all) units should be capable separately of providing all needed cooling, or whether the separate units should be smaller and both (or all) run at the same time, is a matter for technical specifications in specific situations.

"Air conditioning" includes heating as well. In some climates, loss of power can lead to very quick cooling of buildings, and things like frozen and burst pipes can become a problem. Also, most computers have a *lower* limit on operating temperature as well as an upper limit.

Humidity control also is needed. In some climates, low humidity, especially in winter, can present considerable static electricity exposure.

Security personnel should ensure that these and other similar environmental control items have been addressed.

4.1.6.2 Uninterruptible Power Supply

Computers are sensitive to the quality of the power supplied. Low voltages ("brownouts"), sudden, short-term high voltages ("spikes"), and loss of power can be very disruptive to computer equipment. Spikes can cause burnt out chips; brownouts can cause destroyed disks and motors; loss of power means *at least* that whatever is being worked on at the time is lost; sometimes data files can be affected as well. Computers work at speeds much faster than people; by the time a human being notices a problem with power, it's all over for the computer. One solution to this exposure is an "uninterruptible power supply" (UPS).

One aspect of power supply already has been mentioned: Try to supply the computer with a separate source. Large motors, or powerful small motors such as the carriage return in some typewriters, first *drop* the voltage as the motor comes on, then *increase* the voltage as the line readjusts to the sudden change in load. Many computers will react unfavorably to such a surge. While a UPS will avoid this, putting the equipment on a separate power line also avoids the problem, and it may be free or very low in cost.

An uninterruptible power supply can be anything from a short-term backup to allow the computer to "fail soft" (that is, to save files and shut itself off "gracefully," without causing further problems), to a massive installation that will continue to run the computer for a long time.

A common example of a UPS with minimal capability is a battery backup in a clock. Depending on the type of clock, such a backup may hold the correct time for many days. Computers use more power than a clock, naturally, but personal computer users can obtain battery-powered UPSs that will run the computer for 1/2 hour or so. This time should be long enough to finish what was underway and save files, then to shut the machine off until main power returns. A half-hour backup capability can cost as little as about $125, depending on how much power is needed and how long continued operation is required.

The range of UPS equipment can be very wide. Next up from the minimal battery backup mentioned would include a "spike protector," and probably simple filtering provisions too. A spike protector can be a very simple arrangement attached to a "power bar" (low cost), or a more elaborate device capable of handling larger spikes such as lightning surges. A spike protector in a power bar, which is little more than a *fast* fuse, is quite cheap and readily available from retail suppliers. Spike protectors up to the level of handling nearby (not direct!) lightning strikes are common on farms and cost from under $100 to the low hundreds of dollars (one type is called a "ground fault interrupter"). For a personal computer installation, a battery UPS with a spike protector would be all that is normally advisable.

The lower cost retail items usually do not dissipate enough power nor react fast enough to protect most micros. Recommendations include:

- Response time 5 ns or less
- Clamping voltage 156 volts RMS (not more nor less)
- Able to dissipate 90 joules
- Noise filter should attenuate 150 KHz to 30 MHz, to 50 dB or better

A computer that is monitoring an ongoing process, or which maintains medical equipment in a hospital, or that maintains air traffic control, or which is involved in an on-line banking operation, needs something more elaborate. The exposure in such cases can be anything from large monetary losses to loss of life: The computers *must keep running*. (There is, in fact, a significant industry supplying dual, or "tandem," computers so that computer capability remains even if one machine is destroyed.)

A UPS that ensures proper power supply to continue normal operation is more elaborate than a simple fail-soft unit for a personal computer. Large battery packs are common. If long outages are a possibility, the battery pack needs to be supported by an independent generator: When main power dies, the battery pack takes over until the generator is started, then the generator substitutes for the main source until the main source returns. In such an installation, the computer normally runs from an inverter in circuit with batteries; the batteries are charged continuously and the computer always is in the circuit, and there is no "blip" from a changeover. In case of a failure, electronic switching permits a generator to be brought on-line while batteries alone power the equipment. Facilities such as this can be very elaborate and may cost well over $50,000. An installation that needs this sort of backup must also be sure that things such as heating and air conditioning are backed up if necessary.

Professional engineering help, and advice from the manufacturer, would be appropriate if an elaborate system such as described above were under consideration. One thing in which the Security Officer should be involved is ensuring that ongoing procedures include regular maintenance and tests. If the backup power is inoperable during an outage, the money spent for protection was wasted.

This section has had little detail; the variance of power requirements is too wide to be easy to summarize. The basic principle of assessing the assets, the exposures, and the risks should be followed. For example, personal computers, at least the better ones, usually are not exceptionally sensitive to brownouts or spikes; they have some built-in protection. Many people do entirely without power supply protection and never have a problem. A simple backup-plus-spike-protection is relatively cheap insurance, and is advisable if the location is rural or the main power may have known problems.

In Yellowknife, Northwest Territories (a city of about 10,000 in the Canadian Arctic), the city's power supply also powers a large gold mine; when the mine's crusher goes on, the whole town experiences a short brownout. In Yellowknife, even electronic cash registers normally have some form of UPS and spike protection. In Edmonton, Alberta, a city of over 700,000 a few hundred miles south, even some relatively large installations have no backup protection, as the city power supply is very reliable (and in the cited cases, the consequences of a power outage are not life-threatening nor very expensive). Very large installations, and those in places such as hospitals and petroleum refinery complexes, very definitely *do* have backups.

Brownouts—significant periods when the demand on power utilities exceeds their generation capability and voltage drops—have been reported with some frequency, especially in cities on the United States' Eastern Seaboard. If your installation is in one of these locations, a fairly sophisticated UPS may be needed.

4.2 CATASTROPHE, CONTINGENCY, AND CONTINUATION

Webster's dictionary defines "contingency" as:

A possible or not unlikely event or condition

Another possible definition (Shakespeare) could be:

The slings and arrows of outrageous fortune

From the standpoint of information systems security, a "contingency" is something that might happen, which requires a response, and which thus should be planned for. The quotation from Shakespeare suggests the proper planning: Assume things will go wrong, and have a "contingency plan" in place to guide in how to cope. Perhaps the key point in contingency planning is to *have* a contingency plan. When one is in the middle of an emergency situation, whether merely annoying or a real disaster, there is never enough time to cope with immediate needs, much less to reconstruct what should have been in place previously.

Effective risk analysis will lead to identifying many contingencies, things that are "possible or not unlikely." At some point in the carrying out of his or her responsibilities, the Security Officer should have gathered data enabling an assessment of how likely various contingencies are and thus how much time to spend on preparing for them. This will help in deciding how much money to spend: Remember the familiar notion that one should not spend more than the expected loss to avoid the loss.

4.3 CONTINGENCY AND DISASTER PLANNING

At seven minutes after three in the afternoon of a Friday before a holiday weekend in July 1987, Environment Canada issued a tornado warning for Edmonton, Alberta. Most people's reaction was disbelief: Edmonton doesn't *get* tornadoes! By three-thirty, 25 people were dead and hundreds had injuries, some fatal. Hundreds of people were homeless, and dozens of businesses simply were not there any more. The city was totally unprepared for an unprecedented phenomenon (it did have a disaster plan that operated quickly and well and response teams who managed to learn to cope very quickly).

In Houston, a snowstorm paralyzed the city, bringing down power lines, snarling traffic, and destroying buildings. (That snowstorm would barely have been noticed in Edmonton, which *does* expect winter.) Mudslides in Montreal have severed connections and brought down banking computers. Explosions in utility transformers have crippled downtown Toronto. A failed drainage pipe in Chicago in 1992 affected most of the downtown area for months. Floods are common in many river systems. Many places are subject to earthquakes. Florida has hurricanes,

California has mud slides, Oklahoma and Kansas have tornadoes, and so on. Catastrophes happen, even though they may be rare.

This emphasis on major disasters should not blind the reader to the fact that small disasters occur much more frequently. While they may not make the news, incidents like a cup of coffee spilled in the wrong place at the wrong time could impact a business almost as much as a major problem like a fire. Such day-to-day problems properly should be termed *operational contingencies* rather than catastrophes.

If your microcomputer has a hard disk and uses MS-DOS, removing the file COM-MAND.COM from the *root directory* will make it impossible to start up the system unless you have a backup copy of the system, of the correct version, on diskette. Even if COMMAND.COM still exists in another directory, a copy of a recent version of MS-DOS on a diskette is needed before *anything* on the hard disk can be accessed.[2]

Of course, all employees know that one should not FORMAT a hard disk—don't they? What is the contingency plan for that occurrence—it *has* happened.

Because catastrophes *do* happen, contingency planning needs to consider them. If it is a business, backups in separate buildings should exist. Off-site backups across town, or even in another city, may be good insurance. Arrangements for backup computer facilities can be made in advance. Sometimes even duplicated computers are appropriate. Every location has its own exposures to natural and other risks; the contingency plan should use data such as government weather records, flood plain data, earthquake history, and so on to decide what to prepare for. Sometimes this won't help; tornadoes *never* happen in Edmonton—but one did. Thus a catastrophe plan needs to be in place. During or after a disaster is the wrong time to try to come up with a plan.

Things to consider include priorities of activities. For example, probably budget work for next year is lower priority than getting out the payroll at the end of the week. Data and equipment need to be available in places removed from the main computer operation. Some businesses, such as banks or refineries, can be out of business in days without computer capability. The Security Officer should be, or become, aware of common types of catastrophes, especially those common to his or her specific area, and should work with management on creating some catastrophe plan.

Who gets called? Lists of emergency contacts, people and phone numbers, will be needed. These lists must include *current* contact information for people who will be needed to cope with a disaster and subsequent recovery. Some indication of who these people might be is covered in the next section.

An organization coping with a disaster has priorities other than maintaining good security principles and separation of duties. Nevertheless, these issues must be considered. If your data are too sensitive to let janitorial staff look at them during normal operations, should they be exposed to unscreened and unknown people during a problem? What level of contingency still allows what level of controls? (This topic has very different emphases if one is considering *intentional* penetration of a system; a spy may *cause* a catastrophe in order to bypass controls. Such considerations are one reason national security and military security considerations differ from most other environments.) It may be that nothing can be done in many instances; still, the instances should be identified as far as possible. *Most* problems are not catastrophic, yet a very

---

[2]A preventive measure for this operational contingency is to make use of the COMSPEC variable provided in DOS.

common occurrence is breakdown of many security and accounting controls (for example, during a labor dispute).

4.3.1 Stages in a Disaster

The most important thing about a Disaster Recovery plan is that it exists and is current and available. Once the plan exists, people with knowledge and training must be responsible for executing it. These people (and alternates—remember vacations, sickness, injuries, etc.) must be identified and trained as Disaster Recovery Team members.

When a disaster occurs, five stages are usual:

The event itself

> The event probably will be unexpected, and reaction will be the responsibility of whoever is at the site during the event.

The first response

> The *initial response team* needs to handle things like arranging for ambulances, assessing what the damage is, notifying responsible organization management, and so on. If possible, they should be prepared in advance, and they must have current lists of how to reach appropriate people, including emergency services, telephone companies, company executives, etc.

Impact Assessment

> The *impact assessment team* needs to identify losses, and to start recovery processes. This is the time when lists of vendors, locations of backup files and manuals, off-site storage facilities, and the priority list of what needs to be re-started when, become critical.

Startup

> The *startup team* manages re-starting of the operation, or of the part that has survived the event. This team is likely to be larger than the previous groups, and may need special skills such as electronic repair or wiring experience. The startup may be as simple as re-booting a system, or may involve a "hot site," or anything between. It is often complicated by a need for communication link work, and impacted by other organizations affected by the same event.

Full Recovery

> The normal operating team will be back in place at the time of full recovery. (This is a good time to "debrief" and use the results of this event to improve the recovery plan for possible future events.)

If Disaster Recovery Planning is considered in light of these stages, it is clear that different people are involved in the response teams at different phases. For successful recovery, the *Disaster Recovery Planning team* must, during its lifetime, identify the members of the other teams. Due to the sudden nature of most disasters, it is important to have alternates identified, as some primary team members may be ill, on holiday, or injured during the event itself.

The catastrophe plan needs several basic elements, and there are some things which can be done in advance, such as data file, program, and documentation backups. Several stages are common to any disaster, and associated advance preparation is obvious:

4.3.2 Features of a Disaster Plan

With the stages of a disaster in mind, a disaster plan can be formulated. A good disaster plan should include at least the following features:

- A secure site needs to be in use for storage purposes.
- Off-site storage needs to include *everything* needed to restart after a disaster.
- Items stored off-site must be kept up-to-date.
- The data files stored off-site must include current backups.
- Arrangements for back-up hardware must be made, must be *tested* periodically, and must be kept up-to-date.
- Disaster plans must be tested.
- Insurance and other coverage should be reviewed.

The final point is overlooked in many cases. Even if there is adequate insurance, the money will not come to the company until after adjustors and others decide on the loss. The company's need is not money several weeks or months later; it is for replacement equipment *now*. An arrangement for an emergency line of credit can be made with a bank in advance of any problems; this line of credit would bridge the time between a loss and the insurance payment.

Some manufacturers offer plans involving replacement of equipment, or other variations of contingency arrangements. Such alternatives should be explored during consideration of the disaster recovery plan.

Part of the contingency planning process should include at least an outline of what to do if the information center is totally destroyed. During a disaster and the recovery, immediate reaction is necessary.

4.3.3 Testing

At some time, and preferably periodically, backup and contingency plans need to be *tested*. The time to find out that critical phone numbers are not available is *before* an actual emergency when the error can be corrected. Some kinds of plans such as fire evacuation *must* be tested by law; all contingency plans *should* be tested as a matter of professional responsibility and common sense.

The single most important thing about a catastrophe plan is *existence*.

4.3.4 Communication

In addition to the characteristics noted above, the disaster plan must be *communicated* to staff. In the tornado incident in Canada, one provider of ambulance services had just completed an excellent disaster plan—but staff did not know what was in it, or where to find it! Being capable people, they developed, in real time under emergency conditions, many of the elements of the plan. However, the plan itself was wasted effort without communication. The training mentioned in this chapter should include things like contingency plans, and the testing recommended in this chapter will supplement and reinforce such training, as well as lead to improvements.

Select Strategy

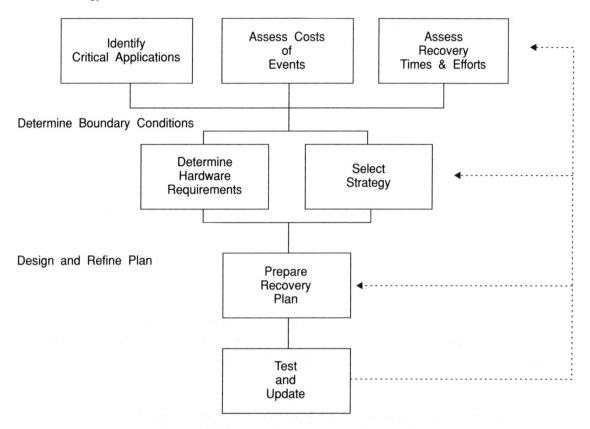

Figure 4.1. Process of Preparing a Contingency Plan

4.4 SECURITY AND CONTROLS IN OFF-SITE BACKUP AND FACILITIES

Any data that were sensitive inside the computer center remain sensitive, at least for some time period, while they are stored outside the center as backup data files, programs, manuals, or in any other form. There are two fundamental control points:

- When backup material is being transferred to the site
- While backup material is stored at the site

An example could be transfer of cash: Guards watch while the transfer is made to an armored vehicle; the vehicle is armored and its route and timing will not be publicized; guards watch while the cash is transferred to a storage area; the storage area itself will be monitored and subject to many rings of protection. The same sort of considerations apply to information systems. It doesn't make much sense to be very careful about disclosure of data in use in the computer, then transfer backup tapes in a van to an unsupervised warehouse.

The backup site itself may need even better protection than the computer center. Data in the backup site are likely not to be used very often, certainly not as often as the computer itself. Problems could go undetected for a long time. More than one company has experienced a problem with a dissatisfied programmer sabotaging the system in use, only to discover that no one checked and the backup tapes are blank. One of the prime reasons computer viruses are such a problem is that backups often are infected as well; when the system is restored from infected backups, the infection cycle begins again.

These and similar considerations often mean that it is cheaper and more effective to contract someone to handle backup storage. The "someone" will be in the business, will be able to spread the cost of expensive security systems over many clients, and probably has a very solid and well-protected storage area that is monitored continuously. These things can be costly for one organization to do on its own.

4.5 BUSINESS AND DP INSURANCE

Many kinds of insurance are available, including equipment replacement, business loss, etc. Insurance does not stop catastrophes, but it *may* help to provide financial and other resources to aid in recovery. Cost-effectiveness is important: Almost anything can be insured, but the cost may be prohibitive. Some kinds of risks may be insurable, but still kill a business; for example, if all data files are destroyed and there are no backups, insurance cannot replace accounts receivable records or customer lists.

One point often overlooked is that there may be a need for money *quickly* after an event. Insurance may take time to provide money unless this is part of the contract. Also, manufacturers may not be able to provide replacement equipment at all quickly.

Wang on DRP

The following material is used with permission of Wang Canada Limited. It represents an example of the sort of arrangements that major vendors, with their ability to take advantage of economies of scale to provide specialized services, may offer their customers. Other vendors offer similar plans.

Note that it requires that the customer contract with the vendor for maintenance, thus eliminating possible third party maintenance agreements. Other significant factors are that it more or less forces the customer to *think* about potential disasters, and it provides a guarantee of very rapid replacement of equipment. This could be significant: Mainframe computer manufacturers normally manufacture to order, and do not maintain stocks of major equipment. Replacement can take several weeks. Certain points related to financing are covered in this plan as well.

FLOOD FIRE HURRICANE

These things happen to computer rooms. If it does, will it mean ? — weeks of downtime while your equipment is being ordered, funds are budgeted, your computer room is being rebuilt, . . .

As a Wang customer you can protect your investment in Wang equipment by subscribing to the new Disaster Protection Plan, which eliminates the casualty exclusion of your current Wang maintenance contract. This unique disaster protection insurance is underwritten by Chubb Canada and offered to Wang customers through Frank B. Hall Insurance Brokers. The plan covers losses from flood, fire, vandalism, *etc.*, and gives protection not previously available from Wang.

Designed to give Customers the solution they need to be up and running quickly after a casualty, the Disaster Protection Plan protects your investment by offering these unique benefits:

- *EXTENDS MAINTENANCE CONTRACT* — Wang Maintenance contract exclusion for casualty losses is eliminated. Wang customers can now buy the total solution to hardware problems from one vendor . . . Wang.

- *HARDWARE REPLACEMENT* — Replacement equipment from Wang will be ready for shipment within 48 hours of your report of a loss, from our U.S. manufacturing facility if replacement is necessary. (Allowances should be made for the additional time to physically ship and install the equipment at the site.)

- *RELOCATION OF PROCESSING ENVIRONMENT* — Wang will establish a temporary environment, to set up replacement equipment should your site be determined unusable.

- *DATA REPRODUCTION AND MEDIA REPLACEMENT* — The Program pays to reload existing backup data onto replacement hardware. It also pays to replace destroyed operating system or Wang application software.

- *ADDITIONAL COVERAGE AT NO EXTRA COST* — Emergency Site use: Should your processing environment be destroyed and immediate processing is a business necessity. During the restoration period, the policy covers the additional expenses associated with the use of a third party "equipped" recovery center,[3] such as declaration fees, travel and personnel accommodations."

The Wang Disaster Protection Plan can be purchased on all new and currently installed Wang manufactured or supplied equipment covered by Wang Maintenance Contracts at a yearly cost of [*a percentage*] of the current list price of the covered product.

This plan does not cover all contingencies: For example, loss of profits and losses caused by power supply problems are not covered. There is a deductible provision in this plan.

Many manufacturers offer similar plans. Critical points in this sort of arrangement with hardware vendors are that *replacement* is covered (Wang Canada has confirmed that they maintain an inventory of equipment to fulfill the replacement commitment within 48 hours); and that provisions for common disaster problems are included. The customer is forced to consider a number of items that often are overlooked (for example, financing of unusual and unbudgeted expenses during the recovery period).

Another significant point is that the companies who may not be large enough to justify having staff with knowledge in such specialized areas as disaster recovery planning, can draw on the expertise of specialists employed by the hardware vendor. This may offer a cost-effective alternative to the use of consultants. Consultants still may be advisable: Employees of vendors normally will offer solutions that involve the vendor, rather than exploring a wider range of possibilities.

Note as well that the vendor in this case, and in most others as well, requires that the customer use the vendor's maintenance services. This makes sense for the vendor for two reasons. First, maintenance can be very profitable (consider an automobile for a comparison: Manufacturers' parts may be priced much higher than jobbers' equivalents). Secondly, in a more favorable light, the vendor is assured that maintenance is performed to standards that the *vendor* controls, rather than to (possibly) lower standards from a third party.

The last point is changing along with a changing business environment. Third-party maintenance has matured considerably and is more common, and more reliable, now than when this policy was created.

---

[3]Author's note: This corresponds to what has been termed a "hot site."

Specialized insurance needs such as this should be discussed with an insurance broker with knowledge of the specific area and of available kinds of insurance. Your lawyer, accountant, or consultant should be able to provide names of brokers, as well as advice and review of brokers' proposals.

Note that, while governments frequently provide special aid in large disasters, normally such aid is *not* provided for losses that could have been insured.

Insurance will be easier to get, and quite possibly cheaper, if the organization has conducted a comprehensive security and control assessment, including risk assessment.

4.6 SOFTWARE ESCROW ARRANGEMENTS

When an organization is dependent on software provided by others, an exposure to the business stability of the software authors exists. Should the author suffer a business failure, the source code for software could become unavailable during the bankruptcy process, possibly causing severe disruption to the user organization. One way to minimize this exposure is to ensure that the source code is held in escrow; that is, a copy is maintained in trust so that it remains available to the using organization even if the author organization fails. (We use the word *escrow* in the legal sense here, as opposed to the technical sense of "key escrow" in Chapter 2.)

Various issues such as confidentiality, software updates, legal title to modified portions of the software, and others arise in escrow arrangements. Legal advice is essential in setting up such a protection.

REFERENCES

Computer Control Guidelines Second Edition, Canadian Institute of Chartered Accountants (CICA), February, 1986.

"EDP Threat assessments: Concepts and Planning Guide," *RCMP Security Information Publications* # 2, January, 1982.

Disaster Recovery Journal, 2712 Meramar Drive, St. Louis, MO 63129. (Perhaps the best of several specialized journals currently published in the contingency planning field.)

Emergency Preparedness Canada, *Guide to the Preservation of Essential Records*, EPC 12/87, December, 1987. 121 pages, French & English.

Gallegos, Frederick, Dana R. (Rick) Richardson, & A. Faye Borthick, *Audit & Control of Information Systems*, South-Western Publishing Company, West. Chicago, IL, 1987.

Lord, Kenniston W., Jr., *The Data Center Disaster Consultant*, QED, Wellesley, MA, 1977.

Parker, Donn B., *Computer Security Management*, Reston Publishing Company, Inc., Reston, VA, 1981.

5. Data Classification

This area deals with procedures for making and communicating decisions about how data is to be handled. It usually involves dividing data into a limited number of classes, all data in a class to be handled similarly, and labeling the data with the name of the set of procedures by which it is to be handled.

The professional is expected to know:

- The elements and objectives of a classification scheme
- The criteria by which data are usually classified
- The procedures that are normally prescribed by such a scheme
- The differences between government and commercial programs
- The limitations of such programs
- How to implement such a program

For example, the professional would be able to:

- Contrast commercial and government schemes
- Distinguish between classification and sensitivity
- In a government context, distinguish "classified" from "sensitive but not classified;
- List the elements (*e.g.*, authorization, custody, reproduction, logging, marking and labeling, filing and safekeeping, etc.) that will normally be prescribed for classified data
- Give examples and advice on the handling for various classes of data
- Be able to identify the criteria (*e.g.*, age, quantity, number of independent associations, scope, useful life, etc.) that are used to classify data
- Give examples of classification schemes
- Identify the roles of users, line managers, and staff in such programs
- Understand the effect of data aggregation on classification
- Describe techniques for avoiding disclosure through inference from small sets
- Other

Classification of data in regards to sensitivity and other criteria is an important element of an information security plan. The key is to identify things that need special handling and label them, in order to allow the system to apply controls of one form or another. Both data and personnel need to be assigned categories: data, their sensitivity, and personnel, the items they need to or are permitted to access.

DEFINITIONS

Access Level

The hierarchical portion of the security level used to identify the sensitivity of data and the clearance or authorization of users. The access level, in conjunction with the non-hierarchical categories, form the sensitivity label of an object. (NCSC-WA-001-85)

Access to Information

The function of providing to members of the public, upon their request, the government information to which they are entitled under law. (A-130)

Access Type

The nature of an access right to a particular device, program, or file (such as read, write, execute, append, modify, delete, and create). (AR 380-380; NCSC-WA-001-85; FIPS PUB 39)

Aggregation

Individual data systems and data elements may be determined to be unclassified and to be of a specific sensitivity category. When those data are combined with other data, the totality of the information may be classified or in a higher sensitivity category, with higher protection requirements. (AFR 205-16)

Asset Granularity

The degree to which assets are considered as individual assets or as a class. (MK)

Authorization

1. The granting to a user, program, or process the right of access. (AR 380-380; NCSC-WA-001-85; FIPS PUB 39)
2. The privilege granted to an individual by a designated official to access information based upon the individual's clearance and need-to-know. (DOE 5636.2A)

Category(ies)

1. Restrictive labels that have been applied to classified or unclassified data as a means of increasing the protection of and further restricting access to the data. Examples include Sensitive Compartmented Information (SCI), Proprietary Information (PROPIN), and NATO. Individuals may be given access to this information only if they have been granted formal access authorization. (AFR 205-16; NCSC-WA-001-85)
2. A grouping of classified or unclassified sensitive information to which an additional restrictive label is applied to signify that personnel are granted access to the information only if they have formal access approval or other appropriate authorization (*e.g.*, proprietary information, For Official Use Only (FOUO), Compartmented Information, Restricted Data [RD]). (DODD 5200.28; CSC-STD-003-85; DOE 5636.2A)

Caution Statement

A statement affixed to computer outputs which contains the highest classification being processed at the time the product was produced and a requirement that any data not requested be controlled at that level and returned immediately to the originating computer center. (AR 380-380)

Classification

A determination that information requires, in the interest of national security, a specific degree of protection against unauthorized disclosure together with a designation signifying that such a determination has been made. Data classification is used along with categories in the calculation of risk index. (CSC-STD-004-85)

Classified Data/Information

1. Information classified pursuant to DODD 5200.1-R in one of the designated security classification categories. (DODD 5200.28)
2. In the private sector, information that has been classified pursuant to a specific set of definitions of categories of sensitivity. (PEF)

Criticality

1. A concept related to the mission the automated system supports and the degree that the mission is dependent upon the system. This degree of dependence corresponds to the effect on the mission in the event of denial of service, modification, or destruction of data or software. (AFR 205-16)
2. A parameter indicating the degree of dependence of the organization on an asset. (RM)

Custodian of Data

The individual or group that has been entrusted with the possession of, and responsibility for, the security of specified data. (WB)

Data

1. A representation of facts, concepts, information, or instructions in a manner suitable for communication, interpretation, or processing by humans or by an AIS. (DODD 5200.28);
2. An asset category consisting of the information handled by the organization. (RM)

Data Integrity

The property that data has not been altered or destroyed in an unauthorized manner. (ISO 7498-2)

Data Level

1. *Level I*. Classified data.
2. *Level II*. Unclassified data requiring special protection; for example Privacy Act, For Official Use Only, technical documents restricted to limited distribution.
3. *Level III*. All other unclassified data. (OPNAVINST 5239.1A)

   Note: Several other levels of security classification of data, for example Classified, Secret, Top Secret, are in use by various U.S. Government agencies.

Data Owner

The statutory authority responsible for a particular type or category of information or the individual or organization responsible for the actual data contained therein. (DODD 5200.28)

Database

An extensive and comprehensive set of records collected and organized in a meaningful manner to serve a particular purpose. (DODD 3200.12)

Default Classification

A temporary classification, reflecting the highest classification being processed in an automated system. The default classification is included in the safeguard statement affixed to the product. (AR 380-380; NCSC-WA-001-85)

Distribution Statement

A statement used in marking a technical document to denote the extent of its availability for distribution, release, and disclosure without additional approvals or authorizations. A distribution statement marking is distinct from and in addition to a security classification marking assigned in accordance with DOD 5200.1-R. (DODD 5230.24)

Documentation

An asset category consisting of the manual, listings, etc. Must also include recovery plans and the result of threat analysis. (RM)

Expected Lifetime

A parameter indicating the length of time an asset is operative or has value to its owners. (RM)

Granularity

1. The relative fineness or coarseness by which a mechanism can be adjusted. The phrase "the granularity of a single user" means the access control mechanism can be adjusted to include or exclude any single user. (DODD 5200.28-STD)
2. An expression of the relative size of a data object, *e.g.,* protection at the file level is considered coarse granularity, whereas protection at the field level is considered to be a finer granularity. (NCSC-WA-001-85)

Information

The terms "data," "information," "material," "documents," and "matter" are considered synonymous and used interchangeably in this order. They refer to all data regardless of its physical form (*e.g.,* data on paper printouts, tapes, disks or disk packs, in memory chips, in random-access memory (RAM), in read-only memory (ROM), on microfilm or microfiche, on communication lines, and on display terminals).[1] (DOE 5636.2A)

Label

1. A piece of information that represents the security level of an object and that describes the sensitivity of the information in the object. (CSC-STD-004-85; NCSC-WA-001-85)

---

[1]Although "data" and similar terms often are used interchangeably with "information," there is a significant distinction. Information is data that have been *processed* in some way, and information has value where data may have little or even negative intrinsic value. For example, padding for purposes of defeating traffic or information flow analysis adds *data* that has a negative value to those interested in the *information* available from traffic analysis.

2. The marking of an item of information to reflect its classification and its set of categories that represent the sensitivity of the information.

   a) *Internal Label.* The marking of an item of information to reflect the classification and sensitivity of the information within the confines of the medium containing the information.

   b) *External Label.* The visible marking on the outside of the medium or the cover of the medium that reflects the classification and sensitivity of the information resident within the medium. (DOE 5636.2A)

Marking

The process of placing a sensitivity designator (*e.g.*, "confidential") with data such that its sensitivity is communicated. Marking is not restricted to the physical placement of a sensitivity designator, as might be done with a rubber stamp, but can involve the use of headers for network messages, special fields in databases, etc. (WB)

Need-to-Know

A determination made by the processor of sensitive information that a prospective recipient, in the interest of national security, has a requirement for access to, knowledge of, or possession of the sensitive information in order to perform official tasks or services. (CSC-STD-004-85)

Object

A passive entity that contains or receives information. Access to an object potentially implies access to the information it contains. Examples of objects are records, blocks, pages, segments, files, directories, directory trees, and programs, as well as bits, bytes, words, fields, processors, video displays, keyboards, clocks, printers, network nodes, etc. (CSC-STD-001-83; AFR 205-16; NCSC-WA-001-85; DCID 1/16-1, Sup.)

Object Reuse

The reassignment to some subject of a medium (*e.g.*, page frame, disk sector, magnetic tape) that contained one or more objects. To be securely reassigned, such media must contain no residual data from the previously contained object(s). (CSC-STD-001-83; NCSC-WA-001-85)

Owner of Data

The individual or group that has responsibility for specific data types and that is charged with the communication of the need for certain security-related handling procedures to both the users and custodians of this data. (WB)

Personal Data

1. Any unique data used in the system of records to locate or retrieve an individual's record. Information subject to the Privacy Act of 1974. (AFR 205-16)

2. Data about an individual including, but not limited to, education, financial transactions, medical history, qualifications, service data, criminal or employment history which ties the data to the individual's name, or an identifying number, symbols, or other identifying particular assigned to the individual, such as a finger or voice print or a photograph. (OPNAVINST 5239.1A)

Privileged Data

Data not subject to usual rules because of some special circumstances. For example, chaplain, legal, and medical files. (AFR 205-16)

Proprietary Data

Data that is created, used, and marketed by individuals having exclusive legal rights. (AFR 205-16)

Sensitive Business Data

Data which requires protection under Title 18, USC 1905, and other data which, by its nature, requires controlled distribution or access for reasons other than that it is classified or personal data. Sensitive business data is recognized in the following categories.

1. *For Official Use Only*—Requiring confidentiality of information derived from inspector general, authority, or other investigative activity.
2. *Financial*—Requiring protection to ensure the integrity of funds or other fiscal assets.
3. *Sensitive Management*—Requiring protection to defend against the loss of property, material, or supplies or to defend against the disruption of operations or normal management practices, etc.
4. *Proprietary*—Requiring protection to protect data or information in conformance with a limited rights agreement or which is the exclusive property of a civilian corporation or individual and which is on loan to the government for evaluation or for its proper use in adjudicating contracts.
5. *Privileged*—Requiring protection for conformance with business standards or as required by law. (Example: government-developed information involving the award of a contract.) (OPNAVINST 5239.1A)

Sensitive Compartmented Information (SCI)

Intelligence information requiring special controls indicating restricted handling. (DODD 5200.28)

Sensitive Data

Data that require protection due to the risk and magnitude of loss or harm that could result from inadvertent or deliberate disclosure, alteration, or destruction of the data. The term includes data whose improper use or disclosure could adversely affect the ability to accomplish a mission, proprietary data, records about individuals requiring protection under the Privacy Act, and data not releasable under the Freedom of Information Act. (A-130)

Sensitive Defense Information

Any information which requires a degree of protection and which should not be made generally available. This type of information includes, but is not limited to that information which must be safeguarded so as to:

1. Prevent damage to national defense and which usually bears a security classification.
2. Assure the individual privacy of U.S. citizens as provided by the Privacy Act of 1974.

3. Maintain the confidentiality of FOUO information derived from the inspector general, an audit, or other investigative activities such as medical or other jurisprudence or disciplinary information derived from records of doctor/patient or lawyer/client relationships.

4. Protect funds, supplies, and material from theft, fraud, misappropriation, or misuse. This includes asset or resource accounting or systems or operations which are involved in the control and distribution of funds or the processing of information which offers the opportunity to divert economically valuable resources.

5. Protect proprietary information which is the exclusive property of an individual or corporation. This proprietary information may be on loan, leased, or purchased by the government or made available to the government for its proper use, to include evaluating or adjudicating contracts.

6. Protect government-developed privileged information involving the award of contracts.

7. Protect information which the commander considers essential for mission accomplishment. (AR 380-380)

Sensitive Information

1. Information that, as determined by a competent authority, must be protected because its unauthorized disclosure, alteration, loss, or destruction will at least cause perceivable damage to someone or something. (CSC-STD-001-83; CSC-STD-003-85; CSC-STD-004-85; NCSC-WA-001-85)

2. Information, classified and unclassified, that requires protection due to the risk and magnitude of loss or harm that could result from inadvertent or deliberate disclosure, modification, or destruction. The term includes information classified pursuant to DODD 5200.1-R in one of the three designated security classification categories. The term also includes records about individuals requiring protection under the Privacy Act, proprietary data, and information not releasable under the Freedom of Information Act, as well as agency data that affects the agency's mission. (DODD 5200.18)

3. Any information which requires a degree of protection and which should not be made generally available. (FIPS PUB 39)

Sensitivity

The characteristic of a resource which implies its value or importance, and may include its vulnerability. (ISO 7498-2)

Special Markings

1. Special Markings are not classification levels [but rather] are used on certain classified documents to indicate that the document has special access or handling requirements. (DOE 5635.1A)

2. Synonymous with Handling Caveats; Dissemination Controls; Dissemination Control Markings; Handling Restrictions.

Split Knowledge

The condition under which two or more parties separately have part of the data, that when combined, will yield a security parameter or that will allow them to perform some sensitive function. (WB)

Technical Data

Classified or unclassified information of any kind that can be used, or adapted for use in the design, production, manufacture, repair, overhaul, processing, engineering, development, operation maintenance, or reconstruction of goods or munitions; or any technology that advances the state-of-the-art or establishes a new art in an area of significant military applicability in the United States. The data may be tangible, such as a model, prototype, blueprint, or an operating manual, or may be intangible, such as a technical service or oral or visual interactions. (DODD 2040.2)

Technical Information

Information, including scientific information, that relates to research, development, engineering, test, evaluation, production operation, use, and maintenance of munitions and other military supplies and equipment. (DODD 5230.24)

Test Data

An asset category consisting of information used to determine the applicability, efficiency, or accuracy of systems. (MK, RM)

5.1 ELEMENTS AND OBJECTIVES OF A CLASSIFICATION SCHEME

In the realm of information security, the purpose of classifying data is simple: to assist in determining what security measures should apply to which data elements. Generally, the higher the classification, the more stringent the security controls that are appropriate.

A data classification scheme must include:

- A security policy that permits categorization of data
- Some means of marking data as to classification level
- Procedures and rules controlling access to data
- Procedures and rules controlling storage, retention, and disposal of data
- Controls such as logs to track access activity and conformance to procedures and rules

Data classification goes along with classification of personnel. Generally, personnel possessing a higher-level clearance will be permitted access to higher levels of data.

5.2 CRITERIA FOR CLASSIFYING DATA

Many types of criteria can be used in classifying data. All lead (in the security realm) to labels such as "confidential," "secret," and so forth. A fundamental issue(see section 5.4.3) is that from a security perspective, almost any data should be classified and protected; from a perspective of ease of use, almost all data should be freely accessible. Tradeoffs in this area must be made on an installation-specific basis and usually will require senior management involvement.

One possible methodology for classifying data involves examining the following characteristics:

- Quantity
- Age

- Number of independent associations
- Criticality
- Scope
- Useful life

5.2.1 Quantity

Clearly, the volume of data has implications on processing. Since classifying data into higher levels of sensitivity implies special attention, the greater the quantity of data classified in higher levels, the greater the impact on normal operations and computer resource requirements.

5.2.2 Age and Useful Life

All data have a useful life. For technical data such as documentation of a specific program, the lifetime may be fairly short or some years; when the program changes materially, prior technical data become useless. Details of a marketing plan may have a quite short useful life; once the program is in place, planning details are no longer relevant. Generally, the older data are, the less valuable they are. A classification scheme should include regular reviews to ensure that data which has outlived its useful lifetime does not continue to hold a high classification.

5.2.3 Scope and Number of Independent Associations

The classification level of data may vary depending on associations with other data. For example, Social Security numbers often are used as identifiers. Where privacy is an issue, the Social Security Number would merit a higher classification because it is associated with many other data elements besides merely a person's name.

5.2.4 Criticality

While criticality more commonly is used to refer to information systems, it also applies to data. In the example of marketing planning information, financial figures could be very critical to an organization. Until the marketing plan is in effect, a competitor who discovers the intended level of resources would have valuable information o guide a counter-strategy. Similar considerations clearly apply to military tactical information.

5.3 STATISTICAL INFERENCE

This sub-section[2] lists exposures and controls related to aggregation and statistical inference. Controls for exposures can affect the classification level appropriate for some kinds of data. For example, some controls include higher levels of classification for apparently innocuous items to prevent disclosure by aggregation.

Exposures and controls related to statistical inference in databases involve complex mathematics that are outside the scope of this work. A much more exhaustive (and perhaps more difficult to read) treatment of this material can be found in the 1982 Denning book, *Cryptography and Data Security* and in several more recent papers (see references for this section).

---

[2]See also section 12.4.

5.3.1 Exposures Related to Statistical Inference

The basic dichotomy in a database is a conflict between disclosure and privacy. The goal is to permit accurate statistics on the overall database without permitting disclosure of information about specific individuals or other significant entities represented in the data base. This goal cannot be attained completely.

Aggregation refers to collection of many individually unimportant statistics, which can reveal an overall picture that should not be disclosed. The classic example is disclosure of a plan of attack from aggregating information about individual combat unit positions.

Statistical inference attacks are the opposite problem: The overall picture *should* be disclosed, but not individual statistics. These attacks may depend on the extent of a penetrator's supplementary knowledge; that is, information about database elements which is gathered from sources other than the database. A list of common statistical attacks on databases would include:

- *Small/large query sets*

  A *query set*, informally, is the number of database entities (records) that are selected by a query. If the number of entities is small the probability of individual disclosure is high (if there is only one member, the probability is unity.) Queries that select small query sets need to be controlled. If a query language permits the operation of complementation, then large query sets must be controlled as their complements could be sensitive small query sets.

- *Trackers*

  Individual, general and union *trackers* exploit the basic principle of padding small query sets with enough extra records that the query sets grow larger than any arbitrary restriction on query set size. The effect of the padding, being known, then can be removed, thus disclosing information about individual records.

- *Key-specified attack*

  If keys are known (Social Security numbers, for instance), then logical queries about groups of records with specified keys may disclose sensitive data associated with individual records.

- *Characteristic attack*

  A generalization of key-specified attacks is *characteristic-specified queries*. By specifying characteristics known to be shared by small numbers of records, successive queries can narrow the query set to small numbers. At the extreme, it may be possible to select individuals this way.

- *Chosen value attack*

  Some *chosen value* (for example, the median of a set of salaries or grade averages) is selected. Queries that define overlapping sets are then proposed to the database. As the overlap in succeeding refined queries decreases, it may be possible to isolate a single record that matches the chosen value. This value is then associated with that record, and individual information has been disclosed. The same principle can be generalized to identifying ranges of values into which individual records fall (salary between $25,000 and $27,500, for example.)

- *Insertion/deletion attack*

  If users can add or delete records from a database, then records that match desired characteristics can be inserted, thus increasing query set sizes to defeat query-set size controls. This is similar to padding in trackers.

5.3.2 Controls Related to Statistical Inference

Although aggregation is not a statistical inference attack, its effect on data classification is considered here to link it with other control methods. About the only thing that can feasibly be done to control attacks that depend on aggregation of many data elements is to assign a higher sensitivity classification to the individual elements. Since there is essentially an infinite number of ways that elements might show a pattern in aggregate that is not evident from individual elements, three strategies are most appropriate:

1. Assign to all individual elements the same data classification held by potential aggregations to be protected from disclosure.
2. Determine which aggregations are to be protected, then assign the same classification to individual elements that the aggregations require.
3. Protect the entire database at the level of most sensitive possible aggregation

None of these approaches is entirely satisfactory. The first approach effectively leads quickly to the third, since it is essentially impossible to predict what aggregations could lead to what disclosures. The only way to be certain is to restrict the entire database. The second approach may allow reasonable access to the database. The risk is that either the set of sensitive aggregations is not complete enough to satisfy security needs (something was overlooked, for instance), or that other sets of individual elements besides those that are identified as leading to the defined sensitive aggregations also may lead to the sensitive areas. Restricting the entire database may control aggregation exposures, at the cost of limiting legitimate use unnecessarily.

Controls usually apply to more than one type of attack, therefore the following list does not correlate precisely with the list of exposures. A list of statistical inference controls would include:

- *Query set size and overlap control*

  The minimum query-set size can be restricted, or controls may restrict overlapping query sets. A minimum query-set is simple to implement, but insufficient. Overlap controls are not feasible in general, as the database would have to remember the history of all previous queries to determine overlap. Use of tracker techniques easily defeats query-set controls.

- *Maximum order control*

  Queries may be restricted to n-order statistics. If it is necessary to determine $n + 1$ attributes to identify individual records, then a restriction to n order statistics will preserve privacy. This may be overly restrictive because many higher-order statistics could be perfectly acceptable for release.

- *Cell suppression*

  Cells containing data that permit derivation of sensitive statistics from a database can be suppressed. An analysis technique is used to suppress (non-sensitive) complementary cells as well, so that distortions of the database are not evident and statistics remain valid for the entire database. A simple example is the n-respondent, $k\%$ dominance rule that implies deleting cells where a small number of respondents contributes to a large percentage of the overall statistics. For example, a table containing gross revenues for Microsoft and all other firms in Seattle producing project-management software would be dominated (probably about 99.9%) by Microsoft. Therefore, the cell containing Microsoft's revenues would have to be suppressed, as would cells containing such totals, to avoid disclosure of several significant (high-order) figures of Microsoft's gross revenues.

Unfortunately, this method becomes computationally infeasible even for relatively small numbers of fields per database record. It is necessary to determine all possible sensitive statistics that can be derived and delete cells and their complements to prohibit this. Such determination is complex and grows rapidly more complex with the number of fields per database record.

- *Implied query*

Theoretical methods allow deduction of all possible "implied query sets" for a statistic. The implied queries are restricted as a control method. For a statistic of order n, there are 2^n implied queries; thus this approach becomes exponentially more complex as the order of statistics grows.

- *Partitioning*

Databases can be partitioned (physically or logically) in such a way as to prevent attacks based on small query sets or insertion/deletion of records. If query sets are constrained to include entire groups rather than subsets, tracker attacks cannot precisely isolate individual entities. While this method offers control, it may be computationally infeasible for databases of practical utility.

- *Noise and perturbation*

One general form of control over statistical inference is to add some form of noise to the database. An analogy is spurious records that pad a data stream to uniform activity, so as to defeat traffic analysis. The noise should be added to the database so as to destroy precision of individual statistics while retaining accurate overall statistics. Noise can be added in the form of additional records or by perturbing data elements directly. Various statistical transformations can be applied so as to distort individual elements while retaining the same overall statistics.

Noise and perturbation usually cannot be used in practical dynamic databases. Too much computing resource is used to apply such transformations dynamically, and the data must not be altered permanently or its functionality could be lost.

- *Random sample queries*

A primary reason for exposure of databases to inference is that the user has control of the composition of each query set. Thus, individual elements can be isolated by using intersecting query sets. *Random sample queries* control this exposure by a combination of prohibiting the user control over the query set and using large samples (on the order of 80% to 90% of the total number of records in the database.) Particularly in a database that is encrypted, this may be implemented efficiently and at a reasonable cost.

5.4 GOVERNMENT CLEARANCES AND DATA SENSITIVITIES

A crucial difference between government and civilian schemes for personnel and data classification is that the government deals in national security arenas. Not only accidental disclosure but also well-funded intentional penetration attempts are expected. Classification schemes are considerably more precise and more strongly enforced than is common in the private sector. In the private sector, intentional disclosure or alteration is industrial espionage; few corporate data are all that sensitive, and the resources and methods applied to industrial espionage seldom approach the level of national security situations.

The following material is adapted from the Department of Defense *Technical Rationale Behind CSC-STD-003-85: Computer Security Requirements*, CSC-STD-004-85, June, 1985, Appendix B

"Detailed Description of Clearances and Data Sensitivities." Other government agencies such as the Department of Energy and the Nuclear Regulatory Commission operate similar schemes; often agencies accept each others' classifications.

5.4.1 Personnel Clearances

System users, including those with direct connections to the system and those who might receive output or generate input to the system, are grouped into levels of clearance:

- Uncleared personnel—access to any information for which there are no specified controls
- Unclassified Information—access to sensitive unclassified information (see 5.3.2 data classifications)
- Confidential Clearance—U.S. citizen and some limited records checking; may require a "National Agency Check (NAC)"
- Secret Clearance—Typically requires a "NAC"
- Top Secret Clearance based on current Background Investigation—requires an investigation extending back 5 to 15 years
- Top Secret Clearance based on current Special Background Investigation—a more stringent investigation than category (e)

The DoD document also describes authorizations for "One Category" and "Multiple Categories."

5.4.2 Data Sensitivities

Increasing levels of data sensitivity are:

- Unclassified—publicly releasable information.
- Not Classified but Sensitive—A category for data or information that are not classified in national security terms but are still controlled. Examples include employment and promotion examination questions and answers, data explicitly exempted under the Freedom of Information Act or other statutes, trade secrets or other financial or commercial information, personal data, and some unclassified technology with military applications.
- Confidential—information, the unauthorized disclosure of which reasonably could be expected to cause damage to the national security.
- Secret—information, the unauthorized disclosure of which reasonably could be expected to cause serious damage to the national security.
- Top Secret—information, the unauthorized disclosure of which reasonably could be expected to cause exceptionally grave damage to the national security.

The DoD document further defines the categories of "One Category" and "Multiple Categories".

5.4.3 Government *versus* Civilian Classification Schemes

A scheme classifying personnel and data to the levels of detail used by the U.S. Department of Defense is not needed nor appropriate for civilian usage, unless the civilian application is as a government contractor in sensitive work.

Consideration of the discussion of statistical inference in section 12.4 will show that to meet high levels of security under a detailed classification scheme such as that of the Department of Defense, nearly all data and information would have to be restricted and/or distorted statistically. In fact, it is common for academically oriented individuals and groups to make the accusation that government data classification schemes have reached a stage of uselessness for exactly this reason. There always will be differences of opinion among different types of users of information; this is in the realm of ethics and there are few "hard and fast" resolutions.

Private sector concerns typically fall between the academic perspective and the government perspective. The private corporation is in a uniquely favorable position between the government with its non-measurable "national security" criterion and the academic with a non-measurable totally free-information perspective: The private firm can measure risk in terms of dollars and profits. Thus risk analysis and cost-benefit considerations may permit the private sector firm to choose a scheme for classification of personnel and data based on a relatively objective criterion. As discussed in this chapter, the private sector organization normally chooses a simpler classification scheme (if any) for personnel and for data.

5.5 PROCEDURES AND MANAGEMENT FOR A CLASSIFICATION SCHEME

We begin by reviewing the six fundamental security requirements that deal with access control:

1. *Security policy*—an explicit and well-defined policy enforced by the system
2. *Marking*—labels must be associated with objects
3. *Identification*—individual entities must be identified
4. *Accountability*—audit trails and so forth must support tracing of actions to individual entities
5. *Assurance*—the system must be capable of independent evaluation to provide assurance that the system enforces the security policy
6. *Continuous protection*—mechanisms must be enforced continuously

Management of a classification scheme lies primarily in the first four of these requirements.

As discussed earlier, a *security policy* must exist that, among other things, defines levels of classification and access privileges. Without this fundamental requirement, no classification scheme (or security program in general) can be very effective.

Marking of objects by classification, and often such characteristics as read-only or levels of clearance permitted access, is essential. For example, hard-copy should have a classification on the front cover, title page, first page and back cover. Magnetic media should be in labelled containers when not mounted (if removable) and internal labels should include classification data. Input and output forms must be marked much as for hard-copy. Only with marking can those who might come across such objects be expected to apply appropriate security measures.

As alluded to in the previous paragraph, all objects must include *labels*. An example would be a classification label in the volume table of contents (VTOC) for a disk drive, or labels on magnetic tape or diskettes.

Marking and labeling can become serious concerns where more than one system is interconnected in a network. If different systems use different marking and labelling schemes, then appropriate controls may not be applied by one system for information that originated elsewhere.

Accountability includes authentication (see Chapter 1), audit trails, logs, and periodic reviews of such data. The principle is that it must be possible to trace actions to entities and, ultimately, to human beings who caused the actions. In the context of classification management, this includes policies and procedures that define authorization, custody, ownership and similar procedures, and mechanisms to monitor and enforce such policies and procedures.

Among the procedures that must be defined in a security policy are those that deal with appropriate controls on reproduction, filing, and storage of data and information. These procedures will vary depending on the classification level and the needs of each individual organization relating to classified data.

REFERENCES

"Controlling Information: Data Classification," *Computer Security*, No. 50: January/February, 1983.

Denning, Dorothy Elizabeth Robling, *Cryptography and Data Security*, Addison-Wesley Publishing Company, Reading, MA, 1983.

"EDP Threat assessments: Concepts and Planning Guide," *RCMP Security Information Publications # 2*, January, 1982.

Koenig, R. C., "Advances in Information Classification," *Computer Security and Privacy Symposium Proceedings*, DM 35, Honeywell Information Systems, Phoenix, AZ, April 15-16, 1980, pp. 119-124.

Lobel, J., *Foiling the System Breakers: Computer Security and Access Control*, McGraw-Hill, NY, 1986

Martin, James, *Security, Accuracy, and Privacy in Computer Systems*, Prentice-Hall, Inc., Englewood Cliffs, NJ, 1973.

"Report on Statistical Disclosure and Disclosure-Avoidance Techniques," U.S. Department of Commerce, U.S. Government Printing Office, Washington, D.C., 1978.

Technical Rationale Behind CSC-STD-003-85: Computer Security Requirements, CSC-STD-004-85, Department of Defense, DoD Computer Security Center, June, 1985.

6. Security Awareness

Security Awareness includes the pro-active steps that management takes to make employees cognizant of their responsibilities for security of corporate assets and the threats to those assets. It focuses on the new or changed behaviors that are necessary to respond to the new technology and media.

The knowledge that the professional must have includes:

- Corporate policies, procedures, and other intentions
- Areas where remedial action is indicated
- Assessment of threats and vulnerabilities
- Technology trends
- Behaviors to be encouraged
- User motives
- Applicable law and regulation
- Available and applicable communication channels and media

For example, the professional should know:

- The user behavior expected and required under applicable law and regulation, policy, classification programs, employee agreements, *etc.*
- The quality of password management and similar procedures within the organization
- The likely effect on user behavior of such new technologies as office automation, LANs, one-time passwords, desk-top computing, *etc.*
- About house organs, bulletin boards, video, film, stickers, *etc.*
- About existing training media available from vendors
- The effects on user behavior of ease of use, management direction, ethical motives, *etc.*

6.1 COMPONENTS OF EDP SECURITY: ADMINISTRATIVE AND ORGANIZATIONAL CONTROLS

6.1.1 Administrative and Organizational Controls

This chapter presents a brief overview of some specific security and control measures that fall into the area of administrative controls (organizational measures relating to security) and awareness. This particular topic area in principle encompasses the entire spectrum of the organization; effectively anything can be considered an administrative or organizational feature. The emphasis here is on broad notions such as "organizational culture," policy statements, company policies defining assets such as trade secrets, elements in the organization responsible for security, changes related to technology, and "how the company does business."

The types of assets which need protection at this broad level are what can be called "soft assets." By this we mean that they are intangible and generally hard to measure in dollar terms. At the level of detail we reach, it is difficult to separate control methods from assets or awareness. For example, the organization's "morale" is an important factor in security and control, is a function of awareness, and is also an asset which is worth protecting, but it is very difficult to put a dollar value on morale. Most of the techniques mentioned in this chapter both support protection of the soft assets and enhance an environment in which control is much easier.

One asset has been mentioned: organization "morale." Are employees generally happy in their jobs, or is there an atmosphere of general mistrust and antagonism? The security problem clearly differs between "happy" and "unhappy" organizations. Similar soft assets are "how the business works"—how does it go about its daily affairs (e. g., do people make extensive use of computers?); the normal functioning of the business (if disrupted, what costs are involved?); the "good name" of the business (how do customers perceive a bank if they cannot get money due to computer problems?). The basic organizational structure of the business is an asset: It has grown to meet needs and to match capabilities of people, and personnel changes or system problems represent costs. Reorganization can present very large costs (for example, the merger of Burroughs and Univac to create Unisys, with layoffs of duplicated headquarters staff, expenses for new logos, forms, new planning efforts, and so on). Training and experience of the employees, and their understanding of each other, and of how each goes about his or her job, are significant assets, difficult and expensive to re-create if changed or disrupted. The last group of representative assets here is the collection of data and information that support the organization's functioning: policies, procedures, manufacturing methods, patents, and the general knowledge base (customer lists and contacts, for instance).

The most basic of all control principles is that an organization which is "happy," which has knowledgeable and capable people, and which is committed to ethical and professional behavior as a culture, is usually a secure and controlled organization. Specific controls still are important to minimize temptations and ensure continued high morale and professionalism. In both information systems and organizations in general, committed people with appropriate skills can make lousy systems work somehow; incompetent or hostile people can and do cause supposedly well-designed systems to fail. Without top management direction on policy and commitment to professional and ethical behavior, the other two factors are directionless. If the organization fails in any of the three basic areas of morale, skilled and committed employees, or top management commitment, security must be imposed; imposed rules are inherently less efficient and effective than committed people.

Effective security and control is not a one-time event. The overall picture needs to be reviewed periodically as much as the budgeting process does. Conditions change; plans need updating. Continual reinforcement through employee awareness programs is essential. The critical element of any good management strategy is continued commitment by the organization, and periodic review and upgrading of system security and control plans is one way to maintain organizational awareness and commitment.

6.1.2 Policies

The issue of security policies has two dimensions: formal policies in the arena of secure systems, and the more general use of "policy." Chapter 16 ("Policy Development") addresses both issues, and the formal sense of policy is treated further in Chapter 7 ("Computer and System Security").

Throughout this book, we emphasize that corporate policies must exist and must be communicated.

6.1.3 Awareness

According to L. LaFleur, of T-Base Research and Development, Inc.:

Training can be a powerful tool that strengthens an existing security awareness program, especially those programs that focus on a marketing approach to get the message to their audiences. A security awareness program needs two techniques for maximum effectiveness:

- A promotional component to introduce, remind, and respond to security issues
- An interactive component to translate concepts into actions, training being one aspect of this component

The key element in a security awareness program is to break the inertia of "doing it the way we always have." Too often, this inertia is broken dramatically, by serious and expensive problems due to a security breach. An effective awareness program should combine passive means of promotional techniques with an interactive component.[1]

The mechanics of delivering security awareness programs do not differ substantially from those of delivering other employee awareness programs. Various passive delivery methods such as in-house newsletters, special topical bulletins (security alerts in this instance), stickers for doors and bulletin boards, classroom instruction, and videos and films are common.

Many sources of information for security awareness programs exist. A list of films and videos from the National Institute of Standards and Technology (NIST) security BBS is provided in Appendix C. (This BBS is open to the public; the phone number is (301) 948-5717, and there are lines for numerous protocols and modem types. Access *via* the InterNet is available on an experimental basis as of late 1992.)

These films and similar materials, especially when combined with interactive components such as having employees participate in development of materials to promote awareness, can be very effective in improving security. These and other methods are examined in the next section.

6.2 ORGANIZATIONAL AND ADMINISTRATIVE CONTROLS

6.2.1 Employee Non-Disclosure Considerations

A non-disclosure agreement is an established form of agreement between employees and a company in which an employee agrees not to disclose trade secrets or other confidential information owned by the company to any unauthorized person. It provides a legal basis for future prosecution of employees who breach security. Thus, employers retain their ability to hire or fire employees and at the same time they maintain their legal right to protect their trade secrets.

A number of specific factors should be considered by the information security specialist in conjunction with the information security attorney. In particular, the establishment of employee agreements and consultant agreements can provide the legal basis for subsequent prosecution in the event of breach of the security guidelines. Some of the significant elements in such agreements are set out below.

- Acknowledgment of the value of trade secrets. There may be a distinction between valuable trade secrets and confidential information without commercial value for the purposes of criminal law and particularly for the purposes of civil remedies available. As a result, the

---

[1] "Training as Part of a Security Awareness Program," *Computer Control Quarterly*, vol 10, #4, Winter, 1992.

agreement may indicate clearly that valuable trade secrets are involved.[2]

- Non-disclosure requirement. This requirement will provide the essential obligation of confidence and secrecy in relation to the trade secrets or other confidential information.

- Non-use requirement. This provision is also often included to as to preclude use of the trade secrets or confidential information by the party restrained. When obligations of confidence are discussed herein, it is assumed a non-use restriction is also included.

- Detail of the scope or definition of the trade secrets. Agreements are more effective when they are certain. As a result, it is an advantage to define with as much precision as possible the confidential information subject to the obligations of confidence. An example might be definition, in a detailed form, of a particular semiconductor design project. The security manager may wish to ensure that the types of activities or the access to certain processes, products, or resources that may constitute confidential information are clearly defined.

- Obligations continuing beyond termination. It is clear that obligations of confidence must continue past the termination of the assignment by the consultant or the employment by the employee. Otherwise, of course, there would be no remedy to deal with the employee who absconded with valuable trade secrets of the former employer. One should also note the necessity of continuing obligations when dealing with general releases of individuals who are fiduciaries (that is, have relationships with high trust such as senior officers or directors of corporations).

- Restraints on duplication of materials. In some circumstances, it may be necessary to provide a clear restraint on an individual's ability to take copies of materials, particularly data and computer programs. These obligations may be important in triggering civil and potentially criminal liability in relation to such unauthorized reproduction of certain materials. These restraints should be clearly integrated into the company's policy in relation to access and use of the firm's computer systems.[3]

- Exit review. At the termination of access or of employment, it is very practical and advisable to conduct a review of the confidential information that the employee or consultant has had access to, and to review the continuing obligations of confidence in relation to that valuable confidential information. Such an exit review performs an educational function and provides some certainty for the employee and employer in ascertaining the information restrained. It should, of course, be in writing and it may be placed in the form of an agreement between the parties.

- Delivery of documents on termination. There should be a clear obligation on the employee or consultant to return all documents upon termination of the employment or engagement. This avoids the prospect of confidential information disclosed in such documents being outside the control of the employer.

Many other terms may exist in such employment or consultant agreements and, in particular, when related to the assignment and ownership of inventions, discoveries, improvements, or works of authorship developed or created by the employee or consultant. It is not within the scope of this text to deal with such additional terms. However, the information security specialist should examine all of these issues in detail with the information security attorney.

In fulfilling employees' obligations under this agreement, employees promise not to disclose

---

[2]See also Chapter 5 on classification schemes.

[3]See also Chapter 5 on classification schemes and handling of classified data.

company trade secrets unless authorized in writing by the company. This agreement should re-main in force even after employment has been terminated. The employee agrees to surrender to company upon termination of employment all notes, records, and documentation that was used, created, or controlled by the employee during employment.[4]

A non-disclosure agreement should stress that an employee should take his or her involve-ment with trade secrets seriously. The agreement must legally bind the signer from disclosing trade secrets. Should the signer disclose the secrets to others, they cannot legally make use of it without facing the possibility of an injunction.

6.2.2 Employee Training

Two kinds of employee training are significant from the security standpoint: orientation and skills. Orientation is training whose intent is to set a climate, convey initial information about a situation, and so on. Employee orientation at the beginning of employment is of interest here. The second kind of training is specific skills training: courses of a few days or weeks' length that help employees upgrade their knowledge and capability or add new knowledge. From the security perspective, orientation relates to employee awareness and organizational culture; and skills training relates to reinforcement of the culture, and the critical need to have competent, know-ledgeable people.

6.2.2.1 Orientation

Every employee hired should learn about the written components of the corporate culture, such as policies, what is considered confidential, rules regarding conflict of interest, and so forth. More mundane knowledge is needed as well, of course: introduction to fellow workers, location of the washrooms and office facilities, formal reporting relationships, union rules and procedures if any, and so forth. The initial employee training sessions should address these areas. A written employee orientation package that is *kept current* is highly recommended, and may be necessary to protect the organization in some kinds of legal disputes.

Employee agreement to such things as acknowledgments of "read and understood" disclosure policies probably has little or no legal value unless it is *informed* agreement. The main thing the SSO needs to ensure is that discussion of just what the company's policies are in regard to secu-rity and control is included in the personnel or human resources department's standard orien-tation programs, and that employees are asked to sign. Signing and acknowledgment should be a condition of hiring and of continued employment.

It is highly recommended that employees review policies regarding confidentiality and secu-rity, and sign new acknowledgments each time there is a material change in employee duties and responsibilities, and in any case periodically (perhaps each six months, or yearly).

Security and control principles include continual reinforcement. Tell employees what is ex-pected "up front," remind them periodically, and the factor of employee awareness will follow.

6.2.2.2 Skills

By far the most frequent cause of losses in any system is employee error. Even though a major part of the effort in any system design project is invested in making the system "bulletproof,"

---

[4][[Remer 84], p. 17]

people make mistakes. Properly trained people make fewer mistakes. Continued employee upgrading, and employee training before new tasks are attempted, are important for economic as well as security and control reasons. Training is not a primary responsibility of the security function, but ensuring that training is available and provided is part of the SSO's responsibility. This is a way to avoid many of the high-occurrence "accidental" threats identified in the risk assessment, as well as one way to help out in the employee morale area. The security people should ensure that training is available, and that new systems developments always include development of employee training programs. Security analyses may include data that will allow managers to assess the true value of training; training can be seen as strictly a cost, and thus avoidable during "lean times," without such data.

Basic control principles suggest that an organization with high morale, with knowledgeable and capable people, and which is committed to professional and ethical behavior, usually is a secure and well-controlled organization. Training both for specific skills and for orientation is an important component in two of the three basic needs.

6.2.3 Telecommuting

Examination of administrative and organizational aspects of security and control would be incomplete without mention of a phenomenon that is growing and may dominate some information industries in the future: "telecommuting." In something resembling in many ways a return to the cottage industry of the early Industrial Revolution, the communication capability of modern information systems, combined with the power of personal computers, has made it possible for people to work at home again. It no longer is necessary to fight traffic to reach the office. It no longer is necessary to have set hours; electronic mail can reach people wherever and whenever they "sign on." It is possible to have complete communication with people (except physical contact) from anywhere there is access to two-way video and computer links. Less complete communication, voice and data but not video, is available from anywhere in the world with a telephone system.

From the security and control perspective, the company that experiments with telecommuting must be aware of some potential new problem areas.

The corporation moving to telecommuting exposes itself to two major risks that may not have been there with employees doing the same tasks in an office, or may have changed in character:

1. Communications exposure

    This is examined in more detail in Chapters 2 and 8. Here, it is enough to say that communicating is necessary to telecommute; the company incurs the exposures relating to information in public networks when it supports telecommuting.

2. Asset exposure

    The assets—data and information, personal computers, and so on—used by the employee, will be in a home environment. Security usually is much looser in people's homes than in even fairly "loose" offices. If there were no other problem, there still will be many locations, rather than just one.

Sensitive company assets, both data and such costly physical assets as personal computers, will be exposed differently, and probably more, with telecommuting than in a single-office environment.

An exposure of the company that does not exist in single-location environments is changed employee relations. Offices serve purposes besides simply collecting people and equipment together; there are social and behavioral and interpersonal factors involved. Telecommuting supports many kinds of information exchange but not groups of people socializing on coffee breaks, for instance. There probably will be significant effects on employee morale for companies which encourage extensive telecommuting. The exact effects are not known for this new phenomenon; the security and control people need to monitor and watch out for morale problems.

Another potential morale problem is employee relations. Cottage industries in the early Industrial Revolution included piecework and other systems that developed into cruel abuse of employees. Although the technology is totally different, the people relation problems and exploitation of workers that prevailed then could recur. There is some evidence (lawsuits in California, for example) that such abuses are resurfacing in telecommuting. Successful examples of telecommuting clearly show that exploitation *need not* be a problem. Lawsuits show that it *may* be. The security and control functions must monitor the situation; not only is the "happy company" at jeopardy, but as well, there is greatly increased exposure.

A discussion of employee morale would be incomplete if it ignored management morale. One problem that occurs in telecommuting is that managers must be sufficiently secure in their own positions to accept employees who are not subject to direct, exact controls. "Management by Walking Around (MBWA)" can be more than slightly difficult when staff could be located in several cities. With cellular telephones and laptop computers, it is entirely possible to work while sunning on the beach. Traditional managers may not find it easy to accept this.

Telecommuting may be a benefit of technology that will free people from traffic, cities from gridlock, and work from "9-to-5 drudgery." It may be a curse that will be used by unscrupulous employers to recreate the exploitation of the early Industrial Revolution. The authors have considerable experience with using world-wide networks and combining people on different continents in the same project; the experience is exhilarating and one wonders how one ever managed without. Others have reported companies using telecommuting to separate workers, deny them interaction with fellows, and impose piecework and monitoring methods that amount to exploitation and invasion of privacy.

6.2.4 Technological Change Effects on Security

The field of information security has undergone drastic changes, paralleling changes in the availability and use of computer. In some senses, "information security" has come to be linked inseparably with "computer security," as computer technology overtakes earlier methods of storing and dealing with information. The changes in computer technology and availability are expected to continue, and changes in information security probably will keep pace.

Differences in the technical environment, applications, and the types and numbers of users have led to fundamental alterations in the nature, use, and abuse of information systems. In this section, we look briefly at technological issues. In section 6.3.5, we look at user issues.

A caution is in order: Some of the current uses and problems were not predicted or expected. In the next decade, we can expect new uses and problems that are different from those now predicted. The information security practitioner has a responsibility to maintain a current awareness of such changes, and to *review* and if necessary *alter* plans to cope with expected problems.

The following material regarding changes in technology, applications, and security threats is based on a study prepared for the Department of Communications in Canada, published in 1991 (see references).

6.2.4.1 Changes in Technology

Obviously, the critical change in technology has been the microcomputer. Less obviously, connectivity has supported and mandated massive changes in work patterns and capabilities.

- The capabilities and availability of information processing technology continue to change at an exponential rate.

- The so-called "paperless office" is not now a reality (and may never be). Nevertheless, increasingly information handling technology has moved from a primary emphasis on paper to a primary emphasis on electronic forms of information. This has raised numerous questions in legal, societal, and other issues, many of which are addressed in this book.

- *Connectivity* refers to the ability to link together many systems, regardless of the physical location, manufacturer, or often even the exact application programs in use. This has led to increasingly dispersed and distributed systems. Both databases and, to some extent, actual programs now may reside in widely separated locations, with increasingly complex software and communications networks providing functional and logical links.

- Increased connectivity has increased not only interconnections among systems within organizations, but also among different organizations. An associated factor is increased dependency of one organization on systems (for example, public carriers such as telephones) developed and maintained by separate organizations.

- As microcomputer technology and application programs drop in price and increase in capability, intelligent workstations are becoming the norm. They are proliferating across organizations and into non-traditional areas like people's homes.

According to the Stevenson, Kellogg report:

> In general, the threats have changed through the combination of two factors. First, the existence of this new network environment. Secondly, the absence of sufficient "network intelligence" to counter both new and long-established threat agents, within the new network environment.

6.2.4.2 Changes in Applications

Thousands of highly sophisticated application programs now exist for microcomputers. These represent added ranges of applications to established applications like payroll and accounting. (Note that these "traditional" applications themselves are quite recent, none more than about 40 to 50 years old and most less than 15 years old.) Some of the key features of this change are:

- A general move towards tool-driven or "local" applications
- Increasing use of semi-structured and unstructured databases
- An expanded perception of the term "data" to include not only alphanumeric representations but also standards for graphics, images, and sound and video images
- Increasing use of re-processed data—data originally created within one system, then captured by another system and reprocessed (one example would be the edited list of videos and films earlier in this chapter)
- Increasing use of extended applications that cross traditional boundaries (for example, technical boundaries for networks involving mainframes and microcomputers, and organizational boundaries for such applications as electronic mail and scheduling systems)

- Use of applications, such as electronic data interchange (EDI), that involve direct computer-to-computer communication between organizations

Many threats have evolved directly from the changes in technology and how it is delivered to users, including:

- Increased use of system hardware and software installation and modification tools (most users have little or no experience or training in this sort of activity)
- Poorly controlled use of widespread communications networks that cannot easily be secured, are vulnerable to failure and penetration efforts, and often are outside the control of users
- Vastly increased ease of access to enormous amounts of data
- Availability of compact and dense portable storage media (this entire book, exclusive of graphics, would fit onto one 2.88 megabyte diskette; hundreds of such books would fit onto one optical disk a few inches in diameter either one would fit easily into a jacket pocket)
- Generally, increasing complexity that makes it difficult even to comprehend systems, much less to implement security measures

6.3 PERSONNEL CONSIDERATIONS

People, or personnel, are the entities who make an organization work, and whose purposes organizations serve. It is also people who protect, or try to penetrate, the organization. According to the RCMP:[5]

> Personnel security includes specifying security requirements in job descriptions, ensuring that incumbents meet these requirements and are provided with adequate security motivation and training. It involves supervising access to and control over system resources through appropriate personnel identification and authorization measures. It further requires attention to hiring and employment termination procedures.

Most organizations of any size have a "human resources department" or a "personnel department," or a group with a similar name. The primary responsibility for people concerns rests with this group. This chapter looks at some specific things that, from the security and control perspective, should be included in those things which the personnel department does.

The assets involved in this section are the "people assets": trained, experienced personnel. First, some of the results relating to why people can be a problem are reviewed. After that, we look at some specific recommendations for security controls that are appropriate in selecting personnel. Some topics related to working conditions—again, from a security and control perspective—will be the next focus, and finally recommendations on maintaining security and control when employees leave will be presented.

This material is not by any means a presentation of "all there is to personnel management." Its purpose is limited to identifying specific security and control measures that relate to personnel security.

---

[5]"EDP Threat assessments: Concepts and Planning Guide," *RCMP Security Information Publications* # 2, January, 1982.

6.3.1 Human Motives for Criminal Action

It has been estimated[6] that perhaps 85% of people are strictly honest: They would not commit crimes regardless of temptation and opportunity. Of the other 15%, perhaps 5% would engage in a dishonest act if they believed there was *no* chance of getting caught; another 5% might risk a small chance, and a final 5% might try even if there were a 50-50 chance of being caught. Regardless of the exact numbers (75%, 85%, 95%, or whatever), the point is that most people are honest, and some are not. The potentially or actually dishonest people are the security concern.

Criminal behavior involves three basic elements:

- Dishonesty
- Opportunity
- Motive

If there is no reason to do something (motive), there is little risk. If there is no opportunity, there is little risk. If the person is one of the 85% who are strictly honest, there is little risk. Almost all of the controls examined so far have been basically preventive: aimed at reducing opportunity or motive. Personnel security in employee selection aims at not hiring dishonest people in the first place. Most administrative controls, and the material in section 6.3.4 on "Working Environment," are in the area of motive: reducing work-related incentives for people to cause problems. Since motives exist outside the workplace (large debts, espionage, gambling problems, and other non-work activities), other controls to be discussed later relate to prevention, detection, and reaction in areas of opportunity.

"Computer crime" probably is an inappropriate term. Crimes have been committed throughout human history, and there is no reason to expect differently of the future. Today, computers often are used in crime, and this is called "computer crime" as though the crime did not exist prior to computers. The actual fact seems to be that computers simply are a tool used by people because they are available. (Some specialized things noted in Chapters 1 and 8 may be new, and Chapter 10 discusses some legislative attempts to define "computer crime.") Most "computer crimes" have been perpetrated by the same sort of people who, for the same sort of reasons, committed crimes a thousand years ago using other tools. If computers have led to anything new, it is probably that more people have opportunity, and the motivational factor of money has increased due to information density and computer speeds.

The largest risk exposure remains employee error. Personnel security measures are aimed at hiring honest, capable employees.

6.3.2 Employee Selection

The first step in hiring an employee is to create an accurate job description. It wastes time, both of applicants and of the people who must sift through resumes, if the nature of the job is not properly defined and communicated to applicants.

Given an accurate job description, the employee recruitment process will lead to many resumes, some interviews, and hopefully a successful placement. Most of this is the responsibility

---

[6]Krauss, Leonard L. and Aileen MacGahan, *Computer Fraud and Countermeasures*, Prentice-Hall, Englewood Cliffs, NJ, 1979. Others have different estimates; philosophical structures and differing cultures seem to condition expectations about honesty.

of the human resources group and the managers who actually will use the employees, rather than anything directly related to a security specialist's duties. There are some simple security and control pointers available to help the primary people to maintain security principles:

- Application forms
- Permissions for investigations
- Reference and document checks
- Security clearances and citizenship

We shall look briefly at each of these. First, there is an important point to make:

No measure will determine that any person is completely honest.

It may be possible to determine that a person previously was *not* honest (criminal record, for instance). There is no way to be sure that a person is now, and forever in the future will be, honest. The points presented in sections 6.2.1 to 6.2.3 relate to minimizing the chance that dishonest people will be hired. The points in section 6.3 relate to keeping them honest.

6.3.2.1 Application forms

All applicants should be required to fill out an application form before being interviewed. The exact nature of the application will vary from position to position; the intent is that all applicants for a position should put relevant data into the same format. This aids in selection, and the information is verifiable. Some suggested components of an application form are:

1. Names

- First, Middle, Last
- Nicknames used frequently
- Was name ever legally changed?
- If so, when, where, and what was the previous name?

2. Date and place born
3. Current address, and previous addresses (for a time period dependent on the type of job)
4. Telephone numbers
5. Employment history, most recent job first

   Note: All time since leaving school must be accounted for, including periods of unemployment. Gaps are significant warning signals.

- Company name, address
- Date hired and terminated
- Job title and nature of job
- Salary or wage
- Name and title of supervisor
- Reason for leaving

6. Education

- School(s) name and address(es)

- Dates attended
- Major field(s) of study
- Degree(s) obtained

7. Health considerations relevant to job performance
8. Credit references
9. Criminal record, if any

Some of these items may be inappropriate or unlawful in some jurisdictions. Questions about health, religion, racial background, criminal record, and so on may be violations of laws regarding privacy (such as the United States Privacy Act 1975 or the Canadian Privacy Act 1974) or of human rights legislation (varies by province and state), or even of the United States Bill of Rights or the Canadian Charter of Rights and Freedoms. The company should not put it itself in the position of violating the law in trying to hire honest employees.

These points are noted from a *security* perspective. A primary goal of the selection process is to evaluate qualifications, which is of course the responsibility of the manager(s) involved.

6.3.2.2 Permissions for Investigations

At the bottom of the standardized form there should be a paragraph like:

I attest that the information provided above is true and complete to the best of my knowledge and belief. I understand that falsification or misrepresentation of any data provided in this application may be grounds for refusing or terminating employment. I authorize (company name) to check any data provided.

Signed _____ Date _____

In addition to the blanket permission of such an acknowledgment, the applicant's permission always should be gained explicitly before checking with references, current employers, credit reporting agencies, educational institutions, or law enforcement agencies. Again, it is emphasized that legal advice is needed; some of these items or checks may be unlawful in some jurisdictions.

One way to avoid potential legal problems is to ask applicants to provide originals or certified copies of such things as birth and citizenship certificates, professional certifications, transcripts, and reference letters. This also may speed up the evaluation process.

The final point in this section is: Check *everything*. It has been estimated that from 10% to 30% of resumes contain misrepresentations or actual falsehoods [Gibb-Clark 1988]. Inconsistencies in data provided (gaps in dates, unusual salaries in previous positions, many previous short jobs, unusual educational qualifications claimed, and similar things) are warning signs, and should be checked out in an interview or separate verification process.

6.3.2.3 Security Clearance and Citizenship

Many jobs involve work on government or other secret projects. Agencies responsible for the projects will have their own requirements; often such data as citizenship, previous or current clearances, and military service will be required (see section 5.4). If it is lawful to ask, such information should be requested on the standard application for companies engaged in such projects: Employees may be transferred, promoted, or otherwise moved from originally non-sensitive positions into sensitive ones.

6.3.2.4 Summary

From a security perspective, all information should be checked. The purpose is to minimize the chance of hiring dishonest employees in the first place. Qualifications also must be checked, but this is the responsibility of the relevant management.

Specific items to watch are:

- Gaps in employment history (Gaps are one of the most common areas of misrepresentation [Gibb-Clark 1988].)
- Frequent job moves
- Unusual previous salaries
- Unusual educational background for previous jobs
- Name changes (check under *all* names)

Items to confirm independently include:

- References
- Previous employment
- Transcripts
- Professional certifications
- Credit record (large debts may indicate risk of blackmail or other pressure)
- Criminal record

It is important to have the procedures and application forms reviewed by the legal department to be sure that the company is not violating laws regarding privacy, human rights, or discrimination.

6.3.3 Professional Certificates

One indicator of a potentially excellent employee is that of holding a professional designation. People who hold them have sworn themselves to codes of conduct and good practice, and may have higher commitment levels than others. They have proven by examination that they possess a defined level of knowledge.

From the security and control perspective, claims of professional certification should be checked out with the certifying agency (as should university degrees and other "pieces of paper"). If the certificate or diploma is valid, the certifying agency or educational institution will be able to provide confirmation that it was issued, and that it is still valid. False claims about certificates and degrees are among the most common falsifications in resumes [Gibb-Clark 1988]. Chapter 15 contains more information regarding certificates, professionalism, and similar activities in North America and elsewhere in the information-processing fields.

People with professional designations have a valuable asset (the certification) that they are very careful to protect. They normally are much less likely to take a chance at crime since the consequences of being caught can be severe. If convicted of a crime or of professionally inappropriate conduct, they can be debarred from their professional society and lose the designation that they have worked hard to obtain. As well, people working towards a professional certificate (such as articling students in an accounting program) are aware that being convicted of committing a crime may wipe out their chances of being admitted to the professional institute.

6.3.4 Working Environment

A "happy" company usually is also well-controlled and reasonably secure, given reasonable control measures. In this section, we look at four components of the working environment important from the security perspective. This is not a complete exposition; much of the responsibility rests with human resources, organization management, and management of specific areas within the organization. The four components that have proven to be especially significant from the security perspective are:

- Vacations and job rotation
- Employee-management relations
- Career path planning
- Remuneration (payment)

6.3.4.1 Vacations and Job Rotation

Vacations and job rotation are important from a security standpoint because they ensure that someone else checks up on employees' work. They have other characteristics as well: People need rest time, vacations often are part of the compensation package, and so on. The main concern from the security perspective is to ensure that employees *do take* vacations. The history is full of instances of dedicated employees who do not take vacations—and are discovered later to have been maintaining frauds that needed continuous attention, or could not bear independent examination.

At least two consecutive weeks of vacation are desirable; ideally, the vacation period should include a month-end or quarter-end closing. Two needs are satisfied by this policy: First, someone besides a single person will be able to take over in an emergency; and second, the refresher aspect of a vacation often will result in an improved error rate and happier staff member.

Job rotation helps ensure backup capability and may also be a factor in improved employee morale; people are challenged to learn new things and to improve their own capabilities. From a security perspective, job rotation has many of the same virtues as vacations; in particular, a new person takes over and a fraud whose continuation requires constant attention might be uncovered quickly.

6.3.4.2 Employee-Management Relations

A "happy" organization works better and gives people fewer motives to engage in undesirable activities. Good employee relations are a function of the overall organizational climate and of individual managers. In some organizations, there may be union or other contracts that set the tone of the relations. The one rule that has been successful in the greatest number of places is that open communication between managers and employees works better. Good employees appreciate feedback; even negative feedback, properly delivered and combined with intelligent corrective measures, minimizes problems. The greatest problems occur when employees do not know what is required or how well they are doing. Perhaps the best single recommendation is "communicate." The security officer has a much easier job in an environment of open communication.

6.3.4.3 Career Path Planning

One element of personnel management is career planning. This primarily is the responsibility of the employee, his or her management, and the human resources department. The major involvement of the security position is to recommend that the company plan for continued upgrading of its employees; frustrated employees tend to leave or even to become a security exposure. This is another area in which the main duty of the security people is to be sure that organizational management are aware that there is an effect on security.

6.3.4.4 Remuneration

Money is not the most important element in Maslow's hierarchy of needs; however, adequate pay for the position, and appropriate raises or bonuses for good performance, are proven motivators. Employees who feel they are reasonably well-paid are less likely to try to "make up the difference" through unlawful activities. The company's pay scales should be on a par with other employers in similar organizations in the relevant area.

Once more, the security people should ensure that management is aware that poor pay, or pay out of line with competitors, can lead to motivational exposures. It is clearly outside the responsibility area of the security staff to set pay rates, but they should know whether material differences exist elsewhere, and keep an eye on employees who may consider themselves drastically under-compensated.

6.3.5 Technological Change Effects on Personnel

Technological change effects on personnel are addressed in many places in this book. They include everything from changes in workplace environments to demands for new skills and demands for continual upgrading to approach the rate of change. Some specific effects include changes in the number and nature of users and new or altered threat agents.

6.3.5.1 Changing Users

Users of computer systems have been seen primarily as specialized relatively junior clerical staff and highly trained technical staff. This is not true today. Typically:

- Users make use of a wide range of applications, from word processors to databases, graphical and desktop publishing tools, and project planning tools
- Many users are non-specialist users who make use of computers as *tools* in the accomplishment of other tasks
- Users frequently make use of information systems from many locations, requiring access from homes, offices, client sites, and even hotels and airports
- Increasingly, users are professional and management-level personnel

A significant organizational impact is the "disappearing middle manager," as senior managers have direct access to processed information for which they previously had to depend on middle management. A related factor is disappearance of "middlemen" who insulated users from direct contact with information systems.

6.3.5.2 Changing Human Threats
Both accidental and intentional human exposures have changed. Accidental threats now include:

- Increased potential for misuse or misrepresentation of semi- or un-structured data
- Problems with poorly trained or unskilled users
- Increased need for direct handling of hardware and software by users
- A general lack of focus on security (this is not new; however, the vastly increased number of users has effected a quantitative change in this area that amounts to a qualitative change)
- Frequently, reduction of separation of duties and responsibilities, increasing exposure to several kinds of frauds
- Increased potential for loss of information through loss of employees (who knows how to use that package now?)

Some of the changes in intentional threats include:

- Frequently, reduction in separation of incompatible duties and responsibilities
- Potential for all forms of assault, both physical and electronic, due to distribution of processes, databases, and workstations
- Increased potential for monitoring communications from microwave and satellite technology (see Chapters 2 and 8)
- Increased potential for theft of hardware, software, and data
- Increased potential for unauthorized modification of data and software
- Increased potential for numerous kinds of direct and indirect attacks, such as computer viruses, traffic analysis, and so forth

The issue of prosecuting those who violate laws is addressed below and in Chapters 10 and 11.

6.3.6 Employee Separation

In normal organizations, employees are hired, move through various positions, and leave. Not all terminations are voluntary. A few security and control principles are important in termination as well as in hiring.

First, any employee found to have falsified or misrepresented information when hired should be terminated. Employees guilty of serious violations of company policy regarding security and controls should be terminated. Employees guilty of unlawful acts should be *prosecuted* as well as terminated. Among other things, such action will provide a highly visible example for employees remaining, demonstrating that management takes security seriously.

Any termination should trigger certain steps, including:

- All company identification, including badges, IDs, business cards, and business-related materials should be collected.
- All keys, cards, signature plates, and other access tools or symbols of authority should be collected.
- All relevant locks, codes, passwords, and access codes must be changed immediately.
- All accounts should be settled (expense accounts, employee loans, etc.).
- Accounts over which the employee had control should be reconciled.
- Other members of the staff should be informed of the termination.

These considerations apply whether the termination is voluntary or involuntary. In addition, if the termination is involuntary, it is recommended that the employee be escorted from the premises and personal effects mailed or delivered later. In involuntary termination, it is critical to be *certain* that access to sensitive resources is denied *immediately* (to ensure that the unhappy former employee cannot sabotage systems, steal critical data or reports, or otherwise create a problem). Many companies use a "termination checklist," listing these and other significant matters; this is a good security practice and is recommended.

The principle of making sure that former employees no longer have access to sensitive resources is *important*. An amazing number of organizations do not do this. It is common to observe situations where, for example, passwords have not been changed, even though people who have not been employed for weeks—or months—previously know them. It should be remembered that employees have training in how to use systems and access that allows them to use the systems. If passwords and such are not changed, *former* employees still have the knowledge and access to do things. Not all former employees are necessarily happy with the organization or with their move; it simply is foolish to allow them to retain access privileges.

Note that, although the procedures recommended here are standard and represent good security practice, there may be severe consequences on morale. Termination, voluntary or otherwise, is a stressful time not only for the employee leaving, but also for those remaining. Great care is needed by management in handling such situations. In particular, a continuing awareness program that includes informing employees of termination procedures and the reasons for them, is essential.

An "exit interview" or "exit review" is recommended in voluntary termination. Since morale is so important, it is important to know why people are leaving. Changes in practices may be appropriate. From a legal and security perspective, the exit interview should also include review of the acknowledgments regarding confidentiality, trade secrets, and similar agreements. At this time, the company should request explicitly that sensitive material be returned. Failure to take this step may make later legal recourse impossible or impractical.

REFERENCES

"Commitment to Security", National Center for Computer Crime Data, NCCCD and RGC Associates, March, 27 1989.

Computer Control Guidelines Second Edition, Canadian Institute of Chartered Accountants (CICA), February, 1986.

Cooper, James Arlin, *Computer-Security Technology*, Lexington Books, Lexington, MA, 1984.

"EDP Threat assessments: Concepts and Planning Guide," *RCMP Security Information Publications* # 2, January, 1982.

The Electronic Vault: Computer Piracy and Privacy (Home of the Future: Industry Research Report series), The Yankee Group, Boston, 1984.

Fites, Philip. E., Martin P. J. Kratz, and Alan F. Brebner, *Control and Security of Computer Information Systems*, W. H. Freeman/Computer Science Press, 1989.

Gallegos, Frederick, Dana R. (Rick) Richardson, & A. Faye Borthick, *Audit & Control of Information Systems*, South-Western Publishing Company, West Chicago, IL, 1987.

Gorrill, B. E., *Effective Personnel Security Procedures*. Dow Jones-Irwin, Inc., Homewood, IL, 1974.

Grant, Kenneth A. et al., "Guidelines for User Requirements for Security in Integrated Communications and Information Systems," report to Department of Communications cat. no. CO22-87/1989E, Stevenson Kellogg Ernst & Whinney, Toronto, 1989.

Krauss, Leonard L. and Aileen MacGahan, *Computer Fraud and Countermeasures*, Prentice-Hall, Englewood Cliffs, NJ, 1979.

Lobel, J., *Foiling the System Breakers: Computer Security and Access Control*, McGraw-Hill, NY, 1986.

Martin, James, *Security, Accuracy, and Privacy in Computer Systems*, Prentice-Hall, Inc., Englewood Cliffs, NJ, 1973.

Parker, Donn B., *Computer Security Management*, Reston Publishing Company, Inc., Reston, VA, 1981.

Straub, Detmar W., "Organizational Structuring of the Computer Security Function," *Computers & Security* 7 (1988), p. 185-195.

7. Computer and System Security

This section describes the things that a member is expected to know about computer, system, and security architectures.

Professionals in the field would understand:

- The principal or common computer organizations, architectures, and designs
- The source and origin of security requirements that arise from the organization of the computer or system, from sharing, or from the relationships of users
- The comparative advantages and disadvantages of the various architectures
- The security features, functions, properties, roles, uses, applications, and responsibilities of the various components and subsystems
- The freedom of choice in the assignment of roles or functions to the various components or subsystems, and the security effect of the choices

For example, the practitioner would be able to:

- Contrast open and closed systems, identify members of each class, sort instances into these classes
- Identify the properties and functions of a trusted system
- Distinguish among the classes of the Trusted Computer System Evaluation Criteria (TCSEC—Orange Book)
- Distinguish between message-object and operator-operand computing; provide examples of each
- Describe the functions of a reference monitor
- Distinguish between single-state and multi-state machines; give examples
- Recognize "binding:" Give examples of early and late binding
- Distinguish between primary and secondary storage
- Distinguish between real and virtual storage
- Distinguish between single- and multi-task; give examples
- Distinguish between multi-programming, multi-tasking and multi-processing
- Recognize isolation and mediation;
- Distinguish between a "ring" and a "state"
- Recognize Bell-La Padula, Clark-Wilson, and Biba
- Distinguish between one-time and reusable passwords; identify strengths and limitations of each
- Contrast an address space and a memory space
- Contrast a real and a virtual machine
- Contrast MVS and VM, Ultrix and VMS, PC-DOS and OS/2, or OS/2 and AIX
- Identify, recognize, or define "kernel"
- Contrast resource manager and reference monitor
- Contrast hardware and software isolation; describe the advantages of each; give examples
- Recognize TOCTU

- Contrast a token value and a parameter, a token value and a capability
- Recognize and distinguish between mandatory and discretionary access controls; give examples
- Distinguish between a compiler and an interpreter; give examples
- Identify browsing, spoofing, and exhaustive attacks
- Identify "strong" in "strongly typed" as in a strongly typed data object
- Recognize "covert channel"
- Recognize "symbolic only addressing"; contrast physical and symbolic addressing
- Compare the security characteristics of LANs and "star-wired through a controller"
- Compare the security requirements of a single-user single-tasking system with those of a multi-user multi-tasking system
- Describe the use of micro-code; describe its potential security uses

DEFINITIONS

Access Control

The prevention of unauthorized use of a resource, including the prevention of use of a resource in an unauthorized manner. (ISO 7498-2)

Access Control List

A list of entities, together with their access rights, which are authorized to have access to a resource. (ISO 7498-2)

Access Mode

A distinct operation recognized by the protection mechanisms as a possible operation on an object. Read, write and append are possible modes of access to a file, while execute is an additional mode of access to a program. (MTR-8201)

Access Type

The nature of an access right to a particular device, program, or file (such as read, write, execute, append, modify, delete, and create). (AR 380-380; NCSC-WA-001-85; FIPS PUB 39)

Accountability

The property that ensures that the actions of an entity may be traced uniquely to the entity. (ISO 7498-2)

Approval/Accreditation

The official authorization that is granted to an ADP system to process sensitive information in its operational environment, based upon comprehensive security evaluation of the system's hardware, firmware, and software security design, configuration and implementation and of the other system procedural, administrative, physical, TEMPEST, personnel, and communications security controls. (CSC-STD-001-83)

Asynchronous Attack

[An] asynchronous attack [. . .] is an attempt to exploit the interval between a defensive act and the attack in order to render inoperative the effect of the defensive act. For instance, an operating task may be interrupted at once following the checking of a stored parameter; the user regains control and malevolently changes the parameter; the operating system regains control and [continues] processing using the maliciously altered parameter. (JL)[1]

Attack

The act of aggressively trying to bypass security controls on an Automated Information System. The fact that an attack is made does not necessarily mean that it will succeed. The degree of success depends on the vulnerability of the system or activity and the effectiveness of existing countermeasures. (NCSC-WA-001-85)

Audit Trail

A set of records that collectively provide documentary evidence of processing used to aid in tracing from original transactions forward to related records and reports, and/or backwards from records and reports to their component source transactions. (CSC-STD-001-83)

Bacterium

A bacterium (also known as a chain letter) is a program which propagates itself by electronic mail to everyone in the victim's mailing list. It may also contain a logic bomb or Trojan horse. (IC)

The term bacterium is a colloquialism referring to one example of a form of malicious code properly called a *worm* (see worm). (PEF)

Bounds Checking

1. Verifying a computer program address for access to storage outside authorized limits. Synonymous with Memory Bounds Checking. (NCSC-WA-001-85; AR 380-380; FIPS PUB 39)
2. The process of checking within a computer program for references outside the declared limits of a storage construct such as an array. Such checking may be performed explicitly by the application program, implicitly by code inserted by a compiler or assembler or interpreter, or not performed. Distinguished from checking for address references outside the bounds of an address space permitted to a process. (PEF)

Bounds Register

A hardware register which holds an address specifying a storage boundary. (FIPS PUB 39)

Capability

In a computer system, an unforgeable ticket that is accepted by the system as incontestable proof that the presenter has authorized access to the object named by the ticket. It is often interpreted by the operating system and the hardware as an address for the object. Each capability also contains authorization information identifying the nature of the access mode (for example read mode, write mode). (MTR-8201)

---

[1]This is one example of the TOC/TOU problem described in section 7.5.

Collusion

The act of two or more agents or perpetrators cooperating or conspiring to perpetrate an intentional event. (MK)

Compartmentalization

The isolation of the operating system, user programs, and data files from one another in main storage in order to provide protection against unauthorized or concurrent access by other users or programs. This term also refers to the division of sensitive data into small, isolated blocks for the purpose of reducing risk to the data. (AR 380-380; FIPS PUB 39)

Computer Abuse

The misuse, destruction, alteration, or disruption of data processing resources. The key aspects of computer related abuse are that it is intentional and improper and it may not involve the violation of a specific law. (NCSC-WA-001-85)

Computer Fraud

Computer-related crimes involving deliberate misrepresentation or alteration of data in order to obtain something of value (usually for monetary gain). A computer system must have been involved in the perpetration or cover-up of the act, or series of acts. A computer system might have been involved through improper manipulation of:

- input data
- output or results
- applications programs
- data files
- computer operations
- communications
- computer hardware, systems software, or firmware (NCSC-WA-001-85)

Configuration Control

1. Management of changes made to a system's hardware, software, firmware, and documentation throughout the development and operational life of the system. (CSC-STD-003-85; CSC-STD-004-85; COE 5636.2A)
2. The process of controlling modifications to the system's hardware, firmware, software, and documentation which provides sufficient assurance the system is protected against the introduction of improper modification prior to, during, and after implementation. (NCSC-WA-001-85)[2]

Confinement

Allowing a process executing a borrowed program (in general, an arbitrary program) to have access to data, while ensuring that the data cannot be misused, altered, destroyed or released. (MTR-8201)

---

[2]The first definition is more general, the second more specifically security-oriented.

Confinement Property

Star Property (*-Property) in the Bell-La Padula security model that constrains subjects from writing down into a dominated security object. (The original Bell-La Padula use included read-up as well as write-down, and the usage has changed.)

Contamination

1. The introduction of data of one sensitivity and need-to-know with data of a lower sensitivity or different need-to-know. This can result in the contaminating data not receiving the required level of protection. (AFR 205-16)
2. The process by which errors in data elements stored in computerized information systems propagate during repeated use, leading to unreliable databases. Examples include any data that are used as input to another process, whose outputs then become unreliable. Also called "corruption." (PEF)

Correctness

In a strict sense, the property of a system that is guaranteed as a result of formal verification activities. Correctness is not an absolute property of a system, rather it implies the mutual consistency of a specification and its implementation. (MTR-8201)

Correctness Proof

A mathematical proof of consistency between a specification and its implementation. It may apply at the security model-to-formal specification level, at the formal specification-to-HOL code level, at the compiler level or at the hardware level. For example, if a system has a verified design and implementation, then its overall correctness rests with the correctness of the compiler and hardware. Once a system is proved correct, it can be expected to perform as specified, but not necessarily as anticipated if the specifications are incomplete or inappropriate. (MTR-8201)

Countermeasure

Any action, device, procedure, technique, or other measure that reduces the vulnerability of an ADP system or activity to the realization of a threat. (OPNAVINST 5239.1A; NCSC-WA-001-85)

Covert Channel

A communication channel that allows two cooperating processes to transfer information in a manner that violates the system's security policy. (NCSC-WA-001-85)

Covert Storage Channel

A covert channel that involves the direct or indirect writing of a storage location by one process and the direct or indirect reading of the storage location by another process. Covert channels typically involve a finite resource (*e.g.*, sectors on a disk) that is shared by two subjects at different security levels. (CSC-STD-001-83; NCSC-WA-001-85)

Covert Timing Channel

A covert channel in which one process signals information to another by modulating its own use of system resources (*e.g.*, CPU time) in such a way that this manipulation affects the real response time observed by the second process. (CSC-STD-001-83; NCSC-WA-001-85)

Criticality

A concept related to the mission the automated system supports and the degree that the mission is dependent upon the system. This degree of dependence corresponds to the effect on the mission in the event of denial of service, modification, or destruction of data or software. (AFR 205-16)

Cryptographic Checkvalue

Information which is derived by performing a cryptographic transformation (see cryptography) on the data unit.

   Note: The derivation of the checkvalue may be performed in one or more steps and is a result of a mathematical function of the key and a data unit. It is usually used to check the integrity of a data unit. (ISO 7498-2)

Cycle (for overwriting memory, disk, etc.)

One overwrite cycle is defined as follows: Write one bit pattern or character, then write the complement of that pattern or character into every addressable location or sector. (CSC-STD-005-85)

Data Contamination

A deliberate or accidental process or act that results in a change in the integrity of the original data. (AR 380-380; FIPS PUB 39).

Data-Dependent Protection

Protection of data at a level commensurate with the sensitivity level of the individual data elements, rather than with the sensitivity of the entire file which includes the data elements. (FIPS PUB 39; AR 380-380)

Discretionary Access Control

A means of restricting access to objects based on the identity of subjects and/or groups to which they belong. The controls are discretionary in the sense that a subject with a certain access permission is capable of passing that permission (perhaps indirectly) on to any other subject (unless restrained by mandatory access control). (DODD 5200.28-STD)

DoD Trusted Computer System Evaluation Criteria

A document published by the National Computer Security Center containing a uniform set of basic requirements and evaluation classes for assessing the effectiveness of hardware and software security controls built into automated information systems. These criteria are intended for use in the design and evaluation of systems that will process and/or store sensitive or classified data. This document is frequently referred to as "The Criteria" or "The Orange Book." (NCSC-WA-001-85) Other acronyms include TCSEC.

Domain

The set of objects that a subject or resources in an automated information system has the ability to access. (NCSC-WA-001-85)

Eavesdropping

The unauthorized interception of information-bearing emanations through the use of methods other than wiretapping. (FIPS PUB 39; AR 380-380)

Executive State

1. One of two generally possible states in which an automated system may operate and in which only certain privileged instructions may be executed. Such privileged instructions may not be executed when the system is operating in the other (user) state. (AR 380-380; NCSC-WA-001-85; FIPS PUB 39)
2. Synonymous with *Supervisor State, Privileged State.*

Exhaustive Attack

[An] exhaustive attack consists of discovering secret data by trying all possibilities and checking for correctness. For a four digit password, one might start with 0000 and move on to 0001, 0002 till 9999. (JL).

Fetch Protection

A system-provided restriction to prevent a program from accessing data in another user's segment of storage. (FIPS PUB 39; AR 380-380; NCSC-WA-001-85) See also Bounds Checking.

Firmware

Software that is permanently stored in a hardware device which allows reading of the software but not writing or modifying. The most common device for firmware is read-only memory (ROM). (AFR 205-16)

Formal Proof

A complete and convincing mathematical argument, presenting the full logical justification for each proof step, for the truth of a theorem or set of theorems. The formal verification process uses formal proofs to show the truth of certain properties of formal specification and for showing that computer programs satisfy their specifications. (CSC-STD-001-83)

Formal Verification

The process of using formal proofs to demonstrate the consistency (design verification) between a formal specification of a system and a formal security policy model or (implementation verification) between the formal specification and its program implementation. (CSC-STD-001-83)

Granularity

1. The relative fineness or coarseness by which a mechanism can be adjusted. The phrase "the granularity of a single user" means the access-control mechanism can be adjusted to include or exclude any single user. (DODD 5200.28-STD)
2. An expression of the relative size of a data object, *e.g.*, protection at the file level is considered coarse granularity, whereas protection at the field level is considered to be a finer granularity. (NCSC-WA-001-85)

Hacker

Originally, a computer enthusiast who spent significant time learning the functions of the computer without benefit of formal training (and often without the technical manuals) by trying combinations of commands at random to determine their effect.

Common usage today is from the press which uses the word to describe people who "break into" computers for various purposes. (BBD)

Handshaking procedures

1. A dialogue between a user and a computer, a computer and another computer, a program and another program for the purpose of identifying a user and authenticating identity. A sequence of questions and answers is used based on information either previously stored in the computer or supplied to the computer by the initiator of the dialogue. (AR 380-380; FIPS PUB 39)

2. The set of communication protocols and codes that allows one computer to exchange information with one or more others. See also hardware handshaking. (PEF)

Hardware Handshaking

The passing of control characters between two devices such as ACK, NAK, XON, XOFF, for the purpose of controlling the flow of information between the devices. (AFR 205-16)

Hash Total

The use of specific mathematical formulae to produce a quantity that is (often appended to and) used as a checksum or validation parameter for the data that it protects. (WB)

Impersonation

An attempt to gain access to a system by posing as an authorized user. (FIPS PUB 39)

Isolation

The containment of users and resources in an automated system in such a way that users and processes are separate from one another as well as from the protection controls of the operating system. (AR 380-380; FIPS PUB 39; NCSC-WA-001-85)

Lattice

A partially ordered set for which every pair of elements has a greatest lower bound and a least upper bound. (CSC-STD-001-83)

Least Privilege

This principle requires that each subject be granted the most restrictive set of privileges needed for the performance of authorized tasks. The application of this principle limits the damage that can result from accident, error, or unauthorized use. (NCSC-WA-001-85; CSC-STD-001-83)

See also Principle of Least Privilege.

Logic Bomb

A resident computer program which, when executed, checks for particular conditions or particular states of the system which, when satisfied, triggers the perpetration of an unauthorized act. (NCSC-WA-001-85)

Malicious Logic

Hardware, software, or firmware that are intentionally included in a system for an unauthorized purpose. An example is a Trojan Horse. (NCSC-WA-001-85; CSC-STD-003-85; CSC-STD-004-85) Also known as *malicious code*.

Mandatory Access Control

A means of restricting access to objects based on the sensitivity (as represented by a label) of the information contained in the objects and the formal authorization (i.e., clearance) of subjects to access information of such sensitivity. (CSC-STD-001-83; CSC-STD-004-85; NCSC-WA-001-85) See also Discretionary Access Control.

Masquerade

The pretence by an entity to be a different entity. (ISO 7498-2)[3]

Memory Bounds

The limits in the range of storage addresses for a protected region in memory. (FIPS PUB 39; AR 380-380)

Memory Bounds Checking

See Bounds Checking.

Non-Discretionary Security

The aspect of DoD security policy which restricts access on the basis of security levels. A security level is composed of a read level and a category set restriction. For read-access to an item of information, a user must have a clearance level greater than or equal to the classification of the information and also have a category clearance which includes all of the access categories specified for the information. (MTR-8201)

Non-Kernel Security-Related Software (NKSR)

Security-relevant software which is executed in the environment provided by a security kernel rather than as a part of the kernel. Processes executing NKSR software may or may not require special privilege to override kernel-enforced security rules. (MTR-8201)

Object

A passive entity that contains or receives information. Access to an object potentially implies access to the information it contains. Examples of objects are records, blocks, pages, segments, files, directories, directory trees, and programs, as well as bits, bytes, words, fields, processors, video displays, keyboards, clocks, printers, network nodes, etc. (CSC-STD-001-83; AFR 205-16; NCSC-WA-001-85; DCID 1/16-1, Sup.)

---

[3]*See* Spoofing, section 7.4.

Operating System

An integrated collection of service routines for supervising the sequencing and processing of programs by a computer. Operating systems control the allocation of resources to users and their programs and play a central role in operating a computer system. Operating systems may perform input or output, accounting, resource allocation, storage assignment tasks, and other system-related functions. Synonymous with Monitor, Executive Control Program and Supervisor. (DODD 5200.28M)

The term *kernel* is used to describe a minimal instruction set essential to the proper functioning of the operating system, as well as in the sense of "security kernel." (PEF)

Penetration Testing

1. The use of teams consisting of data processing, communications, and security specialists to attempt to penetrate a system for the purpose of identifying any security weaknesses. (AR 380-380; FIPS PUB 39)

2. The portion of security testing in which the evaluators attempt to circumvent the security features of a system. The evaluators may be assumed to use all system design and implementation documentation which may include listings of system source code, manuals, and circuit diagrams. The evaluators work under the same constraints applied to ordinary users. (NCSC-WA-001-85; CSC-STD-001-83)

A related term is *tiger team*. (PEF)

Piggy Back

The gaining of unauthorized access to a system via another user's legitimate connection. (NCSC-WA-001-85)

Principle of Least Privilege

The granting of the minimum access authorization necessary for the performance of required tasks. (FIPS PUB 39; AR 380-380) See also Least Privilege.

Privileged Instructions

A set of instructions generally executable only when the automated system is operating in the executive state (such as interrupt handling;) special computer instructions designed to control the protection features on an ADP system (such as storage protection features). (AR 380-380; FIPS PUB 39; NCSC-WA-001-85)

Privileged Process

A process that is afforded (by the kernel) some privileges not afforded normal user processes. A typical privilege is the ability to override the security *-property. Privileged processes are trusted. (MTR-8201)

Privilege Profile

A computer resident record that indicates the resources that a specific user, process, or computer has been explicitly authorized to access. (WB)

Process

1. A program in execution. It is completely characterized by a single current execution point (represented by the machine state) and address space. (CSC-STD-001-83)
2. The active system entity through which programs run. The entity in a computer system to which authorizations are granted; thus the unit of accountability in a computer system. A process consists of a unique address space containing its accessible program code and data, a program location for the currently executing instruction, and periodic access to the processor in order to continue. (MTR-8201)

Read-Only Memory (ROM)

A storage area in which the contents can be read but not altered during normal computer processing. (DODD 5200.28-STD)

Reference Monitor

A security control concept in which an abstract machine mediates accesses to objects by subjects. In principle, a reference monitor should be complete (in that it mediates every access), isolated from modification by system entities, and verifiable. A security kernel is an implementation of a reference monitor for a given hardware base. (MTR-8201)

Reference Monitor Concept

An access control concept that refers to an abstract machine that mediates all accesses to objects by subjects. (NCSC-WA-001-85, CSC-STD-001-83)

Reference Validation Mechanism

An implementation of the reference monitor concept. A security kernel is a particular (but not the only) type of a reference validation mechanism. (NCSC-WA-001-85)

Residue

Data left in storage after processing operations and before degaussing or rewriting has taken place. (FIPS PUB 39; AR 380-380; NCSC-WA-001-85)

Resource

Anything used or consumed while performing a function. The categories of resources are time, information, objects (information containers), or processors (the ability to use information). Specific examples are CPU time; terminal connect time; amount of directly addressable memory; disk space; number of I/O requests per minute, etc. (CSC-STD-001-83)

Resource Encapsulation

A resource must not be directly accessible by a subject but must be protected so that the reference monitor can properly mediate accesses to the resource. A requirement for accurate auditing of resource usage. (NCSC-WA-001-85)

Retro-Virus

A retro-virus is a virus that waits until all possible backup media are infected too, so that it is not possible to restore the system to an uninfected state. (IC)[4]

Security Critical Mechanisms

Those security mechanisms whose correct operation is necessary to ensure the security policy is enforced. The mechanisms may or may not be part of the Trusted Computing Base. (NCSC-WA-001-85; AFR 205-16)

Security Kernel

1. The hardware, firmware, and software elements of a Trusted Computing Base that implement the reference monitor concept. It must mediate all accesses, be protected from modification, and be verifiable as correct. (CSC-STD-001-85; NCSC-WA-001-85)
2. The central part of a computer system (software and hardware) that implements the fundamental security procedures for controlling access to system resources. (FIPS PUB 39)

Seepage

The accidental flow to unauthorized individuals of data or information, access to which is presumed to be controlled by computer security safeguards. (FIPS PUB 39; AR 380-380; NCSC-WA-001-85)

See also Covert Channel. (PEF)

Shoulder Surfing

The stealing of passwords by watching users sign on to systems at their terminals. (TC)

See also Piggy Back.

Softlifting

Illegal copying of licensed software for personal use. (PC/PCIE)

State Variable

A variable that represents either the state of the system or the state of the system resource. (NCSC-WA-001-85)

Subject

An active entity, generally in the form of a person, process, or device that causes information to flow among objects or changes the system state. Technically, a process/domain pair. (CSC-STD-001-83; AFR 205-16; NCSC-WA-001-85; DCID 1/16-1, Sup.)

---

[4]A retro-virus is distinguished from any other virus only by the delay time in the trigger mechanism. Use of this colloquialism should be discouraged, as it cannot be determined when "all possible media are infected. . ." This is also an inaccurate use of the biological analogy implicit in the term "computer virus."

Supervisor State

Synonymous with Executive State.

Technological Attack

An attack which can be perpetrated by circumventing or nullifying hardware and software access control mechanisms rather than by subverting system personnel or other users. (FIPS PUB 39; AR 380-380; NCSC-WA-001-85)

Ticket-Oriented

A computer protection system in which each subject maintains a list of unforgeable bit patterns, called tickets, one for each object the subject is authorized to access. May be contrasted with a list-oriented protection system in which each protected object has a list of all subjects authorized to access it. (NCSC-WA-001-85)

Time Bomb/Time-Bomb

[A] variant of the Trojan horse [. . .], the time bomb [is] where the malicious code is inserted to be [automatically] triggered some time later [. . .]. (JL)

   See also Logic Bomb.

Virus

A program that can "infect" other programs by modifying them to include a, possibly evolved, copy of itself. (Cohen)

Work Factor

An estimate of the effort or time needed to overcome a protective measure by a potential penetrator with specified expertise and resources. (AR 380-380; NCSC-WA-001-85; FIPS PUB 39)

Worm

A program or executable code module which resides in distributed systems or networks. It will replicate itself, if necessary, in order to exercise as much of the system's resources as possible for its own processing. Such resources may take the form of CPU time, I/O channels, or system memory. (NCSC-WA-001-85)[5]

---

[5]Mathematically, a worm is difficult to distinguish from a virus, and a communications network cannot be distinguished from the "network" formed by the buses inside a computer (unless the network includes workstations with independent processing capability, such as microcomputers). Colloquially, a virus alters other "programs" and a worm does not; however, mathematically the environment (sequence of bits in the address space) in which a worm moves is a "program." A virus does not propagate by itself and it modifies other programs; the lack of independence may offer a mathematically definable difference between virus and worm. Dr. F. Cohen has addressed this issue in a recent paper, "A Formal Definition of Computer Worms and Some Related Results," *Computers & Security*, November, 1992. The physical implementation of a network implies very different countermeasures for a worm than for a virus.

A worm or virus need not be malicious code, contrary to media representations in the late 1980s and early 1990s.

7.1 SECURE OPERATING SYSTEMS

7.1.1 History

The history of concern for the security of operating systems follows closely the history of increasing accessibility of computer systems. As time-sharing became common, it became clear that security of some sort was needed to protect users from each others' activities, whether intentional or accidental. Paging systems with protection keys, and virtual storage mechanisms, partially addressed the security need. As charging systems for the use of computer resources became more common, increased security began to be seen as a real need. The explosion of millions of people with training in computer programming, plus the enormous increase in accessibility provided by more and more sophisticated communications, plus the easy availability of significant computer power in the form of microcomputers, has led to several major efforts to address the problem of security in operating systems, and in systems in general.

In the early operating systems, it was all too easy to penetrate the system. The growth of more capable systems usually involved more complexity; the problem of security got worse, as it turned out that very complex systems are not more secure than simpler ones (rather the reverse, usually). Adding communications capability to complex systems allowed many more people the opportunity to try to penetrate already shaky security, and the problem continued to worsen.

It is reasonably well-established by now that complex operating systems, which did not have security as a major design factor, are inherently insecure. Security packages installed with already-developed operating systems, such as IBM's Resource Access Control Facility (RACF) (see Chapter 1), are "add-ons" and help a lot. Unfortunately, the problem is not soluble in general; the add-ons make access from outside and sometimes access inside (legitimate users of the system accessing other users' files, for example) more difficult, but they do not make an originally non-secure system into a secure one.

More than one investigator has concluded that any operating system that allows programming is not secure and cannot be secured; a group in the Netherlands has made a name by publishing successful penetration methods for each new "fix" as it came out. Penetration methods such as those outlined in sections 7.4, 8.2, and 8.6 and in Appendix B, worked on all systems, and still work on all too many systems.

The picture is not totally bleak, however. While operating systems that were not designed for secure operation cannot be made completely secure, the problem has been known for some time. New operating systems designed since about the mid-1970s have had consideration of security as a significant design parameter, and mainframe operating systems that are in common use on today's fourth- and fifth-generation computers are fairly good. Some minicomputer operating systems are reasonably secure as well. (This is not true now for most personal computer operating systems or for all minicomputer systems, however. With the latest machines introduced, and current developments in operating system software for microcomputers, the situation may improve for personal computers as well.)

Results of investigations into the problems of operating-system security, along with a number of well-publicized problems, have led interested parties such as accountants and others to examine security in other aspects of organizations. If the operating system is inherently not secure, then "compensating controls" in other parts of the information system to a large extent can make up for the lack. A major tenet of most security practitioners is that the security problem is not primarily a technical one, and that good organizational measures, such as those recommended previously, can be much more important than technical details.

The investigations into operating system security have been fruitful as well. The concepts of "security kernel" designs and of "trusted computer" systems have led to design of systems that are provably secure, and which have not been penetrated. These are covered in the next section.

Absolute security probably is impossible. Reasonable security combined with reasonably "user-friendly" and usable computer-based information systems is achievable and has been achieved. Most modern computers can be penetrated, but it is much more difficult than it was, and the penetration is likely to be detected by other controls in the information system. Future systems designed for security in the first place will be quite secure indeed. The largest risk today is posed by the 41% of organizations with no security at all, and by general lack of appreciation of the importance of security in the profession and by senior management.[6] Education and reasonable professional standards can help solve this kind of problem.

7.1.2 Concepts: Capabilities, Reference Validations, Kernels

7.1.2.1 Secure Kernels

The word "kernel" has been used for some time to denote the part of the operating system that is memory-resident at all times (as contrasted to less-used parts that are paged in and out as needed). The word has a different meaning in the context of secure operating system design.

In a secure system, the *kernel* is a small module that is a portion of the operating system. *All* references to information and *all* changes to authorizations must pass through the kernel. The kernel needs to meet three basic conditions:

1. Completeness

    All accesses to information must go through the kernel.

2. Isolation

    The kernel itself must be totally protected from any form of unauthorized access or alteration.

3. Verifiability

    The kernel must be small and simple enough that it can be proven that the kernel meets design specifications.

Development and verification of the security kernel uses mathematical concepts and techniques that are beyond the scope of this text.[7]

The development normally includes four important factors:

1. A *mathematical model* defines the rules for demonstrating that system security is preserved.
2. *Formal specifications* bridge the gap between the mathematical model and actual implementation of the kernel. The formal specifications also must be proven mathematically.

---

[6]Survey by Data Processing Management Association, 1987.

[7]*Building a Secure Computer System*, by Morrie Gasser, deals in depth with issues outlined in this text.

3. The kernel is implemented in a *high-order language* that can be verified for correctness mathematically. (This does not mean a "high-level language" such as COBOL or ADA; see below.)
4. *Implementation* of the kernel, using the three elements above, is verified mathematically.

If the three basic conditions are met, and all four elements listed above are present, then the kernel may be considered secure. Since the kernel has been verified, cannot be changed without authorization, and all references must pass through the kernel, the operating system is secure.

There are two points that need to be mentioned here:

1. First, there are reasons in mathematics to question the applicability of this sort of proof; and
2. Second, whether the mathematics is valid or not, using a kernel generally involves greatly increased system overhead.

In theory, the mathematical verification is itself subject to at least some question. Kurt Gödel's work on mathematical consistency indicates some theoretical reasons for this concern. (*Gödel's Proof*, by Ernest Nagel and James Newman, New York University Press, 1967, is a readable treatment of Gödel's work for interested readers with a mathematical background.) It is doubtful whether this theoretical possibility has real existence, but it cannot be determined mathematically, and some question must remain.

The high-order language mentioned must be one of a class of mathematically provable languages that has been developed as part of research into provability of program correctness. One such language is included as part of the Gypsy system for developing secure specifications. These languages are developed by creating canonical forms that are small enough to be proven correct, then combining the canonical forms into more complex language components, using mathematically provable methods such as logical operators. HOL, a language developed at Cambridge University, is another example of a language used in developing and proving secure specifications and systems. Another tool, EVES, is under development in Canada (in 1993). These languages are specialized, and no commonly used computer language meets the provability criterion. ALGOL 68 may have come closest, but it failed to win commercial acceptance, at least in North America.

Even neglecting the rather esoteric consideration of the mathematical strength of the high-order language, there remains the problem of the correctness of the mathematical model itself. Using any computer language, provable or not, to write a program amounts to creating a mathematical model of the process being programmed. There is an extensive history of mathematical models which have proven incorrect or incomplete even after extensive use; Newton's theory of gravitation or Euclidean geometry are examples. The history of incorrect or incomplete computer programs probably includes every program of significant size ever written.

More pragmatically, there is considerable overhead in having all references to any information go through the kernel. Security is gained at the expense of system performance. Given the trend of cheaper hardware, it may be more cost-effective to ensure security by providing non-communicating, separate systems for such things as development, than to have a production machine slowed by a kernel approach. More recent hardware designs and lowered costs for such elements as random access memory permit more system overhead for a security kernel/reference monitor without prohibitive expense or performance degradation. Newer designs that incorporate security features thus are becoming more common and more affordable.

7.1.2.2 Reference Validations and Capabilities

For the purposes of this text, *reference validation* and *capabilities* can be understood sufficiently by considering them as part of a system with a security kernel. (The kernel includes reference validation and may use capabilities and thus is "stronger" than reference validation or capabilities alone—and also involves more overhead.)

One form of reference validation is the storage protection key normally implemented in any paging system. Simplifying, if a process trying to make a reference does not have the proper protect key, the reference is denied (in this case, by the kernel). More complex kinds of reference validation exist.

Capabilities are "tokens" that may be compared to storage protect keys or perhaps to a ticket to enter various areas in a major sporting event. Capabilities are more encompassing than protection keys: They include not only the right to access something, but also what kinds of access are permitted. *Every* physically or logically possible action inside the computer is associated with a capability (under control of the security kernel, capabilities are created, modified, and sometimes revoked, as the computer functions). A capability in computer terms might include information as to whether what is referenced can be *read, written, executed,* or *erased.* For example, a process might have execute capability only for an object module: The process is not allowed to read the object code, erase it, or change it; it can only be run. Another process, presumably with more restricted access itself, may be able to change the module but not to erase it. As an analogy, a sporting event ticket may include access to public viewing areas but not to locker rooms. The ticket would not grant the holder a capability to do other than watch the game. A reporter, on the other hand, would have greater access privileges and the capability to interview athletes, perhaps only in the locker room or perhaps only on the field's sidelines.

The security kernel is responsible to examine the capability presented by a process attempting to access information. The kernel ensures that only actions permitted to processes with that capability (reference, changing, deletion, executing a process, and so on) can occur, and that the capability is permitted by the characteristics of the information referenced. (The information may not have the characteristic of permitting execution even if the process's capability includes execution, for example.) This is *reference validation.*

7.2 PRESENT GUIDELINES AND STANDARDS, TRUSTED COMPUTING BASE

The concept of Trusted computing base is central to the discussion that follows. The Trusted computing base is that portion of a computer system ". . . which contains all elements of the system responsible for supporting the security policy and supporting the isolation of objects (code and data) on which the protection is based."[8]

7.2.1 Present TCB

The TCB evaluation criteria are based on six fundamental security requirements dealing with in-

---

[8]Department of Defense, *Trusted Computer System Evaluation Criteria,* p. 67.

formation systems security and access control:[9],[10]

1. There must be an explicit and well-defined security policy enforced by the system (Security Policy)

2. Access control labels must be associated with objects (Marking)

3. Individual subjects must be identified (Identification)

4. Audit information must be kept and protected so that actions affecting security can be traced to the responsible subject (Accountability)

5. The computer systems must contain hardware and software mechanisms that can be evaluated independently to provide sufficient assurance that the system enforces the security policy (Assurance)

6. The trusted mechanisms that enforce the security policy must be protected continuously against tampering and unauthorized changes (Continuous Protection)

The evaluation criteria are divided into four divisions (D, C, B, and A); divisions C, B, and A are further subdivided into classes. The range is from minimal protection in Division D to the most trustworthy class A1.

The divisions and classes of the TCB are:

Division D: Minimal Protection

This division is reserved for systems that fail to meet standards for any higher evaluation class.

Division C: Discretionary Protection

Classes in this division provide for discretionary (need-to-know) protection and accountability of subjects and the actions they initiate, through inclusion of audit capabilities.

Class C1: Discretionary Security Protection

The TCB of a class C1 system nominally satisfies the discretionary security requirements by providing separation of users and data. Individual users can protect private and project data from accidental reading or alteration by others. The class C1 environment is expected to be one of cooperating users processing data at the same level(s) of sensitivity.

Class C2: Controlled Access Protection

Systems in the class C2 enforce a more finely-grained discretionary access control, making users individually accountable for their actions through log-in procedures, auditing of security-relevant events, and resource isolation.

---

[9]The material in this section is based on Department of Defense, *Technical Rationale Behind CSC-STD-003-85: Computer Security Requirements*, CSC-STD-004-85, DoD Computer Security Center, June, 1985, and Department of Defense, *Trusted Computer System Evaluation Criteria*, DOD 5200.28.STD, Department of Defense Computer Security Center, Fort George G. Meade, Md., December, 1985.

[10]Note that the TCB is an *access-control* schema. Except for certain protections defined for verified processes in higher classes, the TCB provides no protection against such malicious code as virus code, or any other malicious action by an *authorized* user, whether unintentional like a virus or intentional like a deliberate attack. Issues of data *integrity* are addressed by the Clark-Wilson schema, Biba and others; see the papers in the references to this section.

Division B: Mandatory Protection

The notion of a TCB that preserves the integrity of sensitivity labels and uses them to enforce a set of mandatory access control rules is a major requirement of division B. Systems in this division must carry the sensitivity labels with major data structures in the system. The system developer also provides the security policy model on which the TCB is based and furnishes a specification of the TCB. Evidence must be provided to demonstrate that the reference monitor concept has been implemented.

Class B1: Labeled Security Protection

Class B1 systems require all the features required for class C2. In addition, an informal statement of the security policy model, data labeling, and mandatory access control over named subjects and objects must be present. The capability must exist for accurately labeling exported information. Any flaws identified by testing must be removed.

Class B2: Structured Protection

In class B2 systems, the TCB is based on a clearly defined and documented formal security policy model that requires the discretionary and mandatory access control enforcement found in class B1 systems to be extended to all subjects and objects in the computer system. In addition, covert channels are addressed. The TCB must be carefully structured into protection-critical and non-protection-critical elements.[11] The TCB interface is well-defined and the TCB design and implementation enable it to be subjected to more thorough testing and more complete review. Authentication mechanisms are strengthened, trusted facility management is provided in the form of support for system administrator and operator facilities, and stringent configuration management controls are imposed. The system is relatively resistant to penetration.

Class B3: Security Domains

The class B3 TCB must satisfy the reference monitor requirements that it mediate all accesses of subjects to objects, be tamper-proof, and be small enough to be subjected to analysis and tests. To this end, the TCB is structured to exclude code not essential to security policy or enforcement, with significant system engineering during TCB design and implementation directed toward minimizing its complexity. A security administrator is supported, audit mechanisms are expanded to signal security-related events, and system recovery procedures are required. The system is highly resistant to penetration.

Division A: Verified Protection

The critical difference between division A and division B is that formal methods are used, so that mathematical proofs may be applied to analysis[12].

---

[11]The system architecture criterion for level B2 is the first place in the TCB schema that information *integrity* is addressed, as opposed to access. Even here, only integrity of the system is addressed; the TCB schema does not address integrity of data or programs other than the TCB code.

[12]It may be argued that mathematical methods are not appropriate for proving things in the environment of information systems security. Clearly, a proven-secure system is provably secure only within the universe of discourse of the mathematics involved; for example, even a class A1 system provides essentially no protection against loss of data integrity, as the TCB is an access-control domain. Philosophically, the mathematical proof may be comforting but could cause more harm than good if it leads to relaxation of other security means.

This division is characterized by the use of formal security verification methods to assure that the mandatory and discretionary security controls employed in the system can effectively protect classified or other sensitive information stored or processed by the system. Extensive documentation is required to demonstrate that the TCB meets the security requirements in all aspects of design, development, and implementation.

Class A1: Verified Design

Systems in class A1 are functionally equivalent to those in class B3 in that no additional architectural features or policy requirements have been added. The distinguishing feature of systems in this class is the analysis derived from formal design specification and verification techniques and the resulting high degree of assurance that the TCB is correctly implemented.[13]

Figure 7.1 shows the relationships among 27 criteria and the divisions. The divisions are outlined above; the criteria in the chart are partitioned roughly into four categories: documentation, assurance, accountability, and security policy. Readers are referred to Department of Defense, *Trusted Computer System Evaluation Criteria*, DOD 5200.28.STD for details. Many of the criteria are discussed elsewhere in this text; for example, the reference monitor concept is addressed in the first two sections of this chapter.

Systems classified as high as B2 have been offered in the private sector; however, this level of security control interferes with normal use of the system, and such systems have not been well-received commercially.[14] Within the early 1990s, all computer systems used in U.S. federal government projects or connected to U.S. government computer systems will be required to meet or exceed the class C2 TCB evaluation level.

7.2.2 Federal Criteria

In December, 1992, the new U.S. *Federal Criteria for Information Technology Security* (FC) was published for comment. The Federal Criteria are intended to replace the TCSEC material, after a period of comment and revision.

The area of criteria has received considerable attention in North America and Europe, with much duplication of effort being one result. At a meeting of the EC Senior Officials Group for the Security of Information Systems (SOG-IS) in Brussels in February, 1993, a project was started to combine the Canadian (*Canadian Trusted Computer Product Evaluation Criteria* [CTCPEC]) , U.S. (FC), and European *Information Technology Security Evaluation Criteria* (ITSEC) into a single international standard (the "Common Criteria" [CC]).

A draft Common Criteria will be prepared by the spring of 1994. This will be circulated for comment and review, then revised as needed and adopted as a standard by the appropriate bodies in various governments. This work is scheduled for completion by late 1995. Eventually, the Common Criteria document is expected to become an ISO standard.

---

[13]The detailed criteria for class A1 begin to use phrases like "formal systems where possible and informal otherwise". This is a recognition that mathematical proofs are limited and the present state of knowledge does not permit the level of assurance that might be desired. The discussion of TCSEC classes beyond A1 indicates clearly that such are beyond the presently available theory and technology.

[14]For example, IBM submitted RACF version 1.9 for evaluation as a B2 level system in 1990. IBM has designed RACF 1.9 in such a way that it should offer a B2 level if fully implemented, but also so that it can be partially implemented at about the C2 level. Thus commercial viability is maintained.

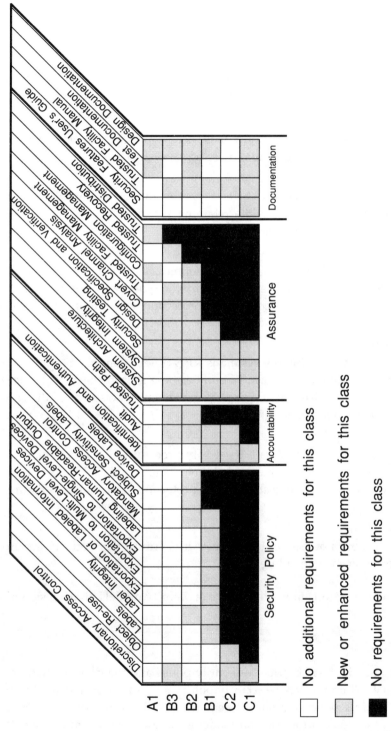

Figure 7.1. Trusted Computer System Evaluation Criteria Summary Chart[15]

___

[15]This chart is from Department of Defense, *Trusted Computer System Evaluation Criteria*, DOD 5200.28.STD, Department of Defense Computer Security Center, Fort George G. Meade, Md., December, 1985.

7.3 DESIGN PRINCIPLES FOR SECURE SYSTEMS

7.3.1 General Criteria

As general principles, several criteria contribute to the design of secure systems that will operate in a secure manner. The following list briefly describes six criteria:

- *Least privilege*

  A process or person should have only those access and operational capabilities that actually are required for effective and approved use of the system.

- *Open design*

  The system should be designed to be *open*; that is, implementing future changes to meet altered operational requirements while retaining security features should be facilitated, and interaction with other systems should be permitted.

- *Fail-safe defaults*

  All systems fail during their operational lifetimes. Particularly for security, failure modes should be designed so as to maintain security requirements (as well as to facilitate easy restarts.) As with the notion of continuous protection, a failure must not violate security requirements.

- *Economy of mechanisms*

  Perhaps the classical rule for any system is KISS (Keep It Simple, Stupid). Security measures can be cumbersome to use, and can be cumbersome to implement. The *simplest* mechanism, and the fewest mechanisms, that correctly implement an element of the security policy are advised for inclusion in the design.

- *Naturalness (human factors)*

  Human beings will use the system. If security procedures are unacceptably cumbersome or interfere excessively with effective work, human beings will find ways to bypass the features. The security system must be usable for full protection with minimal disruption to work requirements.

- *Continuous protection*

  Last in this list, but not least in importance: It is critical that security features provide continuous protection, even in failure modes.

With these general criteria in mind, the role of security models in the design of secure systems can be examined.

7.3.2 Security Models

There is a huge jump in detail between a security policy and the implementation of a system that follows the policy. Without a precise security policy, models are useless (and effective security is hopeless), so a security policy is assumed here. Chapter 16 addresses formal and informal security policies; here we look at the use of a model to help bridge the gap in detail between policy and implementation.

According to Gasser,[16] "a security model has several properties:

---

[16]Gasser, Morrie, *Building a Secure Computer System*, Van Nostrand Reinhold, New York, NY, 1988.

1. It is precise and unambiguous;
2. It is simple and abstract, and therefore easy to comprehend;
3. It is generic: It deals with security properties only and does not unduly constrain the functions of the system or its implementation; and
4. It is an obvious representation of the security policy."

The first two points should be obvious. Point 3 combined with point 4 allow for the fact that the state of security and information technology does not permit formal proofs of complex systems. Therefore, the model must be simple and an obvious representation of the policy so that informal arguments for the security of the system may be sufficient. Point 3 merely states that security models should deal with security issues, and not be confused with implementation or non-security design issues. This is in a sense an instance of the principle of economy of mechanism.

More than one level of model may be appropriate between the security policy and the actual system implementation. By using multiple levels, each level can more closely approach the goals of simplicity and of being an "obvious representation."

Creating a security model involves considerable effort and is worthwhile only if the designer has freedom and resources to design a system with security in mind. If the only alternatives permitted by resource constraints or management policy are to "plug the holes" (make changes here and there to close known vulnerabilities), a security model probably is wasted effort. (As is the plugging of holes; insecure systems normally cannot be made secure this way.)

It may not be necessary to invest the resources to create a new security model in order to achieve a secure system design. Several widely accepted security models already exist, with the Bell-La Padula model being perhaps the best known and most widely used. A more recent formal model called "non-interference" has been used as the basis for developing secure operating systems in some government experiments.

7.3.2.1 Types of Security Models

Two types of security models are relevant here:

1. *State-machine* models
2. *Non-interference* models

Non-interference models involve ways to prevent subjects operating in one domain from affecting one another in ways that violate the system's security policy. These models are a research effort now. While they hold promise for future use, they are not useful for current real design efforts. Therefore, we concentrate on state machine models.

A *state-machine model* describes a system as an abstract mathematical model, with *state variables* representing the state of a system, and *transition functions* defining how the system moves from one state to another. Such models are not feasible for detailed modeling of complex operating systems. Since security models can deal only with security-relevant state variables, a state-machine model for a security system can be far simpler.

One state-machine model is the *access matrix* model. (This general model is used by all of the access control software packages discussed in Chapter 1, although VM Secure has modifications related to differences in the VM system and its virtual machines.) The primary state variable is an array that represents the security state of the system. The array has one row per subject in the system, and one column per subject and object. The entry in each cell specifies the modes of access each subject has to each other subject or object.

A related method of determining access modes between subjects and objects (other than looking up an entry in a large array), is to compare security attributes.

Gasser uses the term *access models* to include all such models based on subject-to-object access.

A variation of the access model is the *information flow model*. In this model, the flow of information from one object to another is constrained according to security attributes of the objects. This book does not address the differences between access models and information flow models. For our purposes, it is sufficient to note that information flow models make covert channel analysis easy, while access models do not.

7.3.2.2 State-machine models

Gasser identifies the following six steps in developing a state-machine model:

1. Define the security relevant *state variables*
2. Define the conditions for a *secure state*
3. Define *state transition functions*
4. Prove that the functions maintain the secure state
5. Define the *initial state*
6. Prove that the initial state is secure in terms of the definition of the secure state

Once things are defined, proving that the initial state is secure and that the state transition functions are secure is sufficient to prove that the system will remain in a secure state.

Perhaps the best way to close the section outlining security models is to quote a paragraph from Gasser:[17]

> You should resist the temptation to beef up your model with additional functions that only serve to make the mapping more nearly complete. Any increase in confidence that you gain by having a fuller mapping is offset by the increased complexity of the mapping and of the proofs of the model. You cannot escape the fact that the informal correspondence process is manual and subjective: Adding excessive detail in an attempt to achieve perfection merely increases the chance for error and confusion. Using a formal specification technique . . . will bridge the code-model gap more soundly than adding detail to the model will.

7.4 COMMON FLAWS AND PENETRATION METHODS

Although computerized information systems have existed only for a few decades, there has been a distressingly large experience with security problems. From "hackers," mostly amateur but often with very high-level skills, to professional penetrations, systems have been subject to attack since information of any value was stored in them. No doubt this will continue. The value of this experience with security in computerized information systems is that several general flaws common to many operating systems have been identified, and several common penetration techniques have been seen repeatedly. If we have learned our lessons well, we will apply now well-understood design and management principles to control the problems.

---

[17] *Ibid.*, p. 159.

Professionals operating in the area of information security should be familiar with the most-often encountered problems. Even now, all too many systems evidence one or more of these well-known flaws, and all too many succumb quickly to one or more of the well-known penetration methods listed later. It can be argued that a professional security practitioner is guilty of negligence (or at least lack of professional competence) if he or she allows a system under his or her control to be vulnerable to these things that ought to have been known by an information security professional.

7.4.1 Common Operating System Flaws

Over time, many methods have been used to penetrate operating systems. Many operating systems share common flaws that make penetration easier than it should be. Some of these vulnerabilities are:

- *Encryption*: Lists of sensitive data such as the table of account and password identifications should be encrypted, so that anyone who manages to access the files cannot read them. This is not always done.

- *Implementation*: There may be a well-designed security system provided in the operating system but not used by the organization, or not implemented properly.

- *Implied sharing*: The system may place sensitive operating-system control information in the user's workspace; under some conditions, the user may be able to read this. (For example, a program error, perhaps deliberately induced, that causes a memory dump may cause a printout of everything in the workspace, including anything the operating system may have stored there.)

- *Incomplete parameter checking*: A system fault which exists when all parameters have not been fully checked for accuracy and consistency by the operating system, thus making the system vulnerable to penetration. (FIPS PUB 39; AR 380-380; NCSC-WA-001-85)

- *Legality checking*: The system may not check on the parameters a user supplies it.

- *Line disconnect*: The user in a time-sharing or other remote system mode may hang up without disconnecting; another user may be able to get in without proper validation. Not all systems "hang up" properly when a line is disconnected.

- *Maintenance hook*: Special instructions in software to allow easy maintenance and additional feature development. These are not clearly defined during access for design specification. Hooks frequently allow entry into the code at unusual points or without the usual checks so they are a serious security risk if they are not removed prior to live implementation. Maintenance hooks are simply special types of trap doors. (NCSC-WA-001-85)

- *Operator carelessness*: Operators may inadvertently mount the wrong disk packs or tapes; some cases have been reported where penetrators telephoned the operator and were able to trick the operator into giving out sensitive information.

- *Passwords*: Passwords may not be used, they may be simple to guess, or the system may allow repeated attempts. (A microcomputer easily can be programmed to try to log on by repeatedly selecting passwords from a list.) The next section looks at passwords in more detail.

- *Repetition*: Systems may allow users an indefinite number of attempts to sign on, thus allowing use of a microcomputer and repeated guesses. The system should disconnect or hang up after some small number of unsuccessful attempts, and the event should be reported to the operator or security officer.

- *Shielding*: As noted in Chapter 8 and elsewhere, wires emit signals that can be detected and analyzed. Unshielded lines with non-encrypted data are a significant exposure in many systems.

- *TOC/TOU*: The acronym TOC/TOU (Time Of Check *versus* Time Of Use) often is used to describe a class of asynchronous attacks. The acronym TOCTU also is used. In essence some control information, or perhaps merely the contents of a file, are changed between the time the system security functions check the contents of variables (or access permissions to files) and the time the variables actually are used during operations. The Between-the-lines, NAK attack, various attacks involving interrupts, and line disconnect in the next list are more specific examples of this class of problem. Many systems have been vulnerable to TOC/TOU class of attacks during I/O processing. Some of the specific attacks described in Chapters 2, 8, and 12 also may be grouped into the TOC/TOU category.

- *Waste*: sensitive printouts may be discarded; more than one system has been penetrated by people who found lists of user identification and passwords in a waste container.

7.4.2 Specific Penetration Techniques: Trojan Horse, Virus, Worm, Salami, Piggyback, Deception, Human Compromise, etc.

Several penetration methods have been used many times to cause successful system penetration. Many of the common methods make use of the flaws noted above. Unfortunately, it still is very common to find that systems are vulnerable to these methods, even though the methods are well-known and often easy to defeat. A security specialist should work with information systems personnel to ensure that at least these common "holes" are plugged.

- *Between-the-lines Entry*: Access obtained through active wiretapping by an unauthorized user to a momentarily inactive terminal of a legitimate user assigned to a communications channel. (AR 380-380; NCSC-WA-001-85; FIPS PUB 39)

  A special terminal is used to tap into the communication line used by a legitimate user while the user is not active. Terminals should never be left signed on and unattended, and lines should be shielded.

- *Browsing*: The act of searching through storage to locate or acquire information without necessarily knowing of the existence or the format of the information being sought. (OPNAVINST 5239.1A; AR 380-380; NCSC-WA-001-85; FIPS PUB 39)

  The user searches through the computer system or through files attempting to locate sensitive information. Such action is controllable through file and other access controls. Commonly, a table listing what the user may access is created, and the user is restricted to only those accesses. Files may be given individual passwords in some systems.

- *Denial of use*: Action or actions that prevent any part of an AIS from functioning in accordance with its intended purpose. This includes any action which causes the unauthorized destruction, modification, or delay of service (DODD 5200.28; NCSC-WA-001-85)

  The user is able to "crash" the system, or hang it up by putting a program into an endless loop. At least one commercial time-sharing system allowed jobs to submit other jobs; it was possible on that system (by submitting a job that submits itself) to fill up the job queue with jobs waiting to be processed so that the computer became unavailable to anyone else.

- *Hidden code*: Programs may contain undocumented code that does things other than what is described in the manuals. Poorly controlled maintenance often allows an opportunity for a programmer to insert a routine that should not be in the program. A program library and controls over maintenance may make this difficult or impossible.

- *Interrupts*: A penetrator may cause program or system interrupts; some operating systems allow a process to enter a privileged mode with more access than usual, while processing an interrupt.

- *Line disconnect*: The user signs off, or the line "goes down," but the system has not yet acknowledged and terminated the user's session. Until this termination occurs, another user may be able to use the session.

- *Logic bomb*: A resident computer program that, when executed, checks for particular conditions or particular states of the system which, when satisfied, triggers the perpetration of an unauthorized act. (NCSC-WA-001-85)

- *Masquerade*:

  An attempt to gain access to a system by posing as an authorized user. (AR 380-380; NCSC-WA-001-85)

  The penetrator obtains identification and passwords and signs on with someone else's account. A user pretending to be someone else by grabbing a line as noted above, is a form of masquerade.

- *NAK attack*: A penetration technique which capitalizes on a potential weakness in an operating system that does not handle asynchronous interrupts properly thus leaving the system in an unprotected state during such interrupts. (FIPS PUB 39)

  NAK and ACK are control codes in communications protocols. In asynchronous processing it is necessary for one device to inform another that processing is complete and more data can be accepted, or that data is about to be transmitted (in synchronous processing this is handled by a clock). If one device does not acknowledge a request ("NAK"), it or the other device may be vulnerable to a spoofing attack or other penetration attempt until the ACK is received. (See also "handshaking" in the definitions at the chapter beginning.)

- *Network weaving*: Network weaving is a technique using different communication networks to gain access to an organization's system. For example, a perpetrator [. . .] makes a call through AT&T, jumps over to Sprint, then to MCI, and then to Tymnet. The purpose is to avoid detection and trace-backs to the source of the call.[18] (TC)

- *Operator deception*: A penetrator may, for example, convince an operator to divulge a password (perhaps by claiming to have just changed the password and miskeyed the new one).

- *Piggyback*: The gaining of unauthorized access to a system via another user's legitimate connection. (NCSC-WA-001-85)

  The penetrator intercepts a communication line and substitutes his or her own messages to the legitimate user and/or to the system (for example, simulates the sign-on program and thus gets the user to give out identification and password information).

- *Salami technique*: In data security, pertains to a fraud spread over a large number of individual transactions, *e.g.*, a program which does not correctly round off figures but diverts the leftovers to a personal account. (MS)

---

[18]The particular pathway in the example also may have saved long-distance telephone charges.

(Not strictly an operating system penetration, but a common fraud): The classic example is a program that accumulates all roundoff figures for a bank's loan calculations into one account. When each amount is rounded to an even penny, there will be small amounts left over.[19] Each such "slice" is less than 1/2 cent and is not noticeable, but for thousands of accounts the cumulative effect can be large.

- *Scavenging*:

  1) Searching through residue for the purpose of unauthorized data acquisition. (FIPS PUB 39; AR 380-380)

  2) Searching through object residue to acquire unauthorized data. (NCSC-WA-001-85)

- *Spoofing*: The deliberate act of inducing a user or a resource into taking an incorrect action. (NCSC-WA-001-85; AR 380-380; FIPS PUB 39)

- *Tampering*: An unauthorized modification which alters the proper functioning of a system or piece of equipment in a manner that degrades the security it provides. (NCSC-WA-001-85)

- *Traffic analysis*: The inference of information from observation of traffic flows (presence, absence, amount, direction, and frequency). (ISO 7498-2)

  Similar to browsing, someone looks at things like how often people are contacted, who is contacted, and what time of the day or week the contacts are. Quite a lot of information about what is underway may be deduced from traffic analysis—without alerting the victim by trying to intercept or change anything.[20]

- *Trap door*: A hidden software or hardware mechanism that permits system-protection mechanisms to be circumvented. It is activated in some innocent appearing manner, *e.g.*, special "random" key sequence at a terminal. Software developers often introduce trap doors in their code that enable them to re-enter the system and perform certain functions. (NCSC-WA-001-85)

- *Trojan horse*: A computer program with an apparently or actually useful function that contains additional (hidden) functions that surreptitiously exploit the legitimate authorizations of the invoking process to the detriment of security. For example, making a "blind copy" of a sensitive file for the creator of the Trojan Horse. (CSC-STD-001-83; NCSC-WA-001-85)

  This is a generic name for the "hidden code" penetration method. Something is in a program that is not supposed to be there, that causes sensitive data to be available. Or, the program does not do what it is supposed to; the name is misleading. It is possible to put a Trojan horse into a system that would, for example, simulate the log-on messages; after collecting user data, the Trojan horse would put the data somewhere accessible to the perpetrator and then remove itself from the system. Familiar kinds of Trojan horses in microcomputers include the freeware or shareware disk-compression utility that spreads a virus as well as compresses data on a disk, and many computer games.

- *Virus* : "A program that can 'infect' other programs by modifying them to include a, possibly evolved, copy of itself." (Cohen) A virus can be considered a delivery mechanism, with an in-

---

[19]This is a well-known kind of fraud, but it is still seen from time to time. Financial institutions are checked by regulators to be sure they don't accumulate all those roundoff errors into the *bank's* account, thus protecting consumers. Standard mathematical techniques are used to ensure that these unavoidable roundoff errors cancel each other out, rather than accumulating *anywhere*.

[20]This topic is addressed in greater detail in Chapters 2 and 8.

fecting process that supports its spread, and a payload that is triggered by some event. When another program is infected, that other program becomes a Trojan horse with at least the non-intended function of propagating the virus, plus any other actions the virus may include.

Viruses are covered in more detail in section 7.5 below.

- *Worm* : A program that moves through an address space by making a copy of itself in a new location. The new location may be any place that the worm can access in any particular invocation. If a copy remains in the previous location and can be invoked again, the worm can replicate into many copies of itself very rapidly, and can cause denial of use by clogging system resources. Benign worms built for such system functions as automatic backups do not leave copies behind, and they save the contents of what may be in the new location and replace any storage they once occupied with its previous contents when a new copy is made.

This is not an exhaustive list; it only is some of the more common penetration methods. The cures generally are rather obvious and often do not cost much money or degrade performance.

Although it is not a technical problem, it should be noted that a favorite way to compromise computer systems is to approach human beings involved in operations, programming, and similar tasks. This exposure is not new, not in the realm of technical problems nor subject to technical solutions, and is not discussed further at this time.

7.5 COMPUTER VIRUS CODE

7.5.1 A Short Introduction to Viruses

Viruses come in many flavors. The most widely accepted classification is into boot-sector, system, and application viruses.[21] The names indicate which types of programs are infected; the names also are indicative of the fact that, so far, almost all virus problems are associated with personal computers.

The first viruses spread very rapidly through bulletin boards and other electronic communications media. This exposure has become much smaller over the years, as operators of BBSs and mail systems have grown aware of the phenomenon and have instituted corrective measures. In the early 1990s, the most common infection vectors seem to be repair shops and swapping of diskettes.

Virus code has been written and demonstrated successfully on mainframe and minicomputers as well as on microcomputers. The security practitioner should not make the error of relegating this phenomenon to the personal computer world. Virus code more or less ignores access-control software, since it is an integrity issue rather than one of authorized access.

Boot sector infectors so far have turned out to be the worst offenders, since they infect a computer before any protective programs can execute and there may be no symptoms until the payload is executed. This is most regrettable, as known boot-sector viruses spread *only* when a computer is booted from an infected disk, which can happen only when several major violations of very basic security precautions occur simultaneously. For a boot-sector virus to spread, an in-

---

[21]There are other classifications that may be more precise but have not achieved such widespread acceptance. A book such as the Fites, Johnston and Kratz work includes more detail than is appropriate here.

fected disk must be in a drive when a computer is turned on; the virus must be loaded; and a diskette must be inserted to which the virus can copy itself. The basic measures of not having disks in drives when the computer is turned on, or scanning all diskettes, or even simply not accepting disks except from trusted sources, usually will avoid infection from boot-sector viruses.[22]

The "boot sector" is a portion of storage on a diskette or hard disk in a personal computer system. All properly formatted personal computer disks and diskettes contain a boot sector; in this sector is code that is loaded and executed when the computer is started ("booted.") The correct code either causes the operating system loading process to begin, or causes the screen to display something like `Non-system disk or disk error; replace and strike any key when ready`. If a virus stores enough of itself in this area to cause the virus to be loaded instead, the system will have the virus running in memory before any software protection that may be installed in the computer can be loaded. Some boot sector (and other) viruses intercept various system calls and display responses indicating that the system is normal when in fact it is infected ("stealth" viruses). Such a virus is very difficult to detect.

This book does not address the mathematical theory of computer viruses in detail. The seminal papers on formal definitions and analysis are by Dr. F. Cohen and Dr. L. Adleman, reproduced in the book by Lance Hoffman in the references for this chapter. Dr. Cohen approaches the virus phenomenon from the perspective of Turing machines, and Dr. Adleman uses recursive function theory. (Dr. Cohen's informal definition is given in the list in the previous section.) The implications of the theory are essentially the same for both approaches.

A significant point in the mathematical work is that there is no concept of "malicious" viruses. "Bad," "good," malicious, and similar concepts are inherently human values and cannot be expressed in the mathematics of computer science. Also, the mathematical concepts necessary to define a "program" or an "environment" (which we discuss briefly in the next paragraph) are not familiar to most non-scientists. The lack of a concept of *good* or *bad* and the difficulty of defining *program* mean that the quite precise discussions among computer scientists may be at variance with common (and highly imprecise) views of the same problems. The security professional should be aware of this and should avoid contributing to the confusion.

Mathematically, a worm is difficult to distinguish from a virus, and a communications network cannot be distinguished from the "network" formed by the buses inside a computer (unless the network includes workstations with independent processing capability, such as microcomputers). Colloquially, a virus alters other "programs" and a worm does not; however, mathematically the environment (sequence of bits in the address space) in which a worm moves is a "program". A virus does not propagate by itself and it modifies other programs; the lack of independence may offer a mathematically definable difference between virus and worm. The physical implementation of a network implies very different countermeasures for a worm than for a virus.

Virus code is not a new idea nor are viruses very interesting mathematically. However, the existence of several thousand different viruses (some for all popular microcomputers), combined with at least 100 million computers exposed, in total comprises a severe problem.

---

[22]In principle, there *are* no "trusted sources"; even shrink-wrapped software shipped directly from manufacturers has been found to contain virus code. However, this is rare, and reported instances have been widely publicized and the problems have been corrected by the manufacturers with dispatch. This is not a major source of infection.

7.5.2 Protection and Recovery from Viruses

The most concise source of advice for non-specialists about protection and recovery from viruses is the most recent update of *Frequently Asked Questions* (FAQ), an electronic publication by numerous contributors to the Virus-L Digest. FAQ is available on many computer systems via anonymous file transfer (ftp) over the InterNet, and usually is distributed (somewhat more slowly) through BBSs. This document is revised several times annually and reflects the most current advice available from people directly involved in virus problems.

Regrettably, the mathematical theory of viruses unambiguously shows that there is no perfect protection, and it is not always possible to recover from an attack. In practice, a fairly simple set of rather basic measures and policies provides total protection against all viruses now known to be "in the wild." Another set of measures, somewhat more complex, permits recovery from most (*not* all) problems caused by currently known viruses.

All of the methods following assume that computer begins in an uninfected state, and discuss how to maintain that state, detect infection, and restore an uninfected state. It must be emphasized again that these measures cannot provide perfect protection or recovery, and new viruses or techniques by the vandals may defeat any of these measures. The security professional is responsible to maintain current knowledge and apply these and other measures intelligently.

7.5.2.1 Protection

Protection invokes two of the three basic security principles of protection, detection, and correction: protection and detection. Trusted sources and scanning of diskettes are protection, in the sense of keeping viruses out of systems. Integrity checking and scanning are detective controls that warn after a virus has entered the system.

- Accept diskettes and programs only from trusted sources.
- Scan all files and diskettes for viruses. Use more than one scanning program. This applies to *all* diskettes and programs, *whatever the source.*
- Make backup copies of clean diskettes, store the originals for safekeeping, and operate from the copies.
- Never boot the computer from a diskette.[23]
- Install one of the memory-resident tools that scans automatically.
- Install some form of integrity checker that will inform you when any sensitive file has been changed. (Sensitive files include executable files, .BAT, .COM, .DLL, .EXE, .OVL, , and similar extensions in DOS-based computers.) A change in a file that should not change may be the result of a virus that defeated all the scans.[24]

More complex measures involving cryptographic techniques have been developed, and may be appropriate in special circumstances. All of these tools and procedures will provide excellent protection, but there is always the possibility of a new virus that all scanners miss, from a trusted source. Therefore, these measures should be combined with corrective controls.

---

[23]Obviously, this is impossible. In some cases, booting from a diskette is necessary; but it should be done only as a rare exceptional case, and utilizing extraordinary precautions.

[24]Integrity shells and checkers pose the problem that one must decide whether a change is intended or not. This knowledge is not in general possible (another regrettable fact of computing science mathematics.) Even in particular instances, few computer users have the technical background to know whether a change is appropriate or not. For example, some programs change themselves during execution. Although integrity checking is in principle a powerful detection control, in practice its usefulness is very questionable.

7.5.2.2 Recovery

Once it is determined that a virus has been active in the computer, some form of recovery is appropriate. We now invoke all three of the principles of security and include correction. Procedures for recovery from a virus attack vary from one computer and operating system to another.

Detailed procedures for PC and Macintosh computers are covered in the Fites, Johnston & Kratz book in the references for this chapter. These procedures outline the only *certain* recovery techniques, essentially restoring the computer to a blank state and rebuilding a clean and uninfected system. This "slash and burn" approach is tricky, time-consuming, and requires proper (and uninfected) backups. Such procedures, however, are *guaranteed* to result in a clean system.

In the following list, we note some pragmatic tools that *usually* will effect a recovery. Some problems *cannot* be corrected; for example, a program, some of whose code has been over-written by a virus, must be re-installed or restored from backups; it cannot be "fixed" by a general-purpose tool. Similarly, data altered by actions of the virus payload cannot be repaired but must be restored from backups. As well, multiple virus infections may make it impossible for a general-purpose tool to restore the system state. One example is the interaction between the Stoned and Michaelangelo viruses; if both have been active simultaneously in a system, no current "repair" program can fix the problem. (For this example, a simple manual procedure using DOS utilities fixes the problem easily.)

1. Ensure that the computer does not currently have a virus active. This means at least turning off the computer to clear volatile memory, then booting from a known *clean, write-protected* startup disk.[25]
2. Use appropriate scanning tools, DEBUG, or whatever is needed to be absolutely sure what virus or viruses have been active.
3. Use appropriate tools to repair programs, rebuild master boot records, boot sectors, or whatever else needs to be done to restore the uninfected state of the machine.
4. Repeat steps 2 and 3 for *every* diskette and program that has been, or could have been, inserted into a drive while the system was infected.
5. Notify any other users who may have been exposed to the infection, so the spread of the virus can be limited. If possible, identify and notify the source of the infection as well.

There is a "sixth step": Install protective and detective measures and expect to repeat the preceding five steps. Experience has shown that if a virus is detected, recovery procedures nearly always miss at least one infected disk or file and the infection process will recur.

The steps outlined in the previous sub-sections are much simpler than low-level formats and rebuilding of systems. However, these steps are risky. If the virus is unknown, or is improperly identified, attempted recovery measures may cause more harm than did the virus. If the recovery tools themselves are, or become, infected, problems can propagate beyond the original. A professional or knowledgeable person may use the short-cuts, but only the "slash and burn" method is guaranteed to work in all cases.

---

[25]If a virus has altered certain system parameters in CMOS, more elaborate measures than merely powering down and restarting may be required.

7.6 COUNTERMEASURES

Much of this book deals with design principles and countermeasures that, properly implemented, can control or prevent exposures to the types of flaws and penetration techniques listed in the previous two sections. For example, file locking can prevent most problems of the TOC/TOU type in some file systems; inference controls (Chapters 2 and 5) can limit exposure to some kinds of database problems; anti-viral software packages and intelligent precautions can minimize or eliminate problems with viruses, and so forth.

Rather than repeat a long list of countermeasures covered elsewhere, we note that secure systems can be obtained by:

- Applying careful design techniques and well-understood software engineering principles during creation of the system itself
- Applying intelligent management of access control and other security measures during implementation and operation
- Practicing intelligent management of procedural and policy issues outside the technical areas of the information system

The many technical controls discussed in appropriate places throughout this book are useful and often necessary, just as are locks on doors. Properly applied, they can improve the security situation materially. Improperly applied, technical measures can be worse than useless, by leading to a false sense of security. The core requirement underlying the three requirements above is *intelligent management*; lacking that element, no information system can be considered secure.

REFERENCES

Attanasio, C. R., P. W. Markstein, and R. J. Phillips, "Penetrating an Operating System: A Study of VM/370 Integrity," *IBM Systems Journal*, Volume 15, Number 1, pp. 102-116.

Bell, D. E., and L. J. La Padula, "Secure Computer Systems: Unified Exposition and MULTICS Interpretation," MTR-2997, rev. 1, Mitre Corporation, Bedford, MA, November, 1973-June, 1974 vols. I-III.

Biba, K. J., "Integrity Considerations for Secure Computer Systems" National Technical Information Service NTIS AD-A039324, Springfield VA, 1977.

Blanc, Robert P., Ed., "An Analysis of Computer Security Safeguards for Detecting and Preventing Intentional Computer Misuse," National Bureau of Standards Special Publication 500-25, 1978.

Clark, D. D. and D. R. Wilson, "A Comparison of Commercial and Military Security Policies" in *Proceedings* of the 1987 Symposium on Security and Privacy, IEEE Computer Society, Washington D.C., 1987.

Cooper, James Arlin, *Computer-Security Technology*, Lexington Books, Lexington, MA, 1984.

Department of Defense, *Technical Rationale Behind CSC-STD-003-85: Computer Security Requirements*, CSC-STD-004-85, DoD Computer Security Center, Fort George G. Meade, MD, June, 1985.

Department of Defense, *Trusted Computer System Evaluation Criteria*, DOD 5200.28.STD, DoD Computer Security Center, Fort George G. Meade, MD, December, 1985.

Fernandez, E. B., R. C. Summers, and C. Wood: *Database Security and Integrity*, Addison-Wesley, Reading, Mass., 1981.

Fites, Philip E., Peter Johnston, and Martin P. J. Kratz, *The Computer Virus Crisis*, second edition, Van Nostrand Reinhold, New York, NY, 1992.

"Guidelines for Computer Security Certification and Accreditation," National Bureau of Standards, FIPS Pub. 102, U.S. Department of Commerce, Springfield, VA, September 27, 1983, P. 12.

Gasser, Morrie, *Building a Secure Computer System*, Van Nostrand Reinhold, New York, NY, 1988.

"Guidelines on User Authentication Techniques for Computer Network Access Control," FIPS Publication 83, U.S. Department of Commerce/National Bureau of Standards, Washington DC, September, 1980.

Hoffman, Lance J., *Rogue Programs: Viruses, Worms and Trojan Horses*, Van Nostrand Reinhold, New York, NY, 1990.

Jacobson, Robert V., et al., "Guidelines for Automatic Data Processing Physical Security and Risk Management," *Federal Information Processing Standards Publication 31*, National Bureau of Standards, 1974.

Karcher, P. A., and R. R. Shell, "MULTICS Security Evaluation: Vulnerability Analysis," ESD-TR-XXX, Electronics Systems Division (AFSC), L. G. Hanscombe Field, Bedford, MA, July 11, 1983.

MULTICS Data Security, GA01-00, Honeywell Information Systems, Phoenix, AZ, 1982.

Pozzo, Maria M., and Terence E. Gray, "Computer Virus Containment in Untrusted Computing Environments," *Information Security: The Challenge*, Pre-prints of papers from the fourth IFIP Security on Information Systems Security, Monte Carlo, December, 1986.

Schmucker, Kurt J., *Fuzzy Sets, Natural Language Computations, and Risk Analysis*, Computer Science Press, 1984.

Spafford, Eugene H., *The InterNet Worm Program: An Analysis*, Purdue University Computer Sciences Dept., November, 1988.

Troy, Eugene F., Stuart W. Katzke, and Dennis D. Steinauer, *Technical Solutions to the Computer Security Intrusion Problem*, National Bureau of Standards, Washington, DC, November, 1984.

White, Steve R., David M. Chess, and Jimmy Kuo, *Coping With Computer Viruses and Related Problems*, IBM Research Report RC 14405, Yorktown Heights, NY, January, 1989.

8. Telecommunications Security

This area describes the things that a professional would be expected to know about how to achieve message integrity and confidentiality for traffic in telecommunications and the control of the use of the telecommunications capacity.

The professional would be expected to know:

- The objectives of telecommunications security
- The hazards and exposures
- The effects of topology, media, protocols, switching
- The hazards and classes of attack
- Defenses and protective measures

For example the professional would be able to:

- Describe the security objectives for telecommunications; identify the key measures
- Describe the most widely used media (*e.g.*, electricity in copper, light in glass and air; radio); describe the applications of each; give an order-of-magnitude cost of attack for each
- Distinguish between star, bus, ring, and mesh; identify strengths and limitations of each
- Distinguish among LAN, WAN, and VAN; describe the applications, features, and vulnerabilities of each
- Identify local loop, local office, LATA
- Distinguish between base-band and broad-band
- Distinguish between CSMA-CA and CSMA-CD
- Contrast CSMA-CD and token-ring
- Describe the use and limitations of physical security and cryptography
- Describe and measure the exposure from the use of network monitors (*e.g.*, DataScope, EtherProbe)

DEFINITIONS

Although these concepts are covered in this chapter, we present some accepted definitions here for comparison.

Aborted Connection

Disconnection which does not follow established procedures. This may occasionally result from a bad phone connection, but more typically results when the user "hangs up" without attempting to issue the disconnect commands.

Note: Some systems are sensitive to aborted connections, and do not detect the disconnect and reset for the next user. Continued aborts are considered [improper] and may result in a warning or revocation of access privileges. (BBD)

Active Wiretapping

The attaching of an unauthorized device, such as a computer terminal, to a communications circuit for the purpose of obtaining access to data through the generation of false signals, or by altering the communications of legitimate users. (FIPS PUB 39)

Asynchronous Attack

An asynchronous attack is an attempt to exploit the interval between a defensive act and the attack in order to render inoperative the effect of the defensive act. For instance, an operating task may be interrupted at once following the checking of a stored parameter; the user regains control and malevolently changes the parameter; the operating system regains control and [continues] processing using the maliciously altered parameter. (JL)

Between-the-lines Entry

Access obtained through active wiretapping by an unauthorized user to a momentarily inactive terminal of a legitimate user assigned to a communications channel. (AR 380-380; NCSC-WA-001-85; FIPS PUB 39)

Call Back

A procedure for identifying a remote terminal. The host system will disconnect the caller and then dial the authorized telephone number of the remote terminal to re-establish the connection. (NCSC-WA-001-85; AR 380-380)

Channel

An information transfer path. (ISO 7498-2)

Communications Security (COMSEC)

1. The protection resulting from all measures designed to deny unauthorized persons information of value which might be derived from the possession and study of telecommunications, or to mislead unauthorized persons in their interpretation of the results of such possession and study. Also called COMSEC. Communications security includes cryptosecurity, transmission security, emission security, and physical security of communications security materials and information. (OPNAVINST 5239.1A; AFR 700-10; AR 380-380)
2. The protection that ensures the authenticity of telecommunications and that results from the application of measures taken to deny unauthorized persons information of value which might be derived from the acquisition of telecommunications. (FIPS PUB 39)

Compromising Emanations

Unintentional data-related or intelligence-bearing signals which, if intercepted and analyzed, disclose the classified information transmission received, handled or otherwise processed by any information processing equipment. TEMPEST is an unclassified short name referring to investigations and studies of compromising emanations. It is sometimes used synonymously for the "compromising emanations." (OPNAVINST 5239.1A; AFR 205-16; AFR 700-10; AR 380-380; NCSC-WA-001-85; DOE 5636.2A)

Covert Channel

1. A communication channel that allows a process to transfer information in a manner that violates the system's security policy. (CSC-STD-001-83; CSC-STD-004-85)
2. A communication channel that allows two cooperating processes to transfer information in a manner that violates the system's security policy. (NCSC-WA-001-85)

Covert Storage Channel

A covert channel that involves the direct or indirect writing of a storage location by one process and the direct or indirect reading of the storage location by another process. Covert channels typically involve a finite resource (*e.g.*, sectors on a disk) that is shared by two subjects at different security levels. (CSC-STD-001-83; NCSC-WA-001-85)

Covert Timing Channel

A covert channel in which one process signals information to another by modulating its own use of system resources (*e.g.*, CPU time) in such a way that this manipulation affects the real response time observed by the second process. (CSC-STD-001-83; NCSC-WA-001-85)

Cross-Talk

An unwanted transfer of energy from one communications channel to another channel. (FIPS PUB 39; AR 380-380)

Dumb Terminal

Terminal (or computer using dumb-terminal software) which allows communications with other computers, but does not enhance the data exchanged, or provide additional features such as upload/download. (BBD)

Eavesdropping

The unauthorized interception of information-bearing emanations through the use of methods other than wiretapping. (FIPS PUB 39; AR 380-380)

Electromagnetic Emanations

Signals transmitted as radiation through the air and through conductors. (FIPS PUB 39; AR 380-380)

Electronic Funds Transfer (EFT)

Electronic funds transfer refers to the movement of value (money) from one party to another by electronic means. (GAO)

Exploitable Channel

Any channel that is usable or detectable by subjects external to the Trusted Computing Base. (CSC-STD-001-83)

Handshaking Procedures

1. A dialogue between a user and a computer, a computer and another computer, or a program and another program for the purpose of identifying a user and authenticating identity. A sequence of questions and answers is used based on information either previously stored in the computer or supplied to the computer by the initiator of the dialogue. (AR 380-380; FIPS PUB 39)
2. The set of communication protocols and codes that allows one computer to exchange information with one or more others. See also Hardware Handshaking. (PEF)

Hardware Handshaking

The passing of control characters between two devices such as ACK, NAK, XON, or XOFF, for the purpose of controlling the flow of information between the devices. (AFR 205-16)

Masquerade

The pretense by an entity to be a different entity. (ISO 7498-2)

Message Authentication Code

A message authentication code (MAC) should be designed so as to ensure that a message cannot be altered during transmission, the originator is known and cannot repudiate the message, and the receiver is known and cannot repudiate reception. Various forms of encipherment are employed in creating MACs. The term usually refers to messages sent among computer devices, although this is not necessary. *Digital signature* is a related concept.[1]

Network

A network is composed of a communications medium and all components attached to that medium whose responsibility is the transference of information. Such components may include AISs, packet switches, telecommunications controllers, key distribution centers, technical control devices, and other networks. (DODD 5200.28; DOE 5636.2A)

Network Weaving

Network weaving is a technique using different communication networks to gain access to an organization's system. For example, a perpetrator [. . .] makes a call through AT&T, jumps over to Sprint, then to MCI, and then to Tymnet. The purpose is to avoid detection and trace-backs to the source of the call. (TC)[2]

Passive Wiretapping

The monitoring and/or recording of data while the data is being transmitted over a communications link. (FIPS PUB 39)

Piggy Back

The gaining of unauthorized access to a system via another user's legitimate connection. (NCSC-WA-001-85)

Protected Wireline Distribution System

A telecommunications system which has been approved by a legally designated authority and to which electromagnetic and physical safeguards have been applied to permit safe electrical transmission of unencrypted sensitive information. Synonymous with approved circuit. (FIPS PUB 39)

---

[1]MACs are discussed in Chapter 2.

[2]The particular pathway in the example also may have saved long-distance telephone charges.

Repudiation

Denial by one of the entities involved in a communication of having participated in all or part of the communication. (ISO 7498-2)

Session

An activity for a period of time; the activity is access to a computer/network resource by a user; a period of time is bounded by session initiation (a form of log-on) and session termination (a form of log-off). (DCID 1/16-1, Sup.)

Spoofing

The deliberate act of inducing a user or a resource into taking an incorrect action. (NCSC-WA-001-85; AR 380-380; FIPS PUB 39)

Stand-Alone, Shared Automated Information System

An Automated Information System that is physically and electrically isolated from all other Automated Information Systems, and is intended to be used by more than one person, either simultaneously (*e.g.*, an Automated Information System with multiple terminals) or serially, with data belonging to one user remaining available to the Automated Information System while another user is using the Automated Information System (*e.g.*, a PC with non-removable storage media such as a hard disk). (NCSC-WA-001-85)

Stand-Alone, Single-User Automated Information System

An Automated Information System that is physically and electrically isolated from all other Automated Information Systems, and is intended to be used by one person at a time, with no data belonging to other users remaining in the Automated Information System (*e.g.*, a PC with removable storage media such as a floppy disk). (NCSC-WA-001-85)

Subcommittee on Telecommunications Security

The NSDD-145 authorizes and directs the establishment, under the NTISSC, of a permanent Subcommittee on Telecommunications Security. The STS is composed of one voting member from each organization represented on the NTISSC. (NCSC-WA-001-85)

Telecommunications

Any transmission, emission, or reception of signs, signals, writing, images, sounds, or other information by wire, radio, visual, or any electromagnetic systems. (FIPS PUB 39)

Teleprocessing

Pertaining to an information transmission system that combines telecommunications, ADP systems, and man-machine interface equipment for the purpose of interacting and functioning as an integrated whole. (FIPS PUB 39)

Teleprocessing Security

The protection that results from measures designed to prevent deliberate, inadvertent, or unauthorized disclosure, acquisition, manipulation, or modification of information in a teleprocessing system. (FIPS PUB 39; AR 380-380)

TEMPEST

1. A short name referring to investigations and studies of compromising emanations. It is sometimes used synonymously for the term "compromising emanations," for example, TEMPEST test, TEMPEST inspections. (AFR 700-10; DOE 5636.2A)
2. The study and control of spurious electronic signals emitted from ADP equipment. (CSC-STD-001-83; AFR 205-16)
3. The study and control of spurious electronic signals emitted from electrical equipment. (NCSC-WA-001-85)

Terminal Identification

The means used to uniquely identify a terminal to an Automated Information System. (NCSC-WA-001-85; AR 380-380; FIPS PUB 39)

Traffic Analysis

The inference of information from observation of traffic flows (presence, absence, amount, direction, and frequency). (ISO 7498-2)

Traffic Flow Security

The protection that results from those features in some crypto-equipment that conceal the presence of valid messages on a communications circuit. This is usually done by causing the circuit to appear busy at all times, or by encrypting the source and destination addresses of valid messages. (FIPS PUB 39; AR 380-380)

Traffic Padding

The generation of spurious instances of communication, spurious data units, and/or spurious data within data units. (ISO 7498-2)

Wiretapping

Cutting in on a communications line to get information.

1. *Active.* The attaching of an unauthorized device, such as a computer terminal, to a communications circuit for the purpose of obtaining access to data through the generation of false messages or control signals, or by altering the communications of legitimate users.
2. *Passive.* The monitoring and/or recording of data which is being transmitted over a communication link. (AR 380-380)

Work Factor

An estimate of the effort or time needed to overcome a protective measure by a potential penetrator with specified expertise and resources. (AR 380-380; NCSC-WA-001-85; FIPS PUB 39)

Worm

A program or executable code module which resides in distributed systems or networks. It will replicate itself, if necessary, in order to exercise as much of the system's resources as possible for its own processing. Such resources may take the form of CPU time, I/O channels, or system memory. (NCSC-WA-001-85)[3]

8.1 TELECOMMUNICATIONS FUNDAMENTALS

Data communications is the transmission and reception of data, often including operations such as *coding*, *decoding*, and *validating* the data.[4] The technology employed is *telecommunications*, or the transmission of signals over some distance (such as by telephone, telegraph, radio or television). The facility by which data communications is accomplished over long distance is the public (or private) *communications network*. The equipment used includes *transmission lines* and equipment, *terminals*, *modems* (signal converters), *control units*, and *computers*. The set of *rules*, *requirements*, *sequences*, and *procedures* for transmitting information between stations in a telecommunications network is known as a *protocol*.

8.1.1 Transmission Media

In this subsection, we review in outline form the types of transmission media and the features of each, in terms of:

- Transmission technologies
- Bandwidth
- Connectivity potential
- Geographical scope
- Noise immunity
- Security
- Applications
- Relative cost

The material is presented in point form. Caution is appropriate in this area, as new developments in communication technologies can dramatically alter cost and other medium characteristics. For example, the Government of Canada has committed to an "MSAT" project that will support satellite communication in the geographically large and sparsely populated Canadian North. Ground stations to receive from the MSAT satellite are more than an order of magnitude smaller and much more than an order of magnitude less costly than those for current satellites. Such changes in cost factors will allow individual vehicles to maintain full computer, voice, and (at a higher cost) video links, thus dramatically altering communications in an area where microwave and long-distance radio have been the only options.

---

[3]Mathematically, a worm is difficult to distinguish from a virus, and a communications network cannot be distinguished from the "network" formed by the buses inside a computer (unless the network includes workstations with independent processing capability, such as microcomputers). Colloquially, a virus alters other "programs" and a worm does not; however, mathematically the environment (sequence of bits in the address space) in which a worm moves is a "program." A virus does not propagate by itself and it modifies other programs; the lack of independence may offer a mathematically definable difference between virus and worm. The physical implementation of a network implies very different countermeasures for a worm than for a virus.

A worm or virus need not be malicious code, contrary to media representations in the late 1980s and early 1990s.

[4]Note the use of *coding* (for example, ASCII coding to represent characters) rather than encryption or enciphering, to create ciphertext from plaintext.

Twisted Pair

The common telephone link is twisted pair, two copper wires. While not ideal, especially for computer links, twisted pair is typically available in all office buildings and reliably supports LANs at up to 1 or 2 megabits per second. Characteristics include:

- Transmission technologies: analog or digital; variety of signal techniques (AM, FM, PM, PCM)
- Bandwidth: Depends on distance, signalling technique, quality of wire pair; up to 1 or 2 megabits; typically 64K bps for PABX
- Connectivity potential: point-to-point and multipoint
- Geographic scope: to 10 miles (16km)
- Noise immunity: variable; can be excellent but typically poor
- Security: poor, easy to tap into and to insert into; better than any broadcast medium
- Applications: PABX, Star networks, Multidrop terminals, some LAN bus networks
- Relative cost: low

Cable Bus

Cable bus technology is found most commonly in cable television systems and higher-speed network links. The basics are:

- Typically Frequency Division Multiplexing of cable bandwidth (CATV 6 MHz, each channel may be further sub-divided)
- Head-end required with inbound and outbound channels (networks or other two-way systems) (two cables, or split frequency bands on same cable; *head-end* performs collision detection and injects external signals)
- Transmission technologies: *baseband* (digital transmission, bit serial, several coding methods, TDM only); *broadband* (Modulated; incoming and outgoing channels; TDM and FDM)
- Bandwidth: *baseband* 3-10 Mbps (to 50 Mbps over short distances); *broadband* 150 Mbps total, usually split (for example into 6 MHz TV channels)
- Connectivity potential: point-to-point and multipoint, can be extended with repeaters
- Geographical scope: *baseband* 1 mile (1.6km); *broadband* approximately 7 miles (11 km)
- Noise immunity: typical *baseband* 50-60 db; typical *broadband* 85-100 db
- Security: difficult to tap without detection, typically impractical to monitor without a tap
- Applications: *baseband*, multidrop signal devices; *broadband*, mixed mode (digital, video, voice)
- Relative cost: twisted pair < coax < fiber optics (depending on distance and subject to change as fiber optics and optoelectronics become more common)

Fiber Optics

- Transmission technologies: typically *baseband*
- Bandwidth: up to 50 Mbps over 10 km
- Connectivity potential: mostly point-to-point but multidrop systems being installed

- Geographical scope: 5-10 miles (8-16 km) without repeaters; essentially unlimited with repeaters
- Noise immunity: unaffected by electromagnetic interference and noise
- Security: excellent (extremely difficult to install undetected tap, essentially impossible to monitor without a tap)
- Applications: transatlantic cables, telephone systems converting, high-capacity local networks of various descriptions
- Relative cost: high relative to twisted pair or coax, but changing with volume production and new developments

(Packet) Radio

- Transmission technologies: spread spectrum signalling techniques
- Bandwidth: typically a few MHz to achieve 200+ Kbps data rate
- Connectivity potential: point-to-point and broadcast
- Geographical scope: tens of miles (limited by Earth curvature to around 70 miles [110 km])
- Noise immunity: varied, generally poor
- Security: not secure unless encryption methods used
- Applications: mobile terminals, cellular telephone
- Relative cost: high but dropping

Infrared (light wave)

There is potential for higher bandwidth using other light frequencies such as ultraviolet. As solid-state lasers are improved for optical fiber applications this technology drops dramatically in price and bulk, etc. of the units. For example, some Hewlett-Packard calculators now communicate with hand-held printers this way.

- Transmission technologies: short pulse with high peak power modulation techniques
- Bandwidth: 10-100 Kbps over 10 miles (16 km), 1.5 Mbps over 1 mile (1.6km)
- Connectivity potential: line of sight (point-to-point), multipoint (reflected) within a room
- Geographical scope: average 1 mile (1.6 km) for high bandwidth, practical maximum 10-20 miles (16-32 km)
- Noise immunity: unaffected by EMI and noise
- Security: as for any broadcast method, none
- Applications: point-to-point, multipoint within a room (specialized uses for portable computer computer-to-peripheral, controls for consumer electronics, communication between portable equipment inside, for example, a warehouse
- Relative cost: high for data communications, low for consumer applications

Figures 8.1 and 8.2 illustrate relative costs for penetration of various technologies, and the use of broadcast *versus* point-to-point methods in complex networks and resulting exposures.

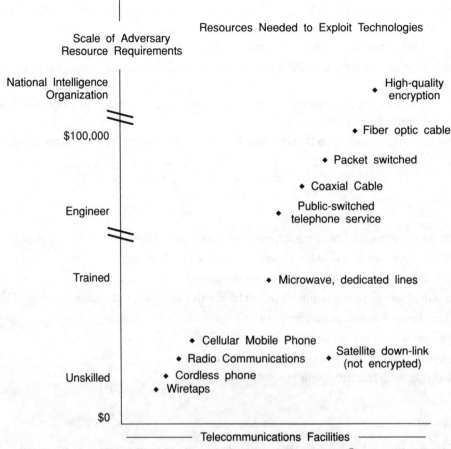

Figure 8.1. Relative Costs of Penetration Efforts[5]

8.1.2 Protocols

The following functions are expected of a transmission facility:

- *Framing*: Delimits data
- *Addressing*: Identifies source and destination of the message
- *Synchronization*: Coordinates state of sender and receiver, ensuring correct data transfer and reception
- *Data Transfer*: Actual transfer of information from sender to receiver, after the above functions have been performed
- *Flow Control*: A mechanism to prevent transmission faster than it can be received

Protocol is a generic term meaning "rules or procedures of operation." The parameters of network transmission protocol are:

- Line directional characteristics
- Line speed

---

[5]This graph is adapted from one published by the U.S. Congress Office of Technology Assessment in *Defending Secrets, Sharing Data*, OTA-CIT-310-1987, 1987.

Vulnerabilities of Telecommunications Facilities

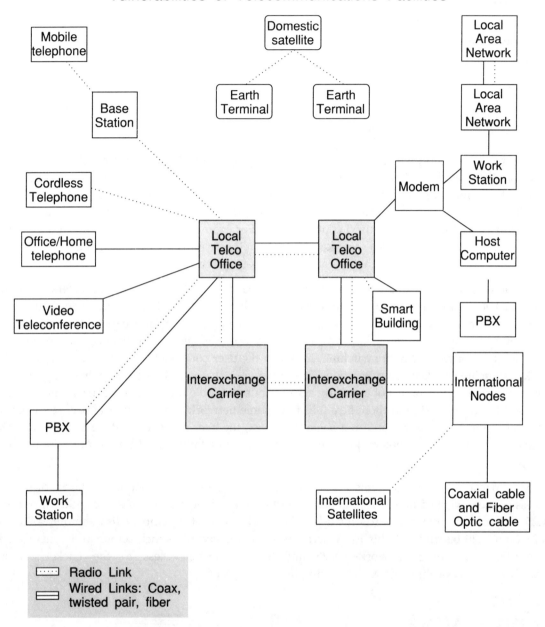

Figure 8.2. Telecommunications Vulnerability[6]

- Message control and code conventions

Protocols for terminal-to-computer systems include:

- Modem control
- Synchronization characters

---

[6]This diagram is from the U.S. Congress Office of Technology Assessment, *Defending Secrets, Sharing Data*, OTA-CIT-310-1987, 1987.

- Message identifiers
- Message block terminators
- Line control
- Error-handling procedures
- Termination procedures

8.1.3 Switching: Circuit, Packet

Circuit switching is simply the connection of two communicating devices over a circuit that is established between them. Typically the circuit is dedicated to that communications task during the term of the connection. This results in two problems: There are physical limits on the number of circuits and the communication system is subject to overload; and considerable capacity is wasted as typical links are not used continuously. (For example, the capacity of a circuit is dedicated even while a user decides what key to press on the terminal, during which time there is no communication). One solution that has arisen is packet switching.

In *packet switching*, data are assembled into packets, typically up to 1,024 characters in length. Each packet contains packet control information such as length and origination/destination addresses. The packet-switching network includes sophisticated computer capability to determine the routing to apply to each packet so as to optimize both the network utilization and response to the user. In contrast to circuit switching, in which the user controls the entire connection length, packet switching makes use of portions of the network that could be monopolized by the user even though that portion is not currently active. Thus available transmission capacity is far better utilized. In addition, should there be a failure in some network component, the packet-switching controller normally will re-route the packet; at most, the user notes a slight delay; normally the user is unaware of any problem. In circuit switching such a failure could disconnect the user entirely.

Most packet-switching systems support the CCITT X.25 protocol, a set of standards for public-access packet-switched networks. Numerous public and private networks worldwide support the X.25 protocol. Related standards include X.3 covering packet assembly/disassembly, X.20 and X.21 (and X.20 bis and X.21 bis for V-series modems) covering asynchronous and synchronous connections to public networks, X.28 and X.29 covering access to the Packet Assembly/Disassembly facility, and X.75 covering internetwork links.

8.2 TYPES OF ATTACK

In this chapter we look at attacks specifically directed at telecommunications systems. Chapter 2 overlaps these somewhat, as encryption, security, and telecommunications are inextricably intertwined. Other attacks are discussed throughout this book, particularly in Chapters 7 and 12.

There are two fundamental types of attack: passive and active. In a passive attack on a telecommunications system, an objective is to avoid detection of the attack. Techniques are restricted to things like eavesdropping and traffic analysis. An active attack involves actually inserting something into the communication stream, or removing or altering something. In a real situation, some combination of passive and active techniques is likely.

8.2.1 Passive: Disclosure, Traffic Analysis, Addition/removal of Nodes

A passive attack on a telecommunications system by definition is restricted to observation or other methods that do not alter the data within the system. Examples include eavesdropping by means of wiretaps, disclosure by observation of a VDT display, and traffic analysis.[7]

Addition of a node to a network may be passive in the sense that it permits the network's data flow to be intercepted without any effect on the data in the network. An action is required to add a node, and in this sense the attack is active. Once a node is added to a network, something like a covert channel has been created. Network information can be analyzed at will once it is intercepted by the node.

Eavesdropping may involve any of many forms of tapping into a channel. The method used varies depending on the type of communication medium, the access to transmission lines and the signal being transmitted.

For twisted-pair transmission, a simple loop of wire around the cabling will pick up magnetic impulses that can be relayed to an analysis unit. The technology involved is very simple and inexpensive. Protection involves encryption, or physical control of access to the cabling. One important element is to control access to cabling within the building or local environment. If the signal leaves the environment subject to physical access control, security is not possible without encryption; the user has no control over the switch paths a public carrier may use. Perhaps paradoxically, this may increase *effective* security, as a penetrator also has no control over what lines are used from time to time and thus which to attack.

Signals transmitted through coaxial cable are much more difficult to intercept. Emissions from the cabling are very low, and a tap involves actually breaking the cable and installing something. Such an action is much easier to detect than the simple placement of a detector near a twisted-pair line. Protection is achieved by physical control over access to the cabling, and continuous electronic monitoring to ensure that characteristics of the cable do not change, possibly reflecting installation of a tap.

Use of fiber optic cable significantly increases resistance of a network to eavesdropping. Not only is it necessary to break the cable to install a tap, as it is with coaxial cable; it also is difficult and requires specialized equipment both to install a tap and to make use of the intercepted signal. Since signals in fiber optic cabling are in the form of laser light pulses, electromagnetic emissions that might be used to tap the line are essentially nonexistent.

Any signal that is transmitted through the air (broadcast), even if on a tight beam, is susceptible to detection and eavesdropping, often from a considerable distance. The directional qualities of various types of antennae and frequencies vary, but all are subject to spreading (lasers and masers the least susceptible). All that is usually needed to eavesdrop on a broadcast signal is a radio receiver of the proper frequency and modulation, and an antenna somewhere within the beam being broadcast. Scanning radios that may monitor hundreds or thousands of frequencies are commonly available from retail outlets. There is little sign to the transmitter that any eavesdropping occurs, and the signal may be recorded and processed at will without further effect on the network. Use of unusual frequencies or modulation techniques may increase the penetrator's work factor, but only high-quality encryption can be considered an effective protection.

---

[7]See also Chapter 2 for discussion of traffic analysis and padding.

In *traffic analysis*, a penetrator may not even need to know the contents of the data in the network; the interest is in who sent to whom, and when. For example, an accounting manager for a local firm who has regular telephone contact with Swiss banks and with known bookies is a potential security risk. No information on message content is needed. Similarly, encrypted messages to known destinations may result in specific events; traffic analysis may determine who sent the messages that caused the events. (See also covert channels, below.) Traffic analysis may be defeated by sending encrypted messages to the same destinations under precise schedules so that the penetrator cannot tell which message (if any) led to a sequence of events. This clearly works only when the number of originators and destinations is fixed and small.

8.2.2 Active: Modification, Insertion, Deletion, Reordering, Replay

Active attacks on networks are those in which data within the network is altered. Alteration could be by modifying existing data, inserting new data, deleting existing data, reordering certain existing data, or replaying a legitimate signal more than the number of times the network expected it.

Attacks such as spoofing involve this sort of penetration. For example, a legitimate user's log-on sequence could be modified to connect another user simultaneously, a legitimate log-on sequence could be replayed by a penetrator, a session-end command could be deleted, a session-end command could be switched with an inserted log-on sequence, or a log-on sequence could be inserted into an established link.

A *playback* attack occurs when something is recorded and then played back into the process for which it was intended. Examples could include sign-on information or access-control information. This is more common in a network than inside a stand-alone computer.

Protection against active attacks involves the standard trio of prevention, detection, and reaction. Access controls and physical controls make it more difficult for a penetrator to insert things into the network, as does use of coaxial cable or fiber optics. Various forms of encryption and authentication make it more difficult for a penetrator to modify or insert data successfully. Time stamps and cryptographic checksums increase the work factor for replays, reordering, and deletion.

8.2.3 Denial of Service

Denial of service is inherently an active method of attack. Denial of service can relate to an individual link—even something as crude as physically cutting wires—or to any larger subset of a network, up to the entire telecommunications system.

Several examples of denial of service were noticed in 1988 and 1989 when instances of malicious code clogged various electronic networks. The InterNet example of November, 1988 may be the best known; a perpetrator introduced a worm program into the InterNet network and the actions of the program in attempting to spread as widely as possible brought numerous nodes to a halt by filling up available storage. Other nodes were subjected to denial as a consequence of coping behaviors when security personnel closed off gateways to the network to stop copies of the worm from attacking (and reproducing) again. Variations of this worm continue to appear from time to time.[8]

---

[8]The InterNet worm was the creation of Robert T. Morris, Jr., then a graduate student at Cornell University. Other examples include the WANK worm and the SPAN worm, both on DEC networks rather than InterNet.

Much less sophisticated programs appear in electronic mail systems from time to time; although not critical now, they seriously clogged worldwide networks when first encountered.[9]

There is no perfect defense against such malicious software. The Computer Emergency Response Team (CERT) set up following the InterNet attack, combined with active monitoring by network managers aware of potential problems, has led to a much lower risk than existed prior to 1988. Various methods of minimizing exposure to malicious code, mostly administrative, lower the risk to an acceptable level. Backups and similar administrative procedures permit recovery in the event of an attack.

Denial of service can be an unintentional side effect of other activities. Telecommunications networks have sufficient capacity to handle only a certain load; during disasters, or even on certain holidays in the case of the telephone system, demand for the service exceeds capacity and denial results. The only protection against this sort of denial is provision of alternate telecommunications capability, or greater capacity. Priority schemes and delay methods may be employed by some networks to contain the problem and ensure communication of highest priority can "bump" others.

In February, 1990, an unexpected software problem in a new switching system caused AT&T to lose most of its long-distance telephone capability for several hours. Ironically, the problem showed up precisely in the alternate path arrangements.

Physical problems such as fire or other events at switching centers have denied access to telephone and data communications services. The largest example to 1990 was the May 1988 fire at the Illinois Bell Central office in Hinsdale, which caused denial of service or serious disruption to hundreds of thousands of voice and data communications lines. Full service was not restored to all customers for as long as 30 days. Defense against this sort of problem involves alternate pathways through networks or other forms of alternate capability, and of course physical and administrative measures for fire prevention, detection, and protection.

Other physical problems that can cause denial of service include various phenomena such as sunspot cycles in the sun. Resulting magnetic and radio interference can seriously impact satellite or other communications links, and the magnetic phenomena have been strong enough to cause widespread power outages. A similar denial can be caused by Electromagnetic Pulse (EMP), an extremely powerful burst of electromagnetic noise caused by detonation of a nuclear explosive or other device designed to generate EMP. TEMPEST grade shielding will protect computer and telecommunications systems from EMP, although broadcast communications will be interrupted. The same level of shielding will minimize problems with other natural phenomena, again with the proviso that broadcast channels may be unusable for the duration of the phenomenon.

8.2.4 Covert Channels

A *covert channel* refers to a way of communicating information that is not intended for such communication. For example, a program might gain access to the value of some classified variable, and cause a loop to repeat a number of times based on the value of that variable. The running time of the program or process then could indicate the value of the classified variable. Similarly, the movement of a tape drive motor or disk drive might be affected, with a consequent (small) ef-

---

[9]The CHRISTMA EXEC and several variations are more-or-less chain letters in electronic mail systems, and can lead to denial of service if run by unsuspecting users.

fect on electrical power demand. Such effect might be measurable from a remote location, thus communicating something covertly along a channel not intended for communication.[10]

A covert channel is a combination of passive and active methods: Something actively causes changes in the channel, but the action of reading the channel is passive in relation to the system under attack. If the process that causes a change to the channel is part of the normal information system operation, the covert channel attack may be entirely passive. Traffic analysis, described earlier, is a form of covert channel attack that is entirely passive.

It is possible to design sophisticated schemes that would pass significant amounts of information along covert channels. There probably is no practical method of controlling all possible covert channels. Control of access to such data as precise power usage and to the facility itself may make the problem of reading the covert channel information more difficult.

8.3 ELECTRONIC EMISSIONS AND TEMPEST

Information systems employing electrical and electronic devices are exposed to several security risks, both accidental and intentional. These include:

- Power disruptions (see section 13.3)
- Noise and other RFI (Radio Frequency Interference, including EMP)
- Emanations

The security professional must be aware that even relatively simple electrical and electronic equipment is subject to emanation risks. Even an electric typewriter generates signals that can be detected at a distance and processed to determine which keys have been activated. Telephone taps are legion and must be considered common knowledge. Personal computers generate signals that visibly interfere with reception of broadcast television; these signals can be detected and processed to reveal what is going on inside the processor. "Dumb terminals" are television monitors that may be eavesdropped upon. Any telecommunications facility that broadcasts a signal is susceptible to interception of the signal.

In many cases, the equipment necessary to perform such electronic eavesdropping is quite simple and inexpensive. A simple microwave receiver within several kilometers of a satellite downlink will detect, and possibly record for later processing, signals sent via satellite to any user of the receiving station. Satellite television dishes can be purchased for less than $2,000, illustrating the easy availability of complete systems for intercepting and processing satellite signals. In other instances, for example with lasers broadcast into air, interception and processing is much more difficult. Any signal broadcast can be considered secure only when effective use is made of high-quality encryption.

Signals that emanate from equipment during the normal course of operation also may be detected and processed. In the case of the electric typewriter, the keys activated can be determined. Even if well-shielded, the power-supply line may show detectable variations that can be processed to show keyboard activity. Similar variations may be exploited to serve as a covert channel in computer systems, for example with the power demand of a tape drive starting and stopping serving to indicate code bits as a program causes the tape to be read from written to. The solution

---

[10]The brief discussion of covert channels in Chapter 7 concentrated on channels internal to the computer; in this chapter the emphasis is on telecommunications, so channels outside the computer are the focus.

to such problems, and also to problems with things like RFI causing "soft" failures of a computer processor, is found in shielding.

Electromagnetic shielding for RFI, incoming or outgoing, is relatively straightforward. For mainframe systems a computer room may have shielding in the floors and walls, interrupters on such potential antennae as water pipes (sprinkler system) and power lines, and similar measures. Work stations may be shielded (although few are) by surrounding the emitting portions with grounded conductors. Filters on power lines and uninterruptible power supplies that isolate the computer or device from direct links to outside power minimize exposure to incoming or outgoing problems.

Details of such shielding are outside the scope of this manual; they are available from any good electronic handbook. The security professional must be aware of the need for such shielding, and that it is critical to pay attention to details to ensure that shielding is not compromised. Specialists may be engaged to "sweep" areas to determine the presence of emanations.

The United States government has a program that assigns a "tempest rating" to devices, dependent on the level of emissions from the device. Details of the TEMPEST program are not readily available, as information about the exact vulnerability and emissions levels of various devices is considered sensitive.

8.4 COMMUNICATIONS

8.4.1 Value-added communications

Value-added communications refers to the product of a telecommunications company that obtains communications capability and then *adds value*, for example in the form of easier access, error correction, sharing or gateways to many information services, and so forth. Simply obtaining high-speed access such as a satellite channel "wholesale" and offering it at "retail" to many people who otherwise could not use such capability is of value all by itself.

Examples of value-added networks include Datapac in Canada, iNet 2000 in Canada and the United States, Tymnet and Telenet in the United States, Janet in the United Kingdom, EARN (European Academic Research Network) in Europe, and others. Commercial services offer electronic mail and other communications, and access to everything from shopping to airline schedules, libraries, newspapers, and no doubt other things between the time this sentence is written and this book is published. (There were over 3,000 value-added networks as of January, 1990—probably *many* more than 3000—many international or world-wide in scope.)

8.4.2 ISO OSI Communications Standard

The *physical* characteristics of transmission devices and media serve both to limit and to enhance our ability to communicate via digital, voice, and video means. *Baseband* (unmodulated) transmission is that which we take for granted as the computer-to-peripheral communication technology, and its use is limited to transmission of *digital* data (as with fiber optic transmission). *Broadband* technology is more difficult to implement and control in a changing environment and is more costly, yet it serves as a means of handling all voice, television, and digital data requirements.

Development efforts of the 1980s and 1990s mostly have been concentrated on the *International Standards Organization/Open System Interconnection* (ISO/OSI) "Universal" communications facility, with the greatest difficulties encountered at the third and fourth network layer, and the Transmission Control Protocol (TCP) the most used *de facto* "standard" implementation.

The International Standards Organization (ISO) was founded in 1946 with 25 charter member countries. Today, it is headquartered in Geneva, Switzerland and is comprised of the national standards bodies of 89 countries. The ISO has had working groups looking at the area of communications standards for many years.

For ease of reference, the table in Figure 8.3 summarizes the seven layers:

1. Physical
2. Data Link
3. Network
4. Transport
5. Session
6. Presentation
7. Application

The seven layers usually are considered in two functional groups, the "Application Service Platform" (layers 5 to 7) and the "Transport Service Platform" (layers 1 to 4). The Transport Service Platform's function is to get error-free data from one system to another; the Application Service Platform's role is to interpret the stream of bits and present it to the user in a form that makes sense to the user.

These layers are illustrated pictorially in Figure 8.4.

8.4.3 ISO/OSI Security Protocols

In 1989, the second part of the ISO/OSI standards was published, the security standards in 7498-2. It is not appropriate to reproduce the entire standard here, but information security practitioners should know what is in 7498-2 and are recommended to the standard itself for details. Here we outline the security services and security mechanisms included in the OSI architecture, and their relation to one another and to the seven layers of the OSI standard.

Layer	Name	Purpose
1	Physical	Transmission of the bit stream to the transmission medium
2	Data Link	Transfer of units of information to the other end of a physical link, responsible for data integrity between nodes
3	Network	Switching and routing of information
4	Transport	End-to-end data integrity and quality of service; assembles and disassembles data packets for Layer 3
5	Session	Coordination of interaction between end-application processes; English language translated into network technology
6	Presentation	Code conversion and data formatting; terminal standards, display rules
7	Application	Application and information content displayed in Layer 6

Figure 8.3. ISO Reference Model for Open Systems Interconnection (OSI)

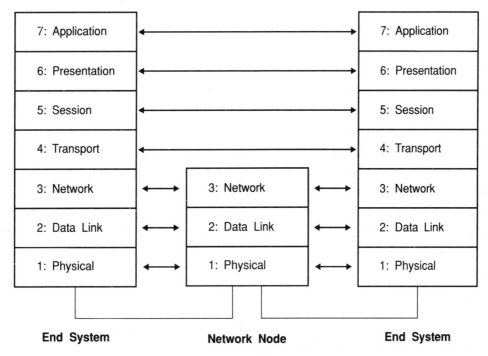

Figure 8.4. ISO/OSI Open Systems Interconnect

Security Services

These are basic security services. In practice, they will be provided by mechanisms that may cover several services, and their location in the framework will vary from installation to installation. There are five groups of services, with sub-classifications in some:

1. Authentication, including:
    *   Peer entity authentication
    *   Data origin Authentication
2. Access control
3. Data confidentiality, including:
    *   Connection confidentiality
    *   Connectionless confidentiality
    *   Selective field confidentiality
    *   Traffic flow confidentiality
4. Data Integrity, including:
    *   Connection integrity with recovery
    *   Connection integrity without recovery
    *   Selective field connection integrity
    *   Connectionless integrity
    *   Selective field connectionless integrity
5. Non-repudiation, including:
    *   Non-repudiation with proof of origin

- Non-repudiation with proof of delivery

Security Mechanisms

Eight mechanisms are defined that may be incorporated into the appropriate layer(s) to provide the services listed previously:

1. Encipherment (see Chapter 2)
2. Digital signature mechanisms
3. Access control mechanisms (see Chapter 1)
4. Data integrity mechanisms
5. Authentication exchange mechanism
6. Traffic padding mechanism (see Chapter 2 and elsewhere in this chapter)
7. Routing control mechanism
8. Notarization mechanism

Pervasive Security Mechanisms

Five mechanisms are classed as "pervasive security mechanisms," those which are not specific to any particular service within the OSI framework:

1. Trusted functionality (described in several places in this book)
2. Security labels
3. Event detection (mechanisms to detect security violations, for example specific security violations, a specific selected event, an overflow on a count of the number of occurrences, and similar events)
4. Security audit trail
5. Security recovery (actions taken to restore or maintain security, as contrasted with continuity planning)

The relationship between services and mechanisms is illustrated in Figure 8.5.

In Figure 8.6, all services are indicated with a "Y" for layer seven, the Application Layer. It is expected that applications (such as operating systems, for example) will provide some security measures themselves. Such application-provided measures are outside the scope of 7498-2.

8.4.4 Integrated Services Digital Network (ISDN)

ISDN is a network architecture that uses digital technology to support integrated services using twisted-pair telephone lines. ISDN is highly compatible with ISO/OSI. The principle is that all communication services currently available will be available not from separate circuits but from a single plug in the wall. Such services include voice telephone, circuit- and packet-switched data communications, switched and non-switched circuits, text messaging services, and facsimile. Proposed uses include voice mail, combined voice and data transmission on one line, caller identification, in-progress statistics such as time and cost, and call-forwarding. Integration will permit such other applications as home telemetry (for example, for security systems and environmental control). New uses no doubt will be invented as the service becomes available; still-frame video combined with simultaneous voice and data communications has been demonstrated, for example.

Other advantages include relative freedom from noise and interference due to the digital signal, and access to many different services through a single line and a small number of interfaces.

Standards for ISDN from CCITT are the I- series of standards. ISDN occupies the lowest three layers of the ISO/OSI framework, Physical, Data Link, and Network.

The future of ISDN is debatable at this writing. The most probable developments appear to be numerous private ISDN installations, linking through the major public networks' ISDN support. More general public access likely will be an evolutionary process, with major urban centers having the first such access and a slow migration to smaller centers. There are potential political and social problems; for example, there is an issue of privacy in caller identification *versus* unlisted telephone numbers.

8.4.5 IEEE 802

The Institute of Electrical and Electronic Engineers (IEEE) instituted Project 802 in February, 1980 to define standards for local area networks. IEEE 802 consists of six standards:

- 802.1, Defining the relationship to ISO/OSI
- 802.2, Defining *logical link control*
- 802.3, CSMA/CD access
- 802.4, Token bus access
- 802.5, Token ring access
- 802.6, Metropolitan Area Network Access

Service	Encipherment	Digital Signature	Access Control	Data Integrity	Authentication Exchange	Traffic Padding	Routing Control	Notarization
Peer Entity Authentication	Y	Y	•	•	Y	•	•	•
Data Origin Authentication	Y	Y	•	•	•	•	•	•
Access Control Service	•	•	Y	•	•	•	•	•
Connection Confidentiality	Y	•	•	•	•	•	Y	•
Connectionless Confidentiality	Y	•	•	•	•	•	Y	•
Selective Field Confidentiality	Y	•	•	•	•	•	•	•
Traffic Flow Confidentiality	Y	•	•	•	•	Y	Y	•
Connection Integrity with Recovery	Y	•	•	Y	•	•	•	•
Connection Integrity without Recovery	Y	•	•	Y	•	•	•	•
Selective Field Connection Integrity	Y	•	•	Y	•	•	•	•
Connectionless Integrity	Y	Y	•	Y	•	•	•	•
Selective Field Connectionless Integrity	Y	Y	•	Y	•	•	•	•
Non-Repudiation, Origin	•	Y	•	Y	•	•	•	Y
Non-Repudiation, Delivery	•	Y	•	Y	•	•	•	Y

Y Yes, the mechanism is considered to be appropriate, either on its own or in combination with other mechanisms.

• The mechanism is considered not to be appropriate.

Figure 8.5. Relation Between Services and Mechanisms

Service / Layer	Physical Layer	Data Link Layer	Network Layer	Transport Layer	Presentation Layer	Traffic Padding	Application Layer
Peer Entity Authentication	•	•	Y	Y	•	•	Y
Data Origin Authentication	•	•	Y	Y	•	•	Y
Access Control Service	•	•	Y	Y	•	•	Y
Connection Confidentiality	Y	Y	Y	Y	•	•	Y
Connectionless Confidentiality	•	Y	Y	Y	•	•	Y
Selective Field Confidentiality	•	•	•	•	•	•	Y
Traffic Flow Confidentiality	Y	•	Y	•	•	•	Y
Connection Integrity with Recovery	•	•	•	Y	•	•	Y
Connection Integrity without Recovery	•	•	Y	Y	•	•	Y
Selective Field Connection Integrity	•	•	•	•	•	•	Y
Connectionless Integrity	•	•	Y	Y	•	•	Y
Selective Field Connectionless Integrity	•	•	•	•	•	•	Y
Non-Repudiation, Origin	•	•	•	•	•	•	Y
Non-Repudiation, Delivery	•	•	•	•	•	•	Y

Y   Yes, service should be incorporated for the layer as a provider option.

•   Not provided.

Figure 8.6. Relation Between Services and OSI Layers

By 1988, 802.2 through 802.5 had been approved by the IEEE Standard Board.

802.2, Logical link control

IEEE 802.2 defines protocols for one or more logical connections to a single medium. Each station attached to the medium uses a common media access method. The control procedures are similar to the CCITT X.25 protocol.

802.3, CSMA/CD access

Carrier Sense Multiple Access with Collision Detection (CSMA/CD) is addressed by IEEE 802.3.

When multiple stations are connected to a single carrier, the possibility of more than one station transmitting simultaneously exists. Such simultaneous transmission without any compensating method would result in signal interference. One method of compensating requires the station to ensure that the medium is free; this is CSMA/CA[11] (Collision *Avoidance*). Ethernet and similar specifications use CSMA/CD; collisions are detected, and measures taken to ensure that re-transmission occurs, in a time frame during which the medium is free.

---

[11]CSMA/CA is Carrier Sense Multiple Access with Collision Avoidance. In essence, no transmission is permitted unless the entire path to the destination is known to be free, and that path is monopolized during transmission. Such networks quickly become clogged at low activity levels and are not commonly seen.

Figure 8.7 summarizes essential characteristics of IEEE 802.3. Figure 8.8 illustrates the relationship between the Open Systems Interconnect layers and IEEE 802.3.

802.4, Token bus access; 802.5, Token ring access

Use of a shared medium may be coordinated by passing a *token*, conferring the right to momentarily control the network to the station receiving the token. The topology of the network is not relevant to the individual station; the token simply follows the network along whatever topology is provided. In all cases, the token passes in descending order of station address. On a ring, information is repeated and sent along by each station not possessing the token (and removed by the originating station); on a bus, the originating station momentarily takes control of the network, relinquishing control when the receiving station signals receipt of the packet of information transmitted.

The IBM token-ring LAN standard is a significant example of IEEE 802.5. Another example is Novell NetWare.

Shared Memory

An experimental technology involving LANs is the sharing of memory, as well as file servers and such devices as printers. Communication requirements are extreme, as workstation performance depends strongly on memory access time and memory access is more frequent than data file access. Problems have been encountered in sharing of memory, and in the similar technology of disk arrays (where the logical disk may reside in several physical locations).

8.5 NETWORK DESIGN

8.5.1 Design Considerations

8.5.1.1 Topology

This section compares advantages and disadvantages of the three basic network topologies (*bus, star,* and *ring*) and their variants (Figure 8.9).

	10BASE5 (standard Ethernet)	10BASE2 (thin Ethernet)	10BROAD36 (broadband Ethernet)	1BASE5 (1MB StarLAN)
Bandwidth	10 Mbps	10 Mbps	10 Mbps	1 Mbps
Media	"Thick" coaxial cable	"Thin" coaxial cable	CATV coaxial cable	Twisted-pair wire
Distance	500 meters	200 meters	3.6 km	500 meters
Topology	bus	bus	bus	star

Figure 8.7. Overview of IEEE 802.3

OSI Reference Model Layers

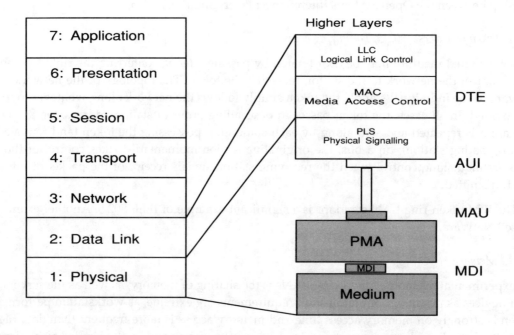

AUI: Attachment Unit Interface   MAU: Medium Attachment Interface
MDI: Medium Dependent Interface   PMA: Physical Medium Attachment

Figure 8.8. OSI Compared with IEEE 802

TOPOLOGY	ADVANTAGES	DISADVANTAGES
BUS	Passive transmission medium Localized failure impact Adaptive utilization	Channel Access techniques (Contention)
STAR	Simplicity Central routing No routing decisions	Reliability of central node Loading of central node
RING	Simplicity Predictable delay No routing decisions	Failure modes with *Global effect*: • Node failure • Token regeneration

Figure 8.9. Network Topology Comparison Table

What the table above does not show is that the primary characteristic of the bus architecture is *contention*.

The primary bus technology in use is IEEE 802.3, with a significant example being *Ethernet*. It is a contention system, and its operating mode is *Carrier Sense, Multiple Access with Collision Detection* (CSMA/CD). A very best Ethernet Local Area Network (LAN) can quickly degrade into as much as 50% retransmission for every device on the bus, for short intervals of time. So long as most of the devices are not dependent upon communication with other devices on the bus, except in a minimal way (as with output print stations), the 802.3 system is effective.

Star Networks

Star, or centralized networks, are those in which primary computing is performed at a central site, with all remote nodes linked to that central site. The nodes may themselves be terminals, intelligent work stations, or other computers.

Hierarchical Networks

Hierarchical networks are those in which computers are linked to other computers in a hierarchy, creating an essentially distributed computational facility. Hierarchies may form part of a central (star) network, or they may be interconnected in a "ring" pattern—or both.

Ring Networks

The ring network is a series of fully-connected computers or computer cluster nodes, forming a closed loop. Ring networks may be diagrammed as nodes linked to form a circle, or they may form a circle with cross-connections. With full interconnection, the ring network permits full operation of all other nodes if a node becomes inoperative.

Local Area Networks

LANs operate in proximity and are characterized by the absence of a central computer dependency. They may be configured with both intelligent and "dumb" terminals.

8.5.1.2 Integration of Countermeasures into Network Design: Cryptographic Checksum; Time Stamp

The ISO/OSI standard 7498-2, discussed in section 8.4.3, indicates where within the OSI model various security measures should be implemented. An example would be use of cryptographic checksums, which would be a mechanism usually related to authentication; this would fit at the network or transport layer.

Cryptographic checksums, time stamps, digital signatures, and similar mechanisms are addressed in Chapter 2.

8.5.1.2 Integration of countermeasures into Protocol Layers: Link-Level Encryption; End-to-End Encryption

Link-level *versus* end-to-end encryption is addressed in section 2.4. In the context of integration of countermeasures, it normally would be placed in the physical layer for full traffic flow confidentiality. Generally, encryption methods relate to the physical layer, and generally there is only one such mechanism needed in one layer. However, there are exceptions to this general rule. For instance, if a high degree of granularity is required along with non-repudiation or selective field protection, then the presentation layer probably would be appropriate. Similar considerations may lead to use of encipherment mechanisms in the transport or network layers.

Provision of encipherment is very much installation-dependent. The key decision factors are requirements for:

- Full traffic flow confidentiality (physical layer)
- High granularity and non-repudiation or selective field protection (presentation layer)
- Bulk protection of end-system to end-system communications, or use of an external encryption device (network layer)

- Integrity with recovery combined with high granularity (transport layer)

If more than one of these factors is required, encipherment in more than one layer may be appropriate.

8.5.2 Assurance

The basic elements of the TCSEC are repeated below for convenience of reference. They are covered in more detail in Chapter 7 and several other places in the book.

8.5.2.1 Concept of trust

The Trusted computing base is that portion of a computer system ". . . which contains all elements of the system responsible for supporting the security policy and supporting the isolation of objects (code and data) on which the protection is based."[12] For networks, the TCB concept has been extended to take into consideration distribution of portions of the TCB over more than one location; see 8.5.2.3 for discussion.

8.5.2.2 Degrees of trustworthiness

The TCB evaluation criteria are based on six fundamental security requirements dealing with information systems security and access control:[13]

1. There must be an explicit and well-defined security policy enforced by the system (Security Policy)
2. Access control labels must be associated with objects (Marking)
3. Individual subjects must be identified (Identification)
4. Audit information must be kept and protected so that actions affecting security can be traced to the responsible subject (Accountability)
5. The computer systems must contain hardware and software mechanisms that can be evaluated independently to provide sufficient assurance that the system enforces the security policy (Assurance)
6. The trusted mechanisms that enforce the security policy must be protected continuously against tampering and unauthorized changes (Continuous Protection)

The evaluation criteria are divided into four divisions (D, C, B, and A); divisions C, B, and A are further subdivided into classes. The range is from minimal protection in Division D to the most trustworthy class A1.

Division D: Minimal Protection

Division C: Discretionary Protection
Classes in this division provide for discretionary (need-to-know) protection and accountability of subjects and the actions they initiate, through inclusion of audit capabilities.

---

[12]Department of Defense, *Trusted Computer System Evaluation Criteria*, p. 67.

[13]The material in this section is based on Department of Defense, *Technical Rationale Behind CSC-STD-003-85: Computer Security Requirements*, CSC-STD-004-85, DoD Computer Security Center, June, 1985, and Department of Defense, *Trusted Computer System Evaluation Criteria*, DOD 5200.28.STD, Department of Defense Computer Security Center, Fort George G. Meade, Md., December, 1985.

- Class C1: Discretionary Security Protection
- Class C2: Controlled Access Protection

Division B: Mandatory Protection

The notion of a TCB that preserves the integrity of sensitivity labels and uses them to enforce a set of mandatory access control rules is a major requirement of division B. Systems in this division must carry the sensitivity labels with major data structures in the system. The system developer also provides the security policy model on which the TCB is based and furnishes a specification of the TCB. Evidence must be provided to demonstrate that the reference monitor concept has been implemented.

- Class B1: Labeled Security Protection
- Class B2: Structured Protection
- Class B3: Security Domains

Division A: Verified Protection

The critical difference between division A and division B is that formal methods are used, so that mathematical proofs may be applied to analysis.

- Class A1: Verified Design

8.5.2.3 Trusted Network Base

The TCSEC classes outlined in the previous section refer to stand-alone systems. A further document from the Department of Defense, the *Trusted Network Interpretation of the Trusted Computer System Evaluation Criteria*, addresses networks and how they may fit within the TCSEC classes.

A network must be considered as partitioned into a set of interconnected components. Each component may have a Network Trusted computing base (NTCB) *partition*, which comprises the security-relevant portions of the NTCB residing in that component. The security-relevant portions of the network as a whole form a TCB, referred to as the NTCB. The network as a whole must have a precisely specified architecture and design.

Two issues arise in networks that are less important in stand-alone systems: potentially vulnerable communications paths, and concurrent, asynchronous operation of network components.[14] The evaluation class of the network as a whole has no *a priori* relationship to the evaluation class(es) of any components. Forcing every component to satisfy a specific TCSEC requirement is neither necessary nor sufficient to ensure that the network as a whole meets that requirement. Components may not provide all of a requirement individually, yet the collection of components could do so; conversely, components may meet all requirements but the interconnections do not.

The Trusted Network Interpretation devotes over 278 pages to details of how NTCB partitions and other factors may be mapped into the TCSEC. Such detail is beyond the intent of this book, and the reader who needs to know is referred to the TNI.

---

[14]Notice that the same issues arise within a single system, particularly when a stand-alone system contains several processors. Mathematically, there is little difference between the "network" inside the box and a network distributed across a continent. Practically, communications channel exposures exist in the network that are minimal or non-existent within a stand-alone system.

The OSI Security Architecture 7498-2 discussed earlier is limited, and is not concerned with security measures needed in end systems, nor with management of security or organizational concerns, except where such issues impact on the choice and placement of services within OSI. The Trusted Network Interpretation and the TCSEC include the OSI 7498-2 standard as a proper subset.

8.5.2.4 Testing

As with any system, networks must be tested. No system can be considered secure (or fully functional) without extensive testing.

Because of the fluid nature of networks and connections, the testing problem is somewhat more difficult than with systems that reside on single machines. Except for the obvious point that security procedures must be included in system testing, there is no real difference in testing due solely to security considerations.

8.5.2.5 Formal Specification and Verification

Given a formal security policy such as the TCSEC and the Trusted Network Interpretation, a formal security model and specifications can be created. The issue of formal specifications is discussed in Chapters 12 and 16. Models are addressed in Chapter 7, and formal and informal security policies are discussed in Chapter 16.

The issue of formal verification is addressed in the TCSEC and in the Trusted Network Interpretation. Appendices A and B of the Trusted Network Interpretation deal with evaluation of network components and rational behind the NTCB (Network Trusted computing base) partitions respectively. Whether formal verification is *required* will depend on the class desired; class A requires formal procedures.

8.6 LOCUS OF ATTACK

Various points of vulnerability exist in any telecommunications network. Figure 8.2 depicts many that are common in any wide-scale network. Depending on its geographic dispersal, a LAN may share many of these points of attack, but it typically will not include radio links or public carriers.

Generally, an attack may be made at any technology employed in the network, or at the endpoints where one technology interfaces with another (for example, wiretaps along the cabling, or at the terminals where twisted pair hooks up to a PABX). Vulnerabilities relate more to the type of information within a channel and the characteristics of the channel than to any other factor. We will discuss briefly some common attacks on networks involving mainframe computers, then spend somewhat more time looking at LANs.

A typical network involving a mainframe computer includes many dumb terminals, connected through a front-end processor (FEP) to the mainframe processor. Communications tasks are handled by the FEP and processing is handled by the mainframe CPU. The typical network topology is a star.

8.6.1 Terminals

Terminals ("dumb terminals") are vulnerable to:

- hardware failure
- eavesdropping on electronic emanations
- wire taps
- modification of signals
- eavesdropping (people looking over your shoulder)
- destruction

Smart terminals or work stations (and any other device that can be programmed) share these and also much the same vulnerabilities as any other processor. Work stations may be more vulnerable than the mainframe, and thus pose an increased risk of penetration into the mainframe than a dumb terminal. Generally if any data or programs can be downloaded to a work station or personal computer, security cannot be assured if data or programs can be uploaded again unless the work station is proven to have the same security level as the mainframe. The risk is greater for data than for programs unless the host uses the same operating system as the work station (a situation that will become common in the 1990s).

8.6.2 Hosts

A host computer in a network is subject to the same list of vulnerabilities as any other computer or device that can be programmed and shares data:

- data corruption
- unauthorized access
- software failure
- hardware failure
- spoofing
- browsing
- modification
- tampering
- logic bomb
- Trojan horse[15]
- emanations
- destruction

Depending on the precise configuration, the order of these exposures may vary. Since the FEP handles communications loads, the host is not directly exposed to things like improper use of tones and codes that may impact the telephone or switching system. Data corruption is the most likely risk in nearly any processor for the simple reason that human entry of data can lead to data corruption by error, by far the most common cause of problems with information systems.

8.6.3 Front-End Processors

The front-end processor (FEP or FECP) is a computer that is optimized for handling the communication load. Typically the FEP will handle many incoming lines, multiplexing signals appro-

---

-alone system.

[15]A virus or worm is either a logic bomb or Trojan horse in this context.

priately for transfer to the host along a channel.[16]

If the FEP can be programmed by an incoming signal, it is subject to the same exposures as the host in addition to an increased exposure to spoofing and unauthorized access. A reasonably secure FEP cannot be programmed by any signal coming in through remote communication lines, but must be altered using special means.

Because the FEP deals with many (perhaps many thousands of) terminals, it is subject to denial of service. It may be subject to the usual problems with software and hardware failure, as well as to spoofing and malicious code; this depends on the capabilities of the FEP.

8.6.4 Gateways

A gateway is the link into a telecommunications facility from the FEP, or from the LAN if such is involved. For mainframe-based telecommunications, the gateway is the FEP. For LANs the gateway is likely to be a modem or other fairly simple device that cannot be programmed.

Most gateways are vulnerable to one or more control codes. These are sequences of signals that are recognized by the gateway to have special meanings, such as "end of packet" or "end of line." There are no general rules other than to be aware that device control codes may constitute a security exposure.

A more complete list would include:

- hardware failure
- emanations
- wire tap
- modification
- eavesdropping
- destruction

Depending on the topology of the network, hardware failure will remove at least one device and perhaps an entire sub-network from access to the host. Emanations and wiretaps are significant because the gateway inevitably has connections between two or more dissimilar systems, thus exposing more links and also more than one system.

8.6.5 Links

The links between elements of a network are exposed to passive and active communications attacks. Characteristics of twisted pair, coaxial cable, packet-switched, optical fiber, and radio links were discussed in section 8.1.

8.6.6 Local Area Networks (LANs)

A LAN offers much the same exposures as any other network with the same topology and physical characteristics. In a mathematical analysis, there is little difference between a "computer system" entirely contained in a single enclosure (such as a multi-CPU parallel processor) and a

---

[16]"Channel" here means a specialized communications link within a mainframe computer configuration, not the general term used so far. Channels handle data transfer between the host and disk drives, databases, communications, and other peripheral devices.

"computer system" spread over any distance. Physical concerns like signal delay times and bandwidth of communication channels imply significant practical differences but do not affect the mathematical analysis. Some exposures and protections are discussed below.

The exposures are characteristic of *devices* such as VDTs, work stations, controllers and servers, gateways, printers, and database managers. The *topology* of the network affects only how signals are shared among devices; for example, tokens are seen by every network device in a token ring network, and thus susceptible to interception, *etc.*, at every node; in a star this exposure is present only at the central node. The characteristics of links between devices determine the physical exposures; for example, short high-speed links like a bus internal to a box are less vulnerable than several hundred meters of coaxial cable linking equivalent units in a LAN. The character of data in the links has an effect, which is controlled by encryption and the inherent sensitivity of the data.

Exposures related to VDTs or terminals, links, and gateways differ little between WANs and LANs. Because a LAN almost always involves work stations and microcomputers, because the physical situation of a LAN typically is far less controlled than access to a mainframe, and because retail products are involved, we look briefly at device-dependent exposures.

Printers

Printers are subject to:

- unauthorized access
- hardware failure
- destruction
- wiretaps
- emanations
- Trojan horses

In a mainframe, access to the printer and to its paper production typically is controlled by a staff and physical access controls. In a LAN environment, such access normally is almost uncontrolled. Thus the printer is subject to the wrong person picking up output. Since printers have moving parts, hardware failure is common relative to other system components like computer chips. Like all other devices, printers emit electromagnetic signals during operation, and wiretaps and other eavesdropping methods may present an exposure.

The last item, Trojan horse, deserves some explanation. Some printers typically connected to LANs are driven by their own microcomputer chips, and may contain printer control languages of various sorts. Any printer on a LAN is a shared device. A printer that supports PostScript or other page description language, or that is programmable on its own, is a device in a shared environment that permits programming, and thus is exposed to the same sorts of malicious code as any other processor.[17] This exposure commonly is overlooked or not understood.

---

[17]For example, a LAN may have a laser printer with a 68000 chip, several megabytes of RAM, and dozens or hundreds of megabytes of disk storage for downloadable fonts and print files. This easily could be the most powerful single device on the LAN. Research has demonstrated that virus code can be created using some printer control languages.

Databases

Issues of database security, including things like inference controls, are addressed in somewhat more detail in Chapters 2, 5, and 12.

In a LAN environment, the most likely exposures of databases are:

- data corruption
- software failure (the DBMS software, usually)
- unauthorized access
- hardware failure
- browsing
- spoofing
- wiretap
- modification
- tampering
- destruction

The only effect of topology on database exposure would be if the database is distributed across several devices; then the tokens or other data transmissions are subject to the same kinds of risks as any other communication.

Exposure of a database or other storage of data in an information system is always greatest to corruption of data, since simple human error is most common and may lead to data corruption. On a LAN, exposure to unauthorized access increases, since the database is on a portable medium, possibly even a diskette that will fit into a shirt pocket or purse. Also, the typical DBMS for a personal computer provides no security facility, thus any access control is the responsibility of the network server as configured by the network manager. Again, the manager is human and all too prone to error in assigning capabilities.

In the following figures the exposures shown for the work stations and for the network server/controller differ, although both usually are programmable computers. Although the server may be physically identical, or nearly identical, to any other work station, the fact that there is but one server per network segment and it normally is subject to closer physical control alters the ordering of risks. (In fact, in many networks risks to the server may be much lower, since the server may not even have a keyboard or monitor attached if it is not normally used as a workstation.)

Bus Network

A bus network is essentially a line to which devices are attached. A signal intended for any device is sent with an address code; devices between the bus head and the intended recipient have access to the signal. On average, signals are read by half of the nodes on the network; however, this average may be misleading as the exposure between any two devices is constant so long as the devices in the path between the bus head and originator are on-line. Loss of a device such as a work station has little effect on other devices. Loss of the bus head or network server means the network is not usable. The bus may gate into other bus (or other topology) networks. Usually, such gateways are relatively simple and do not support significant distributed processing. As noted above, the most common bus protocol IEEE-802.3 is a CSMA/CD; insertion of spurious signals, or higher-than-normal loads, very rapidly can overload the capability of the bus to handle the signals and bring the network to an effective halt.

Control of exposures (Figure 8.10) involves administrative measures, such as personnel clearances and various logs, and technical measures, such as emanation shielding (TEMPEST standards, for example). Control of exposure for devices is the same as for the same device installed anywhere else. The only significant difference is that any device attached to the network must have a card that handles network communication, and this card may be subject to tampering or other alterations, which must be controlled via administrative measures.

The network as a whole may be enclosed in a security-high zone;[18] Figure 8.11 shows two such zones, one for each network segment. Effective encryption of communications is essential for signals that pass through the gateways, unless the link(s) between the two can be shielded to the same standards as the rest of the network. Examples of such controls could include underground bunkers or aircraft, where administrative controls offer a high degree of assurance that personnel are acceptable, and the secure perimeter is relatively easy to set up and extremely difficult to penetrate.

In the absence of such a security perimeter, encryption of signals combined with digital signatures and/or cryptographic checksums and time stamps is necessary to ensure reasonable protection if any penetration attempt is expected.

In a star network the exposure of network signals is much lower (Figure 8.12); any device communicates only to the controller or server, and its signals are not accessible to other devices. This removes the need to encrypt network signals, unless the line to the controller is subject to compromise. Several detailed exposures change somewhat; for example, the database in a star network is assumed to be subjected to more stringent physical controls (probably the same as the host and controller), and thus emanations are not a serious problem. At the same time, the channel to the database must be more capable, since it has to handle requests multiplexed from the controller rather than responding to single requests from network devices; thus the channel becomes exposed.

Since everything is controlled through the controller or FEP, that device and its links to network nodes are the key to security. Failure of the controller or the host makes the network unusable; failure of any other device except the database manager has little effect.

As with a bus network, a secure perimeter around a security-high area is one control method. Personnel clearances, physical access controls, logs and audit trails, and emanation shielding (TEMPEST standards, for example) will ensure reasonable security. Any gateways go through the controller, thus less attention need be applied to the gateway itself since the controller can apply protection. Encryption remains essential for any signals leaving the star network.

---

[18]The mode of operation in which system hardware/software is only trusted to provide need-to-know protection between users. In this mode, the entire system, to include all components electrically and/or physically connected, must operate with security measures commensurate with the highest classification and sensitivity of the information being processed and/or stored. All system users in this environment must possess clearances and authorizations for all information contained in the system. All system output must be clearly marked with the highest classification and all system caveats, until the information has been reviewed manually by an authorized individual to ensure appropriate classifications, and caveats have been affixed. (CSC-STD-003-85)

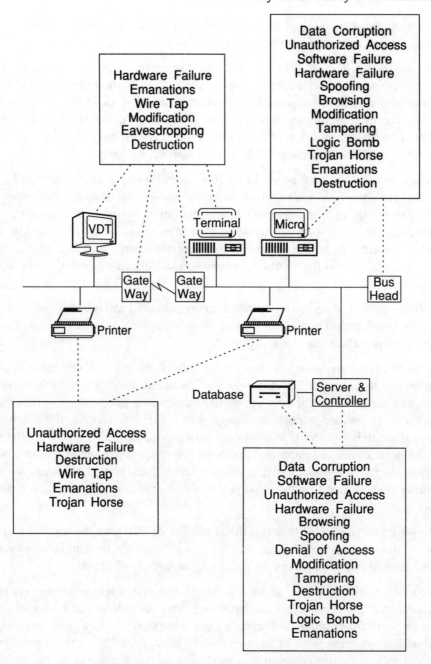

Figure 8.10. Bus Network Exposures

Physical exposure of critical components like the controller, host, and database manager is important.

In the absence of a secure perimeter situation, reasonable security still may be achieved without encryption, by ensuring security of the controller and host and the line between the secure device and the controller. Since no other device sees the network signal, exposure to spurious nodes and such is minimal. The star network (Figure 8.13) is far less subject than a bus to denial of service from spurious signals.

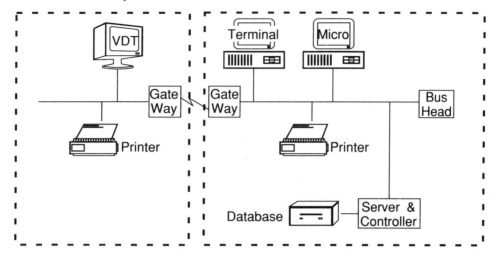

Figure 8.11. Bus Network Control Measures

Star Network

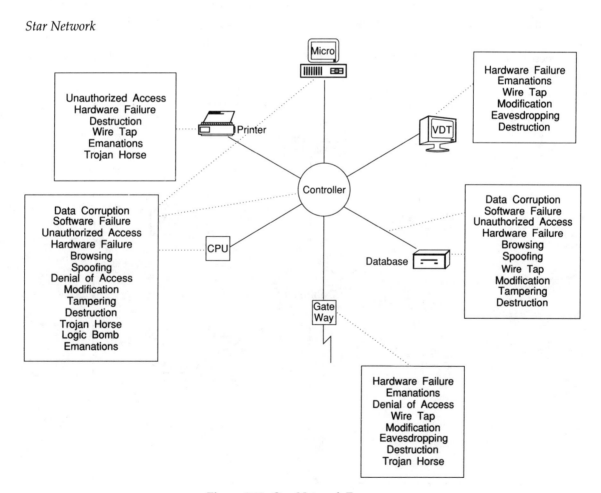

Figure 8.12. Star Network Exposures

Ring Network

The ring network (Figures 8.14 and 8.15) presents much the same exposures as the bus, with two major exceptions. The risk of denial due to introduction of spurious signals or overload is much lower, as the network need not halt while a device responds to a network message. The tokens and packets simply "pass by" and will reach the device on the next pass. This characteristic, however, presents a new risk: Any device may have access to all or most network signals sent by any other device. In the bus, the network is monopolized by the bus head during transmission; in the ring, denial is a lesser risk but disclosure is a much greater risk.

Control of exposures involves administrative measures, such as personnel clearances and various logs, and technical measures, such as emanation shielding (TEMPEST standards, for example). Control of exposure for devices is the same as for the same device installed anywhere else. The only significant difference is that any device attached to the network must have a card that handles network communication, and this card may be subject to tampering or other alterations, which must be controlled via administrative measures.

Since every device attached to the network may see the network signals of every other device, the risk of passive disclosure is at a maximum. As well, any node can introduce a spoofing signal using information contained in the legitimate tokens "passing by." Digital signatures or other authentication measures are essential to enforce security in a ring network not entirely enclosed in a secure perimeter. Encryption alone may not suffice; time-stamps are needed to enforce non-replay.

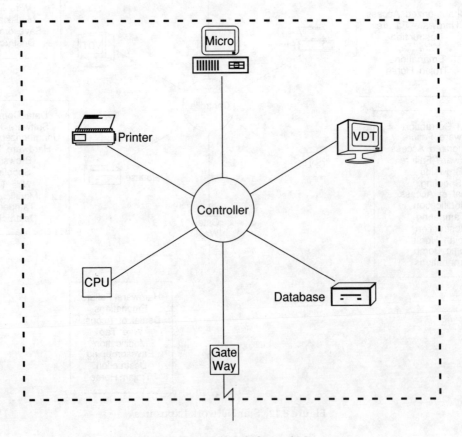

Figure 8.13. Star Network Control Measures

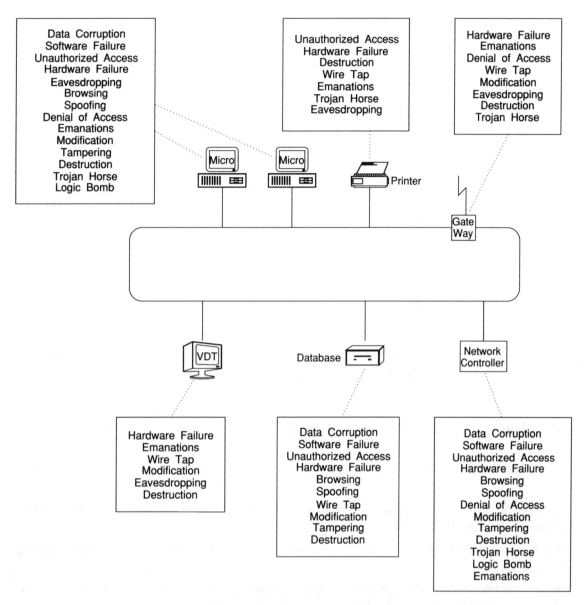

Figure 8.14. Ring Network Exposures

As with other networks, a secure perimeter combined with administrative controls such as personnel clearances, audit logs, and access controls can lead to a secure environment. Every device that can communicate with the network must be enclosed within the perimeter.

As can be seen from the discussion of network attacks in Chapter 8, systems linked together face different problems than isolated systems. Systems that are secure in isolation cannot always be linked into a network, even an internal network of multiple CPUs in a processor, that is secure (composability).

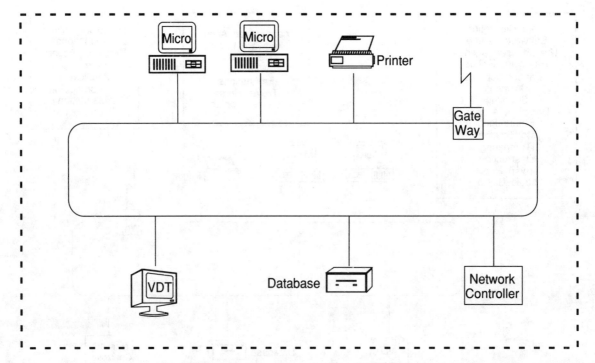

Figure 8.15: Ring Network Control Measures

REFERENCES

Davies, D. W. and W. L. Price, *Security for Computer Networks*, John Wiley & Sons, New York, NY, 1984.

Denning, Dorothy Elizabeth Robling, *Cryptography and Data Security*, Addison-Wesley Publishing Company, Reading, MA, 1983.

Fike, John L., and George E. Friend, *Understanding Telephone Electronics*, Texas Instruments Inc., Dallas, TX, 1983.

Grant, Kenneth A. et al., "Guidelines for User Requirements for Security in Integrated Communications and Information Systems," report to Department of Communications cat. no. CO22-87/1989E, Stevenson Kellogg Ernst & Whinney, Toronto, 1989.

National Computer Security Center, *Trusted Network Interpretation* of the Trusted Computer System Evaluation Criteria, NCSC-TG-005 Version-1, National Computer Security Center, Fort George G. Meade, MD, 31 July 1987.

Shannon, C. E. "Communication Theory of Secrecy Systems," *Bell System Technical Journal*, October 1949.

9. Organization Architecture

This section describes what the information security professional is expected to know about how to organize people to accomplish security objectives.

The professional is expected to know:

- Alternative forms of organization
- How to employ segregation of function and separation of duties
- Where and how to assign line responsibility
- Where and how to assign staff responsibility
- The relationship between information security and related functions:
  - records management
  - risk management
  - plant security
  - information system management
  - personnel
  - other

- The security responsibility of various business functions:
  - payroll
  - payables
  - receivables
  - inventory and other custody functions
  - other

For example, the professional is expected to:

- Recognize "line" and "staff"
- Recognize "matrix management"
- Distinguish between the responsibilities of line and staff
- Distinguish between centralized and decentralized
- Recognize site, establishment and enterprise
- Recognize incompatible responsibilities:
  - finance and data processing
  - origination and approval
  - programming and use
  - other

- Identify the likely reporting points for the information security staff
- Recognize inappropriate reporting points for information security staff
- Be able to allocate duties between line and staff, and between security and other staff functions
- other

DEFINITIONS

Accountability

The property that ensures that the actions of an entity may be traced uniquely to the entity. (ISO 7498-2)

Accountability Information

A set of records, often referred to as an audit trail, that collectively provide documentary evidence of the processing or other actions related to the security of an ADP system. (DOE 5636.2A)

Accreditation

The official authorization granted to an information system to process sensitive information in its operational environment based on comprehensive security evaluation of the system's hardware, firmware, and software security design, configuration, and implementation and of the other system procedural, administrative, physical, TEMPEST, personnel, and communications security controls. (AFR 700-10; CSC-STD-001-83)

Accreditation Authority

An official designated to accredit systems for the processing, use, storage, and production of sensitive defense material. (AR 380-380)

Administrative Security

The management constraints; operational, administrative, and accountability procedures and supplemental controls established to provide an acceptable level of protection for data. (OPNAVINST 5239.1A; FIPS PUB 39; DOE 5636.2A)

Assurance

The hardware, firmware, and software mechanisms of an Automated Information System that can be evaluated to provide sufficient assurance that the system enforces the defined security policy, labelling, identification and auditing capabilities. These mechanisms consist of system architecture, system integrity, security testing, design specification and verification, configuration management, trusted recovery, and trusted distribution. (NCSC-WA-001-85)

Audit

To conduct an independent review and examination of system records and activities in order to test for adequacy of system controls, to ensure compliance with established policy and operational procedures, and to recommend any indicated changes in controls, policy, or procedures. (DODD 5200.28)

1. *Internal Security Audit.* An audit conducted by personnel responsible to the management of the organization being audited.
2. *External Security Audit.* An audit conducted by an organization independent of the one being audited. (OPNAVINST 5239.1A; AR 380-380; FIPS PUB 39)

Authentication Process

The actions involving:

1. Obtaining an identifier and a personal password from an ADP system user
2. Comparing the entered password with the stored, valid password that was issued to, or selected by, the person associated with that identifier
3. Authenticating the identity if the entered password and the stored password are the same

    (Note: If the enciphered password is stored, the entered password must be enciphered and compared with the stored ciphertext or the ciphertext must be deciphered and compared with the entered password.) (FIPS PUB 112)

Authorization Process

The actions involving:

1. Obtaining an access password from an ADP system user (whose identity has already been authenticated, perhaps using a personal password)
2. Comparing the access password with the password associated with the protected data
3. Authorizing access to the data if the entered password and the stored password are the same [see note under Authentication Process]. (FIPS PUB 112)

Caution Statement

A statement affixed to computer outputs which contains the highest classification being processed at the time the product was produced and a requirement that any data not requested be controlled at that level and returned immediately to the originating computer center. (AR 380-380)

Certification

1. A statement based on detailed technical analysis that specifies the extent to which the security measures in the system or facility meet the security requirements. Certification is based on the results of the risk analysis performed. It does not necessarily imply a guarantee that the described system is impenetrable. It is an input to the security accreditation process. (AFR 700-10; AFR 205-16)
2. The technical evaluation of an AIS's security features and other safeguards, made as part of and in support of the accreditation process, that establishes the extent to which a particular AIS design and implementation meet a set of specified security requirements. (DODD 5200.28; CSC-STD-001-83; FIPS PUB 39; AR 380-380)

Certification and Accreditation Program

1. A program designed to ensure that critical decisions regarding the adequacy of AIS security safeguards are made by authorized managers based on reliable technical information. (NCSC-WA-001-85)
2. The process of testing individuals' knowledge and background by an independent organization that then certifies the individual as meeting certain standards and, usually, subscribes to codes of ethics, good practice, and so forth. (PEF)

Closed Security Environment

An environment that includes those systems in which both the following conditions hold true.

1. Application developers (including maintainers) have sufficient clearances and authorizations to provide an acceptable presumption that they have not introduced malicious logic. Sufficient clearance is defined as follows: Where the maximum classification of data to be processed is Confidential or below, developers are cleared and authorized to the same level as the most sensitive data; where the maximum classification of data to be processed is Secret or above, developers have at least a Secret clearance.

2. Configuration control provides sufficient assurance that applications are protected against the introduction of malicious logic prior to and during operation of system applications. (CSC-STD-003-85; CSC-STD-004-85)

Configuration Management

Process of controlling modifications to the system's hardware, firmware, software, and documentation which provides sufficient assurance the system is protected against the introduction of improper modification before, during, and after system implementation. (AFR 205-16)

Contingency Management

Management of all the actions to be taken before, during, and after a disaster (emergency condition), along with a documented, tested procedures which, if followed, will ensure the availability of critical ADP systems and which will facilitate maintaining the continuity of operations in an emergency situation. (DOE 5636.2A)

Contingency Plan

A plan for emergency response, backup operations, and post-disaster recovery maintained by an ADP activity as part of its security program. A comprehensive consistent statement of all the actions (plans) to be taken before, during, and after a disaster (emergency condition), along with documented, tested procedures which, if followed, will ensure the availability of critical ADP resources and which will facilitate maintaining the continuity of operations in an emergency situation. (OPNAVINST 5239.1A; NCSC-WA-001-85)

Continuity of Operations

The maintenance of essential services for an information system after a major failure at an information center. The failure may result from natural causes (such as fire, flood or earthquakes) or from deliberate events (such as sabotage). (GAO)

Controlled Security Mode

The mode of operation that is a type of multilevel security mode in which a more limited amount of trust is placed in the hardware and software base of the system, with resultant restrictions on the classification levels and clearance levels that may be supported. The system may have users who possess neither the security clearance nor the need-to-know for all information in the system; however, access shall be limited to users with a minimal clearance level of one less than the highest classification processed. (NCSC-WA-001-85; CSC-STD-003-85)

Controlled Space

The three-dimensional space surrounding equipment that processes national security information within which unauthorized personnel are

1. Denied unrestricted access
2. Enter escorted by authorized personnel or under continual physical or electronic surveillance (AFR 700-10)

   (Note: This concept also is used in the private sector, with essentially the same meaning. —PEF)

Control Zone

1. The space, expressed in feet of radius, surrounding equipment processing classified information which is under sufficient physical and technical control to preclude a successful hostile intercept attack. (AR 380-380)
2. The space, expressed in feet of radius, surrounding equipment processing sensitive information which is under sufficient physical and technical control to preclude an unauthorized entry or compromise. (NCSC-WA-001-85)

Dedicated Security Mode

A mode of operation wherein all users have the clearance, formal access approval, and need-to-know for all data handled by the AIS. In the dedicated mode, an AIS may handle a single classification level and/or category of information or a range of classification levels and/or categories. (DODD 5200.28; NCSC-WA-001-85)

Designated Approving Authority

A senior policy official who has the authority and the responsibility to make the management decision to accept or not accept the security safeguards prescribed for an AIS; the official who may be responsible for issuing an accreditation statement that records the decision to accept those safeguards. (DODD 5200.28; NCSC-WA-001-85)

Distribution Statement

A statement used in marking a technical document to denote the extent of its availability for distribution, release, and disclosure without additional approvals or authorizations. A distribution statement marking is distinct from and in addition to a security classification marking assigned in accordance with DODD 5200.1-R. (DODD 5230.24)

Fail Safe

Automatic termination and protection of programs and/or processing systems when a hardware or software failure is detected in an automated information system. (NCSC-WA-001-85; AR 380-380; FIPS PUB 39)

Fail Soft

The selective termination of affected non-essential processing when a hardware or software failure is detected in an AIS. (AR 380-380; NCSC-WA-001-85; FIPS PUB 39)

Failure Control

The methodology used to detect and provide fail-safe or fail-soft recovery from hardware and software failures in an automated system. (AR 380-380; FIPS PUB 39; NCSC-WA-001-85)

Individual Accountability

The ability to positively associate the identity of a user with the time, method, and degree of access to an Automated Information System. (NCSC-WA-001-85; AR 380-380)

Information System Security Officer (ISSO)

The Automated Information System Security Officer (ISSO). The title and the division of duties varies between agencies. In this assessment form the term ISSO is intended to apply to the person(s) responsible for automated information security for the information center(s) and Information System(s). The title could be ISSO, ADPSO, ADPSSO, Security Administrator, OISSO, CESSO, CSSO, etc. (GAO)

Least Privilege

This principle requires that each subject be granted the most restrictive set of privileges needed for the performance of authorized tasks. The application of this principle limits the damage that can result from accident, error, or unauthorized use. (NCSC-WA-001-85; CSC-STD-001-83)

Limited ADP Access Security Mode

An ADP system or network is operating in the limited-access security mode when the type of data being processed is categorized as unclassified and requires the implementation of special access controls to restrict the access to the data only to individuals who, by their job functions, have a need to access the data. (OPNAVINST 5239.1A)

Multilevel Security Mode

1. The mode of operation which allows two or more classification levels of information to be processed simultaneously within the same system when some users are not cleared for all levels of information present. (CSC-STD-003-85; NCSC-WA-001-85)

2. An operation under an operating system (supervisor or executive program) which provides a capability permitting various categories and types of classified materials to be stored and processed concurrently in an ADP system, and permitting selective access to such material concurrently by uncleared users having different security clearances and need-to-know is accordingly accomplished by the operating system and associated system software. In a remotely accessed resource-sharing system, the material can be selectively accessed and manipulated from variously controlled terminals by personnel having different security clearances and need-to-know. This mode of operation can accommodate the concurrent processing and storage of:

    a) two or more levels of classified data, or
    b) one or more levels of classified data with unclassified data depending upon constraints placed on the system by the DAA (DODD 5200.28M; OPNAVINST 5239.1A)

Multi-User Security Mode of Operation

This mode of operation is designed for systems which process sensitive unclassified information in which users may not have a need-to-know for all information processed in the system. This mode is also for microcomputers processing sensitive unclassified information which cannot meet the requirements of the stand-alone mode of operation. (AFR 205-16)

Open Security Environment

An environment that includes those systems in which one of the following conditions holds true:

1. Application developers (including maintainers) do not have sufficient clearance or authorization to provide an acceptable presumption that they have not introduced malicious logic.

2. Configuration control does not provide sufficient assurance that applications are protected against the introduction of malicious logic prior to and during the operation of system applications. (CSC-STD-004-85; CSC-STD-003-85; NCSC-WA-001-85)

Operational Site Security Manual

The manual documents the operational requirements, manual security environment, hardware and software configurations and interfaces; all security procedures, measures, and features; and, for computer facilities, the contingency plans for continued support in case of a local disaster. (AFR 205-16)

Penetration Study

A study to determine the feasibility and methods for defeating controls of an Automated Information System. (NCSC-WA-001-85)

Penetration Testing

The portion of security testing in which the evaluators attempt to circumvent the security features of a system. The evaluators may be assumed to use all system design and implementation documentation which may include listings of system source code, manuals, and circuit diagrams. The evaluators work under the same constraints applied to ordinary users. (NCSC-WA-001-85; CSC-STD-001-83)

A related term is *tiger team*. (PEF)

Periods Processing

The processing of various levels of sensitive information at distinctly different times. The Automated Information System must be purged of all information before transitioning from one period to the next whenever there will be new users who do not have clearances and the need-to-know for data processed during the previous period. (NCSC-WA-001-85)

Procedural Security

The management constraints; operational, administrative, and accountability procedures; and supplemental controls established to provide protection for sensitive defense information. (AR 380-380)

Security Audit

An independent review and examination of system records and activities in order to test for adequacy of system controls, to ensure compliance with established policy and operational procedures, to detect breaches in security, and to recommend any indicated changes in control, policy and procedures. (ISO 7498-2)

Security Evaluation

One of two types of evaluations done to assess the degree of trust that can be placed in Automated Information Systems for the secure handling of sensitive information. One type, a product evaluation, is an evaluation performed on the hardware and software features and assurances of a computer product from a perspective that excludes the application environment. The other type, a system evaluation, is done for the purpose of assessing an Automated Information System's security safeguards with respect to a specific operational mission and is a major step in the certification and accreditation process. (NCSC-WA-001-85)

Security Officer

The ADP official, described in OMB Circular A-71, Transmittal Memorandum Number 1 (July 27, 1978), having the designated responsibility for the security of an ADP system. (FIPS PUB 112)

Stand-alone Security Mode of Operation

This mode of operation is meant for microcomputers that are used by only one user at a time. It does NOT apply to microcomputers processing classified, microcomputers with fixed storage if need-to-know does not apply to all users, and microcomputers with active communications or resource sharing. (AFR 205-16)

Stand-alone, Shared Automated Information System

An Automated Information System that is physically and electrically isolated from all other Automated Information Systems, and is intended to be used by more than one person, either simultaneously (*e.g.*, an Automated Information System with multiple terminals) or serially, with data belonging to one user remaining available to the Automated Information System while another user is using the Automated Information System (*e.g.*, a PC with non-removable storage media such as a hard disk). (NCSC-WA-001-85)

Stand-alone, Single-User Automated Information System

An Automated Information System that is physically and electrically isolated from all other Automated Information Systems, and is intended to be used by one person at a time, with no data belonging to other users remaining in the Automated Information System (*e.g.*, a PC with removable storage media such as a floppy disk). (NCSC-WA-001-85)

System High Security Mode

1. The mode of operation in which system hardware/software is only trusted to provide need-to-know protection between users. In this mode, the entire system, to include all components electrically and/or physically connected, must operate with security measures commensurate with the highest classification and sensitivity of the information being processed and/or

stored. All system users in this environment must possess clearances and authorizations for all information contained in the system. All system output must be clearly marked with the highest classification and all system caveats, until the information has been reviewed manually by an authorized individual to ensure appropriate classifications and caveats have been affixed. (CSC-STD-003-85)

2. The mode of operation in which the computer system and all of its connected peripheral devices and remote terminals are protected in accordance with the requirements for the highest security level of material contained in the system at that time. All personnel having access to the Automated Information System have a security clearance but not a need-to-know for all material then contained in the system. (NCSC-WA-001-85)

System Low

The lowest security level supported by a system at a particular time or in a particular environment. (NCSC-WA-001-85)

System Security Officer (SSO)

The person responsible for the security of an ADP system. The SSO is authorized to act in the "security administrator" role as defined in CSC-STD-001-83. Functions that the SSO is expected to perform include auditing and changing security characteristics of a user. (CSC-STD-002-85; CSC-STD-005-85)

Systems Security Steering Group

The NSDD-145 establishes a Steering Group to oversee the NSDD-145 and to ensure its implementation. This group is chaired by the Assistant to the President for National Security Affairs and consists of the Secretary of State, Secretary of Treasury, the Secretary of Defense, the Attorney General, the Director of Office of Management and Budget, and the Director of Central Intelligence. (NCSC-WA-001-85)

9.1 RESPONSIBILITY AREAS, SYSTEM SECURITY OFFICER

An organizational measure that can enhance security is to establish a position or group responsible for administration of security issues. The following material is one suggestion for the characteristics of such a group.

The following sample was provided to the Information System Security Association (ISSA) by Mr. Robert Courtney and is reproduced here with permission of ISSA.

Computer Security Administration

Purpose of Function

Establish, implement, and maintain a computer security program to assist management in the protection of computer resources and associated information assets against accidental or unauthorized modification, destruction, or disclosure.

Major Responsibilities

Establishes appropriate company-wide standards and guidelines for data and physical security safeguards pertaining to information systems.

Administers the implementation and maintenance of data security software that provides controlled access and use of sensitive application systems, computer operating systems, communication networks, and computer hardware.

Administers the implementation and maintenance of critical security measures and control techniques necessary to protect against errors and omissions, fraudulent access, sabotage, natural disasters, and related situations where data processing equipment is used.

Administers monitoring techniques and procedures for detecting, reporting, and investigating breaches in computer security.

Coordinates the development and maintenance of disaster recovery and contingency plans involving computerized systems.

Participates in and provides consultation into technical and application development efforts involving computer data security and integrity issues.

Develops and maintains a computer security manual for use by those responsible for the security of their resources.

Provides a forum for review, counsel, education, and communication of computer security administration procedures to data processing and user personnel.

In conjunction with General Auditing, performs periodic compliance testing to assure adherence to standards, and provides recommendations and remedial action.

Maintains a working relationship with the internal and external auditors and assists management when responding to matters involving security and control of information systems.

Maintains an awareness of existing and proposed legislation and regulatory laws pertaining to information system security and privacy.

9.1.1 Basic Role

One organizational measure that can be taken to implement security and control, is to create the position of System Security Officer (SSO). This position has many alternate names, such as Data Security Administrator or Departmental Security Officer (DSO); in very large organizations there may be several security people responsible for various aspects of security and control (separation of duties). In small organizations, this function typically is part of the System Manager's job. In every organization, some person must have responsibility and be held accountable for security and control (excluding the element of control that is part of any manager's job responsibilities).

It is important to define carefully the responsibilities of the SSO. One way to define responsibilities that has proven of value in many situations is to use a "functional matrix." The risk-management team or other management groups can identify functions related to security (for example, "identify and classify data"; "identify protective controls"; "monitor security and control incidents.") The functions are listed along one side of a matrix. Positions in the organization with responsibilities related to data and information systems are then identified (for example, computer operator, systems manager, new project manager, operations manager, payroll manager).

These positions are listed along a second side of the matrix. The cells defined are then filled in with codes such as "primary responsibility—PR" or "not relevant—N/A." The final result shows who must do what, and who is held accountable. (In real organizations, this exercise usually leads to considerable negotiation the first time it is done, since many managers will become aware that they have responsibilities they didn't fully appreciate previously.)

	Identify Risks	Monitor Operators' Security Practices	Develop & Enforce Security Standards	Evaluate Effectiveness of Security Program
System Security Officer (SSO)	PR	MN	PR	PR
Top Managers	N/A	MN	MN N/A	MN
Systems Development Manager	MC	N/A	MN N/A	MN
Data Center Manager	MC	PR	MC	MN
User	MN N/A	N/A	MC	MC MN
Data Asset Owner	MC	N/A	MN N/A	MN MC

KEY: PR = Primary Responsibility   MN = Must be Notified

MC = Must be Consulted   N/A = Not Applicable

Figure 9.1. (Partial) Functional Responsibility Matrix

Figure 9.1 shows a sample of part of a functional matrix. Notice that this matrix resembles the job exposure matrix in Table 2.1; the logical tool created by laying out functions and positions, then entering relations into cells, is useful in many areas of security and other analyses. In Table 3.4, there was merely an "X" or not, indicating existence of a vulnerability. Degrees of vulnerability, rather than degrees of responsibility as in Figure 9.1, would have given a matrix nearly identical to Table 3.4. (In this *partial* matrix, the abbreviated list of functions does not include areas for which anyone besides the SSO and, in one case, the systems development manager, holds primary responsibility.)

9.1.2 Duties

The specific duties of the SSO, as revealed by this planning tool, normally will vary depending on the organization. The central duty is to be responsible for the security program of the organization's information systems.

A sample of these duties, as reported by Royal Fisher [Fisher 1984] is:

1. Provide direct administrative support for installed security systems to ensure the secure use of all on-line and information systems.

2. Set objectives for future development of security systems for evolving on-line and information systems.

3. Determine special resource requirements such as manpower, training, and equipment and develop plans, schedules, and cost data relative to various security responsibilities.

4. Negotiate with multiple levels of programming support management to assure integration of assigned security objectives with the long-range data processing strategy.

5. Continually review and evaluate security alternatives to determine course of action based upon technical implications, knowledge of business objectives, and corporate asset protection policy, procedures, and requirements.

6. Assure that assigned projects meet corporate security objectives and are completed according to schedule within committed costs; inform management as early as possible of problems that could materially affect objectives, schedules, and costs; recommend alternative solutions.

7. Monitor the use of on-line and information systems to detect and act upon unauthorized access and use of proprietary business data.

8. Interface and coordinate with legal, insurance, and security staff handling internal security investigations on a highly confidential basis.

9. Conduct security audits, participate in security evaluations, and provide guidance and assistance, as requested, to facilitate the implementation of data processing asset protection programs.

10. Supervise documentation efforts associated with internal security systems.

This list is a sample. Items 6 and 9 in particular may cause some problems: Item 6 describes responsibilities normally assigned to a project manager, and item 9 covers many internal audit functions. The specific duties will vary among different organizations. The functional matrix, and the negotiations mentioned in the previous subsection, will help to define the System Security Officer position for any specific situation. Many large organizations have existing policies such as the Canadian Federal Government security policy manual, United States Federal Government manuals, Canadian and United States Department of Defense publications, and similar guides.

All of the ones mentioned have very specific and detailed lists and descriptions of the duties of the SSO or equivalent person.

In performing these or similar duties, the SSO will have to interact with and to understand and be aware of the activities of many groups of people, both within and outside the organization. A sample list might include:

- Suppliers of services
- Users/owners
- Management
- Outsiders such as security guards
- Audit
- Suppliers of computer equipment
- Legal department

In some organizations, this list would be expanded to include, for instance, suppliers of communications services (possibly within the company, possibly outside suppliers). The exact contents of such a list will vary depending on the organization and its normal activities.

9.1.3 Training and Skills for a System Security Officer

To understand and negotiate effectively with diverse groups such as outlined above, the System Security Officer needs a number of basic knowledge sets. Generally, they cover areas of accounting and audit, EDP and other systems, and business knowledge. More specifically, the knowledge sets normally include:

- Organizational knowledge: structure and behavioral
- Technical knowledge (EDP): computers, systems, tools
- Technical knowledge: manual procedures, systems, and tools
- Accounting and audit concepts
- Personnel administration matters
- Law and legislation
- Other business knowledge: strategic and tactical planning, the basic nature of the organization, labor and other negotiating strategies and tactics

Other knowledge sets also can be very useful: Statistics is important in many types of analyses, for example. In working with physical and environmental security, knowledge of building construction and similar areas is an asset. A SSO in a communications environment may need in-depth knowledge of many communications specialties. In a manufacturing company, Material Requirements Planning (MRP) may be needed. In retailing, marketing knowledge may be crucial.

In addition to the rather daunting range of needed knowledge, the SSO needs some specific personal characteristics:

- Honesty
- Tact and politeness
- Oral and written communication skills
- Professionalism and personal maturity

He or she is one of the primary risk exposures, since to do the job properly, virtually complete access is needed, and the training includes how to hide unauthorized events: Unquestioned personal honesty becomes a critical characteristic. As noted in the comment about items 6 and 9 in the sample list of duties, many of the things a SSO does overlap with other managers: Considerable tact and politeness also are needed. Much of the SSO's work involves communicating, either collecting information or being involved in awareness programs, reports to management, and similar presentations: Superior abilities in written and spoken communication are essential. Last, but certainly not least, the individual selected for a SSO position must be highly professional and mature: Not mature in age, but possessing such characteristics as discretion, the ability to command respect, and leadership ability.

Combining all of the needed kinds of knowledge with the range of personal characteristics, a picture of some kind of "superman" or "superwoman" is generated. The requirements described above are ideals; probably, no single person could meet all of them. The knowledge sets alone, in the detail that a SSO needs, would require perhaps 24 years in university (by which time the first knowledge gained would be obsolete). This presentation is to give an idea of the perfect situation. In the real world, one attempts to achieve perfection but must recognize its unattainability and work with available resources and make intelligent allowances for lacks.

9.2 COMMON FORMS OF ORGANIZATIONS

According to Peter Drucker, the five principle organization structures are:

1. Functional structures
2. Federal decentralization
3. Team organization
4. Simulated decentralization
5. The System structure

Functional Structure (Henri Fayol)
Stages of work (such as manufacturing and marketing) and skills (such as accounting) are designed as static; the "work" moves from one stage to another.

Federal Decentralization (Alfred P. Sloane)
This is a result-focused design, with the emphasis on optimum performance. Like a country, the organization consists of relatively autonomous units (usually called "Divisions") under a corporate umbrella. Certain functions are performed centrally, as a country may handle international relations and defense through the national government; certain functions are performed by divisions (usually with duplication among divisions), with examples varying too widely for a useful list. General Motors is the classical example of a federally decentralized corporation. Each Division, for example Chevrolet, Cadillac, and Oldsmobile, has its own manufacturing facilities, marketing, and so forth. In this example, divisions even engage in limited competition, although the degree of competition is controlled centrally.

Team Organization
This differs from the functional organization in that the "work" is conceived as static with "skills" moving to form the specific team that the work, or "task," requires.

"Simulated" Decentralization
Like federal decentralization, simulated decentralization is result-focused. It is considered to be a lesser evil, to be substituted only when the stringent requirements of federal decentralization cannot be met.

System Structure
This is a relations-focused organization principle. This is so because relationships are a generic dimension of management.

9.2.1 Principles of Organization

Management is the concept of a body of knowledge that deals with the orderly integration of people and machines through implementation of task assignments and performance goals. Management exists only in contemplation of performance. It is an organ of the institution and therefore has no function or existence in itself. It is a means—not an end.

Management must perform three tasks to enable the institution in its charge to function and make its contribution:

- Respond to and implement the specific purpose and mission of the institution that it serves
- Make work productive and the worker achieving
- Manage the social impact and the social responsibilities of the enterprise

Management must perform its tasks within the dimension of *time*: past, present, and future.

9.2.2 General Management and Organizational Concepts

9.2.2.1 Business Functions

There are many lists of the general functions that must be performed by all businesses. In this section, we concentrate on the following list:

- Resource Acquisition and Management
- Finance
- Production
- Promotion
- Distribution
- Human Resources
- Management

Resource Acquisition and Management
One function of business management is to ensure that inputs to the processes of the business are available. These *resources* might include land ownership, logging rights in forests, ore bodies or petroleum deposits, trained staff, or whatever else is needed to ensure that the product of the business can be created.

One concept that has been in vogue since the late 1980s is "just-in-time" inventory management. This involves setting up resource acquisition processes in such a way that as a resource is needed it enters the process that uses it. Careful control of processes is essential; if the resource is not at hand when needed, the process may stop, halting a following process and so forth. Examples of this concept include sheet steel entering an automotive production line just in time to be stamped into an appropriate shape. The use of consultants and other practices like part-time work is a form of just-in-time resource management in the service sector. When the practice works well, inventory carrying costs (salaries and benefits in the case of human resources) are minimized. When just-in-time management does not work well, serious consequences may be expected. For example, even a short-term failure of any of many components of the resource stream may shut down production at least for the duration of the failure. The increased exposure to serious consequences (as opposed to maintaining an on-hand inventory) presents issues of security. As well, in the case of just-in-time management in the service sector, many people will be around from time to time who are not long-term employees of the organization, or are not employees of the organization at all in the case of consultants. Again, issues related to security arise, in this case personnel concerns.

Finance

Financial management is a function of senior management. It integrates the planning of financial resources with controls established to meet the institution's objectives. *Controls* are established as a function of management accounting. Control is the responsibility of top-level management; yet it must be exercised at all levels within the organization.

Financial management includes the following:

- Long-range capital planning:
  - Capital budgeting
  - Capital asset acquisition
  - Equity financing
  - Debt financing
  - Tax planning

- Short-run capital planning:
  - Administrative budgeting
  - Sales budgeting
  - Production budgeting

- Inventory management

- Managing production costs

- Interpreting financial statements:
  - Horizontal analysis
  - Vertical analysis
  - Financial ratios analysis
  - Cost volume-profit (CVP) analysis
  - Changes in financial position

Production

Operations is that aspect of management that deals with the repetitive actions of people, machines, and other resources.

Operations management is concerned with the overall planning and coordination of component activities within the organization toward the most efficient, timely, and *optimum* results.

Operations, as a *planning* activity, must use such tools and techniques as are available to measure performance, to determine ways of improving performance, to recommend such changes as are necessary to implement methods of improving performance or results, and to anticipate or predict the yield from such changes.

As a *coordinating* activity, operations must maintain performance or productivity according to the plan and take such actions as are necessary to assure compliance with the organization's objectives.

Where manufacturing is the essential purpose of the enterprise, the manufacturing organization usually follows the *functional structure*, and the management philosophy is usually that of the *Scientific Management* school. Thus the management responsibilities are hierarchical, and the management nodes are the major work stations through which the work flows. In this case both line and staff concepts apply, and supervisory management carries primary responsibility for implementing production goals.

Promotion

The purpose of business is to *serve a customer*. The customer is the foundation of the business, and keeps it in existence. Because its purpose is to serve a customer, the business enterprise has two basic functions: marketing and innovation. Marketing and innovation produce results; all of the rest are costs.

Marketing is the distinguishing, unique function of the business. Marketing performance requires a number of objectives:

- Awareness of existing products and services in existing and present markets
- Abandonment of "yesterday" in product, services, and markets
- Development of new products and services for existing markets
- Development of new markets
- Organization of distribution
- Definition of service standards and service performance
- Definition of credit standards and credit performances; and more

Innovation is the research and development aspect of the business. Without new products, no business can survive long in a changing world.

Distribution

Once the product of the business has been created, whether that product is a physical item like an automobile, a sheet of steel or a computer, or an idea expressed in the form of a book, an available service, or perhaps a database, the product must be distributed.

Distribution channels vary depending on the product. There may be several intermediaries who serve to purchase product in large quantities and repackage for sale in smaller quantities. Issues to be examined include:

- Efficiency and cost of distribution (number of storage sites, transportation mechanisms, etc.)
- Characteristics of customers (retail? sales of steel products to manufacturers? and so forth)

- Pricing at each stage of the distribution channel

At one extreme, a manufacturer of soft drinks likely would not establish thousands of retail soda outlets but would distribute through several layers of middlemen (who would travel to a one-per-region warehouse to buy a can of pop?). The other extreme is likely a firm supplying a unique product to a single, or to a small number, of buyers; the limiting case here is a captive plant supplying one other plant ("just-in-time" inventory's optimum, perhaps); no distribution channel or intermediary is involved.

Human Resources

Organizations are people getting together to accomplish things that can't be accomplished singly. The human resources are what makes a business operate. Several contemporary issues are addressed in section 6.4; the personnel function or department is responsible for management and, to some extent, for acquiring human resources.

Unlike the line organization, in which the chain of authority is uninterrupted from the individual worker to the Chief Executive, the staff organization performs an advisory or supporting role. In terms of increasing authority, staffs may be classified as follows:

- *Advisory* staff—provides special or technical recommendations.
- *Service* staff—provides technical skills and selected services, with a strong influence on line management.
- *Control* staff—develops policies and procedures and defines limits of authority of line management. The control staff advises in technical areas and monitors line activities within the staff's area of authority.
- *Functional* staff—has full line management authority; crosses normal chain-of-command for specific activities.

9.2.2.2 Management Functions

In all of the principal organization structures, Senior (or top-level) management is charged with the following tasks:

- Establish objectives, develop strategies and plans, and make today's decisions for tomorrow's results
- Set standards and examples
- Build and maintain the human organization, making decisions in contemplation of the effect on the entire enterprise
- Establish and maintain major relations with all of the institution's or enterprise's contacts
- Perform ceremonial functions
- Serve as "stand-by" in the event of a major crisis

According to the *Management Process School*, management can be analyzed in terms of specific functions. Within these functions, certain universal principles of general applicability are defined. These principles include Planning, Organization, Staffing, Directing and Controlling activities. Functional areas include:

Marketing
Operations

Manufacturing (or providing a service)

Research and Development

Financial management

Staff support management

Within the functional areas, senior and functional management responsibility vary according to the function or activity to be performed.

Planning

From the days of Frederick W. Taylor and the *Scientific Management School*, planning has been recognized as the fundamental (and primary) task of management and the foundation upon which all other management activities are based. Yehezkel Dror defines planning as:

> the process of preparing a set of decisions for action in the future directed at achieving goals by optimal means.

Planning is a methodology for making schedules. Its purpose is to define, before the fact, all steps that must be taken to achieve the purpose and mission of the enterprise.

The key element of planning is *time*. A *plan* denotes an action, or actions, to be taken at specified time intervals. Actions to be taken must result from positive benefits of the plan, and must (of themselves) contribute to the performance goals of the institution or enterprise.

Planning represents management consideration of both the present and the future—both the short run and the long run. The planning process therefore must include consideration of both present and future resources, and the implementation of the plan must yield both present and future benefits.

There are two reasons why *time* is of particular importance in management's job:

1. The essence of economic and technological progress is that the time span from planning to providing a decision is steadily shortening.
2. Management—almost singularly—has to live in both present and future.

Plans

Planning is influenced, at its inception, by the institution's *creed, nature of business* and *policy*. The creed is conventionally considered to be a statement of the mutually shared convictions of top management (often of questionable social value). It frequently relates the enterprise to its external environment.

The nature of the business or institution is the position that it occupies in the economic community. This self-perspective may be limited or broad in scope.

The *preliminary* steps to planning are:

- Establish objectives.
- List planning assumptions.
- Determine alternate courses of action.
- Evaluate alternate courses of action.
- Select the best course of action.

The next step is *formulation* of the plan itself:

- Identify the *activities* that must be performed to obtain a defined end result.
- Identify the *relationships* among the activities.
- Determine the *type* and *magnitude* of the *resources* required for the performance of each activity.
- Determine major *milestones* and target dates in the implementation of the plan, and identify *activities* that are *critical* in meeting the time constraints presented by the major milestones.
- Prepare *time schedules* for the use of resources corresponding to the time constraints on each activity.

Mission

Business or institutional objectives are stated at two levels:

- Statement of the purpose and objectives of the enterprise—its *mission*
- Statement of the objectives of each managerial unit of the organization as a means of implementing organizational goals subject to the general policy

Policies

Policies are far-reaching, or "sweeping," statements that establish guidelines for decision-making within the organization. They are written statements or general understandings; they represent the selection of a particular course of action that considers future consequences; and they operate as constraints on available options in the operational planning sequence.

Procedures, which are detailed methods for routine handling of future activities, usually are based on general and specific policies and objectives.

Implementing policy and strategy is an extension of the principles involved in their formulation. Tied to the structure and personality of the institution or organization, implementation requires:

- Executive leadership
- Well-defined decision-making process
- A system of "feedback" between levels of management
- A clearly defined planning process
- The involvement of all organizational levels in the decision-making process
- An alert/response system that is active during both planning and implementation of the plan

The Planning Horizon

Because planning inherently involves time, different classifications of planning are defined based on time frame or planning horizon:

- *Strategic planning* deals with the long term. This may be decades or longer (*e.g.,* for forest companies planting trees), or much shorter (three years is a long time in the personal computer industry, for example).
- *Tactical planning* deals with the medium term. For the forest company, tactical planning might involve deciding when to build a lumber mill.

- *Operational planning* refers to a short-term or day-to-day time horizon. Management of the production of a particular model of microcomputer would be operational planning (whether to produce it might be strategic and how many to produce tactical).

In review, the *six steps* in the planning process are:

1. Establish objectives.
2. List planning assumptions.
3. Determine alternate courses of action.
4. Evaluate alternate courses of action.
5. Select the best course of action.
6. Formulate the derivative plan.

Planning is a *continuous* process. The established plan cannot be blindly accepted as the only guide for action; it must be continuously modified when required.

9.2.2.3 Organizing

Organization classifications
The legal organization of groups of people falls into several classifications:

- *Sole proprietorship*, not incorporated and no liability protection—essentially an individual operating as a business.
- *Partnership*, two or more persons operating together; no liability protection; legal dependence of partners on each other and responsibility for each other's business actions.
- *Corporation*, a legal entity separate from any individual; the owners hold shares but have no personal liability.[1]
- *Conglomerate*, a collection of corporations operating as a single entity.
- *Syndicate*, essentially an unincorporated partnership;
- *Joint venture*, a grouping of several entities, incorporated or not, for the purpose of a single activity or project (the entities are separate otherwise).
- *Cooperative*, a group of persons or firms that agree to act cooperatively (for example farmers' cooperatives that buy in bulk and sell to their members at rates less than individuals could get for their smaller purchases).
- *Franchise* refers to an umbrella group, typically a corporation, with an idea; the franchisee purchases the right to use, for example, the trade name McDonalds (and many constraints such as advertising, business location, sole-supplier arrangements and such).

Organization principles
Organization structure should not just "evolve." Organization design and structure require thinking, analysis, and a systematic approach.

The first step is to identify and organize the *building blocks* of an organization. These building blocks are determined by the kind of *contribution* they make.

---

[1]Corporations can be very complex; in many cases, directors and officers may be subject to liability in the case of dishonesty or unlawfulness. The degree of personal liability shielding varies from jurisdiction to jurisdiction.

Structure follows strategy. Organization is unique to each individual business or institution. Therefore, structure, to be effective and sound, must follow strategy.

Formal Specifications

Any "structure" has to satisfy requirements that are grounded in the nature of the structure itself. Thus, organization structure needs to satisfy minimum requirements:

- *Clarity*: Each individual, as a managerial component, must know and understand his or her task responsibilities, reporting responsibilities, and sources of information, cooperation, or decision, and how to get there.

- *Economy*: The minimum effort should be needed to control, supervise, and encourage people to perform.

- *Direction of vision*: Organization structure should direct the vision of individuals and management units toward performance rather than towards efforts; it should direct vision toward results.

- *Understanding* one's *own task* and the *common task*: The individual must understand the specifics of his/her task as it is defined. Everyone should understand the task of the organization.

- *Decision-making*: An organization design should be tested as to whether it impedes or strengthens the decision-making process. A structure that forces a decision to the highest-possible organization level rather than the lowest-possible effective level may be an impediment; so may be the structure that obscures the emergence of the need for crucial decisions, or focuses attention on the wrong issues.

- *Stability and adaptability*: An organization must be able to do its work independently of outside chaos. The organization structure must adapt itself to changing situations, demands, and conditions.

- *Perpetuation and self-renewal*: The organization structure must provide paths of upward migration for individuals; it should be designed for continuous learning and individual achievement. For perpetuation and self-improvement the organization structure must be accessible to new ideas.

Division of labor

The organization structure needs to support division of labor across appropriate units. The classical examples are:

- Horizontal—As in an assembly line, or larger and larger plants to accomplish one task like steel plate production, effort may be applied to parts of closely related activities and achieve economies of scale.

- Vertical—As with "vertical integration" in which a firm may operate mines, steel plants, and toaster assembly lines (or farms, meat processors, and retail stores), the organization may concentrate on all steps in producing a product, gaining economies from control of the total process.

- Specialized—A truer word is probably "other": for example, one-time teams that design, then produce single large items like aircraft or unique outputs of major subsystems within a complex software development effort.

Departmentalization

Just as labor or tasks may be divided, so may the organization establish *departments* with responsibilities for various related activities. Common types of departmentalization are by function and by geography.

By function

• *Marketing*

Marketing involves coordinating demand forecasts, sales efforts, production scheduling, and distribution channels. In some firms, all these and other activities may be handled by one department, thus gaining advantages from having specialists that individual organizational units might not be able to afford.

• *Finance/accounting*

A centralized finance/accounting department may administer many activities like budget processing, payroll, and various accounting tasks. Examples of benefits could include combining the firm's cash resources into one pool, with an investment manager to handle short-term money management so that the larger pool can earn interest or other income until the funds are required for use (a larger pool enables investments that are not practical or available in smaller units, and may more than repay the expense of hiring an investment manager).

• *Production/operations*

Factory planning, production scheduling, and similar activities may be segregated into a department that can specialize, with the usual benefits.

• *Research and development*

R & D is the innovative activity of the enterprise. The typical research and development activity is a *team* organization, in which a variety of "skills" are applied to a particular problem or innovative concept. The two types of research are:

  • *Basic* research, which expands the frontiers of scientific knowledge
  • *Applied* research, which applies scientific knowledge to a commercial objective.

  Development converts the results of basic and applied research to marketable products.

  In the case of research, management is normally at the project level (functional), with minimum supervisory responsibilities. In the case of development, both the team organization and the *System Structure* are implemented to achieve the desired objective.

• *Human resources/personnel*

The department responsible for administering such functions as employee record-keeping, advertising for openings, initial interviews to screen clearly unsuitable candidates, counselling services, and perhaps medical services is usually called personnel or human resources. It is a staff function with some peculiarities caused by needs for confidentiality (even from senior management) in counselling and health care issues. Ensuring that accurate position descriptions exist, ensuring appropriate reviews and so on are functions of human resources; the actual reviews and hiring or promotion decisions naturally are line management responsibilities.

By location/geography

Firms may organize along geographical lines. This may be appropriate for a transnational firm that deals in many countries with differing economic, political, and social conditions; or it may be as simple as locating activities near the customers to improve response and minimize distribution costs.

Other forms of departmentalization include by product or service, and by customer.

By product or service

A diversified firm may find that the activities involved in, for example, handling customer credit and operating retail stores or automobile sales operations, are so different that organizing along the lines of such dissimilar products is justified. Examples include General Motors with its divisions of Chevrolet, Oldsmobile and so on plus EDS (Electronic Data Systems) for data processing services and GMAC (General Motors Acceptance Corporation) for customer financial activities.

By customer

In some instances, particularly where large, unique projects are involved, there may be only one or only a few potential customers. The firm may set up divisions to handle specific customers like a government, or types of customers like the financial services, insurance, or banking industry.

Combination structures

Any or all of the preceding may be combined in appropriate circumstances. The most common reasons are related to organizations where specific projects demand major commitments. For example, an aircraft development project is a complex activity for Boeing that justifies a project including several of the preceding functions. Another example is development of the space shuttle by NASA. In our industry, major software development efforts typically are managed on a project basis, with various teams of personnel with various capabilities attached to the project at appropriate phases (see section 9.4 below for DP Project management).

One model of management relations for project management is so-called matrix management. This refers to the structure that results when people from various reporting relationships are assigned to one or more projects. The reporting relationship to the project manager is by function within the project; however the individual reports permanently to some other management, giving a second dimension. With several projects and several individuals each working on more than one project, the resulting reporting relationships form a matrix.

Scalar principle

The scalar principle refers to the number of persons reporting to a single manager. Historically, military operations have contributed to this concept. The concept is arguably modified to the point of non-validity by the ability of computers in networks to filter and report to managers; it is no longer true that a manager should supervise only seven (or whatever fixed number) employees. The impact of the computer and of connected computers on middle management and *span of control* has only begun; yet already the number of "layers of management" is declining dramatically as senior staff are able to monitor many more subordinates through use of interconnected computers. In organizations where most employee activity involves use of the same or connected computers, computers allow senior managers to monitor employee performance at whatever detail is necessary, thus dispensing with the role of middle manager as an information filter.

Unity of command

In principle, no person should report to more than one master. The disadvantages are in conflicting directives and similar confusion. Project management and matrix reporting structures violate this principle, successfully in some kinds of activities and less successfully for other types of activities.

Line versus staff

With the preceding discussion in mind, it is now possible to view the line and staff concepts in the context of organizational structure and management philosophy.

- The *line* organization is conceived as a chain of authority, much like the military, which places emphasis on a management *hierarchy*.
- The *staff* is conceived as functionally necessary for results that cannot be achieved with line organization along, or through, vertical authority.

Centralization versus decentralization

Centralization and decentralization are authority relationships rather than location or functional relationships. *Decentralization* pertains to assigning of decision-making authority at the lowest level that yields the greatest effectiveness. The degree of decentralization that can be achieved is dependent upon the characteristics and magnitude of the enterprise.

Favorable conditions and arguments for either centralization or decentralization can be made (Peter Drucker):

Factor	Favorable to *Centralization*	Favorable to *Decentralization*
History of Expansion	Internal growth	External Acquisition
Economic size	Small	Large
Policy	Broad, vague	Uniform
Cost of Decision	High	Low
Local Environment	Stable	Dynamic, unstable
Output	Difficult to Measure	Objective standards
Subordinate Managers	Inexperienced	Well-trained

Behavioral influences

Business portfolio concept and strategic business units

A corporation or conglomerate may purchase other businesses. Particularly in cyclical industries, it may make good business sense to have a *portfolio* of businesses whose ups and downs (hopefully) do not coincide. One example might be swimwear manufacturers and ski manufacturers; when sales of one are down sales of the other are up. The principle has been carried to extremes, and some conglomerates have owned dozens or more of other businesses. Management of a portfolio of businesses is difficult and there are many examples of (sometimes spectacular) failure.

In a longer-term sense than the seasonal example, businesses themselves have cycles of startup, maturity, and decline (to over-simplify). One portfolio characterization is:

- *Stars*, winners in every way. Invest and keep them happy.
- *Cash cows*, mature or dying industries. Typically have solid markets and good cash flow; stop maintenance and such "unessential" expenses and milk them (hence the "cow"). Doing this usually transforms them into dogs.
- *Problem children*: Typically a business that turns out not to fit with the conglomerate; it's difficult or impossible to manage and shows no long-term promise for profit, but has promise if some conditions change. Change the conditions or get rid of the business.
- *Dogs*: Losers in every way, no chance of a turnaround and no assets to justify keeping them. Drop them.

- *Appropriate scale versus economies of scale*

In rural parts of the country one may hear the notion that there are two economical sizes for chicken farms: 5 dozen and 5,000 dozen. The idea is that the small number scratch in the yard (no feed cost) and the larger number produce enough eggs to pay for the buildings and feeds necessary at that scale. Similarly, the cost of the plant and equipment to produce computer chips is in the area of hundreds of millions of dollars; the production cost per chip is perhaps $10. The *economy of scale* refers to the low-cost production per unit that a large plant provides; it's an *appropriate scale* if there's a market for the product at a reasonable price. Five dozen chickens will feed a farm family nicely but would not be an *appropriate scale* to earn a living selling eggs, although the cost per egg is much lower at the smaller scale.

- *Leading*

Executive leadership is the bottom line with respect to the present and future prospects of an enterprise. Executive leadership both reflects and influences the quality and substance of an enterprise and the people within it.

- *Influence*

Leadership may be exercised by *influencing*, or persuading people. Certain individuals have "influence"; that is, they are listened to by decision makers, or they are respected, or they otherwise have the ability to cause behavior changes in others.

- *Power*

Leadership may be exercised through the use of *power*. An individual may have the power to promote or fire people, or even to incarcerate them; this person can enforce decisions through the use of this power.

- *Authority*

Authority derives from several sources:

- Position: The "president" has authority.
- Charisma: The person is a "born leader".
- Consensus: The person is agreed to be the leader by the group.
- Knowledge: The person is the only one who knows what's going on.

The source of authority is distinct from the ability to accomplish things and from the style of exercising authority.

- *Styles of leadership*

The role top-level management plays in the organization is discussed above. However the *manner* in which executive authority is exercised, as an aspect of leadership, is critical to the success of the enterprise. An accepted categorization of the manners in which authority is exercised includes:

- Exploitative Authoritative ("My way or the highway")
- Benevolent Authoritative ("This is what's best for you")
- Consultative or collegial ("Tell me your opinion, I decide")
- Participative Group (consensus—everyone must agree)
- Democratic (Voting)
- Laissez-faire ("I hire the right people and leave them alone to do the job.")

The Exploitative Authoritative style of leadership is considered to be best suited to achieve peak performance in the short run. The Participative Group leader is believed to attain the highest productivity and morale over an extended period of time; yet this style of leadership is prone to evolution of a personality cult, and is therefore most vulnerable to the psychological impact of changes in management personnel and style (the "indispensable" manager).

Different styles work better with different groups. Management of technical people often leans towards the laissez-faire approach; management of volunteers often is collegial or by consensus; political management often is more or less democratic.

9.2.3 Centralized Organization

The illustration in Figure 9.2 below indicates one classical view of how to organize a major operation around a mainframe computer. In this and Figures 9.3 and 9.4, it must be kept in mind that as information technology changes, so is the organization of units to make use of that technology. For example, the "minicomputer organization" actually existed in the mid-1980s; that particular organization in 1992 bears little resemblance to the picture of five years previously.

9.2.4 Decentralized Organization

As with other organizational structures, the decentralized organization is undergoing rapid change. Some mainframe organizations now resemble the "office automation" sketch below. Some office automation environments resemble downsized mainframe organizations. (The phenomenon of replacing mainframe MIPS with networks of microcomputers providing similar MIPS and total storage but at perhaps 5% to 10% of the cost is called *downsizing*. The jury is out on how successful it will be. Replacing major centralized staff with something like the decentralized office automation concept saves people and money, but it may leave an organization seriously exposed to reliability problems and without internal staff to cope with technical needs.)

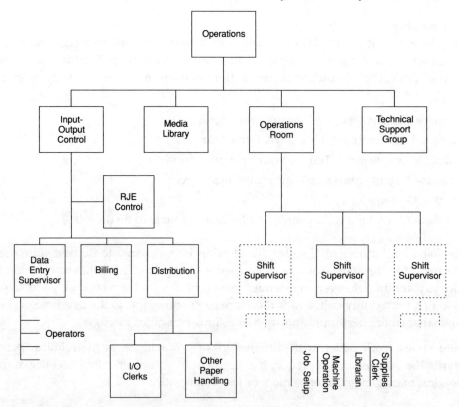

Figure 9.2. Typical Mainframe Organization

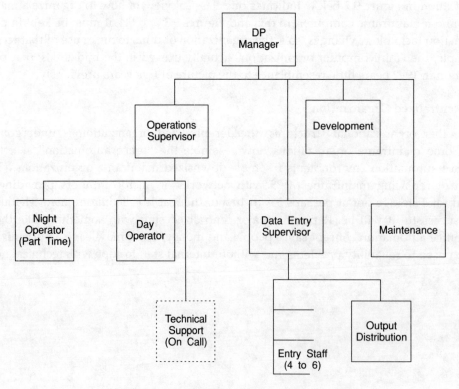

Figure 9.3. Typical Minicomputer Organization

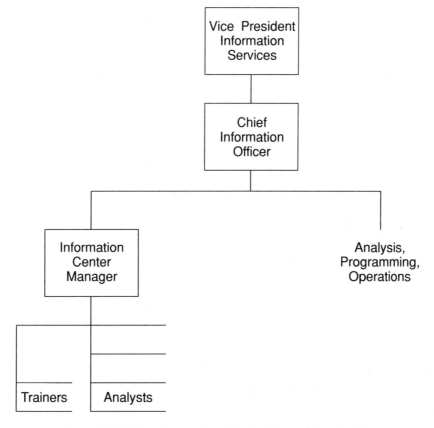

Figure 9.4. Office Automation/Service Center Organization

9.2.5 Line and Staff Responsibilities

Unlike the line organization, in which the chain of authority is uninterrupted from the individual worker to the chief executive, the staff organization performs an advisory or supporting role. In terms of increasing authority, staffs may be classified as follows:

- *Advisory* staff—provides special or technical recommendations
- *Service* staff—provides technical skills and selected services, with a strong influence on line management
- *Control* staff—develops policies and procedures, and defines limits of authority of line management. The control staff advises in technical areas and monitors line activities within the staff's area of authority
- *Functional* staff—has full line management authority; crosses normal chain-of-command for specific activities

9.3 ORGANIZATIONAL CONSIDERATIONS FOR COMPUTER SECURITY INCIDENT RESPONSE

An issue of increasing importance since the late 1980s is response to computer security incidents. Examples of incidents include viruses, worms that may overload an entire network (perhaps international in scale) and many hacker activities. A Computer Security Response Capability (CSIRC) is defined by NIST as:

> . . . that part of a computer security effort that provides the capability to respond to computer security threats rapidly and effectively. A CSIRC is a direct extension of the contingency planning process, due to its explicit preparedness to respond to threats as they occur.[2]

Other issues related to contingency planning and incident response were addressed in Chapter 4. A CSIRC normally would include a Computer Emergency Response Team (CERT). This section discusses issues specifically related both to the CSIR capability and to the team (perhaps an extension of existing contingency team[s]) whose mandate it is to implement the CSIRC. The focus in this section is on organizational issues rather than on the actual operation of a CSIRC or CERT once it is in place. The NIST publication *Establishing a Computer Security Response Capability (CSIRC)*, NIST Special Publication 800-3, which provided the definition quoted above, contains guidelines to operational issues as well as more detail on organizational considerations than the outline here.

Seven primary issues must be addressed in the establishment of a CSIRC:

1. Determine goals
2. Define the CSIRC Constituency
3. Determine the structure
4. Secure management support and funding
5. Create a charter
6. Create an Operations handbook
7. Determine staffing

Determine Goals

NIST suggests the following list of possible CSIRC goals:

- Facilitate centralized reporting of incidents.
- Coordinate response to incidents of a certain type or affecting a certain technology.
- Provide direct technical assistance as needed.
- Perform training and raise security awareness of users and vendors.
- Provide a clearinghouse for relevant computer security information.
- Provide data and other inputs to the contingency planning effort.
- Promote security policies within a constituency.
- Develop or distribute software tools to the constituency.
- Encourage vendors to respond to product-related problems.
- Provide liaisons to legal and criminal investigative groups.

The most important considerations are that goals should be *simple, unambiguous,* and *realistic.*

---

[2]NIST Special Publication 800-3.

Define the CSIRC Constituency

The goals will define the constituency of the CSIRC. The size of the constituency and the scope of the technical focus will constrain the size and expense of the effort. One issue that must be addressed is formal *versus* informal constituencies. If the CSIRC needs to deal with individuals or organizations outside its expected sphere, resource problems can arise.

Determine the Structure

A CSIRC can be provided in a centralized fashion or in any of a number of decentralized modes. Organizational issues relating to centralization and decentralization of technical staff have been addressed already in this chapter.

Secure Management Support and Funding

Without management support and funding, no organizational effort can succeed. In the case of a CSIRC, one issue is uncertainty: Until the operation is in place and has a track record, it may be difficult or impossible to estimate costs precisely. Benefits also may be difficult to assess, even given a track record.

Create a Charter

Legal issues such as negligence can arise during the operation of a CSIRC. A formal charter may help avoid such problems if it states precisely what the CSIRC is and is not planning to do, how it will accomplish its goals, and where the limits on its scope lie.

Such a charter should include something like these sections:

1. Executive Summary
2. Responsibilities
3. Methods
4. Reporting Structure and staffing

The charter needs to be reviewed by legal counsel.

Create an Operations Handbook

The operations handbook is a primary document for reference during daily activities and during incident handling. It should contain:

- Staffing information (particularly contact information)
- Hotline use (numbers, procedures, and on-call information for 24-hour operation)
- Procedures for receiving and sending information from and to constituencies
- Types, contents, review, and handling of incident reports
- Logging, sensitivity considerations, and so forth regarding information handling
- Administration policies, configuration, procedures regarding CSIRC computer equipment
- Administrative procedures (expense reports, travel, security clearances, etc.)
- Contacts within investigative agencies (FBI, Secret Service, RCMP, etc.)
- Dealing with media (press reports, clearance process);
- Vendor contacts
- Other contact information

250 Information Systems Security: A Practitioner's Reference

Such information must be current. As with the charter, legal review of the handbook is advised.

Determine Staffing

Staffing obviously is a function of the scope of the CSIRC and its mandate. The requirement for 24-hour response implies constraints of the personality type and number of people needed. The nature of the response may define a minimum number. Need for specific technical knowledge and capabilities is another determining factor.

9.4 MANAGEMENT OF INFORMATION TECHNOLOGY AND SERVICES

It is questionable whether management of information technology and services differs materially from any other form of general management of an organizational function. Certainly the individual characteristics of staff differ from those of staff in other departments (programmers have relatively low social needs and relatively high growth needs, for example); however so too do the characteristics of accountants differ from, for example, successful sales personnel. The time frames of change in information technology are very short, but other departments also cope with short time frames.

The two key areas where information technology differs from most other management needs are:

1. Information technologies impact on the operations of all other departments, and increasingly so.
2. Most data processing projects have been managed on a project management basis, more like succeeding research projects than like day-to-day operational work.

More and more, information technology forms the backbone of operations for all corporate activities. Whether it is processing of bank transactions, supporting networks of personal work stations using data from a central database to design aircraft, or providing access to accounting records so customer service personnel can answer queries, successful provision of information is critical. Unlike many other activities, the proper functioning of information services has an immediate impact on essentially every corporate activity.

While short time frames are not unique to information technology, the rate of change is extreme in computer hardware. In November, 1989 Compaq corporation announced a 486-based machine for under $25,000 that significantly outperforms minicomputers which sold for $100,000 to $150,000 less than a year before (and in some cases, at the same time). In the fall of 1992, machines with more memory, more secondary storage, and higher processing speeds cost less than $2,500. Organizations that are able to manage information technology to take advantage of this kind of rapid and large change can do new things, or can do older things at much lower costs, than those who that can not take advantage. Although user training and tactical planning are not necessarily primarily the responsibility of IS management, the pervasive influence of information technology combined with the rate of change presents unique challenges and opportunities.

9.4.1 Project Management

A data processing project has the following characteristics:

- Definite and measurable goals
- Onetime cost of undertaking
- Recurring cost *versus* benefits of project results
- A sequence of events leading to completion
- An opportunity for evaluation and improvement after project completion

Executive responsibilities include:

- Project definition
- Assignment of project responsibility
- Provision of personnel and material resources
- Establishing project control parameters as to project duration, major control points for reporting, and reporting procedures
- Exercising go/no-go authority at critical points

The administration or management of regular or routine projects, such as those performed on a daily or periodic basis, is usually accomplished as part of the normal data processing activity. The first-time project, however, requires special attention if it involves a major change in work, a new concept, and a new approach.

Tasks that could qualify as separate projects in implementing a data processing system include the *feasibility study*, the *application study*, the *equipment proposal*, the *equipment selection*, the *equipment installation*, and the final *conversion*.

Project management would include direction and control of any or all of the following tasks:

- The *feasibility study*, which would include a formal statement of measurable goals; an estimate of project cost, and formal justification of the project in terms of cost/benefits.
- The *application study*, which is an extension of the feasibility study and which includes such design concepts as:
  - standardization of terms and procedures
  - close-to-source data capture
  - exception reporting techniques
  - provision of most timely and useful user data format
  - selection of most suitable equipment, software, and procedures to efficiently meet the job requirements

- *Equipment selection*, which includes definition of general and special requirements; qualification of vendors; and evaluation of equipment.

- *Post-project audit and review*, to measure the results of the project either at its completion or at a milestone during the course of the project.

The techniques of project management include:

- Establishing a planning team
- Development of a long-range plan
- Determination of the *critical path*

- Development of contingency or emergency plans
- The use of Gantt Charts, milestone tables, and PERT charts

There are several general steps to implementing an application:

- Develop a "users" training program.
- Assign training responsibility.

  - provide a training model (simulation)
  - test the training model and methods
  - make the necessary corrections

- Install a "test" system for training and "debugging".
- Perform *final* system corrections.
- Develop a conversion plan.
- Coordinate the conversion.
- Perform "live" system testing (in parallel, if possible).
- On user *acceptance*, implement the system.

Finally, note a key characteristic of properly managed projects:

The successful project ENDS!

REFERENCES

"EDP Threat Assessments: Concepts and Planning Guide," *RCMP Security Information Publications # 2*, January, 1982.

"Good Security Practices for Personal Computers," IBM Data Security Support Programs, First Edition (March, 1984).

AFIPS Systems Review Manual on Security, AFIPS Press, Montvale, NJ, 1974.

Computer Control Guidelines Second Edition, Canadian Institute of Chartered Accountants (CICA), February, 1986.

Emergency Preparedness Canada, *Guide to the Preservation of Essential Records*, EPC 12/87, December, 1987. 121 pages, French & English.

Fisher, Royal, *Information Systems Security*, Prentice-Hall, Englewood Cliffs, NJ, 1984.

Fites, Philip. E., Martin P. J. Kratz, and Alan F. Brebner, *Control and Security of Computer Information Systems*, W. H. Freeman/Computer Science Press, 1989.

Gallegos, Frederick, Dana R. (Rick) Richardson, & A. Faye Borthick, *Audit & Control of Information Systems*, South-Western Publishing Company, West. Chicago, IL, 1987.

Gorrill, B. E., *Effective Personnel Security Procedures*, Dow Jones-Irwin, Inc., Homewood, IL, 1974.

Krauss, Leonard L. and Aileen MacGahan, *Computer Fraud and Countermeasures*, Prentice-Hall, Englewood Cliffs, NJ, 1979.

Lobel, J., *Foiling the System Breakers: Computer Security and Access Control*, McGraw-Hill, NY, 1986.

Martin, James, *Security, Accuracy, and Privacy in Computer Systems*, Prentice-Hall, Inc., Englewood Cliffs, NJ, 1973.

Parker, Donn B, *Computer Security Management*, Reston Publishing Company, Inc., Reston, VA, 1981.

Parker, Donn B., *Fighting Computer Crime*, Charles Scribner & Sons, New York, NY, 1983.

Straub, Detmar W., "Organizational Structuring of the Computer Security Function," *Computers & Security* 7 (1988), p. 185-195.

Van Tassel, Dennis, *Computer Security Management*, Prentice-Hall, Inc., Englewood Cliffs, NJ, 1972.

Wack, John P., *Establishing a Computer Security Response Capability (CSIRC)*, NIST Special Publication 800-3, National Institute of Standards and Technology, Gaithersburg, MD, November, 1991.

10. Legal/Regulatory

This section describes in a general way the laws and regulations that the professional is expected to know.

The professional is expected to know:

- Laws and regulations that bind the behavior of his organization
- Those that bind his own behavior
- Those that offer remedies to his constituents
- Others as applicable

For example, the professional is expected to:

- Recognize all applicable federal laws
- Identify applicable federal regulations
- Know the criminal law of the local jurisdictions
- Know applicable civil law
- Recognize landmark cases
- Recognize model laws
- Other.

The purpose of this chapter is to give the information systems security professional a basic understanding and overview of the legal system and some of the particular laws that may be of importance to the information systems security professional's work. The outline provided here sets out basic principles of law. It is important that the reader realize that individual fact situations may result in application of different rules than those general principles described in this chapter. As a result, it is very important that the information systems security professional obtain advice from a competent attorney authorized to practice in the jurisdiction in question in any situation where rights, responsibilities, or interpretation of law may be desired.

This material is intended to help the information systems security professional understand aspects of the legal system that can be used to facilitate a computer security plan and those aspects of the legal system that may cause the information systems security professional some difficulty in enforcing that computer security plan in particular fact situations. It is important for the reader to remember that the law is only a tool, albeit a very important tool, to be used in the development of the security arrangements for any computer system, computer programs.

This chapter addresses some of the legal specifics that relate to computer security and liability. The nature of the legal field is changing rapidly. The professional working in computer security who comes into contact with the law is strongly advised to obtain knowledgeable legal advice.

The intention is to provide a background for the intelligent assessment of legal options in the design of security systems and also to provide a background to the policy issues that may motivate legislative reform. With this understanding, it is anticipated that the security professional may play an active role in the law reform process and ensure that the development of law in this fast-changing industry will be consistent with the needs of that industry.

DEFINITIONS

Some useful definitions in the legal area are covered below. Some definitions from government regulations are provided here; please note that usage varies under differing legislation and jurisdictions. Some of the terms defined here have substantially different meanings depending on the legal context in which they are used. Professional legal advice is encouraged.

Collusion

The act of two or more Agents or Perpetrators cooperating or conspiring to perpetrate an Intentional Event.

Computer Abuse

1. Willful or negligent unauthorized activity that affects the availability, confidentiality, or integrity of computer resources. Computer abuse includes fraud, embezzlement, theft, malicious damage, unauthorized use, denial of service, and misappropriation. Levels of computer abuse are:

   a) Minor abuse—acts that represent management problems, such as printing calendars or running games that do not impact system availability for authorized applications;

   b) Major abuse—unauthorized use (possibly criminal), denial of service, and multiple instances of minor abuse to include waste;

   c) Criminal act—fraud, embezzlement, theft, malicious damage, misappropriation, conflict of interest, and unauthorized access to classified data. (AFR 205-16)

2. The misuse, destruction, alteration, or disruption of data processing resources. The key aspects of computer related abuse are that it is intentional and improper and it may not involve the violation of a specific law. (NCSC-WA-001-85)

Computer Crime

Fraud, embezzlement, unauthorized access, and other "white collar" crimes committed with the aid of or directly involving a computer system and/or network. (GAO)

Computer Fraud

Computer-related crimes involving deliberate misrepresentation or alteration of data in order to obtain something of value (usually for monetary gain). A computer system must have been involved in the perpetration or cover-up of the act, or series of acts. A computer system might have been involved through improper manipulation of:

1. input data
2. output or results
3. applications programs
4. data files
5. computer operations
6. communications
7 computer hardware, systems software, or firmware (NCSC-WA-001-85)

Entrapment

The deliberate planting of apparent flaws in a system for the purpose of detecting attempted penetrations or confusing an intruder about which flaws to exploit. (AR 380-380; FIPS PUB 39; NCSC-WA-001-85)

Investigation(s)

The review and analysis of system security features (*e.g.*, the investigation of system control programs using flow charts, assembly listings, and related documentation) to determine the security provided by the operating system. (OPNAVINST 5239.1A; DODD 5200.28M)

National Security Decision Directive 145

Signed by President Reagan on 17 September, 1984, this directive is entitled, "National Policy on Telecommunications and Automated Information Systems Security." It provides initial objectives, policies, and an organizational structure to guide the conduct of national activities toward safeguarding systems which process, store, or communicate sensitive information, establishes a mechanism for policy development, and assigns implementation responsibilities. (NCSC-WA-001-85)

Notarization

The registration of data with a trusted third party that allows the later assurance of the accuracy of its characteristics such as content, origin, time, and delivery. (ISO 7498-2)

Penetration

The successful act of bypassing the security mechanisms of a system. (NCSC-WA-001-85)

Penetration Profile

A delineation of activities required to effect a penetration. (FIPS PUB 39; AR 380-380)

Penetration Signature

1. The description of a situation or set of conditions in which a penetration could occur or of system events which in conjunction can indicate the occurrence of a penetration in progress. (AR 380-380; FIPS PUB 39)
2. The characteristics or identifying marks that may be produced of an unsuccessful or successful penetration. (NCSC-WA-001-85)

Penetration Study

A study to determine the feasibility and methods for defeating controls of an Automated Information System. (NCSC-WA-001-85)

Privacy

The right of individuals and organizations to control the collection, storage, and dissemination of their information or information about themselves. (FIPS PUB 39)

Privacy Protection

The establishment of appropriate administrative, technical, and physical safeguards to ensure the security and confidentiality of data records and to protect both security and confidentiality against any anticipated threats or hazards that could result in substantial harm, embarrassment, inconvenience, or unfairness to any individual about whom such information is maintained. (FIPS PUB 39)

Proprietary Data

Data that is created, used, and marketed by individuals having[1] exclusive legal rights. (AFR 205-16)

Pseudo-Flaw

An apparent loophole deliberately implanted in an operating system program as a trap for intruders. (FIPS PUB 39; AR 380-380; NCSC-WA-001-85)

Review and Approval

The process whereby information pertaining to the security and integrity of an ADP activity or network is collected, analyzed, and submitted to the appropriate DAA for accreditation of the activity or network. (OPNAVINST 5239.1A)

Security Breach

A violation of controls of a particular information system such that information assets or system components are unduly exposed. (WB)

Security Violation

An instance in which a user or other person circumvents or defeats the controls of a system to obtain unauthorized access to information contained therein or to system resources. (WB)

Softlifting

Illegal copying of licensed software for personal use. (PC/PCIE)

Tampering

An unauthorized modification which alters the proper functioning of a system or piece of equipment in a manner which degrades the security it provides. (NCSC-WA-001-85)

Theft

A peril involving removal of an asset for subsequent use by an agent.

10.1 INTRODUCTION

10.1.1 Theft of Hardware and Copying Software

When computers were first introduced some 50 years ago, business and government were quick to make use of their enormous potential as information-processing machines. About the same

---

[1]More correctly, "claiming to have." The more positive term is retained in this quotation.

time a number of enterprising individuals also saw the potential of these machines for personal gain and began to match their wits against them and find ways to use computers for criminal purposes. It is estimated that the average armed robbery nets less than $7,000[2] and the average computer fraud totals about $109,000.[3] This is a high-yield, low-risk crime.

One area of computer crime is the theft of hardware and software. The outright theft of hardware and software is often reported and identified as the prime motive for a crime. In some instances only parts of the computer are targeted.

Many companies have paid substantial settlements to software vendors for software piracy perpetrated by their employees. In June, 1985, American Brands Company paid an undisclosed amount of cash to Micropro after admitting that some of American Brands' employees had pirated copies of Micropro software. Lotus Development Corporation sued Mueller Company and settled for a large sum for illegal copying and use of Lotus software by Mueller employees, including Mueller's MIS director and a corporate manager of data processing. Companies are becoming more aware that unauthorized software copying by their employees is a continuing problem that must be addressed. The extent of the problem is such that there are severe impacts on the total software development industries of many countries.[4]

10.1.2 Fraud

The computer can create a unique environment in which unauthorized activities can occur. Crimes in this category have many traditional names including theft, fraud, embezzlement, extortion, etc. Computer-related fraud includes the introduction of fraudulent records into a computer system, theft of money by electronic means, theft of financial instruments, theft of services, and theft of valuable data.[5]

10.1.3 Physical Abuse

The computer can be the object of an attack in computer crimes such as the unauthorized use of computer facilities, alteration or destruction of information, data file sabotage, and vandalism against a computer system. Computers have been shot, stabbed, short-circuited, burned, and bombed[6].

10.1.4 Misuse of Information and Privacy

Computer output can be used symbolically to intimidate, deceive, or defraud victims. Attorneys, government agencies, and businesses increasingly use mounds of computer-generated data quite legally to confound their audiences. Criminals also find useful phony invoices, bills, and checks generated by the computer. The computer lends an ideal cloak for carrying out criminal acts by imparting a clean quality to the crime.

---

[2]Royal Canadian Mounted Police figures.

[3][NCCCD 89] Broad estimates of this nature must be considered with caution. Earlier reports have found significant differences among averages in private business, local, and national governmental computer crime incidents. One incident alone in November, 1988 (the "InterNet Worm") involved costs of at least tens of millions. Also, there is much speculation that a majority (perhaps 95%) [Parker 81] of computer crimes go unreported and thus are not included in such estimates.

[4][Wyles 88]. Many articles appear regularly in the trade press describing the impact, or announcing the latest settlements or convictions.

[5][Krauss 79]

[6][NCCCD 89; Whiteside 78]

The computer has made the invasion of our privacy a great deal easier and potentially more dangerous than before the advent of the computer. A wide range of data are collected and stored in computerized files related to individuals. These include banking information, credit information, organizational fund raising, opinion polls, shop-at-home services, driver's licence data, arrest records, and medical records. The potential threats to privacy include the improper commercial use of computerized data, breaches of confidentially by releasing confidential data to third parties, and the release of records to governmental agencies for investigative purposes.

The basic law in the United States that protects privacy is the Fourth Amendment to the U.S. Constitution,[7] which mandates that people have a right to be secure in homes and against unreasonable searches and seizures. In addition a number of laws have been enacted to protect the individual from having damaging information stored in computerized databases.

10.1.5 Issues of Adjudication and Regulation

Traditionally prosecutors have faced a great deal of uncertainty when they attempted to use existing criminal statutes to prosecute offenses. Within the last few years this has changed with the addition to many state and federal codes of computer crime statutes.

Computer crime laws can be seen as a generalized reaction to the many types of computer crime. The goal of these laws is to define the acts that will be punished in the hopes that this will deter computer crime. Some of these acts include the act of trespassing into a computerized system, the invasion of privacy of an individual, the theft of money, service, data or programs from a computerized system, and data alteration or destruction.

Computer laws can also be used to prevent or deter computer-related fraud and the misuse of computerized information. That is to say, the law provides compensation for injuries and, it is hoped, deters wrongdoers by the smooth and efficient operation of the legal system. The law does not generally provide a remedy if no injury has occurred. The law then acts as a shield through its deterrent effect and not in a proactive manner. Where it is vital that the injury does not occur, then the physical and environmental controls described elsewhere in this text[8] must be utilized as additional barriers against the wrongdoer. On the other hand, after a wrongdoer has compromised the physical or environmental security arrangements, the law is generally the only tool available to the information security specialist to minimize the injury already done and to deter, so far as is possible, future wrongdoing.

10.2 LAWS AS TOOLS FOR COMPUTER SECURITY

10.2.1 What Is Law?

Life in complex society gives rise to many forms of individual dispute. A tenant may be angry at a landlord for something the landlord has or has not done. Drivers and pedestrians desire to use the public roadways in a safe and predictable manner. A businessman wishes for certainty and predictability in his or her business relations. The person injured as a result of another's error, mistake, or intentional act seeks redress and compensation.

---

[7]Legislation with similar goals exists in other countries as well.

[8]And others, *eg* [CICA 86]; [Fites and Kratz 89]; [Krauss 79]

The law provides a series of rules establishing the guidelines or parameters for the different relationships that individuals in society enter into. The purpose of these rules is to provide a framework that offers certainty, provides predictability and leads to the resolution of disputes. These rules, which make up the law, also reflect society's concept of justice. This concept of justice has, however, developed over many years so that basic principles of fair play, honesty, truthfulness, and the like are encouraged. The law does not adapt well to very rapid changes in the majority (or minorities') definition of justice or what would be a just result in a particular dispute. The courts tend to take the broader perspective attempting to integrate a particular fashionable viewpoint against a thousand years of legal history and understanding of fundamental human behavior.

Many societies have been overcome and their legal systems overwhelmed by a new concept of how the law should adapt to a particular definition of "justice" that serves the interests of a particular group. An example would be the effect of the rise to power of the National Socialist German Workers' Party in the 1930s and its effect on Germany's legal system. The challenge to our legal system is to adapt swiftly enough to deal with new problems but not so swiftly as to lose sight of the basic principles upon which our society is built.

10.2.2 Common Law

The United States, Canada, England, Australia, New Zealand and many other countries are common-law countries. This means that a large part of their law is as a result of the "common law." The common law encompasses the decisions of countless judges in innumerable cases over the last millennium and generally has developed a sense of practical justice and commercial certainty to resolve conflicts and disputes. The harshness, in isolated cases, of application of rules in fact situations where the application of those rules would be against the prevailing concept of justice is often tempered in such common-law countries by another parallel system of law called *equity*. In most common law countries both the common-law and equity are applied by the same courts.

In common law countries a large amount of the law is developed by the judges interpreting and resolving particular fact situations and disputes. However in modern times a very significant amount of law and regulation issues from the legislative branch of government. Such statute law and regulation provides the regulatory and administrative framework to deal with modern problems, establishes new legal structures to encourage certain political, economic and social policy objectives, and adapts or modifies the pre-existing common-law rules that may be outdated or unsuitable for the more complex problems in our more complex Western societies. The statutory rules and regulations are interpreted and applied by the judges of the various courts to individual fact situations. Those judges are still called upon to develop new common law even in circumstances where a statutory framework may exist so as to deal with internal conflicts in the statute, problems not anticipated by the statute, or inadequacies in the statutory schemes may arise from time to time in particular fact situations.

10.2.3 Civil Law Jurisdictions

In contrast to the common-law countries, other countries have a civil law system based on a fundamental code of law. This approach, for example, is adopted by many countries that rely on the civil code used by the Roman Empire. For example, Germany and France each applies a different civil code to set out the general rules, obligations, and responsibilities that arise from different relationships in the society. Examples of jurisdictions with civil codes also occur as a result of historical development. For example, the State of Louisiana and the Province of Quebec both apply civil codes to deal with certain matters within the jurisdiction of that state or province respectively.

Because the civil codes must deal with and contemplate all possible relationships or business transactions they must be long and complex. Many of the rules in the civil codes are set out as broad principles without the detail that is often found in statutes of common-law countries or the detail of specific judges' decisions in common-law countries. As a result judges in civil law countries often must adapt or interpret those broad principles to meet particular situations.

10.3 CONSTITUTIONAL STRUCTURE

Lastly and again by way of introduction there are two general arrangements for disposition of the legislative power in a country. The first and simplest arrangement is a unitary system. In such a country, England for example, all of the legislative power exists with the English Parliament. Newer countries have developed federal systems to permit the sharing of power among regions, such as the United States, Canada, Australia, and Germany. In a federal system the complete legislative power and authority is divided between the federal level of government and the state or provincial governments as the case may be. It is therefore fundamental in a federal system that there must be a written constitution to delineate the power and authority of the federal government and the state governments. In federal systems the courts play another important role as the final and independent interpreters of those constitutional limits.

This is important for our purposes as legislation, for example, by a state which sets out the rules that operate in an area of federal legislative competence in some circumstances may be held by a court to be invalid as law and *"ultra vires"* the constitutional power of the state. The same procedure applies to review of federal law that may operate in an area of state legislative competence. This is important because in federal systems it gives defendants who may have committed certain harmful acts a possible additional defense in an effort to escape legal responsibility by arguing that the particular provision under which they were charged was unconstitutional.

10.4 BROAD CATEGORIES OF LAW

The information systems security professional needs to be aware that there are three general areas into which the law can be categorized. These three broad areas identify certain of the broad roles that the law plays in governing different relationships in society. These areas are Criminal Law, Civil Law, and Administrative Law. Each of these areas is discussed in more detail below. In addition, two further sub-categories are outlined: Privacy Law and Intellectual Property Law.

10.4.1 Criminal Law

The first area is *criminal law*. Criminal law deals with certain individual conduct that is considered so morally reprehensible that the power of the state's criminal justice apparatus should be brought into play to prosecute the wrongdoer. It has traditionally brought public support for the criminal sanction being applied to certain forms of conduct such as, for example, murder, theft, assault, and the like. However, in more modern times, many types of economic and other conduct have also been criminalized. In a number of cases (for example, some forms of computer abuse) no broad consensus has developed to support the criminalization of the conduct. Not many years ago it was considered an educational exercise by some to attempt to subvert the security controls in many university computer systems. Now such action in many jurisdictions is considered criminal conduct. Because there is not yet broad social support for the full application of these provisions or because the provisions are sometimes so broadly drafted as also to include innocuous conduct, it sometimes may be difficult to obtain convictions. For example, where criminal law may make it an offense to own a satellite scrambler or to tune a scrambled cable signal a number of courts have apparently shown some sympathy to a defendant charged with such offenses and it has been difficult to obtain a conviction in some cases.

The criminal law provisions of primary concern to the information systems security professional are discussed in more detail below.

10.4.2 Civil Law

The second category of law is *civil law*. In this sense civil law is used in a different context than previously discussed. Previously civil law was used in the sense describing a civil code in certain countries as contrasted with common-law countries. Civil law is used in the present context (and throughout the rest of the discussion in this text) to mean the law that governs the relationships between individuals. That law deals with such things as torts (*i.e.*, assaults, battery, trespass, intentional infliction of mental suffering, negligence, and the like), the law of contracts (under which the parties to the contract established the rules that will govern their relationship), property law, and intellectual property law (*i.e.*, copyright, patent, trademark, designs and trade secrets, and the like). Unlike the criminal law these areas of civil law rely upon the plaintiff (the injured party) to bear responsibility for investigating and prosecuting his or her claim. That plaintiff is responsible for the costs of bringing any legal action. On the other hand, however, the plaintiff also has complete control over the conduct of the action. This is not the case with a criminal action where the process is initiated, financed, and supported by the state, but it is also under the control of the state and proceeds whether or not the original victim desires it to stop.

Some civil law provisions that are of interest to the information systems security professional are discussed in more detail below.

10.4.3 Administrative/Regulatory Law

The third major area of law is the *administrative* or regulatory systems of law. These are broad systems of law that generally set out standards of performance and conduct to provide some structure and orderliness in society and some predictability in conduct. These laws may be enacted to protect health, public safety, property, and many other worthwhile goals. Examples are the highway traffic laws that regulate the use of motor vehicles, the law regulating use of aircraft or watercraft, and similarly the laws regulating various governments, governmental departments and agencies' use of their power and assets. We will examine a number of these systems as they may be of some importance to the information systems security professional.

10.4.4 Other General Features of Law

A further factor must be identified as a preliminary matter. Except in very unique cases of threatened wrongdoing, the law generally provides remedies to redress an injury that has *already* occurred. That is to say, the law provides compensation for injuries and, hopefully, deters wrongdoers by the smooth and efficient operation of the legal machinery. The law does not generally provide a remedy if no injury has occurred. The law then acts as a shield through its deterrent effect and not in a proactive manner. Where it is vital that the injury does not occur, then the physical and environmental controls described elsewhere in this text must be utilized as additional barriers against the wrongdoer. On the other hand, after a wrongdoer has compromised the physical or environmental security arrangements, the law is generally the only tool available to the information security specialist to minimize the injury already done and to deter, so far as is possible, future wrongdoing.

By way of example, signing non-disclosure agreements with one's employees *prior* to giving sensitive or secret data or information to such employees serves as an advance warning or reminder to the employees. Since the relationship has been clearly defined, then there will be less potential risk of abuse of the confidential materials. Secondly, having clearly established these legal relationships, enforcement action is less costly and more certain of a successful outcome.

The information security specialist must not rely on legal mechanisms of security (such as creation of rights or obligations) in lieu of the technical and organizational security measures implemented in the environment. There also must be a sense of practicality and sensitivity introduced that will assist in ensuring that employees respect and understand the obligations under which they work. It may be far easier to deter security risks if employees understand their obligations, respect the information security specialist, and understand the consequences of breach of their obligations.

10.4.5 Privacy Laws and Legislation

A further category of law is privacy law. The law enforcement official requires access to a wide range of data and materials in conducting an information abuse investigation. Often, privacy legislation is seen as a barrier to access of information that may be useful in the investigation of such criminal conduct. However, such legislation may also serve as a very useful tool in the protection of data and information. In particular, such legislation provides options for enforcement of rights that may better reflect commercial reality. It is important for the security professional to be involved in the development of these remedies so that there can be a real balance among all of the interests involved.

Loss of privacy is a danger of the proliferation of computerized data banks. The computer's ability to collect, store, and manipulate vast amounts of data and its ability to retrieve selected items from these data banks almost instantaneously allows the collection and distribution of personal information that can affect one's privacy. One of the primary defenses against the loss of individual privacy is the enactment of legislation by national and state legislatures. The basic concern of privacy legislation has been the control and protection of information on or about individuals.

Privacy protection laws have been passed in most developed countries. Early in 1970, the U.S. introduced the Fair Credit and Reporting Act that governs the processing, access, and disclosure of credit information. The U.S. Privacy Act of 1974, and the Canadian Privacy Act 1975 are examples of laws that mandate protection of individual privacy. Other countries also have enacted laws related to individual privacy, including the Swedish Data Act of 1973, the German Federal Data Protection Act of 1977, the French Act on Data Processing of 1978, the Danish Acts on Private Registers, and the Austrian Federal Data Protection Act of 1978. At the international level, the OECD Transborder Data Flow Guidelines address the topic of the flow of information across international borders, perhaps to jurisdictions where privacy laws may differ from the originating venue. The OECD Guidelines are reproduced in section 10.12.

Local or regional jurisdictions such as states and provinces often have laws respecting privacy and disclosure of information. There is too much variation among jurisdictions for any meaningful treatment of these laws in this book; counsel familiar with the jurisdiction's laws should be consulted.

10.4.6 Intellectual Property Laws

Intellectual property law provides protection and exclusive or monopoly rights in relation to certain kinds of innovative activity. Four bodies of intellectual property law discussed below protect different aspects of these ideas and their practical applications.

10.4.6.1 Copyright law

Copyright law provides a very significant legal tool for use in protecting computer software, both before a security breach and certainly after a security breach. This type of breach could deal with misappropriation of data, computer programs, documentation, or similar material. For this reason the information security specialist will want to be familiar with basic concepts related to copyright law.

The United States, United Kingdom, Australia, Canada, and many other countries have amended or revised their copyright legislation to explicitly provide that computer programs are protected by copyright law. Copyright law in the United States is governed by the Copyright Act of 1976 that preempted the field from the states. Formerly the U.S. had a dual state and federal system. In many other countries the reform of copyright law specifically to protect computer programs is actively underway.

10.4.6.2 Trade-Secret Law

A trade secret is a secret, which has some value and usefulness. This law protects the unique and secret aspects of ideas, known only to the discoverer or his confidants. Once disclosed the trade secret is unenforceable as such and can only be protected under one of the following laws. This is very important in the computer field, where even a slight head start in the development of software or hardware may provide a significant competitive advantage.

10.4.6.3 Patent Law

A patent is a registry system that protects inventions whether in products or processes. It is often difficult to obtain a patent (please see discussion below). With computer software, complete disclosure is required; the patent holder must disclose the complete details of the program sufficient to allow another person skilled in programming to build the program. Moreover, a U.S. software invention may be unable to claim patent protection and therefore be unenforceable in other countries.[9]

10.4.6.4 Trademark Law

The name given to the software is often as important as the protection of the software itself and must be protected. Trade names for well known products have gained great value as their com-

---

[9]Such an invention can be protected in Canada.

mercial recognition has increased. Trademark laws exist under both state common laws and federal statutes. Trademark rights arise upon first usage of the trademark in commerce.

Trademarks should be used to protect the names of any software packages. Simply using a trademark gives one common-law rights to continue using it. If the trademark is registered with the Patent and Trademark Office the holder has the rights to use the trademark anywhere business is conducted.

10.5 FEDERAL COMPUTER CRIME LAWS

In addition to a wide range of federal law that may be applicable to a particular fact situation there are certain U.S. federal acts that set out offenses in areas of federal jurisdiction, such as Interstate Commerce. A number of these acts and some of the key provisions in those acts is discussed below.

10.5.1 Computer Fraud and Abuse Act of 1986

The *Computer Fraud and Abuse Act of 1986*, 18 U.S.C. 1001 is an amending act. It amends Title 18 of the United States Code to provide additional penalties for fraud and related activities in connection with access to devices and computers and for other purposes. As a result the following become offenses under Title 18:

Any person commits an offense who:

Intentionally, without authorization to access any computer of the department or agency of the United States, accesses such a computer of that department or agency that is exclusively for the use of the Government of the United States or, in the case of computer non-exclusively for such use, is used by or for the Government of the United States and such conduct effects the use of the Government's operation of such a computer;

Knowingly and with intent to defraud, accesses a federal interest computer without authorization, or exceeds authorized access, and by means of such conduct furthers the intended fraud and obtains anything of value, unless the object of the fraud and the thing obtained consists only of the use of the computer;

Intentionally acts as a federal interest computer without authorization, and by means of one or more instances of such conduct alters, damages, or destroys information in any such federal interest computer, or prevents authorized use of any such computer or information, and thereby:

(a) causes loss to one or more others of a value aggregating $1,000.00 or more during any one year period; or

(b) modifies or impairs, or potentially modifies or impairs, the medical examination, medical diagnosis, medical treatment, or medical care of one or more individuals; or

Knowingly and with intent to defraud traffics . . . in any password or similar information through which a computer may be accessed without authorization, if

(a) such trafficking effects Interstate or Foreign Commerce; or

(b) such computer is used by or for the Government of the United States.

The penalty for commission of the offense is a fine as provided for under the Act or imprisonment for not more than 5 years or both.

"Federal interest computer" is defined specifically to mean:

A computer—

(a)   exclusively for the use of a federal institution or the United States Government, or, in the case of a computer not exclusively for such use, used by or for a financial institution or the United States Government and the conduct constituting the offense affects the use of the financial institution's operations or the Government's operations of such computer; or

(b)   which is one of two or more computers used in committing the offense, not all of which are located in the same State.

A financial institution is likewise defined to mean any bank with deposits insured by the Federal Deposit Insurance Corporation, Federal Savings and Loan Insurance Corporation, National Credit Union Administration, the Federal Reserve, any home loan bank, a broker dealer registered with the Securities Exchange Commission, or an institution of the Farm Credit System.

The term "exceeds authorized use" also is defined to mean to act as a computer with authorization to use such access to obtain or alter information in the computer that the accessor is not entitled so to obtain or alter.

The *Computer Fraud and Abuse Act of 1986*, then, provides some protection where the conduct effects specific computers in which the Federal Government has an interest or where the abuse of conduct occurs as a result of an Interstate telecommunications between the two computers.

The InterNet worm incident is an example of a prosecution under the *Computer Fraud and Abuse Act of 1986*.[10] In that case Robert T. Morris, Jr. intentionally introduced a computer program into a network where that program ultimately shut down thousands of workstations and computers.[11] The damages have been estimated at over $25 million.[12] Mr. Morris would likely never be able to properly compensate all the people and businesses injured by his actions. In such cases criminal sanctions attempt to punish the criminal and deter others from committing similar acts. Morris was charged with computer tampering under the Computer Fraud and Abuse Act of 1986[13] and was convicted after a two-week trial. Morris was also expelled from Cornell University.

Morris created a complex program using his specialized knowledge form previous work experience and his own skills. The program exploited certain known flaws of the InterNet network system and of the UNIX operating system used by most computers linked into InterNet. Among these were parameter passing—the program attempted to send a string longer than the buffer space provided by a utility; if successful, the excess of the string over the buffer length contained instructions that were then executed and ceded privileged access to the worm. Other components of the attack included attempts to use a list of common passwords to log into legitimate accounts,

---

[10]This discussion is adapted from Fites, P., P. Johnston, and M. Kratz, *The Computer Virus Crisis*, ed. 2, Van Nostrand Reinhold, New York, 1992.

[11]Approximately 6,000 computers of the Arpanet and InterNet were affected. These are both UNIX based networks.

[12]First estimates were as high as $250,000,000, but later statistical analyses lowered the probable number of sites affected and thus the best estimate now is between $10 and $25 millions.

[13]18 USC 1030

and a final attempt to use a large spelling dictionary to guess passwords if all other attempts failed. The last penetration method turned out to be the most damaging: The resources consumed in this attack were so great that major nodes of the InterNet were overloaded and had to shut down until the worm was cleared from the entire network. The specific attacks were against two versions of UNIX; the program was constructed to allow other attacks tailored to other computers and versions of UNIX to be added easily.

While Morris claimed that his worm program was only an experiment and that he had not intended to cause the damage that ensued, the conviction is important as it serves to remind others that such conduct shall not be tolerated.

In response to concerns that the Computer Fraud and Abuse Act of 1986 did not specifically deal with the threat of computer virus contamination the Computer Virus Eradication Act[14] was introduced in Congress. This act would have provided specific criminal sanctions for interference with the use of computers through computer virus programs or other programs with hidden commands.[15] Like the Canadian criminal law penalties included a maximum of 10 years imprisonment. A further provision would have permitted victims to recover damages from the vandals. The act did not pass.

10.5.2 Electronic Communications Privacy Act of 1986

The *Electronic Communications Privacy Act of 1986*, 18 U.S.C. 2510, sets out certain federal penalties for interception of communications. It again amends Title 18 of the United States Code. As a result a wide range of interceptions of electronic communications are considered to be offenses and subject to fine and penal sanction under the provision.

Many transmissions readily accessible to the general public are exempted from provisions of the Act. Similarly under the Act it is not unlawful for any person:

(i)   To intercept or access an electronic communication made through an electronic communication system that is configured so that such electronic communication is readily assessable to the general public;

(ii) To intercept any radio communication which is transmitted

(I) by any station for the use of the general public, or that relates to ships, aircraft, vehicles, or persons in distress,

(II) by any governmental, law enforcement, civil defense, private land mobile, for public safety communication system, including police and fire, readily accessible to the general public,

(III) by a station operating on an authorized frequency within the bands allocated to the amateur, citizen band or general mobile radio services, or

(IV) by any marine or aeronautical communication system

. . .

(iv) To intercept any wire or electronic communication the transmission of which is causing harmful interference to any lawfully operating station or consumer electronic equipment, to the extent necessary to identify the source of such interference; or

(v)   For other uses of the same frequency to intercept any radio communications made through a system that utilizes frequencies monitored by individuals engaged in the provision or use of such system, if such communication is not scrambled or encrypted.

---

[14]HR 5061, introduced by Congressman Wally Herger (R -California) in 1988 and re-introduced as HR 55 in 1989.

[15]Essentially this would mean an amendment to the *Computer Fraud and Abuse Act of 1986*, 18 USC 1030.

Furthermore it is not unlawful to use a pen register, trap, or trace device for investigative or diagnostic purposes or for the provider of any electronic communication services to record the fact that a wire or electronic communication was initiated or completed in order to protect such provider, another provider furnishing service towards the completion of the wire or electronic communication, or a user of that service, from fraudulent, unlawful or abusive use of the service.

The *Electronic Communications Privacy Act of 1986* sets out certain positive obligations on any person or entity providing an electronic communication service to the public not to intentionally divulge the contents of any communication while in transmission on that service to any person or entity other than an addressee or intended recipient of such communication or an agent of such addressee or intended recipient. Each of these provisions may result in recovery of civil damages. That relief may include preliminary, equitable or declaratory relief, damages (both to compensate the loss and punitive damages), and reasonable attorney's fees and other litigation costs incurred.

Several new offenses are introduced including unlawful access to stored communications. Subject to certain exceptions an offense is committed by whoever:

1. Intentionally accesses without authorization of facility through which an electronic communication service is provided; or
2. Intentionally exceeds an authorization to access that facility;

    and thereby obtains, alters or prevents authorized access to a wire or electronic communication while it is in electronic storage in such system . . .

The punishment for an offense under the foregoing subsection varies depending on the intent of the offender. If the offense is committed for purposes of commercial advantage, malicious destruction or damage, or private commercial gain then the maximum fine is $250,000 or imprisonment for not more than one year or both for a first offense and a fine or imprisonment for not more than two years or both for subsequent offenses. Where the intent is not for purposes of commercial advantage, malicious destruction or damage, or private commercial gain then the penalty is a fine of not more than $5,000 or imprisonment for not more than six months or both.

Certain exemptions and exceptions are provided in the act to allow for authorized law enforcement, intelligence, and equipment maintenance purposes.

The result of the *Electronic Communications Privacy Act of 1986*, then, is a complex law setting out an arrangement governing the interception of private communications. Similar provisions exist in many other countries. In the United Kingdom it is the *Interception of Communications Act 1985*, c. P. 56 and in Canada the *Privacy Act*, R.S.C., 1985, c. P. 21.

The general concern for security, integrity, and uninterrupted enjoyment of private information particularly on computer systems resulted in enactment of the *Computer Security Act of 1987*. This act is discussed below.

10.5.3 Computer Security Act of 1987

The *Computer Security Act of 1987*, 40 U.S.C. 759, is an administrative act which declares that improving the security and privacy of sensitive information in federal computer systems is in the public interest and creates a means for establishing minimum acceptable security practices for such systems without limiting the scope of security measures already planned or in place.

The act goes on to provide specific purposes assigning responsibility to the National Bureau of Standards for developing standards and guidelines for federal computer systems, including responsibility for developing standards and guidelines needed to assure the cost-effective security and privacy of sensitive information in federal computer systems, drawing on technical advice and assistance (including work products) of the National Security Agency where appropriate. Other purposes of the act include to provide for promulgation of certain standards and guidelines by amending the *Federal Property and Administrative Services Act of 1949*, to require establishment of security plans by all operators of federal computer systems that contain sensitive information, and to require mandatory periodic training of all persons involved in management, use, or operation of federal computer systems that contain sensitive information.

"Sensitive Information" is defined in the act to mean:

Any information the loss, misuse, or unauthorized access to or modification of which could adversely effect the national interest or the conduct of federal programs, or the privacy to which individuals are entitled under section 552a of Title 5, United States Code (the *Privacy Act*), but which has not been specifically authorized under criteria established by an executive order or an act of congress to be kept secret in the interest of National Defense or foreign policy.

Federal agencies are to identify systems that contain sensitive information within six months of the enactment of that act.[16] Within one year of the date of enactment of the Act each such federal agency shall have established a security plan for the security and privacy of each such federal computer system identified with the agency. The security plan is to provide for a security and protection of the computer system but where that level of protection is commensurate with the risk and magnitude of harm resulting from the loss, misuse, or unauthorized access to or modification of the information contained in such federal computer system.

10.6 STATE COMPUTER CRIME LAWS

Each state has enacted some form of criminal law dealing with abuse of computer systems. These states also have laws dealing with forgery, falsifying records, fraud, theft, embezzlement, arson (*e.g.*, burning a building housing a computer), and all other areas of criminal law that may arise in a case of computer abuse.

Most states provide for criminal sanctions in cases of:

1. Unauthorized use of or access to a computer; and
2. Destruction, modification or alteration of data or computer programs.

Each state has its own sanctions and you should review those applicable to your own jurisdiction. A list of these as of January, 1991 concludes this section.

An example of a prosecution under a state computer crime law may be seen in the case of Donald Gene Burleson.[17] Burleson was charged with deleting over 168,000 files from his Fort Worth, Texas, employer's computer by infecting it with a computer virus. The indictment charged that Burleson, a computer programmer, had executed programs "designed to interfere with the normal use of the computer" and that Burleson had committed acts "that resulted in records being deleted." Burleson was charged under a Texas law sometimes referred to as the

---

[16]As noted elsewhere in this text, over 50,000 such sensitive systems had been identified by November, 1989.

[17]*See also* the discussion in Fites, P., P. Johnston, and M. Kratz, *The Computer Virus Crisis*, ed. 2, Van Nostrand Reinhold, New York, 1992.

"harmful access to a computer" law. This law made it a felony to "intentionally and knowingly cause a computer to malfunction or interrupt the operation of a computer; or alter, damage, or destroy a computer program stored, maintained or provided by a computer without the consent of the owner." Burleson was convicted on September 18, 1988 and sentenced to seven years probation and also to pay the former employer compensation for the cost to reconstruct the computer system.[18]

Details of state statutes vary substantially among jurisdictions; the following list should serve as a starting point for practitioners to investigate local considerations.[19]

Code of Alabama Sections 13A-8-100 to 13A-8-103

Alaska Statutes, 11.46.985

Arizona Revised Statutes, Sections 13-2301, 13-2316

Arkansas Criminal Code, Sections 5-41-101 to 5-41-107

California Penal Code, Section 502

Colorado Revised Statutes, Sections 18-5.5-101, 18-5.5-102

Connecticut General Statutes, Sections 53a-250 to 53a-261

Delaware Code, Section 858

Florida Statutes Annotated, Sections 815.01-815.07

Georgia Codes Annotated, Sections 16-9-90 to 16-9-95

Hawaii Revised Statutes Chapter 708

Idaho Code, Chapter 22, Title 18, Section 18-2201, 18-2202

Illinois Criminal Code, Sections 15-1, 16-9

Indiana Code, Sections 35-43-1-4, 35-43-2-3

Iowa Statutes Sections 716A.1 to 716A.16

Kansas Statutes Annotated, Section 21-3755

Kentucky Revised Statutes, Sections 434.840 to 434.860

Louisiana Revised Statutes, Title 14, Sections 73.1 to 73.5

Maine Revised Statutes, Article 27k, Section 357

Laws of Maryland, Sections 146, 45A

Massachusetts General Laws, Chapter 266, Section 30

Michigan Statutes Annotated, Sections 28, 29

Minnesota Criminal Code, Sections 609.87 to 609.89

Mississippi Code Annotated, Sections 97-45-1 to 97-45-13

Missouri Revised Statutes, Sections 569.093 to 569.099

Montana Code Annotated, Sections 45-2-101, 45-6-310, 45-6-311

Revised Statutes of Nebraska, Sections 28-1343 to 28-1348

Nevada Revised Statutes, Sections 205.473 to 205.477

New Hampshire Revised Statutes Annotated, Sections 638:16 to 638:19

NJ Statutes, Chapter 20C, Title 2C, Sections 1, 23-31; Title 2A, Sections 38A-1 to 38A-3

---

[18]For a good summary of the background in this case, see Joyce, E., "Time Bomb Inside the Texas Virus Trial," *1988 Computer Decisions*, p. 38. Speaking technically, the methods Burleson used did not include virus code.

[19]See the current edition of the "Computer Crime Law Reporter" for recent updates.

New Mexico Criminal Offenses, Sections 30-16A-1 to 30-16A-4

New York Penal Law, Sections 156.00 to 156.50

North Carolina, Sections 14-453 to 14-457

North Dakota Century Code, Section 12.1-06.1-01 subsection 3, 12.1-06.1-08

Ohio Revised Code Annotated, Sections 2901, 2913

Oklahoma Session Laws, Title 21, Sections 1951 to 1956

Oregon Revised Statutes, Sections 164.125, 164.377

Pennsylvania Consolidated Statutes Annotated, Section 3933

Rhode Island Criminal Offenses, Sections 11-52-1 to 11-52-4

South Carolina Codes of Laws, Sections 16-16-10 to 16-16-40

South Dakota Codified Laws, Sections 43-43B-1 to 43-43B-8

Tennessee Criminal Offenses, Sections 39-3-1401 to 39-3-1406

Texas Penal Code, Title 7, Sections 33.01 to 33.05

Utah Code Annotated, Sections 76-6-701 to 76-6-704

Code of Virginia, Sections 18.2-152.1 to 18.2-152.14

Revised Code of Washington Annotated, Section 9A.48.100

Wisconsin Statutes Annotated, Section 943.70

Wyoming Statutes, Sections 6-3-501 to 6-3-505

10.7 MODEL COMPUTER CRIME BILLS

From reading many of the above bills, it is apparent that at the state level, legislation is not uniform nor is it consistent. Work needs to be done to strengthen current and proposed legislation at the state level. With this objective in mind, the DPMA has taken an active interest in this effort by calling for the improvement of existing computer crime laws. It has proposed and drafted a "Model Computer Crime Act." The model act incorporates the establishment of civil procedures for redress of victims of computer crime. The DPMA's model act also proposes forfeiture of property, guidelines for what evidence will be considered in a computer crime case (rules of evidence), a good definition of computer crime, suggested punishments including increased penalties for repeated violations and suggestions for jurisdiction.[20] Jurisdiction is a significant problem for the courts since the computer criminal may reside in one state or country while committing a crime in another via data communication systems.

It is important that security practitioners keep abreast of current legislation even though the impact of these laws on the prospective perpetrator of a computer crime may not be great. A review of the literature shows that most researchers believe that the probability of being convicted of a computer crime is low and when convicted the punishments are nominal. Strengthening our existing laws can only have a positive impact and deter a few would-be perpetrators of computer crime.

10.8 INTRODUCTION TO CIVIL LAW

In this section the term *civil law* is used to denote the law governing relationships between individuals such as property law, the law of torts (*i.e.*, negligence), and intellectual property law. As

[20][DPMA 86]

previously mentioned, a number of features are typical of most civil law systems. Particular areas of civil law set out obligations and duties in a particular relationship. It is up to the individuals involved in that relationship to enforce those duties and obligations. In many cases the individual seeking to assert certain rights against another or others is called the plaintiff. The individuals or entities against whom it is desired to enforce certain duties or obligations often is (are) known as the defendant(s).

The plaintiff carries the burden of establishing that a cause of action exists. In other words the plaintiff has to establish all of the elements required to prove that he or she has a case for the court to enforce the particular duty or obligation against the defendant or defendants. The defendant may agree with the plaintiff and, if so, then there is no need for the case to proceed through the legal system. The parties are able to resolve their differences without recourse to the formal court process. If the defendant disagrees with the existence of the duty or obligation or wishes to dispute its enforceability against the defendant for any reason then the defendant normally will file a defense to the plaintiff's claim. That defense must establish a valid defense to the claim made by the plaintiff or set out reasons why the plaintiff's claim should not be enforceable against the defendant (such as an agreement between the plaintiff and defendant or certain conduct of the plaintiff that may disentitle him or her to relief).

The plaintiff has the total responsibility for the investigation and evidence-gathering necessary to establish that he or she has a good cause of action. The plaintiff must marshall his or her witnesses and hire such experts as may be necessary or desirable to establish all of the elements of the action. Together with the responsibility for costs of bringing the action the plaintiff also has complete control of the action and can decide to stop the action or reach a settlement. In fact, a large majority of lawsuits are resolved by settlement between the parties rather than having to proceed all the way through to trial.

The defendant similarly has the obligation to make out all the elements of his or her defense, to marshall the evidence and witnesses necessary for the defense, and to pay for any expert witnesses that may be necessary or desirable to establish a defense.

The structure of the litigation process encourages settlement of lawsuits. The litigation process also tends to result in a refinement and clarification of the issues in dispute between the parties.

In order to succeed in a lawsuit, the plaintiff must establish all of the elements in his or her case on a balance of probabilities. This means, basically, that a judge (or jury) must be convinced that it is more likely that the case presented by the plaintiff case is correct than the case that may have been presented by the defendant. The level of proof, on a balance of probabilities, is sometimes also described as requiring 50+% evidence in order to win. This should be distinguished from the criminal standard of proof which is "beyond a reasonable doubt," a much higher standard of proof.

There are many relationships between individuals or entities that may be of some relevance to the information systems security professional. Typically these areas are within the jurisdictional competence of a state in most federal systems; as a result, the reader is cautioned that the description below sets out general principles and the specific law of the jurisdiction in which you work or that may be relevant to a particular relationship should be examined by an attorney qualified to practice in that particular jurisdiction.

10.8.1 Tort Law

Tort law deals with civil wrongs such as assault, battery, trespass, nuisance, and negligence, among others. Tort law can be divided into two categories depending on whether the conduct complained of was the result of intentional action or merely inadvertence or omission. In the case of non-intentional torts a further classification can be made.

Non-intentional conduct can be divided into:

(a) that conduct for which a certain standard of care is sufficient to escape liability
(b) such conduct for which no level of care is sufficient to escape liability for damage caused as a result of the conduct

This latter category is often called strict or absolute liability. *Strict liability* is often imposed by law where inherently dangerous products or services are used or where the consequences of certain action or inaction may result in very substantial loss, injury, or death.

The area of law that governs unintentional conduct (whether acts or omissions) for which a certain standard of care may result in avoiding liability is generally known as the *law of negligence*.

Some of the rules setting out some of the elements of the intentional torts, elements of negligence and the elements of strict liability are viewed in more detail below.

10.8.1.1 Law of Negligence

Section 307 of the second section of the *Restatement of Torts* states:

> [It] is negligence to use an instrumentality, whether a human being or a thing, which the actor knows, or should know, to be incompetent, inappropriate or defective and that its use involves an unreasonable risk of harm to others.

The use of computers and computer systems, data, and computer programs requires care. Misuse, inappropriate use, or inability to use such systems may cause injury to others.

As a result if, for example, a person, *A*, interfered with a company's computer system so that end users relying on that computer system would receive erroneous results and be damaged through use of that computer system, then not only might the company bring a negligence action against *A* but also those third parties whom *A* should have considered when he or she carried out the abusive conduct. The company also is liable to a negligence action brought by the third parties who will claim that the company had a responsibility to exercise sufficient supervision over the actions of *A* (if *A* is an insider) or to have established sufficient security precautions to preclude *A* from carrying out his or her acts (whether *A* is an insider or outsider).

The law of negligence is therefore very important as it governs many types of conduct.

To be successful in bringing an action for negligence the plaintiff must establish the following elements:[21]

---

[21]Linden, *Canadian Tort Law*, 4th Ed., Butterworths.

1. The claimant must suffer some damage;
2. The damage suffered must be caused by the conduct of the defendant;
3. The defendant's conduct must be negligent, that is, in breach of the standard of care set by law;
4. There must be a duty recognized by law to avoid this damage;
5. The damage should not be too distant or unconnected to the defendant's conduct; and
6. The conduct of the plaintiff should not be such as to bar his recovery, that is, he must not be guilty of contributory negligence and he must not voluntarily assume the risk.

It has been argued that intentional sabotage of computer systems such as, for example, by computer virus contamination or infection, would appear to satisfy all the elements necessary to establish a negligence action against the individual intentionally or negligently introducing the computer virus program or other sabotage to a computer system, (such as a logic bomb, Trojan horse, etc.) not only to the owner of the system but also to the legitimate users of the system.[22]

10.8.1.2 Intentional Torts

Many intentional torts give rise to certain specific responsibilities. These torts are called *intentional* torts because they deal with situations or relationships where the defendant is able to reasonably foresee that injury will be caused to the plaintiff. As a result the law often provides damages above mere compensation to deter such intentional conduct.[23]

One of the intentional torts is *assault*. One commits assault by intentionally causing another to fear either offensive or harmful contact or touching but without the contact or touching occurring. This tort is often associated with the tort of battery that is described below.

The tort of *battery* involves the intentional offensive or harmful touching of another.

Both assault and battery are subject to defences of consent (the defendant consented either expressly or implicitly to the conduct) as well as justification. For example, if an information systems security professional carries out a search of another without obtaining consent the professional may have committed a battery. If the search is threatened then he or she may have committed an assault. If, however, the search is carried out with a consent, either implied through conduct or expressly, then the search is lawful.

An important intentional tort for the information systems security professional to be aware of is that of *false arrest*. False arrest is sometimes also called *false imprisonment*. The essence of this tort is to intentionally restrict or confine either the freedom or movement of another person or persons. The restriction or confinement can occur as a result of actual physical conduct, threatened conduct, or intimidation. Again consent or justification are defences to false imprisonment or false arrest. Often an information systems security professional may wish to detain and question a suspect in respect of certain abusive conduct that may have occurred in respect of a computer system, data, or computer programs. If that confinement occurs without the consent of the suspect or if it turns out that the case is not able to be made out against the suspect then the computer security professional and company which engaged him or her may be subject to a claim of

---

[22]*The Computer Virus Crisis*, Van Nostrand Reinhold, 1989, New York, at pages 116 to 118.

[23]The amounts and guidelines for assessing such *punitive damages* vary widely in differing legal jurisdictions.

false imprisonment or false arrest. For this reason it is very important that the information systems security professional think carefully about his or her conduct in respect of a suspect.

The standard of proof in order to maintain a criminal prosecution for certain abusive conduct in respect of computer system, computer programs or data is "beyond a reasonable doubt" under the criminal law. The standard of proof for civil law, such as a false arrest or false imprisonment action, is only on a "balance of probabilities." As a result the computer security professional must be aware that there may be insufficient evidence to establish proof beyond a reasonable doubt and secure a criminal conviction of the defendant but that failure to obtain such a conviction may give rise to a false imprisonment or false arrest action by the wrongdoer against the business that is easier for the suspect to prove since it is not based on the high level of proof required by the criminal law.

Also of significant importance to the information systems security professional is the intentional tort of *defamation*. Defamation is usually divided into two categories being libel and slander. *Libel* is written defamation whereas *slander* is oral defamation. The essence of the defamation tort is to injure the reputation of another through the publication of false statements about that person. The publication may occur to only one other person and that will be sufficient to give rise to a legal action.

The tort of defamation arises, like the tort of false arrest or false imprisonment, in the investigative role. When a information systems security professional is questioning a suspect he or she must be very careful not to impugn the reputation of that suspect in a way that constitutes defamation. For example, a computer security professional may be called in to determine who carried out certain abusive conduct in respect of a computer system. The information systems security professional may have gathered up evidence that implicates A. If the information systems security professional implicates A in a public way, say by accusing A of committing criminal conduct, then this may be defamation. Of course, truth is a complete defense to a defamation action. Other defences are available where it is claimed that certain communications were made, for example, without malice in certain privileged relationships such as in judicial proceedings.

Another intentional tort that may cause problems for information systems security professionals is that of *malicious prosecution*. One is liable for malicious prosecution if, with malice, one institutes criminal proceedings against another. The essence of this tort is to prevent abuse of the legal system and particularly the criminal justice system for purposes other than bringing a criminal to justice. As a result the computer security professional should be careful that he or she provides complete and unbiased reports, statements of fact, and advice to police, prosecutors, and others involved in the criminal justice system. Generally speaking, without malice it is not possible to establish malicious prosecution.

Just as there are criminal sanctions for certain types of invasion of privacy (such as unauthorized wiretaps) so also in many jurisdictions *invasion of privacy* may also be an actionable tort. The essence of this tort is to intentionally disclose private information about another person, publicly place another person in a false light, or to intrude upon another persons' physical solitude.

Another form of intentional tort that may arise, from time to time, is intentional infliction of mental suffering. The essence of this tort is to intentionally, through either words or conduct, cause emotional or mental suffering or distress to another person. Highly abusive language, for example, can give rise to this cause of action.

10.8.1.3 Strict Liability

As previously mentioned persons who introduce inherently or abnormally dangerous processes, chemicals, objects, or devices into commerce or otherwise to the public may be strictly responsible for all injury or damage that results as a consequence of the inherently dangerous activity. There appears little doubt that introduction of random or intentional damage or injury into computer systems, computer programs, or data without any regard to the consequences or type of computer system results in certain inherent danger to properties and, in certain cases, lives of others. It has been argued that sabotage of computer systems or release of computer virus programs would appear to establish liability under the strict liability theory and possibly also under one of the intentional torts.[24]

10.8.2 Property Law

Property law is divided into two types: dealing with *real property* (such as land or interest in land) and *personal property* (such as individual possessions, intangible rights, and generally moveable things). There are several causes of action that may be brought in respect of dealings with real or personal property. Perhaps most important are the actions of trespass or conversion.

Trespass occurs when an uninvited person invades property or remains on property after permission has been withdrawn. A trespass action allows the owner or person in lawful possession of a building or land to control those who venture onto the land or building.

In many states a person authorized by the owner or person in lawful possession of property is provided with certain powers of arrest to deal with certain types of wrongdoing in respect of the property. There is considerable diversity in these powers of arrest and it is recommended that the reader consult with a competent attorney in the jurisdiction in question for a review of the current provisions in that jurisdiction.

Conversion occurs when a person asserts rights inconsistent with the ownership or lawful use of another in property. For example, a person who took another's property (such as a diskette, computer program, manuals, personal computer, or otherwise) without consent may have committed the tort of conversion and can be sued for return of the property or for the injury caused as a result of loss of the use and enjoyment of the property.

10.8.2.1 Intellectual Property

In addition to real and personal property there is a category of intangible rights in creative or inventive conduct that is sometimes summarized as *intellectual property law*. Intellectual property law consists of the law of patents, copyrights, industrial designs, trade secrets, trademarks, and similar systems. For the purpose of this text we will concentrate primarily on copyright law and trade-secret law principles.

10.8.2.2 Copyright Law

Copyright law protects the form of expression of certain ideas or concepts that are fixed in a tangible form (works). Examples are computer programs, data files, screen displays, written reports, plans, diagrams, and charts. Copyright protects against, among other things, the reproduction of

---

[24]*The Computer Virus Crisis*, Van Nostrand Reinhold, New York, 1989, at page 118. The issue has been raised in recent court proceedings such as the prosecution of Burleson in Texas.

a substantial part of a work, publication of the work, translation of the work, and certain other types of dealings with a work. Given the ease with which computer programs and data may be reproduced, copyright law becomes an important ingredient in the information systems security professional's arsenal of legal weapons.

The traditional view was that copyright, actually a bundle of related rights, was intended to protect forms of creativity. The problem then arose of how to deal with determination of the relative merits of creative works. In a landmark case, *Leiber Code*,[25] the Court held that the law would not rule on the relative merits of a creative work but would protect any work that was an original creation: the product of an author`s labor, skill, and judgment and fixed in a tangible form. Under this rule a wide variety of creative works were protected by copyright law. Examples of such works are:

- Codes consisting of otherwise unintelligible numbers[26]
- Grids of computer generated sequences of letters[27]
- Telegraph Code[28]
- A fixed-odds football pool form[29]
- A timetable index[30]
- A street directory[31]

As a result, it is clear that any data that is an original work of authorship may be protected by copyright law. The implication of this development is that all of the tools available under copyright law may be used in cases where data or software is copied illegally. Similarly, courts have held that selling of pirate materials is fraud[32] and the unauthorized interception of copyright protected materials may be a basis for criminal prosecution or private civil action.[33]

Another requirement of copyright law is that the subject matter be fixed in some tangible form. This may mean that details stored on some magnetic or other media are protected. However, it also means that transitory data, such as may be developed in random memory and which is not yet fixed, may not be protected.

Generally, worldwide copyright law has continued to expand in scope and in the types of works protected. This expansion has been met by a reactionary argument that would see copyright law restricted to its traditional place of protecting artistic forms of creativity.[34] Basically the

---

[25]*D.P. Andreson and Co.* **v.** *The Leiber Code Co.* [1917] 2 K.B. 469 (K.B. Div.)

[26]*D.P. Andreson and Co.* **v.** *The Leiber Code Co.* [1917] 2 K.B. 469 (K.B. Div.)

[27]*Express Newspapers PLC* **v.** *Liverpool Daily Post and Echo PLC* [1985] Fleet Street Reports 306 (Ch. D.)

[28]*Pitman* **v.** *Hine* (1884) 1 T.L.R. 39 (Q.B.) followed in *Canavest House Ltd.* **v.** *Lett* Unreported November 29, 1984 (Ont. H.C.)

[29]*Football League* **v.** *Littlewoods* [1959] Ch. 637; *Ladbroke* **v.** *William Hill* [1964] 1 W.L.R. 273 (H.L.)

[30]*Blacklock* **v.** *Pearson* [1915] 2 Ch. 376

[31]*Kelly* **v.** *Morris* (1966) L.R. 1 Eq. 697

[32]*R* **v.** *Kirkwood* (1983) 148 D.L.R. (3d) 323 (Ontario Court of Appeal) A case involving the sale of pirate video tapes.

[33]*Chartwell Communications Group* **v.** *Westbrook* 637 F. 2d 459 (6th Cir. 1980); *National Subscription Television* **v.** *SALT TV* 644 F. 2D 820 (9TH Cir. 1981)

[34]See for example comments in Case No. 7-0-143/80 (Mannheim District Court); and the defendant's argument in *Apple Computer Inc. and Apple Computer Australia Pty. Ltd.* **v.** *Computer Edge Pty. Ltd. and Michael Suss* Trial decision, not recognizing copyrightability, reported at [1984] 10 F.S.R. 246 *Reversed on Appeal* [1984] 11 F.S.R. 481 (Federal Court of Australia).

argument is that some other form of protection, or no protection at all, should be used for utilitarian forms of creativity. This is basically what the author has previously called the "aesthetic purpose test."[35]

This argument runs counter to the principle, discussed above, in the *Leiber Code* decision. Basically the Court is placed in a situation where it must determine whether or not a work has aesthetic merit. This was the impossible situation that the decision in *Leiber Code* avoided.

Given that copyright law may have application to data as well as to software, the next step is to briefly examine the general elements in copyright law.

Copyright law exists under the appropriate *Copyright Act*[36] and provides a right, in the first creator, to prevent another person from making copies or translations of that creative work without the creator's permission.[37] Note that in some jurisdictions it may be necessary to register or comply with other formalities in order to create these rights.

A copyright is a right that is distinct from the object or work the right relates to. For example, one might purchase a book from a bookstore and have a complete right to possess that book. One may wish to read the book, not to read it, destroy it, throw it away, or give it to another person. Yet, the purchaser of the book does not have all the rights in the book. The copyright holder still retains the copyright. The copyright prevents the purchaser of the book from being able legally to make copies of the book or substantial parts of the book without the copyright holder's permission. Other rights are paternity rights and moral rights. A paternity right is the right of the author of a work to claim authorship of that work. A moral right relates to the alteration or display of a work in a manner that might harm the reputation of the author.

The *Copyright Act* does recognize that certain situations may exist where there should be a limit to a copyright holder's monopoly on copying. As a result there are a number of exemptions under the act under which copying is permissible. Briefly, some of these are:

- Any fair dealing with any work for the purpose of private study, research, criticism, review, or newspaper summary.
- For educational use, short passages suitably acknowledged may be reproduced so long as "not more than two such passages from works by the same author are published . . . within five years."
- Recitation in public of any reasonable extract of a work.

The United States has a broader fair use exemption than the "Fair Dealing" exemption seen in many Commonwealth countries. Under 17 USC, Section 107 states:

Notwithstanding the provisions of Section 106, the fair use of a copyrighted work, including copying of such work by reproduction copies or phonograph records or by any other means specified by that Section, for purposes such as criticism, comment, news reporting, teaching (including multiple copies for classroom use), scholarship, or research, is not an infringement of copyright. In determining whether the use made of a work in any particular case is a fair use, the factors to be considered shall

[35]M. Kratz, "The Creator and the Benefits of Creation: The Protection of Computer Programs in The Information Revolution" (1985) 9:3 *Dalhousie Law Journal* 555

[36]R.S.C. 1970, c.C-30; The Canadian example is used. There are similarities in these basic elements in most advanced legal systems.

[37]A form of copyright notice that is not required by Canadian law or that of other Berne Convention countries but may be required in the United States or under the Universal Copyright Convention.

include:

(1) the purpose and character of the use, including whether such use is of a commercial nature or for non profit educational purposes;
(2) the nature of the copyrighted work;
(3) the amount and substantiality of the portion used in relation to the copyrighted work as a whole; and
(4) the effect of the use upon the potential market for or value of the copyrighted work.[38]

In all cases it should be remembered that a copyright protects only the form of the author's creative expression. The ideas or underlying concepts are not protected by copyright law. Thus, copyright law is generally effective in dealing with software, or data piracy, or direct copying of a computer program or data without permission. However, copyright law is not effective in preventing a competitor from examining the program or data and using the concepts or ideas or other information therein. The competitor cannot make a copy but he or she may be able to use those ideas, concepts, or information in another product.

If copies are made without the permission of the copyright holder, or without the aid of an exemption, then an action may be brought for damages, an accounting for profits, or for an injunction (a court order) ordering the wrongdoer to refrain from continuing to infringe the copyright and also ordering that all copies made without permission be delivered up by the wrongdoer. The copyright holder may also seek to have the summary procedure in the act invoked, in which case the wrongdoer may become liable to pay a fine.

Copyright law becomes a valuable consideration for the information security specialist because many cases of breach of security involving loss of information or data will involve copyright issues. Of particular relevance is the ability to bring both civil or criminal action under many copyright statutes. This makes copyright a very flexible and adaptable tool for the information security specialist.

In summary, copyright law may be effective where identical or substantially similar copies are made of a protected work. The process may be expedited through use of interim injunctions in serious cases and the rights, under the copyright law, apply against all persons in the jurisdiction.

The United States has modified its copyright system with the 1976 reforms and also most importantly in the 1988 reforms. Before 1976 failure to place a copyright notice on a work would result in that work being in the public domain and in loss of the ability to control reproduction, publication, translation, or other dealings with the work. After 1976, however, a defect or even complete failure to provide a copyright notice that was inadvertent and where the copyright is registered within five years of publication, together with legitimate efforts to apply the notice to works that have been released, will not destroy the copyright in the work. As a result internal computer programs, data, reports, and many other works may now be the subject of copyright claims that may be brought against a person who carries out improper dealings with the work.

In addition for works produced or published after March 1, 1989 U.S. residents are able to claim immediate and instant copyright protection under the Berne Artistic Union in most advanced economies in the world. A basic principle of the Berne Artistic Union is that no formalities are required before copyright is recognized on a national treatment basis in the countries of

[38]The leading cases in relation to the interpretation of this section include *Sony Corp. of America* v. *Universal City Studios*, 222 USPQ 665(USSC); *Folsom* v. *Marsh*, 9 FCAS 342 (C CD MASS. 1981); *Grey* v. *Russell*, 10 FCAS 1035 (C CD MASS. 1839).

members of the union. This means, for example, a U.S. copyright will be afforded, without any formalities (including the requirement of copyright notice, registration, or the like), instant and automatic copyright protection in Canada under the Canadian copyright law. The same applies for U.S. copyrights in, for example, Australia, Great Britain, Germany, and the like. In the United States itself, however, the U.S. Library of Congress (which is responsible for administration of the copyright system) has retained a discriminatory two-tier system in respect of U.S. origin works. As a result the previous rule mentioned (relating to defects of notice and requirement of registration within five years) still applies to U.S.-origin works. As a result U.S.-origin works should have a proper copyright notice and should be registered if required under the U.S. Copyright Act.

An important limitation of copyright law is the fact that copyright only protects the *form* of expression and not the underlying ideas or concepts themselves. As a result it is sometimes possible to "reverse-engineer" a work to derive the underlying concepts or ideas and use those concepts or ideas without any legal responsibility to the owner of the copyright. It is important, however, that to avoid liability only the ideas or concepts be used and none of the form of the original work. An example of this approach apparently is found in the extensive reverse-engineering efforts of the Phoenix Corporation in developing the Phoenix BIOS computer program to provide functional compatibility with the IBM BIOS computer program in the IBM PC.

In addition to obtaining damages to compensate the injury done, certain court orders, such as injunctions, which can be used to restrain certain offensive conduct of the defendant, may be obtained. In addition under U.S. copyright law certain types of copyright infringement may result in claims for statutory damages that can, in some cases, be greater than the amount of damages available for pure compensation.

One may be liable for copyright infringement if one commits the infringing act or, also, if one authorizes the committing of the infringing act. As a result, all companies should have a copyright policy that aims to avoid liability of the company for copyright infringement carried out by the employees. A copyright policy also serves an important function for the information systems security professional. Since computer programs and data are often capable of being protected by copyright law, a copyright policy that sets out clear limitations and guidelines on the use, reproduction, and distribution of such materials may achieve positive results. First, users operating subject to those limitations or guidelines are educated as to their responsibilities and most users will comply with the guidelines or limitations. Second, it will be significantly easier to bring a successful copyright infringement action against an abuser of that system. Third, in certain circumstances it will also be significantly easier to bring a criminal prosecution in respect of the offensive conduct.

10.8.3 Trade-Secret Law

Very often a breach of security will involve the misuse or disclosure of confidential business or technical information such as, for example, passwords, client lists, or the like. If a relationship exists between the wrongdoer and the owner of the information then it may be possible to bring action for breach of confidence or misuse of the trade secret. This action also may overlap, to some extent, with other obligations under copyright law or other areas of law.

Trade secret requires a relationship among individuals:

The law of trade secrets is based on a relationship between two or more parties in which there is an express or implied obligation of confidence as pertains to certain information. The roots of this branch of law go back to the Industrial Revolution. Unlike the law of patent or copyright, the law of trade secrets acts *"in personam,"* that is, between the parties and not against all the world.[39]

A trade secret is defined in the U.S. *Restatement of Torts* to consist of:

Any formula, pattern, device or combination of information that is used in one's business, which gives him an opportunity to obtain an advantage over competitors who do not know or use it. The subject matter of a trade secret must be secret . . . so that, except by use of improper means, it would be difficult in acquiring the information. An exact definition of a trade secret is not possible. Some factors to be considered in determining whether given information is one's trade secret: (1) the extent to which the information is known outside the business; (2) the extent to which it is known by employees and others involved in the business; (3) the extent of measures taken by him to guard the secrecy of the information; (4) the value of the information to him in developing the information; . . .; (6) the ease or difficulty with which the information could be properly acquired and duplicated by others.[40]

To establish an action for breach of confidence it is necessary to establish all of the following:

- That the information in question was secret
- That there was an obligation of confidence between the parties either expressed or implied
- That the disclosure has resulted in some detriment or injury

These elements are discussed in more detail below.

A secret must be secret to be protected by law. However the courts will not allow a defendant to rely on his or her breach of confidence to escape liability. Also even where the information may not be generally known in the particular trade or business then even though it may be publicly available in a restricted way it may be that there is sufficient quality of confidence or secrecy to sustain an action.

A very important feature of trade-secret law is the requirement of a *relationship of confidence.* This relationship of confidence may arise expressly such as in a secrecy provision in a license agreement, under a non-disclosure agreement, or a secrecy provision in an employment or other agreement. The obligation of confidence may also arise by implication of law such as, for example, if there is a special relationship between the parties that gives rise to such an obligation (such as attorney-client, doctor-patient, director-company, or the like) or where the circumstances of disclosure give rise to an implied obligation of confidence. This implied obligation of confidence can arise, for example, where disclosure is made under circumstances where it would be reasonable to expect the person or entity receiving the disclosure to treat it as confidential and not disclose it without the consent of the disclosing party.

Since there must be a relationship between the parties to bring a breach of confidence action, it is not possible to bring such an action in many jurisdictions against an industrial spy. An industrial spy generally may be employed by a competitor or foreign government to acquire certain confidential information. Since there is no specific relationship of confidence between the spy and the owner of the confidential information, a breach of confidence action may not be brought. In many jurisdictions, however, such "theft" of confidential information is a criminal offense.

---

[39]*Control and Security of Computer Information Systems,* 1989, Computer Science Press, New York, page 235.

[40]Restatement of Torts, section 757, Comment B (1939).

The third requirement of a breach of confidence action is generally easy to establish. Disclosure of valuable confidential information that results in a competitive advantage almost inevitably results in damage or detriment to the company wishing to preserve the secrecy of the information.

10.8.4 Authorized Use

As will be seen from the provisions of criminal law that deal with computer abuse or computer crime, the concept of *authorized use* often is fundamental to the question of whether a criminal prosecution is likely to result in a conviction of the abuser. The concept of authorized use is also important in respect of civil law remedies that may be available to deal with certain abusive or harmful conduct. If, for example, the particular conduct is authorized or approved then in most cases no action may be brought either under criminal or civil law.

In the computer industry it is common to find that third parties have imposed certain obligations relating to the use of computer systems, computer programs, and/or data that they provide to a company through obligations set out in license agreements. Similarly employees, consultants, and others may often be under non-disclosure obligations (to create express obligations of secrecy). It is therefore important for the information systems security professional to have some understanding of basic concepts involved in license agreements and non-disclosure obligations.

10.8.5 License Agreements

The basic concept of a license agreement is permission from the licensor to carry out certain types of conduct by the licensee. For example in a computer program license the licensor is often the copyright holder. The licensor sets out the guidelines and parameters for use of the copyright protected computer program. Breach of those terms in the license agreement may give rise to either a copyright infringement action or an action for breach of the license or other remedies at law.

Some of the terms that the information systems security professional should be aware of in reviewing license agreements include:

- *The Parties*

  Who are the parties to the license agreement? The licensor provides certain rights to the licensee. Does the licensee have any right to pass any of those privileges onto others? Are the legal identities of the parties correctly stated?

- *Scope of the License*

  The license agreement may provide exclusive or non-exclusive rights in a defined territory for a particular period of time and in relation to certain specific conduct. It is important that the information systems security professional review all of the limitations on the rights granted under the license agreement. The security professional should obtain the assistance of competent attorneys with experience in licensing transactions to assist them in interpreting these rights, obligations, and limits set out under the license agreement.

- *Secrecy Obligations*

  License agreements often contain extensive obligations of secrecy including, in many cases, obligations for employees of the licensee to sign non-disclosure agreements. It is very important for the information systems security professional to be aware of these obligations.

- *Financial Terms*

A license agreement often may provide for payment of royalties or license fees on a periodic basis or, in some cases, as an up-front fee. Failure to make such payments may often result in termination of a license.

- *Termination Provisions*

  Many license agreements will set out a number of situations that may result in default under the license agreement and result in a right of the licensor to terminate the license. It is very important for a licensee to review these provisions carefully so as to prevent termination of the license.

- *Special Notice or Marking Requirements*

  Many license agreements require the licensee to retain certain notices or markings on copies made of, for example, computer programs, data files, records, and the like. It is important for the information systems security professional to review these carefully.

10.8.6 Non-disclosure Considerations

Non-disclosure obligations or restrictions can arise either by implication or expressly, such as through a license agreement, employment agreement, non-disclosure agreement, or other transaction. It is important for the information systems security professional to be aware of the scope of these obligations so as to integrate those obligations into the computer security plan. Some of the important provisions or considerations in non-disclosure obligations include:[41]

- Acknowledgment of the value of trade secrets. There may be a distinction between valuable trade secrets and confidential information without commercial value for the purposes of criminal law and particularly for purposes of civil remedies available. As a result, the agreement may indicate clearly that valuable trade secrets are involved.

- Non-disclosure requirement. This requirement will provide the essential obligation of confidence and secrecy in relation to the trade secrets or other confidential information.

- Non-use requirement. This provision is also often included so as to preclude use of the trade secrets or confidential information by the party restrained. When obligations of confidence are discussed herein, it is assumed that a non-use restriction is also included.

- Detail of the scope or definition of the trade secrets. Agreements are more effective when they are certain. As a result, it is of advantage to define with as much precision as possible the confidential information subject to the obligations of confidence. An example might be definition, in a detailed form, of a particular semiconductor design project. The security manager may wish to ensure that the types of activities or the access to certain processes, products, or resources that may constitute confidential information are clearly defined.

- Obligations continuing beyond termination. It is clear that obligations of confidence must continue past the termination of the assignment by the consultant or the employment by the employee. Otherwise, of course, there would be no remedy to deal with the employee who absconded with valuable trade secrets of the former employer. One should also note the necessity of continuing obligations when dealing with general releases of individuals who are fiduciaries (that is, have relationships with high trust such as senior officers or directors of corporations).

- Restraints on duplication of materials. In some circumstances, it may be necessary to provide a clear restraint on an individual's ability to take copies of materials, particularly data and

---

[41]*Control and Security of Computer Information Systems*, 1989, Computer Science Press, page 238.

computer programs. These obligations may be important in triggering civil and potentially criminal liability in relation to such unauthorized reproduction of certain materials. These restraints should be clearly integrated into the company's policy in relation to access and use of the firm's computer systems.

- Exit review. At the termination of access or of employment, it is very practical and advisable to conduct a review of the confidential information that the employer consultant has had access to, and to review the continuing obligations of confidence in relation to that valuable confidential information. Such an exit review performs an educational function and provides some certainty for the employee and employer in ascertaining the information restrained. It should, of course, be in writing and it may be placed in the form of an agreement between the parties.

- Delivery of documents on termination. There should be a clear obligation on the employer or consultant to return all documents upon termination of the employment or engagement. This avoids the prospect of confidential information disclosed and such documents being outside the control of the employer.

10.8.7 Contracts

Software development contracts can play a contributing role in any security program. The subject of buying and leasing software and hardware can not be explored without some basic knowledge of contract law. Often the user rushes into the contracting stage by signing the supplier's standard form of contract often called the sales order. This is done without documenting claims made by the salesman and without realizing that the sales order is legally binding. If the purchaser is to protect himself fully, he or she must include certain clauses in these contracts.

Room does not allow a complete discussion except for some of the important clauses that are of particular interest to the computer security specialist. The interested reader should refer to one or more of the references listed at the end of this chapter.[42]

Written contracts should always contain a time frame or timetable in which the hardware is to be installed or software completed. Every contract must contain the details about when various parts of a program are to be completed and tested, or likewise when hardware components are to be installed. Functional specifications are needed in which the performance criteria and interface specifications are outlined in detail. The signatures of authorized individuals must be included for both parties of the contract. The method and timing of payments must be specified in detail. The definitions of terms that require clarification should be included in the written contract. The allocation of responsibilities between the two parties involved including what is expected of each other must be clearly specified. If software is to be developed a detailed description of software must be included. The user and supplier must agree that both parties will use all the Uniform Commercial Code rights, duties, and remedies. Contracts should include some form of progress reporting system for hardware installation or the programming of software, include a warranty that the products produced or purchased will perform according to specifications, provide for program maintenance, provide for access to source code via such agreements as a source code escrow.

Detailed specifications are very important in any contract. Put in writing exactly what the program is to do or in the case of hardware how it is to perform. Since the user is the one who

---

[42][Isshiki 82; Mandell 84; Remer 84]

determines the specific adequacies of the product, the more detailed the contract, the better the position user will be in.[43] There must be an agreement on the form and level of performance acceptance tests for hardware or software. These tests should be directly related to the previously mentioned functional specifications. The best solution to obtaining functioning programs is to use care in selecting a programmer or software house that is competent, reliable, and financially sound.

An effective way to protect the user is to formulate a payment schedule so that a payment is made as each phase of installation is completed, tested, and operating properly. Should the project be delayed, the supplier will be responsible for any loss to the user. It also encourages suppliers to meet time schedules and provides some bargaining leverage between the user and the supplier of the hardware or software. Custom-designed programming is more likely to develop problems and take longer to debug. Therefore, users should take this possibility into consideration when negotiating with the contractor.[44]

Provisions should be made for maintenance of hardware and/or software. This should include up-time commitments for hardware and performance specifications for software. The replacement procedures for non-functioning hardware or software "lemons" must be agreed to.

10.8.8 Warranties for Software and Hardware

Comprehensive warranties for any hardware or software leased or purchased should be considered an important element in any security program. As pointed out above, different rights and obligations arise from the sale or lease of computer software and hardware. The sale of a product gives rise to certain warranties by the seller. A warranty is a promise that a particular statement is true, that the software or computer hardware will work as specified. The genesis for warranties is the Uniform Commercial Code (UCC) which divides warranties into two types: express and implied. Few express warranties are used in the sale of computers or software. Implied warranties that imply that a product is fit and proper for the function advertised are very common.

Under the UCC, an express warranty is an affirmation or promise as to the quality of a product to the buyer and becomes a part of the basis of the bargain. Promises and affirmations made by the software developer to the user about the nature and quality of the program can also be classified as express warranties. Programmers or retailers possess the right to define express warranties. Thus, they have to be realistic when they state any claims and predictions about the capabilities, quality, and nature of their software or hardware. Their considerations may include the legal aspects of their affirmative promises, their product demonstrations, and their product description. Every word they say may be as legally effective as though they were stated in writing. Thus, to protect against liability, all agreements should be in writing. A disclaimer of express warranties can free a supplier from being held responsible to any informal, hypothetical statements or predictions made during the negotiation stages.

Implied warranties are also defined by the UCC. These are certain warranties that are provided automatically in every sale. These warranties need not be in writing nor do they need to be verbally stated. They ensure that good title will pass to the buyer, that the product is fit for the purpose sold, and that it is fit for the ordinary purposes for which similar goods are used (merchantability).

---

[43][Hagelshaw 85]

[44][[Mandell 84], p. 7]

10.8.9 Software Escrow

The topic of software escrow is addressed briefly in section 4.6 under the general topic of backup and recovery measures.

10.9 INTRODUCTION TO CRIMINAL LAW

Criminal law, generally, deals with the relationship between the state and individual conduct. In certain situations, individual conduct is considered so reprehensible or otherwise damaging to broad public interest that the full power of the state's criminal justice apparatus should be applied to deal with the conduct.

A criminal prosecution is often started with a formal or informal complaint made to police or prosecuting attorneys. The state carries out the investigation of the alleged conduct, gathers evidence and marshalls the witnesses who may shed light on the incidents in question. All such activities are carried out at the expense of the state (and, of course, the taxpayer). Generally, the prosecutor will make decisions relating to continuing the prosecution whether or not the victim desires the prosecution to continue. In many cases, the victim can still be called as a witness even if he or she does not want to testify or give evidence.

Criminal prosecution often requires two elements. The first element is a physical act (such as unauthorized use of a computer system). The second element is a certain type of intent (such as malice, or intent to injure, etc.) if both the mental and physical element cannot be proved, then it may be impossible to obtain a conviction.

The standard of proof required to obtain a conviction is "beyond a reasonable doubt. While different courts apply different standards to define that principle, it is generally true that this means there can be no credible probability other than that the defendant committed the act.

A criminal conviction may result in a term of imprisonment, fine, community service, or other required conduct on the part of the accused. In some cases, restitution (to the extent possible) may also be ordered.

It is very important for a security professional to be aware that threatening to bring a criminal prosecution to achieve some other result, such as, having an accused deliver up stolen computer programs, data, confess how he or she committed the acts, or the like, may also be committing a criminal offense. It is extortion in many jurisdictions to threaten to bring criminal prosecution to obtain certain types of conduct from another. Information systems security professionals must be *very careful* to avoid committing criminal offenses themselves as they carry out their duties.

In the United States, unlike some other federal systems (Canada for example), the basic criminal law power is at the state level. This leads to a broad diversity of law despite efforts towards that harmonization of law. In addition, the federal government also has legislative competence in the area of criminal activity occurring across state lines or across international borders. As a result, the U.S. criminal law is very complex. Since many types of computer abuse may take place between different states or even different countries, it is possible that an accused may have additional technical defences available basically arguing that he or she was charged under the wrong law.

Because so much abusive conduct occurs at an interstate or international level and because it is beyond the scope of this text to provide a review of individual criminal law in each state, the following section reviews a collected sampling of the federal criminal law provisions relating to certain types of computer abuse.

10.9.1 Theoretical Framework for Computer Crime Laws

Traditionally many types of criminal conduct may involve computer programs, storage media, or data but that are not what is commonly thought of as "computer crime." For example, theft of a system unit or other hardware component is merely theft of a particular physical asset. There is nothing mysterious or unusual about such criminal conduct and the criminal law has a wealth of experience in dealing with that type of criminal activity. The purpose of this material is not to examine this type of activity.

Certain types of conduct have provided difficulty for the established framework of criminal law. Data and computer programs are ephemeral. Considerable damage may be done merely by using or accessing a computer system or by destroying or altering data. Since many of these concepts are new to the criminal justice system, many jurisdictions have found it necessary to enact new, specific, computer crime laws. The purpose of this review, then, is to examine these specific computer crime laws and certain of the general laws that deal with other non-traditional applications for criminal law in relation to the computer industry.

There are several major categories of computer crime, as defined above. These are:

- Unauthorized use of a computer system or computer services.
- Unauthorized use or reproduction of computer programs.
- Unauthorized use or reproduction of data.
- Theft of computer system hardware, programs, or data, or the information contained therein.
- The commission of other offenses (such as theft of other physical assets or destruction of assets) through use of the computer as the medium for committing the offense.
- Denial of access to legitimate users of a computer system, computer services, computer programs, or data.

The particular characteristics in respect of many of the types of computer crime make this area of criminal law particularly difficult for the professional investigator or law enforcement official. Some of these peculiarities are as follows:

- Many computer crimes are undetected. Often use of a computer as the medium by which a particular offense is committed leaves no trail of evidence through which the conduct can be detected. Often it is the discovery of some incidental by-product or activity related to the criminal conduct that results in discovery of the offense (*e.g.*, sudden wealth).
- A wide range of assets is available through representation as data stored in a computer system. Money, monies worth, inventory, and other property may be recorded or represented by data in various computer systems. The ease of manipulation of this data provides the computer criminal with relative ease in manipulating the underlying assets.
- There is a wide geographical area in which computer crime occurs. Through the use of telecommunications access, it is possible for a criminal to institute a chain of events in one jurisdiction, say the State of Texas, U.S., which results in loss or injury in another jurisdiction, say the Province of Ontario, Canada. There are problems of which law, if any, would apply to this particular criminal conduct. Furthermore, there is an additional difficulty of extradition that would complicate prosecution.

- There are innumerable points of access from which the particular abusive conduct may occur. Through the interconnection of many computer systems in local area networks, wide area networks, or otherwise through telecommunication channels, there is a multiplicity of points of access from which the criminal activity can be initiated.

- A contracted time scale may be involved. In many types of traditional crime the criminal conduct may take minutes or even hours to commit. In some cases it may take days or months to commit certain types of crimes. Data or computer programs can be erased, manipulated, or altered in seconds or fractions of a second.

- The range of assets available to the computer criminal is less limited. A few keystrokes may allow the diversion of a significant amount of inventory from a warehouse. A traditional fraud or bank job may deal only with the physical assets that are directly available to the criminal or the victim. The computer and telecommunications system provide a broader range of access to the victim's resources for the computer criminal.

- Software piracy is extremely widespread. The "sharing" of computer programs provides a vector for the transmission of computer virus programs and significantly enlarges the class of potential victims of the abusive conduct. Furthermore the rapid spread of pirate software may lead to rapid dissemination of vulnerable data, such as credit card numbers, confidential telephone numbers, calling card numbers, passwords, or other embedded information. The availability of such sensitive information provides more opportunities for opportunistic criminal activity.

- To the extent that computer security systems are in place, they are often subverted by authorized users of the systems who select easily defeated passwords or otherwise compromise the system security on the basis of maximizing user convenience.

- As well as the points of access provided by interconnection of computers and systems, the widespread proliferation of intelligent devices such as laser printers, facsimile transmission machines, and the like expands the range of entry points for corruption of a computer or telecommunications system.

Many initial matters must be considered and reviewed prior to any in-depth analysis of prosecution experience with enactment of specific computer crime laws. These preliminary matters are, first, the fact that most computer crime laws are based upon the concept of authorization or "colour of right" in respect of the use of computer systems, programs, or data and, second, the fact that there are particular problems in admissibility of computer-generated records. These matters have been discussed earlier.

10.10 CONTROL OF STRATEGIC MATERIALS

Certain materials, know-how, information, devices, plans, blueprints, computer programs, assemblies or parts thereof, in a wide range of areas of advanced technology dealing from composite materials through micro-electronics, semi-conductor design, radar, guidance, communications, laser, or similar fields, are of strategic importance to the security of your country. As a result, most jurisdictions have legislation controlling the import and export of strategic goods and materials. It is important for the information security specialist to make him or herself aware of the provisions of these laws and establish relationships with local customs or special officers enforcing them.

In the event of breach of security at an installation involving strategic goods, information, or other materials whose export may be controlled or restricted, it is important that you notify the appropriate officers so that they may increase their vigilance for attempts to export that strategic technology.

It is very important that the information security specialist be aware that approaches may be made to his company from another friendly country. However, that friendly country may, in some cases, be an inadvertent host for operation of those who wish to divert strategic technology in breach of legislation controlling or prohibiting export of such technology.

If the company is in the business of supplying products or services dealing with such strategic technologies, then a number of indicators may lead to suspicion in relation to a proposed transfer export of such strategic technologies. Some of these indicators or factors are:

- Major new customers who ask to pay in cash.
- Customers who do not want after-service or maintenance contracts.
- Customers who ask for voltage differences from their own country's.
- Customers with unusual shipping instructions, such as requesting crates that do not identify the contents.

The information security specialist may save his company embarrassment and significant liability (both in fines and criminal prosecution) under applicable strategic technology control legislation by being aware of these potential threats and incorporating them into the overall information security plan.

10.11 TRANSBORDER DATA FLOWS

As you read these words electrons speed from country to country along the silver threads of telecommunications networks. Those electrons, by their characteristics, carry information. That information may be temperatures from a weather-reporting service, stock quotations from an exchange, a salesman making a sale and recording the transaction, or the personal comments of a traveller to his loved one separated by so many miles.

Each of these communications and so many others pass through various nodes or links in those telecommunications networks. The information may come from a database in a computer in another country.

The complexity of these transborder data flows, the international nature of the flows, and the ease with which a private individual can gain access to foreign information without passing through any censors or customs bureaus raises a number of problems.

The number of people who have potential or actual access to such information can be large and so there is a need to provide protection from abuse. Actions by one country may be quite ineffective as the information can easily pass through several national telecommunication systems. As a result, some form of international cooperation is required to set standards for the protection of private communications. The Organization of Economic Cooperation and Development (OECD) has begun that process.

The OECD has prepared a set of Guidelines for the handling of private non-data and data communications. These guidelines serve to identify the relative responsibilities of the database operator, the telecommunication system operator, the person assembling the data in the first instance, and also the end user. These are new rules that will eventually provide us all with greater personal privacy in an age when computerization and telecommunications have laid much of our private lives open to view.[45]

Another example of such cooperation is the Canada-United States Free Trade Agreement. In this historic agreement, both countries agree to eliminate certain trade barriers and that future legislation and practice will not increase such barriers, in respect of a wide range of services including computer services.

Computer crime has also entered an age when international cooperation is needed to deal with crimes that may be committed in Texas by a person sitting at a terminal halfway around the world. This problem is complex. In such a case, where did the crime occur? In Texas where the injury was done—or at the terminal in Sweden where the criminal controlled the process? This question becomes important as the law of the place where the crime was committed may be very different.

Pornography and hate literature may be imported through the use of data telecommunications and avoid any border screening by customs officials. At the present time there is no feasible way to intercept all transborder data flows and subject them to scrutiny. In fact the effort to do so would cost so much and create a bureaucracy so large that more serious problems would be created by the solution than by the problem.

The new information based industries must react and act more rapidly today than at any previous time in human history. This is only accomplished when information from the farthest corners of the globe is available to the user without delay and at least cost. This is the age of information industries. To cut the flow of information would be as harmful as it would have been centuries ago to cut the flow of water to a water mill.

The end result is that the citizens of advanced industrialized societies must learn to deal with the added strength and the new problems that arise from transborder data flows. The world continues to become more and more complex. There is no alternative but to adapt to these changes but in a way that serves to strengthen our traditional values and beliefs.

The information security professional must play a role in helping the society interpret and understand the competing needs of personal privacy and secure free flows of data.

10.12 PRIVACY OF DATA—OECD GUIDELINES

The United States, United Kingdom, Canada and other countries are implementing guidelines on the protection of privacy and transborder flows of personal data established by the Organization for Economic Cooperation and Development (OECD) made in Paris 1981. The OECD Council recommendation of September 23, 1980 set out certain guidelines governing the protection of privacy and transborder flows of personal data. These recommendations are set out as follows:[46]

Part 1. General

1.   For the purposes of these guidelines:

---

[45]These guidelines are the result of studies by a group of experts led by Justice M. D. Kirby, Chairman of the Australian Law Reform Commission, and were adopted by the Council of the OECD on September 23, 1980. The text of the guidelines should be reviewed for any detailed study.

[46]Reprinted with permission of the OECD.

(a) "Data Controller" means a party who, according to domestic law, is competent to decide about the contents and use of personal data regardless of whether or not such data are collected, stored, processed or disseminated by that party or by an agent on its behalf;

(b) "Personal Data" means any information relating to an identified or identifiable individual (data subject);

(c) "Transborder Flows of Personal Data" means movements of personal data across national borders.

2. Scope of Guidelines. These guidelines apply to personal data, whether in the public or private sectors, which, because in the manner in which they are processed, or because of their nature with a context in which they are used, impose a danger to privacy and individual liberties.

3. These guidelines should not be interpreted as preventing:

(a) the application, to different categories of personal data, of different protective measures depending on their nature and the context in which they are collected, stored, process of disseminated;

(b) the exclusion from the application of the guidelines of personal data which obviously do not contain any risk to privacy and individual liberty; or

(c) the application of the guidelines only to automatic processing of personal data.

4. Exceptions to the Principles contained in Parts 2 and 3 of these guidelines, including those relating to National Sovereignty, National Security and Public Policy ("*Ordre Public*"), should be:

(a) as few as possible, and

(b) made known to the public.

5. In a particular case of federal countries the observance of these guidelines may be affected by the division of powers in the Federation.

6. These guidelines should be regarded as minimum standards which are capable of being supplemented by additional measures for the protection of privacy and individual liberties.

Part 2. Basic Principles of National Application

1. Collection Limitation Principles

Section 7. There should be limits to the collection of personal data and any such data should be obtained by lawful and fair means and, where appropriate, with the knowledge or consent of the data subject.

2. Data Quality Principle

Section 8. Personal data should be relevant to the purposes for which they are to be used, and, to the extent necessary for those purposes, should be accurate, complete and kept up-to-date.

3. Purpose Specification Principle

Section 9. The purposes for which the personal data are collected should be specified no later than at the time of data collection and the subsequent use limited to the fulfillment of those purposes and such others as are not incompatible with those purposes and as are specified on each occasion of change of purpose.

4. Use Limitation Principle

Section 10. Personal data should not be disclosed, made available or otherwise used for purposes other than those specified in accordance with paragraph 9 except:

(a) with the consent of the data subject; or

(b) with the authority of law.

5. Security Safeguards Principle

Section 11. Personal data should be protected by reasonable security safeguards against such risks as loss or unauthorized access, destruction, use, modification or disclosure of data.

6. Openness Principle

Section 12. There should be a general policy of openness about developments, practices and policies with respect to personal data. Means should be readily available of establishing the existence and nature of personal data, and the main purposes of their use, as well as the identity and usual residence of the data controller.

7. Individual Participation Principle

Section 13. An individual should have the right:

(a) to obtain from a data controller, or otherwise, confirmation or whether or not the data controller has data relating to him,

(b) to have communicated to him, data relating to him

    (i)   within a reasonable time,

    (ii)   at a charge, if any, that is not excessive,

    (iii)   in a reasonable manner, and

    (iv)   in a form that is readily intelligible to him;

(c) to be given reasons if a request made under subparagraphs (a) and (b) is denied, and to be able to challenge such denial; and

(d) to challenge data relating to him and, if the challenge is successful, to have the data erased, rectified, completed or amended.

8. Accountability Principle

Section 14. A data controller should be accountable for complying with measures which give effect to the principle stated above.

Part 3. Basic Principles of International Application

1. Free Flow and Legitimate Restrictions

Section 15. Member countries should take into consideration the implications for other member countries of domestic processing and re-export of personal data.

Section 16. Member countries should take all reasonable and appropriate steps to ensure that transborder flows of personal data, including transit through a member country, are uninterpreted and secure.

Section 17. A member country should refrain from restricting transborder flows of personal data between itself and another member country except where the latter does not yet substantially observe these guidelines or where the re-export of such data would circumvent its domestic privacy legislation. A member country may also impose restrictions in respect of certain categories of personal data for which its domestic privacy legislation includes specific regulations in view of the nature of those data and for which the other member countries provide no equivalent protection.

Section 18. Member countries should avoid developing laws, policies and practices in the name of protection of privacy and individual liberties, which would create obstacles to transborder flows of personal data that would exceed requirements for such protection.

Part 4 of the guidelines sets out the requirement for member countries to establish legal, administrative, or other procedures or institutions for the protection of privacy and individual liberties in respect of personal privacy. Part 5 goes on to require member countries to establish procedures to facilitate information exchange related to guidelines and mutual assistance in the procedural and investigative matters involved, and generally to cooperate towards the development of principles to govern the applicable law in case of transborder flows of personal data.

The member countries of the OECD are Australia, Austria, Belgium, Canada, Denmark, Finland, France, the Federal Republic of Germany, Greece, Iceland, Ireland, Italy, Japan, Luxembourg, the Netherlands, New Zealand, Norway, Portugal, Spain, Sweden, Switzerland, Turkey, the United Kingdom, and the United States. Another example of the implementation of concern of individual privacy is found in the *Privacy Act of 1974*, 5 U.S.C. 522a, Public Law 93-579. This provision is an effort to safeguard individual privacy from misuse of federal records, to provide that individuals be granted access to records concerning them which are maintained by federal agencies, and to establish a privacy protection study commission and related purposes.

From a conceptual level a similar arrangement may be found in Canada's *Privacy Act*, R.S.C. 1985, c. P. 21. In both the United States and Canada the privacy law depends on individual initiative for enforcement action. In other words, an individual who feels aggrieved must bring action or complaint to the Privacy Protection Study Commission or Privacy Commissioner (in Canada) who may then act to investigate and recommend action to the particular governmental agency. Another common feature of these provisions is that they only apply to certain governmental agencies within the jurisdiction or control of the Federal Government.

In Europe, on the other hand, the law is less reliant on individual initiative and contemplates a more proactive state interventionist role. In many European countries a Privacy Commissioner has a positive duty to investigate and bring action when he or she finds instances of abuse or violation of personal data privacy.

Furthermore there are state laws that may also apply additional sanctions or may provide for rights in respect of data relating to private individuals held by a state agency.

REFERENCES

Becker, L. G., *Computer Abuse and Misuse: Assessment of Federal and State Legislative Initiative*, Institute of Defense Analyses, 1801 N. Beauregard Street, Alexandria, VA, IDA Paper P-1798, 1984.

Bill C-19, The House of Commons of Canada.

Bill C-60, "An Act to Amend the Copyright Act and to Amend Other Acts in Consequence Thereof," The House Of Commons Of Canada, 2nd Session 32nd Parliament 1986-87.

"Computer Crime Law Reporter," National Center for Computer Crime Data, 904 Daniel Court, Santa Cruz, CA, 95062, 1989.

"Computer Security Guidelines For Implementing the Privacy Act of 1974," National Bureau of Standards, FIPS-PUB-41, U.S. Department of Commerce, Springfield, VA, May 30, 1975, p. 3.

Datapro Research Corp., "DataPro Reports on Information Security," 1988, Datapro Research Corp., Delran, NJ, current issue.

Davis, G. G., *Software Protection, Practical and Legal Steps to Protect and Market Computer Programs*, Van Nostrand Reinhold, New York, NY, 1985.

Fites, Philip. E., Martin P. J. Kratz, and Alan F. Brebner, *Control and Security of Computer Information Systems*, W. H. Freeman/Computer Science Press, New York, NY, 1989.

Gallegos, Frederick, Dana R. (Rick) Richardson, & A. Faye Borthick, *Audit & Control of Information Systems*, South-Western Publishing Company, West. Chicago, IL, 1987.

"A Guide to the Ethical and Legal Use of Software for Members of the Academic Community," EDUCOM Software Initiative/ADAPSO, 1987.

Hagelshaw, R. Lee, *The Computer User's Legal Guide*, Chilton Book Company, PA, 1985.

Isshiki, Koichiro R., *Small Business Computers, a Guide to Evaluation and Selection*, Prentice-Hall, Englewood Cliffs, NJ, 1982.

Kahin, Brian, "Property and Propriety in the Digital Environment: Towards an Examination Copy License," EDUCOM Software Initiative White Paper, October, 1988.

Kratz, Martin P. J., "Evidentiary Problems of Computer-Generated Materials," in *Technology and the Law for General Practitioners*, Legal Education Society of Alberta, Canada, March, 1987.

Kratz, Martin P. J., "Introduction to Copyright Infringement," in *Technology and the Law for General Practitioners*, Legal Education Society of Alberta, Canada, March, 1987.

Krauss, Leonard L. and Aileen MacGahan, *Computer Fraud and Countermeasures*, Prentice-Hall, Englewood Cliffs, NJ, 1979.

Mandell, Steven L., *Computer Data Processing, and the Law*, West Publishing Company, MN, 1984.

"Model Computer Crime Act," Data Processing Management Association, Park Ridge, IL, 1986.

"OECD Guidelines Governing the Protection of Privacy and Transborder Flows of Personal Data," Recommendations of the council of Europe, adopted at its 523rd meeting on September 23, 1980.

PL-100-235, "The Security Act of 1987", U.S. Congress.

The Privacy Act of 1974, Public Law 93-579, 93rd Cong., S.3418, December, 31, 1974.

Remer, Daniel, *Legal Care for Your Software: A Step by Step Guide for Computer Software Writers*, A Nolo Press Book, Berkeley, CA, 1984.

Richards, T., C. D. Schou, and P. E. Fites, "Information Systems Security Laws and Legislation," in *Information Security Modules*, National Security Agency, 1989.

Sookman, Barry, *Sookman Computer Law: Acquiring and Protecting Information Technology*, Toronto, Canada, 1989.

Whiteside, Thomas, *Computer Capers*, Thomas V. Crowell Co., New York, NY, 1978.

11. Investigation

Information Security includes the requirement to investigate incidents. The practitioner is expected to know how to investigate an incident in such a way as to determine its origin and cause with a high degree of confidence while preserving the integrity of the evidence. This includes knowing how to employ the system and its audit trail, conduct interviews, and document.

Specific knowledge includes:

- Legal requirements for maintaining a trail of evidence
- Interrogation techniques
- Legal limits on interrogation methods permitted

DEFINITIONS

Some useful definitions in the legal area are covered below and in Chapter 10. Some definitions from government regulations are provided here;[1] please note that usage varies under differing legislation and jurisdictions. Some of the terms defined here have substantially different meanings depending on the legal context in which they are used. Professional legal advice is encouraged.

Collusion

The act of two or more Agents or Perpetrators cooperating or conspiring to perpetrate an Intentional Event. (MK)

Computer Abuse

1. Willful or negligent unauthorized activity that affects the availability, confidentiality, or integrity of computer resources. Computer abuse includes fraud, embezzlement, theft, malicious damage, unauthorized use, denial of service, and misappropriation. Levels of computer abuse are:
   a) Minor abuse—acts that represent management problems, such as printing calendars or running games that do not impact system availability for authorized applications
   b) Major abuse—unauthorized use (possibly criminal), denial of service, and multiple instances of minor abuse to include waste
   c) Criminal act—fraud, embezzlement, theft, malicious damage, misappropriation, conflict of interest, and unauthorized access to classified data. (AFR 205-16)
2. The misuse, destruction, alteration, or disruption of data processing resources. The key aspects of computer-related abuse are that it is intentional and improper and it may not involve the violation of a specific law. (NCSC-WA-001-85)

Computer Crime

Fraud, embezzlement, unauthorized access, and other "white collar" crimes committed with the aid of or directly involving a computer system and/or network. (GAO)

---

[1]These are repeated from Chapter 10 for convenient reference in this related chapter.

Computer Fraud

Computer-related crimes involving deliberate misrepresentation or alteration of data in order to obtain something of value (usually for monetary gain). A computer system must have been involved in the perpetration or cover-up of the act, or series of acts. A computer system might have been involved through improper manipulation of:

1. input data
2. output or results
3. applications programs
4. data files
5. computer operations
6. communications
7. computer hardware, systems software, or firmware (NCSC-WA-001-85)

Entrapment

The deliberate planting of apparent flaws in a system for the purpose of detecting attempted penetrations or confusing an intruder about which flaws to exploit. (AR 380-380; FIPS PUB 39; NCSC-WA-001-85)

Investigation(s)

The review and analysis of system security features (*e.g.*, the investigation of system control programs using flow charts, assembly listings, and related documentation) to determine the security provided by the operating system. (OPNAVINST 5239.1A; DODD 5200.28M)

National Security Decision Directive 145

Signed by President Reagan on September 17, 1984, this directive is entitled "National Policy on Telecommunications and Automated Information Systems Security." It provides initial objectives, policies, and an organizational structure to guide the conduct of national activities toward safeguarding systems which process, store, or communicate sensitive information, establishes a mechanism for policy development, and assigns implementation responsibilities. (NCSC-WA-001-85)

Notarization

The registration of data with a trusted third party that allows the later assurance of the accuracy of its characteristics such as content, origin, time, and delivery. (ISO 7498-2)

Penetration

The successful act of bypassing the security mechanisms of a system. (NCSC-WA-001-85)

Penetration Profile

A delineation of activities required to effect a penetration. (FIPS PUB 39; AR 380-380)

Penetration Signature

1. The description of a situation or set of conditions in which a penetration could occur or of system events which in conjunction can indicate the occurrence of a penetration in progress. (AR 380-380; FIPS PUB 39)

2. The characteristics or identifying marks that may be produced of an unsuccessful or successful penetration. (NCSC-WA-001-85)

Penetration Study

A study to determine the feasibility and methods for defeating controls of an automated information system. (NCSC-WA-001-85)

Privacy

The right of individuals and organizations to control the collection, storage, and dissemination of their information or information about themselves. (FIPS PUB 39)

Privacy Protection

The establishment of appropriate administrative, technical, and physical safeguards to ensure the security and confidentiality of data records and to protect both security and confidentiality against any anticipated threats or hazards that could result in substantial harm, embarrassment, inconvenience, or unfairness to any individual about whom such information is maintained. (FIPS PUB 39)

Proprietary Data

Data that is created, used, marketed by individuals having exclusive legal rights. (AFR 205-16)

Pseudo-flaw

An apparent loophole deliberately implanted in an operating system program as a trap for intruders. (FIPS PUB 39; AR 380-380; NCSC-WA-001-85)

Review and Approval

The process whereby information pertaining to the security and integrity of an ADP activity or network is collected, analyzed, and submitted to the appropriate DAA for accreditation of the activity or network. (OPNAVINST 5239.1A)

Security Breach

A violation of controls of a particular information system such that information assets or system components are unduly exposed. (WB)

Security Violation

An instance in which a user or other person circumvents or defeats the controls of a system to obtain unauthorized access to information contained therein or to system resources. (WB)

Softlifting

Illegal copying of licensed software for personal use. (PC/PCIE)

Tampering

An unauthorized modification which alters the proper functioning of a system or piece of equipment in a manner which degrades the security it provides. (NCSC-WA-001-85)

Theft

A peril involving removal of an asset for subsequent use by an agent.

11.1 EVIDENCE—PROOF IN COURT

The elements of a civil action, criminal action, or the elements establishing violation of a regulatory provision need to be proved to the court or tribunal which is hearing the case. As a result the legal system has developed rules of evidence that are intended to ensure that the best available evidence is brought forward and to provide an opportunity that that evidence be tested from the perspectives of credibility, significance, relevance, and reliability.

It is outside the scope of this text to provide a course in the law of evidence. The purpose of this section is merely to provide an introduction to some general principles in this area.

While there are no generally accepted classifications of evidence, evidence can be broken down based on its form or upon the purpose for which it is being introduced.

11.1.1 Purpose of Evidence

In respect of evidence classified in relation to its purpose we may look at direct evidence, indirect or circumstantial evidence, presumptive evidence, original evidence, judicial notice, or agreed statements of facts. Each of these types of evidence is described briefly below.

11.1.1.1 Direct Evidence

Direct evidence is called to prove a specific fact. For example, a licence agreement may be introduced to establish the existence of certain limits on the user's ability to use a computer program.

11.1.1.2 Circumstantial or Indirect Evidence

An excellent description of this type of evidence is:[2]

> On a superficial view, direct or indirect or circumstantial evidence would appear to be distinct species of evidence; whereas these words denote only the different modes in which those classes of evidentiary facts are adduced to produce conviction. Circumstantial evidence is of a nature identically the same with direct evidence; the distinction is, that by direct evidence is intended evidence that applies directly to the fact which forms the subject of inquiry, the *factum probandum*; circumstantial evidence is equally direct in its nature, but, as the name imports, is a direct evidence of a minor fact or facts of such a nature that the mind is led into intuitively, or by a conscious process of reasoning, towards or to the conviction that from it or them some other fact may be inferred. A witness disposes that he saw A inflict on B a wound of which he instantly died; this is a case of direct evidence. B dies of poisoning; A is proved to have had malice and other threats against him, and to have clandestinely purchased poison, wrapped in a particular paper, and of the same kind as that which has caused death, the paper is found in his secret drawer, and the poison gone. The evidence of these facts is direct; the facts themselves constitute indirect and circumstantial evidence as applicable to the inquiry whether a murder has been committed, and whether it was committed by A.

11.1.1.3 Presumptive Evidence

Presumptive evidence differs from circumstantial evidence:[3]

> It implies if not the certainty at least the great probability of some relation between the facts and the inference. Circumstances generally, but not necessarily, lead to particular inferences; for the facts may

---

[2]Wills, *Essays on Principles of Circumstantial Evidence*, 6th ed. London, 1912, pp. 19 to 20.

[3]Wills, *Op. Cit.* page 21.

be indisputable, and yet their relation to the principal fact may be only apparent and not real; and even when the conviction is real, the deduction may be erroneous.

11.1.1.4 Original Evidence

Original evidence arises where it is desired to introduce the facts that a statement or representation was made rather than proving the truthfulness or falsity of that statement. In other words, it may be relevant to prove that there had been a communication of some form between two parties regardless of the truthfulness of that communication.

11.1.1.5 Judicial Notice

Judicial notice is not really a form of evidence. Rather, proof of some facts can be avoided because the fact may be so notorious or well-known that the court is able to take notice of it and accept it as a fact. Example of fact situations in which a court *may* take judicial notice might be as follows: that night follows day; that IBM is a major supplier of computer equipment; that telephone calls may be made across borders; and the like.

There is a related area. Many jurisdictions have laws that allow a court to take judicial notice of certain official government acts, documents, and the like. As a result of those acts it is possible for a court, for example, to accept the Certificate of Incorporation under the Registrar of Corporations seal as conclusive proof that the company in question was incorporated without having to call the Registrar of Corporations to court. A very important provision under such evidence acts are provisions dealing with admissibility of business records made in the ordinary course of business.

11.1.1.6 Agreed Statement of Facts

In certain cases, especially in civil lawsuits, the parties can focus the action on the specific areas of disagreement by agreeing to the existence of certain facts. The parties then provide the court with an Agreed Statement of Facts thus not necessitating proof of those facts to the court.

11.1.2 Form of Evidence

Another means of categorizing evidence is by the *form* of evidence. Evidence may take three forms. These are oral testimony, documentary evidence, or real evidence. Each of these is described briefly below.

11.1.2.1 Oral Evidence

Most evidence is introduced by oral evidence that is the sworn statement of a witness, party or expert. Oral evidence may be either direct or hearsay. Oral testimony is direct when a witness testifies to things that he or she has actually observed, felt, perceived or sensed through his own senses (*i.e.*, sight, hearing, taste, smell, or touch). Hearsay evidence, on the other hand, occurs where a witness is testifying as to what another person has told him. For example, A may testify that B told him that C made six illegal copies of an application program. As a general rule hearsay evidence is inadmissible. There is, however, a number of exceptions to this hearsay rule that allow hearsay (second-hand) evidence to be introduced in special circumstances. One of the most important of those exceptions are the business records provisions of most evidence acts.

The problem introducing business records typically is that the person who made the records (*e.g.*, a clerk or the like) cannot readily be identified or may not be available to give evidence as to the making of the record. As a result for another person in the business (*e.g.*, a department head) to introduce the record as evidence would be introducing hearsay evidence. Business records can, however, usually be introduced if it can be established that they were made in the ordinary course of making the records of the business. Since most modern records are automated this may require a detailed review of the computer system, input, output, processing of records, and steps taken to ensure and maintain the accuracy and reliability of the business records.

11.1.2.2 Documentary Evidence

Evidence is said to be *documentary evidence* when a document is introduced to prove the contents of the document. For example, a license agreement might be introduced to establish contractual restrictions on the user's ability to make copies of a computer program. Documentary evidence is subject to the best evidence rule that requires that the original must be produced. There are some exceptions, however, where the original is not available and copies of secondary evidence may be introduced. Once again, business records are an example of this matter. Often automated systems do not provide original records of a transaction or it may be impossible to introduce the original record (being stored as impulses in a database). As a result it may be possible under business records exemptions under many evidence acts to introduce a printout or report that is not the original document reflecting the transaction. The important issues in reviewing such computer generated records are to determine how much processing has occurred to produce the record and how that processing has affected the accuracy, reliability, or fairness of presentation of the record.

11.1.2.3 Real Evidence

In some cases it is necessary or desirable for a jury or other trier of fact (for example a judge in some cases) to witness the actual scene or representation of a scene, object, or place where events may occur. For example, if the features or functionality of a computer system are brought into issue, the jury or judge may actually observe the functioning of the computer system so as to have real evidence of the circumstances of its functioning.

11.1.3 Testing and Introduction of Evidence

Regardless of the form of evidence that is introduced that evidence must be tested as to its significance to the issues to be determined by the court, the reliability of the evidence and the credibility of the witness. Many of these issues are determined by the process through which the evidence is introduced and tested. Generally, evidence is introduced by, for example, calling a witness and having that witness give direct evidence. The attorney who called the witness asks the witness a number of questions that are designed to assist the witness in setting out his or her evidence.

Once all that evidence has been provided it is tested by cross-examination. In cross-examination the attorney for the competing party (in a civil lawsuit the attorney representing the other party in the action—in a criminal lawsuit the attorney acting as either the defense attorney or prosecutor) proceeds to test the evidence given in the direct examination of the witness by asking a number of probing questions. These questions are provided in an attempt to cast further light or elaboration of the statements made by the witness. For example the witness may have said that he had seen *A* at a particular workstation. In cross-examination it may be discovered that *A* was working at that workstation after normal working hours or that the workstation was not assigned to *A*.

Evidence is usually called before the trier of fact. In many cases the trier of fact is a jury. The judge serves the role of providing rulings on law, including admissibility of evidence and the like, and provides a summary of the applicable law to the jury with which to apply the facts. The jury has the responsibility for determining the facts in the case and therefore is responsible for assessing the credibility, relevance, and significance of all the evidence. In some cases, there is no jury and so the judge also fulfills the role of the jury.

In some special cases evidence can be introduced on the basis of sworn statements called depositions or affidavits. These documents are also subject to cross-examination. Both the direct examination and cross-examination occur under oath. Lying under oath may be a criminal offense in many jurisdictions and subject to additional sanctions including fines and imprisonment.

Generally speaking the opposing attorney will keep a close watch on the type of questions being asked and the type of answers being provided. Evidence may be inadmissible for a number of reasons. An important example of inadmissible evidence is statements of opinion as opposed to statements of fact. (For example, a witness offering his or her opinion about the reliability of a computer system rather than stating facts known to the witness.) Other examples of inadmissible evidence are conclusions of law made by a witness, or hearsay.

Although most witnesses are not entitled to give opinion evidence, expert witnesses may be called to do so. An expert witness typically will be a highly skilled consultant who has been hired by one of the parties to be able to give a conclusion on a complex subject. Expert witnesses are often used in complex litigation or in litigation involving complex subjects, such as relating to complex computer technology and the like. Before the expert witness can give evidence the expert must be qualified. This means that the expert's credentials must be accepted by the court. The attorney who seeks to call the expert introduces the expert and his or her qualifications to the court. The opposing attorney then cross-examines on those qualifications attempting to limit the area in which the expert can be qualified to give an opinion or to show that the expert is not impartial or otherwise to damage or limit the value of the testimony of the expert. Once the expert has been qualified in a particular area (*e.g.*, operation of the UNIX operating system) then the expert is able to give an opinion based on particular facts that relate to his or her area of competence. While the expert is able to give opinion evidence, that evidence is still subject to the other rules of admissibility and relevance.

The opinion of the expert witness may be rejected by the jury or judge. The expert is called to assist the trier of fact and not to replace the function of the trier of fact. In complex cases there may be several conflicting experts and the judge or jury will have to make a determination of which expert's evidence is most likely to be helpful to them.

11.1.4 Admissibility of Computer-generated Records

Since virtually all computer-generated records will have been produced by a third party who may not always be called to testify, *prima facie* the admissibility into evidence of the records may be challenged on the basis of the hearsay rules. In many states the business records provision of the State's Evidence Act may be used, in certain circumstances, to admit those records into evidence. If there is any dispute about admissibility of records or reliability of records, it is recommended that use of computer consultants or experts be considered to assist the Court in resolving such disagreement.

It is not within the scope of the present text to describe the significant evidentiary problems relating to computer-generated records. This subject should be reviewed in any particular fact situation with an attorney qualified in the jurisdiction.

The complexity arises since it is possible for the opposing party to try to attack the admissibility of computer-generated records on the basis that the computer system is not reliable and therefore the records provided by that system may not be reliable or accurate. The opposing party may attack a number of areas, including:

- adequacy of quality control procedures
- adequacy of error detection or error correction processes
- data input errors
- processing errors
- output errors
- the ability of others to introduce changes or errors into the data or processing routines

11.2 AUTHORIZED USE AND A COMPUTER USE POLICY

Computer crime laws dealing with unauthorized use of computer systems, computer programs, or data are premised, fundamentally, on the concept that there is an approved range of permissible activity in relation to the system, programs, or data. Unfortunately in many large (or small) computer installations there is no computer-use policy. As a result, this causes significant difficulty for the prosecutor who must then show that the particular conduct complained of was not authorized by the owner or operator of the computer system. While unauthorized use is easier to show in respect of an outsider gaining access to the computer system, it is a particularly difficult problem when dealing with an insider (*i.e.*, employee or consultant) who has, on a routine basis, access to the computer system, programs, and data.

It is strongly recommended that any system operator or owner of a computer system establish a thorough computer use policy. It is further recommended that the system operator or owner also establish a *computer abuse task force* consisting of, at least, a representative of management with the authority to make decisions about an investigation (who may also have authority to take action based on the results of the investigation or who may report to senior management), an attorney with experience in computer law matters, and an outside computer consultant who may provide an external means of assessing the abuse and analyzing the fact situation underlying the abuse, so as to establish the mode of the abuse, the identify of the abuser(s), and such other information as may be useful in subsequent prosecution.

The computer-use policy is a very important ingredient in any effort to control potential computer abuse. As a result, it is important that such a policy be well thought out and reflect the actual working environment of the particular computer systems, programs, and data. Artificial rules that are routinely broken will not provide the security that is desired from such a computer-use policy. Therefore in addition to the policy being meaningful, the system operator or owner must also do the following:

- Communicate that computer-use policy to all persons who may have access to or use the computer system, programs or data

- Be prepared to take enforcement action to ensure compliance with the computer use policy[4]

The next sections in this chapter contemplate that a computer abuse task force is investigating an actual incident of abuse of a computer system. These factors and considerations will be of assistance not only in the considerations involved in establishing a comprehensive and thorough computer-use policy, but also in providing a basis for civil or criminal prosecutions of the accused.

11.3 COMPUTER ABUSE CHECKLIST

In the event that an incident of computer abuse has been detected it is assumed that the computer abuse task force will immediately respond and attempt to:

- Preserve evidence that may be useful in bringing action, civilly or criminally, against the abuser
- Preserve the rights of the system operator or owner vis-a-vis the abuser
- Identify the means by which the abuse occurred
- Identify the abuser
- Identify and contain any damage resulting from the abuse

In reviewing the facts and physical circumstances of the abuse that may have occurred, the computer abuse task force should review a wide range of considerations. These considerations will be of assistance in building a stronger understanding of the abusive conduct and the events leading to that abuse, and may also provide an indication of means to avoid similar abuse in future cases. This type of information and evidence also may be very important in obtaining a successful prosecution of the abuser. Considerations for the computer abuse task force investigating an actual case of computer abuse include:

- The type of media dealt with (*i.e.*, tape, disk, etc.);
- Whether there was destruction of data or programs and significance of the destroyed portion to the whole;
- Whether there was alteration of data or programs and the significance and effect of the alteration on the whole;
- The value of data or programs destroyed or altered, both to the victim and a market value, if any;
- Whether there was an exchange of value (*i.e.* sale for money or monies worth) with a third party who was acquiring data or programs;
- Whether the defendant had permission, of some kind, to use the computer system (express or implied permission and scope thereof);
- Whether there was a sale or other exchange for value of copyright infringing materials to third parties;
- Whether there was actual detriment (or risk of detriment) to the victim in the form of:
  - financial loss and nature and extent of such loss;

---

[4]See Chapter 16 for further discussion of the policy issue.

- loss of confidence or secrecy of information;
- loss related to the testing or rebuilding of the system;
- other losses (*i.e,.* physical damage, *etc.*);

- How entry into the computer system was effected; whether by legitimate means or by "cracking" the system
- Whether a telecommunication or similar service was utilized as part of the alleged offense
- The actual conduct complained of and the various functions of the computer facility used
- Any physical damage to property
- Any obstruction or interference in access or use of the system
- The level of access obtained
- Whether and which application program(s) were involved
- Whether and which operating system program(s) were involved
- The applicable specific computer crime legislation in the appropriate jurisdiction
- Any applicable general criminal legislation in the particular jurisdiction
- Any copyright legislation in the applicable jurisdiction
- Any trade secret legislation or common-law trade-secret obligations applicable in the jurisdiction
- Where all or any part of the particular conduct occurs
- When all or any part of the particular conduct occurs

The considerations above also may be of assistance to management in establishing a thorough and comprehensive computer use policy.

11.4 REVIEW OF DOCUMENTS

In dealing with a real or a possible case of computer abuse, the computer abuse task force will, of course, have to review in detail the nature of any computer use policy. However, there is a wide range of other documents that establish a framework for further limitations on use of a computer system, computer programs or data.

In an ideal world, all of the documents affecting use of a system operator's or owner's computer system, computer programs or data will have been integrated into the computer use policy. In the real, practical world, however, this is unlikely to have been carried out. This is unfortunate in that the concept of authorized use then becomes more complex to understand and to establish. In the following portion of this manual, it is assumed that the computer abuse task force is dealing with an actual or potential case of computer abuse. As part of the report the computer abuse task force will provide to management an assessment of the ability to obtain successful prosecutions, both under civil law and criminally.

As mentioned previously,[5] the concept of permission, colour of right, or authorized use flows through much of the Criminal Law computer provisions. The computer abuse task force will wish to review all the documents that might relate to the extent of consent to the use of a com-

---

[5]This concept is one of the central points in the area of information security and computer security, and is discussed in several locations, especially Chapter 10 and 11.

puter system that the defendant was entitled to. The computer abuse task force will often be disappointed at the very informal way with which many of these matters are dealt, often by sophisticated systems operators or users. As a result, industry standards and practices should be an important consideration and the use of computer consultants or expert witnesses should be considered for that purpose.

Some of the documents the computer abuse task force may encounter are:

- License agreements providing the terms under which the user has the licensor's consent to use the computer programs and data, and in some cases hardware
- Employment agreements often provide for a legal basis for the introduction of company policies on computer systems and may become part of the employer-employee relationship
- Consulting agreements, like employment agreements, may specify the extent of access or use permitted
- Non-disclosure agreements are often encountered in the computer industry, particularly where system development or design is occurring. These agreements also commonly have restrictions on use of the system and information related to the system
- Invention assignment agreements may be found in many high-technology companies and provide for specific obligations to maintain records and for obligations to deliver up those records under certain circumstances. Many other obligations may be found in such agreements that may be relevant

Restrictive covenants or covenants not to compete may also provide for restrictions on use or disclosure of information or access to the resources of a computer system

Published policies on use may be formal and part of a user's obligations to the system operator. Most policies on use of computer systems are informal and irregularly drafted, if they exist at all. The computer abuse task force should carefully interview as many witnesses as possible to determine what policies or practices might exist:

- in the particular computer center or institution
- in that particular segment of the data processing industry

11.5 REVIEW OF THE ABUSER'S ALLEGED CONDUCT

At some point, hopefully, the computer abuse task force's investigations will identify the individual or individuals who were responsible for creating, planning, and implementing the particular abuse of the computer system, computer programs, or data. In dealing with these individuals, the computer abuse task force must be very cautious in the way in which it proceeds. These individuals have specific rights, both in civil law and criminal law. Imprudent or ill-founded action, such as immediate termination of the individual abuser's employment, may result in civil liability for the employer in this case as a result of a possible wrongful dismissal action. As has been reviewed earlier, this and similar imprudent or ill-founded actions may even leave the organization or security professional open to civil or criminal charges.

It is very important that the computer abuse task force not only clearly identify the computer abusers, but also be able to prove that identity in a court of law.

In this area, as in the review of the legal documents described in the section above, the attorney member of the computer abuse task force will be very important in providing advice both to the computer abuse task force and to senior management.

In addition to understanding the framework of rights and responsibilities not only of the system operator or owner but also of users of the computer system, it is necessary to understand the specific details of the conduct alleged of the individuals identified as being responsible for the particular computer abuse.

The computer abuse task force will want to carefully review the facts in each situation encountered. Obviously, the facts of each case may differ widely. Some considerations the computer abuse task force may look at are:

- The extent to which the abuser's alleged conduct deviates from the normal conduct anticipated in the data processing industry:
    - in time
    - in space
    - in activity
    - in portions of the computer system, programs or data that are accessed
    - to the use made of the computer system, programs or data

- The extent to which the abuser's alleged conduct finds an arguable basis in general industry and educational practice, such as the encouraging of computer science students to break system security in many educational institutions
- Oral permission or consents to use of the computer system, program, or data
- Past conduct of the abuser such as, for example, extensive previous permitted or tolerated access or use of the computer system, program, or data
- Whether the abuser was given any special responsibility or access to the system by way of special access codes, keys, or use of facilities at unusual hours
- The computer abuse task force should always consider the possibility that a third party, possibly unknown, has effected the complained of conduct and, using a sophisticated knowledge of the computer system or programs, manipulated the trail of evidence to point to the suspected abuser

11.6 THE INFORMATION SECURITY SPECIALIST'S ROLE

The information security attorney, as discussed earlier, is an important member of the information security specialist's crisis team. It is important for the information security specialist to establish a team who can immediately investigate a situation of possible wrongdoing, preserve evidence both for the purposes of the investigation and for the purposes of subsequent criminal or civil legal action, and also to protect the company, its assets, and the members of the information security team.

In order to avoid claims of slander, libel, or defamation, the information security specialist must be very careful about making allegations of wrongdoing against any individual or corporation. It will be very important for the information security specialist to fully assess all of the facts and to make accusations only after receiving appropriate legal advice.

It is very important that evidence of wrongdoing be properly preserved so as to avoid exclusion of such evidence because of inappropriate handling, or for several important legal reasons. Again, it is important that the information security specialist obtains appropriate legal advice to preserve the best evidence to maintain the option of criminal or civil action.

The foregoing comments are very important. Imagine you are the information security specialist at an important defense establishment. At 4:00 A.M. you observe one of the employees at the outside gate passing a large box over the fence to another person who quickly drives away. You telephone ahead but the description of the car is common and it is only some ten miles later that the highway patrol pulls over a car of that description containing a box, as you described, with important data from the company. The information security specialist may make the accusation against the employee and feel satisfied that the situation has been encapsulated and resolved so quickly.

However, unfortunately, the information security specialist may also find himself faced, the next morning, with a lawsuit for defamation, wrongful dismissal, malicious prosecution, or any number of other legal actions. In many cases these actions may merely be a smoke screen in an effort to intimidate or threaten the information security specialist or the company into dropping any action against the rogue employee. It is to prevent, or at least minimize, the likelihood of such action that it is important that the information security specialist obtain early and effective legal advice to help ensure that, after a breach of all of the physical and environmental security precautions, the perpetrator is not able to escape upon a legal technicality or a failure to properly preserve evidence for subsequent prosecution.

The information security specialist must also be prepared to act as a witness in criminal or civil actions. Your information security attorney or District Attorney (or Crown Prosecutor) will assist you for your presentation of evidence. There are many basic rules or principles that you must always keep in mind. Remember that the courtroom is also a battlefield and that you must follow very carefully the instructions and directions of your attorney.

- Answer only and precisely the question that you have been asked. If you attempt to elaborate or discuss in broader terms, you may disclose information that would be useful to the defense or upon which they could build an attack on your attentiveness or credibility.

- Do not become emotionally involved. A tactic used by many defense attorneys is to attempt to upset you, get into an argument with you, or otherwise put you off-balance. It is important that you maintain a cool, detached, and professional attitude throughout the presentation of your evidence so that you can avoid being pushed into making foolish and damaging statements.

- Tell the facts as you witnessed them with your own senses. The hearsay rule may preclude admissibility of certain evidence that you obtained from a third party. It is important that you do not make assumptions about your observations.

- If you do not understand a question or if the question is too complicated or contains too many elements, then do not hesitate to ask that the question be repeated or phrased in a manner that does not lead to improper inferences from the way in which the question is asked. For example, the question "Are you still beating your wife?" leaves no satisfactory answer because of the way the question is phrased. If you answer "no," the implication is that you formerly *did* beat your wife. If you suspect that a question has been unfairly stated in an effort to create unfair inferences, then it is most likely that your attorney will object to the question in the form it is phrased. If your attorney does not do so, and you think the question is unfairly phrased, then you should object to it on that basis and request that the question be more fairly phrased.

- Describe your observations in a clear, chronological, and logical sequence. Do not jump ahead or raise tangential or irrelevant matters that will only make it more difficult for a judge or jury to understand your evidence.

In some circumstances, depending upon your experience and training, you may be called upon as an expert witness. An expert witness is entitled to give opinion evidence to a court. Typically, an expert witness will be given a hypothetical fact situation and be asked to provide an opinion based on that hypothetical fact situation.

Normally, an expert witness will have to be qualified before the court (unless having been previously so qualified). This is usually done by submission of the expert witness' resume, textbooks, or articles to the court, and a brief examination of the witness's expertise. In some cases, defense attorneys will attempt to minimize or limit the area in which the expert is qualified to give opinion evidence. They will do this by focusing upon those areas in which the expert witness is truly expert and attempting to limit or minimize those areas. A rough example would be the introduction of a purported expert witness on computer program and system designs. It may be, after examination of the expert witness's qualification, that the expert's qualifications are restricted to experience in a particular environment (such as mainframe or minicomputer and, perhaps, only in relation to specific languages, such as, for example, Pascal and Cobol). However, the dispute before the court may relate to alleged unauthorized use of a computer program, written in C, in a microcomputer environment. In this way, a defense attorney will attempt to minimize or limit the strength or effectiveness of any opinion evidence that might be given by an expert witness.

The information security specialist, in helping to select such expert witnesses, should be aware of the possibility of such limitation, and should ensure that the appropriate expert has been retained for the nature of the specific case.

Furthermore, information security specialists who do become expert witnesses themselves must ensure that they are absolutely candid and frank with the court about their qualifications and their opinions. Any attempt to appear one-sided or to attempt to shift the analysis to favor the client (who after all has paid for the evidence the expert witness is providing), not only will damage the case but also can completely destroy the reputation of the expert witness and end any future likelihood of a career as an expert witness.

The defense attorney may prepare for your testimony by reading your publications or even by obtaining copies of your previous testimony in court in other cases. Any discrepancy between your present evidence and your publications or prior testimony likely will be used by the defense attorney to cast doubt on your present evidence.

The foregoing material has attempted to provide a very basic introduction to a number of legal issues that may be of significant relevance to the information security specialist dealing with advanced technology security concerns, data, computer programs, and the like. It is important that the information security specialist consult with a qualified information security attorney to help in the planning, implementation, and conduct of an appropriate information security plan. This cooperation will result not only in greater likelihood of success for the information security plan, but also greater protection from personal liability for the information security specialist.

It is important for the information systems security professional to gain a general working understanding of the civil law, criminal law, and other law and regulations that may affect his or her employer and the assets being protected. The practitioner should attend continuing education programs in order to upgrade and update this knowledge from time to time. Furthermore, the information systems security professional should develop contacts with competent attorneys who may be able to act as resources in providing advice in the proper carrying out of the information systems security professional's responsibilities to his or her employer.

It is recommended that each company establish a computer abuse task force whose function is to determine policy that may assist in preventing abuse of situations from a occurring, investigating abusive situations that have occurred, and preserving the operations of the company and its computer system and also preserving any evidence that may be necessary or desirable to bring any prosecution at a later date. One other role, obviously, of a computer abuse task force would be to be able to identify the abuser and provide advice to management on options available to deal with the abuser.

As a result, in addition to a properly experienced attorney, the computer abuse task force also may include one or several computer consultants familiar with forensic or investigative work and should have a representative of senior management who would be able to facilitate the operations of the task force (such as entry to buildings, access to computer system, etc.).

It is further recommended that each company or business establish both a clear and meaningful copyright policy and a clear and meaningful computer-use policy. These policies not only must be clear, unequivocal, and meaningful, but also must be communicated to the individuals who should be governed by the policy and must, as appropriate, be enforced. It does no good to have a wonderfully worded policy and never be able to prove that any warnings were given in relation to breaches of the policy or the like. A defense attorney is likely to use such a fact to argue that the policy was not real and that the true operation of the company or business ignored the policy and therefore the policy should be ignored in any lawsuit.

Such a copyright or computer-use policy should be thoughtfully designed and should cover the conduct that is reasonably expected or required of the persons who will be subject to the policy.

Any such policy serves an important educational role in setting out, clearly, the responsibilities of users of the system, such as employees, consultants and others. That educational function is often most important of all since most of such persons will comply with the rules once they are aware that the rules are reasonable, enforced. and meaningful.

REFERENCES

"Case Histories In Computer Security," *Computers & Security*, No. 53, July/August, 1983.

Edelhertz, Herbert, et al., *The Investigation of White-Collar Crime: A Manual for Law Enforcement Agencies*, prepared for the U.S. Department of Justice, Law Enforcement Assistance Administration, Government Printing Office, Washington, DC, 1977.

Fites, Philip. E., Martin P. J. Kratz, and Alan F. Brebner, *Control and Security of Computer Information Systems*, W. H. Freeman/Computer Science Press, New York, NY, 1989.

Gallegos, Frederick, Dana R. (Rick) Richardson, & A. Faye Borthick, *Audit & Control of Information Systems*, South-Western Publishing Company, West. Chicago, IL, 1987.

Kratz, Martin P. J., "Evidentiary Problems of Computer-Generated Materials," in *Technology and the Law for General Practitioners*, Legal Education Society of Alberta, Canada, March, 1987.

Krauss, Leonard L. and Aileen MacGahan, *Computer Fraud and Countermeasures*, Prentice-Hall, Englewood Cliffs, NJ, 1979.

Wills, William D., *Essays on Principles of Circumstantial Evidence*, 6th ed. London, 1912.

12. Application Program Security

Application program security refers to the controls that are included in the application programs. It would include structure of the application to support separation of duties and segregation of function; edits, reconciliations, confirmations, and other feedback; logs, journals, and other permanent records, etc.

The expected knowledge includes the following:

- How controls should be distributed between that application and the system
- The controls available across applications
- Controls specific to key, common, or industry applications
- Criteria for their selection and application
- Tests for their adequacy
- Standards of good practice
- and so on

DEFINITIONS

Acceptance

The condition that exists when a facility or system generally meets the technical performance standards and security requirements. (NCSC-WA-001-85)

Aggregation

Individual data systems and data elements may be determined to be unclassified and to be of a specific sensitivity category. When those data are combined with other data, the totality of the information may be classified or in a higher sensitivity category, with higher protection requirements. (AFR 205-16)

Application

Those portions of a system, including portions of the operating system, that are not responsible for enforcing the security policy. (CSC-STD-003-85; CSC-STD-004-85)

Application Software

Routines and programs designed by, or for system (functional) users and customers. Through the use of available automated system equipment and basic software, application software completes specific, mission-oriented tasks, jobs, or functions. It can be either general purpose packages, such as demand deposit accounting, payroll, machine tool control, and so forth, or specific application programs tailored to complete a single or limited number of user functions, for example, base-level personnel, depot maintenance, missile or satellite tracking, and so forth. Except for general-purpose packages that are acquired directly from software vendors or from the original equipment manufacturers (OEM), this type of software is generally developed by users either with in-house resources or through contract services. (AFR 205-16)

313

Assurance

1. A measure of confidence that the security features and architecture of an AIS accurately mediate and enforce the security policy. If the security features of an AIS are relied upon to handle sensitive information and restrict user access, the features must be tested to ensure that the security policy is uncircumventably enforced during AIS operation. (DODD 5200.28)
2. The hardware, firmware, and software mechanisms of an automated information system that can be evaluated to provide sufficient assurance that the system enforces the defined security policy, labelling, identification and auditing capabilities. These mechanisms consist of system architecture, system integrity, security testing, design specification and verification, configuration management, trusted recovery and trusted distribution. (NCSC-WA-001-85)

Configuration Management

The management of changes made to a system's hardware, software, firmware, and documentation throughout the development and operational life of the system. (NCSC-WA-001-85)

Covert Channel

A communication channel that allows two cooperating processes to transfer information in a manner that violates the system's security policy. (NCSC-WA-001-85)

Covert Storage Channel

A covert channel that involves the direct or indirect writing of a storage location by one process and the direct or indirect reading of the storage location by another process. Covert channels typically involve a finite resource (*e.g.*, sectors on a disk) that is shared by two subjects at different security levels. (CSC-STD-001-83; NCSC-WA-001-85)

Covert Timing Channel

A covert channel in which one process signals information to another by modulating its own use of system resources (*e.g.*, CPU time) in such a way that this manipulation affects the real response time observed by the second process. (CSC-STD-001-83; NCSC-WA-001-85)

Database

An extensive and comprehensive set of records collected and organized in a meaningful manner to serve a particular purpose. (DODD 3200.12)

Data Contamination

1. A deliberate or accidental process or act that results in a change in the integrity of the original data. (AR 380-380; FIPS PUB 39).
2. The process by which errors in data elements stored in computerized information systems propagate during repeated use, leading to unreliable databases. Examples include any data that are used as input to another process, whose outputs then become unreliable; also called "corruption."

Data Integrity

The property that data has not been altered or destroyed in an unauthorized manner. (ISO 7498-2)

Design Verification

The use of verification techniques, usually computer assisted, to demonstrate a mathematical correspondence between an abstract (security) model and a formal system specification. (MTR-8201)

Documentation

An asset category consisting of the manual, listings, etc. Must also include recovery plans and the result of threat analysis. (RM)

File Protection

The aggregate of all processes and procedures established in an automated system and designed to inhibit unauthorized access, contamination, or elimination of a file. (AR 380-380; NCSC-WA-001-85; FIPS PUB 39)

File Security

The means by which access to computer files is limited to authorized users only. (NCSC-WA-001-85)

Granularity

1. The relative fineness or coarseness by which a mechanism can be adjusted. The phrase "the granularity of a single user" means the access control mechanism can be adjusted to include or exclude any single user. (DODD 5200.28-STD)
2. An expression of the relative size of a data object, *e.g.*, protection at the file level is considered coarse granularity, whereas protection at the field level is considered to be a finer granularity. (NCSC-WA-001-85)

Internal Controls

The plan of organization and all of the methods and measures adopted within an agency to safeguard its resources, assure the accuracy and reliability of its information, assure adherence to applicable laws, regulations and policies, and promote operational economy and efficiency. (A-123; DODD 7040.6)

Internal Control Documentation

Written policies, organization charts, procedural write-ups, manuals, memoranda, flow charts, decision tables, completed questionnaires, software, and related written materials used to describe the internal control methods and measures, to communicate responsibilities and authorities for operating such methods and measures, and to serve as a reference for persons reviewing the internal controls and their functioning. (A-123; DODD 7040.6)

Internal Control Review

A detailed examination of internal control to determine whether adequate control measures exist and are implemented to prevent or detect the occurrence of potential risks in a cost effective manner. (A-123; DODD 7040.6)

Privacy

1. The right of an individual to self-determination as to the degree to which the individual is willing to share with others information about himself that may be compromised by unauthorized exchange of such information among other individuals or organizations.
2. The right of individuals and organizations to control the collection, storage, and dissemination of their information or information about themselves. (FIPS PUB 39)

Proprietary Data

Data that is created, used, marketed by individuals having exclusive legal rights. (AFR 205-16)

Sensitive Business Data

Data which requires protection under Title 18, USC 1905, and other data which, by its nature, requires controlled distribution or access for reasons other than that it is classified or personal data. Sensitive business data is recognized in the following categories.

1. *For Official Use Only*—Requiring confidentiality of information derived from Inspector General, authority, or other investigative activity.
2. *Financial*—Requiring protection to ensure the integrity of funds or other fiscal assets.
3. *Sensitive Management*—Requiring protection to defend against the loss of property, material, or supplies or to defend against the disruption of operations or normal management practices, etc.
4. *Proprietary*—Requiring protection to protect data or information in conformance with a limited rights agreement or which is the exclusive property of a civilian corporation or individual and which is on loan to the government for evaluation or for its proper use in adjudicating contracts.
5. *Privileged*—Requiring protection for conformance with business standards or as required by law. (Example: Government-developed information involving the award of a contract.) (OPNAVINST 5239.1A)

Test Data

An asset category consisting of information used to determine the applicability, efficiency, or accuracy of systems. (MK, RM)

Trap Door

A hidden software or hardware mechanism that permits system protection mechanisms to be circumvented. It is activated in some innocent appearing manner, *e.g.*, special "random" key sequence at a terminal. Software developers often introduce trap doors in their code that enable them to re-enter the system and perform certain functions. (NCSC-WA-001-85)

Trojan Horse

1. A computer program with an apparently or actually useful function that contains additional (hidden) functions that surreptitiously exploit the legitimate authorizations of the invoking process to the detriment of security. For example, making a "blind copy" of a sensitive file for the creator of the Trojan horse. (CSC-STD-001-83; NCSC-WA-001-85)
2. A computer program that is apparently or actually useful and that contains a trap door. (FIPS PUB 39)

Work Factor

An estimate of the effort or time needed to overcome a protective measure by a potential penetrator with specified expertise and resources. (AR 380-380; NCSC-WA-001-85; FIPS PUB 39)

12.1 SOFTWARE CONTROLS: DEVELOPMENT

12.1.1 The Real Problem: Bugs and Human Error

"Bugs" are things that go wrong with information and other systems. The term "computer bug" has been attributed to a technician finding a dead moth crushed between the relay contacts of a very early digital computer, which had caused the computer to malfunction. "Debugging" is the process of removing bugs. In essence, there are two reasons computer systems have bugs:

*   The specifications are wrong
*   The implementation does not match the specifications.

By far the largest security exposures are errors and lack of training, not actual deliberate attempts to compromise information systems. When a systems analyst makes an error in describing the proposed system, or when a user forgets that seemingly insignificant but critical item, an error has occurred. This may lead to a system "bug" (as described, a semantic error). When a programmer writes the wrong code by error, this is a program bug (a syntax or implementation error). If all systems analysts were perfect, and all programmers always wrote perfect code, and all users really knew exactly what they needed, then there might be no bugs. In the real world, no one is perfect, and errors occur.

As much as 85% of the total effort in a large data processing shop may be dedicated to "maintenance." Maintenance includes changing programs to reflect new requirements and changed circumstances (this kind of maintenance is addressed later in this chapter). Most maintenance, unfortunately, consists of fixing problems that should not have been allowed to occur in the first place.

From a security and control standpoint, the best idea is to avoid having errors in the systems or programs at all. The best time to effect this is as early as possible in the development process; fixing a system design error may cost easily 1,000 times as much during the "maintenance" period as it would during the design effort and before any code is written.

12.1.2 General Software Engineering Principles: Layering, Modularity

Two basic principles underlie most well-constructed software: layering and modularity.

Layering is the principle of constructing processes in layers, so that each layer deals with a specific kind of activity. Many kinds of layering are possible. Block structured computer languages utilize a form of layering (the concept of data hiding or global *versus* local variables comes into play in this instance.) The formal specifications considered in section 12.4 form a layer between security policy, security model, and implementation. In this instance, the issue is to select layering so that each layer is sufficiently concise and clear to permit convincing proof or argument of correctness, and each layer is relatively "close" to the next in amount of detail, so the correspondence from layer to layer can be demonstrated. Another example of layering is the ISO/OSI protocols and associated security standards. There, the layering is based on physical and logical characteristics of communications facilities.

In secure systems and secure program design, layering leads to definition of levels or security domains, with each level defined by technical characteristics of such elements as a security kernel or trusted filter. Data hiding takes on a different meaning here, with the emphasis on not permitting processes at different classification levels to access data in inappropriate levels. In the case of the most common security models (Bell and La Padula, for example) involving partially-ordered sets and lattices, data hiding is conceptually equivalent to global *versus* local variables.

Modularity refers to breaking activities into small enough segments that individual pieces are understandable and reasonably may be subjected to correctness proofs or exhaustive testing. An example of modularity is discussed in the next section. Another example is found in the design of compilers, where typically the syntax of the language is described in mathematical terms, and a module is created for each primitive element in the formal description.

12.1.3 Structured Methods

An application of the general principles of layering and modularity just discussed is structured analysis and structured programming. These were developed in the 1970s by Constantine and Yourdon, among others. They used "data flow diagrams," and consideration of certain mathematical characteristics of the graphs formed by data flow diagrams, to derive principles that, if followed, minimize the chances of inserting bugs into systems and programs in the first place, and minimize the problems in removing them when discovered. Recently, graphics capabilities of reasonably affordable computers have reached the point that data flow diagrams, linked with data element definitions or data dictionaries, can be handled with a microcomputer in much the same way as numeric data works with a spreadsheet, or a word processor handles text. This sort of enhanced and integrated capability often is referred to as *CASE* (Computer-Assisted System Engineering).

In essence, structured analysis involves identifying activities performed by an organization and the data flows that drive those "processes" (this process is not the same as the technical term used above in discussing secure operating systems). The data flows contain data elements, and when the data flows and data elements are defined, a "data dictionary" results. Programs are written using modular code corresponding to processes (at a very detailed level, of course), and using the data dictionary developed. Modules, in systems or in programs, should not affect each other ("low coupling") and should be reasonably self-contained and perform a single logical function ("high cohesion").

When systems are designed and programs written using these structured concepts, certain mathematical developments apply (coupling and cohesion are English expressions of some of these mathematical concepts from set and graph theory), and programs and systems can be treated to proofs of correctness, mathematical simplifications, and other methods that avoid some of the human problems that make correct systems and programs so difficult to create.

Perhaps most importantly of all, any *defined* means of creating systems, particularly one with a mathematical basis such as structured analysis, allows one to set standards, measure performance against those standards, and correct problems. In principle, an organization should have a business plan, which breaks down into systems and subsystems, which have systems definitions, which are implemented using structured programming techniques. The logical linkage is maintained; senior and user management function within defined responsibilities; users are ensured of involvement in system design and testing; and excellent systems with minimal future problems will be created. (This ideal is not likely ever to be achieved in practice.)

The security personnel's main involvement in this sort of process, which really is the domain of information system management, would be to help ensure that methodologies are followed, approvals requested, procedures in place, and so on. EDP auditors will be allies of security personnel in this area; they are trained to look at such methodologies, or lack of them, during an audit. Involvement of auditors and security personnel during the design of system controls may lead to much better-controlled and more secure systems.

12.1.4 Program Library/Librarian

A control that helps keep intruders and unauthorized changes away from systems under development as well as existing systems, is the use of a program library, usually computer-maintained, and a program librarian whose responsibility it is to ensure that the program library is maintained and controlled according to appropriate policies and procedures.

All copies of data dictionaries, programs, load modules, and documentation would be under the control of the program librarian (in principle; in practice people will retain working copies of some documentation). The program librarian has the responsibility to ensure that programs are not added to the production library until they are properly tested and authorized. Programmers should not be allowed access to production programs; only the program librarian should be able to alter any production program. Thus unauthorized alterations are much less likely.

Whether done by computer or manually, a program library needs to hold *current* versions of programs and documentation. It needs to hold a record of changes made, by whom, when, authorized by whom, and what the changes are. Test data used to verify that changes are done correctly and user signoffs indicating correct testing should be in this library. Much of this can be done nearly automatically when the library is automated, and such an automated program library is highly recommended for any installation of significant size.

12.1.5 Data Dictionary as a Control

When developing programs, programmers may wish, or be forced, to invent names for data elements that are common among several programs. The data dictionary, whether as part of a database management system or as part of a program library, is simply a listing of every data element used in any program, with the data element characteristics, a cross-reference of what programs use the data element and what files it is in, and similar data.

The data dictionary serves as a control, particularly in conjunction with a program library, when programmers are required to use variable names from the program library. This ensures that all programmers use the same name (allowing changes to an element to be made easily, perhaps even automatically, in many programs written by different people), and that there is control over creation of new names (the program librarian).

If the program library is automated, a data dictionary normally will allow copying of definitions into new programs, which saves time and minimizes errors. The same holds true for standard modules in a program library.

12.1.6 Conversion and Implementation

Every new system must be implemented. Most new systems require conversion of data, sometimes a great deal of data, from the format used in a previous system to a new format for the new system. *After thorough testing*, and *user sign-off* that the test system works as it should, conversion can begin.

Controls that applied to the data before the conversion process must be reviewed and the equivalent controls maintained during the conversion. Data entered into the new system must be as complete and as accurate as previously, and converted or new data must retain the integrity of the previous system (at least; ideally, the new system will have higher standards).

During testing and implementation, parallel runs are common. In parallel running, the same data are presented to both systems; hopefully, the same results will be produced, unless different results were part of the design. In practice, results will vary. Do not assume that the new system is in error. As noted in the previous sections, a carefully constructed new system will contain few errors; it is more probable (as much as 90% more) that the discrepancy is caused by an error in the old system that was never discovered. User resistance to acknowledging this is common, and testers need to be prepared to prove their case.

12.2 SOFTWARE CONTROLS: MAINTENANCE

12.2.1 Separation of Duties

Maintenance programming involves changing production programs to fix errors, and modifying programs to produce different results for many reasons (new or revised government regulations or withholding tax changes, for example). To retain control over system security, some separations of duties are needed.

Operators should not be programmers and should not be able to change programs. Programmers should not be able to change production programs directly. Systems analysts normally need not have any access at all to programs, particularly production programs. Users should not have any access to the computer room or to programs. Program librarians are strongly indicated as a control over this area.

The *Computer Control Guidelines, Second Edition* [CICA 1986] indicates that the following roles are incompatible and should be performed by different people or groups:

- Users
- Information system development
- Information systems processing
- Information systems support

Rules such as those given in this section may be difficult or impossible for smaller organizations, where there are fewer staff. In a case where segregation is not possible or is prohibitively costly, compensating controls should exist elsewhere. An example could be a "one-person shop," where the information systems manager is also the analyst, programmer, and operator. There is no control other than such things as professional codes of conduct and standards of good practice in this case; however, if this person has no access to financial assets and cannot cause inventory to be diverted, a compensating control exists that lessens the exposure. A security specialist or at least an accountant should review such situations, to ensure that reasonable control is maintained.

12.2.2 Testing Controls

All changes to any production system need to be tested. User management has the responsibility for the user organization's data, and user management should be required to sign off the results of tests. The program librarian should retain the test data used during implementation of the system, which was the basis for user acceptance signoff; this test data bank can be used to test modifications to be sure the system still works as intended after the changes.

Testing never should be done with production data or files. In a parallel run, a separate copy of production data should be used, with copies of master files rather than production versions. Some organizations go so far as to have a separate computer for testing, or to rent time on someone else's machine. (This can be combined with a test of contingency backup arrangements, thus doing two good things with one action.)

12.2.3 Change Control

One of the common methods to compromise systems has been to insert code into production programs that does something other than what the program is supposed to do (decrease one person's loan account balance, or increase the checking account balance, for example). A change control mechanism needs to be in place that ensures that all changes are:

- Authorized
- Tested to ensure correctness
- Recorded

As noted in 12.2.1, programmers never should have access to production programs, nor should they be allowed to make changes without proper recording and authorization. The best way to ensure this is to use a program library and librarian, plus proper logs and approval forms. The change needs to be *requested*; the change must be *done*; the change must be *documented* in program comments, manuals, operating instructions, and wherever else necessary; the change must be *tested*; the production program must be *modified*. All these events need *recording* and *authorization*.

In some organizations, programmers are not allowed to initiate change requests; the request must come from the user. This can be cumbersome, but it provides an excellent level of control.

There always will be need from time to time for emergency changes. The times will be few if the system is well-designed and tested, but no perfect computer systems have been reported yet. Controls are subject to being relaxed during such events. The Security Officer should work with user and information systems management to ensure that control is maintained as far as possible during emergency modifications, and that emergencies are logged for later review by senior management. Contingency plans (Chapters 4 and 15) need to consider maintenance of as much control as realistically possible.

Ideally, the change process should be a "mini development" process. The development process includes a project proposal, a feasibility study, alternative analysis, system design, program design and construction, testing, approval, implementation, and follow-up. A change to an existing system needs to be considered just as carefully, although some elements of the full system design process may be abbreviated.

A need should be established (the change request), a cost study should consider alternatives, the changes must be planned and program alterations made, the system needs to be tested again using the original test data, etc., and similar sign-off rules apply.

12.3 ASSURANCE

Assurance is the process by which an appropriate authority attests that a system meets specifications. It may involve confirming one or several of the following areas:

- *Integrity*

  Integrity can be formal (Formal integrity policies are addressed in section 12.6) or less so (see the accounting definition in section 12.7.1). Controls must be in place to ensure existing and continued system and data integrity.

- *Testing*

  No system can be considered secure nor assured unless it has been tested thoroughly. Numerous methods of testing, both manual and automated, are part of the classical literature of systems development and implementation.

- *Specification/verification*

  Formal and informal specifications and verification are addressed in section 12.4 and Chapter 16.

- *Facility management*

  Procedures for proper management of the facility must be defined and in place before a system can be assured.

- *Configuration management*

  Procedures for proper management of the hardware configuration must be defined and in place before a system can be assured. Changes in configuration of hardware or software may change the security or integrity status of a system. Typically, any material change will required revisiting of at least part of the assurance process. Note that seemingly minor changes in critical parts of the system, particularly security kernels or other operating system components, may significantly affect integrity or security.

- *Disaster/Contingency Planning*

  Chapter 4 addresses contingency planning in detail. Generally, business continuity planning must be in place before a system can be assured.

- *Compliance/degree of trust*

  Where appropriate, systems may be evaluated according to the Trusted Computer System Evaluation Criteria (TCSEC) and assigned a rating indicating the degree of trust. This has been primarily associated with U.S. Government applications. Under the Computer Security Act of 1987 and succeeding developments, it has become increasingly common to find commercial systems that interact with government systems required to meet TCSEC guidelines at some level of assurance. As EDI, electronic bidding processes and other aspects of connectivity increasingly impact nearly all systems, more commercial systems will have to meet such criteria in the future.

12.4 FORMAL SPECIFICATION AND VERIFICATION

The layering involved in creating a secure system includes policy (an external consideration, expressed formally or informally); a security model, formal specification and verification, and implementation. Policies, both formal and external, are addressed in Chapters 7 and 16. Implementation is the actual code that makes the system run. This section deals with formal specification and verification.

Formal specification and verification methods usually are applied primarily to system software design. The reason is that there is a very significant amount of effort required to specify and verify any software of realistic size. It has been felt necessary to apply such practices to system software since flaws or faulty security here affects everything else. As users can testify, less careful attention commonly is applied to application programs. In fact, specification and verification is a means of maximizing assurance that computer software functions as desired. There is no reason other than resources and cost to consider such methods less applicable to one type of software than to another.

When an application program approaches the complexity and full-featured nature of an operating system, formal methods become more justifiable. A database management system (DBMS) may be one example of such an application program. This is because the DBMS essentially has responsibility for handling all data in a system, and it provides very sophisticated query, programming, and data management capabilities. To most users, the DBMS *is* the operating system.

12.4.1 Purpose of Formal Specification

Morrey Gasser defines the purpose of a formal specification thus:[1] ". . . to describe the functional behavior of the system in a manner that is precise, unambiguous, and amenable to computer processing."

Gasser also regards formal specifications as being unnecessary except in systems that require the highest degree of assurance regarding security.

The basic reason for the phrase "amenable to computer processing," and Gasser's comment that formal specifications are unnecessary except where security needs are highest, is that formal specifications involve a great deal of work. Further, the process of proving properties about a specification is so complex that manual methods simply are not trusted in practice. Because the mathematical formulation of a specification is constrained and (hopefully) well-defined, computer analysis methods can be applied to prove various properties of the specification. (Proof of a specification requires significantly more effort than writing it. Although there is substantial value in writing a specification and informal arguments, *proof* is appropriate only when resources permit, and requirements demand, it.)

[1] *Building a Secure Computer System*

Formal specification and verification would apply equally well to properties other than security, in theory. In practice, because security (ideally) follows from a formal policy and a model, proofs are possible. More general proofs about correspondence of the system with properties other than security are beyond the present state of the art. (And likely to remain that way, for a number of reasons.)

One step in formal verification of a system is proof that the specification conforms to the functions, invariants and constraints of the security model. Another step would be to prove that the implementation of the system corresponds to the formal specification. This final step is beyond present capabilities. Although proof is not feasible, existence of a formal specification simplifies the task of informally demonstrating such correspondence, and may make the informal demonstration seem more trustworthy.

The formal specification serves to provide layers that bridge the great gap in detail between a model and the code that implements a system. Layering concepts were discussed in section 12.1.2.

12.4.2 Formal Specification Techniques

Formally specifying or verifying a system involves use of a set of languages for description and automated tools to handle the detail work. The four most popular such collections are:

- *Gypsy Verification Environment* (GVE) (University of Texas)
- *Formal Development Methodology* (FDM) (Unisys)
- *Hierarchical Development Methodology* (HDM) (SRI International)
- AFFIRM (University of Southern California)

None of these sets of tools is perfect. They are large and complex and differ significantly from one to another. Naturally, their strengths and weaknesses also vary. Work is ongoing in this area, both in academic theoretical approaches and in construction of improved tools for specification and verification.

FDM and HDM view a system as an abstract state machine (see the discussion in Chapter 16 about formal models). Gypsy uses specifications of the inputs and outputs of individual processes in the implementation, and thus more closely resembles the way a system is written. AFFIRM specifies the cumulative effect of a sequence of nested function calls, a form of specification called *algebraic*.

HOL, a language developed at Cambridge University, is an example of a language used in developing and proving secure specifications and systems. Since HOL has been around for some time, and has reasonable support and is reasonably stable, it is used frequently in software verification, including security applications. Another tool, EVES, is under development in Canada (in 1993). Neither of these is a complete system designed for validation and verification in the area of security issues.

12.4.3 Methods of Decomposition

Bridging the detail gap between an implementation and a security model involves a process called *decomposition*. The specification is decomposed into one or more layers, with each layer approaching the detail in implementation more closely (or model, if looked at in the other direction). Three methods are most common:

1. Data structure refinement
2. Algorithmic refinement
3. Procedural abstraction

In *Data structure refinement*, different levels of abstraction are used in different layers. The system is described as a state machine, with information only about the interface with the next level of detail. At the last stage, rather precise interface description is available, although this does not help in designing the internals of the system. Verification involves proving the correctness of the mapping from one layer to the next. The final correspondence demonstration must rely on traditional software engineering techniques. (This concept is closely related to information hiding.)

Algorithmic refinement allows specification of some of the internal structure of the system. The system is viewed as layers, each of which is an abstract state machine that makes a set of functions available for use by the machine above. The implementation of each function in a machine consists of an abstract program that calls functions in the next machine. Proof requires proof of correspondence between the highest-level machine and the model, then successive proofs that the abstract programs (algorithms) in each machine correctly implement their specifications, given the specifications of functions in the next lower machine. The primary difficulty in this approach is that proofs of algorithms are much more difficult than proofs of mappings. (This is alleviated somewhat because the abstract programming language can be formalized and does not have to deal with many details that real programs must handle.)

The third approach is termed *procedural abstraction* by Gasser. (It is the approach used by Gypsy.) Decomposition is done by specifying the functions of every internal procedure in the system and how they manipulate their arguments. The global state of the machine is not considered in the function specification.

As noted for the sets of tools, no one approach is ideal. Their virtues and faults differ, and selection of a specific approach depends very much on specific situations (and resources).

12.5 DATABASE SYSTEMS SECURITY

A database management system (DBMS) is an application program. However, a DBMS often is considered as somehow "more than just an application." This is because the DBMS essentially has responsibility for handling all data in a system, and it provides very sophisticated query, programming, and data management capabilities. To most users, the DBMS *is* the operating system.

A DBMS normally provides such things as a query language, report generator, and a language for specifying database structure and how data elements are to be stored and retrieved. Typically, these languages permit programming capability to support sophisticated queries, reports, or fine-tuning of the DBMS structure and such. The basic purpose of a DBMS is to collect organizational data into one format that permits cross-reference, minimizes duplication of information, and generally optimizes access and use of organizational data. For most users and often even the database administrator, the DBMS is the only component of the operating system they will need or use.

Because of this complexity and sophistication, and particularly because most organizational data is made accessible to most users, a DBMS deserves special attention in the context of information security. For example, data of more than one security classification may be included in the database. Therefore, access control and aggregation and inference controls frequently are provided by the DBMS itself, in addition to whatever access control may be provided by the operating system proper.

12.5.1 Threats

The term *information security*, especially as it applies to control of access to and disclosure of data, almost becomes an oxymoron when used in the context of a DBMS. The very purpose of a DBMS is to provide easy access to a wide range of corporate data. Control over disclosure (other than the obvious control of keeping unauthorized persons entirely away from the system) is at odds with the design and intent of a DBMS.

Regardless of conflicts among design philosophies, the threats that affect data stored and accessed through a DBMS do not differ in kind from threats to any other data. The difference is in degree, as the DBMS makes execution of some penetration efforts much easier than in traditional systems.

A short list of these threats could include:

- Direct disclosure of data
- Unauthorized modification of data
- Data contamination
- Aggregation
- Statistical inference
- Trojan horses and other malicious code
- Covert channels

12.5.1.1 Direct Disclosure of Data

Obviously, direct disclosure of data to unauthorized persons or processes is an exposure. Because the DBMS permits complex queries that combine data elements (perhaps in unexpected ways), the risk may be higher. This is controlled in a DBMS in much the same way as in any other context, through access controls.

12.5.1.2 Modification of Data/Tampering with Data

If the user has the ability to modify data, several threats come into prominence. The obvious is that data could be corrupted or destroyed. Less obvious is the ability to support some kinds of statistical attacks by adding data items.

12.5.1.3 Data Contamination

The issue of data contamination is more critical in a DBMS than in traditional file systems. Here, we use the term to refer to propagation of errors rather than mixing data at different security classifications. The reason this is a worse problem in a DBMS than in a traditional file-management system is that the DBMS supports much greater capabilities to select and combine data elements. If data elements are corrupted for any reason, then reports based on the data will be corrupted. Worse, data elements often may be combined into intermediate constructs which are then combined into more complex constructs, which then form the basis for reports. The propagation of errors in such processes spreads data contamination throughout a DBMS.

Theoretically, there is no control over the spread of data contamination from corrupted data, assuming normal DBMS capabilities. The only possible control is first to avoid entering inaccurate data, and second to audit data to locate inaccuracies and correct them. Once a problem is identified, data contamination effects must be followed as far as feasible, correcting intermediate constructs just described. This is not possible in the common case where intermediate results are created only for the purpose of a query or report, and discarded afterwards.

12.5.1.4 Aggregation Exposures

Aggregation refers to the situation where a collection of individually unimportant data displays a pattern not clear from individual data elements. This exposure and its control are discussed in Chapter 5.

12.5.1.5 Inference Exposures

The inverse of aggregation is statistical inference. Here, data about individual entities is deduced by using statistical attacks such as overlapping queries. Several kinds of inference attacks are addressed in detail in Chapter 5, including:

- Query Set attacks
- Key-specific attacks
- Characteristic attacks
- Trackers
- Insertion/deletion attacks
- Chosen value attacks

12.1.5.6 Trojan Horse

A Trojan horse is a program that contains additional, undocumented functions in addition to its announced purposes, an instance of malicious code. Other than the possibility of a computer virus converting a formerly-trusted DBMS into a Trojan horse, the exposure of a DBMS to a Trojan horse is of greater concern than other application programs only because the DBMS provides such a range of capabilities and handles such a range of data.

12.5.1.7 Covert Disclosure of Data (Covert Channels, etc.)

Covert channels are discussed in several places, including communications issues in Chapter 8 and other types of covert channels in Chapter 7.

12.5.2 Access Controls

Access control is a primary focus of Chapters 1 and 5. A few aspects of access control differ for most DBMSs, and these are outlined briefly in this section.

12.5.2.1 Access Rights and Privileges

Many DBMSs provide their own application-level access controls, including password control to identify users. Some permit definition of capabilities permitted to users, and subsequent control at greater or lesser levels of granularity of such access.

12.5.2.2 Granularity

A database inherently has a granularity equivalent at least to the level of individual data elements. This means that access and other controls may be applied at a very detailed level, much more so than in traditional file management systems. (See section 12.5.4 for comments about storage and performance.)

12.5.2.3 Labels

As with granularity, the individual data element emphasis inherent in the DBMS concept means that labels can be applied to individual elements. In theory, this can support very fine control of security, in at least two ways. Fine access control is discussed below. In addition, assigning labels to individual data elements permits mandatory access control (in the sense of the TCSEC) over these data elements. In principle, and given a sufficiently detailed classification level for the labels, this could support rather sophisticated inference controls as well. (See section 12.5.4 for comments about storage and performance.)

12.5.3 DBMS Controls

12.5.3.1 Access Control Mechanisms

As noted in the previous section, most DBMSs provide a second level of user identification and authentication in addition to whatever may be provided by the operating system. Generally, this is a simple identification/password facility. In principle it could be as sophisticated as any other identification/authentication schema.

Because of the fine granularity inherent in a DBMS, it is possible to assign labels to individual data elements. If this is done, and if the identification process includes user classification information, then the DBMS can control access by individual users to individual data elements.

12.5.3.1 Inference controls

Inference controls include numerous techniques, most of which turn out on analysis not to be feasible or not to be effective, or both. (See Chapters 2 and 5.) There are no universal solutions (other than totally corrupting the database). Some controls offer varying degrees of protection while retaining utility; these controls can be complex, and are discussed in Chapter 5.

12.5.3.3 Accountability Controls

Accountability in a DBMS is not different from any accountability in other process. The issue is to determine who did what, when. If appropriate, it also is nice to save information that allows recovery in the case that the "what" turns out not to be desirable. Most DBMSs save such information, although it may not be easily accessible for security or accounting purposes, since the motive is recovery from problems.

12.5.3.4 Identification and Authentication

The process of identification and authentication requires storage of lists of authorized users and some form of authentication. Passwords typically are used in DBMSs. Since a DBMS may be subject to access by processes from other programs (whose location and security status may be unknown at the time of the attempted access), Message Authentication Codes (MAC) may be used to provide a higher level of control. (See Chapter 2.)

12.5.3.5 Audit

For accountability to function, information about who attempted an action, what action, when, and what the results were, must be logged. The logs must not be subject to tampering or they are useless from a security perspective. A periodic audit should confirm the existence of the logs and, on a sampling basis, confirm that contents reflect what actually happened.

12.5.4 DBMS Design Issues

The very purpose of a DBMS is to provide easy access to a wide range of corporate data. Control over disclosure (other than the obvious control of keeping unauthorized persons entirely away from the system) is at odds with the design and intent of a DBMS. Nevertheless, the design of common DBMSs does permit control, sometimes to a greater extent than most traditional systems allow. The basic reason for this added capability is that the DBMS inherently deals with data elements at a high level of granularity. Controls can be applied to individual users and data elements (at a price in storage usage and/or performance.) Otherwise, approaches to creating trusted operating systems apply equally to creating a trusted DBMS.

12.5.4.1 Protection Approaches

Trusted Kernel

Just as with an operating system, the design approach of creating a small trusted kernel can help support and enforce security policies and rules. (See Chapters 7 and 17 for more detailed discussion of security kernels in operating systems.)

Trusted Filter

A trusted filter is a control that minimizes exposures to statistical inference attacks. In essence, the filter examines queries presented to the DBMS and passes on only those that do not violate rules about things like small or large query sets, or whatever set of constraints is designed into the filter. (See Chapters 2 and 5 for a more detailed discussion.)

Encryption

An apparent solution to several problems regarding disclosure and access in DBMSs is to use encryption. The solution may be more apparent than real. Encryption has significant performance implications at best. More importantly, issues arise such as how and whether to encipher information in the DBMS regarding not the contents of data elements, but relationships with other data elements and logical structures. If such relational information is not enciphered, various attacks similar to traffic analysis in a network are easy (see Chapters 2 and 8). If such information is enciphered, severe performance penalties may result.

Plaintext relational information and data element contents must be protected, particularly if temporary files are used during query processing. If a hardware or software failure (accidental or intentional) occurred and temporary files were left in non-volatile storage, unprotected database contents would be available, and a severe security breach could result.

Encryption will protect the contents of data elements from casual browsing, at the cost of performance impacts on queries that involve combinations of data elements.

12.5.4.1 Performance

Performance of DBMSs may not compare favorably with that of more traditional file systems, depending on the type of query involved. Particularly for a relational DBMS, not only is it necessary to locate relevant data elements, but also considerable processing is implied by many types of queries.

Implementation of various security controls can impact performance of a DBMS severely. Because data element granularity is available (at the extreme), checks through tables of identifications and authorizations could accompany each access to an individual data element. Since it is not uncommon for many thousands of data elements to be involved in a query of any significance, performance of the DBMS can be slowed substantially.

Use of encryption implies key management and all the other trappings discussed in Chapter 2. In addition, performance degradation can be expected as relational information must be deciphered for each data element before its place in a query can be determined. If the query depends on the value of data elements and they are enciphered, then the contents also must be deciphered individually (or at least compared against an enciphered criterion) during the query.

As with any other security analysis, increased security in a DBMS is a tradeoff among cost, performance, and usability issues. A specialized database processor (a computer dedicated to managing the interface to the DBMS and handling issues such as discussed above) may be an answer, albeit a rather costly one.

The exponential increase in computer performance that is impacting all other aspects of computerized information systems also lessens the impact of such performance problems in a DBMS. Performance/cost issues must be examined with care.

12.5.4.3 Storage

Database management systems have been notorious storage hogs for at least 20 years. About the only change is that current relational DBMSs, in addition to using much storage, also use substantial amounts of processor time as they build tables dynamically in response to queries.

One reason for storage problems is that, in addition to storing the data, relationships about the data and how data elements relate to other data elements (and sometimes larger logical structures) must be stored. A common rule of thumb is to allow 2.5 to 2.8 times as much storage for a DBMS as for the total of the individual data elements. The extra 1.5 to 1.8 allows for pointers and similar relational data.

If the data element granularity available is used to provide fine control over access or to attach labels to data elements, this storage problem is compounded. In addition to relational information, security information must be stored.

As with performance, costs of computer storage are decreasing exponentially, and amounts feasible to store are increasing similarly. The issue of inefficient storage may not be a true issue when all cost factors are considered. (Inefficient use of storage, however, profoundly offends many whose attitudes are based on years of training and experience during a long career in informatics.)

12.5.4.4 Assurance

Section 12.3 outlined issues of assurance as applied to application programs in general. These principles apply as well to DBMSs. A higher level of assurance may be required for a DBMS, simply because it deals with a broad range of data and provides sophisticated tools.

12.6 INTEGRITY CONTROLS

An issue that must be addressed is access control *versus* data integrity. This is not because the two are incompatible in any way. Rather, much of the attention to computer security has been invested in consideration of access to and disclosure of information. For example, the TCSEC (Orange Book) is an access-control schema; it does not even address integrity until the B2 level, and then only integrity related to the system itself. Most implementations of security software have been in essence access control software packages.

It may be that the emphasis on access control has been because much of the support for information systems security efforts has been provided by governments, and in particular the U.S. military establishment. As discussed in Chapter 1 and Chapter 15, organizations dealing in national security and military areas tend to concentrate on control of access to and disclosure of information. Therefore, it is natural that access control rather than data integrity would be their primary concern. It is worthy of note that the International Standards Organization's (ISO) security architecture for the OSI (7498-2) places considerable emphasis on data integrity through such mechanisms as message authentication codes (MACs) and encryption. ISO is not a military organization and its emphasis has tended more towards a broader view of information security that includes data integrity.[2]

Two events have focused attention more strongly onto issues relating to data integrity. First, the publication in April of 1987 of David Clark and David Wilson's paper "A Comparison of Commercial and Military Computer Security Policies" has generated great attention in the security community to data integrity issues. Second, the computer virus phenomenon has begun to have a major impact on the operations of most corporations and millions of users of personal computers. Controlling virus constructs is an issue of data integrity; access control software and disclosure policies are essentially irrelevant to the control of computer viruses.

Implementations tend to concentrate on the kinds of controls discussed in section 12.8. Many of these controls derive from accounting controls applied to manual procedures. While frequently effective, these *ad hoc* controls are not part of a formal framework and it is common for gaps and inconsistencies to exist. In early 1993, there is no formal treatment of data integrity that has the sort of widespread awareness and applicability afforded to the TCSEC. In this section, we therefore will concentrate on the Clark-Wilson paper. The professional should be aware that this is an area of ongoing research and new material should be consulted to maintain currency of knowledge.

12.6.1 Integrity Policy

Much as an access control schema depends on a security policy, so does data integrity. As access control eventually is derived from an external policy regarding control and disclosure of information, so also an integrity policy must be based on an external policy. For access control, organizational policies, or laws and directives of the Executive Branch in the case of the TCSEC, are the eventual basis for formal policies, models, and finally implementations.

Integrity policy is not so straightforward as access control. Because "integrity" is considered an abstract virtue, our definition of what the word means is context-sensitive. Although the

---

[2]A comparison of the beginning-of-chapter definitions drawn from 7498-2 with those drawn from military regulations and U.S. government agencies will illustrate this distinction clearly.

TCSEC is a formally defined and well-known access control policy, it is little used outside U.S. government and military circles; the context is wrong. Because "integrity" is more context-sensitive, one may expect that an integrity policy will have even more constrained applicability. This is one area of the ongoing research.

Robert Courtney writes that integrity has two components: data quality and assurance of that quality. "Data quality" consists of five elements:[3]

1. Accuracy
2. Completeness
3. Precision
4. Timeliness
5. Confidentiality

Mr. Courtney goes on to recommend that attention be focused on these characteristics rather than on formal integrity policies. However, it is clear that these five elements may serve to define a framework for implementing the mechanisms of an integrity policy.

12.6.2 Integrity Mechanisms

Mechanisms for implementing an integrity policy are addressed throughout this book. Such techniques as MACs, encryption, edit checks, reasonableness checks, time stamps, logs, and audit trails all can serve to implement facets of the need to assure the five elements of data quality. Nevertheless, if these techniques are included on an *ad hoc* basis, as is common practice in application program construction, major flaws or inconsistencies may be overlooked. Thus there is a need for a model for integrity policy that defines how and when such specific mechanisms should be included.

12.6.3 Integrity Models

Although Clark and Wilson's paper is the major focus of the treatment of integrity in this book, it was not the first attempt to address the issue of data integrity. The best-known of other work was K. Biba's.

Biba

As an offshoot of the work then underway (which led eventually to the TCSEC), Biba and others explored the inverse of the Bell and La Padula access control model, with results published in Biba's 1977 paper, "Integrity Considerations for Secure Computer Systems." Although of some theoretical interest, the Biba integrity framework did not seem to lend itself to practical implementation. (Perhaps also, in 1977 there may have been a general lack of significant interest in integrity issues.)

Bell and La Padula describe a lattice model using partially ordered sets and the *-property to define an access control hierarchy. Control is exerted by forbidding processes at a lower level in the lattice to *read* data at a higher level. Biba's integrity model is in a sense the inverse: The system should prevent lower-level data from contaminating-higher level data. In particular, once a process has accessed lower-level data, that process may not *write* to higher-level data.

---

[3]This paragraph is adapted from Mr. Courtney's comments reproduced in an appendix to the *Report of the Invitational Workshop on Integrity Policy in Computer Information Systems*, October, 1987.

Clark-Wilson

Clark and Wilson's 1987 paper, "A Comparison of Commercial and Military Computer Security Policies" has sparked renewed interest in integrity policy research. Briefly, Clark and Wilson defined a data integrity model that included two integrity classes and two kinds of procedures. Their model then puts forward four enforcement rules and five certification rules.

The two integrity classes are:

1. *Constrained Data Item* (CDI): the data items within the system to which the integrity model must be applied
2. *Unconstrained Data Item* (UDI): untrusted data within the system

The two procedures are:

1. *Integrity Verification Procedure* (IVP): A procedure whose purpose is to confirm that all CDIs within the system conform to integrity specifications at the time the IVP is executed
2. *Transformation Procedure* (TP): A "well-formed transaction," that maintains the integrity state of the system

Integrity assurance has two parts: certification, and enforcement. A security officer certifies and the system enforces. The enforcement rules may be summarized:[4]

E1. Users may operate on CDIs only through operations as specified in rule C2 (TPs), never directly (the concepts of "encapsulation " and "abstract data types").
E2. The system must maintain a list of relations that link users, TPs, and CDIs. (Users may perform operations only if explicitly authorized.)
E3. User identities must be authenticated.
E4. Authorization may be changed only by a security officer. An agent that can certify an entity may not have any execute rights with respect to that entity.

Along with the enforcement rules, Clark-Wilson specifies five related certification rules. These are:

C1. All IVPs must ensure that all CDIs are in a valid state at the time the IVP is run.
C2. All TPs must be certified to be valid. (If a CDI is in a valid initial state, it is in a valid final state after a TP.)[5]
C3. The system must enforce separation of duties.
C4. All TPs must be certified to write to an append-only CDI (the log) all information necessary to permit the nature of the operation to be reconstructed (audit trail).
C5. TPs validate inputs, or reject them. (If a TP takes a UDI as input, the output is a CDI, or rejection of the UDI.) (Usually, input editing.)

Several problems have been identified with this model. For instance, the trivial case of an empty system (no CDIs) is not an acceptable valid initial state, as it is in some other formal models. User identification can pose problems. IVPs inherently are context-sensitive, since the pur-

---

[4]This summary of the rules for enforcement and certifications is adapted from the *Report of the Invitational Workshop on Integrity Policy in Computer Information Systems*, 1988 and from the original Clark-Wilson paper.

[5]Clark and Wilson note that there is an implicit requirement that TPs are not executed concurrently.

pose is not only to verify internal consistency, but also to ensure that data matches some "real-world" situation. (Clark and Wilson use the analogy of an audit or an inventory as examples of IVPs.) Separation of duties is a well-understood concept, but is very difficult to formalize, as it inherently reflects the context of a specific organization.

These problems are not so much a reflection on the Clark-Wilson model as a clarification by the model of some issues in data integrity policy. As discussed earlier, data integrity is inherently context-sensitive. It is difficult-to-impossible to formalize context within a model. Use of models such as Clark-Wilson often pinpoints specific areas where context-sensitive aspects of a system must be given special attention.

12.7 ACCOUNTING AND AUDITING

12.7.1 Segregation of Incompatible Functions

The most basic control is segregation of duties, which essentially limits opportunity and temptation. Segregation of duties can be defined as "separating incompatible functions (giving these duties to two or more people) to strengthen internal control." The activities of a process are split among several people. Mistakes made by one person tend to be caught by the next person in the chain. Unauthorized activities require collusion of at least two people. Since this control is so basic, several variations and implications are presented in the next paragraphs.

In addition to the basic definition (and see also the "official" definition from various accounting and security-oriented texts, below), several elaborations are found in security material provided by computer people. These guidelines help to ensure good internal control and to define "incompatible functions," and include:

1. No Access to Sensitive Combinations of Capabilities

The classic example is control of data about the inventory, and also of the physical inventory. Besides violating segregation of duties, this is an unnecessary temptation: an employee could steal from inventory, then alter the data so the theft is hidden.

2. Prohibit Conversion and Concealment

Another violation of the segregation principle is to put people into a position where they are unsupervised and have access to assets. The lone operator of a night shift is a standard example. This person could copy ("convert") and sell customer lists. Instances have been reported of operators actually using the employer's computer to run a service bureau at night.

3. Same person cannot both originate and approve transactions

Some of the most expensive frauds have occurred when the same person could enter an expense and also authorize it. An expense account is an obvious example. Often, corrections of transactions in error are entered without careful authorization; people have deliberately entered bad data, then re-entered their own corrections, and thus bypassed normal checks and balances.

All of these principles relate to separation of duties. Whether manual or electronic, systems should feature separation of duties and responsibilities. The exact definition of this principle comes from the professional accounting and auditing people (and is found in many security references as well):

This principle actually consists of two parts:

- No single individual must have responsibility for the complete processing of any transaction or group of transactions.
- The perpetration of a fraud must require the collusion of at least two individuals.

Accounting professionals use a somewhat different meaning when they say "control" than computer people use. Accountants and auditors are concerned with protection of an organization's assets and ensuring that assets are used in accordance with the intentions of owners and managers. When an accountant or auditor says "control," it usually is linked with internal control, and relates to this use of assets and to prevention of *fraud*. People from a computer background typically use the word "control" to relate to the predictability, recovery capability, and quaiity of a *computer system*. The uses are not incompatible.

Above, principles from a perspective of computer professionals have been given, followed by the accountant's definition of segregation of duties. In the next paragraph, we list guidelines for segregation of duties from an accounting perspective.

Auditing: An Integrated Approach (Arens, Lobbecke, and Lemon, Prentice Hall, 1987) is a popular text used in accounting courses. Its treatment of segregation of duties includes four guidelines that should be compared to the three guidelines listed above (the *italicized* comments are the authors' comments comparing the previous treatment with this, not a restatement of this book's words):

1. *Separation of Custody of Assets from Accounting*

   (Compare with "No access to sensitive combinations of capabilities.") This auditing text recommends that any person performing an accounting function be denied access to assets which can be converted to personal gain. Similar considerations apply to such EDP examples as programmers who have access to master files containing valuable lists that could be sold, and to other EDP areas (see Chapter 7).

2. *Separation of the Authorization of Transactions from the Custody of Related Assets*

   (Compare with "Same person cannot both originate and approve transactions.") The auditing text uses the example of a person authorizing payment of a vendor invoice and also signing the check for payment. The example under guideline 3 earlier relates to error correction, since it has been a favorite system penetration method in many EDP installations. The relation should be clear.

3. *Separation of Duties within the Accounting Function*

   This manual accounting consideration has little direct *application to computers: Typical EDP accounting systems deliberately* combine *as many accounting functions as possible. (This* combination *creates an exposure that needs controls. This exposure is controlled in a manual accounting system by having different people responsible for the journals and for recording in the subsidiary ledgers. This use of separate journals and ledgers involves repeated entry of the same data, which is inherently inefficient, in a tradeoff for greater control. Typical EDP accounting systems, especially microcomputer accounting packages, normally avoid the inefficiency by having* one *entry, with the computer automatically "posting" to "ledgers" and so on. Controls in such cases are an ongoing concern of EDP and internal auditors.)*

4. *Separation of Operational Responsibility from Record-keeping Responsibility*

   (Compare with "Prohibit Conversion and Concealment," which is a special case.) Record keeping handled by a separate accounting department minimizes the temptation for individual departments to "fudge" data to make themselves look good. The Equity Funding insurance scandal was possible in part because managers using computers were able to violate this guideline.

Segregation of duties and responsibilities must be supplemented by systems that feature:

1. Integrity

   The system does exactly what it should, no more and no less. For every input to the system, the output and response can be predicted. Unidentified inputs should cause error messages and reports and should not cause changes to data files.

2. Auditability

   It must be possible to trace what happened and who caused it to happen. The system should be able to point to a single individual who has responsibility for any transaction. One way is to "time stamp" every transaction with the date, time, and identification of the originator. A detailed transaction list should be available. Good EDP system design, including "before and after" copies of records and transactions (intended mainly to allow recovery from a failure) will serve this purpose, if the originator of the transaction also is identified.

3. Controllability

   The system must do what the managers responsible require of it, and change as they require it to. A system should be broken into precise "modules" for which one person can be held responsible.

The EDP principles of "structured design" and "structured programming" are detail-level applications of this controllability principle, and fit well with the modularity need. The computer professional uses concepts of coupling and cohesion to express the same logical concerns. *Cohesion* refers to the internal unity of a program or system module; high cohesion corresponds to high granularity. *Coupling* refers to interactions *between* modules and to control structures. Low coupling corresponds (approximately) to separation of duties;.

There is a considerable literature on cohesion and coupling in system and program design. The Yourdon Press publishers have a number of books, the most recent of which reflect the latest thinking of the originators of cohesion and coupling in computer system design, Ed Yourdon and Tom deMarco. Lord's *CDP Review Manual: A Data Processing Handbook* [Lord 1986] has an excellent summary; more can be found in Adams, Powers & Owles, *Computer Information Systems Development: Design and Implementation* [Adams 1985], and many other works on systems analysis. Those who need this specialized detail should consult these and other specialized works for details.

The computer programmer usually is working at a detail level where interactions between people and programs are not involved, or have been specified by the system designer. Structured *analysis* and *design* should include considerations of people interactions.

Systems that have integrity, auditability, and controllability are the only ones which any professional should design, or allow.

12.7.2 Computer Control Guidelines

The material on the *Computer Control Guidelines* is presented here because these tend to concentrate on application systems and organizational controls. Earlier discussion of secure systems has been focused primarily on more technical aspects of operating systems or communications networks.

A relatively recent effort of the accounting profession to offer guidance to people who are working with information systems is the Canadian Institute of Chartered Accountants (CICA) *Computer Control Guidelines, Second Edition*, published in 1986. The first edition of this book was accepted widely by accountants and was translated into French, German, Spanish, and Japanese. The Control Objectives and Minimum Control Standards shown in the summary of the CICA *Guidelines* (pages 176-197) are reproduced here, with the permission of the copyright holder, the Canadian Institute of Chartered Accountants, Toronto, Canada.

This manual concentrates on *information systems* security. Accounting concentrates on effective use of an organization's *financial resources*, and controls to prevent fraud and errors. While there is much overlap, there are differences in emphasis.

For readers from a computer background, "control point" is the same for either accounting or computer usage. A "control" in this section is a specific accounting term corresponding to what computer people would mean by using "safeguard."

These guidelines are those proposed by a research study group of the Canadian Institute of Chartered Accountants. Guidelines from other sources may not agree completely. The field is in a state of constant and rapid change, and any security professional will have to become familiar with the latest and best material available, and then exercise *judgment*.

Details on these controls have been a major emphasis throughout this book. Therefore, this section outlines only the major control objectives and minimum control standards. References are provided to sections where more in-depth consideration may be found. (Where appropriate, the primary reference is listed first, then others in order by chapter.)

The format of this section looks like:

Control objectives are indented

Minimum control standards are indented one further level
Cross-references are indented one more level, and are *italicized*.

Responsibility for Control

Control Objective:

A.   To establish control over information and information systems.
Overview, Chapter 1, Chapter 5, Chapter 6, Chapter 9, Chapter 16, Chapter 16.

Minimum Control Standards:

A1.   Senior management should establish policies governing the information systems of the entity.
Chapter 16, Chapter 9.

A2.   Senior management should assign responsibilities for information, its processing and its use.
Chapter 16, Chapter 9.

A3. User management should be responsible for providing information that supports the entity's objectives and policies.
Chapter 16, Chapter 9.

A4. User management should be responsible for the completeness, accuracy, authorization, security and timeliness of information.
Chapter 16, Chapter 9.

A5. Information systems management should be responsible for providing the information systems capabilities necessary for achievement of the defined information systems objectives and policies of the entity.
Chapter 16, Chapter 9, Chapter 14.

A6. Senior management should approve plans for development and acquisition of information systems.
Chapter 9.

A7. Senior management should monitor the extent to which development, operation and control of information systems complies with established policies and plans.
Chapter 16.

Information Systems Development and Acquisition

Control Objective:

B. To ensure that the information systems selected meet the needs of the entity.
Chapter 16, Chapter 9, Chapter 12.

Minimum Control Standards:

B1. The decision to develop or acquire an information system should be made in accordance with the objectives and policies of the entity.
This relates to overall organizational planning, which is not emphasized in this text. Some references occur in Chapter 9 in comments on planning, especially Chapter 4 on Contingency Planning and in the portion of Chapter 12 dealing with system development methodologies.

B2. There should be procedures to determine costs, savings, and benefits before a decision is made to develop or acquire an information system.
Chapter 9, Chapter 3.

B3. Procedures should be established to ensure that the information system being developed or acquired meets user requirements.
Chapter 12, Chapter 9, Chapter 5.

B4. Information systems and programs should be adequately tested prior to implementation.
Section 12.1, comments in several places about program "bugs."

Control Objective:

C. To ensure the efficient and effective implementation of information systems.
In effect, this objective recommends creating a defined planning process, and defined documentation standards. Chapter 9 relates; Chapter 12 discusses signoffs; Chapters 4 and 14 consider contingency planning.

Minimum Control Standards:

C1. Responsibility should be assigned for implementation of information systems.
Chapter 9, Chapter 12.

C2. Standards should be established and enforced to ensure the efficiency and effectiveness of the implementation of information systems.
Chapter 9, Chapter 12.

C3. There should be procedures to ensure that information systems are implemented in accordance with the established standards.
Chapter 9, Chapter 12.

C4. An approved implementation plan should be used to measure progress.
Chapter 9.

C5. Effective control should be maintained over the conversion of information and the initial operation of the information system.
Chapter 12, section 12.1.6.

C6. User management should participate in the conversion of data from the existing system to the new system.
Chapter 12, section 12.1.6

C7. Final approval should be obtained from user management prior to operation of the new information system.
Chapter 9, Chapter 12.

Control Objective:

D. To ensure the efficient and effective maintenance of information systems.
Chapter 9; Chapter 4; Chapter 12, sections 12.2, 12.3; Chapter 14.

Minimum Control Standards:

D1. There should be procedures to document and schedule all planned changes to information systems.
Chapter 12, section 12.2.

D2. There should be procedures to ensure that only change authorization authorized changes are initiated.
Chapter 12, section 12.2; Chapter 14.

D3. Only authorized, tested, and documented changes to information systems should be accepted into production.
Chapter 12, section 12.1.

D4. There should be procedures to report planned information systems changes to information systems management and to the users affected.

Chapter 9; Chapter 12, section 12.2; Chapter 14.
D5. There should be procedures to allow for and to control emergency changes.
Chapter 4; Chapter 14.

D6. There should be procedures to ensure that controls are in place to prevent unauthorized changes to information systems.
This is a major focus of the entire book. Specific mentions are in the index under "configuration management."

Control Objective:

E. To ensure that the development and acquisition of information systems are carried out in an efficient and effective manner.
Other than the peripheral notion that efficiency and effectiveness of systems relates to security, acquisition of information systems is not major focus of this book. Comments about software escrow in Chapters 4 and 10 relate somewhat.

Minimum Control Standards:

E1. Standards should be established and enforced to ensure the efficiency and effectiveness of the systems development and acquisition processes.
Chapter 12.

E2. There should be procedures to ensure that all systems are developed and acquired in accordance with the established standards.

> *Chapter 12, Chapter 16.*

E3. An approved development and acquisition plan (project plan) should be used to measure progress.

> *The topic of information systems planning is not addressed directly in this text, other than mentions of configuration management.*

E4. All personnel involved in systems development and acquisition activities should receive adequate training and supervision.

> *Chapter 6 on personnel selection and training.*

Information Systems Processing

Control Objective:

F. To ensure that present and future requirements of users of information systems processing can be met.

> *Some of the material on the System Security Officer in Chapter 4 relates to this. Standards F4 and F5 have peripheral references in Chapter 14 on operations management. The security function normally is not very involved in this area. It is a normal management responsibility to ensure proper reporting and control, and an information systems management responsibility to monitor changing technology as part of planning.*

Minimum Control Standards:

F1. There should be written agreements between users and information systems processing, defining the nature and level of services to be provided.

F2. There should be appropriate management reporting within information systems processing.

F3. Information systems processing management should keep senior and user management apprised of technical developments which could support the achievement of the objectives and policies of the entity.

F4. There should be procedures to examine the adequacy of information systems processing resources to meet entity objectives in the future.

F5. There should be procedures for the approval, monitoring, and control of the acquisition and upgrade of hardware and systems software.

Control Objective:

G. To ensure the efficient and effective use of resources within information systems processing.

> *Chapter 9, Chapter 14; otherwise, this is another management topic which usually does not involve the security function directly.*

Minimum Control Standards:

G1. A budget for information systems processing should be prepared on a regular basis.

G2. Standards should be established and enforced to ensure efficient and effective use of information systems processing resources.

G3. There should be procedures to ensure that information processing problems are detected and corrected on a timely basis.

> *The control techniques recommended involve recording problems and resolutions, and making sure that historical records are reviewed and reported to senior management.*

Chapter 14 touches on this.

    G4. Users of information systems processing facilities should be accountable for the resources used by them.

Control Objective:

    H. To ensure complete, accurate and timely processing of authorized information systems.
Chapter 14, especially sections 7.3, 7.4, and 7.6; some of Chapter 9; Chapter 12; parts of Chapter 4.

Minimum Control Standards:

    H1. Standards should be established and enforced to ensure complete, accurate and timely processing of authorized information systems.

    H2. There should be operating procedures for all functions of information systems processing.
Written procedures are mentioned in a number of places, including Chapter 14 on operations, Chapter 4 on contingency planning, and in the systems development and implementation part of Chapter 12.

    H3. Information systems processing activities should be recorded and reviewed for compliance with established operating standards and procedures.
This refers mainly to system logs, which are mentioned in several places. Chapter 14, Chapter 9.

    H4. There should be written agreements between users and information systems processing, defining the nature and level of services to be provided.

    H5. Information systems processing activities should be scheduled to ensure that the established user requirements can be met.
Agreements and scheduling are management responsibilities mentioned in Chapter 9.

    H6. Appropriate maintenance should be applied to hardware, systems software and storage media.
Chapter 14, Chapter 4.

    H7. Only authorized, tested and documented new and changed information systems should be accepted into production.
Chapter 12.

Segregation of Incompatible Functions and Security Controls

Control Objective:

    I. To ensure that there is an appropriate segregation of incompatible functions within the entity.
Separation of duties is mentioned frequently. Chapter 14 and Chapter 12, sections 12.6 and 12.7 delve into the topic area in some detail.

Minimum Control Standards:

    I1. The organization structure established by senior management should provide for an appropriate segregation of incompatible functions.
See especially the "typical organization" examples in Chapter 14.

Control Objective:

    J. To ensure that all access to information and information systems is authorized.
Chapter 1, Chapter 5, Chapter 9, Chapter 12.

Minimum Control Standards:

J1. There should be procedures to ensure that information and information systems are accessed in accordance with established policies and procedures.

The control techniques recommended here include 18 specific methods involving security classification of data, communications security, control of access to system utilities, passwords, and so on. Much of Chapters 1, 5, and 12 is devoted to this area.

Control Objective:

K.   To ensure that hardware facilities within information systems processing are physically protected from unauthorized access and from accidental or deliberate loss or damage.

This objective relates to physical security, environmental control, access control. Chapter 13; some of Chapter 14; Chapter 4; and Chapter 1 all touch on this area.

Minimum Control Standards:

K1.   Hardware facilities within information systems processing should be physically separated from other departments in the entity.
Chapter 13.

K2.   Physical access to hardware facilities within the information systems processing should be restricted to authorized personnel.
Chapter 13, Chapter 14.

K3.   There should be procedures to ensure that environmental conditions (such as temperature and humidity) for hardware facilities are adequately controlled.
Chapter 13.

Control Objective:

L. To ensure that information systems processing can be recovered and resumed after operations have been interrupted.

In essence, Chapter 4 is devoted to this objective. The training aspects are mentioned there and in Chapter 6. Part of the control techniques (L1-3 for example) refer to exposure identification, which is a topic of Chapter 3.

Minimum Control Standards:

L1. There should be procedures to allow information systems processing to resume operations in the event of an interruption.
Chapter 4.

L2. Emergency, backup, and recovery plans should be documented and tested on a regular basis to ensure that they remain current and operational.
Chapter 4.

L3. Personnel should receive adequate training and supervision in emergency backup and recovery procedures.
Chapter 4, section 4.4; Chapter 6.

Control Objective:

M.   To ensure that critical user activities can be maintained and recovered following interruptions to normal operations.

This is the user side of the considerations mentioned in the chapters referred to under objective L. The references are the same.

Minimum Control Standards:

M1.   There should be backup and recovery plans to allow users of information systems to resume operations in the event of an interruption.
Chapter 4.

M2.   All information and resources required by users to resume processing should be backed up appropriately.

Chapter 4, Chapter 14.

M3. User personnel should receive adequate training and supervision in the conduct of the recovery procedures.
Chapter 4, Chapter 6.

Application Controls

Control Objective:

N. To ensure that application controls are designed with due regard to the controls relating to segregation of incompatible functions, security, development, and processing of information systems.

> *This refers to the design of controls that are all-encompassing; that is, if there is a weakness in one area such as operations, then there should be a corresponding compensating control elsewhere.*

Minimum Control Standards:

N1. Application controls should be designed with regard to any weaknesses in segregation, security, development and processing controls which may affect the information system.

> *This is a specific instance of the principle of compensating controls. There may be unavoidable weaknesses in one area, such as operating systems; if so, a corresponding application control should ensure that control is maintained elsewhere.*

Control Objective:

O. To ensure that information provided by the information systems is complete, authorized, and accurate.

> *This whole topic area is addressed in Chapter 12 and in a number of other locations in the text. Such things as automatic editing, reasonableness tests, limit tests, suspense account analysis, various reports documenting activities in files, exception reporting, control totals, and generally the sort of system audit trail found in good system design are found in Objective O. Parts of this are referred to many places in the text.*

Minimum Control Standards:

O1. There should be procedures to ensure that all transactions (including those used to change semi- permanent data and to correct errors) are initially recorded.

O2. There should be procedures to ensure that all accepted transactions are authorized.

O3. There should be procedures to ensure that all authorized transactions are recorded accurately.

O4. There should be procedures to ensure that all authorized transactions are processed.

O5. There should be procedures to ensure that all authorized transactions are processed accurately.

O6. There should be procedures to ensure that output is reviewed by users for completeness, accuracy, and consistency.

O7. There should be some method of ensuring that control procedures relating to completeness, accuracy, and authorization are enforced.

Control Objective:

P. To ensure the existence of adequate management trails.

> *See the previous objective.*

Minimum Control Standards:

   P1. Policies and procedures for record retention should be established.

   This topic is covered in passing in parts of the text which discuss backups. The specific sub-topic of record retention and destruction is a specialized area of "Records Management"; legal requirements for records retention are involved as well as computer backup principles and security issues. Related material can be found in Chapter 1, Chapter 4; and Chapter 13.

   P2. There should be some method of identifying and locating the component records involved in the processing of a transaction and in the production of information.

   Time stamps and other means of identifying transactions to permit recovery and audit are mentioned in several places.

12.7.3 Information Systems Audit

There are no "Generally Accepted Auditing Principles" that define either an EDP audit (as a sub-discipline within internal audit) or a security audit. A quote from Charles Cresson Wood illustrates the present situation, particularly for security audits, well:

> The specific controls that constitute a Standard of Due Care have not been documented or agreed-on by any official bodies, although research on the frequency of use of certain information system controls has demonstrated that generally-accepted controls do in fact exits. Certain organizations continue to maintain their own security measure databases, but these are proprietary and not generally available to the practitioner.

> Since little supporting information is available, the practitioner must make do. Accordingly, background information is most often obtained from the practitioner's personal knowledge or that of consultants. This ambiguity and lack of standardization leads to a number of problems . . .

Part of the problem is that the rate of change in computer technology is much greater than the rate at which official bodies, whether government or professional societies, can devise and agree to standards. This phenomenon is not unique to auditing; laws and legal systems (law enforcement, courts, legislatures, and so forth) face very similar problems.

The ISO (committee SC21) is working on a set of guidelines for security audit; this is merely at the stage of a discussion paper as of early 1993. As noted by Cresson Wood, many large organizations have internal guidelines. One source that has reasonably wide availability is the 1988 NIST Special Publication 500-153, *Guide to Auditing for Controls and Security: A System Development Life Cycle Approach*. This source naturally is biased towards specific U.S. laws and government practices; however it provides a useful set of guidelines which may supplement that background information "most often obtained from the practitioner's personal knowledge."

The material in this section is based on the NIST publication, and on Ron Weber's book *EDP Auditing: Conceptual Foundations and Practice*. The reader is referred to that book, or the *Computer Control Guidelines* (see also section 12.7.1), for more detail on EDP audit guidelines.

12.7.3.1 Security Review Objectives

Weber defines EDP auditing this way:

> EDP auditing is the process of collecting and evaluating evidence to determine whether a computer system safeguards assets, maintains data integrity, achieves organizational goals effectively, and consumes resources efficiently.

Thus, Weber would consider the objectives of EDP audit to include examining four items: asset safeguarding, maintenance of data integrity, and efficient use of resources, and effective use of resources. He and other authors include material on security within their works. As with other authors, the material in Weber is not at a level of sophistication or detail sufficient to support a professional practitioner in planning a security audit.[6] To find more detail, the practitioner must consult other sources (such as this book).

NIST Special Publication 500-153 does provide detailed guidelines for planning and conducting an audit of security matters; however its material is closely related to U.S. Government considerations, and the detailed guidelines thus may not be applicable in non-governmental situations. Nevertheless, the objectives provided are summarized below, as they are the most complete available. The practitioner should consider these to be only guidelines, and should adapt as needed to specific situations. We begin with a definition for *Audit of computer security*:

An independent evaluation of the controls employed to ensure:

1. The appropriate protection of the organization's information assets (including hardware, software, firmware, and data) from all significant anticipated threats or hazards;

2. The accuracy and reliability of the data maintained on or generated by an automated data processing system; and

3. The operational reliability and performance assurance for accuracy and timeliness of all components of the automated data processing system.

Note that the EDP audit objective of examining efficient use of resources is not included in this definition. Curiously, many of the detailed objectives below *do* address efficient use of resources. This is one area in particular where the practitioner may deem it appropriate to modify SP 500-153.

The audit objectives in SP 500-13 are organized around a six-stage "System Development Life Cycle:" Initiation, Definition, System Design, Programming and Training, Evaluation and Acceptance, and Installation and Operation.

I. Initiation
    1. User Needs Statement clearly defines the need/problem and justification for implementing that need.
    2. User department(s) management should participate in the project Initiation Phase.
    3. The Feasibility Study document should be clearly defined and documented.
    4. AIS internal control and security vulnerabilities should have been determined, as well as the magnitude of associated threats.
    5. Cost/Benefit Analysis should include all of the cost and benefit considerations associated with the initiation, operation, and maintenance of the AIS.
    6. Management should review the Feasibility Study reports and decide whether to proceed. When the decision is made to proceed, one of the alternatives should be selected as the starting point for the following system development phases.
    7. Validate that an analysis was made prior to programming to determine whether the work could have been done more economically through contracting and/or purchasing off-the-shelf software.

---

[6]In fact, much of the material on security in Weber is quite similar to that in Chapter 3 of this book, though with less detail.

II. Definition

1. A Project Plan should be developed that specifies the strategy for managing the software/AIS development.

2. A definition of existing and new information requirements should be specified with exacting detail.

3. All input requirements should be defined and documented.

4. Output requirements should be defined and documented.

5. Specification for processing steps should be defined and documented.

6. A plan for converting from existing process to new process has been documented.

7. The impact of system failures should be defined and reconstruction requirements specified.

8. The level of service necessary to achieve the processing objectives should be defined and documented.

9. The internal control and security requirements should be defined and documented, per OMB Circular A-130.

10. The user requirements should identify critical/sensitive data and assets, and how those items should be controlled during computer processing.

11. Audit and quality assurance tools and techniques should be planned for the system.

12. The System Decision Paper should include all of the information needed by user management to make a decision on action to be taken regarding the AIS.

III. System Design

1. The revised Project Plan is current and provides the direction needed to effectively and efficiently manage the project.

2. The final system design should be approved by all appropriate levels of management as meeting all predetermined needs.

3. Sufficient data processing and security controls should be incorporated in the detailed design to ensure the integrity of the system.

4. Rules for authorizing transactions should be defined and documented.

5. Documentation suitable for use as audit trails should be incorporated into the detailed design.

6. A vulnerability assessment should be planned and performed in compliance with OMB circulars A-123 and A-130.

7. The system/subsystem, program, and data base specifications should provide the correct architectural solution to meet the documented requirements from the definition phase.

8. The security and internal control related specifications should provide controls adequate for satisfying the control requirements defined in the previous phase.

9. A Validation, Verification, and Testing Plan should be developed and documented.

10. Assure that audit and quality assurance tools and techniques have been included in systems design documents.

11. Assure that the system design has optimized the use of technology.

12. Ensure that the system decision continues to be supported by documents.

IV. Programming and Training

1. Program documentation and programming standards should be enforced to ensure that documentation is maintained in accordance with management policy.

2. Each program should have adequate test data prepared to validate the functioning of the executable source code.

3. Each program should include a detailed narrative description of the processing to be performed and the logic of that processing.

4. All of the source code should be executed during testing.

5. Run manuals for the operators' use should be prepared and adequately documented in an Operations Manual.

6. A Maintenance Manual should be prepared with adequate information on projected maintenance needs and problems.

7. Manuals for users should be prepared and adequately documented.

8. A Training Plan should be prepared and documented in detail. This may be found within or based upon the User Manual and the Operations/Maintenance Manual.

9. Determine that good programming practices have been employed to take advantage of modern software engineering and computer efficiencies.

10. Each program should be tested to ensure that it correctly performs the functions assigned to that unit.

11. An Installation and Conversion Plan should be prepared and adequately documented.

12. An updated System Decision Paper should have been produced at the start of this phase.

13. A change control process should be in place for the User Manual and the Operations/Maintenance Manual.

V. Evaluation and Acceptance

1. Unit, module, and integration testing should be conducted according to the Test Plan and applicable ADP test standards.

2. Test results should be evaluated by data processing management and by user department management to determine that the system functions properly.

3. Test results should be recorded and retained as part of the system documentation.

4. Circumstances under which a parallel run of both existing and new systems is considered desirable should be identified, and criteria for its termination stated.

5. An updated Conversion Plan should be prepared to include assignment of individual responsibilities.

6. Ensure that adequate provisions have been made to assure continuity of processing.

7. Determine that a security evaluation, a certification, and an accreditation have been performed and appropriate documents and statements prepared.

8. Determine that the Installation and Conversion Plan has been updated and currently represents the current status of the AIS.

9. Determine that the User Manual has been updated and currently represents the current status of the AIS.

10. Determine that the Operations/Maintenance Manual has been updated and currently represents the current status of the AIS.

11. Determine that the Project Plan has been updated and represents the current status of the AIS.

12. Determine that the System Decision Paper has been updated and represents the current status of the AIS.

VI. Installation and Operation

(The audit of the life cycle is concluded once the system becomes operational, in the scheme of SP 500-153.)

The Federal Information Processing Standards Publication *Guideline for Computer Security Certification and Accreditation*, FIPS Pub 102, U.S. Department of Commerce/National Bureau of Standards, is referenced several times in the tools and techniques associated with the objectives above. This standard, although somewhat dated, remains a good source of guidance for many specific tasks that need to be performed in the course of certifying a system's security properties. Although it relates to a particular process within the U.S. Government, many of the tasks and rationales apply to other information security situations and to other processes for conducting an information security audit.

12.7.3.2 Evidence Accumulation

In this section, we refer to the evidence needed to support evaluations of controls and to produce audit reports; evidentiary considerations relating to criminal investigation are discussed in Chapter 11. A subtle but significant difference between EDP audit and security audit is in the use to which evidence is put. The traditional EDP audit places great emphasis on the reliability and correct processing of data (data integrity issues.) In a security audit, inconsistencies in files are of interest mainly to the extent that they reveal inadequacies in controls and safeguards.

The purpose of collecting evidence in an EDP audit is the same as for any other audit: to verify the presence and correct operation of controls. The forms of evidence and the method of collection may differ substantially from those traditionally collected during an audit of a manual system. In particular, much of the evidence usually will be in some electronic format, which means that trusted tools and specialized knowledge are required even to read the evidence. As well, as noted in the discussion of the SAFE method in section 3.2.4.3, many of the traditional audit trail elements may not exist in automated systems. Normally, audit software is used to gather evidence during an EDP or security audit. Types and usage of audit software tools are beyond the scope of this book.

Evidence for the existence and correct operation of various controls includes paper documentation as well as electronic formats. For example, several documents are referred to in the objectives above, and part of the evidence for controls is the existence and content of these documents. Similarly, the existence (and currency) of manuals, program listings, and so forth is significant.

In the case of security audit, several methods not usually considered common auditing methods are used from time to time. Generally, these fall into a category that is called "penetration testing." Information flow analysis is a form of penetration testing, where possible covert channels are identified. Another form of penetration testing is actual attempts to circumvent the security of a system, the so-called "tiger team." The appropriateness of such testing varies in different circumstances; such methods as information flow analysis are very expensive, and tiger teams may not be an acceptable method in some organizations.

12.7.3.3 Communication of Control Weaknesses

A sample outline for a typical security audit report is given below. First, it is important to emphasize that the purpose of the report is to communicate the results of a formal process that involves finding flaws, and to suggest corrective actions. It is easy to concentrate on flaws and produce a report very negative in tone, which is not likely to achieve appropriate changes. The report must be accurate, meaningful, and constructive:

- *Accurate*. All judgments must be supported. There must be evidence to justify everything in the final report, and quantitative ratings must explicitly identify assumptions, conditions, methods, and variances.
- *Meaningful*. The report is intended to go to a specific manager, and should lead to action. It is important that the report be laid out and use language in such a way that the recipient has

the best chance of comprehension. As an example, the practitioner may think in terms of disclosure, denial of service, destruction of data, and other concepts in this book; the manager may understand more easily if the results are represented in terms such as fraud, legal exposure, embarrassment of the organization, and so forth.

- *Constructive*. This cannot be emphasized too strongly. The purpose of the evaluation has been to identify things that are wrong. If the report includes only these flaws, it will mis-represent the system: Most systems do many more things right than wrong. A balanced presentation that includes summarization of positive results as well as negative results is needed. As well, recommendations must be realistic and implementable. For example, a recommendation to adopt compensating controls is far more likely to be accepted than a recommendation to shut down a major system due to a single fault.

With the characteristics of accuracy, meaning, and constructiveness in mind, a sample report outline could be:[7]

1. *Introduction and summary*. Briefly describe the application and summarize findings and recommendations.
2. *Background*. This will vary with the situation. The purpose is to identify significant points about the conduct of the security audit. Examples include the boundaries of the applications examined and assumptions about areas outside these boundaries, the security policy that was applied (if any), and similar items.
3. *Major Findings*. There are two parts to this section: controls in place and vulnerabilities discovered. The first part serves the dual purpose of identifying the controls that are in place and their roles in providing security, and of providing the balance referred to above. Roughly speaking, controls in place are things that are right, and vulnerabilities are things that are wrong.
4. *Recommended Corrective Actions*. As noted above, recommendations must be realistic. This means, among other things, that it is necessary to assess the impact of the recommendations: at least a preliminary cost and operational impact statement. In addition to demonstrating a certain realism of the practitioner, such cost and impact statements should make it clear when a recommendation is not feasible and therefore not constructive.
5. *Audit process*. This section summarizes the work done during the security audit. Here is where the mass of evidence is collected, and where the full justification for recommendations is to be found.

The practitioner must retain working papers and records for as long as is necessary. If the audit should be questioned, it must be possible to back up the conclusions. The appropriate retention period will vary depending on individual situations, organizational policies, and perhaps legal considerations.

12.8 SPECIFIC CONTROLS

Specific controls in applications programs vary too much from one program to the next for a long list and detailed treatment to be meaningful. For example, edit of input data is common to all

---

[7]Adapted, rather freely, from *Guideline for Computer Security Certification and Accreditation*, FIPS Pub 102, U.S. Department of Commerce/National Bureau of Standards, September 1983, p. 45-47.

well-designed programs; however, the type and level of editing appropriate for an interactive program controlled through a graphical user interface (GUI) is entirely different from that appropriate for an off-line batch system. The type, timing, and nature of corrective measures also differs vastly. Internal consistency checks also are common to all well-designed programs; however by their nature they may differ totally from one application to the next, or even from one set of subroutines to another set within the same application.

Another issue is the type of corrective measures. Corrective measures involve human beings doing something to correct an identified problem, then re-submitting corrected data for consideration. (This is one of the reasons formal integrity policies are difficult; using the concepts of section 12.6, the IVP includes human intervention or other interaction with an environment external to the system. See also Chapter 14 for discussion of controls involving human input as well as the system.) Further processing, opportunities for fraud through error transaction handling, and similar issues are entirely different in on-line and batch systems.

Keeping in mind the preceding *caveats*, a list of specific controls common to most application programs could include:

- Access controls (passwords, authentication, capabilities and tokens, Read/Write/Execute control, and so forth)
- Edits (syntax, reasonableness, range checks, check digits, . . .)
- Counts (total transactions (number in plus rejects = number out, for example), batch totals, hash totals, balances (credits and debits sum to zero, for example), . . .)
- Logs (who, what system, when)
- Logs (time stamp, before and after images, . . .)
- Internal checks (parameter ranges and data types, valid and legal address references, completion codes, . . .)

REFERENCES

AFIPS Systems Review Manual on Security, AFIPS Press, Montvale, NJ, 1974.

Becker, Hal B., *Information Integrity*, McGraw-Hill, New York, NY, 1983.

Biba, K. J., "Integrity Considerations for Secure Computer Systems" National Technical Information Service NTIS AD-A039324, Springfield VA, 1977.

Clark, D. D. and D. R. Wilson, "A Comparison of Commercial and Military Security Policies," in *Proceedings* of the 1987 Symposium on Security and Privacy, IEEE Computer Society, Washington, DC, 1987.

Computer Control Guidelines, Canadian Institute of Chartered Accountants, Toronto, 1986.

Denning, D., J. Schlorer, and C. Wehrle, "Memoryless Inference Controls for Statistical Databases," *IEEE Computer Security and Privacy Proceedings*, Oakland, CA, April 26-28, 1982, pp. 38-43.

Denning, Dorothy Elizabeth Robling, *Cryptography and Data Security*, Addison-Wesley Publishing Company, Reading, MA, 1983.

Fernandez, E. B., R. C. Summers, and C. Wood, *Database Security and Integrity*, Addison-Wesley, Reading, MA, 1981.

Fisher, Royal, *Information Systems Security*, Prentice-Hall, Englewood Cliffs, NJ, 1984.

Fites, Philip. E., Martin P. J. Kratz, and Alan F. Brebner, *Control and Security of Computer Information Systems*, W. H. Freeman/Computer Science Press, New York, NY, 1989.

Guideline for Computer Security Certification and Accreditation, FIPS Pub 102, U.S. Department of Commerce/National Bureau of Standards, September 1983.

Gallegos, Frederick, Dana R. (Rick) Richardson, and A. Faye Borthick, *Audit & Control of Information Systems*, South-Western Publishing Company, West. Chicago, IL, 1987.

Krauss, Leonard L. and Aileen MacGahan, *Computer Fraud and Countermeasures*, Prentice-Hall, Englewood Cliffs, NJ, 1979.

Martin, James, *Principles of Data Base Management*, Prentice-Hall, Englewood Cliffs, NJ, 1976.

Martin, James, *Security, Accuracy, and Privacy in Computer Systems*, Prentice-Hall, Inc., Englewood Cliffs, NJ, 1973.

Report of the Invitational Workshop on Integrity Policy in Computer Information Systems, Bentley College, Waltham, MA, 1988.

Ruthberg, Zella G., *Guide to Auditing for Controls and Security: A System Development Life Cycle Approach*, NBS Special Publication 500-153, NIST, Gaithersburg, MD, 1988.

Sessions, M. V., "The Security and Privacy of Data Management Systems," Computer Security and Privacy *Proceedings*, MEDW-359-501, Honeywell Information Systems, Phoenix, AZ, April 2-3, 1979, pp. 99-101.

Weber, Ron, *EDP Auditing: Conceptual Foundations and Practice* (Second Edition), McGraw-Hill, New York, NY, 1988.

Whiteside, Thomas, *Computer Capers*, Thomas V. Crowell Co., New York, NY, 1978.

13. Physical Security

Physical security refers to the provision of a safe environment for information processing activities and to the use of the environment to control the behavior of personnel.[1]

The knowledge includes:

- Facility requirements
  - site and building location considerations
  - external characteristics and appearance
  - location of information-processing areas within building
  - construction standards
  - electrical power considerations (service, UPS, motor-generator sets, etc.)
  - protection from rising and falling water
  - traffic and access control
  - air conditioning and exhaust
  - entrances and exits
  - furnishings and other fuel load considerations

- Fire suppression
- Media storage
- Personnel access control
- Other

DEFINITIONS

Backup Procedures

The provisions made for the recovery of data files and program libraries, and for restart or replacement of ADP equipment after a system failure or disaster. (AR 380-380; FIPS PUB 39)

Catastrophe

An event which causes significant restructuring of an environment. (MK)

Clearing

The overwriting of classified information on magnetic media such that the media may be reused. (This does not lower the classification level of the media.) (DOE 5636.2A)

Computer Facility

Physical resources that include structures or parts of structures to house and support capabilities. For small computers, stand-alone systems, and word processing equipment, it is the physical area where the computer is used. (AFR 205-16)

---

[1]This is item 14 in the (ISC)2 Common Body of Knowledge.

Degauss

1. To reduce magnetic flux density to zero by applying a reverse (coercive) magnetizing force. Commonly referred to as demagnetizing. (CSC-STD-005-85; NCSC-WA-001-85)
2. To apply a variable, alternating current (AC) field for the purpose of demagnetizing magnetic recording media. The process involved increases the AC field gradually from zero to some maximum value and back to zero, which leaves a very low residue of magnetic induction on the media. (OPNAVINST 5239.1A; AR 380-380; FIPS PUB 39)

Degausser

An electrical device (AC or DC) or a hand-held magnet assembly which can generate coercive magnetic force for the purpose of degaussing magnetic storage media or other magnetic material. (CSC-STD-005-85; NCSC-WA-001-85)

Destruction

1. The physical alteration of ADP system media or ADP system components such that they can no longer be used for storage or retrieval of information. (DOE 5636.2A)
2. A peril involving the denial of an asset to its owner without acquisition by an agent. (RM)

Environment

The aggregate of external circumstances, conditions, and objects that affect the development, operation, and maintenance of a system. (CSC-STD-004-85; CSC-STD-003-85; NCSC-WA-001-85)

Erasure

A process by which a signal recorded on magnetic media is removed (i.e., degaussed). Erasure may be accomplished in two ways: In AC erasure, the media are degaussed by applying an alternating field which is reduced in amplitude from an initial high value (*i.e.*, AC-powered); in DC erasure, the media are saturated by applying a unidirectional field (*i.e.*, DC-powered or by employing a permanent magnet). (CSC-STD-005-85; NCSC-WA-001-85)

Escort(s)

Duly designated personnel who have appropriate clearances and access authorizations for the material contained in the system and are sufficiently knowledgeable to understand the security implications of and to control the activities and access of the individual being escorted. (OPNAVINST 5239.1A; AR 380-380; DCID 1/16-1; DCID 1/16-1; Sup.; DODD 5200.28M)

Gauss

A unit measure of the magnetic flux density produced by a magnetizing force. (CSC-STD-005-85)

Goods

Any articles, materials, supplies, or manufactured products, including inspection and test equipment. The term excludes technical data. (DODD 2040.2)

Lock-and-Key Protection System

A protection system that involves matching a key or password with a specific access requirement. (FIPS PUB 39; AR 380-380; NCSC-WA-001-85)

Magnetic Field Intensity

The magnetic force required to produce a desired magnetic flux given as the symbol H (see definition of oersted). (CSC-STD-005-85)

Magnetic Flux

Lines of force representing a magnetic field. (CSC-STD-005-85)

Magnetic Flux Density

The representation of the strength of a magnetic field, given as the symbol B (see definition of Gauss). (CSC-STD-005-85)

Magnetic Remanence

A measure of the magnetic flux density remaining after removal of the applied magnetic force. Refers to any data remaining on storage media after removal of the power. (NCSC-WA-001-85)

Magnetic Saturation

The condition in which an increase in magnetizing force will produce or result in little or no increase in magnetic flux. (CSC-STD-005-85)

Media

The peripheral device related physical components used for the storage of data such as tape reels, floppy diskettes, etc. (WB)

Oersted

A unit of measure of the magnetizing force necessary to produce a desired magnetic flux across a surface. (CSC-STD-005-85)

Open Storage

The storage of classified information, not in GSA-approved secure containers, within an accredited facility while such facility is not occupied by authorized personnel. (AR 380-380)

Overwrite

A procedure to remove or destroy data recorded on magnetic storage media by writing patterns of data over or on top of the data stored on the media. (NCSC-WA-001-85)

Overwrite Procedure

A procedure to remove or destroy data recorded on ADP magnetic storage media by recording patterns of unclassified data over or on top of the data stored on the media. (CSC-STD-005-85)

Overwriting

The obliteration of recorded data by recording different data on the same surface. (FIPS PUB 39)

Physical Control Space (PCS)

The spherical space surrounding electronic equipment used to process information which is under sufficient physical control to stop hostile intercept of compromising emanations. It is usually expressed in meters and can be controlled by fences, guards, patrols, walls, and so forth. The exact method of securing the PCS may vary depending upon resources available. (AFR 205-16; OPNAVINST 5239.1A)

Physical Security

The measures used to provide physical protection of resources against deliberate and accidental threats. (ISO 7498-2)

Purging

The orderly review of storage and removal of inactive or obsolete data files and the removal of obsolete data by erasure, overwriting of storage, or resetting of registers. (AR 380-380; NCSC-WA-001-85; FIPS PUB 39)

Remanence

1. The residual magnetism that remains on magnetic storage media after degaussing. (FIPS PUB 39; AR 380-380)
2. A measure of the magnetic flux density remaining after removal of an applied magnetic force. Can also mean any data remaining on ADP storage media after removal of the power. (CSC-STD-005-85)

Restricted Area

Any area to which access is subject to special restrictions or controls for reasons of security or safeguarding of property or material. (AR 380-380; NCSC-WA-001-85)

Sanitization

The elimination of classified information from magnetic media to permit the reuse of the media at a lower classification level or to permit the release to uncleared personnel or personnel without the proper information access authorizations. (DOE 5636.2A)

Sanitize

1. To erase or overwrite classified data stored on magnetic media for the purpose of declassifying the media. (CSC-STD-005-85)
2. To remove sensitive data so that the remaining data is of a lower sensitivity than the original aggregate. (NCSC-WA-001-85)

Sanitizing

The degaussing or overwriting of sensitive information in magnetic or other storage media. Synonymous with Scrubbing. (FIPS PUB 39; AR 380-380)

Security Area

A physically defined space containing classified matter (documents or material) subject to physical protection and personnel access controls. (DOE 5636.2A)

Security Perimeter

The boundary where security controls are in effect to protect assets. (NCSC-WA-001-85)

Survivability

The ability of a system to continue to process critical applications in spite of the fact that it suffered disruptive or damaging events (such as contamination with dust, an earthquake, a bomb, etc.). (WB)

Type 1 Magnetic Media

Magnetic media with coercivity factors not exceeding 325 oersteds. (CSC-STD-005-85)

Type 2 Magnetic Media

Magnetic media with coercivity factors exceeding 325 oersteds, possibly as high as 750 oersteds (also known as high-energy media). (CSC-STD-005-85)

INTRODUCTION

We look first at identification of assets—the "what must be protected." Four physical components are identified here:

1. Facility—Building, rooms, work space, back-up storage area
2. Support—Air conditioning, fire systems, electricity, communications, water, fuel supplies, etc.
3. Physical and Components—Hardware: CPU, printers, disk drives, terminals; desks, chairs, containers, and similar objects
4. Supplies, Materials – tapes, disks, paper supplies, waste material, and so on

	Facility	Support	Supplies, Material & Furn.
Site location	X	X	X
Perimeter security	X	X	X
Construction standards	X	X	
Security containers			X
Drainage water detection	X	X	X
Access control procedures	X	X	X
Doors	X	X	X
Locks, keys, cards	X	X	X
Recognition badges	X	X	X
Access control logs	X	X	X
Maintenance logs		X	
Transportation	X		
Fire protection	X	X	X
Off-site facilities	X	X	X
Waste; disposal			X

Figure 13.1. Physical & Environmental Security—Preventive Techniques/Countermeasures

Note that some of these assets also appear elsewhere. In particular, Chapter 8 deals in more depth with communications-related assets.

The table in Figure 13.1, reproduced from a RCMP presentation, indicates a number of specific protective measures and to which of the asset classes identified above each applies.

The primary vulnerabilities of the classes identified here are:

1. Facility

Destruction
    Accidental (fire, flood, earthquake, wind, snow, construction faults)
    Deliberate (vandalism, sabotage, arson)

2. Support

Destruction
    Accidental (same as above)
    Deliberate (same as above)
Removal
    Accidental (equipment failure, public utility outage, fire, flood, earthquake, wind, snow, con-
        struction faults)
    Deliberate (sabotage, vandalism, arson)
Interruption
    Accidental and Deliberate same as above lists.

3. Supplies, Material, Furniture

Destruction
    Accidental (fire, flood, earthquake, wind, snow, etc.)
    Deliberate (arson, vandalism)
Removal or Disclosure
    Accidental (carelessness)
    Deliberate (theft)
Interruption
    Accidental (fire, flood, etc)
    Deliberate (sabotage, arson, vandalism)

13.1 SITE LOCATION AND CONSTRUCTION

Where the building is, and how it is built, are measures that significantly affect the level of vulnerability to threats. If the security team has the luxury of considering the location and construction of a new (or remodelling a different) building, the following need to be looked at:

- *Vulnerability to crime, riots, and demonstrations*

    Is the area in a high-crime part of a city? Are you planning to construct a nuclear power plant on the San Andreas Fault? Will your staff be comfortable and safe leaving after hours in a dimly lit warehousing district? Is an unlit parking lot hazardous to night staff? These and similar questions need to be asked. Access considerations such as long straight lanes or roads (where a truck could build momentum to crash through a wall) may be relevant if terrorism is a consideration. Nearby police and fire stations also could be factors.

- *Adjacent buildings and/or businesses*

  Does a nearby business attract types of attention you don't want directed towards your information systems facility? If there is an adjacent building, can someone get from it into yours and, if so, is its security as strong as your own? A weak point in many homes is an attached garage; it often is less secure than the house and provides cover and tools for an intruder to spend time getting into the house proper. The same principle applies to adjacent buildings.

- *Emergency support response*

  This already has been referred to: Nearness of fire stations affects how great your fire risk is, for example.

- *Vulnerability to natural disasters*

  Is the proposed location susceptible to earthquake? Tornados or hurricanes? Located below a dam? In the approach path to an airport? All these and other factors need to be considered. Government statistics from groups such as the United States National Weather Bureau help in assessing such threats as weather and other natural phenomena. Flood plain maps, earthquake risk maps, and similar data are available as well. It may be wise to consult an engineer or architect if more detailed information is needed; unless the security person is also qualified in such areas, risks may be missed. (Some guidance to sources of threat information can be found in section 3.2.4 and Chapter 6.)

- *General Building Construction*

  Building construction is a major topic in itself. Obvious points include such things as:

  - Can the structure withstand hurricane-force winds (if relevant)?
  - Is it earthquake-resistant?
  - How many doors does it have, and how strong are they?
  - Will the roof withstand expected snow loading?

Computer room considerations

In 1969, a computer center at Sir George Williams University in Montreal (now Concordia University), which was "on display" behind large glass windows as was popular then, was destroyed by gasoline bombs during a student demonstration. The computer center should be a further protected (point security) area within the building.

Even in an existing building, a computer center can be made fairly secure with little change to the existing structure. Full-height fireproof walls (to close off access through a false ceiling and some fire exposure) often are not especially expensive. (See section 13.6 below, on fire prevention.) Shatterproof glass and good locks on doors are other fairly inexpensive preventive security measures.

If alternatives are available, location of a new building and its construction should be considered in the risk analysis and control program. Even if a new building is out of the question, secure areas for information systems, within existing buildings, usually can be added at a reasonable cost.

13.2 PHYSICAL ACCESS

Some areas, such as computer rooms and rooms where computer media or data are stored, should have restricted access. Such areas need to be identified and marked. "No Admittance" signs do deter many people and are very inexpensive. For greater exposures and potential losses, more expensive measures may be appropriate.

More active measures basically require people, or in some cases expensive automated measures such as a computer-controlled card-access system. The people could be guards or receptionists. In either case, persons wanting to enter restricted areas should be pre-authorized, or accompanied by someone who is authorized. Some system of identification cards or badges normally is required to identify authorized personnel, unless the company is so small that everyone knows everyone else. Disaster planning should consider personnel access as well; many security procedures break down completely for janitors, and are completely useless in stressful situations requiring access by emergency response personnel.

One thing that guards or receptionists should do is ensure that access logs are maintained. Anyone (authorized or not) entering a restricted area should log in and out. Closed circuit TV inside (an "area" control) may be appropriate to detect unwanted inhabitants.

What has been discussed so far are essentially preventive and some detective controls. Reactive or corrective controls also should be included; as mentioned previously, a log of who is inside and when they are inside is not much good unless someone reviews it from time to time. Procedures defining what receptionists should do if someone unauthorized is discovered, should be defined as well.

13.2.1 Access *versus* Security

(See also Chapter 1, Access Control.)

In essence, security is a tradeoff *versus* access. More access implies a lower level of security. Each organization must choose the level of exposure consistent with its desired ease of access. A caution is that if security measures interfere seriously with what is perceived to be "normal" operational activities, people often will defeat the security measure. An example, seen frequently, is a computer room door propped open because the automatic lock interfered with access to something as mundane as a soda dispenser.

13.2.2 Rooms, Windows, Doors, Keys

Passive measures include doors and locks. The doors should be of solid construction; making them fireproof may be a good idea as they will then also be solidly constructed. Reasonably secure locks are fairly inexpensive and often are not provided unless specifically requested. Alarms to indicate that doors are open may be reasonable measures, if someone is monitoring.

More detail on access control, including types of card locks and biometrics, is found in Chapter 1.

13.3 POWER

Computers need electrical power to work. This area is a technical one in which detailed examinations require specific technical training, and an expert should be involved in the design process.

The first level of expert is the manufacturer of the computer(s). Pay attention to what type of power the maker says should be supplied.

Most computers are sensitive to "dirty power." A consideration for microcomputers, for example, could be other office equipment on the same power line. Some electric typewriters generate a fairly powerful short surge when the carriage return is engaged. Such a surge does computer equipment attached to the same power line no good; protection is needed. The first rule of computer power usually is "isolation"—the computer should be on a different line than other office equipment. This rule applies to personal computers as much as to mainframes. (Practically, manufacturers have made personal computers relatively insensitive to this sort of power fluctuation; otherwise no one could use them at home).

The power supply conditions should be monitored. Many automatic devices are available that will keep a record of usage and similar items. From a security perspective, it is wise to consider the building electrical room as well; penetration here could stop the computer as surely as penetration into the computer room itself. Relatively cheap surge protectors and filters can protect from most dirty power problems; a power supply monitor allows the designer to know what sort of filtering is needed.

13.3.1 Spikes, Surges, Brownouts

Computer equipment is vulnerable to many things in the power supply. The most common risks are:

Brownouts or Total Power Loss

The voltage drops or power is lost entirely. Some disk drives and other motors may be very sensitive to low voltage.

Spikes and Surges

When lightning hits outside power lines, or in some other circumstances, a sudden "spike" of high voltage may appear on the power or telephone lines. Computer equipment—*and* modems connected to telephone lines—are very sensitive to high voltage spikes.

Surges are very common on lines with electric motors attached. The voltage drops a bit when a motor starts, then surges a bit when it stops.

Static

Particularly in cold climates, people generate static electricity when moving around. If the humidity is low sparks are common, and a spark can ruin a computer chip or scramble data on a diskette. At a minimum, data currently being processed in the computer can be corrupted.

13.3.2 Costs and Capabilities of Prevention/Protection Equipment

One way to minimize problems with power is to install a "UPS," or Uninterruptible Power Supply. The level of UPS needed can range from batteries that will support the system for a few seconds so that it can "fail soft" (i. e., shut itself down controllably), to elaborate systems including backup generators for systems that must continue to function regardless (air traffic control, or hospital systems, for example). UPSs can cost from one or two hundred dollars (for a small system that will run a personal computer for long enough to finish copying files onto a diskette) to a hundred thousand dollars or more, for elaborate battery systems with automatic backup generators.

When the computer *must* keep running, or when it is convenient to allow a "soft shutdown," some self-contained power-supply units can save a lot of trouble. A UPS can range from a small battery and converter to a massive generator complex.

Protection from most supply problems is fairly inexpensive. Surges are fewer, and interference of several sorts is unlikely, if the computer has its own power line. Unplugging modems from phone lines, and all equipment from power lines during lightning storms will eliminate surge risks. (If lightning gets into the *inside* power lines, you have more problems than just a fried computer!)

Static is minimized by controlling humidity. Anti-static mats under chairs, under machines, and anti-static carpeting definitely are advisable in areas prone to low humidity, such as cities in very cold climates during the winter. Anti-static sprays (marketed to stop clothes from clinging) can help around computers.

A UPS is expensive for anything better than a few seconds' supply to allow you to save files and shut down "softly." The short-term supply needed for this may be available for as little as $150–200 (availability varies locally). A "real" UPS starts in the area of $500 and goes up, quickly, depending on the wattage capacity required. Few microcomputer installations need a "real" UPS. However, a lot of time, trouble, and lost work may be avoided with one of the short-term units. Any "real" UPS also includes filtering of interference, spikes, surges, and so on.

More elaborate UPSs include such capabilities as power-generating facilities that are intended to start up to maintain continuous power after a battery UPS discharges. It is critical that such systems be tested frequently. Such testing must include extreme conditions (for example, a diesel generator outside a building may start perfectly in August, but fail to start at -40 in January).

Manufacturers are aware of the sensitivity of their equipment. The better micros (and more expensive as well, naturally) normally have some built-in protection, and occasionally even some very short-term power backup (to avoid problems with millisecond "blips"). "No-name" units usually skip these features, and may not be as good a buy as they seem for this reason.

It is wise not to buy a computer that is not UL- or CSA-approved. *Never* buy a computer containing a power supply that is not UL- or CSA-approved. UL or CSA approval relates to safety features, not to performance; non-approved equipment may be a hazard, may violate insurance policies, and may be unlawful.

13.4 AIR CONDITIONING

Most large computers require special air conditioning to continue to function properly. This may extend to smaller systems as well; it is not unusual to see someone begin to experience copier problems when a copier is enclosed in an improperly air-conditioned room.

Again, the manufacturer is the first line of expert advice. The maker should specify cooling requirements, and the user should heed the specifications.

As with power, the air conditioning for a computer should be for the computer only. It makes no sense to try to share the load with other, unrelated areas and risk expensive computer hardware.

Air conditioning units require supplies of air and (usually) water. Fire prevention includes making sure the fire won't find a ready entry to the computer through the air conditioner. Water supplies must be controlled to be sure that burst pipes won't destroy the hardware. As electricity-consuming equipment, the air conditioning needs its own power, separate again from the computer. Often, a second cooling unit is appropriate, to be sure that if one fails all cooling is not lost, and the system can continue to function.

Automatic humidity- and temperature-monitoring devices should be installed in climate-controlled computer rooms; the records should be examined regularly to be sure that the climate control is functioning properly.

As solid-state technology continues to improve, the amount of heat generated by computers and the resulting air conditioning need is decreasing. Most personal computers require no more "comfort" than people, and this is also true of many minicomputers and some mainframes. In fact, the primary air conditioning problem found in offices with many microcomputers, is uncomfortable people. A lot of computers collectively generate a considerable amount of heat, as do copiers and even typewriters; offices not designed to handle the load can get to be very uncomfortable workplaces. This does nothing good for productivity; to help keep a "happy company" the risk management team needs to consider cooling the people as well as the computers.

13.5 WATER EXPOSURES AND PROBLEMS

Water exposure problems can be caused by something as simple as a window open during a rainstorm to something as wide-ranging (and outside an individual organization's control) as a collapsed tunnel letting a river into most of downtown Chicago's sub-basement system. A short list of common problems could include:

- flood, whether from weather or municipal facility problems
- basements (water from an upper floor problem tends to wind up in basements)
- roofs (leakage; burst drainpipes during heavy storms; etc.)
- snow load problems
- hurricane and other weather phenomena
- sprinklers (but see Fire Protection, section 13.7)
- air conditioning (often uses water as a coolant or heat transfer fluid)

Careful attention to drainage can help with many of these problems. Location of the computer room may avoid some. Weather precautions vary depending on the local climate. Sprinklers do an excellent job of extinguishing fires, and—*if the water is clean*—may not seriously damage computer equipment. Sometimes, simply drying out the computer is sufficient; sometimes specialized recovery techniques are needed. For events like tunnel collapses in Chicago, insurance may be the only answer, unless location of the data center outside the risk area is feasible.

13.6 FIRE PREVENTION

Fire prevention is not the same as fire protection. *Protection* refers to detecting fire and minimizing damage to people and equipment when it happens. *Prevention* is avoiding the problem in the first place and usually is much less costly and rather more effective in minimizing damage.

Most jurisdictions have fire codes, which will specify legal requirements for minimum fire prevention measures. Expert advice should be sought to ensure that the information systems activities conform to applicable fire code regulations.

Four elements of prevention are outlined here:

1. Computer room construction
2. Employee training
3. Testing
4. Smoking

Construction

The materials used in a computer room should be as fireproof as practical. Combustible material (stacks of paper, for example) should not be stored in computer rooms, or indeed around any other electrical equipment. False ceilings should not be flammable. Rugs, unless specially designed for the purpose, do not belong with computers (for reasons of static electricity as well as flammability).

Magnetic tapes are difficult to ignite when stored in containers, but also difficult to extinguish when ignited, and they produce poisonous combustion products when they burn. If the media storage vault opens onto the computer room (a very common design, for excellent efficiency reasons), special attention is needed to minimize spread of a fire between the equipment and the media vault.

Fire regulations should be known to, and observed by, all employees

Employees should be given training in fire prevention as well as in what to do when a fire does occur. The training should include instructions about exits, extinguishing equipment available, emergency power and other shutoffs.

Fire procedures should be tested periodically with fire drills

(This normally will be required by local regulations as well as being simple common sense.) There is a risk here: Too few fire drills will not maintain familiarity with procedures, too many will create a "boy who cried wolf" situation where real alarms may be ignored.

"No smoking"

For fire risk and other reasons, smoking should not be allowed around computers. This also applies to personal computers—the lifetime of diskettes in environments with cigarette smoke may be very short indeed as the smoke particles can adhere to the media via static and other charges and cause read errors. Smoking also provides a source of ignition. Everyone probably has seen the "worm tracks" in carpets where cigarette smoking is common and ashes fall to the rug; a cigarette dropped into a waste paper box could cause a very destructive fire.

13.7 FIRE PROTECTION

If prevention does not work, fire protection becomes the issue. The first thing is to detect the fire, preferably while it is still small and controllable.

Fire-detection systems are common and inexpensive. Ionization-type smoke detectors react quickly to the charged particles in smoke (remember what charged particles in cigarette smoke can do to oxide surfaces on diskettes). Photoelectric detectors react to light blockage caused by smoke. Heat detectors react to the heat of a fire. Combinations of these detectors can detect a fire very quickly, and often before there is a serious problem. Most local fire codes now require smoke detectors in residences; the mass production of them has brought the costs down drastically. Effective smoke detection, including both ionization and photoelectric detectors, can be had for a small investment.

The first rule after a fire is detected (either by smoke, heat, or other means) is: *Get the people out*. People are the most important asset and are difficult for an organization to replace, as well as having high intrinsic value. Only after all personnel are safe and accounted for is it appropriate to attempt to put out a fire, and then only after calling the fire department.

Many fire extinguishing systems are available. Portable fire extinguishers always should be available near any electrical equipment, including computers. These extinguishers must be examined periodically to be sure they remain useful. For computers, type ABC extinguishers are appropriate, since combustible solids (class A), combustible liquids (class B), and electricity (class C) all are common in computer room fires. Get the people out *first*, then an attempt may be made to extinguish a small fire using portable or other extinguishers. The primary purpose of extinguishers is to make sure that an escape route can be cleared; the fire department always should be called and the people evacuated before any extinguishing attempts are undertaken.

Fixed systems include carbon dioxide extinguishers, with or without directing hoses. The entire computer room may be flooded with carbon dioxide to put out most fires by depriving them of oxygen to support combustion; with hoses, the gas may be directed at specific fire sites. Such systems are expensive and should not be automatic: They deprive people (such as computer operators) of oxygen, as well as fires. Installation of such systems definitely is a job for professional advice and services.

A fire-protection system that is safer for people and that extinguishes fires without irreparably damaging computer equipment uses Halon 1301 gas. This gas has the convenient property of smothering fires without being quickly fatal to people, so automatic systems can kill the fire while allowing people enough time to get out. Halon systems are definitely installations requiring specialized expertise. Professionals should be engaged. Halon systems also are expensive as are tests of the system (a refill can cost over $1,000). Such elaborate fire systems probably are appropriate mainly in mainframe installations. Portable Halon units containing Halon 1301 and Halon 1211 are available and may be appropriate in spite of greater cost (standard fire extinguishers usually will seriously damage equipment they are directed near, while Halon does not). (Halon 1301 and Halon 1211 are trademarks of chemical compounds, owned by Great Lakes Chemical Company Inc. The details of their composition are not relevant in this text and are not public information in any case. Halon 1301 is not self-pressurizing and requires expensive pressure systems for a fire installation; Halon 1211 *is* self-pressurizing, and can be put into a portable extinguisher, either alone or mixed with Halon 1211. Such portable extinguishers have become available as normal retail items.)

With the signing of the Montreal protocol in 1987, Canada, the United States, the European Community, and 23 other nations have agreed to control the production and consumption of certain chlorofluorocarbon compounds (CFCs), including the Halon group. These ozone-depleting substances include some refrigerants and, relevant to this discussion, Halon 1211, Halon 1301, and Halon 2402. These Halons are used primarily in fire-extinguishing applications. The CFC compounds are implicated in the depletion of the ozone layer, a potentially serious global environmental problem.

The timetable for implementation of the Montreal protocols was advanced in 1992, and chlorofluorocarbon fire systems may not be a viable alternative for new, or even existing, installations by the end of the 1990s.

Regulations regarding the use of Halon vary, but typically include the recommendations:

• When planning fire protection for new installations, all alternative options (carbon dioxide, water, etc.) should be fully explored before deciding to use Halon.

• When Halon is used, full-discharge testing should be avoided in favor of alternative test procedures.

Alternative test procedures include a room pressurization test, and the "puff test." Standards for a room pressurization test are available from national fire-protection groups. The puff test involves putting lightweight caps over outlets and using air to ensure that piping is free from obstructions. The professional should ensure that correct procedures and relevant local regulations are known and followed.

It is a good idea to avoid water in computer room fires; automatic sprinkler systems normally use water. First, computer fires usually involve electricity; water conducts electricity. Second, water is likely to damage computer equipment seriously, and may do more damage than small fires. The fact remains however, that water is an excellent way to extinguish fires—one reason it is used by fire departments. In the absence of electrical power, clean water should not damage computer systems, although they must be dried soon and carefully to avoid rust and corrosion problems.

A special problem often overlooked in using water to extinguish fires is how long the water has been "sitting around" in the building's pressurized system. Since fires often disrupt electrical power, building sprinkler systems usually have separate water supplies, not dependent on outside electricity or piping. One way to do this is to have a reservoir somewhere high and separate pipes that are always filled. Another alternative is a separately powered pump system, usually located in a building's basement. (This is called a "wet standpipe" system; in a "dry standpipe" system, water is pumped into the building system from the outside by the fire response units.) Such reservoirs tend to be filled once, then checked for level periodically; it is rare to see checks for purity as well as level. The statement made above that water conducts electricity is not strictly true: *Distilled* water is not a conductor under normal circumstances. However, *tap water*, and especially water that has resided in a reservoir for an unknown time, is *not* distilled water. Some of it can be decidedly contaminated. The main lesson from a security perspective is that computer room fire protection should consider carbon dioxide or Halon, not the building's sprinkler system.

13.8 TAPE AND MEDIA LIBRARIES, RETENTION POLICIES

Computers work with data, and the data, and information into which the data are processed, generally need to be stored. This is the job of magnetic tape, diskettes, and other "media." The list of media is long already, and grows daily. (It also shrinks: Punched cards no longer are common.)

Different media have different characteristics and different capacities. All media contain data, and the data on the media are just as valuable and just as sensitive in movable form as when being used by the computer. Removable media, by definition, also are at least somewhat portable. This presents a security and control risk. It usually is recommended that there be a tape/media library for storing such things.

Depending on the installation, the media library may range in size from a small cabinet up to a rather large warehouse-sized space. Whatever the size, the media storage area should be:

- *Restricted*

  It needs *at least* as careful control as the area in which the data are used. Many computers are not especially portable; removable media are. The equivalent of a small book can fit onto a 3-1/2-inch diskette that will fit easily into a shirt pocket. If the "book" (e. g., the corporate budget) is sensitive, careful protection is needed. All of the access control recommended for any other restricted area also is needed in the media storage area.

- *Controlled*

  Someone should have specific responsibility for keeping records of media entering the library and leaving, and for conducting frequent inventory of the contents. Any discrepancies should be followed up immediately.

- *Locked*

  This is elementary, but frequently ignored. Some form of automatic locking mechanism is preferable, so carelessness cannot lead to a large exposure.

- *Protected from fire*

  Media contain, as an acquired value, information that may be expensive or impossible to replace, and that may be valuable to others as well. The storage area should be separate from the rest of the computer resource and should have its own independent fire protection. This could be elaborate in a large installation, or fairly simple in a small shop.

No general rules on fire and access protection are practical as media vary too much in their characteristics. Punched cards were flammable and had to be kept in humidity-controlled areas to prevent warping, which can cause feed jams. Magnetic tapes are sensitive to heat and burn fiercely but are not especially easy to ignite. Optical storage media are extremely long-lasting and are not fragile (but have very high capacities and may need more careful protection because of the sheer volume of information they hold).

A minimum rule is that any sensitive data should have at least two backups, at least one stored in a different building than all others. There is more on this topic in Chapters 4 and 14.

13.9 DOCUMENT (HARD-COPY) LIBRARIES

Many considerations that apply to storage of media also apply to storage of paper documents. Security considerations are essentially the same, with the exception that the exposure due to unauthorized access is lower since information on paper is far less dense than magnetic media. While the risk of some single document, or small number of documents, being compromised is higher, the risk of loss of enough information to form a coherent overall picture is much lower. (Of course, some single documents may be highly critical, just as some data files may be unusually sensitive.)

In terms of physical storage, paper is more resistant to heat from fires than are magnetic media. Offsetting this, paper is much easier to ignite, and such fire suppressants as water will damage paper seriously when they might not significantly affect magnetic media. Therefore, physical storage for paper documents needs to be:

- larger in volume than for magnetic media
- protected from water damage more carefully
- treated as a fuel repository and kept well separated from more sensitive media

A useful checklist (adapted from *Disaster Planning for Government of Alberta Records*) is:

1. Keep passages unobstructed.
2. Do not store records on the floor.
3. Do not leave original documents on desks overnight.
4. Store cellulose-based nitrate films separately, and treat them as flammable and hazardous goods.
5. Do not pack files too tightly (water can cause swelling and burst packaging).
6. Set materials back slightly from shelf edges to lessen vertical fire propagation.
7. Avoid basement storage.
8. Check areas where condensation may be a problem (pipes, windows, etc.).
9. Install shelving at least 12" from outside walls, 2" from inside walls, and with bottom shelves at least 4" above the floor.
10. Store more valuable material on upper shelves and upper floors.
11. Avoid carpeting in storage areas.

13.10 WASTE DISPOSAL

One of the "classic" computer crimes reported in the literature involved a person gaining accounts and passwords to get into a computer system, and instructions on how to compromise it, by going through a telephone company's waste bins. The security and control principle here is that discarded listings, media, and anything else containing data or information, remain sensitive (if they were in the first place). Control on disposal is needed.

Classified wastes should be:

- Stored in separate containers
- Collected frequently, by security cleared personnel
- Retained in a secure area
- Destroyed by cleared personnel, using an approved and effective method (shredding, incineration, etc.)

Note that the cleaning staff must be cleared, or kept out of areas containing sensitive assets.

Some points should be kept in mind here:

- Most personal computer operating systems do not actually *erase* data files when the operator says "erase" or "delete"; they set a flag indicating the file is "deleted." The flag can be reset, and fragments of data may still exist (some of applications software also does not necessarily destroy data when you "delete" it: For example, many database products don't delete items until the database is "packed"). In fact, programs exist specifically for the purpose of recovering "deleted" files. Degaussing is needed to be sure of erasure (a degausser generates a strong, varying magnetic field that randomizes the magnetic bits used to store data on magnetic media).

Note that formatting a disk on a personal computer may not destroy data (this depends on the operating system and hardware manufacturer.) Overwriting, degaussing, or physical destruction is necessary

- Data stored on commonly available optical media cannot, at the present state of the technology (1992), be erased; the medium must be destroyed thoroughly. (Read/write optical systems do exist and will be common soon. Read/write optical media are erasable. The WORM (Write Once, Read Many) systems acts like read/write, but actually simply makes use of the enormous capacity of an optical disk to store multiple copies of data, one for each version. WORM has advantages where a record of historical changes is needed; the key here is that the data cannot be erased.)

- "Core dumps" generated during program development are sensitive waste. They contain a great deal of information that can be read by trained personnel, sometimes from areas outside the specific program's authorized accesses. Listings must be controlled as classified waste.

- Some kinds of computer memory stay "live" for a long time (up to years) even with the power turned off. An unauthorized user turning on the machine might get access to sensitive information unless the memory is actually written over with zeroes, or some similar destruction method is used.

- As above, data on magnetic media usually are non-volatile. If you put a customer list or proprietary information on a fixed disk, then sell or trade in the computer, format the disk before it leaves your premises.

"Degaussing" is a coined word relating to removing magnetism (a "gauss" is a measure of the strength of a magnetic field). Diskettes should not lean against a telephone; we could add "don't put a diskette on top of a television or audio speaker." A "degausser" is merely something with a strong magnetic field, preferably a "moving" field, which field is not the same as the patterns on storage media. (In computer terms; properly, degaussing *removes* magnetism, and the discussion here is merely of *changing*.) The magnet that rings a telephone bell, or moves the cone in a speaker, or controls the picture tube in a television, induces a magnetic field that is not at all like data on a diskette. Magnetic media are designed to capture and retain imposed fields; the media don't care what the patterns are. The computer decidedly *does* care. Most firms that deal with magnetic tape have bulk tape erasers (it's much faster than doing it with a tape drive, and tape drives have rather more valuable uses). A recent edition of a commercial catalog lists a "Magnetic Bulk Tape/Floppy Disk Eraser" for $34.95. If sensitive material is stored on magnetic media, a degausser can be very cheap insurance, if it is used regularly.

Security personnel should recall that data stored on *optical* media have a very different, non-magnetic, means of recording, and magnetic fields (and degaussers) are irrelevant. Except for future read/write optical media (and some current, very expensive, systems as well), optical disks *cannot be erased*. Even considerable *physical* damage may not destroy the data. One favorite demonstration of optical-disk sales people has been to pour coffee, or cream, or some such, on a disk, then wipe it off and proceed to read it. (This works better with black coffee; you need to use soap and water to remove sugar and other sticky stuff.) To dispose of an optical disk, *physical destruction* is necessary—breaking it into pieces or melting it works best. (See point 2 above.)

When disposing of classified data, more stringent rules may be necessary. "File wipe" programs exist that actually will overwrite media, rather than "delete" the contents. Advances in technology have made it possible to read nearly any magnetic pattern that ever was imposed onto magnetic media; even a file wipe may not be sufficient for classified material. Physical destruction of media may be required.

In the special case of non-removable media that need repairs or are being discarded, consideration must be given to the risk of advanced techniques being used to read the waste. (Of course, advanced techniques are not needed if a disk being repaired has not been wiped, as noted in the fifth point above.) It is common in high-sensitivity situations to destroy any media, removable or not, that must leave a high-security area for any reason.

13.11 OFF-SITE STORAGE

This topic is considered in somewhat more detail in Chapters 4 and 14. For this section, we note that data (or whatever) stored off-site (somewhere outside the normal computer center) must have a level of security and control at least as good as the computer center has. Extremely tight security in the computer center does little good if backup copies of the same data and information are unsupervised in a warehouse without adequate fire or access control. The same considerations apply while media are being transported.

13.12 PHYSICAL ATTACK PARAMETERS

Several observations regarding site selection and building construction have been made in this chapter. In situations of national security or where terrorism may be a factor, careful attention must be given to measures that will lessen vulnerability to physical attacks

Many sources (for example, *Computer Security Risk Management*, Van Nostrand Reinhold and "Target Hardening," *RCMP Security Information Publications # 3*) provide information about typical times for various methods of physical penetration, using various tools. The tactic of putting power poles in the back of a truck and backing it at high speed into a wall has been mentioned (as has the counter of minimizing long straight lanes and roadways). Similarly, chain link fences can be penetrated with minimal damage to vehicles, but can be strengthened substantially simply by attaching a cable to back up the links.

"Typical" times and other considerations vary greatly among these lists, frequently for the same attack using the same tools. Also, introduction of weapons into a situation materially changes things. Nevertheless, such lists can serve as a guide to physical security measures related to site construction and selection. Perhaps the single most important message from the lists is:

Multiple rings of protection, with different preventive measures requiring different tools for penetration at each barrier, can slow an attack significantly, allowing response teams to arrive.

REFERENCES

Bruschweiler, Wallace S. Sr., "Computers as Targets of Transnational Terrorism," in *Computer Security*, J. B. Grimson and H. J. Kugler (eds.), Elsevier Science Publishers, North-Holland, 1985.

"Case Histories In Computer Security," *Computer Security*, No. 53, July/August, 1983.

Disaster Planning for Government of Alberta Records, Records Management Branch, Alberta Public Works Supply and Services, 10442 - 169 Street, Edmonton, Alberta T5P 3X6, 1987.

"EDP Threat assessments: Concepts and Planning Guide," *RCMP Security Information Publications* # 2, January, 1982.

Emergency Preparedness Canada, *Guide to the Preservation of Essential Records*, EPC 12/87, December, 1987. 121 pages, French & English.

Fites, Philip. E., Martin P. J. Kratz, and Alan F. Brebner, *Control and Security of Computer Information Systems*, W. H. Freeman/Computer Science Press, New York, NY, 1989.

Gallegos, Frederick, Dana R. (Rick) Richardson, and A. Faye Borthick, *Audit & Control of Information Systems*, South-Western Publishing Company, West. Chicago, IL, 1987.

"Good Security Practices for Personal Computers," IBM Data Security Support Programs, First Edition (March, 1984).

Jacobson, Robert V., et al., "Guidelines for Automatic Data Processing Physical Security and Risk Management," *Federal Information Processing Standards Publication 31*, National Bureau of Standards, 1974.

Lobel, J., *Foiling the System Breakers: Computer Security and Access Control*, McGraw-Hill, New York, NY, 1986.

Parker, Donn B., *Computer Security Management*, Reston Publishing Company, Inc., Reston, VA, 1981.

Parker, Donn B., *Fighting Computer Crime*, Charles Scribner & Sons, New York, NY, 1983.

Personal Computer Security Considerations (NCSC-WA-002-85), National Computer Security Center, Ft. George G. Meade, MD, December, 1985.

"Small Computer Systems Security," and "Small Systems Questionnaire," *EDP Security Bulletin*, RCMP "T" Directorate, Vol 12 No. 1, July 1987, Pp 4-7. The questionnaire is not copyrighted and may be reproduced for use; it is also in French and English.

"Target Hardening," *RCMP Security Information Publications* # 3, September, 1983.

14. Operations Security

This term is used to identify the controls over hardware, media, and the operators with access privileges to these.[1]

The professional is expected to know:

- The resources that must be protected
- The privileges that must be restricted
- The control mechanisms available
- The potential for abuse of access
- The appropriate controls
- The accepted norms of good practice

For example, the professional should:

- Be familiar with the capabilities provided by the hardware controls, including:
  - initial program load
  - device address modification
  - memory content modification
  - micro-code load and modification
  - hardware content modification
  - system shutdown

- Be familiar with the potential for:
  - accidental interference with intended operation
  - conversion of the system to the operators use
  - corruption of the audit trail

- Understand the use of:
  - access control
  - instruction and training
  - supervision
  - use and application of hardware locks
  - other controls

DEFINITIONS

Access Control List

A list of entities, together with their access rights, which are authorized to have access to a resource. (ISO 7498-2)

---

[1]This is item 15 in the (ISC)[2] Common Body of Knowledge.

Access Control Mechanism(s)

Hardware or software features, operating procedures, management procedures, and various combinations of these designed to detect and prevent unauthorized access and to permit authorized access to an automated system. (AR 380-380; NCSC-WA-001-85; FIPS PUB 39)

Access Control Roster

A list of personnel, users, and so forth, that documents the degree of access and control for each person. (AFR 205-16)

Contrast this basically operational definition with the more general definition of "access control list" above.

Activity Log

A detective countermeasure that keeps track of all, or selected, activities. (RM)

Administrative Security

The management constraints; operational, administrative, and accountability procedures and supplemental controls established to provide an acceptable level of protection for data. (OPNAVINST 5239.1A; FIPS PUB 39; DOE 5636.2A)

Backup Procedures

The provisions made for the recovery of data files and program libraries, and for restart or replacement of ADP equipment after a system failure or disaster. (AR 380-380; FIPS PUB 39)

Closed Shop

A computer operations area set up such that physical access controls restrict programmers, and others who do not have a need to be present, from being in the area. (WB)

Computer Facility

Physical resources that include structures or parts of structures to house and support capabilities. For small computers, stand-alone systems, and word processing equipment, it is the physical area where the computer is used. (AFR 205-16)

Configuration Management

1. Process of controlling modifications to the system's hardware, firmware, software, and documentation which provides sufficient assurance the system is protected against the introduction of improper modification before, during, and after system implementation. (AFR 205-16)
2. The management of changes made to a system's hardware, software, firmware, and documentation throughout the development and operational life of the system. (NCSC-WA-001-85)

Contingency Management

Management of all the actions to be taken before, during, and after a disaster (emergency condition), along with a documented, tested procedures which, if followed, will ensure the availability of critical ADP systems and which will facilitate maintaining the continuity of operations in an emergency situation. (DOE 5636.2A)

Contingency Plan

A plan for emergency response, backup operations, and post-disaster recovery maintained by an ADP activity as part of its security program. A comprehensive consistent statement of all the actions (plans) to be taken before, during, and after a disaster (emergency condition), along with documented, tested procedures which, if followed, will ensure the availability of critical ADP resources and which will facilitate maintaining the continuity of operations in an emergency situation. (OPNAVINST 5239.1A; NCSC-WA-001-85)

Continuity of Operations

The maintenance of essential services for an information system after a major failure at an information center. The failure may result from natural causes (such as fire, flood, or earthquakes) or from deliberate events (such as sabotage). (GAO)

Controlled Access Area

Either part or all of an environment where all types and aspects of an access are checked and controlled. (AFR 205-16)

Control Zone

The space, expressed in feet of radius, surrounding equipment processing classified information which is under sufficient physical and technical control to preclude a successful hostile intercept attack. (AR 380-380)

Escort(s)

Duly designated personnel who have appropriate clearances and access authorizations for the material contained in the system and are sufficiently knowledgeable to understand the security implications of and to control the activities and access of the individual being escorted. (OPNAVINST 5239.1A; AR 380-380; DCID 1/16-1; DCID 1/16-1; Sup.; DODD 5200.28M)

External Security Audit

A security audit conducted by an organization independent of the one being audited. (FIPS PUB 39)

Individual Accountability

The ability to positively associate the identity of a user with the time, method, and degree of access to an Automated Information System. (NCSC-WA-001-85; AR 380-380)

Internal Controls

The plan of organization and all of the methods and measures adopted within an agency to safeguard its resources, assure the accuracy and reliability of its information, assure adherence to applicable laws, regulations, and policies, and promote operational economy and efficiency. (A-123; DODD 7040.6)

Internal Control Documentation

Written policies, organization charts, procedural write-ups, manuals, memoranda, flow charts, decision tables, completed questionnaires, software, and related written materials used to describe the internal control methods and measures, to communicate responsibilities and authorities for operating such methods and measures, and to serve as a reference for persons reviewing the internal controls and their functioning. (A-123; DODD 7040.6)

Internal Control Review

A detailed examination of internal control to determine whether adequate control measures exist and are implemented to prevent or detect the occurrence of potential risks in a cost-effective manner. (A-123; DODD 7040.6)

Internal Security Audit

A security audit conducted by personnel responsible to the management of the organization being audited. (FIPS PUB 39)

Open Security Environment

An environment that includes those systems in which *one* of the following conditions holds true:

1. Application developers (including maintainers) do not have sufficient clearance or authorization to provide an acceptable presumption that they have not introduced malicious logic.
2. Configuration control does not provide sufficient assurance that applications are protected against the introduction of malicious logic prior to and during the operation of system applications. (CSC-STD-004-85; CSC-STD-003-85; NCSC-WA-001-85)

Open Storage

The storage of classified information, not in GSA-approved secure containers, within an accredited facility while such facility is not occupied by authorized personnel. (AR 380-380)

Operational Data Security

The protection of data from either accidental or unauthorized, intentional modification, destruction, or disclosure during input, processing, or output operations. (AR 380-380; NCSC-WA-001-85)

Operational Site Security Manual

The manual documents the operational requirements, manual security environment, hardware and software configurations and interfaces; all security procedures, measures, and features; and, for computer facilities, the contingency plans for continued support in case of a local disaster. (AFR 205-16)

Operational Security (OPSEC) Indicators

Actions or classified or unclassified information, obtainable by an (OPSEC) adversary, that would result in adversary appreciations, plans, and actions harmful to achieving friendly intentions and preserving friendly military capabilities. (AFR 700-10)

Periods Processing

1. The processing of various levels of sensitive information at distinctly different times. The Automated Information System must be purged of all information before transitioning from one period to the next whenever there will be new users who do not have clearances and the need-to-know for data processed during the previous period. (NCSC-WA-001-85)
2. Processing data of a given classification level during a period of time and data of a different classification during a different period of time. Also applies to changing security mode of operation. (AR 380-380; OPNAVINST 5239.1A)

Personnel Security

1. The procedures established to ensure that all personnel who have access to any sensitive information have the required authorities as well as all appropriate clearances. (FIPS PUB 39; AR 380-380; NCSC-WA-001-85; DOE 5636.2A)
2. The procedures established to ensure that each individual has a background which indicated a level of assurance of trustworthiness which is commensurate with the value of ADP resources which the individual will be able to access. (OPNAVINST 5239.1A)

Real-Time Reaction

A response to a penetration attempt which is detected and diagnosed in time to prevent the actual penetration. (FIPS PUB 39; AR 380-380)

Recovery Procedures

The actions necessary to restore a system's computational capability and data files after a system failure or penetration. (FIPS PUB 39; AR 380-380; NCSC-WA-001-85)

Secure Configuration Management

The use of procedures appropriate for controlling changes to a system's hardware and software structure for the purpose of ensuring that such changes will not lead to decreased data security. (AR 380-380; NCSC-WA-001-85; FIPS PUB 39)

Secure Working Area

An accredited facility which is used for handling, discussing, or processing sensitive defense information. (AR 380-380; NCSC-WA-001-85)

Security Perimeter

The boundary where security controls are in effect to protect assets. (NCSC-WA-001-85)

System High Security Mode

The mode of operation in which the computer system and all of its connected peripheral devices and remote terminals are protected in accordance with the requirements for the highest security level of material contained in the system at that time. All personnel having access to the Automated Information System have a security clearance but not a need-to-know for all material then contained in the system. (NCSC-WA-001-85)

System Manager

The ADP official who is responsible for the operation of an ADP system. (FIPS PUB 112)

System Security Officer (SSO)

The person responsible for the security of an ADP system. The SSO is authorized to act in the "security administrator" role as defined in CSC-STD-001-83. Functions that the SSO is expected to perform include auditing and changing security characteristics of a user. (CSC-STD-002-85; CSC-STD-005-85)

14.1 ORGANIZATION OF COMPUTER OPERATIONS

This topic is expanded from the discussion in Chapter 9, "Organization Architecture."

The phenomenon of replacing mainframe MIPS with networks of microcomputers providing similar MIPS and total storage but at perhaps 5% to 10% of the cost is called *downsizing*. A related term that has begun to see use and may be legitimized in the future is *rightsizing*, or selecting the proper size of computer (perhaps a mainframe, perhaps a network of microcomputers) for the task at hand. The jury is out on how successful downsizing will be.

Replacing major centralized staff with something like the decentralized office automation concept saves people and money, but it may leave an organization seriously exposed to reliability problems and without internal staff to cope with technical needs. Although individual microcomputers usually are more reliable than mainframes, in 1992 networks of microcomputers are *not* more reliable than networks managed by "traditional" mainframe communication technology. The combination of new kinds of problems (new for most organizations, that is) inherent in networks of microcomputers with fewer centralized staff to support the networks can lead to serious operational problems.

In addition to problems with system reliability, problems arise in the area of separation of duties. Often, while the microcomputer network does provide appropriate MIPS at a much lower cost than the mainframe-supported network, much of the savings is offset because security and control of the network is much more difficult without centralized operation.

14.1.1 Mainframes

Mainframes, and some minicomputers as well (so-called "superminis" in particular), can be large computers, both physically and in terms of the amount of work they can handle. They are found in environments where there is a great deal to do, and they handle a very great amount of information. Today, "mainframe" computers also may be quite small; the technology, and the meaning of what a mainframe is, are changing very rapidly. Regardless of the size of the machine, the mainframe is a complex environment. There is far too much work within this environment for a single individual or even a small group of individuals. "Computer operations" in this area means several groups of people who do things like:

- Enter data into computer-readable form
- Deliver output to users
- Check input for obvious errors
- Check output for obvious errors

- Mount tapes and disk packs and run production jobs
- Put paper into printers, change ribbons, and other maintenance jobs
- Monitor the functioning of communications links
- Decollate and burst multiple-copy forms produced during the run
- Order supplies such as paper
- Schedule operators and jobs

This list is not exhaustive (nor unchanging: The data-entry function is being replaced by automated scanning and departmental computing very rapidly). The point is that this environment is complex. There well may be hundreds or even thousands of users and great numbers of batch and on-line jobs, some of which may take up so much computer capability that special scheduling is needed. To make cost-effective use of what may be several million dollars invested in hardware, it is common to schedule operations for three shifts to service users any time they need the machine (and often from anywhere in the world they may be located as well). The organization of such an operation reflects the complexity of what is being done.

An organization chart is presented in Figure 14.1, that identifies many positions which have been found to be needed in the sort of environment typical of mainframes and large minicomputers.

Basically, the operation is split into three components: input-output control, actual operations, and support functions such as technical support and the media library.

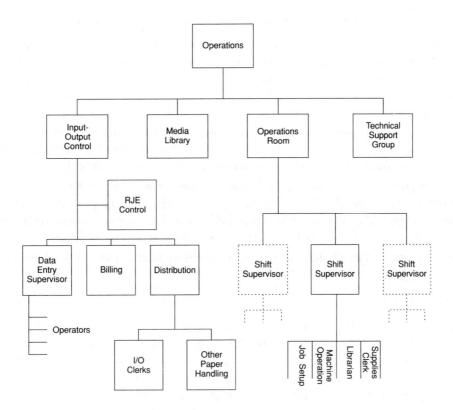

Figure 14.1. Mainframe Computer Operations

Input-output control includes people who are responsible for data entry from manual forms into computer-readable form, and people who are responsible for distributing the resulting output. In some cases, more direct connections may bypass the usual data entry function (for example, entry of purchases from terminals rather than filling out a form manually). Distribution of bills to users for use of computer resources may be included within this group as well, since the distribution function already has the necessary channels set up. Many mainframes support remote job entry (RJE); this function likely also would be found in I/O control.

A mainframe normally includes a large collection of machines that requires a special room or rooms. With many machines depending partly on mechanical processes, some break. Frequently, there will be a technical support group either on call or actually in the operations area at all times, to fix problems. A second support group is those people in charge of the media library. There may be thousands of magnetic tapes, and the media librarian(s) record who signs them out, for what purpose, and their return. The media library also would be responsible for such things as erasing tapes at the end of the retention period. (See section 13.10 for details on disposal.)

The actual operation of the equipment—mounting tapes and disks, putting paper into printers and removing reports, controlling scheduling of batch jobs, and general "trouble-shooting"—falls under the operations room group. There may be two or three shifts with identical staffing, or there may be variations in staffing due to differences in workload for different shifts.

This whole process is complex, and many people are needed to accomplish all the work. However, the critical principle of separation of duties is enforced by having large jobs split up into several small jobs. More on separation of duties will come to light in section 14.2.

In the near future, this sort of organization will change very dramatically for three reasons:

1. More and more functions of the operation of the computer are being automated. There has been little use of automation in the actual operation of the computer (perhaps partly because the job of computer operator has been seen as an entry-level position leading to "better things"). In the late 1980s and early 1990s, the increasing speed and capability of mainframe computers, the shrinkage in their sizes, and changes in characteristics of what is done, have led to experimentation with automating many of the things traditionally done by an operator. Often, the results have been significant improvements in operations effectiveness. This is particularly evident in an on-line communications-oriented environment.

2. The mainframe computer often is evolving towards essentially a database manager and communications processor. With a myriad of local work stations providing data entry and printing capability, as well as removable and fixed disk storage, many of the traditional functions of a mainframe operations staff are performed at remote locations.

3. Downsizing essentially replaces the mainframe entirely with a network, with major effects on operations organization.

14.1.2 Minicomputers

Discounting the special-purpose machine (minicomputers often are responsible for process control such as petroleum refineries, for example), a minicomputer operation is pretty much the same as a mainframe—but not as large. The same functions need to be performed, but a mini normally has far fewer users (perhaps only a dozen or two), so fewer people are required. As well, minicomputers have fewer things to go wrong, so less technical and operator attention is required. The functions of librarian, output control, and operator well may be combined into one person.

Adequate separation of duties for control purposes can be difficult to achieve with the smaller number of people.

A sample organization of a minicomputer installation is shown in Figure 14.2. This shop had two HP-3000 minicomputers, with a number of terminals scattered among several buildings and about a hundred users. The output control function was small enough that only one person, during a day shift, was needed; the technical support was handled on an "on-call" basis (from a city 600 air miles away). Data entry was a separate functional group. There was one operator at a time, with limited technical support capabilities as part of this person's function.

As the capacity and capability of microcomputers increases, and particularly as networks proliferate, the notion of "minicomputer" is changing. Some have claimed that the minicomputer will disappear entirely, except for specialized applications like process control. Certainly, high-end work stations provide computing capability that overlaps into what only a few years ago was considered to be "minicomputer territory."

14.1.3 Microcomputer/Office Automation

By definition, an organization includes more than one person working together. A microcomputer is also called a "personal computer" and, in business, has a major use as an approach to a "manager's work station"; if only one person is using it, there is no organization. All functions —data entry, operations, output control, and so on—still need to be handled; however this usually is done by one person (with, obviously, no separation of duties at all).

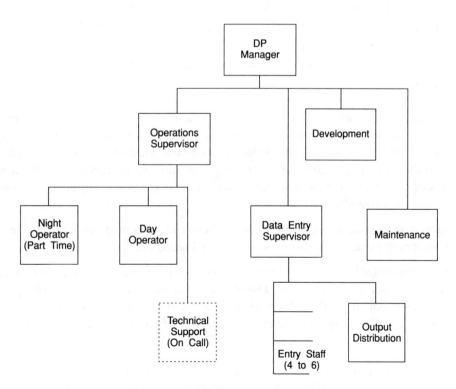

Figure 14.2. Minicomputer Operations

Microcomputers are far more reliable than mainframes have been. Operators and technical support functions are not needed on a regular or frequent basis. For example, mean time between failures in one organization was 2-1/2 weeks, with 128 micros, for an expected value per micro of 320 weeks of continuous (24-hour) operation. This reliability difference is related to complexity and to certain other technical factors, and the difference is decreasing as the size of mainframes decreases. Also, since that reported reliability experience, microcomputers have become yet more reliable.[2]

This lack of need for several people to run the computer raises a number of security and control problems; microcomputers today easily may have more complex data and programs than many mainframes of 1966, and *some* control is appropriate. There is no way to determine how much time is lost due to, for example, inadequate backup, but it certainly must be considerable.

When many microcomputers are in use in an organization, the control problem can become extraordinarily difficult. Managers may each produce impressive-looking printouts in meetings, based on different data—with disastrous effects on productive meeting-time usage. These and other problems—of compatibility both of different brands of equipment and of databases; of a need to help users learn to use packaged programs; and similar issues—have led to some reasonably common and workable solutions. (Denying purchase of micros is not a workable solution: Managers have been known to list them as "electronic typewriters" to sneak into an uncontrolled budget category. When the denial does work, the organization in the longer term loses out to competitors who have the benefit of micros.)

There are five fundamental issues in using microcomputers in large organizations:

1. Deployment (who gets them)
2. Role of the existing data processing center
3. Design responsibility (who ensures proper, cost-effective use of the tools?)
4. Limits of centralized responsibility
5. Networking (how microcomputers link with one another and with mainframes, and how to control and manage the resulting systems)

A number of other problems arise in various circumstances; Thomas Madron's *Microcomputers in Large Organizations* addresses these issues in some detail. Computer technology is changing rapidly and there are no universal solutions for all problems. Most of these other problems really do not fall into the area of "security and control"; use of information centers and "in-house computer stores" does in that it helps to address the issues of coordination, support, and responsibility to use the tools in a cost-effective manner.

Two solutions to standard microcomputer problems in organizations are the "information center" and what may be called "in-house stores." (See Figure 14.3.)

The information center is staffed with people who have business knowledge as well as knowledge of how to use micros and packages. Users often may buy "non-standard" computers—but they will not get support from the information center staff. The basic purpose here is to allow people to use micros effectively while keeping some sort of control of equipment and data. An

---

[2]This comment refers to hardware. The combined hardware *and software* system fails more often than would be tolerated by a competent operations and support staff in a large mainframe operation. Also, *networks* of microcomputers so far have not proven as reliable as similar communications nets supported by mainframes.

example of this organization is illustrated in Figure 14.3. Linking the micros into a network can help to add some control to the problem of differing databases mentioned earlier (and raises its own problems; complex networks have organizational needs for support staff similar to main-frames).

Another proven way to minimize some of the problems with microcomputers is to establish an "internal store" which "sells" microcomputers and software. A variation of this approach is an "approved supplier" list. This technique has proven useful in very large organizations: Potential users of the computers have a fairly good selection to choose from, at reasonable prices since the supplier knows many will be purchased and gives discounts, and all the choices are supported by information center staff.

Control problems and the five fundamental issues apply in large organizations. There are no universal solutions. In smaller organizations, the problems are of a different nature and generally simpler; following hints given in this text will result in reasonable levels of security and control in most situations.

14.2 SEPARATION OF DUTIES

Probably the most fundamental principle of security and control is separation of duties Because of its importance, we repeat the two parts of the principle here (see Chapters 4 and 12 for more details and discussion):

No single individual must have responsibility for the complete processing of any transaction or group of transactions

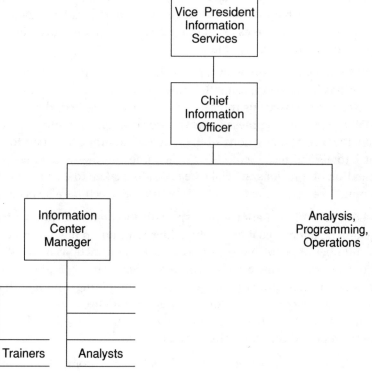

Figure 14.3. "Office Automation" Operations

The perpetration of a fraud must require the collusion of at least two individuals.

From this principle comes the important rule that the functions of computer operation and programming should be divided between two or more individuals. If both these duties were performed by one individual, he or she would have the ability to revise production programs and run these programs on live data to perpetrate or conceal a fraud.

The ideal type of person to hire as an operator should not have programming aptitude or knowledge (but see the comment at the end of this section about reality *versus* ideals.) He or she will be using production programs and data files, and a lack of programming knowledge and aptitude, plus lack of access to detailed documentation, will keep the operator from altering programs fraudulently.

Since programmers have a detailed understanding of the application programs and data, they could alter these easily if allowed to perform operations functions. Keeping the programmers out of the computer room will be a solution in a batch, off-line system. However, when there is on-line programming, additional controls are required. For example, password control mechanisms should allow programmers to access only *test* programs and data, not production programs or live data. Some large organizations go to the length of having development done on separate computers, with no connection whatever to production machines or data.

In addition to separating system design and programming from operations, it is desirable to have an independent data control group and a separate media library. Sensitive media (such as payroll files) should be released from the library only to the operators, and only at the time scheduled for a particular run (for example, payroll check printing). This would reduce opportunities for unauthorized changes.

The data control group, also known as the "input-output control group," reconciles control totals, record counts, and hash totals (see below for more detail on hash totals), and follows up any errors or discrepancies. This serves as an independent check on processing and thus the control group must be separate from the operator.

A favorite way to penetrate systems in the past has been in the handling of rejected transactions. One way that has been used frequently to defraud systems (manual as well as computerized) is to enter deliberately erroneous transactions. These are rejected; the perpetrator (who usually has responsibility for handling these "rejects"—for example, a night operator) then replaces them with seemingly correct transactions—but with, for example, the "pay to" account number changed. The batch totals and record counts stay the same, but the wrong person gets the money. In analyzing separation of functions, special care should be taken to ensure that this sort of intentional distortion cannot be perpetrated by one individual: Corrections also need approvals.

The sheer amount of work and appropriate specialization tends towards adequate separation of duties in large organizations. Smaller organizations tend not to have so much work, nor to be able to afford the number of people necessary to separate all functions as would be desirable. At the limit, if only one person is using a microcomputer, there is no separation at all. Perhaps there is no need for separation here—but what if the person is preparing a budget that will be used to make critical decisions? Is there no need for an independent check on the results? (Lack of such an independent check in a situation very similar to this budget scenario led to a company losing millions in one of the reported computer supported frauds.)

In companies with poor or no segregation (such as the microcomputer example above), there should be increased supervision and careful analysis of output by management.

The guidelines stated in the revised *Computer Control Guidelines, Second Edition* [CICA 1986], from the accounting profession, are summarized throughout this book where they apply to specific topic areas. These guidelines have details of recommended separation of duties in many circumstances.

Many of the specific comments above violate what has been said in Chapter 6 about training: Operators are denied a career path into programming that has been traditional, for instance. The extreme of doing development on a separate machine, even when combined with use of that machine as a hot site backup, is an expensive practice. Other costs, in personnel and management time as well as in dollars, arise from ideal separation of duties. Company management, supported by the risk analysis, must decide what to implement when.

Separation of duties is an ideal, to which any accountant or auditor will subscribe. The reality is a need for effective management of a tradeoff between risk of fraud and cost of the controls (extra personnel, for example). The risk analysis process described in Chapter 3 should have identified and valued assets that are exposed; consideration of separating functions can be costed out, and the cost compared to the potential loss.

14.3 CONTROLS AT INTERFACES

Computer and other information systems deal with data entered into them, and produce some form of information as output. The points where things enter a system or leave it are called "interfaces." If the analysis is at a general level, interfaces include such entities as the data entry clerk, or the output clerk, or a terminal connected to a system. At a more in-depth level of analysis, each program could be a "system," where the interface is the point at which a data file from another program is accepted. An example at the detailed level might be an "integrated" accounting system that passes transaction files between programs, or the edited transaction file from an entry program going on to the master file update program. (Another term for these interfaces is "control points." This phrase can be confusing since accounting professionals use it in one sense and computer professionals often intend a slightly different meaning; "interface" will be used in this text.)

Controls at *all* interfaces to systems are crucial to a secure and controlled environment. If someone can alter the file of "edited data" mentioned in the previous paragraph, system security and control checks may be bypassed. This is the "integrity" property of data addressed in Chapter 12.

Data that enter systems must be complete and accurate, and integrity must be maintained, to ensure control. *Complete* means that *all* data crossing an interface must be recorded and must successfully cross the boundary. None may be lost, and none may be added; otherwise, security and control may be breached. Ways to ensure completeness include many very sophisticated techniques; however, one very simple means is available and effective: Count how many transactions there are (record counts). At every interface, transaction counts on each side need to be maintained to ensure proper control and completeness. Procedures to use this (detective) control include having people or programs ensure that record counts are consistent. Results of processing offer opportunities here as well: The number of entries in the old master, added to the number of new entries, less the number deleted, must be the total in the new master. Similar basic counts need to be established at every interface. (See below and Chapters 3 and 12 for more on these application controls and some that apply to on-line systems as well.)

On-line systems pose more complex problems in ensuring completeness. Since transactions across interfaces happen at random rather than in neat batches, batch totals and batch record counts are not appropriate. Probably the only method that will ensure completeness in an on-line system is to record *every* transaction in the system and "time-stamp" it. The transaction is copied, and the originator and timing recorded; thus, "who did it when" is available, and recovery from "system crashes" is feasible. More elaborate schemes involve copying "old" and "new" versions of every data element changed as well. Combining all of these can ensure that completeness is maintained, and that auditability in the sense of identifying "who, what, where, when" also is maintained. (Auditability in the sense used by public auditors may not be maintained, and there remains the risk of sophisticated criminals altering the records of their fraudulent transactions.) Using such an elaborate mechanism also adds considerably to system development and operating costs; intelligent management will compare such increased costs with the exposures identified in the risk analysis before making decisions.

The second characteristic that data must possess is *accuracy*. Since this is dependent on individual systems' needs, no universal rules can be given, save one: Editing routines must check *every data element entered in every transaction. Nothing* can be assumed; experience clearly shows that **all** data must be checked. Reasonableness checks and others are part of the standard elements in programmed checking.

Once accuracy is determined, it must be maintained: This is the *integrity* part of data across interfaces. Every program must check every data input to ensure that it has not been changed in an unauthorized manner while "between programs." Every batch transferred from one person to another must be checked. (See the discussion of integrity in Chapter 12.) Detective controls include recording and checking record counts, batch totals, hash totals, check digits on numbers, and others. In computer operations, the emphasis is on detecting changes in data while it is not under the control of the system and ensuring that no bad data gets across interfaces without detection and appropriate action.

Hash totals involve adding things like account numbers to get some number that should not change. For example, the sum of the employee numbers in a payroll run could be calculated, and recalculated at each control point. If an employee number is altered between control points (for instance, to pay the wrong person), the *sum* of the employee numbers will change even though the number of transactions and perhaps the total dollars stay the same.

Check digits are arithmetic relations built into numbers; if an employee number with a check digit were altered, the new number would have to have a correct check digit or it would be caught immediately. Credit card numbers, Social Insurance numbers and Social Security numbers, and bank account numbers contain check digits for this reason.

One operational method of helping to ensure completeness, accuracy, and integrity is the Input-Output Control Group mentioned earlier. Integrity *inside* the computer is the responsibility of good systems and programs. Data entering is counted, entered, and edited. It then goes into the computer as a "black box." Once the computer is finished, reports are generated; these reports should include printing of the appropriate control totals, and the output clerk would compare with the input counts and totals. Output then is directed to the appropriate recipients.

Specific recommendations to ensure that output reaches the proper people include the following:

- Restricting access to the printed output storage areas

- Printing heading and trailing banners with recipients' names and locations
- Requiring signed receipt acknowledgments before releasing output
- Printing "no output," with banners, when the report is empty

The I/O clerk also should check that control totals and record counts are appropriate, and inform management of discrepancies.

Note that the effect of these recommendations is to ensure separation of duties, and to ensure that different people check, as part of their normal job responsibilities, interface controls. Again, we emphasize that in a small shop, this level of separation may not be practical; management must be aware of the risks and security and control issues involved, and make an intelligent decision: Is a high level of control worth the cost? The risk analysis should indicate the potential loss, making the cost comparison simple: Do not spend more to avoid a problem than the problem would cost if it occurred.

14.4 MEDIA CONTROLS

Tapes, removable disks, diskettes, and even punched cards and paper backup copies of original transactions, are valuable data and information resources in any organization. In computer operations in any reasonably sized organization, there will be a tape and/or disk or diskette library. These "media"—magnetic tape, magnetic disk, diskette, perhaps optical disks or other storage media — need some specific controls in a good operation.

First, volume labels are an absolute requirement before any other control measure can be effective. Every volume (reel of tape, disk pack, diskette, optical disk, or whatever, containing data stored on media) must be labeled, both in human-readable form and in machine-readable form. Both labels should indicate:

- Date created
- Date to be destroyed (or retention period)
- Who created it
- Name of the volume/file(s) is(are)
- Version of the volume/file(s)
- Security control classifications

Many other items, such as length of files, may also be appropriate. Periodic checks should be made to ensure that human-readable labels on the outside of the volume match the machine-readable labels on the media themselves. Any discrepancies naturally must be reported and followed up.

An interesting variation sometimes found is use of color-coded media. Diskettes and tapes can be purchased with containers in different colors. If a coding scheme is used, such as "black for backup, red for production files, no yellow or blue media in this shop," then inappropriate uses can be detected very rapidly by sight.

Data volumes need to be stored somewhere. While the "somewhere" may be different for a 3-1/2-inch diskette or a 2,400-foot reel of magnetic tape, any data relating to a computer needs to be stored in an identified place, with characteristics appropriate for safe storage of the media which will go into the storage area. Ideally, there should be logs of entry, removal, replacement (another interface, really). The locations of all storage areas should be included in operations and backup and contingency planning documentation.

There is a different level of need in small organizations than in an organization storing perhaps hundreds of thousands of magnetic tapes; security needs will vary as well. The key is to *have* a defined storage area ("library"), and to apply appropriate controls to ensure that what is stored there is labelled, and that it is possible to trace who "checked it out" when.

It is especially important to emphasize the need for careful labeling and for control of media in an office automation or personal computer environment. Many people using microcomputers do not have a data processing background and may not be aware of the value of the data on their diskettes, nor of the methods developed by computer professionals to minimize problems. One of the virtues of a risk analysis procedure is that the value of the data on diskettes should be identified. People who may not have been aware of the actual value previously often will initiate their own controls once they realize what their data assets are worth and how much disruption could be caused in case of loss. The control techniques recommended above are neither new nor especially sophisticated; they do work, *if* they are used.

(See section 13.10 for more detail on issues related to disposal of media.)

14.5 BACKUP PROCEDURES

This section is inserted here mainly to emphasize that backups should be done. Details of how often to do backups and other procedures are covered in Chapters 4 and 15 as part of contingency planning and operations management.

In the office automation environment, people may not realize how important it is to keep current backups. Diskettes are sensitive: Leave one leaning on a telephone when it rings, and the magnetic fields created in ringing the bell may make the diskette unreadable. Data on diskettes are valuable. The risk analysis identifies how valuable. Backup procedures are included here simply to emphasize that backup is important.

Three (or more) copies of every file are recommended. One would be the original, in use. A second copy would be of the original, stored away from the computer, but on-site. The third copy should not even be in the same building. (A fourth copy is needed for complete safety while transporting the second and third backups, so there is no risk of losing the only two backups while in the same vehicle, and also losing the original due to some computer problem.)

14.6 CONSOLE CAPABILITIES

As noted in the Common Body of Knowledge segment at the beginning of this chapter, operations security involves risks related to the capabilities of the hardware in the computer room. Although the capabilities at the console are different from one computer to another, a typical outline of such exposures might include:

- Initial Program Load (IPL): The program that actually starts the operating system is controlled from the console. An operator has an opportunity to load the wrong program (accidentally or intentionally), possibly seriously compromising operations or security.

- Device address modification: The address of a device could be altered, thus effectively re-routing input or output and perhaps compromising security.

- Memory content modification: In some systems, it is possible to modify memory directly from the console, bypassing any software controls.

- Micro-code load and modification: Most hardware is controlled at a level deeper than the operating system by micro-code. This code defines such things as precisely what actions are to be caused by specific machine instructions. Loading the wrong micro-code could interfere seriously with the computer or pose a serious security exposure, again bypassing any possible software controls. (This exposure is more to a systems engineer than to an operator, as micro-code is a very specialized area and loading it is not a typical operator duty.)

- Hardware content modification: An operator typically can re-assign the mapping between logical and physical devices as noted above. Another exposure to operations personnel is hardware modification: physically removing, altering, or replacing components. Examples could include insertion of transmitters that would constitute a covert channel, replacement of a large disk in a microcomputer with a small one (probably for personal gain), and similar activities.

- System shutoff is handled from the console or operations area, just as is IPL. Whether the concern is for accidental or intentional inappropriate shutdown, this capability is a potential exposure.

These and similar capabilities are necessary to run the system and recover from failures of one sort or another, and cannot be restricted without severely impacting on system reliability. Personnel controls and appropriate separation of duties are the most useful in controlling misuse of the capabilities of the hardware in the operations realm. Physical control measures (such as not permitting staff to bring unauthorized electronic equipment into the computer room) are appropriate as well.

14.7 PERSONNEL CONTROLS

Computer operations rooms contain expensive, sensitive equipment. In some cases, data and information in the room are even more valuable than the hardware. Controls on the people inside computer rooms are needed. The level of control depends on the specific environment: A personal computer at someone's desk is not at much risk of anything (except being picked up and carried away) if the diskettes with software and data are locked up (and there is no hard disk included). A minicomputer will be larger physically and may be in a separate, climate-controlled room; more control is needed here. A mainframe computer typically has a secure and climate-controlled room with very restricted access. If national secret projects are under way in the computer, very stringent controls indeed may be needed, even for personal computers. There are no universal detailed rules.

There are two general principles that will apply nearly anywhere, though:

1. Hire competent personnel.
2. Restrict access to people who actually need it.

The first principle applies everywhere in any organization. Incompetent personnel are an obvious security and control problem anywhere. Chapter 6 detailed a number of principles and specific controls in personnel areas, which if followed should minimize problems in computer operations.

Computers, and any other valuable or sensitive assets, should be accessible to, and used by, only people who actually have a valid reason. For mainframe computers with special rooms, this translates to careful access controls such as locked doors, no-admittance signs, receptionists and even guards. The same would apply to sensitive or large minicomputer installations. Every person other than regular staff who enters or leaves the computer area should be recorded: who, why, when in, when out. In large or very sensitive operations, such things can be done automatically with (expensive) computer-controlled card-lock systems. Less expensive is a system with a receptionist who in addition to secretarial duties ensures people use sign-in logs appropriately. In any case, each person should have an identification card, with his or her photograph and access permissions attached; use and display of this card should be required in sensitive areas.

Separation of duties also is a "personnel control." Another is alertness on the part of supervisors and fellow employees. Any large change in someone's behavior may indicate problems that could lead to security and control exposures. (Of course, in any case it is good management practice to be sensitive to personal problems of employees.) Such things should be checked out.

The basic principles of controlling personnel in computer operations are simply to have competent staff and to keep unauthorized people out. Many ways to accomplish these objectives are available.

14.8 DOCUMENTATION CONTROLS

It is not appropriate to depend on secrecy of documentation as a control of access to system program or other restricted functions. Just as in cryptanalysis the attacker is assumed to know the algorithms employed, it is prudent to assume that penetrators have access to all documentation relating to the operating system or application program. This includes so-called "undocumented functions," which are actually trap doors in a sense. Many operating systems are famous—or notorious—for the undocumented functions available. (These are discussed as maintenance hooks above.) Sometimes these are intentional: tools that make it easy for system maintainers to perform unusual functions. If such intentional functions are included with malicious intent, they would be classified as trap doors or Trojan horses. Most operating systems and application programs also include *unintentional* functions, commonly known as "bugs."

Both documented and undocumented functions, of course, are implicit in the actual code that implements programs. Tools exist (and are being improved continually) to analyze existing code in the context of maintenance of some billions or trillions of lines of code in existing, operating, poorly documented application systems. Even if we consider that copies of the documentation for a sensitive program are tightly controlled, these analysis tools can be applied to the analysis of operating system code just as well as to analysis of application program code.

REFERENCES

"Case Histories In Computer Security," *Computer Security*, No. 53, July/August, 1983.

Computer Control Guidelines Second Edition, Canadian Institute of Chartered Accountants (CICA), February, 1986.

Fisher, Royal, *Information Systems Security*, Prentice-Hall, Englewood Cliffs, NJ, 1984.

Fites, Philip. E., Martin P. J. Kratz, and Alan F. Brebner, *Control and Security of Computer Information Systems*, W. H. Freeman/Computer Science Press, New York, NY, 1989.

Gallegos, Frederick, Dana R. (Rick) Richardson, and A. Faye Borthick, *Audit & Control of Information Systems*, South-Western Publishing Company, West. Chicago, IL, 1987.

"Good Security Practices for Personal Computers," IBM Data Security Support Programs, First Edition (March, 1984).

Gorrill, B. E., *Effective Personnel Security Procedures*, Dow Jones-Irwin, Inc., Homewood, IL, 1974.

Lobel, J., *Foiling the System Breakers: Computer Security and Access Control*, McGraw-Hill, New York, NY, 1986.

Madron, Thomas, *Microcomputers in Large Organizations*, Prentice-Hall, New York, NY, 1983.

Parker, Donn B, *Computer Security Management*, Reston Publishing Company, Inc., Reston, VA, 1981.

"Small Computer Systems Security," and "Small Systems Questionnaire," *EDP Security Bulletin*, RCMP "T" Directorate, Vol 12 No. 1, July 1987, pages 4-7. The questionnaire is not copyrighted and may be reproduced for use; it is also in French and English.

15. Information Ethics

Information ethics can be described as the study or philosophy of right conduct with respect to information. A member is expected to know:[1]

- Duties with respect to information; for example, duties owed by:
  - the collectors of data to the data subject
  - data custodians to data owners
  - data users to owners and subjects
  - system users to system managers, sponsors, or owners
  - system managers to users
  - users to other users
  - other

- Origins of those duties, for example:
  - the common good or community interest
  - legitimate national interest
  - individual or civil rights
  - enlightened self-interest
  - criminal law
  - tort law
  - contract
  - patents
  - copyrights
  - professional ethics or practice
  - generally accepted standards of good practice
  - other public policy
  - tradition and culture
  - religion
  - other concepts of fairness, justice, or equity

15.1 ETHICAL DECISION-MAKING

Privacy

The right of individuals to control or influence what information related to them may be collected and stored and by whom and to whom that information may be disclosed.

Note: Because this term relates to the right of individuals, it cannot be very precise and its use should be avoided except as a motivation for requiring security. (ISO 7498-2)

---

[1]This is item 16 in the (ISC)² Common Body of Knowledge.

This definition of privacy, from the standard ISO 7498-2 *Open Systems Interconnection Basic Reference Model Security Architecture*, illustrates one of the dilemmas that arise when attempting to incorporate ethical considerations into a technical discussion of information systems security. In this example, the inherent imprecision of the term is emphasized. In the discussion in Chapter 1, it was noted that academics hold a value system which stresses the concept of free dissemination of information, while military and national security agencies hold a value system that generally stresses precisely the opposite. Here, two different but equally valid perspectives collide.

The *duties* of custodians of information to the owners of the information are straightforward and have been addressed in several places already. These duties are defined by accepted norms of behavior and such things as client contracts and national laws. As noted in the (ISC)² Common Body of Knowledge, the origins of these duties include defined areas like:

- criminal law
- laws and regulations relating to civil and individual rights
- tort law
- contracts
- patents
- copyright considerations

Another straightforward origin for such duties is defined company policy. As a first approximation, a professional should follow such clear guidelines unless ethical considerations override them.

Less straightforward sources of concepts of information ethics arise from less well-defined areas such as:

- the "common good," or community interest
- "legitimate national interest"
- tradition and culture
- religion
- "enlightened self-interest"

Each of the items in the list above is subject to interpretation, and each item varies in differing circumstances. It can be argued that a principle that varies in different cultures, or according to differing circumstances, is not an ethical principle, but merely a guideline. A guideline of such a nature can and should be violated if it conflicts with ethical principles.

Clearly, the "common good" (or perhaps the greatest good of the greatest number, to choose another formulation) is amorphous. In particular, who decides? How does one measure the common good? Over what time frame? What about actions that are *expected* to improve the common good but *certainly* will impact severely and detrimentally some individuals? The common good argument has been used to justify genocidal policies, with the contention that the human race is improved overall if certain groups are removed from the gene pool.

"Legitimate national interest" may offer a justification for over-riding normal ethical principles. One obvious example is that it may be considered in the legitimate national interest in time of war to kill, an action that otherwise seldom is considered ethical except in self-defense. Again, the question arises: Who defines "legitimate?" Trials after the Second World War demonstrated that the societies which now form the Western democracies considered defeated enemies not to have been ethical even though the enemies followed legitimate national interest (as defined by their governments) and performed actions intended to be for the common good of a community.

Tradition and culture clearly vary from place to place and from time to time. They would seem to be poor determiners of ethical principles that do not change over time or in differing situations. Religions that vary from monotheistic to polytheistic to nearly non-theistic offer a very wide range of ethical prescriptions and proscriptions.

Enlightened self-interest may be an excellent guideline for an individual or individual organization in deciding on how to handle information ethics questions. It hardly can be considered a foundation of ethical principles.

One may argue that a primary source of guides for ethical behavior for an information system security practitioner is professional ethics and generally accepted standards of good practice. There is much to this argument. Unfortunately, there *are* no generally accepted standards of good practice in the informatics industry in general, much less for a specialized area such as information systems security. Organizations like ICCP and (ISC)[2] have defined professional codes and standards (some are noted in the next major section); however there are no universally accepted standards or codes. To some extent, this simply reflects a new field of human endeavor. (Since existing codes for legal and accounting professions, some of which have been in place with little change for centuries, are called into question daily due to the effects of technological change, one can not blame the informatics profession for such a lack.)

Nevertheless, several principles seem to cross many different societies, religions, professional codes, and laws:

- There are hierarchies of ethical principles. One has a higher duty to some principles than to others. For example, a duty to legitimate national interest may override normal laws or contracts, but may not override a religious duty.
- Ethical behavior may not be lawful, and behavior may not be ethical even though it is lawful.
- Professionals are expected to know and to abide by relevant laws and contractual agreements, as well as professional codes and guidelines.
- Unless a higher ethical principle applies, laws and contracts should guide conduct. If a higher principle is deemed to apply, the professional must accept responsibility and expect sanctions to be applied by authorities.
- A professional should be guided in the first instance by available codes of conduct and standards of good practice.
- A general principle is to "do no harm." A professional must act in the best interests of the client.
- A general principle is that, if harm or unethical behavior is suspected, inaction is unethical.
- A professional has a duty to avoid deception, particularly of clients or the general public. This includes such areas as accepting work without being competent to do so, misleading clients intentionally or by omission, and disclosure of actual or potential conflict of interest.
- Particularly in informatics, protection of individual privacy and the privacy of the client-consultant relationship is a strong ethical requirement. Protection of confidential information is a requirement second only to protection of privacy.

Such broad principles appear in codes and guidelines that have been adopted by various organizations, even though they may not be generally accepted principles. Specific issues such as religion and culture have been avoided purposefully in the preceding.

Although such surveys fall into the category of tradition and culture, the two editions of *Ethical Conflicts in Computer Science and Technology*, reporting studies by Donn Parker and others in 1977 and 1987 (see References) are excellent sources of information documenting how groups responded to ethically-questionable situations, and how the responses changed in ten years. Studies done using surveys in academic and business environments have shown that in many instances perceptions of ethical behavior held by students and academics differ markedly from those held in the business world. Just as academics and military differ on issues of dissemination of information, so others differ on other issues. The principles in the preceding list may be shared by most. Certainly they are found in one form or another in many codes from many organizations in different countries. The differences found in surveys and workshops demonstrate clearly that the question of ethical behavior appropriate for informatics professionals has not been resolved.

One goal of the efforts of groups like (ISC)^2 is precisely to fill a void in the arena of ethical behavior involving information systems, and to bring together enough people within the informatics profession to approach the criterion of "generally accepted." Hopefully, such efforts will bear fruit.

15.2 PROFESSIONAL SOCIETIES

Many organizations, both governmental and professional societies, are interested in issues of information systems security. In this chapter, we list some of the best-known professional societies and North American governmental activities. These lists are not exhaustive, but are intended to sketch a picture of the breadth of resources available. The professional should maintain contacts with local and relevant broader-scale groups as part of his or her continuing education responsibility. In addition, such groups offer an opportunity to further the development of the field of information systems security, and to help educate the public in security issues.

Many professional societies are involved in activities related to information systems or to information systems security, although only (ISC)^2 concentrates solely on information systems security and represents more than one professional group. Information about a number of professional societies is presented in this section to show something of the range of professional societies and some of the activities they undertake.

Of all the groups listed below, only CSI, ISSA, and (ISC)^2 are specialized in information systems security. For other major groups the connection is through some special interest group or similar construct.

A primary way to encourage the human motivational characteristics necessary to have dedicated and secure personnel is the development of a sense of "professionalism." As with doctors, lawyers, accountants, and engineers, computer professionals should share a common background and expectation of behavior.

People with professional designations have a valuable asset (the certification) that they are very careful to protect. They normally are much less likely to take a chance at crime since the consequences of being caught can be severe. If convicted of a crime or of professionally inappropriate conduct, they can be debarred from their professional society and lose the designation that they have worked hard to obtain. (Some designations require seven years of education and job experience, in addition to examinations. All of those described below require at least five years of education and job experience, in addition to success in demanding professional examinations.) As well, people working towards a professional certificate (such as articling students in an accounting program) are aware that being convicted of committing a crime may wipe out their chance of being admitted to the professional institute.

The dictionary defines a *profession* as, "a calling requiring specialized knowledge and often long and intensive preparation." In practice, however, the general recognition and acceptance of a particular occupation as being a profession is the determinant.

First, we review the notion of professionalism. Aspects of a profession include:

- Image in the public mind
- Codified body of knowledge
- Accredited education program
- Uniform examinations and certification of knowledge
- Apprenticeship or internship
- Code of ethics
- Code of Conduct and good Practice
- Oversight by society (governments)

15.2.1 American Society for Industrial Security (ASIS)

American Society for Industrial Security , 1655 North Fort Meyers Drive, Suite 1200, Arlington, VA, 22209, 703/522-5800.

The American Society for Industrial Security (ASIS) was founded in 1955 in the United States. It presently has a membership exceeding 24,000 in 22 countries. ASIS is an "organization of security professionals who are dedicated to protecting the people, property and information assets of a diverse group of private and public organizations."[2] ASIS is organized on local, regional, and international levels in a global network of over 180 chapters.

ASIS provides programs that enable members to update and exchange information. Efforts include a certification program, seminars, meetings, conferences, a series of professional publications, 29 standing committees (including one for information system security), and a monthly magazine. ASIS is not primarily dedicated to *information systems* security, although an active subgroup (somewhat like the CIPS or DPMA security SIGs) exists. Many of its members are current or former law enforcement personnel.

15.2.2 British Computer Society (BCS)

British Computer Society, 13 Mansfield Street, London W1M 0BP, England, 71/637-0471.

The British Computer Society (BCS) was founded in 1957. It has grown so that it now contains over 30,000 members in over 40 local groupings in the United Kingdom and other Commonwealth countries. In July of 1984, the Society was incorporated under a Royal Charter. The BCS is comparable in size to DPMA in the United States, but operates more internationally.

---

[2]The quotes in this section are from public material describing ASIS.

The British Computer Society publishes examination regulations and an examination syllabus, much as ICCP and others do in North America. They are similar in that each contains the rules under which examinations will be held and marked, and each syllabus (or "Official Study Guide") has a detailed outline of the contents of every examination section lists of references for study and review.

The BCS has all of the trappings of professionalism noted above, including a Code of Ethics and Codes of Practice, formal examinations, prescribed curricula of study, and rather greater visibility through the Royal Charter than DPMA, CIPS, and ICCP have yet achieved in North America.

The BCS material is not immediately relevant in Canada or the United States, but as it derives from the British legal system it was adopted by CIPS as the pattern to follow for the Canadian professional certification Information Systems Professional (ISP). The Data Processing Management Association has agreed to work with the BCS in a joint management development program. Other Commonwealth countries that share the British legal heritage can be expected to consider both the ICCP and BCS patterns, as Canada has done.

15.2.3 Canadian Information Processing Society (CIPS)

Canadian Information Processing Society, 243 College Street, Toronto, ON, M5V 2S9, 416/593-4040.

CIPS is the Canadian Information Processing Society. It was founded in 1958 and grew from interest mainly in Canadian universities to become the largest single information processing group in Canada. CIPS now has over 5,000 members in Canada. CIPS is the official Canadian representative to ICCP and the International Federation for Information Processing (IFIP).

The investigation of professionalism is of interest especially in Canada. In December, 1985, Bill C21 *The Professions and Occupations Registration Act* was passed in Alberta; this law allows professional societies who can prove they represent 25% of the members of a profession and who can meet other criteria to be established as provincial controlling bodies. There is a similar law in Ontario. While these are not licensing powers, this clearly is a first step on the road towards licensing.

CIPS has a National Security Special Interest Group, and a number of local organizations with more or less close affiliations to CIPS and the national organization. The CIPS National Security-SIG is one of the founding organizations of (ISC)².

CIPS introduced the Information Systems Professional (ISP) program in 1989 (section 15.5.6).

15.2.4 Computer Professionals for Social Responsibility (CPSR)

Computer Professionals for Social Responsibility, Inc., P.O. Box 717, Palo Alto, CA, 94301, 415/322-3778.

An organization for computer professionals concerned about social issues. There are active chapters around the world. They produce a newsletter. Issues related to computer security are addressed regularly; however, CPSR provides no certification programs or other similar activities.

15.2.5 Computer Security Institute

Computer Security Institute, Miller Freeman Publications, 500 Howard St., San Francisco, CA, 94105, (415) 267-7651.

The Computer Security Institute is one of the founding members of (ISC)^2. It is a for-profit corporation in California, operating since the late 1970s and acquired by Miller Freeman in 1990. CSI presents conferences, a quarterly review, and a monthly newsletter. Several special-purpose publications such as a *Computer Security Handbook* are prepared from time to time. CSI is the only group listed in this section that is for-profit; CSI meets the needs of some several thousand (over 3,500 in early 1990) members well enough to co-exist with the various not-for-profit societies.

15.2.6 Data Processing Management Association (DPMA)

Data Processing Management Association, 505 Busse Highway, Park Ridge, IL, 60068-3191, 708/825-8124.

The Data Processing Management Association (DPMA) was founded in 1950 in the United States (as the National Machine Accountants' Society). Today, there are some 25,000 members, in Canada and the United States, and many in other countries.

DPMA is an ICCP member, and in fact developed the CDP program and started ICCP. An important component of DPMA's contribution to professionalism in informatics is the Special Interest Group for Certified Professionals (SIG-CP). Through SIG-CP, a network of "Region Certification Ambassadors" has been established in each DPMA Region and in Canada. These people aid local chapters in matters related to the CDP and other ICCP examinations, and in interaction with ICCP.

DPMA includes several Special Interest Groups (SIGs). In 1987, the SIG-CS for Computer Security was created, and this SIG has over 200 members from the general DPMA membership. Like other similar SIGs (see CIPS), DPMA SIG-CS draws on the large resources of the parent group to offer a level of service to members that may exceed what could be offered by a single-interest group. DPMA SIG-CS is a unified body that links members across North America, unlike the CIPS Security-SIG program where very loosely associated local bodies are the primary emphasis.

SIG-CS and SIG-CP are among the founding organizations of (ISC)^2.

15.2.7 EDP Auditors' Foundation (EDPAF)

EDP Auditors' Association, P. O. Box 88180, 455 Kehoe Boulevard, Suite 106, Carol Stream, IL, 60188-0180, 708/682-1200.

The EDP Auditors' Association was founded in 1969. It presently has over 7,000 members, with chapters in major cities worldwide. The Association fosters the professionalism of its members in many ways, including:

- Education (seminars, conferences, other professional forums)
- Information transfer (facilitating communication among members)
- Communication (publishing new developments to the auditing community at large)
- Research

The EDPAA serves members and the public through a newsletter and a bookstore, as well as in the ways noted above.

The EDPAA includes chapters and regions, and has a sister organization in the EDPAF.

The EDP Auditors' Foundation, Inc. (EDPAF) operates the Certified Information Systems Auditor (CISA) certification program, another certificate of significance both to accounting and informatics professionals.

In the absence of clearly recognized information systems security professionals, it is common for the auditor to be called upon to assess security as well as more traditional auditing tasks. This is especially true of the EDP auditor, and the interests of EDPAA and content of the Body of Knowledge and the CISA examination reflect the need for security knowledge.

15.2.8 Information Systems Security Association (ISSA)

Information Systems Security Association, Inc., P. O. Box 809107, Chicago, IL, 60680-9107, 312/644-6610

ISSA was founded in 1982, and is incorporated as a not-for-profit corporation in California. As the name indicates, this organization concentrates specifically on issues of computer security. ISSA currently has at least 24 active chapters, including Ottawa and Toronto Canada, and over 2,000 members. As with the other organizations mentioned in this part of Chapter 15, ISSA serves members and the public through publications, seminars, conferences, and other educational opportunities, and in other ways.

ISSA is a founding organization of (ISC)².

15.2.9 Institute for Certification of Computer Professionals (ICCP)

Institute for Certification of Computer Professionals, 2200 E. Devon Avenue, Suite 268, Des Plaines, IL, 60018, 708/299-4227

The ICCP operates the oldest certification program, including now the CDP, CSP, ACP (Associate Computer Professional), and CCP (Certified Computer Programmer).

The Institute for Certification of Computer Professionals (ICCP) was founded in 1973 by DPMA (U.S.) and was given the CDP program and the responsibility to administer it. The ICCP programs are the most long-lived in the information processing industry.

ICCP has representatives of over 13 groups. These groups collectively represent over 200,000 computer professionals in North America. CIPS was involved, as the Canadian representative, in the creation (in 1975) of ICCP as it now exists. New members join ICCP regularly, and the membership list changes frequently.

15.2.10 International Information Systems Security Certification Consortium, Inc. (ISC)²

(ISC)², P. O. Box 98, Spencer, MA, 01562-0098.[3]

The International Information Systems Security Certification Consortium, Inc. or (ISC)² was formed as a cooperative effort by representatives of several organizations interested in a professional-level certification program for information systems security certification. The mission of (ISC)² is straightforward:

To support a program for the certification of information systems security professionals.

---

[3]Some of this material is reproduced from the Introduction so that it will be collected within this section on professional societies as well as discussed separately.

(ISC)^2 was established in July 1989 as a non-profit corporation with a mission to develop a process including a comprehensive examination to certify individuals in the information systems security specialty.

As this chapter hints, the number of data processing organizations, the proliferation of letters certifying, qualifying, and otherwise designating skill levels has become so complex it is difficult to keep track of all the players. Some work was started by several of the Consortium members several years ago toward certification of computer security practitioners. This work was conducted independently and largely without knowledge of each others' efforts. After discovering the work of each other, the groups felt it was in their best interest to combine and offer a single examination leading to the awarding of a single certificate designation, the Certified Information Systems Security Practitioner (CISSP). The Consortium approach involves many organizations, avoids the wasted effort of competing programs, and helps to ensure the acceptance of the certification. To realize the benefits of support from multiple organizations, (ISC)^2 the Consortium was created. (ISC)^2 is a nonprofit corporation chartered in the Commonwealth of Massachusetts dedicated solely to its stated mission. It operates independently of all computer security groups, companies and organizations.

(ISC)^2 was formed by representatives from the following groups: (Listed alphabetically)

Canadian Information Processing Society (CIPS)

Computer Security Institute (CSI)

Data Processing Management Association—Special Interest Group for Computer Security (DPMA SIG-CS)

Idaho State University (ISU)

Information Systems Security Association (ISSA)

International Federation for Information Processing (IFIP)

Representatives from each of these groups hold positions as officers or members of the board of directors, although in their capacity as (ISC)^2 representatives they are committed solely to the goals of (ISC)^2. These individuals are volunteers, without compensation.

Control and overview of the Consortium takes place through the vehicle of an Advisory Committee. Positions on the Advisory Committee are held by representatives of the groups who formed the Consortium, recognized industry experts selected by the board of directors, and representatives of organizations that qualify as significant corporate contributors.

15.2.11 Related Organizations

There are hundreds of professional societies not mentioned above. They range from large and significant groups like the Association for Computing Machinery (ACM) and the Association for Systems Management (ASM) to specialized, new, or small organizations. With the interest in information systems security created by several widely reported problems in 1988 and 1989, new organizations are founded regularly. The purpose of this part of Chapter 15 has been to identify a selection to show something of the range of professional societies and some of the activities they undertake.

15.3 CANADIAN SYSTEM SECURITY CENTRE

Canadian System Security Centre, Communications Security Establishment, P.O. Box 9703, Terminal, Ottawa, Ontario, K1G 3Z4

As the address indicates, the Canadian System Security Centre is an operation of the Communications Security Establishment of the Government of Canada. As with the U.S. government organizations discussed below, this non-classified operation helps to disseminate security information and to develop solutions to perceived information systems security problems. CSSC presents a conference annually in Ottawa, similar to the National computer Security Conference in Baltimore.

A related activity is the Canadian Advisory Council on Information Technology Security (CACITS), a group that works with the Canadian Standards Association and international bodies such as IFIP Working Group TC11.

15.4 NATIONAL COMPUTER SECURITY CENTER

National Security Agency, 9800 Savage Road, Ft. George G. Meade, MD 20755-6000, Stop S94

The Department of Defense Computer Security Initiative was established in 1978 by the Assistant Secretary of Defense for Communications, Command, Control and Intelligence with a goal of ensuring the widespread availability of trusted ADP systems for use within the DoD.[4]

In January, 1981, the National Computer Security Center (NCSC) was established and assumed responsibility for the activities of the Initiative. The Center encourages the development of trusted computing systems and develops computer security guidelines for interested users. The Center also sponsors basic research in this emerging and vital field. Such research and developing products will help all users protect their vital information.

One of the effects of the Computer Security Act of 1987 was to transfer responsibility for such non-classified operations as NCSC to NIST. As this is written (May 1993), the NCSC still has a skeleton staff at the contact address above. Over the next few years, this operation will be transferred totally to NIST.

15.5 NATIONAL INSTITUTE OF STANDARDS AND TECHNOLOGY

The Computer Security Act of 1987 caused, among other things, a change in name from the National Bureau of Standards to the National Institute of Standards and technology (NIST). More important from the perspective of information systems security, the unclassified and non-national-security aspects of information systems security that had been handled by the National Computer Security Center operation of NSA became the responsibility of NIST.[5]

NIST maintains the National Computer Systems Laboratory (NCSL), which develops standards and test methods, conducts research on computers and related telecommunications systems, and provides technical assistance.

---

[4]These two paragraphs are adapted from the 12th National Computer Security Conference conference brochure, co-sponsored by NCSC and NIST (October 1989). Consideration of the references in this manual may give an idea of the impact of NSA and NCSC on information systems security. Nevertheless, the CISSP program is not a U.S. government program, and thus NCSC perhaps receives less recognition in this manual than it deserves. The Communications Security Establishment in Ottawa, an agency that like NSA does not seek notoriety, is another supporter of (ISC)², and also is mentioned less in this manual than it may deserve.

[5]The following information is accurate at October 1989. Since the effect of the CSA '87 really began to be felt in late 1988, numerous changes have occurred within NIST, and more are expected in the 1990s. The functions mentioned are still performed in 1993, with few changes at this high level so far.

NIST also maintains a Computer Security Division. The CSD contact address is A216, Bldg. 225, NIST, Gaithersburg, MD, 20899, 301/975-2929.

The Computer Security Division program has four primary components:

1. Security technology (identification, non-classified cryptography, secure O/S, PC security, database security, and network architecture)

2. Management and evaluation (guidance in the application of risk management techniques, computer security management, contingency planning, and audit)

3. Planning and assistance (aid to government agencies in computer security planning, training and related activities)

4. Research and development (identification technologies, computer virus code, network security mechanisms, operating system security, cryptography, and related areas)

Other divisions of NIST include:

- Information Systems Engineering Division
- Systems and Software Technology Division
- Systems and Network Architecture Division
- Advanced Systems Division

NIST has representatives in the management structure of (ISC)[2].

15.6 PROFESSIONAL CERTIFICATIONS

There are many professional certification programs within the field of information systems. Probably the range is illustrated best by the contrast between the ICCP examination program and the BCS program; therefore, these two are covered in some detail. The general philosophy of all examinations is similar, with a body of knowledge, codes of ethics and practice, varying experience requirements, and an examination process. The specifics of examinations vary depending on subject matter. Rules regarding re-certifying vary from none (an accountant is a CA or CPA for life) to significant requirements for ongoing practice and training (for example, a medical doctor). Some programs offer different levels of certification, from para-professional to very senior.

The CISSP program of (ISC)[2] that has provided the structure of this text falls in the expected range of this group, with a recertification requirement and an experience requirement.

15.6.1 Certificate in Data Processing (CDP), Certified Systems Professional (CSP), Certified Computer Programmer (CCP) [ICCP Examinations]

During 1988 and 1989, the ICCP extensively revised the certification program. The status of the CDP and ICCP certification programs in general continued to be under intense review in 1992, and future changes may be expected. One probable change is replacement of the designations, including the CDP, with another program. The designations of CCP, CDP, CSP, and ACP as of 1990 are part of an overall framework, with a core of material that all candidates must pass and nine specialty examinations.

Some facts about the CDP are:

- The first exam was administered in 1962 by DPMA.

- In 1975, the exam was administered by the new ICCP organization.
- More than 30,000 persons now hold CDPs.
- There are about 160 testing centers in countries all over the world.
- In 1985, the CSP program developed by ASM was given to ICCP; there are now over ,7000 CSP holders as well.

The ICCP examination structure now is divided into a core examination and several specialty modules, including:

1. Systems Development
2. Business Information Systems
3. Management
4. Office Information Systems
5. Communications
6. Procedural Programming
7. Software Engineering
8. Scientific Programming
9. Systems Programming
10. Computer Security

Specialty modules are added or deleted from time to time.

The core covers the following topics:

- Technology
- Data and Information
- Human and Organizational Aspects
- Systems Concepts
- Systems Development
- Associated Disciplines

All sections of the core must be taken and passed at one sitting.

Objectives of the Programs[6]

Certified Computer Programmer (CCP)
The CCP program has the following objectives:

1. Develop a generally accepted examination program which will measure knowledge and experience appropriate to senior-level computer programmers and analysts.
2. Establish a method for distinguishing those individuals who have sufficient knowledge and experience to qualify as senior-level computer programmers/analysts.

Certified Data Processor (CDP)
The CDP program has the following objectives:

---

[6]The remainder of section 15.5.1 is reproduced with permission from the *1990 ICCP Official Study Guide*, with no changes other than formatting.

1. Establish a method to measure knowledge appropriate to the management of information processing.
2. Establish a method whereby society can identify those individuals having knowledge considered important to the management of information processing.
3. Lay a firm foundation for the continued growth of the information processing field and for personnel within the field seeking to attain positions of leadership.
4. Establish high standards for information processing personnel by emphasizing a broad educational framework and practical knowledge in the field as desirable personal objectives.

Certified Systems Professional (CSP)
The CSP program has the following objectives:

1. Identify systems practitioners who have attained a specified level of knowledge and experience in the principles and practices of information systems development, information resource management, and other related disciplines.
2. Provide tools, guidelines, and assessment methods necessary to achieve professional status.
3. Foster continuing professional development.
4. Delineate, and encourage adherence to, professional standards for those in the information systems profession.

Holders of the Certified Computer Programmer, Certified Data Processor and Certified Systems Professional are entitled to use the designations "CCP," "CDP," and "CSP," respectively after their names. The Councils endorse the use of these terms as meaning that the individual has achieved the ICCP credential, having met all of the requirements pertaining to it.

Examinations Required for Designations

In recognition of the increasing degree of specialization among information systems and information technology professionals, the ICCP certification examinations are structured into a Core exam and a set of Specialty exams.

To satisfy the examination requirements for the CCP, CDP or CSP designation a candidate must pass:

- the Core examination, plus
- a required Specialty exam, plus
- any other Specialty exam.

The Specialty exams offered in 1990 are:

- Procedural Programming   (Required for CCP)
- Management   (Required for CDP)
- Systems Development   (Required for CSP)

- Business Information Systems
- Communications
- Office Information Systems
- Scientific Programming

- Software Engineering
- Systems Programming

The ICCP certification programs are directed to senior level personnel in the information processing industry.

Any person may take the examination. However, they will not receive their certificate and be entitled to the use the corresponding designation until the following experience requirement is met.

Experience

A candidate must have at least 60 months of full-time (or part-time equivalent) direct experience in computer-based information systems. The 60 months need not be consecutive or in a single position. Acceptable forms of experience include that in data processing systems, programming, management, and teaching computer-based information systems. Systems and programming experience gained while employed by computer equipment manufacturers, service centers, management consulting firms, or educational institutions may be applied toward this requirement. Clerical, data-entry, or experience gained in connection with formal class work will not be considered acceptable.

Type of Examination

The ICCP examinations are multiple-choice examinations. The number of questions ranges from 200 to 100 for various core and specialty examinations.

ICCP undertook a massive restructuring of its examination program for 1990 and following years. The designations are now earned by passing a core examination and one of several available specialties. The choice of specialties determines the certificate earned. Changes are continuing into the 1990s (amid considerable controversy.)

15.6.2 Certified Information Systems Auditor (CISA)

The CISA examination is administered under the auspices of the EDP Auditors' Foundation, to test suitability of information systems auditors.

The examination itself covers the following areas of EDP auditing:

- Application Systems Control
- Security
- Data Integrity
- System Software
- Systems Development Life Cycle
- Maintenance
- Application Development
- Data Processing Resource Management
- General Operational Procedures and Controls
- Information Systems Audit Management

15.6.3 Certified Information Systems Security Practitioner (CISSP)

At this writing details about the CISSP examination had not been finalized by (ISC)². The body of knowledge (CBK) to be tested includes these seventeen categories:

1. Access Control
2. Cryptography
3. Risk Management
4. Business Continuity Planning
5. Data Classification
6. Security Awareness
7. Computer and System Security
8. Telecommunications Security
9. Organization Architecture
10. Legal and Regulatory Considerations
11. Investigation
12. Application Program Security (change control, etc.)
13. System Program Security
14. Physical Security
15. Operations Security
16. Information Ethics
17. Policy Development

Throughout this text, details of the CBK are included to begin each chapter.

15.6.4 Fellow of the British Computer Society (FBCS)

The BCS operates in the UK and in a number of Commonwealth countries such as Hong Kong & Singapore and administers various degrees of Fellow of the BCS (FBCS).

The BCS examinations are in two parts, aptly named "Part I" and "Part II." Part I has a general examination section (a several-hour examination given under controlled circumstances, testing knowledge similar to that described in more detail for the CDP in section 13.2); a "Part I Paper" that must demonstrate the candidate's understanding of informatics; and a "Report of Project," which must demonstrate the successful achievement of a significant project proving that the candidate has the skills and experience to be considered a professional. The BCS considers that the level of ability and learning demonstrated by successful completion of the Part I examination is roughly equivalent to a four-year college degree in North America. Part II of the BCS examinations is examination in depth in one or another specialization. The BCS considers that the candidate should demonstrate a depth of knowledge in the specialization equivalent to a Master of Science in the area.

As with the ICCP, the BCS has developed review courses and other educational materials, and accredits courses for their examinations and recertification.

Type of Examination

The ICCP and BCS examinations occupy extremes of the range of professional certification examinations. The ICCP examinations are multiple-choice, and as described above the BCS examinations are in essay form.

15.6.5 Information Systems Professional (ISP)

The Canadian Information Processing Society (CIPS) opened applications for the designation of Information Systems Professional in March, 1989. By 1992, some 2000 professionals in Canada held the designation (many by means of "grandfathering during the initial phase of the program.) CIPS members who paid the application fee and met one or more of the following five combinations of education and experience were granted the ISP certification during 1989:

Education	Years
Accredited university degree (B.Sc.)	2
Non-accredited university degree (B.Sc.)	4
ICCP Certificate, CDP, CSP, CCP (since 1984)	5
Non-accredited 2 or 3 year or technical school program	6
Other	10

Re-certification, with continuing education a required component, is required every five years to retain the ISP designation.

Clearly, the initial certification requirements were at one end of the range described, as no examination is required and the combination of education and experience is significantly lower than for some other certifications.

REFERENCES

Behrman, Jack H., *Essays on Ethics in Business and the Professions*, Prentice-Hall, Englewood Cliffs NJ, 1988.

Brownoski, J., *Science and Human Values*, Harper & Row, New York, NY, 1956.

Burnham, David, *The Rise of the Computer State*, Random House, New York, NY, 1983.

"Case Histories In Computer Security," *Computers & Security*, No. 53, July/August, 1983.

"A Guide to the Ethical and Legal Use of Software for Members of the Academic Community," EDUCOM Software Initiative/ADAPSO, 1987.

Kahin, Brian, "Property and Propriety in the Digital Environment: Towards an Examination Copy License," EDUCOM Software Initiative White Paper, October, 1988.

Kratz, Martin P. J., "Introduction to Copyright Infringement," in *Technology and the Law for General Practitioners*, Legal Education Society of Alberta, Canada, March, 1987.

Martin, James, *Security, Accuracy, and Privacy in Computer Systems*, Prentice-Hall, Inc., Englewood Cliffs, NJ, 1973.

"OECD Guidelines Governing the Protection of Privacy and Transborder Flows of Personal Data," Recommendations of the council of Europe, adopted at its 523rd meeting on September 23, 1980.

Parker, Donn B., *Ethical Conflicts in Computer Science and Technology*, Arlington, VA., AFIPS Press 1981.

Parker, Donn B., *Ethical Conflicts in Information and Computer Science, Technology and Business*, QED Information Sciences Inc., Wellesley MA, 1991. (An update of the 1977 study published in 1981.)

Parker, Donn B., *Fighting Computer Crime*, Charles Scribner & Sons, New York, NY, 1983.

Scalet, Elizabeth, *VDT Health and Safety: Issues and Solutions*, Ergosyst Associates, Ergosyst/Report Store, Old Post Road, Brookfield, VT, 05036, December, 1987.

Westin, A. F., *Privacy and Freedom*, Atheneum, New York, NY, 1967.

16. Policy Development

Policy is used to identify whatever manifestation management makes of its intentions. Policy Development is the articulation and representation of that intent.[1]

The information security professional is expected to know how to articulate such intent and the content that it should have to achieve effective and efficient treatment of the data.

For example, the professional is expected to know that policy should:

- Have a long life
- Be jargon free
- Be independent of jobs, titles or positions
- Set objectives
- Fix responsibility
- Provide resources
- Allocate staff
- Be implemented using standards and guidelines

DEFINITIONS

Assertion

A compound predicate concerning the values of attributes of certain specified entities, and/or the existence of certain relationships among them. (ET, MA)

Bell-La Padula Model

A formal state transition model of computer security policy that describes a set of access control rules. In this formal model, the entities in a computer system are divided into abstract sets of subjects and objects. The notion of a secure state is defined and it is proven that each state transition preserves security by moving from secure state to secure state; thus inductively proving that the system is secure. A system state is defined as "secure" if the only permitted access modes of subjects to objects are in accordance with a specific security policy. In order to determine whether or not a specific access mode is allowed, the clearance of a subject is compared to the classification of the object and a determination is made as to whether the subject is authorized for the specific access mode. See *-Property. (NCSC-WA-991-85; CSC-STD-001-83)

Conceptual Entity

Anything about which we might want to say something. Examples of conceptual entities are physical objects, scenes, processes, and IF-THEN rules. (ET, MA)

Correctness

In a strict sense, the property of a system that is guaranteed as a result of formal verification activities. Correctness is not an absolute property of a system, rather it implies the mutual consistency of a specification and its implementation. (MTR-8201)

---

[1]This is item 17 in the (ISC)[2] Common Body of Knowledge.

Correctness Proof

A mathematical proof of consistency between a specification and its implementation. It may apply at the security model-to-formal specification level, at the formal specification-to-HOL code level, at the compiler level or at the hardware level. For example, if a system has a verified design and implementation, then its overall correctness rests with the correctness of the compiler and hardware. Once a system is proved correct, it can be expected to perform as specified, but not necessarily as anticipated if the specifications are incomplete or inappropriate. (MTR-8201)

Design Verification

The use of verification techniques, usually computer-assisted, to demonstrate a mathematical correspondence between an abstract (security) model and a formal system specification. (MTR-8201)

Discretionary Access Control

A means of restricting access to objects based on the identity and need-to-know of subjects and/or groups to which they belong. The controls are discretionary in the sense that a subject with a certain access permission is capable of passing that permission (perhaps indirectly) on to any other subject. (NCSC-WA-001-85; CSC-STD-001-83; CSC-STD-004-85)

Dominate

Security level S1 is said to *dominate* security level S2 if the hierarchical classification of S1 is greater than or equal to that of S2 and the non-hierarchical categories of S1 include all of those of S2 as a subset. (CSC-STD-001-83)

Formal Proof

1. A complete and convincing mathematical argument, presenting the full logical justification for each proof step, for the truth of a theorem or set of theorems. The formal verification process uses formal proofs to show the truth of certain properties of formal specification and for showing that computer programs satisfy their specifications. (CSC-STD-001-83)

2. A complete and convincing mathematical argument, presenting the full logical justification for each proof step, for the truth of a theorem or set of theorems. (NCSC-WA-001-85)

Formal Security Policy Model

1. A mathematically precise statement of a security policy. To be adequately precise, such a model must represent the initial state of a system, the way in which the system progresses from one state to another, and a definition of a "secure" state of the system. To be acceptable as a basis for a TCB, the model must be supported by a formal proof that if the initial state of the system satisfies the definition of a "secure" state and if all assumptions required by the model hold, then all future states of the system will be secure. Some formal modelling techniques include: state transition models, temporal logic models, denotational semantics models, algebraic specification models. An example is the model described by Bell and La Padula. (CSC-STD-001-83; NCSC-WA-001-85)

2. See Bell-La Padula Model; Security Policy Model.

Formal Verification

The process of using formal proofs to demonstrate the consistency (design verification) between a formal specification of a system and a formal security policy model or (implementation verification) between the formal specification and its program implementation. (CSC-STD-001-83)

Identity-based Security Policy

A security policy based on the identities and/or attributes of users, a group of users, or entities acting on behalf of the users and the resources/objects being accessed. (ISO 7498-2)

Implementation Verification

The use of verification techniques, usually computer-assisted, to demonstrate a mathematical correspondence between a formal specification and its implementation in program code. (MTR-8201)

Lattice

A partially ordered set for which every pair of elements has a greatest lower bound and a least upper bound. (CSC-STD-001-83)

Least Privilege

This principle requires that each subject be granted the most restrictive set of privileges needed for the performance of authorized tasks. The application of this principle limits the damage that can result from accident, error, or unauthorized use. (NCSC-WA-001-85; CSC-STD-001-83)

Logical Completeness Measure

A means for assessing the effectiveness and degree to which a set of security and access control mechanisms meet the requirements of security specifications. (FIPS PUB 39; AR 380-380; NCSC-WA-001-85)

Mandatory Access Control

A means of restricting access to objects based on the sensitivity (as represented by a label) of the information contained in the objects and the formal authorization (i.e., clearance) of subjects to access information of such sensitivity. (CSC-STD-001-83; CSC-STD-004-85; NCSC-WA-001-85) See also Discretionary Access Control.

Object

A passive entity that contains or receives information. Access to an object potentially implies access to the information it contains. Examples of objects are records, blocks, pages, segments, files, directories, directory trees, and programs, as well as bits, bytes, words, fields, processors, video displays, keyboards, clocks, printers, network nodes, etc. (CSC-STD-001-83; AFR 205-16; NCSC-WA-001-85; DCID 1/16-1, Sup.)

Policy

Administrative decisions which determine how certain security-related concepts will be interpreted as system requirements. All such policy decisions must eventually be interpreted formally and implemented. (MTR-8201)

Principle of Least Privilege

The granting of the minimum access authorization necessary for the performance of required tasks. (FIPS PUB 39; AR 380-380)

Profiles

A detailed security description of the physical structure, equipment components, equipment locations and relationships, and general operating environment of the automated system. (AR 380-380)

Rule-based Security Policy

A *security policy* based on global rules imposed for all users. These rules usually rely on a comparison of the sensitivity of the resources being accessed and the possession of corresponding attributes of users, a group of users, or entities acting on behalf of users. (ISO 7498-2)

Secure State

A condition where no subject can access any object in an unauthorized manner. (NCSC-WA-001-85)

Security Policy

The set of criteria for the provision of security services (see also *identity-based* and *rule-based* security policy). (ISO 7498-2)

Security Policy Model

An informal presentation of the security policy supported by the system. It must identify the sets of laws, rules, and practices that regulate how a system manages, protects, and distributes sensitive information. (NCSC-WA-001-85)

Simple Security Condition

A Bell-La Padula security model rule allowing a subject read access to an object only if the security level of the subject dominates the security level of the object. (DODD 5200.28-STD)

*-Property (Star Property)

A Bell-La Padula security model rule allowing a subject write access to an object only if the security level of the subject is dominated by the security level of the object. Also known as the Confinement Property. (CSC-STD-001-83; NCSC-WA-001-85)

Subject

An active entity, generally in the form of a person, process, or device that causes information to flow among objects or changes the system state. Technically, a process/domain pair. (CSC-STD-001-83; AFR 205-16; NCSC-WA-001-85; DCID 1/16-1, Sup.)

Verification

The process of comparing two levels of system specification for proper correspondence (*e.g.*, security policy model with top-level specifications, top-level specification with source code, or source code with object code). This process may or may not be automated. (NCSC-WA-001-85; CSC-STD-001-83)

16.1 FORMAL SECURITY POLICY CONSIDERATIONS

Formal security models were discussed in Chapter 7, and specifications in Chapter 12. These are bridges between the enormous differences in level of detail between an implementation and the highest level of the security hierarchy, the security policy. A distinction needs to be made: a security policy has the ultimate goal of controlling people, is intended to guide human behavior, and often reflects requirements external to the organization; a *formal* security policy model is an implementation of a security policy that is stated in terms susceptible to mathematical proofs and verification.

According to ISO (7498-2):

Essentially a security policy states, in general terms, what is and is not permitted in the field of security during the general operation of the system in question. Policy is usually not specific; it suggests what is of paramount importance without saying precisely how the desired results are to be obtained. Policy sets the topmost level of a security specification.

16.1.1 Authorization

A statement as to what constitutes authorization must be embodied in the security policy. To the extent that there are permissible variations in the rules relating to authorization (for example, discretionary access control *versus* mandatory access control), the policy must define clearly those variations and the circumstances in which they apply.

There are two basic types of security policy, based on the nature of the authorization provided: *identity-based security policy* and *rule-based security policy*. Most real implementations combine aspects of both, with the combination being strongly organization-specific.

16.1.2 Identity-based Security Policy

Identity-based security policies involve authorization criteria based on specific, individualized attributes. Some attributes may be assumed to be permanently linked to the entities to which they apply; some may be passed on to other entities. Privileges and capabilities are an example of attributes that are possessions and may be passed on (see Chapter 7). Access-control lists are examples of attributes that remain permanently attached to an entity.

In the realm of telecommunications and networks that may include different systems, with different security policies and labels, identity-based policies can pose serious or insurmountable problems. The granularity of entities assigned attributes may vary dramatically from one system to the next, and correspondingly so would the precise form of the attributes and the security policy criteria linked to those attributes.

16.1.3 Rule-based Security Policy

Rule-based security policies use rules based on a small number of general attributes or sensitivity classes, that are enforced universally. Data and/or resources are marked with security labels. Processes acting on behalf of human users may acquire the security label appropriate to their originators. Rules define the kinds of access and use that are authorized based on these labels. To a large degree, a mandatory access control policy falls into the realm of a rule-based security policy.

In the realm of telecommunications and networks that may include different systems, with different security policies and labels, a rule-based policy may be easier to deal with. This is because there is a relatively small number of rules and sensitivity classes that must be resolved among differing systems.

16.2 INFORMAL SECURITY POLICY

There must be an explicit and well-defined security policy. This policy should focus attention on those aspects of security that the highest level of authority considers important. In the case of a formal policy model as discussed above, the policy forms the highest level of the security system, with the model (Chapter 7), then specifications (Chapter 12) forming a bridges to the details of implementation.

Informal policies still must be explicit and focused, and naturally must be communicated effectively. Subjects that should be covered include:

- Responsibility and authority
- Access control
- The extent to which formal verification is required
- Discretionary/Mandatory control (most relevant in government situations or formal policies)
- Marking/labeling
- Control of media
- Import and export of data
- Security and classification levels
- Treatment of system outputs

All of these issues have been addressed in some detail throughout this book. In the following sub-sections we outline these considerations again, to emphasize their position in the discussion of policy. Later sections in this chapter address publication and present several sample security policies from various organizations.

16.2.1 Intent of Policy

The intent of a security policy is to delineate what is expected of an organization in the realm of information security, as defined by the organization's highest authority. This normally will include norms for expected behavior, control of access to information, control of use and dissemination of information, a mandate that systems should remain available, and provision for business continuity in the event of problems (security-related or otherwise).

16.2.2 Laws and Regulations

One necessity for any reasonable policy is to reflect any relevant laws and regulations that impact on the organization's use of information. As noted in Chapter 10, privacy is a particular concern (and may involve international obligations and treaties). Legal advice is needed for this element of security policy, as laws and regulations vary from one jurisdiction to another.

16.2.3 Company Policy: Trade Secrets

Trade Secrets, Employee Agreements, Conflict of Interest

Trade secrets relate to the ways a company does business, or to things unique to and of value to the company. There is a legal definition and a great number of legal decisions relating to trade secrets; these technicalities will be avoided here. (More detail on legal aspects is contained in Chapter 10.) For the purposes of this text, a trade secret is an asset that needs protecting. To have legal protection, it is necessary both that the asset is a trade secret, and that the company *treat* it as such. Specifically, employees must be made aware of the secrecy and the company and its employees must not publish it (in conversations over coffee at conferences, for instance).

Specific control measures that help to protect trade secrets (computer programs, manufacturing techniques, or whatever) are:

1. A company policy regarding confidentiality.
2. Have each employee sign both agreements to keep confidential things secret, and acknowledgments that he/she understands that "x" is a confidential trade secret.

Without both elements, losses may not be recoverable through legal processes. In the Canadian case *Regina* v. *Tannis* (Dome Petroleum), a departing employee retained copies of programs. The company attempted to have the former employee held accountable for breach of trade secrets but was unable to establish that the employee knew the items in question were controlled, or that he knew they were trade secrets, or that the company had made any attempt to recover material on termination.

The acknowledgments should be read and signed both before employment and periodically while employed, and reviewed when the employee leaves.

Acknowledgments such as referred to here are one example of a detail item that would be part of employee awareness. More about the topic of awareness is found in Chapter 6.

Another example of a detailed supporting element of a policy, is conflict of interest rules. The company should have a policy that defines whether, for instance, spouses may work in the same department, or may report to one another. Both separation of duties and simple common sense come into play here. A married couple are not normally at "arms length" in a business sense; duties split between them may not be truly separated. If a spouse reports to another, could the company depend on performance appraisals? Again, rules should be made, communicated, and acknowledged by employees.

16.2.4 Mandatory and Discretionary Security

This topic is included with the discussion of policies to place a cross-reference. "Mandatory" and "discretionary" are used to describe specific processes related to the TCSEC criteria. Over time, their use has acquired a specialized meaning in the context of the TCSEC criteria different from the usual English language usage.

16.2.5 Accountability: Identification, Authentication, Audit Capability

As with mandatory and discretionary security, this topic is included with the discussion of policies to place a cross-reference. Topics of accountability are addressed in Chapters 6 and 12.

16.3 PUBLICATION AND STAFF ACKNOWLEDGMENT

As with most security considerations, the overall climate of the organization, or its "culture," is crucial. Every organization will have unwritten rules that "x" is "simply not done," or that "y" is "done this way here." A key point in security and control is to make sure that the organizational culture includes norms that lead to professional behavior.

The methods used in working with organizational culture are many and varied (there is an entire field of study called "Organizational Development" which deals primarily in this area). Obvious ways culture is communicated include:

1. *Perception and observation*

   What does senior management do? If the owner regularly uses company funds for personal expenses, it is possible that secretaries may see nothing wrong with raiding petty cash.

2. *Employee Training*

   The initial orientation and subsequent "refreshers" should tell people what is considered acceptable.

The main point here is that employees must know what is expected of them. Rather than depending on more or less uncontrolled "osmosis," a security and control (and good management) principle is to *tell* people what you want. A secondary point also should be obvious: Don't try to tell people things which they will observe for themselves are not true.

The lesson from these observations is that security and control first must consider the organization and its norms and expectations. The control program must be designed with this in mind, and it must be communicated: Employee awareness must be generated.

These comments lead to the principle that security must come from the top. Employees must be able to recognize a clear top management commitment, or any security effort is likely to fail. The most workable way to meet this need is to have a clear policy of the company regarding security. This policy must be:

1. Simple and clear
2. Known to employees
3. Supported and adhered to by top management

Section 16.4.1 contains an example of a policy in an educational institution. It is short, clear, and "comes from the top." Managers have the responsibility to fill in details (such as trade secret agreements noted above) to ensure that the policy is carried out.

Note that this policy explicitly recognizes that in an educational environment people must be relatively free to experiment.

16.4 MODEL COMPUTER SECURITY POLICIES

It is desirable that policies (and legislation) adopted by organizations in similar industries should share common characteristics. Each organization may have individual requirements not shared with others. Within broad categories such as particular industries, local government, and so forth, similar activities are undertaken, and similar security needs should lead to similar policies. It is doubtful whether this is the case in the 1990s.

Professional societies that deal with questions of information systems security may be the best available source of model policies, from which a specific policy for an individual organization may be derived. Examples of such model policies include educational institution examples, the Data Processing Management Association "Corporate Computer Security Policy Statement," and others.[2]

16.4.1 Educational Institution Security Policy

The following policy is adapted from one developed by the authors for a private trade school with two-year training programs for various aspects of programming and computer operations.

Information Systems Security Policy

This organization is committed to conducting its affairs at all times in accordance with the law and the highest ethical standards. The reputation that we enjoy is based not on a list of detailed rules but on the example set by management and the character and good judgment of each employee and the reputation of our graduates. It is expected that employees at all levels will conduct themselves so that their actions will not embarrass themselves, their families or their organizations, and that students will conduct themselves in accordance with the student conduct guidelines. The following principles are stated to furnish general guidelines in a variety of situations relating to information systems:

1. Integrity is an essential element of every business relationship; with our employees, with our students, with our suppliers, and with our shareholders and the general public.

2. In the course of normal business operations, employees and students have access to the "XYZ" computer facilities and to privileged information. All employees and students are expected to avoid any actions which might harm the interests of any users of the computer facilities besides themselves. This includes, but is not limited to, affecting the availability of the computer capabilities, integrity of data and information, disclosure of data or information not belonging to the student or employee, or any other action which is unlawful or harmful to others.

3. No employee will knowingly fail to comply with all applicable laws and regulations of federal, state, and local governments in the conduct of the business.

4. Detailed guidelines and standards regarding professional conduct and release of information about students will be adhered to strictly by all employees.

5. Ethical business conduct is a condition of employment, and of continued employment, for all employees of this organization.

6. As this is an educational institution and experimentation is part of the learning process, some student violations of the standards of conduct will be subject to warnings before actual suspension; however, deliberate damage to others, or disclosure of sensitive information for personal gain, will be cause for immediate expulsion from the academic program; knowing violations of federal, state, or local laws will also be grounds for immediate expulsion.

---

[2]Some of the following examples contain definitions and usages that are not completely compatible with those used elsewhere in this text, nor indeed necessarily with one another. The policies are reproduced exactly as provided by the various organizations; incompatibilities may illustrate the present poorly-standardized state of information security policy.

7. It is the responsibility of the President and the Information Systems Manager to put in place systems and controls which will ensure minimal exposure of privileged information and the computer facilities, and of all employees and students to follow the relevant portions of those guidelines.

8. It is the responsibility of the Director of Academics to put in place detailed standards of student conduct which will support this policy.

Computer uses, such as "playing games," which might be totally inappropriate in a secret government project, are condoned in this policy. Students are allowed to experiment, within the limits of not harming others or making the system unavailable to authorized users. Detailed guidelines, procedures, and standards involved in implementing this policy will include warnings prior to suspensions; in other environments termination, or even police attention, might accompany the same rule violations.

16.4.2 DPMA Model Policy

The Data Processing Management Association (DPMA)[3] includes some 25,000 members from all aspects of the informatics professions. In October, 1987, the DPMA Executive Council approved the following:[4]

DPMA Model Corporate Computer Security Policy Statement

The DPMA Model Corporate Computer Security Policy is intended to serve as an example policy statement. Organizations should tailor it to fit the nature of the organization and to retain consistency with other organization policies.

The policy statement is a brief description of the major objectives, value, and intended use of computer resources and information. It is not intended to provide specific procedures for the implementation of the policy.

Procedures should be place in a separate—and more detailed—document containing such things as:

*   the levels of information in the computer system and the types of information requiring protection;
*   the required user clearance level and the individuals able to access various pieces of information;
*   control measures; and
*   assignments of various security responsibilities.

Here is the complete text of the DPMA Model Corporate Computer Security Policy Statement:

The computer system and information contained therein are essential to the daily operations and future success of our organization. The computer systems serving (organization name) provide and support various business functions and manage proprietary information assets.

It is the responsibility of (organization name) management and each of its area managers to assess and effectively manage the degree of risk regarding:

*   the protection of proprietary information, and
*   the ability to process critical business applications.

---

[3]See section 15.2.

[4]This Model Policy was developed by a team chaired by Mr. Richard Cashion. He and other members of the team went on to help in the creation of the DPMA Special Interest Group for Computer Security, also established in 1987. The material presented here is reproduced from the *DPMA Position Statements Handbook*, revised January, 1989. At this writing, August, 1992, the policy is under review.

The primary objective of managing such risks to corporate computer resources is to prevent, contain and recover from man-made and/or natural harms.

It is the policy of (organization name) to protect its proprietary information assets and allow the use, access and disclosure of such information only in accordance with corporate interests and applicable laws and regulations.

Proprietary information is any data of (organization name) which it does not wish to freely disclose or lose control of, and governed by copyright and/or trade regulations. The term also includes the computer resources and information of others in the possession of (organization name) which is subject to restrictions on its use or further disclosure.

The protection of proprietary information—regardless of the medium of storage—must be part of the overall business plan and computer system design.

Data center and systems management assumes a responsibility to know and comply with the usage and access controls required by the proprietary and/or criticality identification specified by the owner/ originator.

Critical business applications are those programs, functions, activities and data, the loss, interruption or misuse of which would have a significant impact on the products and/or services provided by (organization name) and/or would materially impair the capacity of the organization to carry out its mission.

Each employee—as the originator, custodian and/or user of data—must ensure that corporate data under his/her direction and/or control is properly identified and safeguarded according to its sensitivity, proprietary nature, and criticality.

As users of corporate data, each employee must strictly adhere to the specific security measures and controls that have been established. Any unauthorized use of the organization's computer resources for personal purposes—or any other purpose not related to the organization—is strictly forbidden. Employees are only permitted to use the computer resources and information for which they are authorized. Employees must be granted use of the computer system—from proper authority—for approved outside and personal activities. These activities should be in no way detrimental to the companies best interests.

Violations or suspected violations of computer security measures or controls must be reported at once to management and/or those with the responsibility for computer security.

Procedures developed to support this policy shall be communicated to management and personnel. This will provide management the capabilities for oversight and properly inform personnel of their responsibilities as users of corporate computer resources and information.

16.4.3 Information Systems Security Association (ISSA) Sample Policies

16.4.3.1 Corporate Information Security Policy and Data Security Policy

The following Corporate Information Security Policy and Data Security Policy were developed in 1986 by the Los Angeles Chapter of Information Systems Security Association. These are general patterns, like the DPMA Model policy reproduced above.

CORPORATE INFORMATION SECURITY POLICY

I. Purpose & Scope
The purpose of this policy is to establish responsibility and custodial roles for the protection of corporate in-

formation. This policy applies to all operations within the company.

II. Policy
Information is a vital organization asset requiring protection commensurate with its value. Measures shall be taken to protect these assets against accidental or unauthorized modification, disclosure, or destruction, as well as to assure the security, reliability, integrity and availability of information.

III. Responsibilities
Management is responsible for identifying, defining and granting access to information assets and the protection of information within their assigned area of management control. Management is also responsible for the protection of information accessed by non-employees in the course of company business. They are responsible for implementing this policy consistent with sound business practice and any standards and procedures set forth.

Information Security Administration is responsible for the establishment, implementation and maintenance of an information protection program to assist management in the protection of their assigned assets. Security Administration shall develop and publish such standards, procedures and guidelines necessary to assure adequate security in all areas within the scope of this policy.

IV. Compliance
This policy and all supporting standards, procedures and guidelines issued in support of this policy shall serve as a standard to be applied by management, and will be a basis for compliance monitoring and review.

A violation of standards, procedures or guidelines established in support of this policy shall be brought to the attention of management for appropriate action and could result in termination of employment.

V. Definitions

Corporate Information is all information used by the company for the conduct of its business.

Data are aggregations of facts used to run an organization (a telephone directory contains data).

Information is extracted from data in response to specific needs (a telephone number is information). *Information systems* provide the means of entering, storing, processing and communicating data so that information can be extracted and presented in response to a particular need.

Data integrity refers to the completeness, accuracy, and honesty of the data.[5]

Data security is the safety of data from accidental or intentional disclosure, modification or destruction.

Responsibility and *custodial* roles are each distinctly different concepts. An understanding of those differences is important to understanding this policy statement.

Primary responsibility for any particular aggregation of data is held by the manager charged with their acquisition, maintenance and integrity.

Secondary responsibility for data is with anyone authorized access to that data by the manager with primary responsibility for it.

Custody of data is held by any person or group charged with the storage, processing, communication or presentation of that data.

All employees are responsible for information protection and will be held accountable for the accuracy, integrity and confidentiality of the information to which they have access. They shall use information resources only for authorized company business.

---

[5](Author's footnote) See other definitions at the beginnings of chapters in this book.

DATA SECURITY POLICY

I. Purpose
To establish the basic policy of the Corporation for the use, protection and preservation of computer-based information systems.

To provide management with the legal basis of action in the event of misuse or loss of corporate information assets.

II. Scope
This policy applies to all operating units of the Corporation and to all information processed by mainframe computers, minicomputers and microcomputers.

III. Policy
Computer resources and associated corporate data are vital company assets requiring protection appropriate to its value. Measures shall be taken to protect these assets against accidental or unauthorized disclosure, modification or destruction, as well as to ensure their security, accuracy, reliability, availability and integrity.

IV. Responsibilities

Information Security Function

The information security function shall establish and implement this policy and such standards, procedures and guidelines as necessary to insure the security of information assets. It shall have a consulting and review role in all matters affecting information security and provide necessary support to management, owners, custodians, and users in the performance of their responsibilities.

Management

Management is responsible for the identification and protection of information assets within their operational areas. They shall insure employee awareness of this policy and supporting procedures, standards and guidelines and shall also review employee compliance with established security controls.

Owner

Owners shall specify security requirements commensurate with the value of the information asset. They shall authorize access and assign custody as appropriate.

Custodian

Custodians shall insure that entrusted assets are appropriately maintained, processed, secured, archived and available as directed by the information owner. They shall convey to the user all security requirements specified by the owner.

User

Users of information assets shall comply with all established security controls and procedures. Information assets shall be used only for authorized company business. Consultants, contractors and other non-employees who are users of the company's information assets must comply with all sections of this policy.

V. Compliance
Failure to comply with this policy and all supporting information security policies, procedures, standards and guidelines will be presented to appropriate management for disciplinary action, which may include dismissal and/or legal action.

VI. Definitions

    Assets—Any property of the company, including facilities, equipment, data, storage media, software, and electronic transmissions.

    Owner—The manager with authority for acquiring, creating or maintaining the asset.[6]

    Custodian—The person responsible for the physical possession of the asset.

    User—The person utilizing the asset for an authorized business function.

16.4.3.2 Sample Security Administration, Corporate Policy Letter, Data Security Policy

The following three samples were provided to ISSA by Mr. Robert Courtney and are reproduced here with permission of ISSA. "Computer Security Statement of Policy" is the policy statement of a major insurance company. "Sample Corporate Policy Letter" is a sample useful as a starting point. "Data Security" is the policy statement of a major, multi-division national organization, with centralized MIS.

COMPUTER SECURITY STATEMENT OF POLICY

Computer resources and associated corporate data are vital company assets requiring protection appropriate to its value. Measures shall be taken to protect these assets against accidental or unauthorized modification, disclosure, or destruction, as well as to assure the security, reliability, and integrity of information processing activity.

Scope

This policy applies to all information systems of the Company which access, process, or have custody of corporate data. This applies equally to mainframe, minicomputer, and microcomputer environments of the Company. The policy intent is applicable to all Divisions and associated personnel of the Company, including product line and service divisions as well as Information Services, Systems Development, and Management Services.

Standard

This policy and all supporting standards, procedures, and guidelines issued in support of this policy shall serve as a standard to be applied by management, and can be a basis for compliance monitoring and review.

Responsibilities

Line management retains primary responsibility for identifying and protecting information and computer assets within their assigned area of management control. They are responsible for implementing this policy consistent with sound business practice and any standards and procedures set forth.

    Computer Security Administration is responsible for the establishment, implementation, and maintenance of a computer security program to assist responsible management in the protection of their assigned assets. Security Administration shall develop and publish such standards, procedures, and guidelines necessary to assure adequate security in all areas within the scope of this policy.

Enforcement

A violation of standards, procedures, or guidelines established in support of this policy shall be brought to the attention of management for appropriate action and could result in termination of employment.

SAMPLE CORPORATE POLICY LETTER

The continuing increase in the dependence of (company name) on computer-based systems requires a delineation of corporate policy relative to data processing asset protection. The purpose of this letter is to provide

---

[6]See earlier note about compatible definitions.

a statement of that policy.

Our holdings in data and our capabilities to process those data constitute a major corporate asset. Anything which denies us continuing access to these assets jeopardizes our ability to conduct the business in a timely and profitable manner. Because this situation exists, it is therefore essential that the duties and responsibilities of the protection of data and the means for processing security are these:

> To ensure the integrity and accuracy of data;
>
> To provide for the privacy of proprietary, trade secret, personal, privileged, or otherwise sensitive data;
>
> To protect and preserve corporate assets from physical hazards, such as fire, flood, and civil unrest, and from misappropriation, misapplication, conversion, and vandalism;
>
> To ensure the ability to survive hazards;
>
> To protect employees from unnecessary temptation to default on their responsibilities;
>
> To protect employees from suspicion in the event that another individual defaults on his responsibilities; and
>
> To protect management from charges of imprudence if any compromise of security occurs.

The data processing centers are support organizations to the functional area of the corporation. The functional area managers not the data processing center management, must assume primary responsibilities for the integrity of their respective areas, including data processing support. To this end, the functional area managers are charged to secure sufficient support from the management of the data processing functions to permit adequately precise identification of their security exposures and to identify and implement, again with data processing management support, the necessary safeguards.

The cost of security should be borne by the respective functional areas in direct relation to the costs imposed on the data processing operation and their own area by their particular security needs. Functional areas needing the greatest security should not be allowed to impose the costs of that security on other using functions whose security needs are more modest.

Finally, all managers must assume responsibility for the awareness by the persons reporting to them that continuing sensitivity to the need for the data security and rigid compliance with the procedures and practices supportive of that goal are conditions of employment and, as such, are neither optional nor negotiable.

CORPORATE POLICY STATEMENT
DATA SECURITY

Background

_ has for many years been among the industry leaders in the use of computer-based systems for the efficient and effective management of complex retail operations. Rapid and continuing technical advances in electronic data processing have increased the dependence of each functional area of the business on these systems and the data used in them. For that reason, these data and the ability to process them must be recognized as major corporate assets and treated accordingly.

Data which are stored in the central computers and accessed by terminals in the work areas, data which are acquired, stored, and processed locally on micro-computers, and the material generated by word processing systems are vulnerable to a variety of threats against which they must be protected.

Purpose

This policy establishes primary and secondary responsibility and custodial roles for the protection of data on magnetic media and in printed form to the end that the respective roles of the contributors, users, technical data processing people, auditors and security personnel in the safeguarding of data are fully understood.

Definitions

1. *Data* are aggregations of facts which we use to run the business (A telephone directory contains data).

2. *Information* is extracted from data in response to specific needs (a particular telephone number is information). Information systems provide the means of entering, storing, processing, and communicating data so that information can be extracted and presented in response to a particular need.

3. *Data security* is the safety of data from accidental or intentional disclosure, modification, or destruction.

4. In an information systems environment, *security controls* are those things which are put in place to assure the integrity of data and of the means of processing them. These controls include hardware, programs, procedures, policies, practices, and physical safeguards, such as locks and fire extinguishers.

5. Ownership, responsibility, and custodial roles are each distinctly different concepts. An understanding of those differences is important to understanding this policy statement.

    Ownership of all data within __is solely by __and is not assigned or delegated in any way.

    Primary responsibility for any particular aggregation of data is held by the manager charged with their acquisition, maintenance, and integrity.

    Secondary responsibility for data is with anyone authorized access to those data by the manager with primary responsibility for them.

    Custody of data is held by any person or group charged with the storage, processing, communication, or presentation of those data.

Classification and marking of data and information is a means for informing all persons having authorized or unauthorized access to them that __considers them to be proprietary and their disclosure to unauthorized persons to be improper. Classification refers only to sensitivity to disclosure. Virtually all data are sensitive to illicit modification or destruction. Therefore, lack of classification does not imply insensitivity to security problems.

Protection of Classified Data

1. The Corporate Chief Financial Officer has responsibility for the review and approval of guidelines prepared by Information Services for the classification of data and the protection of classified data. He has oversight responsibility for compliance with those guidelines by corporate headquarters staff.

2. The Chief Financial Officer of each division has oversight responsibility for compliance by that division with the guidelines on classified data.

Information Services Roles and Responsibilities in Data Security

1. Information Services will establish guidelines for security controls for all common and division-particular systems in all divisions and including new systems.

2. Information Services will establish guidelines for the conduct by the divisions of assessments of the risk of security losses involving their data and the means of processing those data.

3. Information Services will monitor compliance with security guidelines to establish their effectiveness and to identify need for additions, modifications, or deletions to them.

4. Information Services has custodial responsibility for all data and programs supporting common systems from their initial communication to IS and including processing and storage.

5. The security afforded data in its custody by Information Services will reflect due regard for the security concerns identified to them by the corporate or division manager with primary responsibility for those data.

6. Information Services will have primary responsibility for all computer programs supporting IS equipment, the security of the data communications network, of division-level equipment integral to common systems, and of the data base.

Division Responsibilities

1. Divisions, through the appropriate functional area managers, retain primary responsibility for their data whether the data are in their custody or in the custody of others to whom they have transmitted them for whatever purpose.

2. Division personnel with primary responsibility for the security of data will convey to all persons or organizations given access to them the appropriate instructions for the protection of those data and their classification, if any.

3. Persons acquiring rights of access to data or to systems from persons with primary responsibility for them have secondary responsibility for the protection of those data through compliance with the instructions of the persons primarily responsible, whether within the same division or not, and with all appropriate guidelines and procedures.

4. Divisions will provide security in keeping with the requirements of the corporate guidelines and augmented by such additional controls as may be required by local circumstances. Compliance by each division with the guidelines for quantitative risk assessments is expected.

5. The management of any functional area with primary responsibility for data must conduct such reviews and evaluations of those data as may be required to see that they are as timely, complete, accurate, precise, and relevant as is required to properly support the uses made of them.

6. Persons in the possession of data in whatever form are charged with appropriate protection of those data. Appropriate protection is defined by persons with primary responsibility for those data.

7. Employees whose normal duties require or permit access to sensitive data, not just classified data, will be required to sign annually a Standards of Conduct statement which includes their responsibilities for the protection of data.

8. The division security management is responsible for monitoring compliance with asset protection and loss prevention procedures appropriate to data and computing equipment and with the provision of appropriate physical security safeguards for them.

9. Divisions are responsible for the review and approval of the adequacy of business controls described in the functional specifications for each new system.

10. Divisions are responsible for the inclusion into all division-peculiar systems of all appropriate security controls and for the compliance of such systems with appropriate corporate standards and guidelines for security.

Internal Audit

The General Auditor is responsible for assessing, throughout __ , compliance with security-related specifications, standards, guidelines, and generally accepted business practices.

REFERENCES

Computer Control Guidelines, Second Edition, Canadian Institute of Chartered Accountants (CICA), February, 1986.

"EDP Threat assessments: Concepts and Planning Guide," *RCMP Security Information Publications* # 2, January, 1982.

Fites, Philip. E., Martin P. J. Kratz, and Alan F. Brebner, *Control and Security of Computer Information Systems*, W. H. Freeman/Computer Science Press, New York, NY, 1989.

Gallegos, Frederick, Dana R. (Rick) Richardson, and A. Faye Borthick, *Audit & Control of Information Systems*, South-Western Publishing Company, West Chicago, IL, 1987.

Krauss, Leonard L. and Aileen MacGahan, *Computer Fraud and Countermeasures*, Prentice-Hall, Englewood Cliffs, NJ, 1979.

Lobel, J., *Foiling the System Breakers: Computer Security and Access Control*, McGraw-Hill, New York, NY, 1986.

Parker, Donn B., *Computer Security Management*, Reston Publishing Company, Inc., Reston, VA, 1981.

Appendix A: References

This appendix lists all the references from the ends of chapters in the text body, in alphabetical order by author.

AFIPS Systems Review Manual on Security, AFIPS Press, Montvale, NJ, 1974.

AFIPS, Security: "Checklist for Computer Center Self-Audits," AFIPS Press, Washington, DC, 1979.

Attanasio, C. R., P. W. Markstein, and R. J. Phillips, "Penetrating an Operating System: A Study of VM/370 Integrity," *IBM Systems Journal*, Volume 15, Number 1, pp. 102-116.

Bacic, Eugene Mate, "Computer Viruses," Government of Canada Communications Security Establishment, S312-6-7, Ottawa, December 19, 1988.

Becker, Hal B., *Information Integrity*, McGraw-Hill, New York, NY, 1983.

Becker, L. G., *Computer Abuse and Misuse: Assessment of Federal and State Legislative Initiative*, Institute of Defense Analyses, 1801 N. Beauregard Street, Alexandria, VA, IDA Paper P-1798, 1984.

Behrman, Jack H., *Essays on Ethics in Business and the Professions*, Prentice-Hall, Englewood Cliffs NJ, 1988.

Beker, Henry and Fred Piper, *Cipher Systems*, John Wiley & Sons, New York, NY, 1982.

Bell, D. E., and L. J. La Padula, "Secure Computer Systems: Unified Exposition and MULTICS Interpretation," MTR-2997, rev. 1, vols. I-III, Mitre Corporation, Bedford, MA, November, 1973-June, 1974.

Biba, K. J., "Integrity Considerations for Secure Computer Systems," National Technical Information Service NTIS AD-A039324, Springfield, VA, 1977.

Bill C-60, "An Act to Amend the Copyright Act and to Amend Other Acts in Consequence Thereof," The House Of Commons Of Canada, 2nd Session 32nd Parliament 1986-87.

Blanc, Robert P., ed., "An Analysis of Computer Security Safeguards for Detecting and Preventing Intentional Computer Misuse," National Bureau of Standards Special Publication 500-25, Gaithersburg, MD, 1978.

Bosworth, Bruce, Codes, *Ciphers and Computers*, Hayden Book Company, New York, NY, 1982.

Brandstad, Dennis K., Ed., *Computer Security and the Data Encryption Standard*, National Bureau of Standards Special Publication 500-27, NY, 1978.

Brownoski, J., *Science and Human Values*, Harper & Row, New York, 1956.

Bruschweiler, Wallace S. Sr., "Computers as Targets of Transnational Terrorism," in *Computers & Security*, J. B. Grimson and H. J. Kugler (eds.), Elsevier Science Publishers, North-Holland, 1985.

Burnham, David, *The Rise of the Computer State*, Random House, New York, NY, 1983.

"Case Histories In Computer Security," *Computers & Security*, No. 53, July/August, 1983.

Clark, D. D., and Wilson, D. R., "A Comparison of Commercial and Military Security Policies" in *Proceedings* of the 1987 Symposium on Security and Privacy, IEEE Computer Society, Washington, DC, 1987.

Cohen, Fred, *Computer Viruses*, 1985. Unpublished doctoral thesis.

Cohen, Fred, "Computer Viruses: Theory and Experiments," 7th DOD/NBS Computer Security Conference, September, 1984.

Computer Control Guidelines, Canadian Institute of Chartered Accountants, Toronto, 1986.

"Computer Crime Law Reporter," National Center for Computer Crime Data, 904 Daniel Court, Santa Cruz, CA 95062, 1989.

Computer Data Authentication, Federal Information Processing Standards Publication 113, National Institute of Standards and Technology, Washington, DC.

"Computer Security Guidelines For Implementing the Privacy Act of 1974," National Bureau of Standards, FIPS-PUB-41, U.S. Department of Commerce, Springfield, VA, May 30, 1975, p. 3.

"Controlling Information: Data Classification," *Computer Security*, No. 50: January/February, 1983.

Cooper, James Arlin, *Computer-Security Technology*, Lexington Books, Lexington, MA, 1984.

Data Encryption Standard, Federal Information Processing Standards Publication 46-1, National Institute of Standards and Technology, Washington, DC, 1988.

"Datapro Reports on Information Security," 1988, Datapro Research Corp., Delran, NJ 08075, 800/328-2776.

Davies, D. W., and W. L. Price, *Security for Computer Networks*, John Wiley & Sons, New York, NY, 1984.

Davis, G. G., *Software Protection, Practical and Legal Steps to Protect and Market Computer Programs*, Van Nostrand Reinhold, New York, NY, 1985.

Deavours, Cipher A., and Louis Kruh, *Machine Cryptography and Modern Cryptanalysis*, Artech House, Dedham, MA, 1985.

Denning, Dorothy Elizabeth Robling, *Cryptography and Data Security*, Addison-Wesley Publishing Company, Reading, MA, 1983.

DES Modes of Operation, Federal Information Processing Standards Publication 81, National Institute of Standards and Technology, Washington, DC, 1980.

Diffie, W., and M. Hellman, "New Directions in Cryptography," *IEEE Transactions on Information Theory*, Vol. IT-22(6), November, 1976, p. 644-654.

Disaster Planning for Government of Alberta Records, Records Management Branch, Alberta Public Works Supply and Services, 10442 - 169 Street, Edmonton, Alberta T5P 3X6, 1987.

Disaster Recovery Journal, Systems Support, Inc., P. O. Box 510110, St. Louis, MO 63151. Perhaps the best of several specialized journals currently published in the contingency planning field.

Edelhertz, Herbert, et al., *The Investigation of White-Collar Crime: A Manual for Law Enforcement Agencies*, U.S. Department of Justice, Law Enforcement Assistance Administration, Government Printing Office, Washington, DC, 1977.

"EDP Threat assessments: Concepts and Planning Guide," *RCMP Security Information Publications* # 2, January, 1982.

The Electronic Vault: Computer Piracy and Privacy (Home of the Future: Industry Research Report series), The Yankee Group, Boston, 1984.

Emergency Preparedness Canada, *Guide to the Preservation of Essential Records*, 121 pages, French & English, EPC 12/87, December, 1987.

Fernandez, E. B., R. C. Summers, and C. Wood: *Database Security and Integrity*, Addison-Wesley, Reading, MA, 1981.

Fike, John L., and George E. Friend, *Understanding Telephone Electronics*, Texas Instruments Inc., Dallas, TX, 1983.

"Financial Institution Message Authentication X9.9," American National Standards Committee X9- Financial Services, American Bankers Association, Washington, DC, April 13, 1982.

Fisher, Royal, *Information Systems Security*, Prentice-Hall, Englewood Cliffs, NJ, 1984.

Fites, Philip E., Peter Johnston, and Martin P. J. Kratz, *The Computer Virus Crisis*, second edition, Van Nostrand Reinhold, New York, NY, 1992.

Fites, Philip. E., Martin P. J. Kratz, and Alan F. Brebner, *Control and Security of Computer Information Systems*, W. H. Freeman/Computer Science Press, New York, NY, 1989.

Gallegos, Frederick, Dana R. (Rick) Richardson, and A. Faye Borthick, *Audit & Control of Information Systems*, South-Western Publishing Company, West. Chicago, IL, 1987.

Garfinkel, Simon, and Eugene Spafford, *Practical UNIX Security*, O'Reilly & Associates, Inc., 632 Petaluma Avenue, Sebastopol, CA, 95472, 1991.

Gasser, Morrie, *Building a Secure Computer System*, Van Nostrand Reinhold, New York, NY, 1988.

"Good Security Practices for Personal Computers," IBM Data Security Support Programs, First Edition White Plains, NY, March, 1984.

Gorrill, B. E., *Effective Personnel Security Procedures*, Dow Jones-Irwin, Inc., Homewood, IL, 1974.

Grant, Kenneth A. et al., "Guidelines for User Requirements for Security in Integrated Communications and Information Systems," report to Department of Communications cat. no. CO22-87/1989E, Stevenson Kellogg Ernst & Whinney, Toronto, 1989.

Greenberger, M., "Method in Randomness," *Communications of the ACM*, vol 8 #3, March, 1965, p. 177.

"A Guide to the Ethical and Legal Use of Software for Members of the Academic Community," EDUCOM Software Initiative/ADAPSO, 1987.

"Guidelines for Automatic Data Processing Physical Security and Risk Management," FIPS Publication 31, U.S. Department of Commerce/National Bureau of Standards, Washington, DC, June, 1974.

"Guidelines for Computer Security Certification and Accreditation," National Bureau of Standards, FIPS Pub. 102, U.S. Department of Commerce, Springfield, VA, September 27, 1983.

"Guidelines for Implementing and Using the NBS Data Encryption Standard," FIPS Publication 74, U.S. Department of Commerce/National Bureau of Standards, Washington, DC, April, 1981.

"Guidelines on User Authentication Techniques for Computer Network Access Control," FIPS Publication 83, U.S. Department of Commerce/National Bureau of Standards, Washington, DC, September, 1980.

Hagelshaw, R. Lee, *The Computer User's Legal Guide*, Chilton Book Company, Radnor, PA, 1985.

Henderson, Stuart C., "A Comparison of Data Access Control Packages: Part I," *Computer Security Journal*, Computer Security Institute, Vol. IV # 2, 1989; and ". . .: Part II," Vol. V # 1, 1989.

Hersh, H. M., Caramazza, A., and Brownell, H. H., "Effects of Context on Fuzzy Membership Functions," in *Advances in Fuzzy Set Theory and Applications*, Gupta, M. M., Ragade, R. K., and

Yager, R. R. (eds.), Elsevier, New York, NY, 1979.

Hersh, H. M. and Caramazza, A., "A Fuzzy Set Approach to Modifiers and Vagueness in Natural Language," *Journal of Experimental Psychology: General*, vol. 105, no. 3, 1976, p. 254-276

"Human Error," AD-689 365, U.S. Department of Commerce, Springfield, VA.

IBM, *OS/VS2 MVS RACF General Information*, document GC28-0722-xx (xx is the number of the current release).

IBM, *RACF 1.8.1 Overview*, July 1988

IBM, *RACF Auditor's Guide System Reference Library*, document SC28-1342-xx.

IBM, *RACF GAC and Generics Use*, document GG22-9375-xx.

IBM, *RACF Security Administrator's Guide*, document SC28-1340-xx.

Isshiki, Koichiro R., *Small Business Computers, a Guide to Evaluation and Selection*, Prentice-Hall, Englewood Cliffs, NJ, 1982.

Jacobson, Robert V., et al., "Guidelines for Automatic Data Processing Physical Security and Risk Management," Federal Information Processing Standards Publication 31, National Bureau of Standards, Gaithersburg, MD, 1974.

Johnson, Deborah G., *Computer Ethics: A Guide for the New Age*, Prentice-Hall, Englewood Cliffs, NJ, 1985.

Kahin, Brian, "Property and Propriety in the Digital Environment: Towards an Examination Copy License," EDUCOM Software Initiative White Paper, October 1988.

Karcher, P. A., and R. R. Shell, "MULTICS Security Evaluation: Vulnerability Analysis," ESD-TR-XXX, Electronics Systems Division (AFSC), L. G. Hanscombe Field, Bedford, MA, July 11, 1983.

Katzen, Harry J., *The Standard Data Encryption Algorithm*, Petrocelli Books, New York, NY, 1977.

Koenig, R. C., "Advances in Information Classification," *Computer Security and Privacy Symposium Proceedings*, DM 35, Honeywell Information Systems, Phoenix, AZ, April 15-16, 1980, pp. 119-124.

Kratz, Martin P. J., "Evidentiary Problems of Computer-Generated Materials," in *Technology and the Law for General Practitioners*, Legal Education Society of Alberta, Edmonton, AB, March, 1987.

Kratz, Martin P. J., "Introduction to Copyright Infringement," in *Technology and the Law for General Practitioners*, Legal Education Society of Alberta, Edmonton, AB, March, 1987.

Krauss, Leonard L. and Aileen MacGahan, *Computer Fraud and Countermeasures*, Prentice-Hall, Englewood Cliffs, NJ, 1979.

Landreth, Bill, with Howard Rheingold, *Out of the Inner Circle: A Hacker's Guide to Computer Security*, Microsoft Press, Bellevue, WA, 1985.

Lobel, J., *Foiling the System Breakers: Computer Security and Access Control*, McGraw-Hill, New York, NY, 1986.

Lord, Kenniston W., Jr., *The Data Center Disaster Consultant*, QED, Wellesley, MA, 1977.

Mandell, Steven L., *Computer Data Processing, and the Law*, West Publishing Company, Minneapolis, MN, 1984.

Martin, James, *Principles of Data Base Management*, Prentice-Hall, Inc., Englewood Cliffs, NJ, 1976.

Martin, James, *Security, Accuracy, and Privacy in Computer Systems*, Prentice-Hall, Inc., Englewood Cliffs, NJ, 1973.

Meyer, Carl H., and Stephen M. Matyas, *Cryptography: A New Dimension in Computer Security*, John Wiley & Sons, New York, NY, 1982.

"Model Computer Crime Act," Data Processing Management Association, Park Ridge, IL, 1986.

MULTICS Data Security, GA01-00, Honeywell Information Systems, Phoenix, AZ, 1982.

Murray, W. H., "The Application of Epidemiology to Computer Viruses," *Computers & Security* 7 (1988), pp. 139-150.

National Center for Computer Crime Data, "Commitment to Security", NCCCD and RGC Associates, March 27 1989.

National Computer Security Center, *Trusted Network Interpretation of the Trusted Computer System Evaluation Criteria*, NCSC-TG-005 Version-1, National Computer Security Center, Fort George G. Meade, MD, July, 1987

National Technical Information Service, *Risk Analysis Methodology*, AD-A072-249, U.S. Department of Commerce, Springfield, VA, 1979.

"OECD Guidelines Governing the Protection of Privacy and Transborder Flows of Personal Data," Recommendations of the Council of Europe, adopted at its 523rd meeting on September 2#, 1980.

Parker, Donn B., *Computer Security Management*, Reston Publishing Company, Inc., Reston, VA, 1981.

Parker, Donn B., *Ethical Conflicts in Computer Science and Technology*, Arlington, VA., AFIPS Press, 1981.

Parker, Donn B., *Ethical Conflicts in Information and Computer Science, Technology and Business*, QED Information Sciences Inc., Wellesley MA, 1991. (An update of the 1977 study published in 1981.)

Parker, Donn B., *Fighting Computer Crime*, Charles Scribner & Sons, New York, NY, 1983.

Password Management Guideline, CSC-STD-002-85, Department of Defense Computer Security Center, Fort George G. Meade, MD, April, 1985.

Password Usage, Federal Information Processing Standards Publication 112, National Bureau of Standards, Gaithersburg, MD, May 30, 1985.

Personal Computer Security Considerations (NCSC-WA-002-85), National Computer Security Center, Ft. George G. Meade MD, December, 1985.

Peters, Donald, "The InterNet Crash", Government of Canada Communications Security Establishment S600-19-1, December 20, 1988.

Pozzo, Maria M., and Terence E. Gray, "Computer Virus Containment in Untrusted Computing Environments," *Information Security: The Challenge*, Preprints of papers from the fourth IFIP Security on Information Systems Security, Monte Carlo, December, 1986.

The Privacy Act of 1974, Public Law 93-579, 93rd Cong., S.3418, December 31, 1974.

Reed, Susan K., "Automatic Data Processing Risk Assessment," National Bureau of Standards NBSIR 77-1228, Gaithersburg, MD, 1977.

Remer, Daniel, *Legal Care for Your Software: A Step by Step Guide for Computer Software Writers*, A Nolo Press Book, Berkeley, CA, 1984.

Report of the Invitational Workshop on Integrity Policy in Computer Information Systems, Bentley College, Waltham, MA, 1988.

"Report on Statistical Disclosure and Disclosure-Avoidance Techniques," U.S. Department of Commerce, U.S. Government Printing Office, Washington, DC, 1978.

Rhee, Man Y., *Error Correction Coding Theory*, McGraw-Hill, New York, NY, 1990.

Richards, T., Schou, C. D. and Fites, P.E. "Information Systems Security Laws and Legislation," in *Information Security Modules*, National Security Agency, Gaithersburg, MD, 1991.

Rivest, R. L., A. Shamir, and L. Adleman, "A Method for Obtaining Digital Signatures and Public-Key Cryptosystems," *Communications of the ACM*, vol. 21(2), pp. 120-126, February, 1978.

Ruthberg, Zella G., *Guide to Auditing for Controls and Security: A System Development Life Cycle Approach*, NBS Special Publication 500-153, NIST, Gaithersburg, MD, 1988.

Scalet, Elizabeth, *VDT Health and Safety: Issues and Solutions*, Ergosyst Associates, Ergosyst/Report Store, Old Post Road, Brookfield, VT 05036, December, 1987.

Schmucker, Kurt J., *Fuzzy Sets, Natural Language Computations, and Risk Analysis*, Computer Science Press, Reston, VA, 1984.

"The Security Act of 1987", PL-100-235.

Sessions, M. V., "The Security and Privacy of Data Management Systems," Computer Security and Privacy *Proceedings*, MEDW-359-501, Honeywell Information Systems, Phoenix, AZ, April 2-3, 1979, pp. 99-101.

Shannon, C. E. "Communication Theory of Secrecy Systems," *Bell System Technical Journal*, October 1949.

"Small Computer Systems Security," and "Small Systems Questionnaire," *EDP Security Bulletin*, Royal Canadian Mounted Police "T" Directorate, Vol 12 No. 1, July 1987, Pp 4-7. The questionnaire is NOT COPYRIGHTED and may be reproduced for use; it is also in French and English.

Sookman, Barry, *Sookman Computer Law: Acquiring and Protecting Information Technology*, Carswell, Toronto, Canada, 1989.

Spafford, Eugene H., *The InterNet Worm Program: An Analysis*, Purdue University Computer Sciences Department, November, 1988.

Straub, Detmar W., "Organizational Structuring of the Computer Security Function," *Computers & Security* 7 (1988), pp. 185-195.

Sykes, D. J., "Generating Secure System Specifications," *Computer Security and Privacy Symposium Proceedings*, DF 84, Honeywell Information Systems, Phoenix, AZ, April 7-8, 1981, pp. 91-93.

Systems Center, Inc., *VMSECURE Directory Manager's Guide*, Reston, VA, August, 1989.

Systems Center, Inc., *VMSECURE Messages and Codes*, Reston, VA, August, 1989.

Systems Center, Inc., *VMSECURE Rules Facility Guide*, Reston, VA, August, 1989.

Systems Center, Inc., *VMSECURE System Administrator's Guide and Reference*, Reston, VA, August, 1989.

"Target Hardening," *RCMP Security Information Publications # 3*, September, 1983.

Technical Rationale Behind CSC-STD-003-85: Computer Security Requirements, CSC-STD-004-85, Department of Defense Computer Security Center, Fort George G. Meade, MD, June, 1985.

Troy, Eugene F., Stuart W. Katzke, and Dennis D. Steinauer, *Technical Solutions to the Computer Security Intrusion Problem*, National Bureau of Standards, Washington, DC, November, 1984.

Trusted Computer System Evaluation Criteria, DOD 5200.28.STD, Department of Defense Computer Security Center, Fort George G. Meade, MD, December, 1985.

Validation Systems Requirements and Procedures, NBS Special Publication 500-156, NIST, Washington, DC, 1988.

Van Tassel, Dennis, *Computer Security Management*, Prentice-Hall, Inc., Englewood Cliffs, NJ, 1972.

Wack, John P., *Establishing a Computer Security Response Capability (CSIRC)*, NIST Special Publication 800-3, National Institute of Standards and Technology, Gaithersburg, MD 20899, November, 1991.

Weber, Ron, *EDP Auditing: Conceptual Foundations and Practice* (Second Edition), McGraw-Hill, New York, NY, 1988.

Westin, A. F., *Privacy and Freedom*, Atheneum, New York, NY, 1967.

White, Steve R., David M. Chess, and Jimmy Kuo, *Coping with Computer Viruses and Related Problems*, IBM Research Report RC 14405, Yorktown Heights NY, January, 1989.

Whiteside, Thomas, *Computer Capers*, Thomas V. Crowell Co., New York, NY, 1978.

Appendix B: Attacks

This appendix, somewhat as Appendix A does for references, collects all the types of attack considered in this book. The index shows where the attacks and related countermeasures are addressed in the text body.

There is much overlap among categories of attack. Some of the attacks below are repeated in more than one category. Most of them may fall into more than one category depending on the specific instance in question.

B.1 GENERAL DEFINITIONS

Some general definitions common to all attacks are reproduced here.

Threat

A *threat* is any circumstance or event with the potential to cause harm to a system in the form of destruction, disclosure, modification of data, and/or denial of service. (NCSC-WA-001-85)

Common usage today is from the press, which uses the word to describe people who "break into" computers for various purposes. (BBD)

Attack

Action or actions that prevent any part of an Automated Information System from functioning in accordance with its intended purpose. This includes any action which causes the unauthorized destruction, modification, or delay of service (DODD 5200.28; NCSC-WA-001-85)

The act of aggressively trying to bypass security controls on an AIS. The fact that an attack is made does not necessarily mean that it will succeed. The degree of success depends on the vulnerability of the system or activity and the effectiveness of existing countermeasures. (NCSC-WA-001-85)

Asynchronous Attack

[An] asynchronous attack [. . .] is an attempt to exploit the interval between a defensive act and the attack in order to render inoperative the effect of the defensive act. For instance, an operating task may be interrupted at once following the checking of a stored parameter; the user regains control and malevolently changes the parameter; the operating system regains control and [continues] processing using the maliciously altered parameter. (JL)[1]

Exhaustive Attack

[An] exhaustive attack consists of discovering secret data by trying all possibilities and checking for correctness. For a four-digit password, one might start with 0000 and move on to 0001, 0002 till 9999. (JL).

Denial of Use
The user is able to "crash" the system, or hang it up by putting a program into an endless loop.

---

[1]This is one example of the TOC/TOU problem described in section B.5.

At least one commercial time-sharing system allowed jobs to submit other jobs; it was possible on that system (by submitting a job that submits itself) to fill up the job queue with jobs waiting to be processed so that the computer became unavailable to anyone else.

Denial of service is inherently an active method of attack. Denial of service can relate to an individual link—even something as crude as physically cutting wires—or to any larger subset of a network, up to an entire telecommunications system.

Data Contamination

A deliberate or accidental process or act that results in a change in the integrity of the original data. (AR 380-380; FIPS PUB 39). (See also the second meaning in a different context in section B.4.)
Hacker

Originally, a computer enthusiast who spent significant time learning the functions of the computer without benefit of formal training (and often without the technical manuals) by trying combinations of commands at random to determine their effect.

B.2 CRYPTOGRAPHY ATTACKS

Cryptanalysis is the art and science of reading enciphered messages without the encryption key. Several types of specialized attack are recognized. Details are in Chapter 2.

Hacker

Originally, a computer enthusiast who spent significant time learning the functions of the computer without benefit of formal training (and often without the technical manuals) by trying combinations of commands at random to determine their effect.

Ciphertext-Only Attack

The analyst has only the ciphertext from which to determine the key.

Chosen-Plaintext Attack

The analyst is able to obtain ciphertext corresponding to selected plaintext. This is the most favorable case for the analyst. One way to obtain such plaintext-ciphertext pairs is to insert elements into a database, then observe the changes in the stored ciphertext.

Known-Plaintext Attack

The cryptanalyst knows some plaintext-ciphertext pairs. For instance, if the ciphertext represents a computer program, one may reasonably expect that words like *begin, end, do, while, if, then* and so forth appear with some frequency. More precisely, the analyst may *know* that the first portion of the ciphertext relates to a signon message and contains the characters "LOGON".

Chosen-Ciphertext Attack

With public-key systems, the inverse of the chosen-plaintext attack becomes feasible. The analyst may be able to deduce the private key.

Other cryptographic attacks include things like masquerading, playback, spoofing, traffic analysis, and insertion/deletion of blocks or records. These are addressed in section 7.4.

B.3 COMMUNICATIONS ATTACKS

Many attacks on information systems exploit vulnerabilities in telecommunications. Some of the most common are listed under the communications category. Details are discussed in Chapter 8.

A *passive attack* on a telecommunications system by definition is restricted to observation or other methods that do not alter the data within the system. Examples include eavesdropping by means of wiretaps, disclosure by observation of a VDT display and traffic analysis.

Active attacks on networks are those in which data within the network is altered. Alteration could be by modifying existing data, inserting new data, deleting existing data, reordering certain existing data, or replaying a legitimate signal more than the number of times the network expected it.

Between-the-lines Entry

Access obtained through active wiretapping by an unauthorized user to a momentarily inactive terminal of a legitimate user assigned to a communications channel. (AR 380-380; NCSC-WA-001-85; FIPS PUB 39)

A special terminal is used to tap into the communication line used by a legitimate user while the user is not active. Terminals should never be left signed on and unattended, and lines should be shielded.

Compromising Emanations

Unintentional data-related or intelligence-bearing signals which, if intercepted and analyzed, disclose the classified information transmission received, handled, or otherwise processed by any information processing equipment. TEMPEST is an unclassified short name referring to investigations and studies of compromising emanations. It is sometimes used synonymously for the term "compromising emanations." (OPNAVINST 5239.1A; AFR 205-16; AFR 700-10; AR 380-380; NCSC-WA-001-85; DOE 5636.2A)

Covert Channel

A communication channel that allows two cooperating processes to transfer information in a manner that violates the system's security policy. (NCSC-WA-001-85)

Covert Storage Channel
A covert channel that involves the direct or indirect writing of a storage location by one process and the direct or indirect reading of the storage location by another process. Covert channels typically involve a finite resource (*e.g.*, sectors on a disk) that is shared by two subjects at different security levels. (CSC-STD-001-83; NCSC-WA-001-85)

Covert Timing Channel
A covert channel in which one process signals information to another by modulating its own use of system resources (*e.g.*, CPU time) in such a way that this manipulation affects the real response time observed by the second process. (CSC-STD-001-83; NCSC-WA-001-85)

Cross-Talk

An unwanted transfer of energy from one communications channel to another channel. (FIPS PUB 39; AR 380-380)

Eavesdropping

The unauthorized interception of information-bearing emanations through the use of methods other than wiretapping. (FIPS PUB 39; AR 380-380)

Eavesdropping may involve any of many forms of tapping into a channel. The method used varies depending on the type of communication medium, the access to transmission lines and the signal being transmitted.

Line Disconnect

The user in a time-sharing or other remote system mode signs off without disconnecting; or the line "goes down," but the system has not yet acknowledged and terminated the user's session. Until this termination occurs, another user may be able to use the session without proper validation. Not all systems "hang up" properly when a line is disconnected.

NAK Attack

A penetration technique which capitalizes on a potential weakness in an operating system that does not handle asynchronous interrupts properly and thus, leaves the system in an unprotected state during such interrupts. (FIPS PUB 39)

NAK and ACK are control codes in communications protocols. In asynchronous processing it is necessary for one device to inform another that processing is complete and more data can be accepted, or that data is about to be transmitted (in synchronous processing this is handled by a clock). If one device does not acknowledge a request ("NAK"), it or the other device may be vulnerable to a spoofing attack or other penetration attempt until the ACK is received.

Network Weaving

A technique using different communication networks to gain access to an organization's system. For example, a perpetrator makes a call through AT&T, jumps over to Sprint, then to MCI, and then to Tymnet. The purpose is to avoid detection and trace-backs to the source of the call. (TC)

Playback

A *playback* attack occurs when something is recorded and then played back into the process for which it was intended. Examples could include signon information or access control information. This is more common in a network than inside a stand-alone computer.

Repudiation

Denial by one of the entities involved in a communication of having participated in all or part of the communication. (ISO 7498-2)

Traffic Analysis

The inference of information from observation of traffic flows (presence, absence, amount, direction, and frequency). (ISO 7498-2)

Similar to browsing, someone looks at things like how often people are contacted, who is contacted, and what time of the day or week the contacts are. Quite a lot of information about what is underway may be deduced from traffic analysis—without alerting the victim by trying to intercept or change anything.

Wiretapping

1. *Active*. The attaching of an unauthorized device, such as a computer terminal, to a communications circuit for the purpose of obtaining access to data through the generation of false messages or control signals, or by altering the communications of legitimate users. (AR 380-380)

2. *Passive*. The monitoring and/or recording of data while the data is being transmitted over a communications link. (FIPS PUB 39)

B.4 ATTACKS ON DATA AND DATABASES

Data and databases are subject to simple attacks like browsing and sometimes-sophisticated attacks like statistical inference. Chapter 5 addresses these and other topics.

Aggregation

Aggregation refers to collection of many individually unimportant statistics, which can reveal an overall picture that should not be disclosed. The classic example is disclosure of a plan of attack from aggregating information about individual combat unit positions.

Individual data systems and data elements may be determined to be unclassified and to be of a specific sensitivity category. When those data are combined with other data, the totality of the information may be classified or in a higher sensitivity category, with higher protection requirements. (AFR 205-16)

Statistical Inference

Statistical inference attacks are the opposite problem: The overall picture *should* be disclosed, but not individual statistics. These attacks may depend on the extent of a penetrator's supplementary knowledge; that is, information about database elements which is gathered from sources other than the database. A list of common statistical attacks on data bases would include:

1. Query Set attacks
2. Key-specific attacks
3. Characteristic attacks
4. Trackers
5. Insertion/deletion attacks
6. Chosen value attacks

Small/Large Query Sets

A *query set*, informally, is the number of database entities (records) that are selected by a query. If the number of entities is small the probability of individual disclosure is high (if there is only one member, the probability is unity.) Queries that select small query sets need to be controlled. If a query language permits the operation of complementation, then large query sets must be controlled as their complements could be sensitive small query sets.

Key-Specified Attack

If keys are known (Social Security numbers, for instance), then logical queries about groups of records with specified keys may disclose sensitive data associated with individual records.

Characteristic Attack

A generalization of key-specific attacks is *characteristic-specified queries*. By specifying characteristics known to be shared by small numbers of records, successive queries can narrow the query set to small numbers. At the extreme, it may be possible to select individuals this way.

Trackers

Individual, general, and union *trackers* exploit the basic principle of padding small query sets with enough extra records that the query sets grow larger than any arbitrary restriction on query set size. The effect of the padding, being known, then can be removed, thus disclosing information about individual records.

Insertion/Deletion Attack

If users can add or delete records from a database, then records that match desired characteristics can be inserted, thus increasing query set sizes to defeat query-set size controls. This is similar to padding in trackers.

Chosen Value Attack

Some *chosen value* (for example, the median of a set of salaries or grade averages) is selected. Queries that define overlapping sets are then proposed to the database. As the overlap in succeeding refined queries decreases, it may be possible to isolate a single record that matches the chosen value. This value is then associated with that record, and individual information has been disclosed. The same principle can be generalized to identifying ranges of values into which individual records fall (salary between $25,000 and $27,500, for example.)

Browsing

The act of searching through storage to locate or acquire information without necessarily knowing of the existence or the format of the information being sought. (OPNAVINST 5239.1A; AR 380-380; NCSC-WA-001-85; FIPS PUB 39)

The user searches through the computer system, or through files, attempting to locate sensitive information. Such action is controllable through file and other access controls. Commonly, a table listing what the user may access is created, and the user is restricted to only those accesses. Files may be given individual passwords in some systems.

Contamination

The introduction of data of one sensitivity and need-to-know with data of a lower sensitivity or different need-to-know. This can result in the contaminating data not receiving the required level of protection. (AFR 205-16)

This definition relates to security levels rather than to the sense of the definitions under "data contamination."

Data Contamination

The process by which errors in data elements stored in computerized information systems propagate during repeated use, leading to unreliable data bases. Examples include any data that are used as input to another process, whose outputs then become unreliable. Also called "corruption."

Residue

Data left in storage after processing operations and before degaussing or rewriting has taken place. (FIPS PUB 39; AR 380-380; NCSC-WA-001-85)

Scavenging

Searching through residue for the purpose of unauthorized data acquisition. (FIPS PUB 39; AR 380-380)

Seepage

The accidental flow to unauthorized individuals of data or information, access to which is presumed to be controlled by computer security safeguards. (FIPS PUB 39; AR 380-380; NCSC-WA-001-85)

See also covert channel.

Waste

Sensitive printouts may be discarded; more than one system has been penetrated by people who found lists of user identification and passwords in a waste container.

Searching through object residue to acquire unauthorized data. (NCSC-WA-001-85)

B.5 OPERATING SYSTEM ATTACKS

One category of attack exploits vulnerabilities common to most operating systems. Chapters 7 addresses these issues.

Legality Checking

The system may not check on the parameters a user supplies it.

Implied Sharing

The system may place sensitive operating system control information in the user's workspace; under some conditions, the user may be able to read this. (For example, a program error, perhaps deliberately induced, that causes a memory dump may cause a printout of everything in the workspace, including anything the operating system may have stored there.)

Incomplete Parameter Checking

A system fault which exists when all parameters have not been fully checked for accuracy and consistency by the operating system, thus making the system vulnerable to penetration. (FIPS PUB 39; AR 380-380; NCSC-WA-001-85)

Interrupts

A penetrator may cause program or system interrupts; some operating systems allow a process to enter a privileged mode with more access than usual, while processing an interrupt.

Password

Passwords may not be used, they may be simple to guess, or the system may allow repeated attempts. (A microcomputer easily can be programmed to try to log on by repeatedly selecting passwords from a list.)

Repetition

Systems may allow users an indefinite number of attempts to sign on, thus allowing use of a microcomputer and repeated guesses. The system should disconnect or hang up after some small number of unsuccessful attempts, and the event should be reported to the operator or security officer.

TOC/TOU

The acronym *TOC/TOU* (Time Of Check *versus* Time Of Use) often is used to describe a class of asynchronous attacks. The acronym TOCTU also is used. In essence some control information, or perhaps merely the contents of a file, is changed between the time the system security functions check the contents of variables (or access permissions to files) and the time the variables actually are used during operations. The Between-the-lines, NAK attack, various attacks involving interrupts, and line disconnect in the next list are more specific examples of this class of problem. Many systems have been vulnerable to TOC/TOU class of attacks during I/O processing.

B.6 MALICIOUS CODE

A general name for programs that are intended to cause harm or otherwise defeat security measures is *malicious code*. Although it is a misnomer (people can be malicious; code is neutral), the term is gaining recognition.

Logic Bomb

A resident computer program that, when executed, checks for particular conditions or particular states of the system which, when satisfied, triggers the perpetration of an unauthorized act. (NCSC-WA-001-85)

Malicious Logic

Hardware, software, or firmware that are intentionally included in a system for an unauthorized purpose. An example is a Trojan Horse. (NCSC-WA-001-85; CSC-STD-003-85; CSC-STD-004-85) Also known as *malicious code*; the word *logic* includes things like hardware and firmware that usually are not thought of as "code."

Hidden code

Programs may contain undocumented code that does things other than those described in the manuals. Poorly controlled maintenance often allows an opportunity for a programmer to insert a routine that should not be in the program. A program library and controls over maintenance may make this difficult or impossible.

Maintenance hook

Special instructions in software to allow easy maintenance and additional feature development. These are not clearly defined during access for design specification. Hooks frequently allow entry into the code at unusual points or without the usual checks so they are a serious security risk if they are not removed prior to live implementation. Maintenance hooks are simply special types of *trap doors*. (NCSC-WA-001-85)

Salami Technique

In data security, pertains to a fraud spread over a large number of individual transactions, *e.g.,* a program which does not correctly round off figures but diverts the leftovers to a personal account. (MS)

The classic example is a program that accumulates all roundoff figures for a bank's loan calculations into one account. When each amount is rounded to an even penny, there will be small amounts left over. Each such "slice" is less than 1/2 cent and is not noticeable, but for thousands of accounts the cumulative effect can be large.

Time Bomb

A logic bomb where the trigger is recognition of a particular time reached or interval elapsed.

Trap Door

A hidden software or hardware mechanism that permits system protection mechanisms to be circumvented. It is activated in some innocent appearing manner, *e.g.,* special "random" key sequence at a terminal. Software developers often introduce trap doors in their code that enable them to re-enter the system and perform certain functions. (NCSC-WA-001-85)

Trojan Horse

1. A computer program with an apparently or actually useful function that contains additional (hidden) functions that surreptitiously exploit the legitimate authorizations of the invoking process to the detriment of security. For example, making a "blind copy" of a sensitive file for the creator of the Trojan horse. (CSC-STD-001-83; NCSC-WA-001-85)
2. A computer program that is apparently or actually useful and that contains a trap door. (FIPS PUB 39)

This is a generic name for the "hidden code" penetration method. Something is in a program that is not supposed to be there, that causes sensitive data to be available. Or, the program does not do what it is supposed to; the name is misleading. It is possible to put a Trojan horse into a system that would, for example, simulate the logon messages; after collecting user data the Trojan horse would put the data somewhere accessible to the perpetrator and then remove itself from the system. Familiar kinds of Trojan horses in microcomputers include the freeware or shareware disk compression utility that spreads a virus as well as compresses data on a disk, and many computer games.

Virus

A computer *virus* is a program that can "infect" other programs by modifying them to include a (possibly evolved) copy of itself. When another program is infected, that other program becomes a Trojan horse with at least the non-intended function of propagating the virus, plus any other actions the virus may include.

Virus code is not a new idea nor are viruses very interesting mathematically. However, the existence of several thousand different viruses (some for all popular microcomputers), combined with at least 75 million computers exposed, in total comprises a severe problem.

Viruses come in many flavors. The most widely accepted classification is into boot sector, system, and application viruses. The names indicate which types of programs are infected. Boot sector infectors so far have been the worst, since they infect a system before any protective programs can execute. This is most regrettable, as known boot sector viruses spread *only* when a computer is booted from an infected disk, which can happen only when several major violations of very basic security precautions occur simultaneously.

Virus code has been written and demonstrated successfully on mainframe and minicomputers as well as on microcomputers. The security practitioner should not make the error of relegating this phenomenon to the personal computer world. Virus code more or less ignores access control software, since it is an integrity issue rather than one of authorized access.

Worm

A program that moves through an address space by making a copy of itself in a new location. The new location may be any place that the worm can access in any particular invocation. If a copy remains in the previous location and can be invoked again, the worm can replicate into many copies of itself very rapidly, and can cause denial of use by clogging system resources. Benign worms built for such system functions as automatic backups do not leave copies behind, and they save the contents of what may be in the new location and replace any storage they once occupied with its previous contents when a new copy is made.

B.7 CONSOLE AND OPERATIONS ROOM ATTACKS

Some kinds of attack require access to operations facilities or personnel, or make use of special capabilities provided by the operator's console that are not available elsewhere (or anywhere through software alone.)

Device Address Modification

The address of a device could be altered, thus effectively re-routing input or output and perhaps compromising security.

Hardware Content Modification

An operator typically can re-assign the mapping between logical and physical devices. Another exposure to operations personnel is hardware modification: physically removing, altering, or replacing components (tampering). Examples could include insertion of transmitters that would constitute a covert channel, replacement of a large disk in a microcomputer with a small one (probably for personal gain), and similar activities.

Initial Program Load (IPL)

The program that actually starts the operating system is controlled from the console. An operator has an opportunity to load the wrong program (accidentally or intentionally), possibly seriously compromising operations or security.

Memory Content Modification

In some systems, it is possible to modify memory directly from the console, bypassing any software controls.

Micro-code Load and Modification

Most hardware is controlled at a level deeper than the operating system by micro code. This code defines such things as precisely what actions are to be caused by specific machine instructions. Loading the wrong micro-code could interfere seriously with the computer or pose a serious security exposure, again bypassing any possible software controls. (This exposure is more to a systems engineer than to an operator, as micro-code is a very specialized area and loading it is not a typical operator duty.)

Operator Carelessness

Operators may inadvertently mount the wrong disk packs or tapes; some cases of operator deception have been reported where penetrators telephoned the operator and were able to trick the operator into giving out sensitive information.

System Shutoff

System shutoff is handled from the console or operations area, just as is IPL. Whether the concern is for accidental or intentional inappropriate shutdown, this capability is a potential exposure.

Tampering

An unauthorized modification which alters the proper functioning of a system or piece of equipment in a manner which degrades the security it provides. (NCSC-WA-001-85)

For example, addition of a node to a network may be passive in the sense that it permits the network's data flow to be intercepted without any effect on the data in the network. An action is required to add a node, and in this sense the attack is active. Once a node is added to a network, something like a covert channel has been created. Network information can be analyzed at will once it is intercepted by the node.

These and similar capabilities are necessary to run the system and recover from failures of one sort or another, and cannot be restricted without severely impacting on system reliability. Personnel controls and appropriate separation of duties are the most useful in controlling misuse of the capabilities of the hardware in the operations realm. Physical control measures (such as not permitting staff to bring unauthorized electronic equipment into the computer room) are appropriate as well.

B.8 PHYSICAL ATTACKS

This last category of attack is labelled "physical attacks" because in general some actual contact by a person is involved (for instance talking to an operator, or looking over someone's shoulder.) Some of the attacks, such as a masquerade, do not require a physical presence.

Another category of attack could include such physical actions as throwing bombs, shooting at computers, cutting communications cables, using magnets near magnetic media, and similar things (all of which have happened). This kind of attack is not a major focus of this book and generally is not covered except as an example.

Impersonation

An attempt to gain access to a system by posing as an authorized user. (AR 380-380; NCSC-WA-001-85)

Masquerade

An attempt to gain access to a system by posing as an authorized user. (FIPS PUB 39)

The pretense by an entity to be a different entity. (ISO 7498-2)

The penetrator obtains identification and passwords and signs on with someone else's account. A user pretending to be someone else by grabbing a line as noted above, is a form of masquerade.

Operator Deception

A penetrator, for example, may convince an operator to divulge a password (perhaps by claiming to have just changed the password and miskeyed the new one).

Although it is not a technical problem, a favorite way to compromise computer systems is to approach human beings involved in operations, programming, and similar tasks. This exposure is not new and not in the realm of technical problems nor subject to technical solutions.

Piggy Back

The gaining of unauthorized access to a system via another user's legitimate connection. (NCSC-WA-001-85)

Shoulder Surfing

The stealing of passwords by watching users sign on to systems at their terminals. (TC)

Spoofing

The deliberate act of inducing a user or a resource into taking an incorrect action. (NCSC-WA-001-85; AR 380-380; FIPS PUB 39)

For example in communications, the penetrator intercepts a communication line and substitutes his or her own messages to the legitimate user and/or to the system. (For example, simulates the signon program and thus gets the user to give out identification and password information.)

Appendix C: Security Videos

This list of films and videos is from the National institute of Standards and Technology ;(NIST) security BBS. (This BBS is open to the public; the phone number is (301) 948-5717, and there are lines for numerous protocols and modem types. Access *via* the InterNet is available on an experimental basis as of early 1993.) Repeats of addresses for the same organization have been edited out to save space.[1]

Title: ADP Security for Security Inspectors

   Length: 8 Minutes

   Date: October 1985

      Organization: Allied Signal Inc.
      Bendix Kansas City Division
      P.O. Box 419159
      Kansas City, MO 64141-6159

   Cost: Free with blank tape

   Description: This videotape was made for the Physical Security Department and deals with computer security concerns of security inspectors.

Title: ASIS Safeguarding Proprietary Information

   Program: Computers

   Length: 12-15 Minutes

   Date: 1985

      Organization: American Society for Industrial Security

   Cost: $219.00

   Description: The vulnerabilities of computers are addressed concerning unauthorized access or abuse by authorized employees.

Title: ASIS Safeguarding Proprietary Information

   Program: Document Manager

   Length: 12-15 Minutes

   Date: 1985

      Organization: American Society for Industrial Security

   Cost: $219.00

   Description: Describes how to classify, store, distribute, declassify, and destroy a variety of documents.

Title: ASIS Safeguarding Proprietary Information

   Program: The Electronic Office

      Length: 12-15 Minutes

   Date: 1985

---

[1]The edited version of this list was published in the *SIG-CS Newsletter* in March, 1991. This list was compiled in 1988; some information listed may be outdated. Prices vary from free or nominal to several hundred or over a thousand dollars. These prices are subject to change and have been included merely to show a comparison.

Organization: American Society for Industrial Security

Cost: $219.00

Description: Looks at the security problems faced in the electronic office as opposed to a paper-oriented office and suggests ways to deal with these problems.

Title: ASIS Safeguarding Proprietary Information

Program: Industrial Espionage

Length: 12-15 Minutes

Date: 1985

Organization: American Society for Industrial Security

Cost: $219.00

Description: The growing dangers of loss through espionage are examined and the methods that can provide protection.

Title: ASIS Safeguarding Proprietary Information

Program: Overview

Length: 12-15 Minutes

Date: 1985

Organization: American Society for Industrial Security

Cost: $219.00 (Discounts available)

Description: This overview presents a general picture of the need for information security and the kinds of information that need to be protected throughout various departments.

Title: ASIS Safeguarding Proprietary Information

Program: Policy

Length: 12-15 Minutes

Date: 1985

Organization: American Society for Industrial Security

Cost: $219.00 (Discounts available)

Description: This video describes six principles that should be followed in creating an information security policy. Included are suggestions about the distribution policy, enforcement of it, and reviews.

Title: ASIS Safeguarding Proprietary Information

Program: Product Development

Length: 12-15 Minutes

Date: 1985

Organization: American Society for Industrial Security

Cost: $219.00 (Discounts available)

Description: Product development focuses on special requirements needed for information security when a product is being developed. Physical security safeguards are discussed, need-to-know policies are reviewed, and the importance of continually keeping employees aware of security needs is described.

Title: ASIS Safeguarding Proprietary Information

Program: Program Development

Length: 12-15 Minutes

Date: 1985

    Organization: American Society for Industrial Security

Cost: $219.00 (Discounts available)

Description: This video shows how to implement an information security program and includes advice on how to sell the program to an organization. How to prepare, distribute, and review the proposed program are also shown.

Title: ASIS Safeguarding Proprietary Information

    Program: Research

    Length: 12-15 Minutes

    Date: 1985

        Organization: American Society for Industrial Security

    Cost: $219.00 (Discounts available)

    Description: This video looks at the unique security concerns during a research and development effort. The components of an effective information protection policy are detailed.

Title: Billion Dollar Bubble

    Length: 60 Minutes

    Date: 1979

        Organization: Films Incorporated
        5547 N. Ravenswood
        Chicago, IL 60640
        (800) 323-4222

    Cost: $450.00 video, $900.00 film, $200.00 rental

    Description: The Equity Funding Fraud is dramatized in this account of a computer used to cover up the largest corporate fraud ever. Considered a classic by many computer security professionals.

Title: Chip Mykrp Meets the Wizard

    Length: 15 Minutes

    Date: September 1984

        Organization: Allied Signal Inc.
        Bendix Kansas City Division

    Cost: Free, just send a blank Beta videotape

    Description: This video was produced by DOE/AL and addresses personal computer security. Originally shown to ACSSOs/ACPPMs and others.

Title: Cloak and Data

    Length: 24 Minutes

    Date: 1983

        Organization: Vision Film Associates
        85 Scollard Street
        Toronto, ON M5R 1G5 Canada
        (416) 960-1636

    Cost: $700.00 plus $10.00 shipping and handling

Description: Awareness is highlighted in this fictitious story of how a security officer up-grades security practices and catches a dishonest employee. The need to protect passwords and hard copy, and to use computer resources for official business purposes only is emphasized.

Title: Computer Security

Length: 22 Minutes

Date: 1985

> *Organization:* Coronet/MTI Film and Video Division of Simon and Schuster School
> 108 Wilmot Road
> Deerflies, IL 60015
> (800) 621-2131

Cost: $445.00 video, $95.00 rental

Description: A general computer-security training video that emphasizes the responsibilities people have with regard to computers.

Title: Computer System Security: Access Control

Length: 17 Minutes

Date: 1985

> *Organization:* National Computer Security Center
> National Security Agency
> ATTN: E-23
> 9800 Savage Road
> Fort George G. Meade, MD 20755-6000
> (301) 859-4502

Cost: Free, include a blank VHS or Beta tape

Description: Shows how to control access to a computer system and how to prevent crime on the system from occurring.

Title: Computer System Security: Access The Ins and Outs

Length: 20 Minutes

Date: 1985

> *Organization:* National Computer Security Center National Security Agency

Cost: Free, include a blank VHS or Beta tape

Description: Computer crime is broken down into who, what, where, why, and how.

Title: Computer Systems Security: It's Your Move

Length: 19 Minutes

Date: 1986

> *Organization:* AT&T Data Securities Services
> Room 5BA
> 9333 South John Young Parkway
> Maitland, FL 32819-8619
> (800) 447-0012

Cost: $195.00 to own, $35.00 to preview

Description: This video encourages employees to promote security and information integrity by not leaving passwords in sight, always wearing I.D. badges, shredding sensitive data, and remembering to implement contingency plans in the event of an emergency.

Title: Data Security: Be Aware or Beware

Length: 20 Minutes

Date: 1985

Organization: Commonwealth Films, Inc.
223 Commonwealth Avenue
Boston, MA 02116
(617) 262-5634

Cost: $400.00 plus $5.00 or $150.00 for a 3-day rental plus $10.00

Description: This video is aimed at the orientation of new employees. It humorously presents its message concerning what end-users need to know about computer security.

Title: Electronic Delinquents

Length: 14 Minutes

Date: 1983

Organization: Coronet/MTI Film and Video Division of Simon and Schuster School

Cost: $265.00 video, $290.00 film, or $50.00 for 3-day rental.

Description: This film is from ABC's 20/20 program and deals with the vulnerability of computer systems to an experienced hacker. Also discusses society's attitude that big businesses are legitimate game for attacks by hackers.

Title: Goodbye Gutenberg

Length: 85 Minutes

Date: 1982

Organization: Films Inc.

Cost: $695.00 video, $1,050.00 film, $250.00 rental

Description: Computers are seen to have had more of a dramatic impact on society than the printing press in this BBC production. A variety of topics are discussed along with privacy.

Title: High Tech Trail to Moscow

Length: 50 Minutes

Date: 1985

Organization: Films Incorporated

Cost: $495.00

Description: The KGB cleverly bribes U.S. officials for access to high-tech secrets using credit information obtained from computers.

Title: Information Asset Protection Overview

Length: None Specified

Date: None Specified

Organization: IBM Corporation
Information Systems Management Institute
One IBM Plaza, 19th Floor

Chicago, IL 60611
(800) 426-2468

Cost: none

Description: This video deals with the importance of disaster-recovery planning to protect data from misuse or loss.

Title: Information: Handle With Care

Length: 10 Minutes

Date: 1982

> *Organization:* Modern Talking Pictures

Cost: none

Description: This film shows what can happen from errors, carelessness, or deliberate attempts to penetrate or damage a system.

Title: Information Security: Protecting Our Major Asset

Length: 45 Minutes

Date: 1985

> *Organization:* Southwestern Bell Telephone Co.
> Room 22-H-8, One Bell Center
> St. Louis, MO 63101-3099
> (314) 235-3027

Cost: $20.00

Description: This video focuses on information security needs and issues. The format of this production is a tutorial-type overview.

Title: Introduction to the Unclassified Computer Security Program—DOE Order 1360.2

Length: 19 Minutes

Date: February, 1988

> *Organization:* U.S. Department of Energy
> Office of ADP Management
> MA24, Room F-315 GTN
> Washington, DC 20545
> FTS 233-3307

Cost: none

Description: This video is designed to help CPPMs implement DOE Order 1360.2

Title: I Shouldn't Be Telling You This But

Length: 23 Minutes

Date: 1980

> *Organization:* Coronet/MTI Film and Video Division of Simon and Schuster School

Cost: $650.00 video, $695.00 film, or $165.00-a-week rental

Description: This video emphasizes the need for employees to follow policies and procedures concerning computer access responsibilities. A part of POPI—Protection of Proprietary Information program.

Title: Let There Be Light

Length: 11 Minutes

Date: 1983

> *Organization:* Sales Graphics
> 30 Irving Place
> New York, NY 10003
> (212) 505-0910

Cost: $320.00

Description: A general security video that deals not only with computer security but also with general office security. Discusses why security is important.

Title: Locking the Door

Length: 20 Minutes

Date: 1987

Organization: Commonwealth Films, Inc.

Cost: none

Description: This video shows six incidents of breaches of computer data security, based on actual cases. Emphasizes restricted data access to authorized users, secure and backup diskettes, and other physical hazards.

Title: Memo from a Grateful Spy

Length: 10 Minutes

Date: 1981

Organization: Coronet/MTI Film and Video Division of Simon and Schuster School

Cost: $265.00 video, $290.00 film, or $50.00 for a 3-day rental

Description: This film deals with information security more than computer security. Motivating employees and establishing good procedures are discussed.

Title: The New Ecology

Length: 10 Minutes

Date: None Specified

> *Organization:* AT&T American Transtech
> 2600 Maitland Center Parkway
> Suite 390
> Maitland FL 32751
> (800) 477-0012

Cost: $195.00 to own, $35.00 to preview

Description: This video focuses on the need by people, particularly top management, to protect their organization's information from disasters, employee error, or sabotage.

Title: An Ounce of Prevention

Length: 12 Minutes

Date: 1984

> *Organization:* Modern Talking Pictures
> 3520 Progress Drive, Suite C
> Cornwells Heights, PA 19020
> (215) 639-6540

Cost:

Description: This film presents a scenario showing the importance of information security in office systems. Comes with a guide for discussion.

Title: Proper Use of Computers

Length: 8 Minutes

Date: July 1982

> *Organization:* Allied Signal Inc.
> Bendix Kansas City Division

Cost: Free, just send blank Beta tape

Description: This video covers computer security and the proper use of government computers.

Title: Spies in the Wires

Length: 50 Minutes

Date: 1984

> *Organization:* Films Incorporated

Cost: $495.00

Description: Shows methods that are used to steal information from a computer. Emphasis is placed on the importance of computer security by the end-user.

Title: Throw Away the Key

Length: 28 Minutes

Date: 1986

> *Organization:* Info Pro Division of Bell Canada
> 16E2
> 700 Rue de la Gauchetiere O
> Montreal, PQ H3B 4L1 Canada
> (514) 870-5566

Cost: none

Description: Reviews security measures for computerized information systems. Outlines the threats associated with the computer environment and explores the array of measures that should be taken to minimize the risk of computer crime and property losses.

Title: Time Bomb

Length: 33 Minutes

Date: 1982

> *Organization:* Visucom Productions
> P.O. Box 5472
> Redwood City, CA 94063
> (415) 364-5566

Cost: $695.00 plus $7.50 to own, or $150.00 plus $7.50 to rent

Description: The video deals with a former employee who wants revenge and writes a program that will sabotage the computer. Emphasizes the need for computer security, including physical security and auditing a system.

Title: Training for Computer Security Officers of Microcomputers

> *Length:* 23 Minutes

> *Date:* 1986

>> *Organization:* Oak Ridge National Laboratory
>> ATTN: Michael Sheppard
>> P.O. Box Y
>> Bldg. 9766, MS 2
>> Oak Ridge, TN 37831-6109
>> (615) 574-1639

> *Cost:* $20.00

Description: A video to define the duties and responsibilities of the System Computer Security Officer to protect his/her microcomputer system and all classes of information.

Title: Was It Something I Said?

> *Length:* 13 Minutes

> *Date:* 1985

>> *Organization:* Coronet/MTI Film and Video Division of Simon and Schuster School

> *Cost:* $225.00 video, $325.00 film, $75.00 rental

Description: This video looks at the responsibility of employees at all levels to protect proprietary or classified information.

Title: You Do Make A Difference

> *Length:* 12 Minutes

> *Date:* 1986

>> *Organization:* Bank of America
>> Box 37000
>> Dept. 3183
>> San Francisco, CA 94137
>> (415) 622-5599

> *Cost:* $400.00

Description: This general computer security video emphasizes individual responsibility and need to backup.

Index

*-Property, 151, 156, 411, 414. *See also* Star property
7498-2. *See* ISO 7498-2
A-123, ix, 315, 316, 346, 375, 376
A-130, ix, 114, 118, 346
A5 encipherment, 46
ABC extinguishers, 365
Aborted connection, 181
Abstract program, 325
Acceptance, 313, 341
Access
    level, 113
    matrix, 169
    mode, 148, 411
    model, 170
    privileges, 126
    type, 114, 148
Access control, 14, 126, 148, 199, 200, 327
    list, 148, 373
    mechanism, 413, 374
    package, 14
    roster, 374
    software, 14, 15, 16, 169, 175, 331, 446
Access to Information Act, 114
Accessibility, 69, 160
Accidental threats, 143
Accountability, 2, 126, 127, 148, 220
Accreditation, 220, 347
    authority, 220
Accumulated depreciation, 67
Accuracy, 338, 386

ACF-2, 14
Acknowledgment, 133, 387, 417
ACM, 401
ACP, 403
Acquired value, 57, 61, 62, 67, 71, 367
Acquired Value Worksheet, 63
Acquisition, 339, 340
Active attacks, 439
Active wiretapping, 181
Activity log, 374
Address space, 149, 176
Adleman, 176
Administrative
    controls, 82
    security, 220, 374
AFFIRM, 324
AFR 205-16, ix
AFR 700-10, ix
Aggregation, 114, 121, 122, 123, 313, 327, 441
Air conditioning, 102, 103, 104
ALE, 50
ALGOL 68, 162
Algorithmic refinement, 325
American Society for Industrial Security (ASIS), 397
Annual Loss Expectancy (ALE), 50
Anonymous file transfer, 177
ANSI X9.9, 45
Application form, 139, 141
Application software, 313

Appropriate scale, 244
Approval, 319, 321, 322, 339, 340, 384
Approval/Accreditation, 148
AR 380-380, ix
ASIS, 397
ASM, 401
Assertion, 411
Asset(s)
    category, 50
    data and information, 61
    granularity, 114
    intangible, 57
    people skills and training, 58
    physical, 58
    software, 60
    tangible, 57
    valuation, 62, 63
Asset-based risk analysis, 84
Association for Computing Machinery (ACM), 401
Association for Systems Management (ASM), 401,
    404
Assurance, 126, 220, 323
Asymmetric key. See Public key encryption
Asynchronous Attack, 149, 182, 437
Attack, 149, 437
Audit, 220
    of computer security, 345
    objectives, 345
    software, 348
    trail, 149, 332, 346, 348
Auditability, 336, 386
Authentication, 33, 127, 199, 328
    exchange, 200
    process, 221
Authenticity requirement, 25
Authorization, 114, 221, 338
Authorized transactions, 343
Availability, 50, 54, 56, 61, 62, 63, 67, 71, 72, 419

Backup, 96, 97, 98, 99, 101, 102, 103, 104, 106, 108,
    109, 110, 142, 174, 321, 342, 361, 362, 367, 370,
    382, 385, 387, 388, 446
    computer, 98. See also tandem
    control point, 109
    documentation, 99, 108
    frequency, 99
    offsite, 106, 109
    online, 98
    procedure, 95, 97, 98, 342, 353, 374
    UPS, 103, 104
Backup computer, 106. See also Tandem
Bacterium, 149
Banyan Vines, 17
Batch total, 384, 386

BBD, ix, 154, 181, 183, 437
BCS, 397
    examinations, 407
"Before" image, 98
Behavior, 102, 130, 134, 231, 390, 396, 418
Bell and La Padula, 151, 169, 318, 332, 412, 414
Bell-La Padula model, 411
Between-the-lines, 172, 182, 439, 444
Bill of Rights, 140
Biometrics, 4, 360
Block
    chaining, 30
    cipher, 30
    mode, 29
Block structured computer languages, 318
Book value, 67
Boot sector, 176
    infectors, 175
Bounds checking, 149, 153, 155
    register, 149
British Computer Society (BCS), 398, 407
Brownout, 103, 104, 105
Browsing, 172, 174, 441, 442
Budget, 340
Bugs, 390
Bulletin boards (BBS), 175
Burleson, G., 270
Business continuity planning, 322

CACITS, 402
Calculations, 73
Call back, 182
Canadian Advisory Council on Information
    Technology Security (CACITS), 402
Canadian Information Processing Society (CIPS),
    398, 401, 408
Canadian Standards Association, 402
Canadian System Security Centre, 401
Canadian Trusted Computer Product Evaluation
    Criteria (CTCPEC), 166
Capability, 149, 163
CASE, 318
Cash
    cow, 244
    flow, 244
Catastrophe, 96, 98, 106, 353
    plan, 108. See also Contingency plan; disaster
        plan
Category, 114
Caution Statement, 114, 221
CC, 166
CDI, 333
CDP, 400, 403, 404, 405
Cell suppression, 123

Cellular telephones, 47
Centralization, 243
CERT, 79, 248
Certification, 140, 141, 221, 396, 397, 400
Certification
    and Accreditation Program, 221
    Ambassadors, 399
    Canada, 398
Certified Information Systems Auditor (CISA), 400
Certified Information Systems Security Practitioner
    (CISSP), 401
Chained block cipher, 44
Change authorization, 339
Change control, 90, 321, 347
Channel, 182
Characteristic attacks, 327
Characteristic-specified queries, 122, 442
Charter of Rights and Freedoms, 140
Checksum, 44, 154
Chip, 244
Chlorofluorocarbon, 366
Chosen-ciphertext attack, 32, 438
Chosen-plaintext attack, 32, 438
Chosen value attacks, 122, 327, 442
Cipher block, 32
    chaining, 30, 32
Ciphertext, 21, 25, 30
Ciphertext-only attack, 32, 438
CIPS, 398, 401, 408
CISA, 400, 406
CISSP, 401, 407
Clark-Wilson, 334
Classes of threat, 72
Classified data/information, 114, 115
Clearing, 353
Cleartext, 22, 24, 31
Clipper Chip, 45, 46
Closed security environment, 222
Closed shop, 374
Code system, 22
Coercivity, 357
Cohen, F., ix, 159, 176
Cohesion, 318, 336
Collusion, 150, 256, 297
Color coding, 387
Common Body of Knowledge, xvii, xxiii-xxvi, 388,
    394
Common Criteria, 166
Communications, 59
Communications security (COMSEC), 182
Compartmentalization, 150
Compensating controls, 160, 321, 343
Completeness, 161, 338, 385, 386
Complexity, 69, 70, 160, 382
Composability, 217
Compression, 174, 446

Compromising Emanations, 182, 439
Computationally
    infeasible, 25, 31, 43, 44
    secure, 31
Computer Control Guidelines, 337
Computer
    abuse, 150, 256, 297
    Assisted System Engineering (CASE), 318
    crime, 256, 297
    facility, 353, 374
    fraud, 150, 256, 298
    laws
        Computer Virus Eradication Act, 268
        Computer Fraud and Abuse Act of 1986, 267
        Computer Security Act of 1987, 402
    security response capability, 248
Computer Emergency Response Team (CERT), 248
Computer Professionals for Social Responsibility
    (CPSR), 398
Computer Security Institute (CSI), 399, 401
Conceptual entity, 411
Confidentiality, 54, 56, 63, 67, 71, 72, 82, 133, 145,
    417
Configuration
    control, 150
    management, 222, 314, 322, 374
Confinement property, 150, 151, 414
Conflict of interest, 133, 417
Connection
    confidentiality, 199
    integrity with recovery, 199
    integrity without recovery, 199
Connectionless
    confidentiality, 199
    integrity, 199
Connectivity, 136
Consequential damages, 101
Constrained Data Item (CDI), 333
Consultant, 234
Containment, 90
Contamination, 151, 442
Contingency
    management, 96, 222, 374
    plan, 96, 99, 105, 106, 108, 222, 322, 338, 375, 388.
        See also Catastrophe plan; Disaster plan
Continuity of operations, 96, 222, 375
Continuous protection, 126, 168
Control, 83, 84, 346, 348
Control objective, 337
Control point, 71, 72, 109, 337, 385, 386
    analysis, 82
Control total, 386, 384, 387
Control zone, 223, 375
Controlled access area, 375
Controlled security mode, 222
Controlled space, 223

Conversion, 339
  plan, 347
COPS, 79
Copyright law
  examples of works protected, 278
  exemptions, 279
  formalities, 279
  moral rights, 279
  nature of right, 279
  protection of ideas, 280
  registration, 279
Corrective control, 87, 90, 142, 360
Correctness proof, 151, 411, 412
Corruption, 70, 72, 73, 151, 314, 443
Cost/benefit analysis, 338, 345
Cost exposure matrix, 72, 76, 77, 86
  worksheet, 73
Cost/loss multiplier, 76
Countermeasure, 151
Coupling, 318, 336
Covert channel, 151, 158, 170, 182, 314, 439, 443
  storage 151, 183, 314, 439
  timing 151, 183, 314, 439
CP1 (Data Gathering) – CP11 (Data Disposition),
  83
CPSR, 398
Creative output, 100
Criminal law, 268
Criticality, 96, 99, 101, 115, 152
Cross-talk, 183, 440
Cryptanalysis, 31, 390
Cryptographic checksum, 44, 152, 205
Cryptographic system, 31, 46
Cryptography, 22, 46, 47
CSC-STD-001-83, ix
  -002-85, ix
  -003-85, ix
  -004-85, ix
  -005-85, ix
CSP, 400, 403, 404, 405
Culture, 129, 130, 133, 418
Custodian
  of data, 2, 115
  of information, 394
Cycle, 152

Data
  computer-readable, 61
  contamination, 152, 314, 326, 327, 438, 443
  control group, 384. *See also* input-output
    control group
  integrity, 14, 22, 115, 200, 315, 322, 331, 348
  owner, 115
Data (in disaster recovery)
  re-entry, 100
  recovery, 101
Data (programming)
  dictionary, 318, 319, 320
  flow diagrams, 318
  hiding, 318
  structure refinement, 325
Data authentication algorithm, data authentication
    code, 45
Database, 116, 314
Database management system, 323, 325. *See also*
    DBMS
Data-Dependent protection, 152
Data Encrypting Key, 22
Data Encryption Standard, 33. *See also* DES
Data origin authentication, 199
Data Processing Management Association
    (DPMA), 84, 399
Data Security Administrator, 228
DBMS, 323, 325, 326, 327, 328, 329, 330
DCID 1/16-1, ix
DCID 1/16-1, Sup., ix
Decentralization, 232, 233, 243
Deciphering transformation, 24, 25
Decipherment, 22
Decomposition, 324
Decryption, 21, 25
Dedicated security mode, 223
Default classification, 116
Degauss, 354, 356, 369
Degree of membership, 78
Denial of service, 50, 172, 349, 437
Density, 69, 138
Departmental Security Officer (DSO), 228
Department of Defense Directive. *See* DODD
DES, 26, 27, 29, 32, 33, 43, 45, 46, 47
Designated approving authority, 223
Design verification, 315, 412
Destruction, 72, 97, 98, 102, 354, 358, 369, 370
Detection, 50, 89, 90, 363, 386
Detective controls, 87, 89, 360, 385, 386
Device address modification, 389, 446
Digital signature, 23, 33, 45, 205
  mechanisms, 200
Disaster
  plan, 105, 108
  communication, 108
  stages, 107
  testing, 108
Disclosure, 46, 72, 109, 133, 349, 358, 419
Discretionary access control, 152, 155, 412, 415
Dishonesty, 138
Distortion, 384
Distribution statement, 116, 223
Documentation, 116, 315, 346, 347, 390
DODD (Department of Defense Directive)

2040.2, ix
3200.12, ix, 116, 314
5200.1-R, ix
5200.28, x
5200.28-STD, x
5200.28M, x
5215.1, x
5230.24, x
5230.25, x
7040.6, x
DODI 5215.2, x
DOE
    5635.1A, x
    5636.2A, x
Dog, 244
Dollars as a measure, 62
Domain, 152
Dominate, 412
DOS, xxviii, 147
Downsizing, 245, 378, 380
DPMA, 84, 86, 397, 399
Drucker, Peter, 232, 243
Dry standpipe, 366
DSO, 228
Dumb terminal, 183

Eavesdropping, 153, 183, 440
Economy
    of mechanism, 168, 169
    of scale, 244
EDI, 47, 137
Edit check, 332
EDP audit, 344, 345, 348
EDP Auditors' Association (EDPAA), 399
EDP Auditors' Foundation (EDPAF), 400, 406
EFT, 183
Electromagnetic emanations, 183
Electronic data interchange (EDI), 47, 137
Electronic funds transfer (EFT), 183
Embarrassment, 349
Emergency changes, 339
EMP, 196
Employee awareness, 88, 133, 417, 418
Enciphering transformation, 25
Encipherment, 23, 46, 184, 200, 205, 206
Encode, 23
Encryption, 21, 23, 25, 47, 171, 329, 330, 331, 332
    advantages, 46
    advice, 46
    disadvantages, 46
    end-to-end. See End-to-end encryption
    key, 21, 26, 27
    link. See Link encryption
    password table, 171

performance degradation, 46
    unit, 21
End-to-end encryption, 23, 205
Entities, 148, 338
Entrapment, 257, 298
Environment, 354
Environmental
    conditions, 342
    control, 102, 103, 342
Equity Funding fraud, 451
Erasure, 354, 369
Error-correcting codes, 32
Error-detecting codes, 32
Escort, 354, 375
Escrow, 46
Estimation methods, 63
ET, x
Evaluation, 251
Event, 76, 90, 105
    security breach, 171, 444
Evidence, 348
Executive state, 153, 159
Exhaustive attack, 153, 437
Exit review, 145
Expected lifetime, 116
Expected value, 78
Expert witness, 310
Exploitable channel, 183
Exposure, 50, 69, 70, 71, 72, 76, 77, 82, 84, 91, 103,
    104, 135, 138, 172, 335, 342, 420
    ranking, 64
External security audit, 375
Extinguisher, 365
Eye blood vessel, 4

Facility, 59, 357, 358, 359
    management, 322
Fail safe, 223
    defaults, 168
Fail soft, 223
Failure control, 224
FAQ, 177
Fayol, H., 232
FBCS, 407
FC, 166
FDM, 324
Feasibility study, 251
Federal Criteria for Information Technology
    Security (FC), 166
Fellow of the BCS (FBCS), 407
Fetch protection, 153
File
    protection, 315
    security, 315

FIMA, 45
Fingerprint, 4
FIPS publications
    39, x
    102, 347
    112, x
    113, 45
Fire
    prevention, 363, 364
    protection, 363, 364, 365, 366, 367
Firmware, 153
Formal
    development methodology, 324
    integrity policies, 322
    proof, 153, 412
    security
        models, 415
        policy, 208
        policy model, 412, 413, 415
    specification, 151, 153, 323, 413
    verification, 151, 153, 208, 323, 411, 413
Fraud, 349
Free Trade Agreement, 291
Freeware, 174, 446
Frequency of backups, 99
Frequently Asked Questions (FAQ), 177
ftp, 177
Functional matrix, 228, 230
Fuzzy metrics, 77, 78, 79, 87
Fuzzy sets, 77, 78

Galois fields, 44
Game, 174, 446
Gantt chart, 252
GAO (General Accounting Office), x
Gauss, 354
Generally Accepted Accounting Principles
    (GAAP), 67
Generally Accepted Auditing Principles, 344
General value analysis of system assets, 86
Geometric characteristics, 4
Gödel, K., 162
Goods, 354
Granularity, 116, 153, 205, 206, 315, 328, 329, 330
Graphical user interface (GUI), 350
Guessing attack, 30
GUI, 350
GVE, 324
Gypsy, 162, 324, 325
Gypsy Verification Environment (GVE), 324

Hacker, 154, 170, 438

Halon
    1211, 365
    1301, 365
    2402, 366
Hand measurements, 4
Handshaking procedures, 154, 183
Hardware, 60
    content modification, 389, 446
    handshaking, 184
Harmful access to a computer, 271
Hash total, 89, 154, 384, 386
Hazards, 345
HDM, 324
Hidden code, 172, 174, 445
Hierarchical Development Methodology (HDM),
    324
High Order Language (HOL), 162
HOL, 151, 412
Hot-standby, 96
Human factors, 168
Human rights, 140, 141

IC, x
ICCP, 400
Identification, 126
Identity-based security policy, 413
IFIP, 401, 402
Image, 397
Impersonation, 154, 448
Implementation, 230, 322, 338, 341, 415
    of available tools, 171
    of the kernel, 161, 162
    plan, 339
    step in system development, 320, 321
    verification, 413
Implied query, 124
    set, 124
Implied sharing, 171, 443
In-house, 382
Incompatible functions, 320, 334, 341, 343
Incomplete parameter checking, 171, 444
Individual accountability, 224, 375
Inference control, 212, 328
Information center, 108, 382, 383
Information flow model, 170
Information hiding, 325
Information security specialist
    attorney, 308
    expert witness, 310
    role of, 308
    witness in court, 309
Information System Security Officer (ISSO), 224.
    See also DSO, SSO
Information Systems Professional (ISP), 408

Information Systems Security Association (ISSA), 84, 400, 401
Information Technology Security Evaluation Criteria (ITSEC), 166
Initial permutation, 33, 35
Initial Program Load (IPL), 388, 447
Initial state, 412
Input-output, 380
    control group, 379, 384, 386
Insertion/deletion attack, 122, 327, 442
Institute for Certification of Computer Professionals (ICCP), 400
Insurance, 101
Intangible asset, 57, 63, 71, 129
    physical, 59
Integrity (data), 44, 54, 55, 56, 67, 71, 72, 175, 320, 322, 336, 385, 386, 419, 446
Integrity policy, 332
Integrity Verification Procedure (IVP), 333
Intentional threats, 144
Interface, 385, 386, 387, 388
Internal control, 315, 375
    documentation, 315, 376
    review, 316, 376
Internal security audit, 376
International Federation for Information Processing (IFIP), 401
International Information Systems Security Certification Consortium, 400. *See* (ISC)²
International Standards Organization. *See* ISO
InterNet, 177, 267
Interpersonal skills, 135
Interruption, 72, 73, 342, 358
Interrupts, 172, 173, 444
    handling, 156
Intrinsic value, 57, 62, 67, 71, 365
Investigation, 257
Invisibility, 91
I/O control, 380
IPL, 388, 389, 447
(ISC)², xvii, 400, 401
ISO, 166, 344, 415
ISO 7498-2 document, x, 198
ISO/OSI, 17
    protocols, 318
    standards, 198
Isolation, 154, 161, 361
ISP, 398
ISSA, 84, 86, 400, 401
ISSO, 224
ITSEC, 166
IVP, 333, 334

Job exposure matrix, 230
Job exposures, 81

Kernel, 156, 161, 162, 163
    capabilities, 163
    overhead, 162
    proof of, 161
    operating system general, 161
    reference validation, 161, 162, 163
Key, 23. *See also* Encipherment; Encryption
    escrow, 45
    management, 23, 27, 46, 330
    schedule, 33, 36
    schedule calculation, 41
    stream, 30
Key-specified attack, 122, 327, 442
Known-plaintext attack, 30, 32, 438

Labels, 116, 126, 387, 388
Laissez-faire, 245
LAN, 181, 188, 203, 204, 208, 210, 211, 212
Lattice, 154, 318, 413
Layering, 317, 318, 323
Layers of protection, 90, 91
Leadership style, 245
Leading, 244
Least privilege, 2, 154, 156, 168, 224, 413
Legal exposure, 349
Legality checking, 171, 443
Levels of classification, 126
Librarian, program, 319
Library (), 384, 388. *See also* Media library; Program library
Likelihood, 71, 72, 73, 76
Limited ADP access security Mode, 224
Line disconnect, 171, 172, 173, 440, 444
Link-by-link encipherment, 24
Link encryption, 23, 205
Local variables, 318
Logic bomb, 154, 159, 173, 444
Lock-and-key protection system, 355
Logical
    asset, 57
    completeness measure, 413
    controls, 71, 230, 318, 319, 336
    operators, kernel validation, 162
Loss multiplier, 76, 86
Lucky guess, 25

MAC, 45, 48, 184, 328, 331, 332
Magnetic
    field intensity, 355
    flux, 355
        density, 354, 355
    media, 353, 354, 368, 369, 370
    remanence, 355
    saturation, 355
Mainframe operations staff, 380
Maintenance, 339, 341
Maintenance hook, 171, 390, 445
Malicious code, 155, 159, 194, 195, 210, 211, 444
Mandatory access control (MAC), 152, 155, 413,
    415, 416
Manuals, 348
Marking, 117, 126
Masquerade, 32, 155, 173, 184, 439, 448
Mathematical
    consistency, 162
    verification, 162
Matrix, 228
Maximum order control, 123
Mechanisms, 199
Media, 46, 60, 69, 70, 83, 97, 341, 355, 360, 364, 366,
    367, 368, 369, 370, 384, 387, 388
    erasure, 369
    library, 379, 380, 384, 387
    magnetic, type 1 magnetic, 357, 369
    optical, 369
Memory Bounds, 149, 155
Memory content modification, 389, 447
Message authentication code (MAC), 45, 48, 184,
    328, 331
Metric, 67
    fuzzy, 87. See also Fuzzy metric
Micro-code load and modification, 389, 447
Minimum control standard, 337
MIPS, 378
MK, x
Modularity, 317, 318
Morale, 129, 130, 134, 135, 142, 145, 245
Morris, Robert T., Jr., 267
Motivation, 137, 138, 142
MS, x
MSAT, 187
MTR-8201, x
Multilevel security mode, 224
Multi-user security mode of operation, 225
Multiplier, 77

NAK attack, 172, 173, 440, 444
National Bureau of Standards, 402
National Center for Computer Crime Data
    (NCCCD), 84

National Computer Security Center (NCSC), 402
National Computer Systems Laboratory (NCSL),
    402
National Institute of Standards and Technology
    (NIST), 45, 402, 449
    security BBS, 131
National security, 47, 79, 289, 370
    suspicious factors, 290
National Security Decision Directive 145, 257, 298
NCCCD, 84
NCSC, 402
NCSC-WA-001-85, x
NCSL, 402
Need-to-know, 117
Negligence, 171
Network, 184, 267, 378
    layer (ISO/OSI), 205
    weaving, 173, 184, 440
Network Trusted Computing Base (NTCB), 207,
    208
NIST, 248, 344, 345, 402, 403
    security BBS, 449
NKSR, 155
Noise and perturbation, 124
Non-discretionary security, 155
Non-interference, 169
Non-Kernel Security-Related software (NKSR), 155
Non-repudiation, 205
Notarization, 24, 200, 257, 298
Novell Netware, 17
NP-complete, 31
NSDD-145, x, 185, 227
NTCB, 207, 208
    partitions, 207

Object, 117, 152, 155, 413
    reuse, 117
Objectives, 338
OECD, 290
    transborder data flow guidelines, 290
Oersted, 355, 357
Office automation, 378, 388
Off-site storage, 108
Off-the-shelf software, 345
One-time pad, 31
One-way function, 24
Onion skin, 91
Open design, 168
Open security environment, 225, 376
Open storage, 355, 376
Operating system, 156
Operational
    contingencies, 106
    data security, 376

planning, 239
    security (OPSEC) indicators, 376
    site security manual, 225, 376
operations/maintenance manual, 347
Operator
    carelessness, 171, 447
    deception, 173, 448
OPNAVINST 5239.1A, xi
Opportunity, 138, 160, 172, 334, 445
OPSEC, 376
Optical media, 369
Orange Book, 147, 152, 331
Organization of Economic Cooperation and
    Development (OECD), 290
Organizational structure, 243
Originator, 336, 386
OSI, 205, 208, 331
OSI Security Architecture, 208
Output control, 380, 381
Overcontrol, 84
Overwriting, 355, 356, 369, 370
Owner, 26, 56, 231, 335, 418
    of data, 117
    of information, 394
Ownership, 1, 2, 72

Padding, 122, 442
Parallel run, 252, 347
Paralysis by analysis, 69, 79
Partially ordered set, 154, 318
Passive
    attack, 439
    threat, 51
    wiretapping, 184
Password, 4, 5, 6, 46, 88, 171, 173, 328, 384, 444, 448
    communicating, 6
    creation, 5
    guessing, 4, 5, 171, 444
    selection, 26
    table encryption, 171
PC/PCIE, xi, 158, 258, 299
Peer entity authentication, 199
Penetration, 257, 298
    methods, 160, 172, 175
    profile, 257, 298
    signature, 257, 298
    study, 225, 257, 299
    testing, 156, 225, 348
Peril, 51
Periods processing, 225, 377
Permutation function, 33, 38
Permuted input block, 35, 36
Personal computer security, 451
Personal data, 117

Personal Identification Numbers (PIN), 46
Personnel controls, 377, 389, 447
Perturbation, 124
Physical, 71, 72, 92, 134, 163, 231, 342, 357, 370
    access, 342
    asset, 57, 58, 60
    control space, 356
    layer, 205
    security, 356
Piggyback attack, 156, 158, 184, 173, 448
PIN, 46
Plaintext, 21, 24, 25, 30, 46, 329
Playback attack, 32, 194, 439, 440
Policy, 90, 129, 130, 133, 144, 230, 323, 337, 338, 342,
    346, 413, 417, 418, 420
    example, 418
Power, 244
Preoutput, 35, 36
Presentation layer, 205
Prevention objective, 88, 89, 90
Preventive control, 87, 88, 138, 359, 360
Primitive functions, 38, 39
    function P, 39
    functions S1, S2, . . ., S8, 38
Principle of least privilege, 154, 156, 414
Privacy, 47, 55, 122, 257, 258, 299, 316, 393
Privacy Act, 140
Private key, 25, 26, 43, 45
Private transformation, 45
Privileged
    data, 118
    instructions, 153, 156
    process, 156
    state, 153
Privilege Profile, 156
Probability, 76, 97
Problem child, 244
Procedural abstraction, 325
Procedural security, 225
Procedures, 341
Process, 151, 154, 157, 439
Processing
    controls, 343
    value, 54
Productivity, 235, 245
Professionalism, 130, 141, 231, 396, 397, 399
Profiles, 414
Program librarian, 319, 320, 321
Program library, 173, 319, 320, 321, 445
Project plan, 340
Proprietary data, 118, 258, 299, 316
Protected wireline distribution system, 184
Protection, 88
Pseudo-flaw, 258, 299
Pseudo-random numbers, 26
Public key encryption, 25, 26, 43, 45

Public transformation, 45
Purging, 356
Purloined letter, 91

Quality assurance, 346
Query set, 122, 441
    attacks, 327
    size and overlap control, 123
Questionnaire, 86

RACF, 14, 160
Radio Frequency Interference (RFI), 196
Random numbers, 26
Random sample queries, 124
Rate of change, 99
Re-synchronization, 32
Reaction, 90
Reactive, 90
Read-Only Memory (ROM), 157
Real-time processes, 100
Real-time reaction, 377
Reasonableness checks, 332, 386
Receiver, 26
Record count, 384, 385, 386, 387
Record retention, 344
Recovery procedures, 96, 342, 343, 377
Recursive function theory, 176
Reference check, 88
Reference
    monitor, 157, 158
    validation, 157, 163
Relational DBMS, 330
Remanence, magnetic, 356
Remote job entry (RJE), 380
Removal, 72, 73, 358, 388
Repetition, 171, 444
Replacement cost, 67
Replay, 30
Repudiation, 24, 45, 185, 440
Residue, 157, 443
Resource encapsulation, 157
Responsibilities, 337
Restricted area, 356
Resume, 138, 140, 141
Retina prints, 4
Retro-virus, 158
Review and approval, 258, 299
RFI, 196, 197
Rightsizing, 378
Rings of protection, 91, 109
Risk, 51
    assessment, 51

level of occupations, 81
maps, 359
analysis team, 51, 385
    data processing, 56
    members, 56
    users, 57
management, 51, 71, 72, 80, 88
    process, 68, 84
    team, 56, 57, 87, 90, 228, 363
Rivest, Shamir, and Adleman (RSA), 43, 44. *See also*
    Public key encryption
RJE, 380
RM, xi
ROM, 157
Routing control, 200
Royal Charter, 397, 398
RSA, 21, 26, 43
Rule-based security policies, 414, 415
Rule of least privilege, 2

S-boxes, 43
SAFE, 71, 83, 84, 348
Safeguard, 52, 337
Salami technique, 173, 445
Sanitization, 356
Scalar measures, 63, 64
Scavenging, 174, 443
Scenario analysis, 52, 82, 384
SCI, 118
Secrecy of documentation, 390
Secrecy requirements, 25
Secure
    configuration management, 377
    data transmission, 21
    state, 170, 411, 414
    working area, 377
Security
    area, 357
    audit, 226, 344, 348
        report, 348
    breach, 258, 299
    domains, 318
    evaluation, 226, 347
    films, 131, 449
    kernel, 156, 157, 158, 161
    mechanisms, 200
    model, 168, 169, 323
    officer, 104, 106, 171, 226, 321, 444. *See also* DSO;
        ISSO; SSO
    perimeter, 357, 377
    policy, 126, 153, 411, 412, 414, 415
    requirement, 25
    safeguards, 52
    services, 199

videos, 131, 449
violation, 258, 299
vulnerabilities, 345
Security-critical mechanisms, 158
Seepage, 158, 443
Segregation of duties, 334, 335, 336, 343, 384
Selection function, 33
Selective field
    confidentiality, 199
    connection integrity, 199
    connectionless integrity, 199
    protection, 205
Self-synchronous stream cipher, 30, 32, 44, 100
Sensitive business data, 118
Sensitive compartmented information, 118
Sensitive defense information, 118
Sensitivity, 52, 119
    analysis, 80
    assessment, 52
    and criticality, 52
Separation of duties, 106, 228, 320, 334, 335, 336,
    341, 380, 381, 383, 385, 384, 387, 389, 390, 417,
    447
Session, 185
Session key, 28
Shareware, 174, 446
Shielding, 172
Shoulder surfing, 158, 448
SIG-CS, 399, 401
Simple security condition, 414
Sloane (school of management thought), 232
Soft asset, 129, 130
Softlifting, 158, 258, 299
SOG-IS, 166
SP 500-13, 345
SP 500-153, 345, 347
Span of control, 242
Special Interest Group for Computer Security
    (SIG-CS), 401
Special markings, 119
Special Publication 500-153, 344, 345
Spike-protection, 103, 104
Split knowledge, 119
Splitting, 91
Spoofing, 32, 439, 448
SRI, 84, 86
SSO, 99, 102, 104, 133, 227, 228, 230, 231, 232, 321,
    378
Stages of a disaster, 108
Stand-alone
    security mode of operation, 226
    shared automated information system, 185, 226
    single-user automated information system, 185,
        226
Standards, 161, 319, 320, 338, 339, 340, 341, 346, 347
Star Property, 151, 414. *See also* *-Property

State machine, 169, 324, 325
    variables, 169, 170
State transition, 411
    function, 170
    models, 412
State variable, 158, 169
Statistical attacks on databases, 122, 441
Statistical inference, 121, 122, 124, 327, 441
Stealth, 176
Storage, off-site, 108, 110
Strategic
    materials: national security, 289
    planning, 238
Stream cipher, 30
Strength of cipher, 32
Structured
    analysis, 318, 319, 336
    design, 336
    programming, 318, 319, 336
Subcommittee on Telecommunications Security,
    185
Subject, 152, 158, 414
Substitution, 30
Superuser, 17
Supervisor state, 153, 159
Supplementary knowledge, 122, 441
Supplies, materials, 59, 357
Support, 59, 230, 320, 357, 358, 359, 379, 380, 381,
    382, 383
Survivability, 357
Synchronous stream cipher, 30
System
    audit records, 101
    design, 346
    development, 339
    manager, 378
    Security Officer, 99, 102, 104, 105, 106, 227, 228,
        230, 231, 321, 340, 378
    security steering group, 227
    shutoff, 389, 447
System Development Life Cycle (SDLC), 345
"System high" security mode, 226, 377
"System low" security mode, 227

Tactical planning, 238
Tampering, 174, 258, 299, 447
Tandem processing, 100, 104
Tangible asset, 55, 57, 58, 60, 67, 71
Taylor, 237
TC, xi
TCB, 163, 164, 165, 166, 206, 207, 412
TCSEC, 14, 16, 147, 152, 166, 207, 208, 322, 328, 331,
    332, 417
Technical information, 120

Technological attack, 159
Telecommunications, 46, 185
Telecommuting, 134, 135
Teleprocessing security, 185
TEMPEST, 186
Temptation, 130, 334
Terminal identification, 186
Termination, 137, 144, 145, 417, 420
    checklist, 145
Test data, 120, 316
Testing, 108, 322, 338, 347
    contingency plans, 342
Texas law, 270
Theft, 258, 299
Theoretically secure, 31
Threat, 52, 70, 71, 72, 73, 82, 345
    agent, 53
    analysis, 53, 76
    classes, 73
    event, 53
    information—outside sources, 86
    monitoring, 53
Threat-based risk analysis, 84
Ticket, 149, 159
Tiger team, 156, 225, 348
Time bomb, 159, 445
Time stamp, 205, 332, 386
TOC/TOU, 172, 444
TOCTU, 147
Tokens, 163
Top Secret, 14
TP, 333
Trackers, 122, 327, 442
Trade secrets, 129, 145, 417, 418
    acknowledgment of value, 131
    exit review, 132
    non-disclosure requirement, 132
    non-use requirement, 132
Traffic flow
    analysis, 24, 32, 144, 174, 186, 329, 439, 440
    confidentiality, 199, 205
    padding, 24, 186, 200
    security, 186
Training, 250, 252, 340, 342, 343, 347
Transborder data flows, 291
Transformation Procedure (TP), 333
Transition function, 169
Transport layer, 206
Trap door, 174, 316, 390, 445
Trojan horse, 159, 174, 175, 317, 327, 390, 445, 446
Trusted
    filter, 329
    kernel, 329
    source, 176
Trusted Computer System Evaluation Criteria
    (TCSEC), 14, 152, 147, 322

Trusted Computing Base (TCB), 14, 158, 163, 206
Trusted Network Interpretation (TNI), 207, 208
Turing machine, 176
Turnaround, 244
Type 1 magnetic media, 357
Type 2 magnetic media, 357

UDI, 333
Unauthorized access, 342
Unconstrained Data Item (UDI), 333
Undocumented functions, 390
Uninterruptible power supply (UPS), 102, 103, 361
Unisys, 324
UNIX, 17, 79
UPS, 103, 104, 105, 361
User
    management, 339
    requirements, 338
    manual, 347
User exit, 16
Utility, 174, 446

Validation, verification, and testing plan, 346
Value-added communications, 197
Value analysis, 54
Vandal, 268
Verifiability, 161
Verification, 325, 414
Victim, 268
Vigenère cipher, 31
Virus, 144, 159, 172, 174, 176, 327, 445, 446
Virus-L Digest, 177
VM Secure, 14, 169
Voice
    patterns, 4
    print, 4
Volume label, 387
Vulnerability, 21, 53, 70, 80, 82, 230, 358, 359
Vulnerability assessment, 53, 346

Waste, 172, 357, 364, 368, 369, 443
WB, xi
Weak keys, 42
Wet standpipe, 366
Wiretapping, 186, 441
Work
    factor, 44, 159, 186, 317
    function, 31
Work station, 235, 250, 381

Worm, 102, 149, 159, 172, 174, 175, 176, 186, 267, 268, 445, 446
Worst case, 78, 79
Written agreements, 340, 341